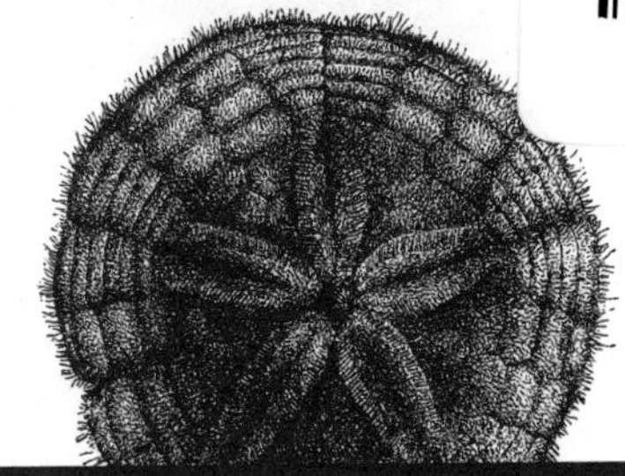

JAVA™ ENTERPRISE IN A NUTSHELL

A Desktop Quick Reference

THE JAVA™ SERIES

Exploring Java™

Java™ Threads

Java™ Network Programming

Java™ Virtual Machine

Java™ AWT Reference

Java™ Language Reference

Java™ Fundamental Classes Reference

Database Programming with JDBC™ and Java™

Java™ Distributed Computing

Developing Java Beans™

Java™ Security

Java™ Cryptography

Java™ Swing

Java™ Servlet Programming

Java™ I/O

Java™ 2D Graphics

Enterprise JavaBeans™

Also from O'Reilly

Java™ in a Nutshell

Java™ in a Nutshell, Deluxe Edition

Java™ Examples in a Nutshell

Java™ Enterprise in a Nutshell

Java™ Foundation Classes in a Nutshell

Java™ Power Reference: A Complete Searchable Resource on CD-ROM

JAVA™ ENTERPRISE IN A NUTSHELL

A Desktop Quick Reference

David Flanagan, Jim Farley, William Crawford & Kris Magnusson

O'REILLY®

Beijing · Cambridge · Farnham · Köln · Paris · Sebastopol · Taipei · Tokyo

Java™ Enterprise in a Nutshell

by David Flanagan, Jim Farley, William Crawford, and Kris Magnusson

Published by O'Reilly & Associates, Inc., 101 Morris Street, Sebastopol, CA 95472.

Editor: Paula Ferguson

Production Editor: Mary Anne Weeks Mayo

Printing History:

September 1999: First Edition.

ISBN: 1-56592-483-5 [10/00]
[M]

Table of Contents

Preface .... *xi*

Part I: Introducing the Java Enterprise APIs

Chapter 1—Introduction *3*

Enterprise Computing Defined 3
Enterprise Computing Demystified 4
The Java Enterprise APIs 5
Enterprise Computing Scenarios 11
Java Enterprise APIs Versus Jini 14

Chapter 2—JDBC *15*

JDBC Architecture 15
JDBC Basics 16
JDBC Drivers 18
Connecting to the Database 20
Statements 21
Results 23
Handling Errors 26
Prepared Statements 27
Metadata 29
Transactions 32
Stored Procedures 34
Escape Sequences 36
JDBC 2.0 37

Chapter 3—Remote Method Invocation *43*
Introduction to RMI 43
Defining Remote Objects 51
Creating the Stubs and Skeletons 55
Accessing Remote Objects as a Client 56
Dynamically Loaded Classes 60
Remote Object Activation 64
RMI and Native Method Calls 75
RMI over IIOP 78

Chapter 4—Java IDL *82*
The CORBA Architecture 83
Creating CORBA Objects 87
Putting It in the Public Eye 98
Finding Remote Objects 103
What If I Don't Know the Interface? 111

Chapter 5—Java Servlets *114*
The Servlet Life Cycle 115
Servlet Basics 116
Servlet Chaining 126
Custom Servlet Initialization 128
Thread Safety 130
Server-Side Includes 133
Cookies 135
Session Tracking 136
Databases and Non-HTML Content 139
The Servlet API 2.1 141

Chapter 6—JNDI *143*
JNDI Architecture 144
A JNDI Example 145
Introducing the Context 146
Looking Up Objects in a Context 148
The NamingShell Application 149
Listing the Children of a Context 154
Creating and Destroying Contexts 159
Binding Objects 161
Accessing Directory Services 162
Modifying Directory Entries 167

Creating Directory Entries 169
Searching a Directory 170

Chapter 7—Enterprise JavaBeans *174*

A Note on Evolving Standards 175
EJB Roles 176
Transaction Management 182
Implementing a Basic EJB Object 186
Implementing Session Beans 191
Implementing Entity Beans 196
Deploying an Enterprise JavaBeans Object 213
Using an Enterprise JavaBeans Object 219
Changes in EJB 1.1 Specification 222

Part II: Enterprise Reference

Chapter 8—SQL Reference *227*

Relational Databases 228
Data Types 229
Schema Manipulation Commands 230
Data Manipulation Commands 233
Functions 239
Return Codes 241

Chapter 9—RMI Tools *245*

rmic 245
rmiregistry 247
rmid 247
serialver 248

Chapter 10—IDL Reference *250*

IDL Keywords 251
Identifiers 252
Comments 253
Basic Data Types 253
Constants and Literals 255
Naming Scopes 258
User-Defined Data Types 259
Exceptions 268

Module Declarations 271
Interface Declarations 271

Chapter 11—CORBA Services Reference *281*

Naming Service 282
Security Service 282
Event Service 282
Persistent Object Service 283
Life Cycle Service 283
Concurrency Control Service 284
Externalization Service 284
Relationship Service 284
Transaction Service 285
Query Service 286
Licensing Service 286
Property Service 287
Time Service 287
Trading Service 287
Collection Service 288

Chapter 12—Java IDL Tools *289*

idltojava 289
tnameserv 291

Part III: API Quick Reference

How to Use This Quick Reference *295*

Chapter 13—The java.rmi Package *304*

Chapter 14—The java.rmi.activation Package *313*

Chapter 15—The java.rmi.dgc Package *322*

Chapter 16—The java.rmi.registry Package *324*

Chapter 17—The java.rmi.server Package *327*

Chapter 18—The java.sql Package *339*

Chapter 19—The javax.ejb Package *361*

Chapter 20—The javax.ejb.deployment Package *369*

Chapter 21—The javax.jms Package *373*

Chapter 22—The javax.naming Package *398*

Chapter 23—The javax.naming.directory Package *416*

Chapter 24—The javax.naming.spi Package *426*

Chapter 25—The javax.servlet Package *430*

Chapter 26—The javax.servlet.http Package *437*

Chapter 27—The javax.sql Package *444*

Chapter 28—The javax.transaction Package *451*

Chapter 29—The javax.transaction.xa Package *458*

Chapter 30—The org.omg.CORBA Package *461*

Chapter 31—The org.omg.CORBA.DynAnyPackage Package *506*

Chapter 32—The org.omg.CORBA.ORBPackage Package *508*

Chapter 33—The org.omg.CORBA.portable Package *510*

Chapter 34—The org.omg.CORBA.TypeCodePackage Package *517*

Chapter 35—The org.omg.CosNaming Package 519

Chapter 36—The org.omg.CosNaming.-NamingContextPackage Package 531

Chapter 37—Class, Method, and Field Index 540

Index 567

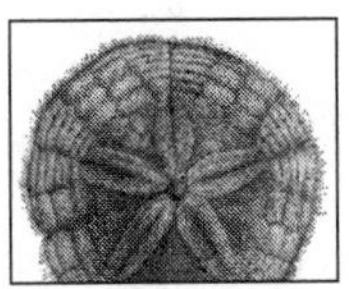

Preface

This book is a desktop quick reference for Java programmers who are writing enterprise applications. The first part of the book provides a fast-paced introduction to the key Java Enterprise APIs: JDBC™, RMI, Java IDL (CORBA), servlets, JNDI, and Enterprise JavaBeans™. These chapters are followed by a quick-reference section that succinctly details every class of those APIs, as well as a few other Enterprise APIs.

This book complements the best-selling *Java in a Nutshell* and the forthcoming *Java Foundation Classes in a Nutshell*. *Java in a Nutshell* introduces the Java programming language itself and provides an API quick reference for the core packages and classes of the Java platform, while *Java Foundation in a Nutshell* offers a fast-paced tutorial on the Java APIs that comprise the Java Foundation Classes (JFC) and provides corresponding quick-reference material.

Contents of This Book

This book is divided into three parts:

Part I: Introducing the Java Enterprise APIs
: The chapters in this part introduce the key Enterprise APIs and provide enough information so that you can start using them right away.

Part II: Enterprise Reference
: This part contains two reference chapters that help you work with technologies key to the Enterprise APIs: SQL and IDL. It also contains chapters that cover the tools provided with Sun's Java Development Kit for RMI and Java IDL.

Part III: API Quick Reference
: This part is a quick reference for the Java Enterprise APIs; it forms the bulk of the book. Please be sure to read the *How To Use This Quick Reference* section, which appears at the beginning of this part. It explains how to get the most out of this book.

Related Books

O'Reilly & Associates publishes an entire series of books on Java programming. These books include *Java in a Nutshell* and *Java Foundation Classes in a Nutshell*, which, as mentioned above, are companions to this book.

A related reference work is the *Java Power Reference*. It is an electronic Java quick-reference on CD-ROM that uses the *Java in a Nutshell* style. But since it is designed for viewing in a web browser, it is fully hyperlinked and includes a powerful search engine. It is wider in scope but narrower in depth than the *Java in a Nutshell* books. *Java Power Reference* covers all the APIs of the Java 2 platform, plus the APIs of many standard extensions. But it does not include tutorial chapters on the various APIs, nor does it include descriptions of the individual classes.

You can find a complete list of O'Reilly's Java books at *http://java.oreilly.com*. Books of particular interest to enterprise programmers include the following:

Java Servlet Programming, by Jason Hunter with William Crawford
: A guide to writing servlets that covers dynamic web content, maintaining state information, session tracking, database connectivity using JDBC, and applet-servlet communication.

Java Distributed Computing, by Jim Farley
: A programmer's guide to writing distributed applications with Java.

Database Programming with JDBC and Java, by George Reese
: An advanced tutorial on JDBC that presents a robust model for developing Java database programs.

Enterprise JavaBeans, by Richard Monson-Haefel
: A thorough introduction to EJB for the enterprise software developer.

Java Programming Resources Online

This book is designed for speedy access to frequently needed information. It does not, and cannot, tell you everything you need to know about the Java Enterprise APIs. In addition to the books listed in the previous section, there are several valuable (and free) electronic sources of information about Java programming.

Sun's main web site for all things related to Java is *http://java.sun.com*. The web site specifically for Java developers is *http://developer.java.sun.com*. Much of the content on this developer site is password-protected and access to it requires (free) registration.

Some of the Enterprise APIs covered in this book are part of the core Java 2 platform, so if you have downloaded the JDK, you have the classes for APIs such as

JDBC, RMI, and Java IDL. Other APIs are standard extensions, however, so if you want to use, say, JNDI or servlets, you have to download the classes separately. The best way to get the latest APIs is to start on Sun's Products and APIs page at *http://java.sun.com/products/* and find the appropriate API from there.

Sun distributes electronic documentation for all Java classes and methods in its *javadoc* HTML format. Although this documentation is rough or outdated in places, it is still an excellent starting point when you need to know more about a particular Java package, class, method, or field. If you do not already have the *javadoc* files with your Java distribution, see *http://java.sun.com/docs/* for a link to the latest available version.

Finally, don't forget O'Reilly's Java web site. *http://java.oreilly.com* contains Java news and commentary and a monthly tips-and-tricks column by O'Reilly Java author Jonathan Knudsen.

Examples Online

The examples in this book are available online and can be downloaded from the home page for the book at *http://www.oreilly.com/catalog/jentnut*. You may also want to visit this site to see if any important notes or errata about the book have been published there.

Conventions Used in This Book

The following formatting conventions are used in this book:

Italic
: Is used for emphasis and to signify the first use of a term. Italic is also used for commands, email addresses, web sites, FTP sites, file and directory names, and newsgroups.

Bold
: Is occasionally used to refer to particular keys on a computer keyboard or to portions of a user interface, such as the **Back** button or the **Options** menu.

`Letter Gothic`
: Is used in all Java code and generally for anything that you would type literally when programming, including options, keywords, data types, constants, method names, variables class names, and interface names.

`Letter Gothic Oblique`
: Is used for the names of function arguments, and generally as a placeholder to indicate an item that should be replaced with an actual value in your program.

Franklin Gothic Book Condensed
: Is used for the Java class synopses in Part III. This very narrow font allows us to fit a lot of information on the page without a lot of distracting line breaks. This font is also used for code entities in the descriptions in Part III.

Franklin Gothic Demi Condensed
Is used for highlighting class, method, field, property, and constructor names in Part III, which makes it easier to scan the class synopses.

Franklin Gothic Book Compressed Italic
Is used for method parameter names and comments in Part III.

We'd Like to Hear from You

We have tested and verified the information in this book to the best of our ability, but you may find that features have changed (or even that we have made mistakes!). Please let us know about any errors you find, as well as your suggestions for future editions, by writing to:

O'Reilly & Associates, Inc.
101 Morris Street
Sebastopol, CA 95472
1-800-998-9938 (in the U.S. or Canada)
1-707-829-0515 (international or local)
1-707-829-0104 (FAX)

You can send us messages electronically. To be put on the mailing list or request a catalog, send email to:

info@oreilly.com

To ask technical questions or comment on the book, send email to:

bookquestions@oreilly.com

We have a web site for the book, where we'll list examples, errata, and any plans for future editions. You can access this page at:

http://www.oreilly.com/catalog/jentnut/

For more information about this book and others, see the O'Reilly web site:

http://www.oreilly.com

Acknowledgments

This book is an outgrowth of the best-selling *Java in a Nutshell*. We'd like to thank all the readers who made that book a success and who wrote in with comments, suggestions, and praise.

The authors would like to say a big thank you to the book's technical reviewers, whose constructive criticism has done much to improve this work: Andy Deitsch, Jason Hunter, William Smith, and Gary Letourneau.

David Flanagan

Java Enterprise in a Nutshell is a book I've wished I could write for some time now. Time constraints and my own lack of expertise in enterprise computing have kept me from doing it myself, and so I am deeply grateful to Jim Farley, William Crawford, and Kris Magnusson, who are experts and who did all the hard work to make this book a reality. I owe an extra thanks to Jim Farley for taking the time to help me understand Enterprise JavaBeans and the JTA and JTS transaction APIs. Paula Ferguson also earns my sincere thanks: she had the unenviable task of editing material from four independent authors and fitting it seamlessly together into a single book.

Jim Farley

A writing project of any kind requires a much larger cast of characters than those listed on the cover. Paula Ferguson deserves mention above all, not only for doing her usual excellent editing job, but also for roping in four disobedient authors, as opposed to the usual one disobedient author. I'd like to thank David Flanagan for putting together the API listings and the introductory chapter, as well as providing great technical review comments, all of which helped integrate this into the "Java ... Nutshell" set. Technical reviewers are the unsung heroes of writing projects such as this one, so many thanks to Andy Deitsch, Bill Smith, Jason Hunter, and Gary Letourneau.

To my wife Sandy Mallalieu, who has somehow not only accepted the fact that her husband enjoys spending much of his free time on writing projects like this, but is also supportive and inspiring through it all—well, what else is there to say? My extended family, and the folks at the Harvard Business School, were supportive as always, and getting through efforts such as this makes me appreciate them both all the more. And for the late-night inspiration, my undying gratitude to Madeline and to Declan MacManus.

William Crawford

Writing projects would be impossible without the support of everyone at Invantage, especially Martin Streeter, Nicholas Riley, and Stephen Braverman. Jason Hunter's knowledge of servlet programming was a boon to Chapter 5. I would also like to thank the staff of the Emotion Cybernet Cafe in Hanoi, Vietnam, where I wrote most of the class summaries for the `java.sql` package, paying six cents a minute for computer time. And we wouldn't be here without David Flanagan.

I have enjoyed support, encouragement, and grudging tolerance from William F. Crawford, William E. Crawford, Francine Crawford, and Faith Crawford, as well as from Joel Pomerantz, Sam Carner, and Isaac Kohane.

Finally, my heartfelt thanks goes to our editor, Paula Ferguson, for her extreme patience with me over the last year and a half.

Kris Magnusson

I found a good deal of pleasure in writing the JNDI-related material for this book. And I have many people to thank for the opportunity—too many to list here. But some deserve special mention.

In particular I thank my partner and wife Kristen Dalzen for all her support, without which my work would not have been possible. She is the Empress of the Blue People, and she has enriched my life beyond description. She has been brave to bear the abandonment.

At O'Reilly, David Flanagan provided invaluable assistance in writing my portions of this book; clearly he is an asset to the entire Java community. My editor, Paula Ferguson, was equally invaluable; she tightened up my language and code like a vise. And my other editor, Mike Loukides, is a good sport for giving me time off from my other book to work on this one.

My Novell experience has been a period of immense personal growth for me. My officemates Bruce "Stocks" Bergeson, Jim Sermersheim, and Kent Boogert have been key players in that drama, as were Alan Landes, Alvin Tedjamulia, Chris Stone, Don Lavange, Don Thomas, Ed Lane, Erni Messenger, Michael J. Simpson, Mike Flathers, Mike MacKay, Ric Buhler, Scott Pead, Steve Holbrook, Steve Weitzeil, and Trisha Turner. Here's to a fruitful second act.

Outside of work, Don Yacktman and Dr. Sean Luke were instrumental in sharing their object-oriented architecture expertise over the years. And Yan Fang and her support for my computer and other habits helped immensely with my transition from fresh economics graduate to software guy.

Thanks, everyone!

PART I

Introducing the Java Enterprise APIs

Part I is an introduction to the key Enterprise APIs. These chapters provide enough information for you to get started using these APIs right away.

Chapter 1, *Introduction*
Chapter 2, *JDBC*
Chapter 3, *Remote Method Invocation*
Chapter 4, *Java IDL*
Chapter 5, *Java Servlets*
Chapter 6, *JNDI*
Chapter 7, *Enterprise JavaBeans*

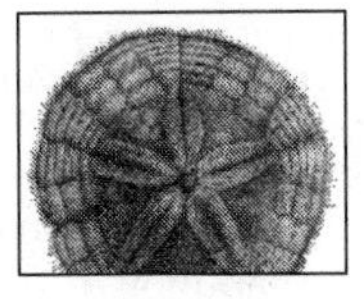

CHAPTER 1

Introduction

This book is an introduction to, and quick reference for, the Java Enterprise APIs. Some of these APIs are a core part of the Java platform, while others are standard extensions to the platform. Together, however, they enable Java programs to use and interact with a suite of distributed network services that are commonly used in enterprise computing.

Just before this book went to press, Sun announced a new Java platform for enterprise computing. Java 2 Platform, Enterprise Edition, or J2EE, is the standard Java 2 platform with a number of extensions for enterprise computing. As of this writing, J2EE is still in its alpha stages; it will be some time before a complete specification and implementation are delivered. From the preliminary specifications, however, it appears that most of the enterprise-computing technologies that will be part of J2EE are already documented in this book. In the months ahead, you will undoubtedly hear quite a bit about Java 2 Platform, Enterprise Edition. Although you won't find that name used explicitly here, you can rest assured that this book documents the building blocks of J2EE.

Enterprise Computing Defined

Before we go any further, let's be clear. The term *enterprise computing* is simply a synonym for distributed computing: computation done by groups of programs interacting over a network.

Anyone can write distributed applications: you don't have to work for a major corporation, university, government agency, or any other kind of large-scale "enterprise" to program with the Java Enterprise APIs. Small businesses may not have the same enterprise-scale distributed computing needs large organizations have, but most still engage in plenty of distributed computing. With the explosive growth of the Internet and of network services, just about anyone can find a reason to write distributed applications. One such reason is that it is fun. When distributed computing is used to leverage the power of the network, the results can be amazingly cool!

So, if the Java Enterprise APIs aren't used exclusively by enterprises, why aren't they called the Java Distributed Computing APIs? The reasons are simple. First, enterprise is a hot buzzword these days—everyone in the networking industry wants to be doing enterprise something. Second, large enterprises have lots of money to spend on costly hardware for running their expensive network server software. Since the enterprise is where the money is, we get the word enterprise in the APIs.

Enterprise Computing Demystified

Enterprise computing has a reputation for complexity and, for the uninitiated, it is often surrounded by a shroud of mystery. Here are some reasons enterprise computing can seem intimidating:

- Enterprise computing usually takes place in a heterogeneous network: one in which the computers range from large mainframes and supercomputers down to PCs (including both top-of-the-line Pentium IIIs and outdated 386s). The computers were purchased at different times from a variety of different vendors and run two or three or more different operating systems. The only common denominator is that all the computers in the network speak the same fundamental network protocol (usually TCP/IP).
- A variety of server applications run on top of the heterogeneous network hardware. An enterprise might have database software from three different companies, each of which defines different, incompatible extensions.
- Enterprise computing involves the use of many different network protocols and standards. Some standards overlap in small or significant ways. Many have been extended in various vendor-specific, nonstandard ways. Some are quite old and use a vocabulary and terminology that dates back to an earlier era of computing. This creates a confusing alphabet soup of acronyms.
- Enterprise computing has only recently emerged as an integrated discipline of its own. Although enterprise development models are today becoming more cohesive and encompassing, many enterprises are still left with lots of "legacy systems" that are aggregated in an ad-hoc way.
- Enterprise programmers, like many of us in the high-tech world, tend to make their work seem more complicated that it actually is. This is a natural human tendency—to be part of the "in" group and keep outsiders out—but this tendency seems somehow magnified within the computer industry.

Java helps to alleviate these intimidating aspects of enterprise computing. First, since Java is platform-independent, the heterogenous nature of the network ceases to be an issue. Second, the Java Enterprise APIs form a single, standard layer on top of various proprietary or vendor-enhanced APIs. For example, the JDBC API provides a single, standard, consistent way to interact with a relational database server, regardless of the database vendor and regardless of the underlying network protocol the database server uses to communicate with clients. Finally, recall that many enterprise protocols and standards were developed before the days of object-oriented programming. The object-oriented power and elegance of the Java language allow the Java Enterprise APIs to be simpler, easier to use, and easier to understand than the non-Java APIs upon which they are layered.

The messages you should take away from this discussion are:

- Enterprise computing is for everyone.
- Any programmer can write distributed applications using the Java Enterprise APIs.

With that said, it is important to understand that distributed computing actually is somewhat more complicated than nondistributed computing. Just as using threads in a program introduces complexities that do not exist in single-threaded programs, using network services in a program introduces complexities that do not exist in programs that run entirely on one computer. While multithreaded programs have to deal with the issues of thread synchronization and deadlock, distributed applications have to deal with the possibilities of network failure and the complexities of distributed transaction processing. Do not fear, however: the complexities of distributed computing are not overwhelming, and, with a little study, any programmer can master them.

The Java Enterprise APIs

The Java Enterprise APIs provide support for a number of the most commonly used distributed computing technologies and network services. These APIs are described in the sections that follow. The APIs are building blocks for distributed applications. At the end of the chapter, I'll present some enterprise computing scenarios that illustrate how these separate APIs can be used together to produce an enterprise application.

JDBC: Working with Databases

JDBC is the Java Enterprise API for working with relational database systems. JDBC allows a Java program to send SQL query and update statements to a database server and to retrieve and iterate through query results returned by the server. JDBC also allows you to get meta-information about the database and its tables from the database server.

The JDBC API is independent of vendor-specific APIs defined by particular database systems. The JDBC architecture relies upon a `Driver` class that hides the details of communicating with a database server. Each database server product requires a custom `Driver` implementation to allow Java programs to communicate with it. Major database vendors have made JDBC drivers available for their products. In addition, a "bridge" driver exists to enable Java programs to communicate with databases through existing ODBC drivers.

The JDBC API is found in the `java.sql` package, which was introduced in Java 1.1. Version 1.2 of the Java 2 platform adds a number of new classes to this package to support advanced database features. Java 1.2 also provides additional features in the `javax.sql` standard extension package. `javax.sql` includes classes for treating database query results as JavaBeans, for pooling database connections, and for obtaining database connection information from a name service. The extension package also supports scrollable result sets, batch updates, and the storage of Java objects in databases.

The JDBC API is simple and well-designed. Programmers who are familiar with SQL and database programming in general should find it very easy to work with databases in Java. See Chapter 2, *JDBC*, for details on JDBC, and Chapter 8, *SQL Reference*, for a quick reference to SQL.

RMI: Remote Method Invocation

Remote method invocation is a programming model that provides a high-level, generic approach to distributed computing. This model extends the object-oriented programming paradigm to distributed client-server programming; it allows a client to communicate with a server by invoking methods on remote objects that reside on the server. You invoke remote methods using the same syntax you would use to invoke methods of a normal local object. This model for distributed computing can be implemented in a number of ways. One of those ways is the Java Remote Method Invocation (RMI) API. RMI is implemented in the `java.rmi` package and its subpackages, which were introduced in Java 1.1 and have been enhanced for Version 1.2 of the Java 2 platform.

The Java RMI implementation is full-featured, but still simple and easy to use. It gains much of its simplicity by being built on top of a network-centric and dynamically extensible platform, of course. But it also gains simplicity by requiring both client and server to be implemented in Java. This requirement ensures that both client and server share a common set of data types and have access to the object serialization and deserialization features of the `java.io` package, for example. On the other hand, this means that RMI cannot be used with distributed objects written in languages other than Java, such as objects that exist on legacy servers.* It also means that servers written using RMI can be used only by clients written in Java. In practice, RMI is an excellent distributed object solution for situations where it is clear that clients and servers will always be written in Java. Fortunately, there are many such situations.

The `java.rmi` package makes it easy to create networked, object-oriented programs. Programmers who have spent time writing networked applications using lower-level technologies are usually amazed by the power of RMI. By making RMI so easy, `java.rmi` points the way to future applications and systems that consist of loose groups of objects interacting with each other over a network. These objects may act both as clients, by calling methods of other objects, and as servers, by exposing their own methods to other objects. See Chapter 3, *Remote Method Invocation (RMI)*, for a tutorial on using RMI.

---

* One way to work around this restriction is to use native methods to create Java wrappers that interface directly with the legacy objects that are written in other languages.

Java IDL: CORBA Distributed Objects

As we've just seen, RMI is a distributed object solution that works well when both client and server are written in Java. It does not work, however, in heterogenous environments where clients and servers may be written in arbitrary languages. For environments like these, the Java 2 platform includes a CORBA-based solution for remote method invocation on distributed objects.

CORBA (Common Object Request Broker Architecture) is a widely used standard defined by the Object Management Group (OMG). This standard is implemented as a core part of the Java 2 platform in the `org.omg.CORBA` package and its subpackages. The implementation includes an Object Request Broker (ORB) that a Java application can use to communicate, as both a client and a server, with other ORBs, and thus with other CORBA objects.

The interfaces to remote CORBA objects are described in a platform- and language-independent way with the Interface Description Language (IDL). Sun provides an IDL compiler (in "early access" release at the time of this writing) that translates an IDL description of a remote interface into the Java stub classes needed for implementing the IDL interface in Java or for connecting to a remote implementation of the interface from your Java code.

A number of Java implementations of the CORBA standard are available from various vendors. This book documents Sun's implementation, known as Java IDL. It is covered in detail in Chapter 4, *Java IDL*. The syntax of the IDL language itself is summarized in Chapter 10, *IDL Reference*.

JNDI: Accessing Naming and Directory Services

JNDI (Java Naming and Directory Interface) is the Java Enterprise API for working with networked naming and directory services. It allows Java programs to use name servers and directory servers to look up objects or data by name and search for objects or data according to a set of specified attribute values. JNDI is implemented in the `javax.naming` package and its subpackages as a standard extension to the Java 2 platform.

The JNDI API is not specific to any particular name or directory server protocol. Instead, it is a generic API that is general enough to work with any name or directory server. To support a particular protocol, you plug a service provider for that protocol into a JNDI installation. Service providers have been implemented for the most common protocols, such as NIS, LDAP, and Novell's NDS. Service providers have also been written to interact with the RMI and CORBA object registries. JNDI is covered in detail in Chapter 6, *JNDI*.

Enterprise JavaBeans

Enterprise JavaBeans do for server-side enterprise programs what JavaBeans do for client-side GUIs. Enterprise JavaBeans (EJB) is a component model for units of business logic and business data. Thin client programming models that take business logic out of the client and put it on a server or in a middle tier have many advantages in enterprise applications. However, the task of writing this middleware has always been complicated by the fact that business logic must be mixed in with code for handling transactions, security, networking, and so on.

The EJB model separates high-level business logic from low-level housekeeping chores. A bean in the EJB model is an RMI remote object that implements business logic or represents business data. The difference between an enterprise bean and a run-of-the-mill RMI remote object is that EJB components run within an EJB container, which in turn runs within an EJB server. The container and server may provide features such as transaction management, resource pooling, lifecycle management, security, name services, distribution services, and so on. With all these services provided by the container and server, enterprise beans (and enterprise bean programmers) are free to focus purely on business logic. The particular set of services provided by an EJB server is implementation-dependent. The EJB specification is strongest in the areas of transaction management and resource pooling, so these are features that are expected in all EJB server implementations.

The EJB specification is a document that specifies the contracts to be maintained and conventions to be followed by EJB servers, containers, and beans. Writing EJB components is easy: you simply write code to implement your business logic, taking care to follow the rules and conventions imposed by the EJB model.

Unlike the other Java Enterprise APIs, EJB is not really an API; it is a framework for component-based enterprise computing. The key to understanding Enterprise JavaBeans lies in the interactions among beans, containers, and the EJB server. These interactions are described in detail in Chapter 7, *Enterprise JavaBeans*. There is, of course, an API associated with the EJB application framework, in the form of the `javax.ejb` and `javax.ejb.deployment` packages. You'll find complete API quick-reference information for these packages in Part III of this book.

Servlets

A *servlet* is a piece of Java code that runs within a server to provide a service to a client. The name servlet is a takeoff on applet—a servlet is a server-side applet. The Java Servlet API provides a generic mechanism for extending the functionality of any kind of server that uses a protocol based on requests and responses.

Right now, servlets are used primarily by web servers. On the growing number of web servers that support them, servlets are a Java-based replacement for CGI scripts. They can also replace competing technologies, such as Microsoft's Active Server Pages (ASP) or Netscape's Server-Side JavaScript. The advantage of servlets over these other technologies is that servlets are portable among operating systems and among servers. Servlets are persistent between invocations, which gives them major performance benefits over CGI programs. Servlets also have full access to the rest of the Java platform, so features such as database access are automatically supported.

The Servlet API differs from many other Java Enterprise APIs in that it is not a Java layer on top of an existing network service or protocol. Instead, servlets are a Java-specific enhancement to the world of enterprise computing. With the advent of the Internet and the World Wide Web, many enterprises are interested in taking advantage of web browsers—a universally available thin-client that can run on any desktop. Under this model, the web server becomes enterprise middleware and is responsible for running applications for clients. Servlets are a perfect fit here. The user makes a request to the web server, the web server invokes the appropriate servlet, and the servlet uses JNDI, JDBC, and other Java Enterprise APIs to fulfill the request, returning the result to the user, usually in the form of HTML-formatted text.

The Servlet API is a standard extension to the Java 2 platform, implemented in the `javax.servlet` and `javax.servlet.http` packages. The `javax.servlet` package defines classes that represent generic client requests and server responses, while the `javax.servlet.http` package provides specific support for the HTTP protocol, including classes for tracking multiple client requests that are all part of a single client session. See Chapter 5, *Java Servlets*, for details on servlet programming.

JMS: Enterprise Messaging

JMS (Java Message Service) is the Java Enterprise API for working with networked messaging services and for writing message-oriented middleware (fondly referred to as MOM).

The word "message" means different things in different contexts. In the context of JMS, a message is chunk of data that is sent from one system to another. The data serves as a kind of event notification and is almost always intended to be read by a computer program, not by a human. In a nondistributed system, an `Event` object notifies the program that some important event (such as the user clicking a mouse button) has occurred. In a distributed system, a message serves a similar purpose: it notifies some part of the system that an interesting event has occurred. So you can think of a networked message service as a distributed event notification system.

Like JNDI and JDBC, JMS is an API layered on top of existing, vendor-specific messaging services. In order to use JMS in your applications, you need to obtain a JMS provider implementation that supports your particular message server.

Although JMS is an important part of the Java Enterprise APIs, its use is not nearly as universal as APIs such as JDBC and JNDI, so this book does not contain a tutorial chapter on JMS. Chapter 21, *The javax.jms Package*, does contain a complete API quick reference for the `javax.jms` package, however.

JTA: Managing Distributed Transactions

The JTA, or Java Transaction API, is a Java Enterprise API for managing distributed transactions. Distributed transactions are one of the things that make distributed systems more complicated than nondistributed programs. To understand distributed transactions, you must first understand simple, nondistributed transactions.

A *transaction* is a group of several operations that must behave *atomically*—as if they constituted a single, indivisible operation. Consider a banking application that allows a user to transfer money from a checking account to a savings account. If the two account balances are stored in a database, the application must perform two database updates to handle a transfer: it must subtract money from the checking account and add money to the savings account. These two operations must behave atomically. To see why, imagine what would happen if the database server crashed after money had been subtracted from the checking account but before it had been added to the savings account. The customer would lose money!

To make multiple operations atomic, we use transactions. In our banking example, we first begin a transaction, then perform the two database updates. While these updates are in progress, no other threads can see the updated account balances. If both updates complete successfully, we end the transaction by *committing* it. This makes the updated account balances available to any other clients of the database. On the other hand, if either of the database updates fails, we *roll back* the transaction, reverting the accounts to their original balances. Other clients are again given access to the database, and they see no changes in the account balances. The JDBC API supports transactions on databases. The database server is required to do some complex work to support transactions, but for the application programmer, the API is easy: simply begin a transaction, perform the desired operations, and then either commit or rollback the transaction.

Distributed transactions are, unfortunately, quite a bit more complex than the simple transactions just described. Imagine, for example, a program that transfers money from an account stored in one database to another account stored in a different database running on a different server. In this case, there are two different servers involved in the transaction, so the process of committing or rolling back the transaction must be externally coordinated. Distributed transactions are performed using a complex procedure known as the *two-phase commit protocol*; the details of the protocol are not important here. What is important is that we could write our account transfer code so that it implements the two-phase commit protocol itself, coordinating the entire distributed transaction with the two database servers. This would be tedious and error-prone, however. In practice, distributed transactions are coordinated by a specialized distributed transaction service.

This brings us, finally, to the JTA. The JTA is a Java API for working with transaction services. It defines a Java binding for the standard XA API for distributed transactions (XA is a standard defined by the Open Group). Using the JTA, we can write a program that communicates with a distributed transaction service and uses that service to coordinate a distributed transaction that involves a transfer of money between database records in two different databases.

Unfortunately, however, using the JTA in this way is still complex and error-prone. Modern enterprise applications are typically designed to run within some kind of application server, such as an Enterprise JavaBeans server. The server uses JTA to handle distributed transactions transparently for the application. Under this model, JTA becomes a low-level API used by server implementors, not by typical enterprise programmers. Therefore, this book doesn't include a tutorial chapter on JTA. It does, however, contain a complete API quick reference for the `javax.transaction` and `javax.transactions.xa` packages (see Chapters 28 and 29).

Enterprise Computing Scenarios

The previous sections have been rapid-fire introductions to the Java Enterprise APIs. Don't worry if you didn't understand all the information presented there: the rest of the chapters in this Part cover the APIs in more detail. The important message you should take from this chapter is that the Java Enterprise APIs are building blocks that work together to enable you to write distributed Java applications for enterprise computing. The network infrastructure of every enterprise is unique, and the Java Enterprise APIs can be combined in any number of ways to meet the specific needs and goals of a particular enterprise.

Figure 1-1 shows a network schematic for a hypothetical enterprise. It illustrates some of the many possible interconnections among network services and shows the Java Enterprise APIs that facilitate those interconnections. The figure is followed by example scenarios that demonstrate how the Java Enterprise APIs might be used to solve typical enterprise computing problems. You may find it useful to refer to Figure 1-1 while reading through the scenarios, but note that the figure does not illustrate the specific scenarios presented here.

Enabling E-Commerce for a Mail-Order Enterprise

CornCo Inc. runs a successful catalog-based mail-order business selling fresh flavored popcorn. They want to expand into the exciting world of electronic commerce over the Internet. Here's how they might do it:*

- A customer visits the company's web site, *www.cornco.com*, and uses a web browser to interact with the company's web server. This allows the customer to view the company's products and make selections to purchase.
- The web server uses a shopping-cart servlet to keep track of the products the customer has chosen to buy. The HTTP protocol is itself stateless, but servlets can persist between client requests, so this shopping-cart servlet can remember the customer's selections even while the customer continues to browse the web site.
- When the customer is done browsing and is ready to purchase the selected products, the web server invokes a different checkout servlet. This servlet performs a number of important tasks, using several Enterprise APIs.
- The checkout servlet uses JDBC to retrieve the list of products to be purchased (stored in a database by the shopping-cart servlet).
- Next, the servlet queries the customer for a shipping address, a billing address, and other required information, and then uses JDBC again to store this information in a customer database. This database can be used, for example, by the CornCo marketing department for direct mail purposes.

* This example is intended to illustrate only how the Java Enterprise APIs can be used together. I have ignored efficiency considerations, so the resulting design might not actually be practical for a large-scale e-commerce web site.

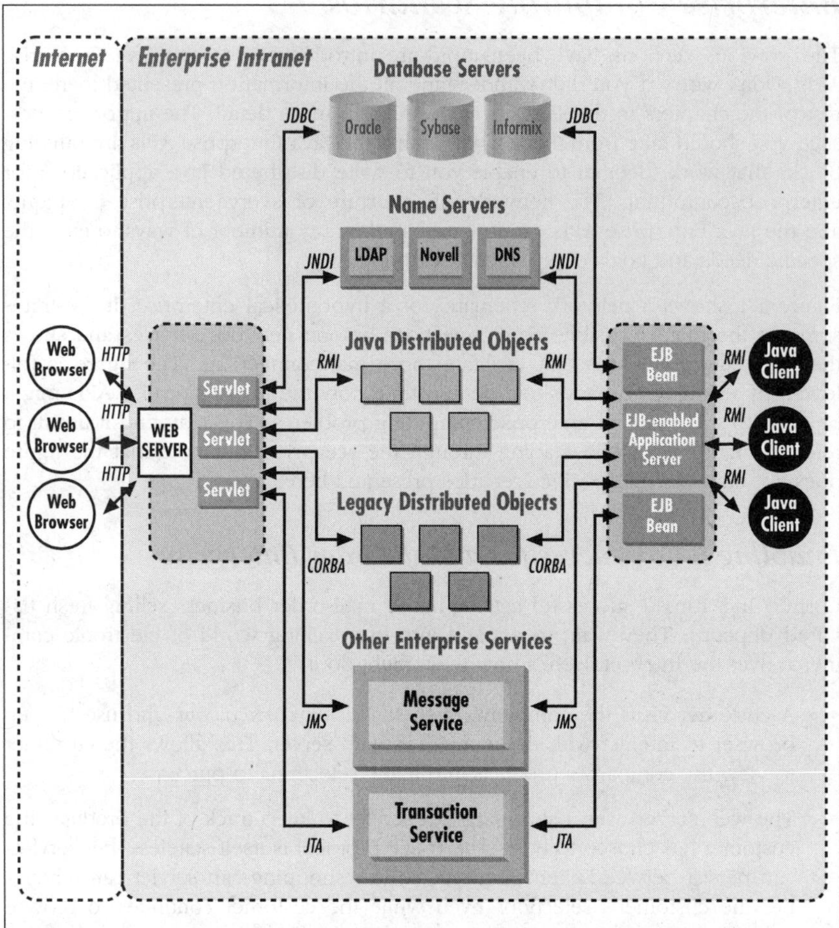

Figure 1-1: The distributed computing architecture of a hypothetical enterprise

- The servlet then sends the customer's billing address and total purchase price to the billing server. This server is a legacy application, specific to CornCo, that has a nonstandard interface. Fortunately, however, the billing server exports itself as a CORBA object, so the servlet can treat the entire server as a CORBA remote object and invoke the necessary methods on it.
- In order to ensure the very freshest product, CornCo maintains warehouses throughout the world. CornCo is a growing company, so the list of warehouses is frequently updated. The checkout servlet uses JNDI to contact a directory server and then uses the directory server to find a warehouse that is close to the customer and has the customer's requested products in stock.
- Having located a warehouse that can fulfill the customer's order, the checkout servlet uses JMS to contact the company's enterprise messaging service. It uses this service to send the customer's order to the selected warehouse in

the form of a message. This message is delivered to and queued up on the local computer at the warehouse.

Updating CornCo with Enterprise JavaBeans

You may have noticed a flaw in the previous scenario. The checkout servlet sends billing information to one server, and then sends fulfillment information to another server. But it performs these two actions independently, without any attempt to maintain transactional integrity and make them behave atomically. In other words, if a network failure or server crash were to occur after the billing information had been sent, but before the fulfillment information had been sent, the customer might receive a bill for popcorn that was never shipped.

The designers of the e-commerce system described in the previous section were aware of this problem, but since distributed transactions are complex, and CornCo did not own a transaction management server, they simply chose to ignore it. In practice, the number of customers who would have problems would be small, and it was easier for the original programmers to let the customer service department sort out any irregularities.

But now, CornCo has hired a new Vice President of Information Systems. She's tough as nails, and likes all her i's dotted and her t's crossed. She won't stand for this sloppy state of affairs. As her first official act as VP, she buys a high-end application server with Enterprise JavaBeans support and gives her e-commerce team the job of revamping the online ordering system to use it. The modified design might work like this:

- The customer interacts with the web server and the shopping-cart servlet in the same way as before.
- The checkout servlet is totally rewritten. Now it is merely a frontend for an Enterprise JavaBeans component that handles the interactions with the ordering and fulfillment servers and with the marketing database. The servlet uses JNDI to look up the enterprise bean, and then uses RMI to invoke methods on the bean (recall that all enterprise beans are RMI remote objects).
- The major functionality of the checkout servlet is moved to a new checkout bean. The bean stores customer data in the marketing database using JDBC, sends billing information to the billing server using CORBA, looks up a warehouse using JNDI, and sends shipping information to the warehouse using JMS. The bean does not explicitly coordinate all these activities into a distributed transaction, however. Instead, when the bean is deployed within the EJB server, the system administrator configures the bean so that the server automatically wraps a distributed transaction around all of its actions. That is, when the `checkout()` method of the bean is called, it always behaves as an atomic operation.
- In order for this automatic distributed transaction management to work, another change is required in the conversion from checkout servlet to checkout bean. The checkout servlet managed all its own connections to other enterprise services, but enterprise beans do not typically do this. Instead, they rely on their server for connection management. Thus, when the checkout

bean wants to connect to the marketing database or the enterprise messaging system, for example, it asks the EJB server to establish that connection for it. The server doesn't need to know what the bean does with the connection, but it does need to manage the connection, if it is to perform transaction management on the connection.

Java Enterprise APIs Versus Jini

Jini™ is the latest networking initiative from Sun. It is related to, but mostly incompatible with, the Java Enterprise APIs. Jini is a next-generation networking system designed to enable instantaneous networking between unrelated devices, without external communication. Jini is a system for distributed computing; it includes a name service, a distributed transaction service, and a distributed event service. Although these services overlap with JNDI, JTS, and JMS, Jini is fundamentally different from the Java Enterprise APIs. The Enterprise APIs are designed to bring Java into existing enterprises and to interoperate with existing protocols and services. Jini, on the other hand, is a next-generation networking system that was designed from scratch, with no concern for compatibility with today's distributed systems. Jini is a powerful and interesting technology, but covering it is beyond the scope of this book.

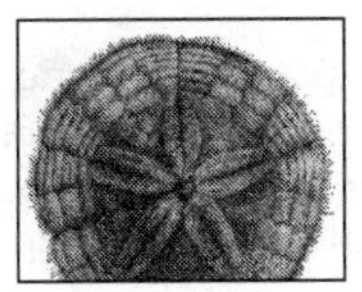

CHAPTER 2

JDBC

The JDBC* API provides Java applications with mid-level access to most database systems, via the Structured Query Language (SQL). JDBC is a key enterprise API, as it's hard to imagine an enterprise application that doesn't use a database in some way. This chapter starts by demonstrating the central concepts and classes that comprise the original JDBC API (JDBC 1.0), which was introduced as an add-on to Java 1.0 and included as part of the core Java 1.1 API. It concludes with an introduction to the new JDBC 2.0 features that are provided as part of Version 1.2 of the Java 2 platform.

A word of caution: while the `java.sql` package is less complicated than, say, the RMI packages, it does require grounding in general database concepts and the SQL language itself. This book does include a brief SQL reference (see Chapter 8, *SQL Reference*), but if you have never worked with a relational database system before, this chapter is not the place to start. For a more complete treatment of JDBC and general database concepts, I recommend *Database Programming with JDBC and Java* by George Reese (O'Reilly).

JDBC Architecture

Different database systems have surprisingly little in common: just a similar purpose and a mostly compatible query language. Beyond that, every database has its own API that you must learn to write programs that interact with the database. This has meant that writing code capable of interfacing with databases from more than one vendor has been a daunting challenge. Cross-database APIs exist, most notably Microsoft's ODBC API, but these tend to find themselves, at best, limited to a particular platform.

* According to Sun, JDBC is not an acronym for Java Database Connectivity, although most people assume it is.

JDBC is Sun's attempt to create a platform-neutral interface between databases and Java. With JDBC, you can count on a standard set of database access features and (usually) a particular subset of SQL, SQL-92. The JDBC API defines a set of interfaces that encapsulate major database functionality, including running queries, processing results, and determining configuration information. A database vendor or third-party developer writes a JDBC *driver*, which is a set of classes that implements these interfaces for a particular database system. An application can use a number of drivers interchangeably. Figure 2-1 shows how an application uses JDBC to interact with one or more databases without knowing about the underlying driver implementations.

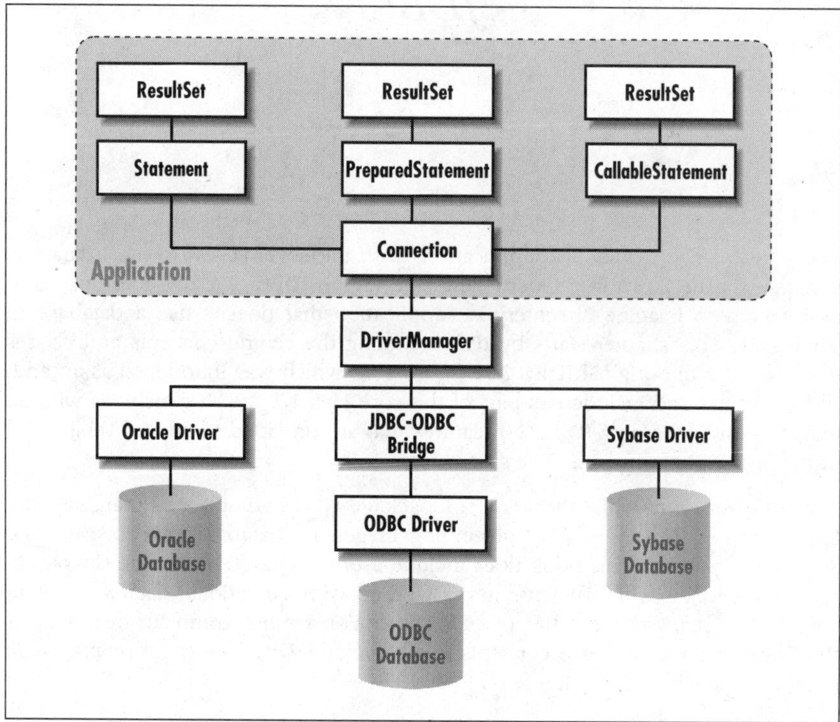

Figure 2-1: JDBC-database interaction

JDBC Basics

Before we discuss all of the individual components of JDBC, let's look at a simple example that incorporates most of the major pieces of JDBC functionality. Example 2-1 loads a driver, connects to the database, executes some SQL, and retrieves the results. It also keeps an eye out for any database-related errors.

Example 2-1: A Simple JDBC Example

```
import java.sql.*;

public class JDBCSample {
```

Example 2-1: A Simple JDBC Example (continued)

```
  public static void main(java.lang.String[] args) {
    try {
      // This is where we load the driver
      Class.forName("sun.jdbc.odbc.JdbcOdbcDriver");
    }
    catch (ClassNotFoundException e) {
      System.out.println("Unable to load Driver Class");
      return;
    }

    try {
      // All database access is within a try/catch block. Connect to database,
      // specifying particular database, username, and password
      Connection con = DriverManager.getConnection("jdbc:odbc:companydb",
                                                   "", "");

      // Create and execute an SQL Statement
      Statement stmt = con.createStatement();
      ResultSet rs = stmt.executeQuery("SELECT FIRST_NAME FROM EMPLOYEES");

      // Display the SQL Results
      while(rs.next()) {
        System.out.println(rs.getString("FIRST_NAME"));
      }

      // Make sure our database resources are released
      rs.close();
      stmt.close();
      con.close();

    }
    catch (SQLException se) {
      // Inform user of any SQL errors
      System.out.println("SQL Exception: " + se.getMessage());
      se.printStackTrace(System.out);
    }
  }
}
```

Example 2-1 starts out by loading a JDBC driver class (in this case, Sun's JDBC-ODBC Bridge). Then it creates a database connection, represented by a `Connection` object, using that driver. With the database connection, we can create a `Statement` object to represent an SQL statement. Executing an SQL statement produces a `ResultSet` that contains the results of a query. The program displays the results and then cleans up the resources it has used. If an error occurs, a `SQLException` is thrown, so our program traps that exception and displays some of the information it encapsulates.

Clearly, there is a lot going on in this simple program. Every Java application that uses JDBC follows these basic steps, so the following sections discuss each step in much more detail.

JDBC Drivers

Before you can use a driver, the driver must be registered with the JDBC `DriverManager`. This is typically done by loading the driver class using the `Class.forName()` method:

```
try {
  Class.forName("sun.jdbc.odbc.JdbcOdbcDriver");
  Class.forName("com.oracle.jdbc.OracleDriver");
}
catch (ClassNotFoundException e) {
  /* Handle Exception */
}
```

One reason most programs call `Class.forName()` is that this method accepts a `String` argument, meaning that the program can store driver selection information dynamically (e.g., in a properties file).

Another way to register drivers is to add the driver classes to the `jdbc.drivers` property. To use this technique, add a line like the following to *~/.hotjava/properties* (on Windows systems this file can be found in your Java SDK installation directory):

```
jdbc.drivers=com.oracle.jdbc.OracleDriver:foo.driver.dbDriver:com.al.AlDriver;
```

Separate the names of individual drivers with colons and be sure the line ends with a semicolon. Programs rarely use this approach, as it requires additional configuration work on the part of end users. Every user needs to have the appropriate JDBC driver classes specified in his properties file.

JDBC drivers are available for most database platforms, from a number of vendors and in a number of different flavors. There are four categories of drivers:

Type 1 JDBC-ODBC Bridge Drivers
: Type 1 drivers use a bridge technology to connect a Java client to an ODBC database system. The JDBC-ODBC Bridge from Sun and InterSolv is the only extant example of a Type 1 driver. Type 1 drivers require some sort of non-Java software to be installed on the machine running your code, and they are implemented using native code.

Type 2 Native-API Partly Java Drivers
: Type 2 drivers use a native code library to access a database, wrapping a thin layer of Java around the native library. For example, with Oracle databases, the native access might be through the Oracle Call Interface (OCI) libraries that were originally designed for C/C++ programmers. Type 2 drivers are implemented with native code, so they may perform better than all-Java drivers, but they also add an element of risk, as a defect in the native code can crash the Java Virtual Machine.

Type 3 Net-protocol All-Java Drivers
: Type 3 drivers define a generic network protocol that interfaces with a piece of custom middleware. The middleware component might use any other type of driver to provide the actual database access. BEA's WebLogic product line (formerly known as WebLogic Tengah and before that as jdbcKona/T3) is an

example. These drivers are especially useful for applet deployment, since the actual JDBC classes can be written entirely in Java and downloaded by the client on the fly.

Type 4 Native-protocol All-Java Drivers

Type 4 drivers are written entirely in Java. They understand database-specific networking protocols and can access the database directly without any additional software. These drivers are also well suited for applet programming, provided that the Java security manager allows TCP/IP connections to the database server.

When you are selecting a driver, you need to balance speed, reliability, and portability. Different applications have different needs. A standalone, GUI-intensive program that always runs on a Windows NT system will benefit from the additional speed of a Type 2, native-code driver. An applet might need to use a Type 3 driver to get around a firewall. A servlet that is deployed across multiple platforms might require the flexibility of a Type 4 driver.

A list of currently available JDBC drivers is available at *http://java.sun.com/products/jdbc/jdbc.drivers.html.*

JDBC URLs

A JDBC driver uses a JDBC URL to identify and connect to a particular database. These URLs are generally of the form:

```
jdbc:driver:databasename
```

The actual standard is quite fluid, however, as different databases require different information to connect successfully. For example, the Oracle JDBC-Thin driver uses a URL of the form:

```
jdbc:oracle:thin:@site:port:database
```

while the JDBC-ODBC Bridge uses:

```
jdbc:odbc:datasource;odbcoptions
```

The only requirement is that a driver be able to recognize its own URLs.

The JDBC-ODBC Bridge

The JDBC-ODBC Bridge ships with JDK 1.1 and the Java 2 SDK for Windows and Solaris systems. The bridge provides an interface between JDBC and database drivers written using Microsoft's Open DataBase Connectivity (ODBC) API. The bridge was originally written to allow the developer community to get up and running quickly with JDBC. Since the bridge makes extensive use of native method calls, it is not recommended for long-term or high-volume deployment.

The bridge is not a required component of the Java SDK, so it is not supported by most web browsers or other runtime environments. Using the bridge in an applet requires a browser with a JVM that supports the JDBC-ODBC Bridge, as well as a properly configured ODBC driver and data source on the client side. Finally, due to different implementations of the native methods interface, the bridge does not work with some development environments, most notably Microsoft Visual J++.

The JDBC URL subprotocol *odbc* has been reserved for the bridge. Like most JDBC URLs, it allows programs to encode extra information about the connection. ODBC URLs are of the form:

```
jdbc:odbc:datasourcename[;attribute-name=attribute-value]*
```

For instance, a JDBC URL pointing to an ODBC data source named `companydb` with the `CacheSize` attribute set to 10 looks like this:

```
jdbc:odbc:companydb;CacheSize=10
```

Connecting to the Database

The `java.sql.Connection` object, which encapsulates a single connection to a particular database, forms the basis of all JDBC data-handling code. An application can maintain multiple connections, up to the limits imposed by the database system itself. A standard small office or web server Oracle installation can support 50 or so connections, while a major corporate database could host several thousand. The `DriverManager.getConnection()` method creates a connection:

```
Connection con = DriverManager.getConnection("url", "user", "password");
```

You pass three arguments to `getConnection()`: a JDBC URL, a database username, and a password. For databases that do not require explicit logins, the user and password strings should be left blank. When the method is called, the `DriverManager` queries each registered driver, asking if it understands the URL. If a driver recognizes the URL, it returns a `Connection` object. Because the `getConnection()` method checks each driver in turn, you should avoid loading more drivers than are necessary for your application.

The `getConnection()` method has two other variants that are less frequently used. One variant takes a single String argument and tries to create a connection to that JDBC URL without a username or password. The other version takes a JDBC URL and a `java.util.Properties` object that contains a set of name/value pairs. You generally need to provide at least *`username=value`* and *`password=value`* pairs.

When a `Connection` has outlived its usefulness, you should be sure to explicitly close it by calling its `close()` method. This frees up any memory being used by the object, and, more importantly, it releases any other database resources the connection may be holding on to. These resources (cursors, handles, and so on) can be much more valuable than a few bytes of memory, as they are often quite limited. This is particularly important in applications such as servlets that might need to create and destroy thousands of JDBC connections between restarts. Because of the way some JDBC drivers are designed, it is not safe to rely on Java's garbage collection to remove unneeded JDBC connections.

The JDBC 2.0 standard extension, discussed later in this chapter, provides a facility for *connection pooling*, whereby an application can maintain several open database connections and spread the load among them. This is often necessary for enterprise-level applications, such as servlets, that may be called upon to perform tens of thousands of database transactions a day.

Statements

Once you have created a Connection, you can begin using it to execute SQL statements. This is usually done via Statement objects. There are actually three kinds of statements in JDBC:

Statement
: Represents a basic SQL statement

PreparedStatement
: Represents a precompiled SQL statement, which can offer improved performance

CallableStatement
: Allows JDBC programs complete access to stored procedures within the database itself

We're just going to discuss the Statement object for now; PreparedStatement and CallableStatement are covered in detail later in this chapter.

To get a Statement object, you call the createStatement() method of a Connection:

```
Statement stmt = con.createStatement();
```

Once you have created a Statement, you use it to execute SQL statements. A statement can either be a query that returns results or an operation that manipulates the database in some way. If you are performing a query, use the executeQuery() method of the Statement object:

```
ResultSet rs = stmt.executeQuery("SELECT * FROM CUSTOMERS");
```

Here we've used executeQuery() to run a SELECT statement. This call returns a ResultSet object that contains the results of the query (we'll take a closer look at ResultSet in the next section).

Statement also provides an executeUpdate() method, for running SQL statements that do not return results, such as the UPDATE and DELETE statements. executeUpdate() returns an integer that indicates the number of rows in the database that were altered.

If you don't know whether a SQL statement is going to return results (such as when the user is entering the statement in a form field), you can use the execute() method of Statement. This method returns true if there is a result associated with the statement. In this case, the ResultSet can be retrieved using the getResultSet() method and the number of updated rows can be retrieved using getUpdateCount():

```
Statement unknownSQL = con.createStatement();
if(unknownSQL.execute(sqlString)) {
  ResultSet rs = unknownSQL.getResultSet();
  // display the results
```

```
    }
    else {
      System.out.println("Rows updated: " + unknownSQL.getUpdateCount());
    }
```

It is important to remember that a Statement object represents a single SQL statement. A call to executeQuery(), executeUpdate(), or execute() implicitly closes any active ResultSet associated with the Statement. In other words, you need to be sure you are done with the results from a query before you execute another query with the same Statement object. If your application needs to execute more than one simultaneous query, you need to use multiple Statement objects. As a general rule, calling the close() method of any JDBC object also closes any dependent objects, such as a Statement generated by a Connection or a ResultSet generated by a Statement, but well-written JDBC code closes everything explicitly.

Multiple Result Sets

It is possible to write a SQL statement that returns more than one ResultSet or update count (exact methods of doing so vary depending on the database). The Statement object supports this functionality via the getMoreResults() method. Calling this method implicitly closes any existing ResultSet and moves to the next set of results for the statement. getMoreResults() returns true if there is another ResultSet available to be retrieved by getResultSet(). However, the method returns false if the next statement is an update, even if there is another set of results waiting farther down the line. To be sure you've processed all the results for a Statement, you need to check that getMoreResults() returns false and that getUpdateCount() returns -1.

We can modify the previous execute() example to handle multiple results:

```
Statement unknownSQL = con.createStatement();
unknownSQL.execute(sqlString);
while (true) {
  rs = unknownSQL.getResultSet();
  if(rs != null)
    // display the results
  else
    // process the update data

 // Advance and quit if done
  if((unknownSQL.getMoreResults() == false) &&
     (unknownSQL.getUpdateCount() == -1))
    break;
}
```

Statements that return multiple results are actually quite rare. They generally arise from stored procedures or SQL implementations that allow multiple statements to be executed in a batch. Under SyBase, for instance, multiple SELECT statements may be separated by newline (\n) characters.

Results

When a SQL query executes, the results form a pseudo-table that contains all rows that fit the query parameters. For instance, here's a textual representation of the results of the query string "SELECT NAME, CUSTOMER_ID, PHONE FROM CUSTOMERS":

```
NAME                             CUSTOMER_ID PHONE
-------------------------------- ----------- -------------------
Jane Markham                               1 617 555-1212
Louis Smith                                2 617 555-1213
Woodrow Lang                               3 508 555-7171
Dr. John Smith                             4 (011) 42 323-1239
```


This kind of textual representation is not very useful for Java programs. Instead, JDBC uses the `java.sql.ResultSet` interface to encapsulate the query results as Java primitive types and objects. You can think of a `ResultSet` as an object that represents an underlying table of query results, where you use method calls to navigate between rows and retrieve particular column values.

A Java program might handle the previous query as follows:

```
Statement stmt = con.createStatement();
ResultSet rs = stmt.executeQuery(
  "SELECT NAME, CUSTOMER_ID, PHONE FROM CUSTOMERS");

while(rs.next()) {
  System.out.print("Customer #" + rs.getString("CUSTOMER_ID"));
  System.out.print(", " + rs.getString("NAME"));
  System.out.println(", is at " + rs.getString("PHONE");
}
rs.close();
stmt.close();
```

Here's the resulting output:

```
Customer #1, Jane Markham, is at 617 555-1212
Customer #2, Louis Smith, is at 617 555-1213
Customer #3, Woodrow Lang, is at 508 555-7171
Customer #4, Dr. John Smith, is at (011) 42 323-1239
```

The code loops through each row of the `ResultSet` using the `next()`method. When you start working with a `ResultSet`, you are positioned before the first row of results. That means you have to call `next()` once just to access the first row. Each time you call `next()`, you move to the next row. If there are no more rows to read, `next()` returns `false`. Note that with the JDBC 1.0 `ResultSet`, you can only move forward through the results and, since there is no way to go back to the beginning, you can read them only once. The JDBC 2.0 `ResultSet`, which we discuss later, overcomes these limitations.

Individual column values are read using the `getString()` method. `getString()` is one of a family of `getXXX()` methods, each of which returns data of a particular type. There are two versions of each `getXXX()` method: one that takes the case-insensitive `String` name of the column to be read (e.g., `"PHONE"`, `"CUSTOMER_ID"`) and one that takes a SQL-style column index. Note that column indexes run from

1 to *n*, unlike Java array indexes, which run from 0 to *n*–1, where *n* is the number of columns.

The most important `getXXX()` method is `getObject()`, which can return any kind of data packaged in an object wrapper. For example, calling`getObject()` on an integer field returns an `Integer` object, while calling it on a date field yields a `java.sql.Date` object. Table 2-1 lists the different `getXXX()` methods, along with the corresponding SQL data type and Java data type. Where the return type for a `getXXX()` method is different from the Java type, the return type is shown in parentheses. Note that the `java.sql.Types` class defines integer constants that represent the standard SQL data types.

Table 2–1: SQL Data Types, Java Types, and Default getXXX() Methods

SQL Data Type	*Java Type*	*GetXXX() Method*
CHAR	String	getString()
VARCHAR	String	getString()
LONGVARCHAR	String	getString()
NUMERIC	java.math.BigDecimal	getBigDecimal()
DECIMAL	java.math.BigDecimal	getBigDecimal()
BIT	Boolean (boolean)	getBoolean()
TINYINT	Integer (byte)	getByte()
SMALLINT	Integer (short)	getShort()
INTEGER	Integer (int)	getInt()
BIGINT	Long (long)	getLong()
REAL	Float (float)	getFloat()
FLOAT	Double (double)	getDouble()
DOUBLE	Double (double)	getDouble()
BINARY	byte[]	getBytes()
VARBINARY	byte[]	getBytes()
LONGVARBINARY	byte[]	getBytes()
DATE	java.sql.Date	getDate()
TIME	java.sql.Time	getTime()
TIMESTAMP	java.sql.Timestamp	getTimestamp()

Note that this table merely lists the default mappings according to the JDBC specification, and some drivers do not follow these mappings exactly. Also, a certain amount of casting is permitted. For instance, the `getString()` method returns a `String` representation of just about any data type.

Handling Nulls

Sometimes database columns contain `null`, or empty, values. However, because of the way certain database APIs are written, it is impossible for JDBC to provide a method to determine before the fact whether or not a column is `null`.* Methods that don't return an object of some sort are especially vulnerable. `getInt()`, for instance, resorts to returning a value of -1. JDBC deals with this problem via the `wasNull()` method, which indicates whether or not the last column read was `null`:

```
int numberInStock = rs.getInt("STOCK");
if(rs.wasNull())
  System.out.println("Result was null");
else
  System.out.println("In Stock: " + numberInStock);
```

Alternately, you can call `getObject()` and test to see if the result is `null`:†

```
Object numberInStock = rs.getObject("STOCK");
if(numberInStock == null)
  System.out.println("Result was null");
```

Large Data Types

You can retrieve large chunks of data from a `ResultSet` as a stream. This can be useful when reading images from a database or loading large documents from a data store, for example. The relevant `ResultSet` methods are `getAsciiStream()`, `getBinaryStream()`, and `getUnicodeStream()`, where each method has column name and column index variants, just like the other `getXXX()` methods. Each of these methods returns an `InputStream`. Here's a code sample that retrieves an image from a `PICTURES` table and writes the image to an `OutputStream` of some kind (this might be a `ServletOutputStream` for a Java servlet that produces a GIF from a database):

```
ResultSet rs =
  stmt.executeQuery("SELECT IMAGE FROM PICTURES WHERE PID = " +
                    req.getParameter("PID"));

if (rs.next()) {
  BufferedInputStream gifData =
    new BufferedInputStream(rs.getBinaryStream("IMAGE"));
  byte[] buf = new byte[4 * 1024];  // 4K buffer
  int len;
  while ((len = gifData.read(buf, 0, buf.length)) != -1) {
    out.write(buf, 0, len);
  }
}
```

The JDBC 2.0 API includes `Blob` and `Clob` objects to handle large data types; we discuss these objects later in this chapter.

---

* The driver can figure this out after reading the object, but since some driver implementations and database connection protocols allow you to reliably read a value from a column only once, implementing an `isNull()` method requires the `ResultSet` to cache the entire row in memory. While many programs do exactly this, it is not appropriate behavior for the lowest-level result handler.

† Some drivers, including early versions of Oracle's JDBC drivers, don't properly support this behavior.

Dates and Times

JDBC defines three classes devoted to storing date and time information: `java.sql.Date`, `java.sql.Time`, and `java.sql.Timestamp`. These correspond to the SQL `DATE`, `TIME`, and `TIMESTAMP` types. The `java.util.Date` class is not suitable for any of them, so JDBC defines a new set of wrapper classes that extend (or limit) the standard `Date` class to fit the JDBC mold.

The SQL `DATE` type contains only a date, so the `java.sql.Date` class contains only a day, month, and year. SQL `TIME` (`java.sql.Time`) includes only a time of day, without date information. SQL `TIMESTAMP` (`java.sql.Timestamp`) includes both, but at nanosecond precision (the standard `Date` class is incapable of handling more than milliseconds).

Since different DBMS packages have different methods of encoding date and time information, JDBC supports the ISO date escape sequences, and individual drivers are required to translate these sequences into whatever form the underlying DBMS requires. The syntax for dates, times, and timestamps is:

```
{d 'yyyy-mm-dd'}
{t 'hh:mm:ss'}
{ts 'yyyy-mm-dd hh:mm:ss.ms.microseconds.ns'}
```

A `TIMESTAMP` only needs to be specified up to seconds; the remaining values are optional. Here is an example that uses a date escape sequence (where `dateSQL` is a `Statement` of some sort):

```
dateSQL.execute("INSERT INTO FRIENDS(BIRTHDAY) VALUES ({d '1978-12-14'})");
```

Handling Errors

Any JDBC object that encounters an error serious enough to halt execution throws a `SQLException`. For example, database connection errors, malformed SQL statements, and insufficient database privileges all throw `SQLException` objects.

The `SQLException` class extends the normal `java.lang.Exception` class and defines an additional method called `getNextException()`. This allows JDBC classes to chain a series of `SQLException` objects together. `SQLException` also defines the `getSQLState()` and `getErrorCode()` methods to provide additional information about an error. The value returned by `getSQLState()` is one of the ANSI-92 SQL state codes; these codes are listed in Chapter 8. `getErrorCode()` returns a vendor-specific error code.

An extremely conscientious application might have a `catch` block that looks something like this:

```
try {
  // Actual database code
}
catch (SQLException e) {
  while(e != null) {
    System.out.println("\nSQL Exception:");
    System.out.println(e.getMessage());
    System.out.println("ANSI-92 SQL State: " + e.getSQLState());
```

```
        System.out.println("Vendor Error Code: " + e.getErrorCode());
        e = e.getNextException();
      }
    }
```

SQL Warnings

JDBC classes also have the option of generating (but not throwing) a SQLWarning exception when something is not quite right, but at the same time, not sufficiently serious to warrant halting the entire program. For example, attempting to set a transaction isolation mode that is not supported by the underlying database might generate a warning rather than an exception. Remember, exactly what qualifies as a warning condition varies by database.

JDBC

SQLWarning encapsulates the same information as SQLException and is used in a similar fashion. However, unlike SQLException objects, which are caught in try/catch blocks, warnings are retrieved using the getWarnings() methods of the Connection, Statement, ResultSet, CallableStatement, and PreparedStatement interfaces. SQLWarning implements the getMessage(), getSQLState(), and getErrorCode() methods in the same manner as SQLException.

If you are debugging an application, and you want to be aware of every little thing that goes wrong within the database, you might use a printWarnings() method like this one:

```
void printWarnings(SQLWarning warn) {
  while (warn != null) {
    System.out.println("\nSQL Warning:");
    System.out.println(warn.getMessage());
    System.out.println("ANSI-92 SQL State: " + warn.getSQLState());
    System.out.println("Vendor Error Code: " + warn.getErrorCode());
    warn = warn.getNextWarning();
  }
}
```

Then you could use the printWarnings() method as follows:

```
// Database initialization code here
ResultSet rs = stmt.executeQuery("SELECT * FROM CUSTOMERS");
printWarnings(stmt.getWarnings());
printWarnings(rs.getWarnings());
// Rest of database code
```

Prepared Statements

The PreparedStatement object is a close relative of the Statement object. Both accomplish roughly the same thing: running SQL statements. PreparedStatement, however, allows you to precompile your SQL and run it repeatedly, adjusting specific parameters as necessary. Since processing SQL strings is a large part of a database's overhead, getting compilation out of the way at the start can significantly improve performance. With proper use, it can also simplify otherwise tedious database tasks.

As with Statement, you create a PreparedStatement object from a Connection object. In this case, though, the SQL is specified at creation instead of execution, using the prepareStatement() method of Connection:

```
PreparedStatement pstmt = con.prepareStatement(
      "INSERT INTO EMPLOYEES (NAME, PHONE) VALUES (?, ?)");
```

This SQL statement inserts a new row into the EMPLOYEES table, setting the NAME and PHONE columns to certain values. Since the whole point of a PreparedStatement is to be able to execute the statement repeatedly, we don't specify values in the call to prepareStatement(), but instead use question marks (?) to indicate parameters for the statement. To actually run the statement, we specify values for the parameters and then execute the statement:

```
pstmt.clearParameters();
pstmt.setString(1, "Jimmy Adelphi");
pstmt.setString(2, "201 555-7823");
pstmt.executeUpdate();
```

Before setting parameters, we clear out any previously specified parameters with the clearParameters() method. Then we can set the value for each parameter (indexed from 1 to the number of question marks) using the setString() method. PreparedStatement defines numerous setXXX() methods for specifying different types of parameters; see the java.sql reference material later in this book for a complete list. Finally, we use the executeUpdate() method to run the SQL.

The setObject() method can insert Java object types into the database, provided that those objects can be converted to standard SQL types. setObject() comes in three flavors:

```
setObject(int parameterIndex, Object x, int targetSqlType, int scale)
setObject(int parameterIndex, Object x, int targetSqlType)
setObject(int parameterIndex, Object x)
```

Calling setObject() with only a parameter index and an Object causes the method to try and automatically map the Object to a standard SQL type (see Table 2-1). Calling setObject() with a type specified allows you to control the mapping. The setXXX() methods work a little differently, in that they attempt to map Java primitive types to JDBC types.

You can use PreparedStatement to insert null values into a database, either by calling the setNull() method or by passing a null value to one of the setXXX() methods that take an Object. In either case, you must specify the target SQL type.

Let's clarify with an example. We want to set the first parameter of a prepared statement to the value of an Integer object, while the second parameter, which is a VARCHAR, should be null. Here's some code that does that:

```
Integer i = new Integer(32);
pstmt.setObject(1, i, Types.INTEGER);
pstmt.setObject(2, null, Types.VARCHAR);
// or pstmt.setNull(2, Types.VARCHAR);
```

Metadata

Most JDBC programs are designed to work with a specific database and particular tables in that database; the program knows exactly what kind of data it is dealing with. Some applications, however, need to dynamically discover information about result set structures or underlying database configurations. This information is called *metadata*, and JDBC provides two classes for dealing with it: `DatabaseMetaData` and `ResultSetMetaData`. If you are developing a JDBC application that will be deployed outside a known environment, you need to be familiar with these interfaces.

JDBC

DatabaseMetaData

You can retrieve general information about the structure of a database with the `java.sql.DatabaseMetaData` interface. By making thorough use of this class, a program can tailor its SQL and use of JDBC on the fly, to accommodate different levels of database and JDBC driver support.

Database metadata is associated with a particular connection, so `DatabaseMetaData` objects are created with the `getMetaData()` method of `Connection`:

```
DatabaseMetaData dbmeta = con.getMetaData();
```

`DatabaseMetaData` provides an overwhelming number of methods you can call to get actual configuration information about the database. Some of these return `String` objects (`getURL()`), some return `boolean` values (`nullsAreSortedHigh()`), and still others return integers (`getMaxConnections()`). The full list is given in Chapter 17, *The java.rmi.server Package*.

A number of other methods return `ResultSet` objects. These methods, such as `getColumns()`, `getTableTypes()`, and `getPrivileges()`, generally encapsulate complex or variable-length information. The `getTables()` method, for instance, returns a `ResultSet` that contains the name of every table in the database and a good deal of extra information besides.

Many of the `DatabaseMetaData` methods take string patterns as arguments, allowing for simple wildcard searching. A percent sign (%) substitutes for any number of characters, and an underscore (_) calls for a single character match. Thus, `%CUSTOMER%` matches `NEW_CUSTOMERS`, `CUSTOMER`, and `CUSTOMERS`, while `CUSTOMER%` matches only `CUSTOMER` and `CUSTOMERS`. All of these patterns are case-sensitive.

Example 2-2 shows a simple program that displays some basic database characteristics, a list of tables, and a list of indexes on each table. The program assumes a JDBC driver with full support for all the `DatabaseMetaData` commands.

Example 2-2: DBViewer Program

```
import java.sql.*;
import java.util.StringTokenizer;

public class DBViewer {

  final static String jdbcURL = "jdbc:odbc:customerdsn";
  final static String jdbcDriver = "sun.jdbc.odbc.JdbcOdbcDriver";
```

Example 2-2: DBViewer Program (continued)

```
  public static void main(java.lang.String[] args) {

    System.out.println("--- Database Viewer ---");

    try {
      Class.forName(jdbcDriver);
      Connection con = DriverManager.getConnection(jdbcURL, "", "");

      DatabaseMetaData dbmd = con.getMetaData();

      System.out.println("Driver Name: " + dbmd.getDriverName());
      System.out.println("Database Product: " + dbmd.getDatabaseProductName());
      System.out.println("SQL Keywords Supported:");
      StringTokenizer st = new StringTokenizer(dbmd.getSQLKeywords(), ",");
      while(st.hasMoreTokens())
        System.out.println(" " + st.nextToken());

      // Get a ResultSet that contains all of the tables in this database
      // We specify a table_type of "TABLE" to prevent seeing system tables,
      // views and so forth
      String[] tableTypes = { "TABLE" };
      ResultSet allTables = dbmd.getTables(null,null,null,tableTypes);
      while(allTables.next()) {
        String table_name = allTables.getString("TABLE_NAME");
        System.out.println("Table Name: " + table_name);
        System.out.println("Table Type: " + allTables.getString("TABLE_TYPE"));
        System.out.println("Indexes: ");

        // Get a list of all the indexes for this table
        ResultSet indexList = dbmd.getIndexInfo(null,null,table_name,false,false);
        while(indexList.next()) {
          System.out.println(" Index Name: "+indexList.getString("INDEX_NAME"));
          System.out.println(" Column Name:"+indexList.getString("COLUMN_NAME"));
        }
        indexList.close();
      }

      allTables.close();
      con.close();
    }
    catch (ClassNotFoundException e) {
      System.out.println("Unable to load database driver class");
    }
    catch (SQLException e) {
      System.out.println("SQL Exception: " + e.getMessage());
    }
  }
}
```

Here's some sample output when this program is run against a Microsoft Access database via the JDBC-ODBC bridge (snipped slightly to prevent several pages of uninteresting text):

```
--- Database Viewer ---
Driver Name: JDBC-ODBC Bridge (odbcjt32.dll)
Database Product: ACCESS
SQL Keywords Supported:
 ALPHANUMERIC
```

```
  AUTOINCREMENT
  BINARY
  BYTE
  FLOAT8
  ...
 Table Name: Customers
 Table Type: TABLE
 Indexes:
  Index Name: PrimaryKey
  Column Name:CustNo
  Index Name: AddressIndex
  Column Name:Address
  ...
```

JDBC

ResultSetMetaData

The `ResultSetMetaData` interface provides information about the structure of a particular `ResultSet`. Data provided by `ResultSetMetaData` includes the number of available columns, the names of those columns, and the kind of data available in each. Example 2-3 shows a short program that displays the contents of a table and shows the data type for each column.

Example 2-3: TableViewer Program

```
import java.sql.*;
import java.util.StringTokenizer;

public class TableViewer {

  final static String jdbcURL = "jdbc:oracle:customerdb";
  final static String jdbcDriver = "oracle.jdbc.OracleDriver";
  final static String table = "CUSTOMERS";

  public static void main(java.lang.String[] args) {

    System.out.println("--- Table Viewer ---");

    try {
      Class.forName(jdbcDriver);
      Connection con = DriverManager.getConnection(jdbcURL, "", "");
      Statement stmt = con.createStatement();
      ResultSet rs = stmt.executeQuery("SELECT * FROM "+ table);

      ResultSetMetaData rsmd = rs.getMetaData();
      int columnCount = rsmd.getColumnCount();
      for(int col = 1; col <= columnCount; col++) {
        System.out.print(rsmd.getColumnLabel(col));
        System.out.print(" (" + rsmd.getColumnTypeName(col)+")");
        if(col < columnCount)
          System.out.print(", ");
      }
      System.out.println();

      while(rs.next()) {
        for(int col = 1; col <= columnCount; col++) {
          System.out.print(rs.getString(col));
          if(col < columnCount)
            System.out.print(", ");
        }
```

Example 2-3: TableViewer Program (continued)

```
        System.out.println();
      }

      rs.close();
      stmt.close();
      con.close();
    }
    catch (ClassNotFoundException e) {
      System.out.println("Unable to load database driver class");
    }
    catch (SQLException e) {
      System.out.println("SQL Exception: " + e.getMessage());
    }
  }
}
```

The key methods used here are `getColumnCount()`, `getColumnLabel()`, and `getColumnTypeName()`. Note that type names returned by `getColumnTypeName()` are database-specific (e.g., Oracle refers to a string value as a `VARCHAR`; Microsoft Access calls it `TEXT`). Here's some sample output for `TableViewer`:

```
--- Table Viewer ---
CustNo (SHORT), CustName (VARCHAR), CustAddress (VARCHAR)
1, Jane Markham, 12 Stevens St
2, Louis Smith, 45 Morrison Lane
3, Woodrow Lang, 4 Times Square
```

Transactions

A *transaction* is a group of several operations that must behave atomically, or as if they are a single, indivisible operation. With regards to databases, transactions allow you to combine one or more database actions into a single atomic unit. If you have an application that needs to execute multiple SQL statements to fulfill one goal (say, an inventory management system that needs to move items from an `INVENTORY` table to a `SHIPPING` table), you probably want to use JDBC's transaction services to accomplish the goal.

Working with a transaction involves the following steps: start the transaction, perform its component operations, and then either commit the transaction if all the component operations succeed or roll it back if one of the operations fails. The ability to roll back a transaction is the key feature. This means that if any one SQL statement fails, the entire operation fails, and it is as though none of the component operations took place. Therefore it is impossible to end up with a situation where, for example, the `INVENTORY` table has been debited, but the `SHIPPING` table has not been credited.

Another issue with transactions and databases concerns when changes to the database become visible to the rest of the system. Transactions can operate at varying levels of isolation from the rest of the database. At the most isolated level, the results of all the component SQL statements become visible to the rest of the system only when the transaction is committed. In other words, nobody sees the reduced inventory before the shipping data is updated.

The `Connection` object in JDBC is responsible for transaction management. With JDBC, you are always using transactions in some form. By default, a new connection starts out in transaction auto-commit mode, which means that every SQL statement is executed as an individual transaction that is immediately committed to the database.

To perform a transaction that uses multiple statements, you have to call the `setAutoCommit()` method with a `false` argument. (You can check the status of auto-commit with the `getAutoCommit()` method.) Now you can execute the SQL statements that comprise your transaction. When you are done, you call the `commit()` method to commit the transaction or the `rollback()` method to undo it. Here's an example:

```
try {
  con.setAutoCommit(false);
  // run some SQL
  stmt.executeUpdate("UPDATE INVENTORY SET ONHAND = 10 WHERE ID = 5");
  stmt.executeUpdate("INSERT INTO SHIPPING (QTY) VALUES (5)");
  con.commit();
}
catch (SQLException e) {
  con.rollback(); //undo the results of the transaction
}
```

When auto-commit is set to `false`, you must remember to call `commit()` (or `rollback()`) at the end of each transaction, or your changes will be lost.

JDBC supports a number of transaction isolation modes that allow you to control how the database deals with transaction conflicts—in other words, who sees what when. JDBC defines five modes, some of which may not be supported by all databases. The default mode varies depending on the underlying database and driver. Higher isolation levels yield poorer performance. Here are the five standard options, which are defined as integer constants in the `Connection` interface:

`TRANSACTION_NONE`
: Transactions are either disabled or not supported.

`TRANSACTION_READ_UNCOMMITTED`
: Minimal transaction support that allows dirty reads. In other words, other transactions can see the results of a transaction's SQL statements before the transaction commits itself. If you roll back your transaction, other transactions may be left with invalid data.

`TRANSACTION_READ_COMMITTED`
: Transactions are prevented from reading rows with uncommitted changes, or in other words, dirty reads are not allowed.

`TRANSACTION_REPEATABLE_READ`
: Protects against repeatable reads as well as dirty reads. Say one transaction reads a row that is subsequently altered (and committed) by another transaction. If the first transaction reads the row again, the first transaction does not get a different value the second time around. The new data is visible to the first transaction only after it calls `commit()` and performs another read.

`TRANSACTION_SERIALIZABLE`
: Provides all the support of `TRANSACTION_REAPEATABLE_READ` and guards against row insertions as well. Say one transaction reads a set of rows, and then another transaction adds a row to the set. If the first transaction reads the set again, it does not see the newly added row. Put another way, this level of isolation forces the database to treat transactions as if they occurred one at a time.

Transaction isolation modes are set by the `setTransactionIsolation()` method. For example:

```
con.setTransactionIsolation(TRANSACTION_READ_COMMITTED);
```

You can use the `DatabaseMetaData` class to determine the transaction support of the underlying database. The most useful methods are `getDefaultTransactionIsolation()`, `supportsTransactions()`, `supportsTransactionIsolationLevel()`, and `supportsDataDefinitionAndDataManipulationTransactions()` (which may very well be the longest method name in the Java API).

An application that uses transactions is a prime candidate for also using a connection pool (available in JDBC 2.0). Since each database transaction requires its own Connection object, an application that performs multiple simultaneous transactions (for instance, spawning threads that perform database updates) needs multiple connections available. Maintaining a pool of connections is much more efficient than creating a new one whenever you need a new transaction.

Stored Procedures

Most RDBMS systems include some sort of internal programming language (e.g., Oracle's PL/SQL). These languages allow database developers to embed procedural application code directly within the database and then call that code from other applications. The advantage of this approach is that the code can be written just once and then used in multiple different applications (even with different platforms and languages). It also allows application code to be divorced from the underlying table structure. If stored procedures handle all of the SQL, and applications just call the procedures, only the stored procedures need to be modified if the table structure is changed later on.

Here is an Oracle PL/SQL stored procedure:*

```
CREATE OR REPLACE PROCEDURE sp_interest
(id IN INTEGER
bal IN OUT FLOAT) IS
BEGIN
SELECT balance
INTO bal
FROM accounts
WHERE account_id = id;

bal := bal + bal * 0.03;
```

* If it looks familiar, that's because it is from George Reese's *Database Programming with JDBC* (O'Reilly).

```
UPDATE accounts
SET balance = bal
WHERE account_id = id;

END;
```

This PL/SQL procedure takes two input values, an account ID and a balance, and returns an updated balance.

The `CallableStatement` interface is the JDBC object that supports stored procedures. The `Connection` class has a `prepareCall()` method that is very similar to the `prepareStatement()` method we used to create a `PreparedStatement`. Because each database has its own syntax for accessing stored procedures, JDBC defines a standardized escape syntax for accessing stored procedures with `CallableStatement`. The syntax for a stored procedure that does not return a result set is:

```
{call procedure_name[(?[,?...])]}
```

The syntax for a stored procedure that returns a result is:

```
{? = call procedure_name[(?[,?...])]}
```

In this syntax, each question mark (?) represents a placeholder for a procedure parameter or a return value. Note that the parameters are optional. The JDBC driver is responsible for translating the escape syntax into the database's own stored procedure syntax.

Here's a code fragment that uses `CallableStatement` to run the `sp_interest` stored procedure:

```
CallableStatment cstmt = con.prepareCall("{call sp_interest(?,?)}");
cstmt.registerOutParameter(2, Types.FLOAT);
cstmt.setInt(1, accountID);
cstmt.setFloat(2, 2343.23);
cstmt.execute();
out.println("New Balance:" + cstmt.getFloat(2));
```

In this example, we first create a `CallableStatement` using the `prepareCall()` method and passing in the appropriate escape syntax for the stored procedure. Since this stored procedure has an output parameter (actually, in this case, an `IN OUT` parameter, which means it also serves as an input parameter), we use the `registerOutParameter()` method to identify that parameter as an output of type `FLOAT`. Note that just as with prepared statements, substituted parameters are numbered from 1 to *n*, left to right. Any time you have an output parameter in a stored procedure, you need to register its type using `registerOutParameter()` before you execute the stored procedure.

Next we set the two input parameters, the account ID and the balance, using the appropriate `setXXX()` methods. Finally, we execute the stored procedure and then use the `getFloat()` method to display the new balance. The `getXXX()` methods of `CallableStatement` are similar to those of the `ResultSet`.

You need to use `CallableStatement` only with stored procedures that have output values, such as the one we just saw. You can use either of the other statement objects to execute stored procedures that take parameters but don't return anything.

Escape Sequences

Escape sequences allow JDBC programs to package certain database commands in a database-independent manner. Since different databases implement different features (especially scalar SQL functions) in different ways, in order to be truly portable, JDBC needs to provide a way to access at least a subset of that functionality in a standard way. We've already seen escape sequences twice: with the various SQL date and time functions, and with the `CallableStatement` object.

A JDBC escape sequences consists of a pair of curly braces, a keyword, and a set of parameters. Thus, `call` is the keyword for stored procedures, while `d`, `t`, and `ts` are keywords for dates and times. One keyword we haven't seen yet is `escape`. This keyword specifies the character that is used to escape wildcard characters in a `LIKE` statement:

```
stmt.executeQuery(
   "SELECT * FROM ApiDocs WHERE Field_Name like 'TRANS\_%' {escape '\'}");
```

Normally, the underscore (_) character is treated as a single-character wildcard, while the percent sign (%) is the multiple-character wildcard. By specifying the backslash (\) as the escape character, we can match on the underscore character itself. Note that the `escape` keyword can also be used outside wildcard searches. For example, SQL string termination characters (such as the single quote) need to be escaped when appearing within strings.

The `fn` keyword allows the use of internal scalar database functions. Scalar functions are a fairly standard component of most database architectures, even though the actual implementations vary. For instance, many databases support the `SOUNDEX(string)` function, which translates a character string into a numerical representation of its sound. Another function, `DIFFERENCE(string1, string2)`, computes the difference between the soundex values for two strings. If the values are close enough, you can assume the two words sound the same ("Beacon" and "Bacon"). If your database supports `DIFFERENCE`, you can use it by executing a SQL statement that looks like this:

```
{fn DIFFERENCE("Beacon", "Bacon")}
```

Available scalar functions differ depending on the database being used. In addition, some drivers, such as Oracle's, do not support the `{fn}` escape mechanism at all.

The last escape keyword is `oj`, which is used for outer joins. The syntax is simply:

```
{oj outer-join}
```

Outer joins are not supported by some databases and are sufficiently complex (and unrelated to the JDBC API per se) as to be beyond the scope of this chapter. For more information, consult the SQL documentation for your database.

Note that when performance is an issue, you can use the `setEscapeProcessing()` method of `Statement` to turn off escape-sequence processing.

JDBC 2.0

The original JDBC API (JDBC 1.0) was first introduced as an add-on package for JDK 1.0, and it became a part of the core Java API with Java 1.1. In May 1998, Sun released the specification for JDBC 2.0. This new version of the API provides support for extended result handling, Java-aware databases, BLOB fields, and other minor improvements. All in all, there are enough new features in JDBC 2.0 to warrant a separate section in this chapter. The new version of the API is backward-compatible; code written for JDBC 1.0 compiles and runs just fine under JDBC 2.0.

The updated API ships with Version 1.2 of the Java 2 platform and is also available for download separately. As of early 1999, there are very few JDBC 2.0-compliant drivers available, although Sun and InterSolv are working towards an updated version of the JDBC-ODBC Bridge.

Results Handling

With JDBC 1.0, the functionality provided by the `ResultSet` interface is rather limited. There is no support for updates of any kind and access to rows is limited to a single, sequential read (i.e., first row, second row, third row, etc., and no going back). JDBC 2.0 supports scrollable and updateable result sets, which allows for advanced record navigation and in-place data manipulation.

With scrolling, you can move forward and backward through the results of a query, rather than just using the `next()` method to move to the next row. In terms of scrolling, there are now three distinct types of `ResultSet` objects: forward-only (as in JDBC 1.0), scroll-insensitive, and scroll-sensitive. A scroll-insensitive result set generally does not reflect changes to the underlying data, while scroll-sensitive ones do. In fact, the number of rows in a sensitive result set does not even need to be fixed.

As of JDBC 2.0, result sets are also updateable. From this perspective, there are two different kinds of result sets: read-only result sets that do not allow changes to the underlying data and updateable result sets that allow such changes, subject to transaction limitations and so on.

To create an updateable, scroll-sensitive result set, we pass two extra arguments to the `createStatement()` method:

```
Statement stmt = con.createStatement(ResultSet.TYPE_SCROLL_SENSITIVE,
                                     ResultSet.CONCUR_UPDATABLE);
```

If you do not pass any arguments to `createStatement()`, you get a forward-only, read-only result set, just as you would using JDBC 1.0. Note that if you specify a scrollable result set (either sensitive or insensitive), you must also specify whether or not the result set is updateable. After you have created a scrollable `ResultSet`, use the methods listed in Table 2-2 to navigate through it. As with JDBC 1.0, when you start working with a `ResultSet`, you are positioned before the first row of results.

Table 2-2: JDBC 2.0 Record Scrolling Functions

Method	*Function*
`first()`	Move to the first record.
`last()`	Move to the last record.
`next()`	Move to the next record.
`previous()`	Move to the previous record.
`beforeFirst()`	Move to immediately before the first record.
`afterLast()`	Move to immediately after the last record.
`absolute(int)`	Move to an absolute row number. Takes a positive or negative argument.
`relative(int)`	Move backward or forward a specified number of rows. Takes a positive or negative argument.

The JDBC 2.0 API also includes a number of methods that tell you where you are in a `ResultSet`. You can think of your position in a `ResultSet` as the location of a cursor in the results. The `isFirst()` and `isLast()` methods return `true` if the cursor is located on the first or last record, respectively. `isAfterLast()` returns `true` if the cursor is after the last row in the result set, while `isBeforeFirst()` returns `true` if the cursor is before the first row.

With an updateable `ResultSet`, you can change data in an existing row, insert an entirely new row, or delete an existing row. To change data in an existing row, you use the new `updateXXX()` methods of `ResultSet`. Let's assume we want to update the `CUSTOMER_ID` field of the first row we retrieve (okay, it's a contrived example, but bear with me):

```
Statement stmt = con.createStatement(ResultSet.TYPE_SCROLL_SENSITIVE,
                                     ResultSet.CONCUR_UPDATABLE);
ResultSet rs = stmt.executeQuery("SELECT NAME, CUSTOMER_ID FROM CUSTOMERS");

rs.first();
rs.updateInt(2, 35243);
rs.updateRow();
```

Here we use `first()` to navigate to the first row of the result set and then call `updateInt()` to change the value of the customer ID column in the result set. After making the change, call `updateRow()` to actually make the change in the database. If you forget to call `updateRow()` before moving to another row in the result set, any changes you made are lost. If you need to make a number of changes in a single row, you can do that with multiple calls to `updateXXX()` methods and then a single call to `updateRow()`. Just be sure you call `updateRow()` before moving on to another row.

The technique for inserting a row is similar to updating data in an existing row, with a few important differences. The first step is to move to what is called the insert row, using the `moveToInsertRow()` method. The *insert row* is a blank row associated with the `ResultSet` that contains all the fields, but no data; you can think of it as a pseudo-row where you can compose a new row. After you have moved to the insert row, use `updateXXX()` methods to load new data into the insert row and then call insertRow() to append the new row to the ResultSet and the underlying database Here's an example that adds a new customer to the database:

```
ResultSet rs = stmt.executeQuery("SELECT NAME, CUSTOMER_ID FROM CUSTOMERS");
rs.moveToInsertRow();
rs.updateString(1, "Tom Flynn");
rs.updateInt(2, 35244);
rs.insertRow();
```


Note that you do not have to supply a value for every column, as long as the columns you omit can accept null values. If you don't specify a value for a column that cannot be null, you'll get a SQLException. After you call insertRow(), you can create another new row, or you can move back to the ResultSet using the various navigation methods shown in Table 2-2. One final navigation method that isn't listed in the table is moveToCurrentRow(). This method takes you back to where you were before you called moveToInsertRow(); it can only be called while you are in the insert row.

Deleting a row from an updateable result set is easy. Simply move to the row you want to delete and call the deleteRow() method. Here's how to delete the last record in a ResultSet:

```
rs.last();
rs.deleteRow();
```

Calling deleteRow() also deletes the row from the underlying database.

Note that not all ResultSet objects are updateable. In general, the query must reference only a single table without any joins. Due to differences in database implementations, there is no single set of requirements for what makes an updateable ResultSet.

As useful as scrollable and updateable result sets are, the JDBC 2.0 specification does not require driver vendors to support them. If you are building middleware or some other kind of system that requires interaction with a wide range of database drivers, you should avoid this functionality for the time being. The extended JDBC 2.0 DatabaseMetaData object can provide information about scrolling and concurrency support.

Batch Updates

The original JDBC standard isn't very efficient when it comes to loading large amounts of information into a database. Even if you use a PreparedStatement, your program still executes a separate query for each piece of data inserted. If your software is inserting 10,000 rows into the database, there may be performance problems.

The new addBatch() method of Statement allows you to lump multiple update statements as a unit and execute them at once. You call addBatch() after you create the statement and before execution:

```
con.setAutoCommit(false);      // If some fail, we want to rollback the rest
Statement stmt = con.createStatement();
```

```
stmt.addBatch("INSERT INTO CUSTOMERS VALUES (1, "J Smith", "617 555-1323");
stmt.addBatch("INSERT INTO CUSTOMERS VALUES (2, "A Smith", "617 555-1132");
stmt.addBatch("INSERT INTO CUSTOMERS VALUES (3, "C Smith", "617 555-1238");
stmt.addBatch("INSERT INTO CUSTOMERS VALUES (4, "K Smith", "617 555-7823");

int[] upCounts = stmt.executeBatch();
con.commit();
```

Notice that we turn transaction auto-commit off before creating the batch. This is because we want to roll back all the SQL statements if one or more of them fail to execute properly. After calling addBatch() multiple times to create our batch, we call executeBatch() to send the SQL statements off to the database to be executed as a batch. Batch statements are executed in the order they are added to the batch. executeBatch() returns an array of update counts, where each value in the array represents the number of rows affected by the corresponding batch statement. If you need to remove the statements from a pending batch job, you can call clearBatch(), as long as you call it before calling executeBatch().

Note that you can use only SQL statements that return an update count (e.g., CREATE, DROP, INSERT, UPDATE, DELETE) as part of a batch. If you include a statement that returns a result set, such as SELECT, you get a SQLException when you execute the batch. If one of the statements in a batch cannot be executed for some reason, executeBatch() throws a BatchUpdateException. This exception, derived from SQLException, contains an array of update counts for the batch statements that executed successfully before the exception was thrown.

The addBatch() method works slightly differently for PreparedStatement and CallableStatement objects. To use batch updating with a PreparedStatement, create the statement normally, set the input parameters, and then call the addBatch() method with no arguments. Repeat as necessary and then call executeBatch() when you're finished:

```
con.setAutoCommit(false);        // If some fail, we want to rollback the rest
PreparedStatement stmt = con.prepareStatement(
                          "INSERT INTO CUSTOMERS VALUES (?,?,?)");

stmt.setInt(1,1);
stmt.setString(2, "J Smith");
stmt.setString(3, "617 555-1323");
stmt.addBatch();

stmt.setInt(1,2);
stmt.setString(2, "A Smith");
stmt.setString(3, "617 555-1132");
stmt.addBatch();

int[] upCounts = stmt.executeBatch();
con.commit();
```

This batch functionality also works with CallableStatement objects for stored procedures. The catch is that each stored procedure must return an update count and may not take any OUT or INOUT parameters.

Java-Aware Databases

Java is object-oriented; relational databases are not. As a result, it's decidedly difficult to shoehorn a Java object into a stubbornly primitive-oriented database table. Luckily, the wind is changing, and newer database systems, including object-oriented database management systems (OODBMS) and Java-relational database management systems,* provide direct support for storing and manipulating objects. Where a regular relational database can store only a limited number of primitive types, a JDBMS system can store entire, arbitrary Java objects.

JDBC

Say we want to store a customized Java `Account` object in the `ACCOUNTS` table in a database. With a standard DBMS and JDBC 1.0, we have to pull each piece of data (account number, account holder, balance, etc.) out of the `Account` object and write it to a complicated database table. To get data out, we reverse the process. Short of serializing the `Account` object and writing it to a binary field (a rather complex operation), we're stuck with this clumsy approach.†

With JDBC 2.0, the `getObject()` method has been extended to support these new Java-aware databases. Provided that the database supports a Java-object type, we can read the `Account` object just like any primitive type:

```
ResultSet rs = stmt.executeQuery("SELECT ACCOUNT FROM ACCOUNTS");
rs.next();
Account a = (Account)rs.getObject(1);
```

To store an object, we use a `PreparedStatement` and the `setObject()` method:

```
Account a = new Account();
// Fill in appropriate fields in Account object

PreparedStatement stmt = con.prepareStatement(
                          "INSERT INTO ACCOUNTS (ACCOUNT) VALUE (?)");
stmt.setObject(1, a);
stmt.executeUpdate();
```

A column that stores a Java object has a type of `Types.JAVA_OBJECT`. The JDBC API does not take any special steps to locate the bytecodes associated with any particular class, so you should make sure that any necessary objects can be instantiated with a call to `Class.forName()`.

BLOBs and CLOBs

Binary large objects (BLOBs) and character large objects (CLOBs) store large amounts of binary or character data. Different database vendors have different names for these fields. For example, on Oracle7 systems, they are known as `LONG` and `LONG RAW` fields, while Microsoft Access refers to them as OLE object fields. Oracle8 introduces actual `BLOB` and `CLOB` types. JDBC 1.0 makes programs retrieve

---

* This is Sun's term. I have yet to see any packages actually marketed as Java-relational databases, but many newer packages, including Personal Oracle, are capable of storing Java classes. A number of these products also use Java as a trigger language, generally in a JDBC structure.

† There is a commercial product, called Java Blend, that automatically handles mapping objects to database records and vice versa. See *http://www.javasoft.com/products/java-blend/index.html* for more information.

BLOB and CLOB data using the getBinaryStream() or getAsciiStream() methods (a third method, getUnicodeStream(), has been deprecated in favor of the new getCharacterStream() method, which returns a Reader).

In JDBC 2.0, the ResultSet interface includes getBlob() and getClob() methods, which return Blob and Clob objects, respectively. The Blob and Clob objects themselves allow access to their data via streams (the getBinaryStream() method of Blob and the getCharacterStream() method of Clob) or direct-read methods (the getBytes() method of Blob and the getSubString() method of Clob).

In addition, you can set Blob and Clob objects when you are working with a PreparedStatement, using the setBlob() and setClob() methods. There are update methods for streams, but no updateBlob() and updateClob()methods. Note that the lifespan of a Blob or Clob object is limited to the transaction that created it.

The JDBC Standard Extension

The javax.sql package is a standard extension for JDBC 2.0 that includes support for a variety of enterprise-development activities. For example, the standard extension lets you use JNDI for connecting to a database, making it possible to obtain the name of a database from a name service, rather than using a hardcoded name. Another key feature is the ability to treat the results of a database query as a JavaBeans component, using the RowSet interface. The PooledConnection interface offers connection-pooling functionality, so that your application can have a cache of open database connections. The standard extension also provides support for distributed transactions by allowing a JDBC driver to utilize the standard two-phase commit protocol used by the Java Transaction API (JTA), which facilitates the use of JDBC in Enterprise JavaBeans components.

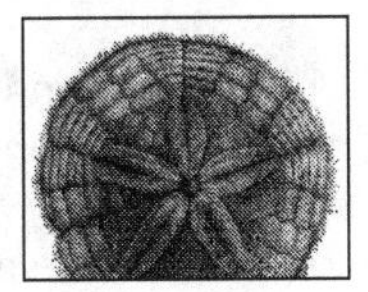

CHAPTER 3

Remote Method Invocation

RMI

This chapter examines the Java Remote Method Invocation (RMI) API—Java's native scheme for creating and using remote objects. Java RMI provides the following elements:

- Remote object implementations
- Client interfaces, or stubs, to remote objects
- A remote object registry for finding objects on the network
- A network protocol for communication between remote objects and their client
- A facility for automatically creating (activating) remote objects on-demand

Each of these elements (except the last one) has a Java interface defined for it within the `java.rmi` package and its subpackages, which comprise the RMI API. Using these interfaces, you can develop remote objects and the clients that use them to create a distributed application that resides on hosts across the network.

Introduction to RMI

RMI is the distributed object system that is built into the core Java environment. You can think of RMI as a built-in facility for Java that allows you to interact with objects that are actually running in Java virtual machines on remote hosts on the network. With RMI (and other distributed object APIs we discuss in this book), you can get a reference to an object that "lives" in a remote process and invoke methods on it as if it were a local object running within the same virtual machine as your code (hence the name, "Remote Method Invocation API").

RMI was added to the core Java API in Version 1.1 of the JDK (and enhanced for Version 1.2 of the Java 2 platform), in recognition of the critical need for support for distributed objects in distributed-application development. Prior to RMI, writing a distributed application involved basic socket programming, where a "raw" communication channel was used to pass messages and data between two remote processes. Now, with RMI and distributed objects, you can "export" an object as a remote object, so that other remote processes/agents can access it directly as a Java object. So, instead of defining a low-level message protocol and data transmission format between processes in your distributed application, you use Java interfaces as the "protocol" and the exported method arguments become the data transmission format. The distributed object system (RMI in this case) handles all the underlying networking needed to make your remote method calls work.

Java RMI is a Java-only distributed object scheme; the objects in an RMI-based distributed application have to be implemented in Java. Some other distributed object schemes, most notably CORBA, are language-independent, which means that the objects can be implemented in any language that has a defined binding. With CORBA, for example, bindings exist for C, C++, Java, Smalltalk, and Ada, among other languages.

The advantages of RMI primarily revolve around the fact that it is "Java-native." Since RMI is part of the core Java API and is built to work directly with Java objects within the Java VM, the integration of its remote object facilities into a Java application is almost seamless. You really can use RMI-enabled objects as if they live in the local Java environment. And since Java RMI is built on the assumption that both the client and server are Java objects, RMI can extend the internal garbage-collection mechanisms of the standard Java VM to provide distributed garbage collection of remotely exported objects.

If you have a distributed application with heterogeneous components, some of which are written in Java and some that aren't, you have a few choices. You can use RMI, wrapping the non-Java code with RMI-enabled Java objects using the Java Native Interface (JNI). At the end of this chapter, we discuss this first option in some detail, to give you a feeling for where it could be useful and where it wouldn't. Another option is to use another object distribution scheme, such as CORBA, that supports language-independent object interfaces. Chapter 4, *Java IDL*, covers the Java interface to CORBA that is included in the Java 2 SDK. A third option involves the new RMI/IIOP functionality that allows RMI objects to communicate directly with remote CORBA objects over IIOP. We also discuss this option in some detail at the end of this chapter.

RMI in Action

Before we start examining the details of using RMI, let's look at a simple RMI remote object at work. We can create an `Account` object that represents some kind of bank account and then use RMI to export it as a remote object so that remote clients (e.g., ATMs, personal finance software running on a PC) can access it and carry out transactions.

The first step is to define the interface for our remote object. Example 3-1 shows the `Account` interface. You can tell that it's an RMI object because it extends the `java.rmi.Remote` interface. Another signal that this is meant for remote access is that each method can throw a `java.rmi.RemoteException`. The `Account` interface includes methods to get the account name and balance and to make deposits, withdrawals, and transfers.

Example 3-1: A Remote Account Interface

```
import java.rmi.Remote;
import java.rmi.RemoteException;
import java.util.List;

public interface Account extends Remote {
  public String getName() throws RemoteException;
  public float getBalance() throws RemoteException;
  public void withdraw(float amt) throws RemoteException;
  public void deposit(float amt) throws RemoteException;
  public void transfer(float amt, Account src) throws RemoteException;
  public void transfer(List amts, List srcs) throws RemoteException;
}
```

The next step is to create an implementation of this interface, which leads to the `AccountImpl` class shown in Example 3-2. This class implements all the methods listed in the `Account` interface and adds a constructor that takes the name of the new account to be created. Notice that the `AccountImpl` class implements the `Account` interface, but it also extends the `java.rmi.UnicastRemoteObject` class. This RMI class provides some of the basic remote functionality for server objects.

Example 3-2: Implementation of the Remote Account Interface

```
import java.rmi.server.UnicastRemoteObject;
import java.rmi.RemoteException;
import java.util.List;
import java.util.ListIterator;

public class AccountImpl extends UnicastRemoteObject implements Account {
  private float mBalance = 0;
  private String mName = "";

  // Create a new account with the given name
  public AccountImpl(String name) throws RemoteException {
    mName = name;
  }

  public String getName() throws RemoteException {
    return mName;
  }
  public float getBalance() throws RemoteException {
    return mBalance;
  }

  // Withdraw some funds
  public void withdraw(float amt) throws RemoteException {
    mBalance -= amt;
    // Make sure balance never drops below zero
    mBalance = Math.max(mBalance, 0);
  }

  // Deposit some funds
  public void deposit(float amt) throws RemoteException {
    mBalance += amt;
  }
```

Example 3-2: Implementation of the Remote Account Interface (continued)

```
  // Move some funds from another (remote) account into this one
  public void transfer(float amt, Account src) throws RemoteException {
    src.withdraw(amt);
    this.deposit(amt);
  }

  // Make several transfers from other (remote) accounts into this one
  public void transfer(List amts, List srcs) throws RemoteException {
    ListIterator amtCurs = amts.listIterator();
    ListIterator srcCurs = srcs.listIterator();
    // Iterate through the accounts and the amounts to be transferred from
    // each (assumes amounts are given as Float objects)
    while (amtCurs.hasNext() && srcCurs.hasNext()) {
      Float amt = (Float)amtCurs.next();
      Account src = (Account)srcCurs.next();
      this.transfer(amt.floatValue(), src);
    }
  }
}
```

Once the remote interface and an implementation of it are complete, you need to compile both Java files with your favorite Java compiler. After this is done, you use the RMI stub/skeleton compiler to generate a client stub and a server skeleton for the `AccountImpl` object. The stub and skeleton handle the communication between the client application and the server object. With Sun's Java SDK, the RMI compiler is called *rmic*, and you can invoke it for this example like so:

```
% rmic -d /home/classes AccountImpl
```

The stub and skeleton classes are generated and stored in the directory given by the `-d` option (*/home/classes*, in this case). This example assumes that the `AccountImpl` class is already in your `CLASSPATH` before you run the RMI compiler.

There's just one more thing we need to do before we can actually use our remote object: register it with an RMI registry, so that remote clients can find it on the network. The utility class that follows, `RegAccount`, does this by creating an `AccountImpl` object and then binding it to a name in the local registry using the `java.rmi.Naming` interface. After it's done registering the object, the class goes into a `wait()`, which allows remote clients to connect to the remote object:

```
import java.rmi.Naming;

public class RegAccount {
  public static void main(String argv[]) {
    try {
      // Make an Account with a given name
      AccountImpl acct = new AccountImpl("JimF");

      // Register it with the local naming registry
      Naming.rebind("JimF", acct);
      System.out.println("Registered account.");
    }
    catch (Exception e) {
      e.printStackTrace();
```

```
            }
        }
    }
```

After you compile the RegAccount class, you can run its main() method to register an Account with the local RMI registry. First, however, you need to start the registry. With Sun's Java SDK, the registry can be started using the *rmiregistry* utility. On a Unix machine, this can be done like so:

```
objhost% rmiregistry &
```

Once the registry is started, you can invoke the main() method on the RegAccount class simply by running it:

```
objhost% java RegAccount
Registered account.
```

Now we have a remote Account object that is ready and waiting for a client to access it and call its methods. The following client code does just this, by first looking up the remote Account object using the java.rmi.Naming interface (and assuming that the Account object was registered on a machine named *objhost.org*), and then calling the deposit method on the Account object:

```
import java.rmi.Naming;

public class AccountClient {
  public static void main(String argv[]) {
    try {
      // Lookup account object
      Account jimAcct = (Account)Naming.lookup("rmi://objhost.org/JimF");

      // Make deposit
      jimAcct.deposit(12000);

      // Report results and balance.
      System.out.println("Deposited 12,000 into account owned by " +
                         jimAcct.getName());
      System.out.println("Balance now totals: " + jimAcct.getBalance());
    }
    catch (Exception e) {
      System.out.println("Error while looking up account:");
      e.printStackTrace();
    }
  }
}
```

The first time you run this client, here's what you'd do:

```
% java AccountClient
Deposited 12,000 into account owned by JimF
Balance now totals: 12000.0
```

For the sake of this example, I've assumed that the client process is running on a machine with all the necessary classes available locally (the Account interface and the stub and skeleton classes generated from the AccountImpl implementation). Later in the chapter, we'll see how to deal with loading these classes remotely when the client doesn't have them locally.

RMI Architecture

Now that we've seen a complete example of an RMI object in action, let's look at what makes remote objects work, starting with an overview of the underlying RMI architecture. There are three layers that comprise the basic remote-object communication facilities in RMI:

- The *stub/skeleton* layer, which provides the interface that client and server application objects use to interact with each other.
- The *remote reference* layer, which is the middleware between the stub/skeleton layer and the underlying transport protocol. This layer handles the creation and management of remote object references.
- The *transport protocol* layer, which is the binary data protocol that sends remote object requests over the wire.

These layers interact with each other as shown in Figure 3-1. In this figure, the server is the application that provides remotely accessible objects, while the client is any remote application that communicates with these server objects.

In a distributed object system, the distinctions between clients and servers can get pretty blurry at times. Consider the case where one process registers a remote-enabled object with the RMI naming service, and a number of remote processes are accessing it. We might be tempted to call the first process the server and the other processes the clients. But what if one of the clients calls a method on the remote object, passing a reference to an RMI object that's local to the client. Now the server has a reference to and is using an object exported from the client, which turns the tables somewhat. The "server" is really the server for one object and the client of another object, and the "client" is a client and a server, too. For the sake of discussion, I'll refer to a process in a distributed application as a server or client if its role in the overall system is generally limited to one or the other. In peer-to-peer systems, where there is no clear client or server, I'll refer to elements of the system in terms of application-specific roles (e.g., chat participant, chat facilitator).

As you can see in Figure 3-1, a client makes a request of a remote object using a client-side stub; the server object receives this request from a server-side object skeleton. A client initiates a remote method invocation by calling a method on a stub object. The stub maintains an internal reference to the remote object it represents and forwards the method invocation request through the remote reference layer by *marshalling* the method arguments into serialized form and asking the remote reference layer to forward the method request and arguments to the appropriate remote object. Marshalling involves converting local objects into portable form so that they can be transmitted to a remote process. Each object is checked as it is marshaled, to determine whether it implements the `java.rmi.Remote` interface. If it does, its remote reference is used as its marshaled data. If it isn't a `Remote` object, the argument is serialized into bytes that are sent to the remote host and reconstituted into a copy of the local object. If the argument is neither `Remote` nor `Serializable`, the stub throws a `java.rmi.MarshalException` back to the client.

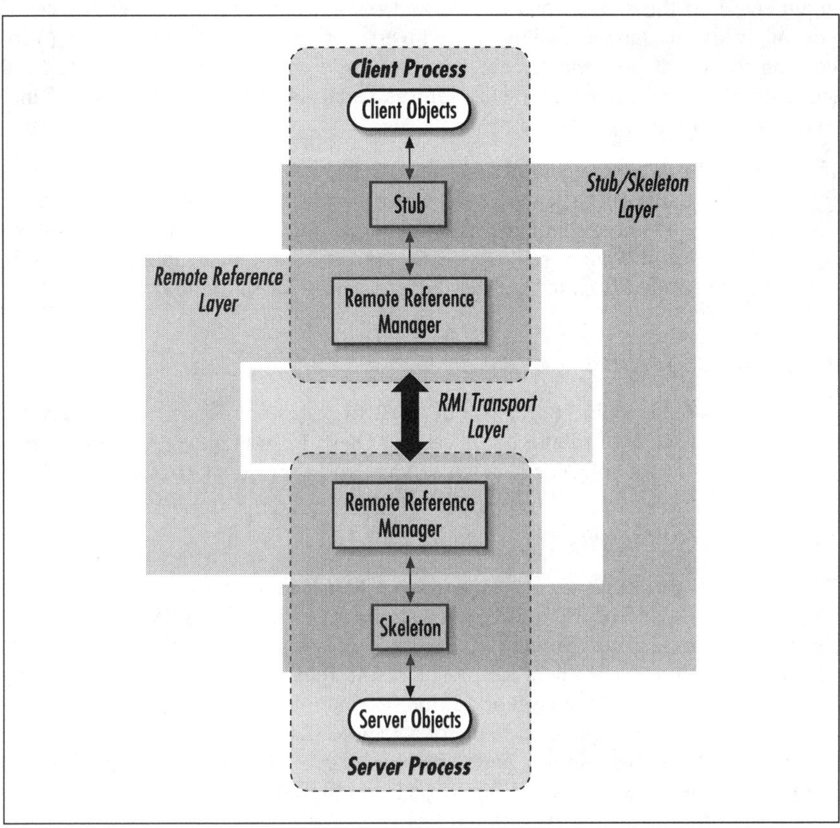

Figure 3-1: The RMI runtime architecture

If the marshalling of method arguments succeeds, the client-side remote reference layer receives the remote reference and marshaled arguments from the stub. This layer converts the client request into low-level RMI transport requests according to the type of remote object communication being used. In RMI, remote objects can (potentially) run under several different communication styles, such as point-to-point object references, replicated objects, or multicast objects. The remote reference layer is responsible for knowing which communication style is in effect for a given remote object and generating the corresponding transport-level requests. In the current version of RMI (Version 1.2 of Java 2), the only communication style provided out of the box is point-to-point object references, so this is the only style we'll discuss in this chapter. For a point-to-point communication, the remote reference layer constructs a single network-level request and sends it over the wire to the sole remote object that corresponds to the remote reference passed along with the request.

On the server, the server-side remote reference layer receives the transport-level request and converts it into a request for the server skeleton that matches the referenced object. The skeleton converts the remote request into the appropriate method call on the actual server object, which involves *unmarshalling* the method arguments into the server environment and passing them to the server object. As you might expect, unmarshalling is the inverse procedure to the marshalling process on the client. Arguments sent as remote references are converted into local stubs on the server, and arguments sent as serialized objects are converted into local copies of the originals.

If the method call generates a return value or an exception, the skeleton marshals the object for transport back to the client and forwards it through the server reference layer. This result is sent back using the appropriate transport protocol, where it passes through the client reference layer and stub, is unmarshaled by the stub, and is finally handed back to the client thread that invoked the remote method.

RMI Object Services

On top of its remote object architecture, RMI provides some basic object services you can use in your distributed application. These include an object naming/registry service, a remote object activation service, and distributed garbage collection.

Naming/registry service

When a server process wants to export some RMI-based service to clients, it does so by registering one or more RMI-enabled objects with its local RMI registry (represented by the `Registry` interface). Each object is registered with a name clients can use to reference it. A client can obtain a stub reference to the remote object by asking for the object by name through the `Naming` interface. The `Naming.lookup()` method takes the fully qualified name of a remote object and locates the object on the network. The object's fully qualified name is in a URL-like syntax that includes the name of the object's host and the object's registered name.

It's important to note that, although the `Naming` interface is a default naming service provided with RMI, the RMI registry can be tied into other naming services by vendors. Sun has provided a binding to the RMI registry through the Java Naming and Directory Interface (JNDI), for example. See Chapter 6, *JNDI*, for more details on how JNDI can be used to look up objects (remote or otherwise).

Once the `lookup()` method locates the object's host, it consults the RMI registry on that host and asks for the object by name. If the registry finds the object, it generates a remote reference to the object and delivers it to the client process, where it is converted into a stub reference that is returned to the caller. Once the client has a remote reference to the server object, communication between the client and the server commences as described earlier. We'll talk in more detail about the `Naming` and `Registry` interfaces later in this chapter.

Object activation service

The remote object activation service is new to RMI as of Version 1.2 of the Java 2 platform. It provides a way for server objects to be started on an as-needed basis. Without remote activation, a server object has to be registered with the RMI registry service from within a running Java virtual machine. A remote object registered this way is only available during the lifetime of the Java VM that registered it. If the server VM halts or crashes for some reason, the server object becomes unavailable and any existing client references to the object become invalid. Any further attempts by clients to call methods through these now-invalid references result in RMI exceptions being thrown back to the client.

The RMI activation service provides a way for a server object to be activated automatically when a client requests it. This involves creating the server object within a new or existing virtual machine and obtaining a reference to this newly created object for the client that caused the activation. A server object that wants to be activated automatically needs to register an activation method with the RMI activation daemon running on its host. We'll discuss the RMI activation service in more detail later in the chapter.

Distributed garbage collection

The last of the remote object services, distributed garbage collection, is a fairly automatic process that you as an application developer should never have to worry about. Every server that contains RMI-exported objects automatically maintains a list of remote references to the objects it serves. Each client that requests and receives a reference to a remote object, either explicitly through the registry/naming service or implicitly as the result of a remote method call, is issued this remote object reference through the remote reference layer of the object's host process. The reference layer automatically keeps a record of this reference in the form of an expirable "lease" on the object. When the client is done with the reference and allows the remote stub to go out of scope, or when the lease on the object expires, the reference layer on the host automatically deletes the record of the remote reference and notifies the client's reference layer that this remote reference has expired. The concept of expirable leases, as opposed to strict on/off references, is used to deal with situations where a client-side failure or a network failure keeps the client from notifying the server that it is done with its reference to an object.

When an object has no further remote references recorded in the remote reference layer, it becomes a candidate for garbage collection. If there are also no further local references to the object (this reference list is kept by the Java VM itself as part of its normal garbage-collection algorithm), the object is marked as garbage and picked up by the next run of the system garbage collector.

Defining Remote Objects

Now that you have a basic idea of how Java RMI works, we can explore the details of creating and using distributed objects with RMI. As I mentioned earlier, defining a remote RMI object involves specifying a remote interface for the object, then providing a class that implements this interface. The remote interface and implementation class are then used by RMI to generate a client stub and server skeleton for your remote object. The communication between local objects and remote objects is handled using these client stubs and server skeletons. The relationships among stubs, skeletons, and the objects that use them are shown in Figure 3-2.

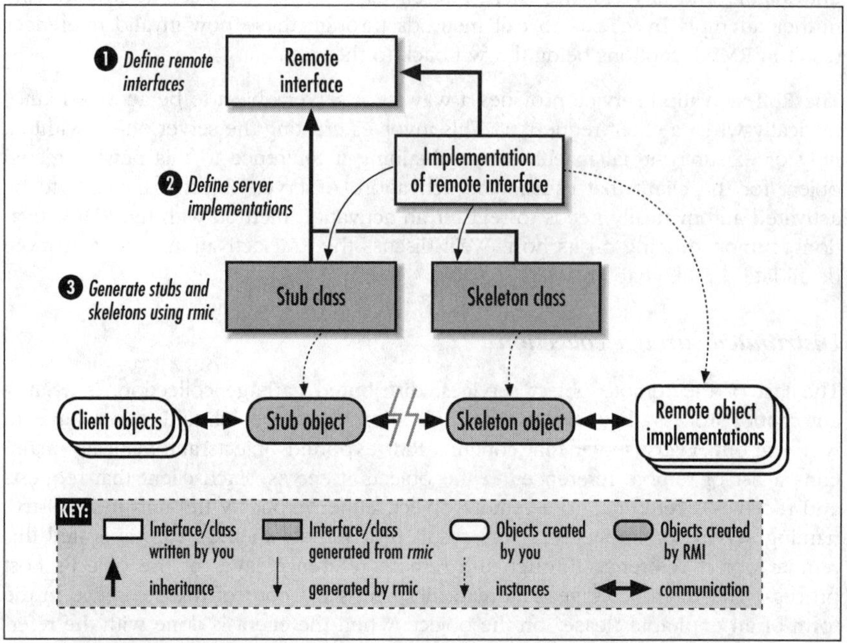

Figure 3-2: Relationships among remote object, stub, and skeleton classes

When a client gets a reference to a remote object (details on how this reference is obtained come later) and then calls methods on this object reference, there needs to be a way for the method request to get transmitted back to the actual object on the remote server and for the results of the method call to get transmitted back to the client. This is what the generated stub and skeleton classes are for. They act as the communication link between the client and your exported remote object, making it seem to the client that the object actually exists within its Java VM.

The RMI compiler (*rmic*) automatically generates these stub and skeleton classes for you. Based on the remote interface and implementation class you provide, *rmic* generates stub and skeleton classes that implement the remote interface and act as go-betweens for the client application and the actual server object. For the client stub class, the compiler generates an implementation of each remote method that simply packages up (marshals) the method arguments and transmits them to the server. For the server skeleton class, the RMI compiler generates another set of implementations of the remote methods, but these are designed to receive the method arguments from the remote method call, unpackage them, and make the corresponding method call on the object implementation. Whatever the method call generates (return data or an exception), the results are packaged and transmitted back to the remote client. The client stub method (which is still executing at this point) unpackages the results and delivers them to the client as the result of its remote method call.

So, the first step in creating your remote objects is to define the remote interfaces for the types of objects you need to use in a distributed object context. This isn't much different from defining the public interfaces in a nondistributed application, with the following exceptions:

- Every object you want to distribute using RMI has to directly or indirectly implement an interface that extends the `java.rmi.Remote` interface.
- Every method in the remote interface has to declare that it throws a `java.rmi.RemoteException` or one of the parent classes of `RemoteException`.*

RMI imposes the first requirement to allow it to differentiate quickly between objects that are enabled for remote distribution and those that are not. As we've already seen, during a remote method invocation, the RMI runtime system needs to be able to determine whether each argument to the remote method is a `Remote` object or not. The `Remote` interface, which is simply a tag interface that marks remote objects, makes it easy to perform this check.

The second requirement is needed to deal with errors that can happen during a remote session. When a client makes a method call on a remote object, any number of errors can occur, preventing the remote method call from completing. These include client-side errors (e.g., an argument can't be marshaled), errors during the transport of data between client and server (e.g., the network connection is dropped), and errors on the server side (e.g., the method throws a local exception that needs to be sent back to the remote caller). The `RemoteException` class is used by RMI as a base exception class for any of the different types of problems that might occur during a remote method call. Any method you declare in a `Remote` interface is assumed to be remotely callable, so every method has to declare that it might throw a `RemoteException`, or one of its parent interfaces.

Example 3-3 shows a simple remote interface that declares two methods: `doThis()` and `doThat()`. These methods could do anything that we want; in our `Account` example, we had remote methods to deposit, withdraw, and transfer funds. Each method takes a single `String` argument and returns a `String` result. Since we want to use this interface in an RMI setting, we've declared that the interface extends the `Remote` interface. In addition, each method is declared as throwing a `RemoteException`.

Example 3-3: The ThisOrThatServer Interface

```
import java.rmi.Remote;
import java.rmi.RemoteException;

public interface ThisOrThatServer extends Remote {
  public String doThis(String todo) throws RemoteException;
  public String doThat(String todo) throws RemoteException;
}
```

With the remote interface defined, the next thing we need to do is write a class that implements the interface. Example 3-4 shows the `ThisOrThatServerImpl` class, which implements the `ThisOrThatServer` interface.

* Note that prior to Java 1.2, the RMI specification required that every method on a remote interface had to throw `RemoteException` specifically. In Java 1.2, this has been loosened to allow any superclass of `RemoteException`. The reason for this change is to make it easier to define generic interfaces that support both local and remote objects.

Example 3-4: Implementation of the ThisOrThatServer

```
import java.rmi.server.UnicastRemoteObject;
import java.rmi.RemoteException;

public class ThisOrThatServerImpl
  extends UnicastRemoteObject implements ThisOrThatServer {

  public ThisOrThatServerImpl() throws RemoteException {}

  // Remotely accessible methods
  public String doThis(String todo) throws RemoteException {
    return doSomething("this", todo);
  }

  public String doThat(String todo) throws RemoteException {
    return doSomething("that", todo);
  }

  // Non-remote methods
  private String doSomething(String what, String todo) {
    String result = "Did " + what + " to " + todo + ".";
    return result;
  }
}
```

This class has implementations of the `doThis()` and `doThat()` methods declared in the `ThisOrThatServer` interface; it also has a nonremote method, `doSomething()`, that is used to implement the two remote methods. Notice that the `doSomething()` method doesn't have to be declared as throwing a `RemoteException`, since it isn't a remotely callable method. Only the methods declared in the remote interface can be invoked remotely. Any other methods you include in your implementation class are considered nonremote (i.e., they are only callable from within the local Java virtual machine where the object exists).

Key RMI Classes for Remote Object Implementations

You probably noticed that our `ThisOrThatServerImpl` class also extends the `UnicastRemoteObject` class. This is a class in the `java.rmi.server` package that extends `java.rmi.server.RemoteServer`, which itself extends `java.rmi.server.RemoteObject`, the base class for all RMI remote objects. There are four key classes related to writing server object implementations:

`RemoteObject`

: `RemoteObject` implements both the `Remote` and `Serializable` interfaces. Although the `RemoteObject` class is in the `java.rmi.server` package, it is used by both the client and server portions of a remote object reference. Both client stubs and server implementations are subclassed (directly or indirectly) from `RemoteObject`. A `RemoteObject` contains the remote reference for a particular remote object.

  `RemoteObject` is an abstract class that reimplements the `equals()`, `hashCode()`, and `toString()` methods inherited from `Object` in a way that makes sense and is practical for remote objects. The `equals()` method, for example, is implemented to return `true` if the internal remote references of the two

`RemoteObject` objects are equal, (i.e., if they both point to the same server object).

`RemoteServer`
: `RemoteServer` is an abstract class that extends `RemoteObject`. It defines a set of static methods that are useful for implementing server objects in RMI, and it acts as a base class for classes that define various semantics for remote objects. In principle, a remote object can behave according to a simple point-to-point reference scheme; it can have replicated copies of itself scattered across the network that need to be kept synchronized; or any number of other scenarios. JDK 1.1 supported only point-to-point, nonpersistent remote references with the `UnicastRemoteObject` class. The Java 2 SDK 1.2 has introduced the RMI activation system, so it provides another subclass of `RemoteServer`, `Activatable`.

`UnicastRemoteObject`
: This is a concrete subclass of `RemoteServer` that implements point-to-point remote references over TCP/IP networks. These references are nonpersistent: remote references to a server object are only valid during the lifetime of the server object. Before the server object is created (inside a virtual machine running on the host) or after the object has been destroyed, a client can't obtain remote references to the object. In addition, if the virtual machine containing the object exits (intentionally or otherwise), any existing remote references on clients become invalid and generate `RemoteException` objects if used.

`Activatable`
: This concrete subclass of `RemoteServer` is part of the new RMI object activation facility in Java 1.2 and can be found in the `java.rmi.activation` package. It implements a server object that supports persistent remote references. If a remote method request is received on the server host for an `Activatable` object, and the target object is not executing at the time, the object can be started automatically by the RMI activation daemon.

RMI

Creating the Stubs and Skeletons

After you define the remote Java interface and implementation class, you compile them into Java bytecodes using a standard Java compiler. Then you use the RMI stub/skeleton compiler, *rmic*, to generate the stub and skeleton interfaces that are used at either end of the RMI communication link, as was shown in Figure 3-1. In its simplest form, you can run *rmic* with the fully qualified classname of your implementation class as the only argument. For example, once we've compiled the `ThisOrThatServer` and `ThisOrThatServerImpl` classes, we can generate the stubs and skeletons for the remote `ThisOrThatServer` object with the following command (Unix version):

```
% rmic ThisOrThatServerImpl
```

If the RMI compiler is successful, this command generates the stub and skeleton classes, `ThisOrThatServerImpl_Stub` and `ThisOrThatServerImpl_Skel`, in the current directory. The *rmic* compiler has additional arguments that let you specify where the generated classes should be stored, whether to print warnings, etc. For example, if you want the stub and skeleton classes to reside in the directory */usr/local/classes*, you can run the command using the `-d` option:

```
% rmic -d /usr/local/classes ThisOrThatServerImpl
```

This command generates the stub and skeleton classes in the specified directory. A full description of the *rmic* utility and its options is given in Chapter 9, *RMI Tools*.

Accessing Remote Objects as a Client

Now that we've defined a remote object interface and its server implementation and generated the stub and skeleton classes that RMI uses to establish the link between the server object and the remote client, it's time to look at how you make your remote objects available to remote clients.

The Registry and Naming Services

The first remote object reference in an RMI distributed application is typically obtained through the RMI registry facility and the `Naming` interface. Every host that wants to export remote references to local Java objects must be running an RMI registry daemon of some kind. A registry daemon listens (on a particular port) for requests from remote clients for references to objects served on that host. The standard Sun Java SDK distribution provides an RMI registry daemon, *rmiregistry*. This utility simply creates a `Registry` object that listens to a specified port and then goes into a wait loop, waiting for local processes to register objects with it or for clients to connect and look up RMI objects in its registry. You start the registry daemon by running the *rmiregistry* command, with an optional argument that specifies a port to listen to:

```
objhost% rmiregistry 5000 &
```

Without the port argument, the RMI registry daemon listens on port 1099. Typically, you run the registry daemon in the background (i.e., put an `&` at the end of the command on a Unix system or run `start rmiregistry [`*`port`*`]` in a DOS window on a Windows system) or run it as a service at startup.

Once the RMI registry is running on a host, you can register remote objects with it using one of these classes: the `java.rmi.registry.Registry` interface, the `java.rmi.registry.LocateRegistry` class, or the `java.rmi.Naming` class.

A `Registry` object represents an interface to a local or remote RMI object registry. The `bind()` and `rebind()` methods can register an object with a name in the local registry, where the name for an object can be any unique string. If you try to `bind()` an object to a name that has already been used, the registry throws an `AlreadyBoundException`. If you think that an object may already be bound to the name you want to register, use the `rebind()` method instead. You can remove an object binding using the `unbind()` method. Note that these three methods (`bind()`, `rebind()`, and `unbind()`) can be called only by clients running on the same host as the registry. If a remote client attempts to call these methods, the client receives a `java.rmi.AccessException`. You can locate a particular object in the registry using the `lookup()` method, while `list()` returns the names of all the objects registered with the local registry. Note that only Remote objects can be bound to names in the Registry. Remote objects are capable of supporting remote references. Standard Java classes are not, so they can't be exported to remote clients through the Registry.

The LocateRegistry class provides a set of static methods a client can use to get references to local and remote registries, in the form of Registry objects. There are four versions of the static getRegistry() method, so that you can get a reference to either a local registry or a remote registry running on a particular host, listening to either the default port (1099) or a specified port. There's also a static createRegistry() method that takes a port number as an argument. This method starts a registry running within the current Java VM on the given local port and returns the Registry object it creates.

Using the LocateRegistry and Registry interfaces, we can register one of our ThisOrThatServerImpl remote objects on the local host with the following code:

```
ThisOrThatServerImpl server = new ThisOrThatServerImpl();
Registry localRegistry = LocateRegistry.getRegistry();
try {
  localRegistry.bind("TTServer", server);
}
catch (RemoteException re) { // Handle failed remote operation }
catch (AlreadyBoundException abe) { // Already one there }
catch (AccessException ae) { // Shouldn't happen, but... }
```

If this operation is successful (i.e., it doesn't raise any exceptions), the local registry has a ThisOrThatServerImpl remote object registered under the name "TTServer." Remote clients can now look up the object using a combination of the LocateRegistry and Registry interfaces, or take the simpler approach and use the Naming class.

The Naming class lets a client look up local and remote objects using a URL-like naming syntax. The URL of a registered RMI remote object is typically in the format shown in Figure 3-3. Notice that the only required element of the URL is the actual object name. The protocol defaults to *rmi:*, the hostname defaults to the local host, and the port number defaults to 1099. Note that the default Naming class provided with Sun's Java SDK accepts only the *rmi:* protocol on object URLs. If you attempt to use any other protocol, a java.net.MalformedURLException is thrown by the lookup() method.

If we have a client running on a remote host that wants to look up the ThisOrThatServerImpl we registered, and the ThisOrThatServerImpl object is running on a host named *rmiremote.farley.org*, the client can get a remote reference to the object with one line of code:

```
ThisOrThatServer rmtServer =
  (ThisOrThatServer)Naming.lookup("rmi://rmiremote.farley.org/TTServer");
```

If we have a client running on the same host as the ThisOrThatServerImpl object, the remote reference can be retrieved using the degenerate URL:

```
ThisOrThatServer rmtServer = (ThisOrThatServer)Naming.lookup("TTServer");
```

Alternately, you can use the LocateRegistry and Registry interfaces to look up the same object, using an extra line of code to find the remote Registry through

Figure 3-3: Anatomy of an RMI object URL

the `LocateRegistry` interface:

```
Registry rmtRegistry = LocateRegistry.getRegistry("rmiremote.farley.org");
ThisOrThatServer rmtServer =
        (ThisOrThatServer)rmtRegistry.lookup("TTServer");
```

When you look up objects through an actual `Registry` object, you don't have the option of using the URL syntax for the name, because you don't need it. The hostname and port of the remote host are specified when you locate the `Registry` through the `LocateRegistry` interface, and the RMI protocol is implied, so all you need is the registered name of the object. With the `Naming` class, you can reduce a remote object lookup to a single method call, but the name must now include the host, port number, and registered object name, bundled into a URL. Internally, the `Naming` object parses the host and port number from the URL for you, finds the remote `Registry` using the `LocateRegistry` interface, and asks the `Registry` for the remote object using the object name in the URL.

The principal use for the `Registry` and `Naming` classes in an RMI application is as a means to bootstrap your distributed application. A server process typically exports just a few key objects through its local RMI registry daemon. Clients look up these objects through the `Naming` facility to get remote references to them. Any other remote objects that need to be shared between the two processes can be exported through remote method calls.

Remote Method Arguments and Return Values

As I've already mentioned, a critical element of executing a remote method call is the marshalling and unmarshalling of the method arguments and, once the method has executed, the reverse marshalling and unmarshalling of the method's return value. RMI handles this process for you automatically, but you need to understand how different types of objects are transmitted from the method caller to the server object and back again and, more importantly, you need to know which types of objects can't be used in remote method calls at all.

When you call a method on a remote object, the arguments to the method have to be serializable. That is, they need to be primitive Java data types (like `int`, `float`, etc.) or Java objects that implement `java.io.Serializable`. The same restriction applies to the return value of the remote method. This restriction is enforced at runtime, when you actually make the remote method call, rather than at compile time, when you generate the stubs and skeletons using the *rmic* compiler.

The RMI stub/skeleton layer decides how to send method arguments and return values over the network, based on whether a particular object is `Remote`, `Serializable`, or neither:

- If the object is a `Remote` object, a remote reference for the object is generated, and the reference is marshaled and sent to the remote process. The remote reference is received on the other end and converted into a stub for the original object. This process applies to both method arguments and return values.
- If the object is `Serializable` but not `Remote`, the object is serialized and streamed to the remote process in byte form. The receiver converts the bytes into a copy of the original object.
- If the method argument or return value is not serializable (i.e., it's not a primitive data type or an object that implements `Serializable`), the object can't be sent to the remote client, and a `java.rmi.MarshalException` is thrown.

RMI

The principal difference between remote and nonremote objects is that remote objects are sent *by reference*, while nonremote, serializable objects are sent *by copy*. In other words, a remote reference maintains a link to the original object it references, so changes can be made to the original object through the remote stub. If the server object calls update methods on an argument to a remote method, and you want the updates to be made on the original object on the client side, the argument needs to be a `Remote` object that automatically exports a stub to the server object. Similarly, if the return value of a remote method call is intended to be a reference to an object living on the server, the server implementation needs to ensure that the object returned is a `Remote` object.

Factory Classes

When a reference to a remote object is obtained through the RMI registry and then used to request additional remote references, the registered remote object is often referred to as a *factory class*.

Factory classes are useful in distributed applications that use remote objects because in most cases you can't predict beforehand the kind and number of remote objects that will need to be shared between two processes. To make a remote object visible to clients through the RMI registry service, you need to explicitly create the object inside a Java VM on the server and then register that object using the `bind()` or `rebind()` method on the `Registry`. Using remote references obtained through method calls on factory objects, however, the client application can dynamically request the creation of new remote objects, without the objects being registered individually with the server registry.

As an example, suppose we're building a remote banking system, using the `Account` object we saw earlier in the chapter. We want to set up a centralized server that provides account services to remote clients running on PCs, embedded in ATMs, etc. On the server, we could run an RMI registry, create an `Account` object for every account we have on record, and register each one with the RMI registry service using the account name. In this scheme, registering accounts with the RMI registry goes something like this:

```
Registry local = LocateRegistry.getRegistry();
local.bind("Abrams, John", new AccountImpl("John Abrams"));
local.bind("Barts, Homer", new AccountImpl("Homer Barts"));
  .
  .
  .
```

As you can imagine, this is quite unwieldy in practice. Starting the server can take a long time, as thousands of accounts need to be registered, many of them unnecessarily, since many accounts may not see any activity before the next downtime. More importantly, accounts that are created or closed during the server's lifetime somehow need to be added or removed from the RMI registry, as well as from the bank's database of accounts. A much more sensible approach is to define a factory class for `Account` objects, along the lines of the following interface:

```
import java.rmi.Remote;
import java.rmi.RemoteException;

public interface AccountManager extends Remote {
  public Account getAccount(String name) throws RemoteException;
  public boolean newAccount(Account s) throws RemoteException;
}
```

The `AccountManager` lets a client ask for an account by name, using the `getAccount()` remote method. The method returns a reference to an `Account` object that corresponds to the account. Once the client has the `Account` reference, transactions against the account can be done through method calls on the `Account` object. The `AccountManager` also has a `newAccount()` method that allows clients to add new accounts to the manager's underlying database.

The server implementation of the `getAccount()` method simply needs to look up the named account in the account database, create an `AccountImpl` object to represent the account, and return the object to the remote client as a remote reference. Since `Account` objects are `Remote` objects, the RMI remote reference layer automatically creates a remote reference for the `Account` object, and the client that called the `getAccount()` method receives a stub for the `Account` object on the server.

Using the factory object to find accounts is more manageable than using the RMI registry. The bank maintains a database of accounts and their status, so the server implementation of the `AccountManager` can access that database directly to find accounts and create corresponding `Account` remote objects. Trying to keep the RMI registry in sync with the bank database makes the registry an unnecessary shadow of the main database of accounts, giving the bank two databases to maintain.

Dynamically Loaded Classes

The RMI runtime system has a dynamic class-loading facility that loads the classes it needs while executing remote method calls. In some situations, you don't need to worry much about how your application classes are obtained by the various agents in an RMI application. This is especially true if you have direct access to all hosts involved in the distributed system (i.e., if you can install your application classes in the local CLASSPATH for each machine participating in the application). For instance, when discussing the earlier Account example, I assumed that all the relevant classes (Account, AccountImpl, stub, and skeleton classes) were installed on both the client and the server. However, if your distributed application involves remote agents running on hosts that are not directly under your control, you need to understand how RMI loads classes at runtime, so you can ensure that each remote agent can find the classes it needs in order to run.

As with any Java application, the Java runtime system is responsible for loading the classes needed to initiate an RMI session. Starting an interaction with a remote object means loading the RMI API classes themselves, as well as the base interface for the remote object and the stub class for the remote interface. On the server side, the skeleton class for the remote object and the actual implementation class need to be loaded in order to run the server object that is being remotely exported.

The classes that are referenced directly by a given Java class are normally loaded by the same class loader that loaded the class itself. So, in an RMI client that does a Naming lookup to find a remote object, the stub interface for the remote object is loaded using the class loader for the class doing the lookup. If the RMI client is a Java application (started using the *java* command to invoke the main() method on an object), the default (local) class loader tries to find the remote interface locally, from the local CLASSPATH. If the RMI client is an applet loaded in a web page, the AppletClassLoader tries to look for the remote interface on the applet's host, in the codebase of the applet.

The RMI runtime system provides its own class loader, the RMIClassLoader, to augment the default class loading process I just described. The RMIClassLoader loads stubs and skeleton classes for remote interfaces, as well as the classes for objects used as remote method arguments or return values. These classes usually aren't explicitly referenced by your RMI application itself, but they are needed by the RMI runtime system for generating remote references and marshalling/unmarshalling method arguments and return values.

When it's loading the bytecodes for class definitions, the RMI runtime system first attempts to use the default class loader for the local context (i.e., an AppletClassLoader for an applet or the system class loader for a Java application). If the referenced class isn't found using the default local class loader, the RMIClassLoader tries to load the class bytecodes remotely according to the procedures explained next.

Configuring Clients and Servers for Remote Class Loading

When the RMI runtime system marshals a remote object stub, method argument, or return value, it encodes a URL in the marshaled bytestream to tell the process on the receiving end of the stream where to look for the class file for the marshaled object. If the class for the object being marshaled was loaded by a nondefault class loader (e.g., the AppletClassLoader or the RMIClassLoader), the codebase of that class loader is encoded in the marshaled stream. If the class was loaded by the default class loader from the local CLASSPATH, the value of the java.rmi.server.codebase property for the Java VM marshalling the object is sent in the stream. This property is not set by default in the Java VM, so you need to make sure that it's set to a URL that points to the location of the necessary class files. One way to do this is to include a command-line argument when starting the Java VM, as in:

```
% java -Djava.rmi.server.codebase=http://objhost.org/classes/RMIProcess
```

Here we're starting a Java process with its codebase set to *http://objhost.org/classes/*. This means that any remote process that needs to load classes for objects received from this process during an RMI session should use this HTTP URL in order to find them (if the classes can't be found on the local CLASSPATH, that is). This applies either if *RMIProcess* is serving remote objects itself through an RMI registry or if *RMIProcess* is passing objects into methods it is calling on other remote objects. In the first case, a remote client that needs to load the stub classes for the objects exported by *RMIProcess* uses the codebase to find these classes. In the second case, a remote process uses the codebase to load the classes for method arguments that *RMIProcess* is passing into remote method calls it makes.

If an RMI runtime system is trying to unmarshal an object stub, method argument, or return value and it doesn't find the class using the default class loader (e.g., the system class loader, which looks on the local CLASSPATH first), the RMIClassLoader can use the URL in the marshal stream to look for the class bytecodes remotely. The RMIClassLoader takes the URL from the marshaled bytestream and opens a URL connection to the specified host to load the needed classes. If both the local class search and this remote URL search fail to find the required classes, the unmarshal operation generates an exception, and the remote method call fails.

Note that in order for a Java runtime system to even attempt to load classes remotely, it has to have a security manager installed that allows remote class loading. The java.rmi.RMISecurityManager can be used for this. In both your RMI object server and clients, include the following line before any RMI calls:

```
System.setSecurityManager(new RMISecurityManager());
```

If you don't set the security manager, the Java VM is allowed to look for classes only locally, and your RMI calls will work only if all of the required classes can be found on the local CLASSPATH.

Another issue with dynamically loading remote classes is that the default Java security policy doesn't allow all the networking operations required to resolve a class from a remote host. So, if you have an RMI client or server that needs to resolve classes remotely, you need to use a policy file that opens up network permissions to allow this. I'm not going to go into the details of network policies here or the syntax of the security policy file,* but you will need to add the following line to the policy file on the RMI client:

```
permission java.net.SocketPermission "objhost.org", "accept,connect";
```

* For details on Java security policies and policy files, see *Java Security*, by Scott Oaks (O'Reilly).

This line gives the RMI object server *objhost.org* the permission to open connections to the local machine. This is needed to bypass the stricter rules imposed by the RMISecurityManager. Once you've made a modified policy file, you can specify it on the command line when you start your RMI process, in a similar way to setting the codebase property:

```
% java -Djava.security.policy=mypolicy.txt RMIProcess
```

As a simple example, suppose we want to use our earlier Account example to export an Account object on one host and access that Account on another host where the only class available locally is the Account interface class itself. On the server, we start an RMI registry* and run the RegAccount class as before, but since we want remote clients to be able to load the stub classes remotely, we need to set the codebase property to where the clients can find these classes:

```
% java -Djava.rmi.server.codebase=http://objhost.org/classes/ RegAccount
Registered account.
```

RMI

We've setting the codebase to *http://objhost.org/classes/*, so we have to make sure that an HTTP server is running on the *objhost.org* machine and that the necessary class files (e.g., the AccountImpl stub class) are in the *classes* directory of that HTTP server's document root.

Now we can run the AccountClient class on the remote client as before, but the client's host machine doesn't have the stub class for the Account remote object available locally. When the AccountClient tries to look up the remote Account object, we want the stub class to be loaded remotely. Two simple changes to our Account example make this possible. First, add a line to the AccountClient main() method that sets the RMISecurityManager, in order to allow for remote class loading:

```
import java.rmi.Naming;
import java.rmi.RMISecurityManager;

public class AccountClient {
  public static void main(String argv[]) {
    try {
      // Set the RMI security manager,
      // in case we need to load remote classes
      System.setSecurityManager(new RMISecurityManager());

      // Lookup account object
      Account jimAcct = (Account)Naming.lookup("rmi://objhost.org/JimF");
      .
      .
      .
```

The other change is to use a more lenient policy file when running AccountClient so the necessary network operations can be performed. Again, I won't discuss the syntax of the policy file here, but assuming we've put the required policy settings into a file named *rmipolicy.txt*, we can start the client like so:

---

* Note that in order for the RMI registry to recognize and pass along the codebase property you specify, it has to be started in such a way that it can't find any of the remotely loaded classes on its CLASSPATH. So start your RMI registry with a CLASSPATH that doesn't include the stub/skeleton classes, etc., then run your RMI server with a CLASSPATH that includes all required classes.

```
% java -Djava.security.policy=rmipolicy.txt AccountClient
Deposited 12,000 into account owned by JimF
Balance now totals: 12000.0
```

Loading Classes from Applets

Virtually all the steps I just outlined for running an RMI client to allow it to remotely load classes apply to applets as well. The only difference is that the classes for applets are loaded using an `AppletClassLoader`, which checks the applet's codebase for any classes required to run the applet. The default security policy for applets already allows for remote loading of classes, since this is how an applet works in the first place, so there's no need to change the security policy when using RMI within an applet. All you need to do to ensure that the applet finds the remote interface and stub class for the RMI object is to put them in the server directory that corresponds to the applet's codebase.

Remote Object Activation

Automatic activation of remote objects is a new feature in RMI as of Java 1.2. The activation subsystem in RMI provides you with two basic features: the ability to have remote objects instantiated (activated) on-demand by client requests, and the ability for remote object references to remain valid across server crashes, making the references persistent. These features can be quite useful in certain types of distributed applications.

For example, think back to the `AccountManager` class we discussed when we talked about factory objects. We might not want to keep the `AccountManager` running on our server 24 hours a day; perhaps it consumes lots of server resources (memory, database connections, etc.), so we don't want it running unless it is being used. Using the RMI activation service, we can set up the `AccountManager` so that it doesn't start running until the first client requests an `Account`. In addition, after some period of inactivity, we can have the `AccountManager` shut down to conserve server resources and then reactivated the next time a client asks for an `Account`.

If a remote object is made activatable, it can be registered with the RMI registry without actually being instantiated. Normally, RMI remote objects (based on the `UnicastRemoteObject` interface) provide only nonpersistent references to themselves. Such a reference can be created for a client only if the referenced object already exists in a remote Java VM. In addition, the remote reference is valid only during the lifetime of the remote object. The remote object activation service adds support for persistent remote references that can be created even if the remote object is not running at the time of the request and that can persist beyond the lifetime of an individual server object.

The key features provided by the RMI activation service include:

- The ability to automatically create remote objects, triggered by requests for references to these objects.

- Support for activation groups, in which groups of activatable remote objects are executed in the same Java VM, which is automatically started by the activation service if needed.
- The ability to restart remote objects if they exit or are destroyed due to a system failure of some kind. This can add a certain degree of fault tolerance to RMI applications.

In the RMI activation system, activatable objects belong to activation groups, and each activation group runs within its own Java VM. If you don't group your activatable objects, simply assigning a new activation group to each activatable object you create, then each object runs inside a separate Java VM.

You typically define an activatable remote object by:

- Subclassing your remote object implementation from the `Activatable` class provided in the `java.rmi.activation` package
- Providing activation constructors in the server implementation
- Registering the object and its activation method with the activation service

If you want remote clients to directly access your activatable object, you also need to register the object with the RMI registry, so that it can be found by name on the network. You can register an activatable class with the registry without actually creating an instance of the remote object, as we'll see shortly.

You can also create an activatable object without subclassing the `Activatable` class. This might be necessary if you need to extend another class and the Java single-inheritance limit keeps you from also extending `Activatable`. For most of this section, we'll just discuss the case where you're subclassing `Activatable`; I'll only mention this other approach when needed.

Persistent Remote References

The primary difference between an activatable remote object and a nonactivatable one is that a remote reference to an activatable object doesn't need to have a "live" object behind it. If an activatable object is not running (e.g., it hasn't been constructed yet, or it has been garbage-collected by its Java VM, or its VM has exited), a remote reference to the object can still be exported to a client. The client receives a stub, as usual, and can make remote method invocations through the stub. When the first method is invoked, the activation service running on the server sees that the object is not active and goes about activating the object for the client. If the object doesn't have a VM to run in, the activation system starts one. The object is then activated using information that has been registered with the activation system. This information includes the object's class name, a URL that can load the class bytecodes if they're not found in the local `CLASSPATH`, and data to pass into the object's activation constructor. Once the object has been activated, the method invocation takes place, and the results are marshaled and sent back to the client.

As long as the object stays running, future method requests are handled as usual. If the object stops running for some reason (e.g, it is garbage-collected, or its VM dies), the next method request triggers the activation service again, and the object is reactivated. This is what is meant by persistent remote references: remote references to activatable objects can persist across multiple lifetimes of the actual server object.

Defining an Activatable Remote Object

Naturally, before you can register and use an activatable object with the RMI activation system, you need to define the remote interface and the server implementation for the object. The `java.rmi.activation` package provides the classes you need to define an activatable remote object. You usually define a remote object as activatable by subclassing it from `Activatable` and defining a special constructor that activates the object. You also have to register the object with the activation service on the server host.

Other than that, the implementation of an activatable remote object is similar to that of a nonactivatable one. You start with a remote interface that contains the methods you want to export from your object. The interface should extend `Remote`, and each method should throw a `RemoteException` (or, as of Java 1.2, any parent of `RemoteException`). The server implementation implements this interface and extends a concrete implementation of the `java.rmi.server.RemoteServer` class. Since you're defining an activatable remote object, you typically extend `java.rmi.activation.Activatable` directly and use its constructors to initialize, register, and activate your remote object. If you choose not to extend `Activatable` directly, you have to use the static `exportObject()` methods on the `Activatable` class to register your object with the activation runtime system.

The Activatable class

The `Activatable` class has four constructors. Here are signatures for two of them:

```
protected Activatable(String src, MarshalledObject data,
   boolean restart, int port) throws RemoteException
protected Activatable(String src, MarshalledObject data,
   boolean restart, int port, RMIClientSocketFactory csfactory,
   RMIServerSocketFactory ssfactory) throws RemoteException
```

These two constructors are *initialization* constructors. You use them when you decide to proactively create one of your remote objects and register it with the RMI activation service. In this case, the object already exists when a client first makes a method request on it, but if the object is destroyed, the next client request causes the object to be reactivated. These constructors register an object with the local activation service and export the object so that it can receive remote method requests. Both constructors have the following arguments in common:

- The `String` parameter is a URL that indicates where class bytecodes required by this object can be located. This information is exported to a remote client so it can dynamically load classes required to unmarshal method return values, for example.

- The `MarshalledObject` parameter provides initialization data for the object; this parameter is necessary because data is typically sent from the activation daemon's VM to the VM designated to run the activatable object and the two might not be the same (more on this later).
- The `boolean` flag indicates whether the object should be automatically recreated when its home VM or its activation group is restarted (e.g., after a server restart).
- The `int` parameter specifies the port on which the object is exported. A port of zero tells the RMI runtime system to export the object on a random open port.

The second initialization constructor takes custom client and server socket factories that create socket communications between the server and the clients of the object. Customized socket factories are a new feature in RMI as of the Java 2 SDK 1.2. I won't discuss them in this chapter, but you can consult the RMI API reference in Part III for more details.

RMI

The other two `Activatable` constructors have the following signatures:

```
protected Activatable(ActivationID id, int port) throws RemoteException
protected Activatable(ActivationID id, int port,
   RMIClientSocketFactory csfactory, RMIServerSocketFactory ssfactory)
   throws RemoteException
```

These constructors are *(re)activation* constructors. The activation system uses them to activate a remote object that has received a remote method request, but isn't currently active. The `ActivationID` is a persistent ID issued by the activation system for the remote object, and the port number is the port that exports the remote object. The second constructor again takes custom server and client socket factories.

The `Activatable` class also has a set of `exportObject()` methods that correspond to the constructors I've just described. You can use these methods when an activatable object doesn't directly extend the `Activatable` class. You call the appropriate `exportObject()` methods from within the constructors of the class, so they serve the same function as calling the `Activatable` constructors during initialization of an `Activatable` subclass.

Implementing an activatable object

As I already mentioned, you can implement an activatable remote object in two ways: derive the remote object from the `Activatable` class directly and make the required calls to the `Activatable` constructors in its constructors, or have the class implement a `Remote` interface and make the required calls to the static `exportObject()` methods in its constructors.

In either case, when the activation system activates a remote object, it looks for a constructor on the class that takes two arguments: an `ActivationID` and a `MarshalledObject`. The activation system calls this constructor, passing in an `ActivationID` it generates for the object and the `MarshalledObject` registered for the activatable object by the first constructor we just discussed.

This means you have to provide a constructor with this signature in your implementation of an activatable object. In this constructor, you should call either one of the (re)activation constructors on the Activatable parent class (if your class extends Activatable), or the corresponding Activatable.exportObject() method (if you didn't extend Activatable). In this call, you pass on the ActivationID issued by the activation system and you specify the port for the exported remote object (a port number of 0 causes the object to be exported on a random open port).

In addition to this required constructor, you can define other constructors for your remote object implementation as needed. If you want your object to be reactivatable, any additional constructors should call one of the initialization constructors on Activatable (using super()) or the corresponding exportObject() method, passing in a valid source URL and a MarshalledObject to be used as an argument if the object is reactivated. If the object is destroyed at some point, and a subsequent remote method request is received for it, the activation system reactivates the object by calling the required (re)activation constructor on the object's class, passing in this MarshalledObject argument.

Example 3-5 shows an activatable implementation of the ThisOrThatServer interface from Example 3-3. The primary differences between this implementation and the nonactivatable one in Example 3-4 are that this new implementation extends the java.rmi.activation.Activatable class instead of UnicastRemoteObject, and its constructors support the activation system. This implementation also includes a name that identifies the server.

Example 3-5: An Activatable Version of the ThisOrThatServer

```
import java.rmi.activation.*;
import java.rmi.MarshalledObject;
import java.rmi.RemoteException;
import java.io.IOException;

public class ActivatableThisOrThatServerImpl
  extends Activatable implements ThisOrThatServer {

  // Name for server
  private String myName = "";

  // "Regular" constructor used to create a "pre-activated" server
  public ActivatableThisOrThatServerImpl(String name, String src, int port)
      throws RemoteException, ActivationException, IOException {
    // Register and export object (on random open port)
    super(src, new MarshalledObject(name), false, port);
    // Save name
    myName = name;
    System.out.println("Initialization constructor called.");
  }

  // Constructor called by the activation runtime to (re)activate
  // and export the server
  protected ActivatableThisOrThatServerImpl(ActivationID id,
      MarshalledObject arg) throws RemoteException {
    // Export this object with the given activation id, on random port
    super(id, 0);
    System.out.println("Activating a server");
```

Example 3-5: An Activatable Version of the ThisOrThatServer (continued)

```
    // Check incoming data passed in with activation request
    try {
      Object oarg = arg.get();
      if (oarg instanceof String) {
        myName = (String)oarg;
      }
      else {
        System.out.println("Unknown argument received on activation: " +
                           oarg);
      }
    }
    catch(Exception e) {
      System.out.println("Error retrieving argument to activation");
    }
    System.out.println("(Re)activation constructor called.");
  }

  // Remotely-accessible methods
  public String doThis(String todo) throws RemoteException {
    String result = doSomething("this", todo);
    return result;
  }

  public String doThat(String todo) throws RemoteException {
    String result = doSomething("that", todo);
    return result;
  }

  // Non-remote methods
  private String doSomething(String what, String todo) {
    String result = myName + ": " + what + " " + todo + " is done.";
    return result;
  }
}
```

The first constructor for `ActivatableThisOrThatServerImpl` is a public one, used to construct a server with a given name. The constructor registers the new object with the activation system, passing in a URL that acts as a codebase for finding the classes required for this class. It also passes in the name given to the server, wrapped in a `MarshalledObject`. This ensures that the server is given the same name if it needs to be reactivated later.

The second constructor is the required one used by the activation system. If an object of this type needs to be activated (or reactivated after a crash of some sort), this constructor is called to create the remote object. The constructor takes an `ActivationID`, issued by the activation system, and the `MarshalledObject` registered for the object with the activation system. The constructor exports the object by calling the second constructor on the `Activatable` class, then initializes itself with the data from the `MarshalledObject`.

Registering Activatable Objects

There are several ways to register an activatable object with its local activation system. In each case, the activation system needs to be told how to create (or recreate) the object. The information the activation system needs to activate an object is encapsulated in the ActivationDesc class. An ActivationDesc object contains the name of the class for the remote object, a URL with the network location of the bytecodes for the class, a MarshalledObject to be used as the initialization data for the object, and the group assignment for the object.

The simplest way to register an Activatable object is to create an instance of the object. In our example, we've derived our server implementation from the Activatable class, so the public constructor on the ActivatableThisOrThatServerImpl class registers the object by calling the necessary constructor on Activatable. Thus, we can create and register one of these as follows:

```
// Make an activation group for the object
ActivationGroupDesc gdesc = new ActivationGroupDesc(null, null);
ActivationGroupID gid = ActivationGroup.getSystem().registerGroup(gdesc);
ActivationGroup.createGroup(gid, gdesc, 0);

// Make a server object, which registers it with activation system
ThisOrThatServer server =
    new ActivatableThisOrThatServerImpl(serverName, codebaseURL, 0);

// Register with naming service
LocateRegistry.getRegistry().rebind(serverName, server);
```

The first four lines are required to create an activation group for our activatable object. We'll talk more about activation groups shortly. For now, all you need to know is that this code creates the default activation group for the current VM. Any remote object that isn't specifically assigned to a group is placed in this default group.

The activatable object itself is created by simply calling the public ActivatableThisOrThatServerImpl constructor. This constructor registers the object with the activation system by calling the appropriate Activatable constructor, as we've already discussed. Since we haven't specified an activation group for the object, it is placed in the default group we just created. If we hadn't created that default group, the activation system would throw an exception here, when the object is registered.

Aside from the creation of the activation group, this example looks a lot like our other examples of registering RMI objects. The difference here is that if the registering process dies off at some point, the activation system can reactivate the activatable object in a new Java VM using the information provided in the ActivationDesc for the object. In this case, we're relying on the Activatable constructor (which is called by our ActivatableThisOrThatServerImpl constructor) to create and register an ActivationDesc for our object.

When an object needs to be activated, the activation system first looks up the ActivationDesc for the object and then looks for the class referenced in the ActivationDesc, using the URL to load the class bytecodes. Once the class has been loaded, the activation system creates an instance of the class by calling the activation constructor, which takes an ActivationID and a MarshalledObject as arguments. The ActivationID is issued by the activation system, and the MarshalledObject contains the data previously registered with the ActivationDesc. In our activatable ThisOrThatServer in Example 3-5, the activation system calls the second constructor on our ActivatableThisOrThatServerImpl class. The new object passes the ActivationID up to the Activatable constructor so that it can be recorded, and the name of the server is pulled from the MarshalledObject. The Activatable constructor takes care of creating and registering an ActivationDesc for the object and exporting the object with the activation system.

Registering an activatable object without instantiating

A more complicated, but often more useful way to register a remote object is to create an ActivationDesc for it and then register the information directly with the activation system, *without* creating an instance of the object. The static Activatable.register() method accepts an ActivationDesc object and registers it with the activation system directly. Here's how we can do that:

```
// Make a codebase and activation argument for the object
String src = "http://objhost.org/classes";
MarshalledObject actArg = new MarshalledObject("MyServer");

// Create the ActivationDesc and get a stub for the object
ActivationDesc desc =
  new ActivationDesc("ActivatableThisOrThatServerImpl", src, actArg);
ThisOrThatServer serverStub =
  (ThisOrThatServer)Activatable.register(desc);
```

When we create the ActivationDesc for the object, we specify the name of the class to use for creating the object, a codebase for finding the class, and a MarshalledObject that is passed to the object when it's activated. The ActivationDesc is used in the call to the Activatable.register() method, which returns a RemoteStub for the activatable object. Since we know this stub is for an object that implements the ThisOrThatServer interface, we can safely cast it to a ThisOrThatServer. We can also use this reference to register the remote object with the local RMI naming registry:

```
LocateRegistry.getRegistry().bind("ThisOrThatServer", serverStub);
```

Although I haven't shown it here, note that you also have to create an activation group for the object, just like we did in our earlier example, before you can register it with the activation service.

So, to recap, we've registered a remote object with the activation system and the RMI naming registry without actually creating the object itself. When a client tries to look up the object, it gets back a remote stub, with no active object behind it on the server. When the client calls a method on the stub, however, the activation system on the server creates the object, using the information in the ActivationDesc we provided.

Passing data with the MarshalledObject

The way you can pass arguments to activatable objects before they are activated is through the MarshalledObject contained within the ActivationDesc for the object. However, once the ActivationDesc is registered with the activation system, you can't dynamically update the contents of the MarshalledObject. One way to have the arguments to an activatable object be dynamic is to bundle a filename or

URL into the MarshalledObject. At the point that the object is activated, it can read data from the file or URL and use that data during activation.

Activation Groups

Every activatable RMI object belongs to an activation group. Each group of activatable objects runs within the same Java VM on the server host. In essence, activation groups are a way of defining collections of activatable remote objects that should share the same physical address space. We've already seen how to set up an activation group, since we had to do this before registering our activatable object with the activation system. In this section, we'll take a look at creating activation groups in a bit more detail and discuss what the activation group is actually doing for you.

Activation groups in RMI are more than just a way of organizing remote objects. Each activation group is responsible for monitoring, activating, and reactivating the objects it contains. The objects involved in maintaining an activation group are shown in Figure 3-4. Note that you don't normally need to interact with the underlying objects themselves. You simply set up your ActivationGroup objects and assign activatable objects to them; the activation system does the rest for you.

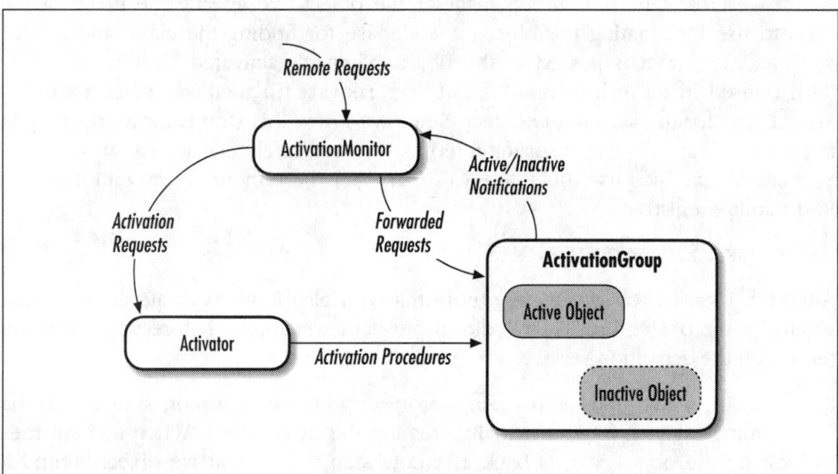

Figure 3-4: The components of the activation system

An ActivationGroup is created when the first object in the group needs to be activated. The Activator is responsible for creating a VM for the ActivationGroup to run in, and for starting the ActivationGroup using the information in the registered object's ActivationGroupDesc, if it has one. If the remote object doesn't have a specified group, a default one is created. The new ActivationGroup object is then told to activate the requested remote object, by calling its newInstance() method. The arguments the Activator passes into this method are the ActivationID for the new object and the ActivationDesc that the Activator has registered for the object.

The ActivationDesc gives an ActivationGroup everything it needs to activate the remote object. The ActivationGroup takes the class name for the object and looks for the class bytecodes. First it checks the local CLASSPATH, and if that pulls up nothing, it uses the URL in the ActivationDesc to load the class from the given URL. Once the class is loaded, an instance of the class is created by calling the activation constructor on the class (e.g., the constructor that has an ActivationID argument and a MarshalledObject argument). The ActivationID and MarshalledObject come from the call to the newInstance() method. The new, active remote object is returned to the Activator as a serialized MarshalledObject. This is done for two reasons. First, the Activator runs in a separate Java VM, so the active object reference needs to be transferred from one VM to another, and the easiest way to do this is to serialize it and transmit it in that form. Second, since the object has been bundled into a MarshalledObject, the Activator doesn't need to load the object's bytecodes unless absolutely necessary. In most cases, the Activator doesn't need to interact directly with the object itself, so it doesn't need to waste time loading unnecessary bytecodes.

Each ActivationGroup has an ActivationMonitor associated with it. The ActivationGroup has to tell the ActivationMonitor whenever an object becomes active or inactive. An activatable object is responsible for informing its ActivationGroup when it becomes active and inactive, by calling the group's activeObject() and inactiveObject() methods, respectively. The ActivationGroup, in turn, passes the information on to the ActivationMonitor by calling identical methods on the monitor object. When the object becomes inactive, the ActivationMonitor makes note of it and arranges for the object to be reactivated the next time a method request comes in for it. If an entire ActivationGroup becomes inactive, the ActivationMonitor is informed through its inactiveGroup() method. The next request for an object in that group causes the Activator to recreate the group.

Registering activation groups

An ActivationGroup is registered with the activation system in roughly the same way as an activatable object. You have to create an ActivationGroupDesc object that contains the name of the class for the group, the URL where the class bytecodes can be loaded, and a MarshalledObject that is given to the ActivationGroup as initialization data. Unlike activatable objects, though, the class of a group has to be a concrete subclass of ActivationGroup. You register the ActivationGroupDesc by calling the static ActivationSystem.registerGroup() method, passing in the ActivationGroupDesc. The ActivationSystem returns an ActivationGroupID that can assign specific objects to the group.

Assigning activatable objects to groups

You assign an activatable object to a group by specifying the group ID in the ActivationDesc registered with the activation system. The ActivationGroupID returned by the ActivationSystem.registerGroup() method can be passed into the ActivationDesc constructor.

Before you can register a remote object with the activation system, you need to create a group for it. For our activatable ThisOrThatServer example, we can run

Java code along the following lines on the object server (note I've left out the exception handling):

```
// Make an activation group for the object
ActivationGroupDesc gdesc = new ActivationGroupDesc(null, null);
ActivationGroupID gid =
  ActivationGroup.getSystem().registerGroup(gdesc);
ActivationGroup.createGroup(gid, gdesc, 0);

// Set up ActivationDesc for object
String codebaseURL = "http://objhost.org/classes";
String serverName = "Fred";
MarshalledObject activationArg = new MarshalledObject(serverName);
ActivationDesc desc =
  new ActivationDesc(gid, "ActivatableThisOrThatServerImpl",
                     codebaseURL, activationArg);
ThisOrThatServer serverRef =
  (ThisOrThatServer)Activatable.register(desc);
LocateRegistry.getRegistry().rebind(serverName, serverRef);
```

Here we're using the `ActivatableThisOrThatServerImpl` class and registering a remote object with the activation system without actually instantiating it. Before we register our remote object, we create an `ActivationGroupDesc`, then use it to register and create a new activation group with the activation system. After we create the activation group (using the `ActivationGroup.createGroup()` method), we use the `ActivationGroupID` for our new group to make an `ActivationDesc` for our remote object, and we use that to register the object with the activation system. The activation system generates a remote stub for our object, and we register that with the RMI naming registry.

Since each `ActivationGroup` is started within its own VM if it's initially activated by the activation system, grouping objects is a convenient way to partition your remote objects into shared address spaces on your server. For more details on the activation group interfaces in RMI, consult the `java.rmi.activation` reference material in Chapter 14, *The java.rmi.activation Package*.

The Activation Daemon

The heart of the RMI activation system is the activation daemon, which runs on the host for an activatable object. The activation daemon is responsible for intercepting remote method requests on activatable objects and orchestrating the activation of the object, if needed.

The activation daemon provided with the Java SDK, *rmid*, runs a Java VM that includes a `java.rmi.activation.Activator` object. The `Activator` is responsible for keeping a registry of activatable objects, along with the information needed to activate them. This information is in two parts: an `ActivationDesc` object and an optional `ActivationGroupDesc`. The `ActivationGroupDesc` identifies the group of activatable objects to which the object should be added and describes how to start the group if it doesn't exist. The `ActivationDesc` includes all information needed to activate the object itself. An activatable object has to be registered with the activation system in one of the ways described earlier to be started automatically by the `Activator`.

If a remote method request is received by the RMI runtime system on a host, and the target object hasn't been created yet, the Activator is asked to activate it. The Activator looks up the ActivationDesc (and ActivationGroupDesc, if present) for the object. If the object has an ActivationGroup assigned to it, and the ActivationGroup doesn't exist yet, a Java VM is started for the group, and the ActivationGroupDesc data is used to start an ActivationGroup object within the new VM. If the object has no ActivationGroup associated with it, it's given its own ActivationGroup running in its own VM. The group is then asked to start the requested object, using the ActivationDesc object registered for the object. Once the ActivationGroup activates the object within its VM, the Activator is notified, and the now-active remote reference is returned to the RMI runtime system. The RMI runtime system forwards the remote method request through the reference to the object, and the return value is exported back to the client as usual.

The daemon's dual personality

When you start the *rmid* daemon, it creates an Activator and then listens on the default port of 1098 for activation requests. There is also a -port command-line option that lets you specify a different port for the VM to use. In addition to running the Activator, the *rmid* daemon also runs its own RMI Registry. If needed, you can register local objects with the daemon's internal Registry by specifying the daemon's port when you call the bind() or rebind() method of the Registry. For example, if *rmid* is running on its default port of 1098:

```
RemoteObject server = ...
Registry local = LocateRegistry.getRegistry(1098);
local.bind(server, "Server");
```

This way, you can consolidate your activation system and your naming service into one VM on your server.

RMI and Native Method Calls

As I mentioned at the beginning of this chapter, RMI is a Java-only remote object scheme, so it doesn't provide a direct connection between objects implemented in different languages, like CORBA does. But, using Java's Native Interface API, it is possible to wrap existing C or C++ code with a Java interface and then export this interface remotely through RMI.

To demonstrate, let's suppose we have some (legacy) native code that implements a service we want to export through RMI to remote clients. We can create an implementation of our ThisOrThatServer interface that uses this native code to implement the doSomething() method on our remote interface. The implementation for a NativeThisOrThatServerImpl is shown in Example 3-6. The only significant difference between this implementation and our original ThisOrThatServerImpl is that the doSomething() method is declared native, so the method body is left empty.

Example 3-6: Remote Object Using a Native Method Implementation

```
import java.rmi.server.UnicastRemoteObject;
import java.rmi.RemoteException;

public class NativeThisOrThatServerImpl
  extends UnicastRemoteObject implements ThisOrThatServer {

  public NativeThisOrThatServerImpl() throws RemoteException {}

  // Remotely-accessible methods
  public String doThis(String todo) throws RemoteException {
    return doSomething("this", todo);
  }

  public String doThat(String todo) throws RemoteException {
    return doSomething("that", todo);
  }

  // Natively-implemented method
  native private String doSomething(String what, String todo);
}
```

We can compile this RMI class and generate the stubs and skeletons for it using the RMI compiler, just like with our other RMI examples. But once this is done, we need to provide a native implementation for the `doSomething()` method. To start, we can generate a C/C++ header file for the native method using the *javah* tool:

```
% javah -jni -d . NativeThisOrThatServerImpl
```

The `-jni` option tells the *javah* tool to generate JNI-compliant header files (as opposed to header files based on the earlier native method interface that shipped with Java 1.0). Invoking this command generates a JNI C/C++ header file that looks something like the following:

```
/* DO NOT EDIT THIS FILE - it is machine generated */
#include <jni.h>
/* Header for class NativeThisOrThatServerImpl */
#ifndef _Included_NativeThisOrThatServerImpl
#define _Included_NativeThisOrThatServerImpl
#ifdef __cplusplus
extern "C" {
#endif
/*
 * Class: NativeThisOrThatServerImpl
 * Method:    doSomething
 * Signature: (Ljava/lang/String;Ljava/lang/String;)Ljava/lang/String;
 */
JNIEXPORT jstring JNICALL Java_NativeThisOrThatServerImpl_doSomething
  (JNIEnv *, jobject, jstring, jstring);
#ifdef __cplusplus
}
#endif
#endif
```

The only details worth noting in this header file are the inclusion of the *jni.h* header file, which is provided with the Java SDK, and the single method declaration. The *jni.h* header file provides declarations and definitions for all of the data structures and utility methods provided by the JNI API. The method declaration has a signature that corresponds to the native method declared on our Java class. When you invoke the doSomething() method on the NativeThisOrThatServerImpl, the Java VM looks for a native method that matches this signature.

Now all we need to do is implement the C/C++ function declared in our JNI-generated header file. This is where we tie our Java method to some legacy native code. In this case, suppose the native code is wrapped up in a single C/C++ function called doSomethingNative(). This function is available in a native library on the server platform (e.g., a DLL file on Windows or a shared library on Unix). We want to use our Java method to invoke this native function, so we can implement the Java_NativeThisOrThatServerImpl_doSomething() function along these lines:

```
#include <jni.h>
#include "NativeThisOrThatServerImpl.h"
#include "nativeDoSomething.h"
#ifdef __cplusplus
extern "C" {
#endif
/*
 * Native implementation for method doSomething() on class
 * NativeThisOrThatServerImpl.
 */
JNIEXPORT jstring JNICALL Java_NativeThisOrThatServerImpl_doSomething
  (JNIEnv * env, jobject me, jstring what, jstring todo) {
  // Convert the Java strings to native strings
  const char* whatStr = (*env)->GetStringUTFChars(env, what, 0);
  const char* todoStr = (*env)->GetStringUTFChars(env, todo, 0);

  // Call the native method
  char* result = doSomethingNative(whatStr, todoStr);

  // Convert result back to Java string
  jstring res = (*env)->NewStringUTF(env, result);
  return res;
}
#ifdef __cplusplus
}
#endif
#endif
```

The first part of the function just converts the Java strings (passed in as C jstring data structures) into native char* strings. Then it passes the string arguments into the native doSomethingNative() function, converts the result back into a jstring, and returns it. The JNI system handles the conversion of the jstring into a Java String object in the VM environment.

Once we compile this C/C++ code (linking with the native library that contains the doSomethingNative() function), we can export remote NativeThisOrThatServerImpl objects. Then remote clients can call the doThis() or doThat() methods. These remote method calls in turn cause the invocation of native code on the server, when the object implementation calls its native doSomething() method.

Note that in order for the server object to find its native method, the native library containing the doSomethingNative() function has to be loaded into the server object's VM using the System.loadLibrary() method. You can do this in the application code that uses the native method or by adding a static initializer to the class, you can have the library loaded automatically when the `NativeThisOrThatServerImpl` class is referenced:

```
static { System.loadLibrary("methods"); }
```

The `System.loadLibrary()` method automatically converts the library name that you provide to a platform-specific file name. So if the previous example is run on a Solaris machine, the Java VM looks for a library file named *libmethods.so*. On a Windows machine, it looks for *methods.dll*.

RMI with JNI Versus CORBA

There are pros and cons to using RMI and JNI to export legacy native code using Java remote objects, as opposed to using CORBA. With CORBA, a CORBA object implemented in the same language as the native code (C/C++ for our example) is created and exported on the server. Remote Java clients can get a Java stub to this CORBA object using JavaIDL, or any third-party Java CORBA implementation (see Chapter 4 for details).

One obvious advantage of the CORBA approach is that you don't need to have Java on the server. Since this is presumably a legacy server, perhaps a mainframe of some sort, finding a stable Java VM and development kit for the platform may be a problem. If a Java implementation isn't available or if installing additional software on the legacy server isn't desirable, CORBA is your only option.

An advantage of the RMI/JNI approach is that you're running Java at both ends of the remote communication and avoiding the use of CORBA entirely. CORBA is a very rich distributed object API, but it may be overkill for your application. Using the simpler RMI API and keeping your code development strictly in Java (with some minimal C/C++ to interface to the legacy code) might be an advantage to you in this case.

RMI over IIOP

A new and exciting possibility for connecting RMI objects to non-Java objects is the ability for RMI objects to communicate directly with remote CORBA objects using IIOP, the CORBA network interface protocol.* The standard RMI implementation provided with Java uses an RMI-specific protocol, JRMP, to communicate over the network. RMI/IIOP allows RMI objects to use the CORBA network protocol, IIOP, to communicate with other objects. This means that an RMI object using RMI/IIOP can communicate with a remote CORBA object, regardless of the implementation language of the CORBA object. Likewise, a CORBA object can interact with your Java RMI objects directly. This really gives you the best of both worlds, since you can then implement your remote clients using RMI and use either CORBA or RMI/JNI on the server to interface to any native legacy code.

In order to convert your RMI objects to use IIOP, there are some changes you need to make:

---

* The RMI-IIOP tools and classes are an extension to the standard Java platform that has to be downloaded separately from *http://java.sun.com/products/rmi-iiop/*.

- Any implementation classes should extend the `javax.rmi.PortableRemoteObject` class, rather than `java.rmi.server.UnicastRemoteObject`.
- All your stub and skeleton classes need to be regenerated using the updated *rmic* compiler provided with the RMI/IIOP installation. This updated compiler has an `-iiop` option that produces stubs and ties (*ties* refers to skeletons in the CORBA vernacular). These stubs and ties handle the link between client and server objects, but using IIOP rather than JRMP.
- All use of the RMI `Naming` registry has to be converted to use JNDI to talk to a CORBA Naming Service. Objects that you export are bound to names in the CORBA Naming Service through the JNDI context, and remote objects you look up are accessed from the Naming Service through the JNDI context.
- Instead of using the standard Java casting operator on remote objects you look up, you should use the `javax.rmi.PortableRemoteObject.narrow()` method.

RMI

To give you a taste for how to use RMI/IIOP with your RMI classes, let's convert our first `Account` example to use RMI/IIOP. First, we need to update the `AccountImpl` class to extend `PortableRemoteObject`. The following fragment of the `IIOPAccountImpl` class does that:

```
import javax.rmi.PortableRemoteObject;
import java.rmi.RemoteException;
import java.util.List;
import java.util.ListIterator;

public class IIOPAccountImpl extends PortableRemoteObject implements Account {
  // Remainder of implementation is identical
```

We can compile the updated `IIOPAccountImpl` using the regular Java compiler, then use the extended *rmic* compiler included with RMI/IIOP to generate IIOP stubs and ties:

```
% rmic -iiop -d /home/myclasses IIOPAccountImpl
```

This generates an *IIOPAccountImpl_Stub* class and an *IIOPAccountImpl_Tie* class, which act as the IIOP stub and tie for the remote object.

In the CORBA world, remote objects are looked up using the CORBA Naming Service, so we need to update the `RegAccount` class to use JNDI to register an `Account` object with a CORBA Naming Service, rather than the RMI registry. The updated `IIOPRegAccount` class looks like this:

```
import javax.naming.*;
import java.rmi.*;

public class IIOPRegAccount {
  public static void main(String argv[]) {
    try {
      // Make an Account with a given name
      IIOPAccountImpl acct = new IIOPAccountImpl("JimF");

      // Get a reference to CORBA naming service using JNDI
      Hashtable props = new Hashtable();
      props.put("java.naming.factory.initial",
```

```
                "com.sun.jndi.cosnaming.CNCtxFactory");
      props.put("java.naming.provider.url", "iiop://objhost.org:900");
      Context ctx = new InitialContext(props);

      // Register our Account with the CORBA naming service
      ctx.rebind("JimF", acct);
      System.out.println("Registered account.");
    }
    catch (Exception e) {
      e.printStackTrace();
    }
  }
}
```

Refer to Chapter 6, *JNDI*, for details on the properties used to create the JNDI context and what they mean. All you need to glean from this is that we're trying to connect to a naming service running on *objhost.org*, listening to port 900. Once we are connected, we register the new `IIOPAccountImpl` object with the naming service using the `Context.rebind()` method.

Finally, we need to update our client so that it works with RMI/IIOP. Instead of using an RMI registry to look up the remote `Account` object, the client needs to use JNDI to connect to the same CORBA Naming Service that now hosts our `Account` object and ask for the `Account` by name. The updated `IIOPAccountClient` is shown here. Notice that we've also changed the client to use the `PortableRemoteObject.narrow()` method, instead of just casting the object returned from the lookup:

```
import javax.naming.*;
import java.rmi.RMISecurityManager;

public class IIOPAccountClient {
  public static void main(String argv[]) {
    try {
      // Lookup account object
      Hashtable props = new Hashtable();
      props.put("java.naming.factory.initial",
                "com.sun.jndi.cosnaming.CNCtxFactory");
      props.put("java.naming.provider.url", "iiop://objhost.org:900");
      Context ctx = new InitialContext(props);
      Account jimAcct =
        (Account)PortableRemoteObject.narrow(ctx.lookup("JimF"),
                                             Account.class);

      // Make deposit
      jimAcct.deposit(12000);

      // Report results and balance.
      System.out.println("Deposited 12,000 into account owned by " +
                         jimAcct.getName());
      System.out.println("Balance now totals: " + jimAcct.getBalance());
    }
    catch (Exception e) {
      System.out.println("Error while looking up account:");
      e.printStackTrace();
    }
  }
}
```

In order to register the server object, we need a CORBA Naming Service running, just like we need an RMI registry with standard RMI. The RMI/IIOP package includes a special naming service that is started using the *tnameserv* utility. This tool is similar to the naming service provided with Java IDL (and discussed in Chapter 4), but this version is a CORBA Naming Service that also provides JNDI access. On *objhost.org*, we need to start the naming service like so:

```
objhost% tnameserv -ORBInitialPort 900
```

Now we can run `IIOPRegAccount` to register the `Account` object with the naming service, then run our `IIOPAccountClient` to access the `Account` and make a deposit. All network communications are now taking place using IIOP rather than the RMI protocol.

Accessing RMI Objects from CORBA

Since our `Account` object is now speaking IIOP, we can also access it from other, non-Java CORBA clients. First, we need to get an IDL interface for the `Account` interface, which can be done using the *rmic* compiler provided with RMI/IIOP. The `-idl` option generates an IDL mapping of a Java RMI interface using the Java-to-IDL mapping defined by the CORBA standard. With this IDL mapping, we can generate language-specific stubs that lets any CORBA client talk to our Java remote object. See Chapter 4 for more details on using IDL and generating language-specific interfaces from it.

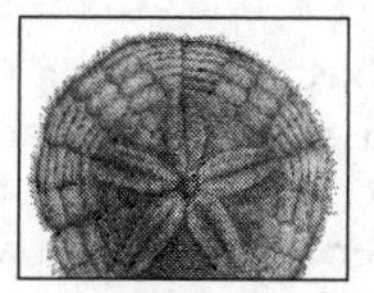

CHAPTER 4

Java IDL

The Java IDL API, introduced in Version 1.2 of the Java 2 platform, provides an interface between Java programs and distributed objects and services built using the Common Object Request Broker Architecture (CORBA). CORBA is a standard defined by the Object Management Group (OMG). It describes an architecture, interfaces, and protocols that distributed objects can use to interact with each other. Part of the CORBA standard is the Interface Definition Language (IDL), which is an implementation-independent language for describing the interfaces of remote-capable objects. There are standard mappings defined by the OMG for converting IDL interfaces into C++ classes, C code, and Java classes, among other things. These generated classes use the underlying CORBA framework to communicate with remote clients and give you the basis for implementing and exporting your own distributed objects. Java IDL is an implementation of the standard IDL-to-Java mapping and is provided by Sun with the standard Java SDK in the `org.omg.CORBA` and `org.omg.CosNaming` packages and their subpackages.*

Like RMI, Java IDL gives you a way to access remote objects over the network. It also provides the tools you need to make your objects accessible to other CORBA clients. If you export a Java class using Java IDL, you can create an instance of that class and publish it through a naming/directory service. A remote client can find this object, call methods on it, and receive data from it, just as if it were running on the client's local machine. Unlike RMI, however, objects that are exported using CORBA can be accessed by clients implemented in any language with an IDL binding (C, C++, Ada, etc.).

The CORBA standard is extensive, to say the least. In addition to the basic remote object architecture and the syntax of IDL, it also includes specifications for several distributed object services, like an object naming service, a security policy service, and persistent object services. It would be foolhardy to attempt to cover all these

* The version of Java IDL shipped with Version 1.2 of Java 2 is compliant with the CORBA 2.x specification.

topics completely in one chapter, so I won't. Instead, I'll just cover the basic features of the CORBA architecture and the IDL syntax. We'll also look at the Naming Service, which is key to almost every CORBA application because it provides a standard way to find remote CORBA objects on the network. With that under our belts, we'll take a look at the Java IDL API and the *idltojava* compiler and how together they give you an interface from your Java code to CORBA objects and services. They also give you the tools you need to create your own CORBA objects, implemented in Java.

The rest of this chapter is broken down roughly into three parts. In the first part, we'll look at an overview of the CORBA architecture and how it allows you to create, export, access, and manage remote objects. In the second part, we'll explore the details of creating your own CORBA objects. Finally, we'll look at how clients can remotely access your CORBA objects.

The CORBA Architecture

At its core, the CORBA architecture for distributed objects shares many features with the architecture used by Java RMI. A description of a remote object is used to generate a client stub interface and a server skeleton interface for the object. A client application invokes methods on a remote object using the client stub. The method request is transmitted through the underlying infrastructure to the remote host, where the server skeleton for the object is asked to invoke the method on the object itself. Any data resulting from the method call (return values, exceptions) is transmitted back to the client by the communication infrastructure.

But that's where the similarities between CORBA and RMI end. CORBA was designed from the start to be a language-independent distributed object standard, so it is much more extensive and detailed in its specification than RMI is (or needs to be). For the most part, these extra details are required in CORBA because it needs to support languages that have different built-in features. Some languages, like C++, directly support objects, while others, like C, don't. The CORBA standard needs to include a detailed specification of an object model so that nonobject-oriented languages can take advantage of CORBA. Java includes built-in support for communicating object interfaces and examining them abstractly (using Java bytecodes and the Java Reflection API). Many other languages do not. So the CORBA specification includes details about a Dynamic Invocation Interface and a Dynamic Skeleton Interface, which can be implemented in languages that don't have their own facilities for these operations. In languages that do have these capabilities, like Java, there needs to be a mapping between the built-in features and the features as defined by the CORBA specification.

The rest of this section provides an overview of the major components that make up the CORBA architecture: the Interface Definition Language, which is how CORBA interfaces are defined; the Object Request Broker (ORB), which is responsible for handling all interactions between remote objects and the applications that use them; the Naming Service, a standard service in CORBA that lets remote clients find remote objects on the network; and the inter-ORB communication that handles the low-level communication between processes in a CORBA context.

Interface Definition Language

The Interface Definition Language provides the primary way of describing data types in CORBA. IDL is independent of any particular programming language. Mappings, or bindings, from IDL to specific programming languages are defined and standardized as part of the CORBA specification. At the time of this writing, standard bindings for C, C++, Smalltalk, Ada, COBOL, and Java have been approved by the OMG. Chapter 10, *IDL Reference*, contains a complete description of IDL syntax.

The central CORBA functions, services, and facilities, such as the ORB and the Naming Service, are also specified in IDL. This means that a particular language binding also provides the bindings for the core CORBA functions to that language. Sun's Java IDL API follows the Java IDL mapping defined by the OMG. This allows you to run your CORBA-based Java code in any compliant Java implementation of the CORBA standard, provided you stick to standard elements of the Java binding. Note, however, that Sun's implementation includes some nonstandard elements; they are highlighted in this chapter where appropriate.

Object Request Broker

The core of the CORBA architecture is the Object Request Broker, as shown in Figure 4-1. Each machine involved in a CORBA application must have an ORB running in order for processes on that machine to interact with CORBA objects running in remote processes. Object clients and servers make requests through their ORBs; the ORB is responsible for making the requests happen or indicating why they cannot. The client ORB provides a stub for a remote object. Requests made on the stub are transferred from the client's ORB to the ORB servicing the implementation of the target object. The request is passed onto the implementation through its skeleton interface.

The Naming Service

The CORBA Naming Service provides a directory naming structure for remote objects. The tree always starts with a root node, and subnodes of the object tree can be defined. Actual objects are stored by name at the leaves of the tree. Figure 4-2 depicts an example set of objects* registered within a Naming Service directory. The fully qualified name of an object in the directory is the ordered list of all of its parent nodes, starting from the root node and including the leaf name of the object itself. So, the full name of the object labeled "Fred" is "living thing," "animal," "man," "Fred," in that order.

Each branch in the directory tree is called a *naming context*, and leaf objects have *bindings* to specific names. The `org.omg.CosNaming.NamingContext` interface represents each branch in the naming directory. Each `NamingContext` can be asked to find an object within its branch of the tree by giving its name relative to that

* Example adapted from *Categories*, by Aristotle. Please pardon the categorization "man," as opposed to "human." This is the typical translation of Aristotle's original Greek, perhaps because political correctness wasn't in fashion in 350 B.C.

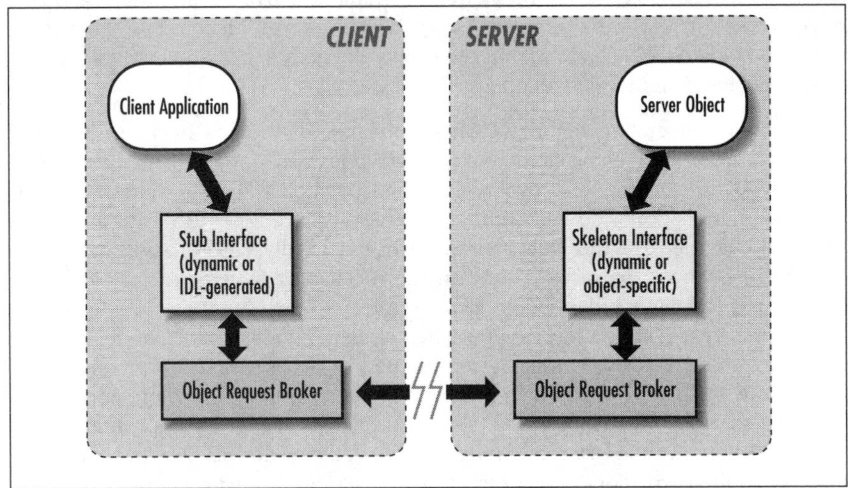

Figure 4-1: Basic CORBA architecture

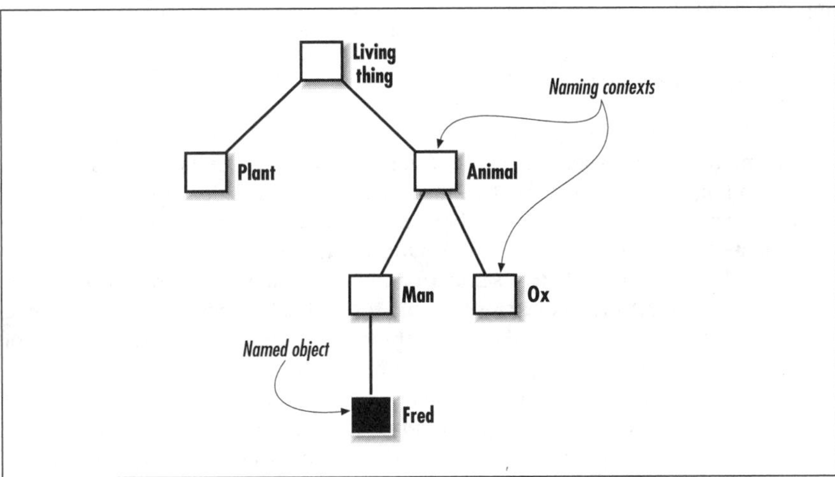

Figure 4-2: A naming directory

naming context. You can get a reference to the root context of the naming directory from an ORB using the `resolve_initial_references()` method. The standard name for the Naming Service is "NameService", so the following code snippet gets the root `NamingContext`:

```
ORB myORB = ORB.init(...);
org.omg.CORBA.Object nameRef =
        myORB.resolve_initial_references("NameService");
NamingContext nc = NamingContextHelper.narrow(nameRef);
```

Note that we have to narrow the `Object` reference to a `NamingContext` reference using the `NamingContextHelper.narrow()` method. Even though Java has a cast operation in its syntax, there's no guarantee in the Java IDL binding that the object reference returned by the `resolve_initial_references()` method is the correct type, since there's no guarantee that the local environment has access to the language-specific definition of the object's interface.

This `narrow()` operation highlights one of the key differences between RMI and CORBA. In the Java environment, class bytecodes are portable, and all remote object types are objects that can be specified by their full class names. An RMI client can automatically download the bytecodes for a remote stub from the object server, if the class for the stub cannot be found locally (see Chapter 3, *Remote Method Invocation*, for more details on the mechanics of remote class loading). CORBA is a language-independent remote object scheme, so there is no portable way to specify a remote object's type when a client obtains a stub reference. As a result, the stub reference is initially represented by a basic `ObjectImpl` object that knows how to forward methods requests to its server object. The client application is forced to "cast" this stub to the correct local type, using the appropriate `narrow()` method. In the Java mapping of IDL, this means calling the `narrow()` method on the corresponding helper class. The `narrow()` method converts the reference, making a type-specific stub interface that also includes the remote object reference information needed to forward method requests to the actual object implementation.

Inter-ORB Communication

Version 2.0 (and later) of the CORBA standard includes specifications for inter-ORB communication protocols that can transmit object requests between various ORBs running on the network. The protocols are independent of the particular ORB implementations running at either end of the communication link. An ORB implemented in Java can talk to another ORB implemented in C, as long as they're both compliant with the CORBA standard and use a standard communication protocol. The inter-ORB protocol is responsible for delivering messages between two cooperating ORBs. These messages might be method requests, return types, error messages, etc. The inter-ORB protocol also deals with differences between the two ORB implementations, like machine-level byte ordering and alignment. As a CORBA application developer, you shouldn't have to deal directly with the low-level communication protocol between ORBs. If you want two ORBs to talk to each other, you just need to be sure that they both speak a common, standard inter-ORB protocol.

The Internet Inter-ORB Protocol (IIOP) is an inter-ORB protocol based on TCP/IP. TCP/IP is by far the most commonly used network protocol on the Internet, so IIOP is the most commonly used CORBA communication protocol. There are other standard CORBA protocols defined for other network environments, however. The DCE Common Inter-ORB Protocol (DCE-CIOP), for example, allows ORBs to communicate on top of DCE-RPC.

Creating CORBA Objects

Now that you understand the various parts of the CORBA architecture, let's walk through the creation of CORBA objects using Java IDL. In order to distribute a Java object over the network using CORBA, you have to define your own CORBA-enabled interface and it implementation. This involves doing the following:

- Writing an interface in the CORBA Interface Definition Language
- Generating a Java base interface, plus a Java stub and skeleton class, using an IDL-to-Java compiler
- Writing a server-side implementation of the Java interface in Java

An IDL Primer

This section provides a quick overview of writing a CORBA interface in IDL. A full reference on IDL syntax is provided in Chapter 10, if you need more details.

The syntax of both Java and IDL were modeled to some extent on C++, so there are a lot of similarities between the two in terms of syntax. Interfaces in IDL are declared much like classes in C++ and, thus, classes or interfaces in Java. The major differences between IDL and Java are:

- IDL is a declaration language. In IDL, you declare only the names and types for interfaces, data members, methods, method parameters, etc. Method implementations are created in the implementation language you choose (in this case Java), after you've used an IDL compiler to convert your IDL interface to your target language.
- IDL, like C++, includes non-class data structure definitions, like structs, unions, and enumerations.
- Method parameters in IDL include modifiers that specify whether they are input, output, or input/output variables. In Java, all primitive data types are passed by value, and all object data types are passed by reference.
- An IDL file can include multiple public interfaces. Java allows multiple inner classes within a single public class definition and multiple nonpublic classes per file, but only a single public class can be defined in a given Java file.
- Modules, which are similar to Java packages, can be nested within other modules in the same IDL file, and interfaces in multiple distinct modules can be defined in the same IDL file. In Java, you can define a class only within a single package in a single Java file.

Modules

Modules are declared in IDL using the `module` keyword, followed by a name for the module and an opening brace that starts the module scope. Everything defined within the scope of this module (interfaces, constants, other modules) falls within the module and is referenced in other IDL modules using the syntax *module-name*`::x`. Suppose that you want all your classes to be contained in a module called corba, which is part of a larger module called jen (an acronym for the title of this book). In IDL this is declared as follows:

```
// IDL
module jen {
  module corba {
    interface NeatExample ...
  };
};
```

If you want to reference the NeatExample interface in other IDL files, use the syntax jen::corba::NeatExample, which may look familiar to readers who have done C++ programming. Java programmers should note the semicolons following the closing braces on the module definitions, which are required in IDL but not in Java. A semicolon is also required after the close of an interface definition.

Interfaces

Interfaces declared in IDL are mapped into classes or interfaces in Java. As I mentioned before, IDL is used only to declare modules, interfaces, and their methods. Methods on IDL interfaces are always left abstract, to be defined in the programming language you use to implement the interfaces.

The declaration of an interface includes an interface header and an interface body. The header specifies the name of the interface and the interfaces it inherits from (if any). Here is an IDL interface header:

```
interface PrintServer : Server { ...
```

This header starts the declaration of an interface called PrintServer that inherits all the methods and data members from the Server interface. An IDL interface can inherit from multiple interfaces; simply separate the interface names with commas in the inheritance part of the header.

Data members and methods

The interface body declares all the data members (or attributes) and methods of an interface. Data members are declared using the attribute keyword. At a minimum, the declaration includes a name and a type (see Chapter 10 for a complete list of the basic data types available in IDL and the mapping to Java types). The declaration can optionally specify whether the attribute is read-only or not, using the readonly keyword. By default, every attribute you declare is readable and writable (for Java, this means that the IDL compiler generates public read and write methods for it). Here is an example declaration for a read-only string attribute:

```
readonly attribute string myString;
```

You declare a method by specifying its name, return type, and parameters, at a minimum. You can also optionally declare exceptions the method might raise, the invocation semantics of the method, and the context for the method call (see Chapter 10 for more details). Here is the declaration for a simple method that returns a string:

```
string parseString(in string buffer);
```

This declares a method called `parseString()` that accepts a single `string` argument and returns a `string` value.

A complete IDL example

Now let's tie all these basic elements together. Here's a complete IDL example that declares a module within another module, which itself contains several interfaces:

```
module OS {
  module services {
    interface Server {
      readonly attribute string serverName;
      boolean init(in string sName);
    };

    interface Printable {
      boolean print(in string header);
    };

    interface PrintServer : Server {
      boolean printThis(in Printable p);
    };
  };
};
```

The first interface, `Server`, has a single read-only `string` attribute and an `init()` method that accepts a `string` and returns a `boolean`. The `Printable` interface has a single `print()` method that accepts a string header. Finally, the `PrintServer` interface extends the `Server` interface (hence inheriting all its methods and attributes) and adds a `printThis()` method that accepts a `Printable` object and returns a `boolean`. In all cases, we've declared our method arguments as input-only (i.e., pass-by-value), using the `in` keyword.

Turning IDL Into Java

Once you've described your remote interfaces in IDL, you need to generate Java classes that act as a starting point for implementing those remote interfaces in Java using an IDL-to-Java compiler. Every standard IDL-to-Java compiler generates the following Java classes from an IDL interface:

- A Java interface with the same name as the IDL interface. This can act as the basis for a Java implementation of the interface (but you have to write it, since IDL doesn't provide any details about method implementations).
- A *helper* class whose name is the name of the IDL interface with "Helper" appended to it (e.g., `ServerHelper`). The primary purpose of this class is to provide a static `narrow()` method that can safely cast CORBA `Object` references to the Java interface type. The helper class also provides other useful static methods, such as `read()` and `write()` methods that allow you to read and write an object of the corresponding type using I/O streams.

- A *holder* class whose name is the name of the IDL interface with "Holder" appended to it (e.g., `ServerHolder`). This class is used when objects with this interface are used as `out` or `inout` arguments in remote CORBA methods. Instead of being passed directly into the remote method, the object is wrapped with its holder before being passed. When a remote method has parameters that are declared as `out` or `inout`, the method has to be able to update the argument it is passed and return the updated value. The only way to guarantee this, even for primitive Java data types, is to force `out` and `inout` arguments to be wrapped in Java holder classes, which are filled with the output value of the argument when the method returns.

The *idltojava* tool provided by Sun* can also generate two other classes:

- A client *stub* class, called `_interface-nameStub`, that acts as a client-side implementation of the interface and knows how to convert method requests into ORB requests that are forwarded to the actual remote object. The stub class for an interface named `Server` is called `_ServerStub`.

- A server *skeleton* class, called `_interface-nameImplBase`, that is a base class for a server-side implementation of the interface. The base class can accept requests for the object from the ORB and channel return values back through the ORB to the remote client. The skeleton class for an interface named `Server` is called `_ServerImplBase`.

So, in addition to generating a Java mapping of the IDL interface and some helper classes for the Java interface, the *idltojava* compiler also creates subclasses that act as an interface between a CORBA client and the ORB and between the server-side implementation and the ORB. Chapter 12, *Java IDL Tools*, provides a complete reference for Sun's *idltojava* compiler. We use this IDL-to-Java tool in the examples in this chapter. Remember, though, that any Java mapping of the CORBA standard should include its own IDL-to-Java compiler to generate these Java classes from the IDL interfaces you write. In addition, the Java that these tools generate should be compliant with the standard IDL mapping for Java, published by the OMG in the CORBA standard.

A simple server class

The IDL interface shown in Example 4-1 is the IDL equivalent of the Java class we defined in Example 3-3 in the RMI chapter. The interface, named `ThisOrThatServer`, declares two methods, `doThis()` and `doThat()`. As in the earlier RMI example, each method accepts a string that specifies what to do and returns a string that indicates what was done. Since this is IDL, the string data type is `string`, and the parameters are declared as `in` arguments, since we want them to be passed into the remote method by value.

---

* Although Java IDL is a standard part of Java 1.2, Sun still offers only the early-access version of its *idltojava* compiler, which you have to download separately from *http://developer.java.sun.com/developer/earlyAccess/jdk12/idltojava.html*.

Example 4-1: A ThisOrThatServer Declared in IDL

```
interface ThisOrThatServer {
  string doThis(in string what);
  string doThat(in string what);
};
```

We can run the *idltojava* compiler on this IDL interface using the following command line (Windows version):

```
D:\>idltojava -fno-cpp ThisOrThatServer.idl
```

This command creates the five Java classes I just described: a Java version of the interface, a helper class, a holder class, a client stub, and a server skeleton. I had to use the `-fno-cpp` option on my machine because I don't have a C preprocessor installed for *idltojava* to use; this option tells the IDL compiler to use an alternate parsing scheme while it converts the IDL to Java (see Chapter 12 for complete details on the command-line arguments for *idltojava*).

The compiler creates the Java interface shown in Example 4-2, in a file named *ThisOrThatServer.java*. The mapping is fairly straightforward for this simple example. The interface declaration is mapped directly to a Java interface declaration, with the interface extending the `org.omg.CORBA.Object` interface. If we had included any module definitions in our IDL specification, they would have been mapped into a `package` statement at the beginning of the Java file. The IDL `string` type is converted into the Java `String` type, and, since they don't require any special handling in a remote method call, the `in` method parameters in IDL are mapped into regular Java input arguments.

Example 4-2: Java Interface for ThisOrThatServer

```
/*
 * File: ./THISORTHATSERVER.JAVA
 * From: THISORTHATSERVER.IDL
 * Date: Thu Apr 15 21:42:40 1999
 *   By: C:\JDK12~1.1\BIN\IDLTOJ~1.EXE Java IDL 1.2 Aug 18 1998 16:25:34
 */

public interface ThisOrThatServer
    extends org.omg.CORBA.Object {
    String doThis(String what)
;
    String doThat(String what)
;
}
```

You might notice that the IDL compiler has put the semicolons following the method declarations on separate lines. To my knowledge, there's no good reason for this; it's just a quirk of the *idltojava* tool provided by Sun.

The helper class

The compiler also generates a helper class, called `ThisOrThatServerHelper`, as shown in Example 4-3. As I mentioned earlier, the helper class has methods that let you read and write `ThisOrThatServer` objects to and from CORBA I/O streams, get the TypeCode for a ThisOrThatServer object, and, most importantly, safely narrow a CORBA Object reference into a ThisOrThatServer reference.

Example 4-3: Helper Class for the ThisOrThatServer

```
/*
 * File: ./THISORTHATSERVERHELPER.JAVA
 * From: THISORTHATSERVER.IDL
 * Date: Thu Apr 15 21:42:40 1999
 *   By: C:\JDK12~1.1\BIN\IDLTOJ~1.EXE Java IDL 1.2 Aug 18 1998 16:25:34
 */

public class ThisOrThatServerHelper {
    // It is useless to have instances of this class
    private ThisOrThatServerHelper() { }

    public static void write(org.omg.CORBA.portable.OutputStream out,
                             ThisOrThatServer that) {
        out.write_Object(that);
    }
    public static ThisOrThatServer
      read(org.omg.CORBA.portable.InputStream in) {
        return ThisOrThatServerHelper.narrow(in.read_Object());
    }
   public static ThisOrThatServer extract(org.omg.CORBA.Any a) {
     org.omg.CORBA.portable.InputStream in = a.create_input_stream();
     return read(in);
   }
   public static void insert(org.omg.CORBA.Any a, ThisOrThatServer that) {
     org.omg.CORBA.portable.OutputStream out = a.create_output_stream();
     write(out, that);
     a.read_value(out.create_input_stream(), type());
   }
   private static org.omg.CORBA.TypeCode _tc;
   synchronized public static org.omg.CORBA.TypeCode type() {
          if (_tc == null)
             _tc = org.omg.CORBA.ORB.init().create_interface_tc(id(),
                   "ThisOrThatServer");
      return _tc;
   }
   public static String id() {
       return "IDL:ThisOrThatServer:1.0";
   }
   public static ThisOrThatServer narrow(org.omg.CORBA.Object that)
            throws org.omg.CORBA.BAD_PARAM {
        if (that == null)
            return null;
        if (that instanceof ThisOrThatServer)
            return (ThisOrThatServer) that;
        if (!that._is_a(id())) {
            throw new org.omg.CORBA.BAD_PARAM();
        }
        org.omg.CORBA.portable.Delegate dup =
          ((org.omg.CORBA.portable.ObjectImpl)that)._get_delegate();
        ThisOrThatServer result = new _ThisOrThatServerStub(dup);
        return result;
   }
}
```

In the implementation of the narrow() method, we can see how the helper class converts a CORBA Object reference to a reference to a specific type. First, the narrow() method checks to see if the Object parameter is already a ThisOrThatServer object (using the Java instanceof operator), then it checks to see if the object passed in is a null pointer. If neither case is true, the Object should contain a *delegate* of a ThisOrThatServer object. Every CORBA stub for a remote object contains an internal Delegate object (from the org.omg.CORBA.portable package) that's used by the stub to invoke remote requests. If the object's delegate is a ThisOrThatServer (checked using the objects's _is_a() method), the delegate is used to create a new ThisOrThatServer stub. We'll take a look at the ThisOrThatServer stub class in a bit. If the object doesn't contain a delegate, the is_a() method returns false, and the narrow() method throws a BAD_PARAM exception.

The holder class

The compiler generates a holder class for the ThisOrThatServer class, as shown in Example 4-4. The holder class, called ThisOrThatServerHolder, is a wrapper used when ThisOrThatServer objects are called for as out or inout arguments in an IDL method. All holder classes implement the Streamable interface from the org.omg.CORBA.portable package. An ORB knows to pass Streamable objects in method calls using the _read() and _write() methods of the Streamable object; these methods handle whatever serialization the object needs.

Example 4-4: Holder Class for the ThisOrThatServer

```
/*
 * File: ./THISORTHATSERVERHOLDER.JAVA
 * From: THISORTHATSERVER.IDL
 * Date: Thu Apr 15 21:42:40 1999
 *   By: C:\JDK12~1.1\BIN\IDLTOJ~1.EXE Java IDL 1.2 Aug 18 1998 16:25:34
 */

public final class ThisOrThatServerHolder
     implements org.omg.CORBA.portable.Streamable{
    //  instance variable
    public ThisOrThatServer value;
    //  constructors
    public ThisOrThatServerHolder() {
        this(null);
    }
    public ThisOrThatServerHolder(ThisOrThatServer __arg) {
        value = __arg;
    }

    public void _write(org.omg.CORBA.portable.OutputStream out) {
        ThisOrThatServerHelper.write(out, value);
    }

    public void _read(org.omg.CORBA.portable.InputStream in) {
        value = ThisOrThatServerHelper.read(in);
    }

    public org.omg.CORBA.TypeCode _type() {
        return ThisOrThatServerHelper.type();
    }
}
```

A holder contains a single instance of a CORBA object (a ThisOrThatServer, in this example). When a holder object is passed into a remote method call as an inout argument, its _write() method is invoked. This method takes the object contained by the holder class, serializes it, and streams it through the ORB to the remote object server. When the remote method call returns, the holder's _read() method is invoked to read the (possibly updated) object from the remote object server, and the holder object replaces its internal value with the updated object.

As an example of using the holder class, let's define another IDL interface that includes a method that uses a ThisOrThatServer as an inout parameter:

```
// IDL
interface ServerManager {
  boolean updateServer(inout ThisOrThatServer server);
};
```

The Java interface generated from this IDL interface uses the holder class for the ThisOrThatServer as the type for the corresponding Java method parameter:

```
// Java
public interface ServerManager
    extends org.omg.CORBA.Object {
    boolean updateServer(ThisOrThatServerHolder server)
;
}
```

The ThisOrThatServerHolder class has public constructors that let you create a holder from an existing ThisOrThatServer object, so that you can easily pass the object into this kind of method.

The client and server stubs

The *idltojava* compiler generates two more classes from our interface definition: a client stub (_ThisOrThatServerStub) and a base class for a server implementation (_ThisOrThatServerImplBase). The client stub, shown in Example 4-5, implements the generated ThisOrThatServer Java interface and acts as a client-side proxy for a remote ThisOrThatServer object. The stub has implementations of the doThis() and doThat() methods from the interface. Each implementation just generates a request to the ORB to make a remote method call on the server-side object that this stub is a proxy for. The method arguments are bundled up and passed along with the request to the ORB. I'm not going to go into the details of the stub's method implementations because you shouldn't have to worry much about them, but it is enlightening to look at the source code to see how your remote objects do what they do in detail, using the core CORBA functions.

Example 4-5: ThisOrThatServer Stub Class Generated by IDL Compiler

```
/*
 * File: ./_THISORTHATSERVERSTUB.JAVA
 * From: THISORTHATSERVER.IDL
 * Date: Thu Apr 15 21:42:40 1999
 *   By: C:\JDK12~1.1\BIN\IDLTOJ~1.EXE Java IDL 1.2 Aug 18 1998 16:25:34
 */

public class _ThisOrThatServerStub
```

```
        extends org.omg.CORBA.portable.ObjectImpl
        implements ThisOrThatServer {

    public _ThisOrThatServerStub(org.omg.CORBA.portable.Delegate d) {
          super();
          _set_delegate(d);
    }

    private static final String _type_ids[] = {
        "IDL:ThisOrThatServer:1.0"
    };

    public String[] _ids() { return (String[]) _type_ids.clone(); }

    //  IDL operations
    //      Implementation of ::ThisOrThatServer::doThis
    public String doThis(String what)
 {
           org.omg.CORBA.Request r = _request("doThis");
           r.set_return_type(org.omg.CORBA.ORB.init().get_primitive_tc(
               org.omg.CORBA.TCKind.tk_string));
           org.omg.CORBA.Any _what = r.add_in_arg();
           _what.insert_string(what);
           r.invoke();
           String __result;
           __result = r.return_value().extract_string();
           return __result;
   }
    //      Implementation of ::ThisOrThatServer::doThat
    public String doThat(String what)
 {
           org.omg.CORBA.Request r = _request("doThat");
           r.set_return_type(org.omg.CORBA.ORB.init().get_primitive_tc(
               org.omg.CORBA.TCKind.tk_string));
           org.omg.CORBA.Any _what = r.add_in_arg();
           _what.insert_string(what);
           r.invoke();
           String __result;
           __result = r.return_value().extract_string();
           return __result;
   }
};
```

When a Java client gets a reference to a remote `ThisOrThatServer` object, it is given one of these stub objects. The client can make method calls on the stub object, and the stub converts these calls into corresponding requests to the ORB to invoke the methods on the remote object and send back the results.

The base class for the server implementation, shown in Example 4-6, accepts requests that are intended for the server implementation from the ORB. The base class converts a request into a method call on the server object and then takes the result of the call and gives it back to the ORB to send to the client stub. All this work is done in the server skeleton's `invoke()` method. The `invoke()` method figures out which method is being called, unpacks the method arguments (if any) from the request, and calls the method directly on itself.

Note that the server skeleton doesn't have implementations of the doThis() or doThat() methods declared in the interface. The *idltojava* compiler doesn't do everything for you; you still need to create a server implementation for your interface.

Example 4-6: Implementation Base Class for ThisOrThatServer

```
/*
 * File: ./_THISORTHATSERVERIMPLBASE.JAVA
 * From: THISORTHATSERVER.IDL
 * Date: Thu Apr 15 21:42:40 1999
 *   By: C:\JDK12~1.1\BIN\IDLTOJ~1.EXE Java IDL 1.2 Aug 18 1998 16:25:34
 */

public abstract class _ThisOrThatServerImplBase extends
    org.omg.CORBA.DynamicImplementation implements ThisOrThatServer {
    // Constructor
    public _ThisOrThatServerImplBase() {
         super();
    }
    // Type strings for this class and its superclasses
    private static final String _type_ids[] = {
        "IDL:ThisOrThatServer:1.0"
    };

    public String[] _ids() { return (String[]) _type_ids.clone(); }

    private static java.util.Dictionary _methods = new java.util.Hashtable();
    static {
      _methods.put("doThis", new java.lang.Integer(0));
      _methods.put("doThat", new java.lang.Integer(1));
     }
    // DSI Dispatch call
    public void invoke(org.omg.CORBA.ServerRequest r) {
       switch (((java.lang.Integer) _methods.get(r.op_name())).intValue()) {
           case 0: // ThisOrThatServer.doThis
              {
              org.omg.CORBA.NVList _list = _orb().create_list(0);
              org.omg.CORBA.Any _what = _orb().create_any();
              _what.type(org.omg.CORBA.ORB.init().get_primitive_tc(
                  org.omg.CORBA.TCKind.tk_string));
              _list.add_value("what", _what, org.omg.CORBA.ARG_IN.value);
              r.params(_list);
              String what;
              what = _what.extract_string();
              String ___result;
                            ___result = this.doThis(what);
              org.omg.CORBA.Any __result = _orb().create_any();
              __result.insert_string(___result);
              r.result(__result);
              }
              break;
           case 1: // ThisOrThatServer.doThat
              {
              org.omg.CORBA.NVList _list = _orb().create_list(0);
              org.omg.CORBA.Any _what = _orb().create_any();
              _what.type(org.omg.CORBA.ORB.init().get_primitive_tc(
                  org.omg.CORBA.TCKind.tk_string));
              _list.add_value("what", _what, org.omg.CORBA.ARG_IN.value);
              r.params(_list);
```

Example 4-6: Implementation Base Class for ThisOrThatServer (continued)

```
          String what;
          what = _what.extract_string();
          String ___result;
                        ___result = this.doThat(what);
          org.omg.CORBA.Any __result = _orb().create_any();
          __result.insert_string(___result);
          r.result(__result);
          }
          break;
        default:
          throw new org.omg.CORBA.BAD_OPERATION(0,
              org.omg.CORBA.CompletionStatus.COMPLETED_MAYBE);
      }
  }
}
```

Writing the Implementation

So, we've written an IDL interface and generated the Java interface and support classes for it, including the client stub and the server skeleton. Now we need to create concrete server-side implementations of all of the methods on your interface. We do this by subclassing from the _*xxx*`ImplBase` class generated by the *idltojava* compiler. For our example, we need to subclass `_ThisOrThatServerImplBase` and implement the `doThis()` and `doThat()` methods. The `ThisOrThatServerImpl` class in Example 4-7 does just that. Note that we've mimicked the method implementations from the RMI example in Chapter 3. The only real difference is that this `ThisOrThatServerImpl` class extends `_ThisOrThatServerImplBase`, while the one in Chapter 3 extends the `UnicastRemoteObject`.

Example 4-7: Server-Side Implementation of ThisOrThatServer Interface

```
public class ThisOrThatServerImpl extends _ThisOrThatServerImplBase {

  public ThisOrThatServerImpl() {}

  // Remotely-accessible methods
  public String doThis(String what) {
    return doSomething("this", what);
  }

  public String doThat(String what) {
    return doSomething("that", what);
  }

  // Non-remote methods
  private String doSomething(String todo, String what) {
    String result = todo + " " + what + " is done.";
    System.out.println("Did " + todo + " to " + what);
    return result;
  }
}
```

Java IDL

Putting It in the Public Eye

We still need to do some work to make the Java implementation of our IDL interface available to remote clients. There are two ways a client gets a reference to a remote object: it can get an initial object reference using the `ORB.resolve_initial_references()` method and somehow find a reference to the object through method calls on the initial object, or it can get a "stringified" reference to the remote object (an Interoperable Object Reference) and convert it locally to a live object reference.

For the first case, the remote object needs to be registered in some way with a server-side ORB. In order for you to register a remote object, you first have to get a reference to an ORB. We'll look at how to do that first, then look at registering the remote object with a Naming Service. We discuss the stringified object reference technique later in this chapter, when we look at how clients can access remote objects.

Initializing the ORB

Since the ORB is so central to everything in a CORBA environment, the first thing any CORBA process needs to do is get a reference to a local or remote ORB that it can use to find other objects, access CORBA services, and handle remote method calls. A CORBA participant initializes its ORB reference by calling one of the static `init()` methods on the ORB interface. Each of these methods returns an `ORB` object that can find CORBA objects and services. The standard `init()` methods provided on an ORB are as follows (Sun's Java IDL supports all of these standard initialization methods):

`public static ORB ORB.init()`
: Returns a shared (static) ORB instance. Each call within the same runtime environment returns the same ORB reference. If used within an applet context, the ORB has limited abilities.

`public static ORB ORB.init(String[] args, Properties props)`
: Creates a new ORB using the given arguments and properties, as discussed in the following paragraphs.

`public static ORB ORB.init(Applet applet, Properties props)`
: Creates a new ORB within an applet context. The applet's codebase and host are used by the ORB as the source of various services, such as the Naming Service.

There are two standard properties defined for an ORB that can be set in the call to `init()`, using either the `String` arguments array or a `Properties` object. These are the `ORBClass` and `ORBSingletonClass` properties, which specify the Java classes to use to create ORBs when an `init()` method is called. (`ORBSingletonClass` is a shared ORB instance that is used mainly by generated classes to do things like create `TypeCode` objects that identify the types of CORBA objects, while `ORBClass` is a fully functional ORB.) You can use these properties to specify a custom ORB implementation. You may want to override the default ORB implementation (`com.sun.CORBA.iiop.ORB` in Java IDL) with one of your own that has particular performance characteristics. Or you may be running your CORBA code within an applet and want to ensure that a valid ORB is available no matter what browser version your applet encounters.

Sun's Java IDL also adds two nonstandard properties: `ORBInitialHost` and `ORBInitialPort`. By default, each `ORB.init()` method initializes an ORB that looks for its services locally. The current version of the Java IDL API includes a single service, the Naming Service, and the `ORB.init()` methods assume that the Naming Service is listening to port 900 on the local host. Java IDL adds these two nonstandard properties to allow your local ORB to defer its services (naming, trading, etc.) to a remote ORB running on a given host and listening on a given port. Be careful before you decide to depend on these properties in your application or applet. They are only honored within Sun's Java IDL implementation of the CORBA standard. If you want your CORBA application to be portable to any implementation of the standard IDL-to-Java binding, and you want to use a remote Naming Service, you should stick to using a stringified reference to the remote service, obtained through a secondary communication channel, as we'll discuss shortly.

Any of these properties can be specified within a `Properties` object or as a command-line option to a Java application. As an example, if you want to specify a different host to use for finding services like the Naming Service, one way to do this is to specify the host explicitly in the code that initializes the ORB, using a `Properties` object:

```
Properties orbProps = new Properties();
orbProps.put("org.omg.CORBA.ORBInitialHost", "remote.orb.com");
ORB myOrb = ORB.init((String[])null, orbProps);
```

Alternately, you can take command-line arguments passed into your Java code and pass them to the `ORB.init()` method to be parsed. Say we have a class named `InitRemote` with a main method implemented as follows:

```
public class InitRemote {
  public static void main(String[] argv) {
    try {
      ORB myOrb = ORB.init(argv, null);
      ...
    }
  }
}
```

In this case, we can specify any ORB properties on the command line using specific argument names:

```
orbhost% java InitRemote -ORBInitialHost remote.orb.com
```

Note that you can use the second `ORB.init()` method with both a `String` arguments array and a `Properties` list specified, even though the examples here haven't shown that.

Registering with a Naming Service

One way to make a server object available to remote clients is to register it with the local CORBA Naming Service under a specific name. A remote client can then get a reference to the root NamingContext for the Naming Service and ask for the server object by name.

Example 4-8 shows a class whose main() method creates an instance of our ThisOrThatServer implementation and then registers the object with the Naming Service. The program starts by getting a reference to the local ORB. Then it asks the ORB for a reference to the Naming Service (using the standard name "NameService") with the resolve_initial_references() method. This reference is actually the root NamingContext, so we narrow the object reference using NamingContextHelper. We register the ThisOrThatServer with the Naming Service by building an array of NameComponent objects and then calling the rebind() method on the NamingContext. With the object registered, we go into a wait state, waiting for client requests.

Example 4-8: Registering an Object with the Naming Service

```
import org.omg.CORBA.*;
import org.omg.CosNaming.*;

public class ServerNamingInit {
  public static void main(String[] argv) {
    try {
      // Obtain ORB reference
      ORB myORB = ORB.init(argv, null);

      // Make a ThisOrThatServer object to register with the ORB
      ThisOrThatServer impl = new ThisOrThatServerImpl();

      // Get the root name context
      org.omg.CORBA.Object objRef =
        myORB.resolve_initial_references("NameService");
      NamingContext nc = NamingContextHelper.narrow(objRef);

      // Register the local object with the Name Service
      NameComponent ncomp = new NameComponent("ThisOrThatServer", "");
      NameComponent[] name = {ncomp};
      nc.rebind(name, impl);

      // Go into a wait state, waiting for clients to connect
      System.out.println("Waiting for clients...");
      java.lang.Object dummy = new String("I wait...");
      synchronized (dummy) {
        dummy.wait();
      }
    }
    catch (Exception e) {
      System.out.println("Error occurred while initializing server object:");
      e.printStackTrace();
    }
  }
}
```

Note that Example 4-8 imports the org.omg.CORBA and org.omg.CosNaming packages, which are the two main packages in Java IDL. Because of the naming collision between java.lang.Object and org.omg.CORBA.Object, we have to use the fully qualified names of these two classes when we use them in CORBA applications that import org.orm.CORBA. Finally, note that this example binds the ThisOrThatServer object within the root NamingContext using the name

"ThisOrThatServer". We'll see shortly how to create subcontexts and bind objects within them.

Before running this initialization of our CORBA object, we need to start a Naming Service on the host for the object. A Naming Service daemon listens for Naming Service requests on a specific port and provides access to the named object directory it manages. In Java IDL, the Naming Service is started using the *tnameserv* command:

```
objhost% tnameserv &
```

With that done, we can run our initialization method to register our server object with the ORB:

```
objhost% java ServerNamingInit
```

Adding Objects to a Naming Context

Initially, a CORBA naming directory is empty, with only its root `NamingContext` and no objects. The `bind()` method on a `NamingContext` object binds a server object to a name within the context. The `bind_new_context()` method creates new subcontexts within a given `NamingContext`. Using a file directory analogy, calling `bind_new_context()` on a `NamingContext` object is like making a new subdirectory, while calling `bind()` puts a new file into a directory.

The Java IDL mapping uses arrays of `NameComponent` objects to represent the names of subcontexts within a naming directory. Each `NameComponent` represents a component of the path to the named object. A `NameComponent` contains `id` and `kind` string fields that serve to label the component in the path. Only the `id` field is significant in determining name uniqueness. So a `NameComponent` with `id` set to "student" and `kind` set to an empty string conflicts with a `NameComponent` with an `id` of "student" and `kind` "doctoral," if both `NameComponent` objects are relative to the same subcontext. The `NameComponent` class has a constructor that takes the `id` and `kind` values as arguments. Here's how to create a single `NameComponent`:

```
NameComponent comp1 = new NameComponent("student", "doctoral");
```

A complete name path can be composed as an array of these objects:

```
NameComponent path[] = { comp1, comp2, ... };
```

The `bind()` method takes two arguments: an array of `NameComponent` objects as the relative name for the object you're putting into the Naming Service and the server object itself. If you're binding a server object using the root context of the Naming Service, the name is also the absolute name of the object in the overall naming directory. If an object is already bound to the name, you can use the `rebind()` method with the same arguments, causing the existing object bound to that name to be replaced by the new object. Note that since the Naming Service is a CORBA service that can be accessed remotely by other CORBA clients, the objects it contains need to be exportable to these remote clients. This means that only `org.omg.CORBA.Object` references can be bound to names within a `NamingContext`.

The following code binds a few of our `ThisOrThatServer` objects to names within the root context of a Naming Service:

```
// Get the root naming context
ORB myORB = ORB.init(...);
org.omg.CORBA.Object ref =  myORB.resolve_initial_references("NameService");
NamingContext rootNC = NamingContextHelper.narrow(ref);

// Create a few servers
org.omg.CORBA.Object ref1 = new ThisOrThatServerImpl();
org.omg.CORBA.Object ref2 = new ThisOrThatServerImpl();

// Bind them to names in the Naming Service
NameComponent name1 = new NameComponent("server1", "");
NameComponent path1[] = { name1 };
NameComponent name2 = new NameComponent("server2", "");
NameComponent path2[] = { name2 };
rootNC.bind(path1, ref1);
rootNC.bind(path2, ref2);
```

Before you can bind an object to a name with multiple components, all the subcontexts (subdirectories) have to be created using the `bind_new_context()` method on a `NamingContext`. The `bind_new_context()` method takes an array of `NameComponent` objects as the relative path of the new context and a reference to the `NamingContext` object to bind to that location in the overall directory. A new `NamingContext` object can be created from an existing one by calling its `new_context()` method. If a context already exists at the target name, you can use the `rebind_context()` method to replace the existing context with a new one. This is useful for emptying out an entire subcontext without removing each object individually.

Here is an example that binds some objects within various subcontexts:

```
// Get the root context, as before
NamingContext rootNC = ...;

// Create the components to the subcontext name
NameComponent comp1 = new NameComponent("servers", "");
NameComponent ttComp = new NameComponent("ThisOrThat", "");
NameComponent otherComp= new NameComponent("misc", "");

// Create each subcontext within the root context and bind them
// to their appropriate names
// Create a new context, bind it to the name "servers"
// off the root NamingContext
NamingContext context1 = rootNC.new_context();
NameComponent path1[] = { comp1 };
rootNC.bind_context(path1, context1);
// Create another context, bind it to the name "servers, ThisOrThat"
NamingContext ttDir = rootNC.new_context();
NameComponent path2_1[] = { comp1, ttComp };
rootNC.bind_context(path2_1, ttDir);
// Create another context, bind it to the name "servers, misc"
NamingContext otherDir = rootNC.new_context();
NameComponent path2_2[] = { comp1, otherComp };
rootNC.bind_context(path2_2, otherDir);

// Now we can bind servers to a name within any of the new subcontexts
org.omg.CORBA.Object ttRef = new ThisOrThatServerImpl();
org.omg.CORBA.Object otherRef = new SomeOtherServerImpl();
```

```
// Bind the other server to the "misc" branch of the "servers" dir.
NameComponent yetAnotherComp = new NameComponent("SomeOtherServer", "");
NameComponent otherPath[] = { comp1, otherComp, yetAnotherComp };
rootNC.bind(otherPath, otherRef);

// Bind the ThisOrThatServer to the appropriate branch under "servers"
NameComponent tt1Comp = new NameComponent("server1", "");
NameComponent ttPath[] = { comp1, ttComp, tt1Comp };
rootNC.bind(ttPath, ttRef);
```

If you try to bind an object or a subcontext to a name within a context that hasn't been created yet, a `org.omg.CosNaming.NamingContextPackage.NotFound` exception is thrown.

Note that names used in the `bind()` or `rebind()` methods are relative to the `NamingContext` object that they're called on. This means we can bind our `ThisOrThatServer` object in the previous example to the same absolute name within the directory by replacing the last two lines of the example with the following:

```
NameComponent relObjPath[] = { tt1Comp };
ttDir.bind(relObjPath, ttRef);
```

The `ttDir` context is bound to the {"servers", "ThisOrThat"} subdirectory, so binding an object to the name {"server1"} within this context is equivalent to binding it to the full path {"servers", "ThisOrThat", "server1"} from the root context. You can use similar shorthand when binding new contexts within a directory. In other words, you can bind a context to a relative name within a subcontext, instead of an absolute name within the root context.

Java IDL

Finding Remote Objects

Now that we have registered our remote object with an ORB, it is available to CORBA client applications. This means we are done with the setup of the remote object and can turn our attention to client applications that want to use the object. As I said earlier, every CORBA process needs a reference to an ORB. Once a client application has access to an ORB, the next thing for it to do is find remote objects to interact with. But before we can discuss finding remote objects, we need to talk a bit about what remote object references look like under CORBA.

The whole point of CORBA is to be able to distribute objects across the network and then use them from any point on the network. In order for a local process to make requests of a remote object, it needs to have some kind of reference to that remote object. This object reference needs to contain enough information for the local ORB to find the ORB serving the target object and send the request to the remote ORB using an agreed-upon protocol.

In most situations, a CORBA client has a reference to a remote object in the form of an object stub. The stub encapsulates the actual object reference, providing what seems like a direct interface to the remote object in the local environment. If the client is implemented in C++, Java, or some other object-oriented language, the object stub is a native object in that language. Other, nonobject languages represent remote object references in whatever way is dictated in the CORBA language binding for that language.

CORBA includes its own root object class, since some object programming languages may have different inheritance structures. In the Java binding for CORBA, all CORBA object references (local or remote) implement the `org.omg.CORBA.Object` interface. So, when a client of a remote CORBA object receives a stub for the object, it actually gets an `org.omg.CORBA.Object` that serves as a proxy for the remote object. The `org.omg.CORBA.portable.ObjectImpl` class provides default implementations for the methods defined on `org.omg.CORBA.Object`. Java stubs and implementations for CORBA objects are actually subclassed from the `ObjectImpl` class. Internally, `ObjectImpl` deals with delegating requests on the object to the proper target object, whether it is a remote object or a local one. `ObjectImpl` implements the `org.omg.CORBA.Object` interface and extends the `java.lang.Object` class, so it truly provides a joining point between the CORBA and Java object environments.

A reference to an `org.omg.CORBA.Object` object that is connected to a remote object is all a client needs to invoke methods on a remote object. Using the Dynamic Invocation Interface defined by the CORBA standard, you can create method requests and send them to the remote object through the `Object` interface, as we'll discuss later in this chapter. If your client has the actual Java interface for the remote object available at compile time, however, you probably want to convert the `Object` reference into a reference of that type, so that you can use the interface to call remote methods directly.

Converting an `org.omg.COBRA.Object` to a specific remote interface is done by narrowing the object reference to the corresponding interface type, using type-specific helper classes to do the narrowing. We've already seen how the Java IDL compiler, *idltojava*, creates a helper class from an IDL interface (e.g., `ThisOrThatServerHelper`). The helper class includes a `narrow()` method that converts an `org.omg.CORBA.Object` reference to a reference of the given type. If the object reference you pass into the `narrow()` method is not the type the helper expects, an `org.omg.CORBA.BAD_PARAM` exception is thrown. This is a `RuntimeException`, so it doesn't have to be caught by your code, unless you're trying to test the type of a CORBA reference for some reason.

With that background material out of the way, let's discuss actually finding remote object references. There are many ways that an object reference can find its way through the ORB into a client application, but they all boil down to one of these methods:

- Getting an initial reference directly from the ORB
- Getting an object reference through a method call on another remote object reference
- Using a stringified object reference obtained through a secondary channel and converting it to a live object reference

Initial ORB References

In addition to providing core object communication services, an ORB can also provide additional services, such as a Naming Service, a Trading Service, a Security Service, etc. These services are represented as CORBA objects and are available through the ORB automatically, based on how it is configured. The ORB interface provides the `resolve_initial_references()` method for obtaining references to these initial objects. Each CORBA service the ORB supports is represented by one or more object interfaces, and these objects can be asked for using standard names. As we saw earlier when we registered a remote object, the standard name for the Naming Service is "NameService."

Once you've initialized your ORB reference, you can ask the ORB for a list of the names of its initial objects using the `list_initial_services()` method:

```
String names[] = myORB.list_initial_services();
```

This method returns an array of `String` objects that contains the names of all initial objects in the ORB. These names can then be used to get references to the objects through the `resolve_initial_references()` method.

Here's how we used `resolve_initial_references()` to obtain a reference to the Naming Service in Example 4-8:

```
ORB myORB = ORB.init(...);
org.omg.CORBA.Object nameRef =
        myORB.resolve_initial_references("NameService");
```

Although the `list_initial_services()` and `resolve_initial_references()` methods are a standard element of the ORB interface, how the ORB implements these initial object references is not standardized. Sun's Java IDL implementation stores an ORB's initial object references as root objects in its Naming Service.

Getting Objects from Other Remote Objects

In addition to getting remote objects directly from an ORB reference, a client can obtain remote objects from other remote objects. A common variation on this approach is to get a reference to a Naming Service object and then look up objects in the naming directory by name. Another variation (that we won't cover in detail in this section) is to obtain an application-specific object reference, either directly from the ORB or through the Naming Service, and use this initial reference to request other objects. An object used in this way in a distributed application is sometimes called a *factory* object.

Using a naming context

Once you have a reference to a Naming Service that you can narrow to a `NamingContext` reference, you can look up objects within the context by passing names to its `resolve()` method. As before, when we were binding objects, a name is represented by an ordered array of `NameComponent` objects. Each `NameComponent` (both the `id` field and the `kind` field) must exactly match the path to an object within the context in order to successfully find the object. If an object is not found at a specified name, an org.omg.CosNaming.NamingContextPackage.NotFound exception is thrown.

So, if a client wants to find the object we stored in the last binding example, it needs to do the following (assuming that it already has a reference to the root naming context of the Naming Service):

```
// Set up path
NameComponent comp1 = new NameComponent("servers", "");
NameComponent comp2 = new NameComponent("ThisOrThat", "");
NameComponent serverName = new NameComponent("server1", "");
NameComponent objPath[] = { comp1, comp2, serverName };

// Find the object in the directory
org.omg.CORBA.Object objRef = rootNC.resolve(objPath);
ThisOrThatServer server = ThisOrThatServerHelper.narrow(objRef);
```

Note the use of the narrow() method on ThisOrThatServerHelper to "cast" the generic object reference to a ThisOrThatServer object.

You can also use the resolve() method on a NamingContext to get a reference to a subcontext. Just use the path to the context itself and narrow() it to a NamingContext reference:

```
NameComponent ttPath[] = { comp1, comp2 };
org.omg.CORBA.Object ncRef = rootNC.resolve(ttPath);
NamingContext ttContext = NamingContextHelper.narrow(ncRef);
```

Using multiple naming services

Suppose there are objects stored in multiple Naming Services (representing, for example, multiple organizations offering CORBA-based services) that you want to access from your client. One way to do this is to initialize an ORB reference for each one. Sun's Java IDL lets you specify an initial host and port for an ORB when you initialize it. So, if each independent Naming Service has its own ORB behind it, you can simply get a reference to each ORB and ask it for a reference to its Naming Service:

```
String host1 = "orbhost1.net";
int port1 = 1234;
String host2 = "orghost2.net";
int port2 = 2345;

// Initialize the first ORB reference
Properties props = new Properties();
props.put("org.omg.CORBA.ORBInitialHost", host1);
props.put("org.omg.CORBA.ORBInitialPort", String.valueOf(port1));
ORB orb1 = ORB.init((String[])null, props);

// Initialize another ORB reference
props.put("org.omg.CORBA.ORBInitialHost", host2);
props.put("org.omg.CORBA.ORBInitialPort", String.valueOf(port2));
ORB orb2 = ORB.init((String[])null, props);

// Get references to the Naming Services
org.omg.CORBA.Object nc1Ref =
        orb1.resolve_initial_references("NameService");
```

```
org.omg.CORBA.Object nc2Ref =
        orb2.resolve_initial_references("NameService");

// Narrow the Naming Service references to NamingContexts and use them
...
```

The only problem with this approach is that it depends on using a nonstandard feature of Sun's Java implementation of the CORBA standard. If you try using this same code against a different Java implementation of CORBA, it probably won't work.

Another option is to have one Naming Service hold references to other Naming Services located elsewhere on the network. As we've seen, the interface to a Naming Service is a `NamingContext` object reference that represents the root of the naming tree for that name directory. Since the `NamingContext` is itself a CORBA-exported object, one Naming Service can hold a reference to a `NamingContext` from another Naming Service, acting as a bridge to the other Naming Service and its objects. To do this, you first have to run some code on the server that is going to act as the bridge. This code gets a reference to the local Naming Service and stores references to remote Naming Services in the local directory:

```
// Get the local ORB and main NamingContext
ORB myORB = ORB.init(...);
org.omg.CORBA.Object ncRef =
  orb.resolve_initial_references("NameService");
NamingContext localNC = NamingContextHelper.narrow(ncRef);

// Create a new subcontext to hold the remote contexts
NameComponent nodeName = new NameComponent("RemoteContexts", "");
NameComponent path[] = {nodeName};
NamingContext ncNode = localNC.bind_new_context(path);

// Get a reference to a remote Naming Service
// using Sun's non-standard ORB properties
Properties remoteORBProps = new Properties();
remoteORBProps.put("org.omg.CORBA.ORBInitialHost", "remote.orb.com");
ORB remoteORB = ORB.init((String[])null, remoteORBProps);
org.omg.CORBA.Object remoteNCRef =
  remoteORB.resolve_initial_references("NameService");
NamingContext remoteNC = NamingContextHelper.narrow(remoteNCRef);

// Store the remote reference in the local context
NameComponent sub = new NameComponent("Naming1", "");
NameComponent path2[] = {nodeName, sub};
localNC.bind(path2, remoteNC);
```

With this done, a remote client can get a reference to the main Naming Service directory and then look up other remote directories within the bridge directory:

```
public class NamingClient {
  public static void main(String argv[]) {
    ORB orb = ORB.init(argv, null);
    org.omg.CORBA.Object ref = null;
    try {
      ref = orb.resolve_initial_references("NameService");
    }
    catch (InvalidName invN) {
      System.out.println("No primary NameService available.");
```

```
      System.exit(1);
    }
    NamingContext nameContext = NamingContextHelper.narrow(ref);
    NameComponent topNC = new NameComponent("RemoteContexts", "");
    NameComponent subNC = new NameComponent("Naming1", "");
    NameComponent path[] = {topNC, subNC };
    try {
      org.omg.CORBA.Object ref2 = nameContext.resolve(path);
      NamingContext nameContext2 = NamingContextHelper.narrow(ref2);
      System.out.println("Got secondary naming context...");
    }
    catch (Exception e) {
      System.out.println("Failed to resolve secondary NameService:");
      e.printStackTrace();
    }
  }
}
```

Using one Naming Service as a bridge to other remote named object directories is a useful tool to help manage a constellation of remote objects, but the same question arises: how do we get references to the remote `NamingContext` objects in order to store them in the bridge directory? In the previous bridge example, we're still using the nonstandard ORB properties provided by Sun's Java IDL implementation to initialize references to multiple remote ORBs (and their Naming Services). What we really want to do is initialize the bridge directory in a way that falls within the CORBA standard. One way is to do this is to use stringified object references, which are the topic of the next section.

Stringified Object References

As we've seen, Sun's implementation of Java IDL provides a nonstandard way to initialize an ORB to reference a remote Naming Service, so that one of the ORB's initial references is to the root context of the remote Naming Service. But what do you do if you want an object from a remote Naming Service, and your Java IDL implementation doesn't provide a way to directly initialize a reference to the remote service? Or, worse yet, what if the object that you want isn't stored in a Naming Service or available through any other CORBA service? How can your client get a reference to the object?

The CORBA standard comes to the rescue again. Part of the standard, called Interoperable Object References (IORs), includes a syntax for representing a remote object reference in the form of a printable string of characters. This stringified object reference includes enough information for a remote CORBA client to locate the object's home ORB and convert the string to a runtime stub reference to the object. Two methods on the `ORB` interface, `object_to_string()` and `string_to_object()`, let you convert a CORBA object reference to string form and back again.

Example 4-9 shows how to create an instance of our server implementation of the `ThisOrThatServer` interface, register it with the ORB, and generate a stringified object reference from the CORBA server object. A stringified reference to a remote object is called an Interoperable Object Reference (IOR) because it uses a format for object references that can be freely distributed between ORBs running a cross the network. In order for the IOR you generate to be acceptable to another ORB, both your ORB and the remote ORB have to be using the same inter-ORB communication protocol (IIOP, DCE-CIOP, etc.). In this example, our client and host are both running IIOP.

Example 4-9: Registering an Object/Getting Its Stringified Object Reference

```
import org.omg.CORBA.*;

public class ServerInit {
  public static void main(String[] argv) {
    try {
      // Obtain ORB reference
      ORB myORB = ORB.init(argv, null);

      // Make a ThisOrThatServer object to register with the ORB
      ThisOrThatServer impl = new ThisOrThatServerImpl();

      // Register the local object with the ORB
      myORB.connect(impl);

      // Get a stringified reference to the object
      String sor = myORB.object_to_string(impl);
      System.out.println("ThisOrThatServer IOR: " + sor);

      // Go into a wait state, waiting for clients to connect
      java.lang.Object dummy = new String("I wait...");
      synchronized (dummy) {
        dummy.wait();
      }
    }
    catch (Exception e) {
      System.out.println("Error occurred while initializing server object:");
      e.printStackTrace();
    }
  }
}
```

The `ServerInit` class contains a `main()` method that is intended to be run on the server host for our remote object. The `main()` method first initializes a connection to the local ORB and then creates an instance of the `ThisOrThatServerImpl` class. This instance serves as the server implementation of our remote object. We create a stringified reference to the object using the `object_to_string()` method on the ORB and then output the stringified reference, so that it can be copied and sent to clients. Finally, by doing a synchronous `wait()` on a local object, the `main()` method goes into a wait state. This `wait()` is necessary to keep the ORB running so that it can respond to client requests. If we let the `main()` method exit, the server object we created is destroyed, and the IOR we generated is no longer valid.

A sample client for our object is shown in Example 4-10. The client accepts a stringified object reference as a command-line argument to its `main()` method. Then it initializes a local ORB reference and uses its `string_to_object()` method to convert the stringified reference to a live object reference. To do this, the ORB parses the encoded information in the stringified reference, makes a connection with the remote ORB serving the object, and generates a CORBA object reference for the client.

Example 4-10: A Client Utilizing a Stringified Object Reference

```
import org.omg.CORBA.*;

public class ServerStringClient {
  public static void main(String[] argv) {
    // Get the stringified reference from our command-line arguments
    String sor = null;
    if (argv.length > 0) {
      sor = argv[0];
    }
    else {
      System.out.println("You forgot the object reference...");
      System.exit(1);
    }

    try {
      // Obtain ORB reference
      ORB myORB = ORB.init(argv, null);

      // Convert the stringified reference into a live object reference
      org.omg.CORBA.Object objRef = myORB.string_to_object(sor);

      // Narrow the object reference to a ThisOrThatServer
      // using the ThisOrThatServerHelper
      ThisOrThatServer server = ThisOrThatServerHelper.narrow(objRef);

      // Invoke some methods on the remote object through the stub
      server.doThis("something");
      server.doThat("something else");
    }
    catch (Exception e) {
      System.out.println("Error occurred while initializing server object:");
      e.printStackTrace();
    }
  }
}
```

Before we can run the client, the remote object has to be registered with its ORB, so that we can get the stringified object reference:

```
objhost% java ServerInit
ThisOrThatServer IOR: IOR:000000000000002349444c3a6a656e2f636f7262612f546869
734f72546861745365727665723a312e30000000000001000000000000003000010000000000
0a6c6f63616c686f737400043200000018afabcafe00000002496bb469000000080000000000
000000
```

Somehow, you have to get this IOR to the client host. You could embed the stringified object reference within a hidden field in a HTML page, so that a Java client can access it using a `URL` object. Or you could set up a simple server on a given port on your host that broadcasts the stringified object reference to whoever makes a socket connection. Or you could email the string to a colleague, and she can type the stringified reference into the startup command for her CORBA client. In any case, the client is invoked with the IOR as a command-line option:

```
clienthost% java ServerStringClient IOR:000000000000002349444c3a6a656e2f636f
7262612f546869734f72546861745365727665723a312e300000000000010000000000000030
000100000000000a6c6f63616c686f737400043200000018afabcafe00000002496bb4690000
00080000000000000000
```

The client uses the argument to reconstitute a remote reference to the server object, so that it can invoke methods on the remote object.

What If I Don't Know the Interface?

In the examples we've seen so far, we've always assumed that the Java interfaces for the remote objects are available at compile time. But what happens if they aren't? You might get a reference to a CORBA `Object` from a Naming Service, for example, and not know what interface that object implements. I mentioned earlier that you can use an `org.omg.CORBA.Object` reference directly to make requests and exchange data with its remote object.

The CORBA standard defines two complementary APIs for this purpose: the Dynamic Invocation Interface (DII) that a client can use to make remote method requests of a server object, and the Dynamic Skeleton Interface (DSI) that a server-side skeleton can use to forward method invocations to its server implementation object. Both of these APIs provide the same essential function: a dynamic interface to an object whose interface is not known at compile time. The DII offers this functionality to clients of CORBA objects, and the DSI provides it to the server-side skeletons that bridge the object implementation with the ORB.

The DII and DSI may seem like sidebar topics in the CORBA world, but in reality they are at the heart of CORBA and how it works. When we generate Java stubs and skeletons from IDL interfaces, the code that is generated uses the DII and DSI to execute remote method calls. The details of how this is done are shielded from you, the developer, by the Java interface you use to interact with the remote object. But it's still worthwhile to understand how CORBA objects implement their distributed nature, especially in situations where the Java interface for the remote object is not there, and you need to deal directly with these details.

In this section, we take a look at how the DII works and how you might use it in a client. We won't cover the DSI in this book, since its practical uses are even more limited for the average developer. Note, however, that the API of the DSI is analogous to that of the DII, so you shouldn't have much trouble mapping the following explanation to the DSI as well.

Dynamic Invocation Interface

The Dynamic Invocation Interface provides abstract representations of remote method requests and their arguments. In simple terms, this means it includes objects that represent remote method requests and parameters that are passed with these method requests. Methods on these objects allow you to set the parameters to the request, make the request, and get the results. DII's central classes are:

`Request`
: A request to invoke a method on a remote object. Created by the client and issued through the ORB to the server object.

NamedValue
: A named parameter to a method request. Conceptually, this is a name tied to an Any value. The name of the value must match the name of the parameter as specified in the IDL interface the remote object satisfies.

NVList
: A list of NamedValue parameters used to represent an argument list passed into a remote method request.

Any
: A general argument value. An Any object can contain the Java equivalent of any basic IDL type or an Object that can be described in IDL.

Context
: A list of NamedValue objects used to specify any details of the client environment that shouldn't be passed as method arguments.

Once you get an org.omg.CORBA.Object reference to a remote object (using any of the approaches we've already covered), you can create and issue a method request to the object by building a parameter list for the method call, making a NamedValue object to hold the result, making a Context object and putting any useful environment values in it, and then using all of these items to create a Request object that corresponds to a particular method on the object. Example 4-11 shows a sample DII client that gets a reference to a remote object through a Naming Service and then makes a dynamic call to its doThis() method.

Example 4-11: Client Using DII to Make Remote Method Call

```
import org.omg.CORBA.*;
import org.omg.CosNaming.*;

public class DIISimpleClient {
  public static void main(String argv[]) {
    ORB myORB = ORB.init(argv, null);
    ORB singleORB = ORB.init();
    try {
      // Get a reference to the object
      org.omg.CORBA.Object ncRef =
        myORB.resolve_initial_references("NameService");
      NamingContext nc = NamingContextHelper.narrow(ncRef);
      NameComponent nComp = new NameComponent("ThisOrThatServer", "");
      NameComponent[] path = {nComp};
      org.omg.CORBA.Object objRef = nc.resolve(path);

      // Now make a dynamic call to the doThis method.  The first step is
      // to build the argument list. In this case, there's a single String
      // argument to the method, so create an NVList of length 1.  Next
      // create an Any object to hold the value of the argument and insert
      // the desired value.  Finally, wrap the Any object with a NamedValue
      // and insert it into the NVList, specifying that it is an input
      // parameter.
      NVList argList = myORB.create_list(1);
      Any arg1 = myORB.create_any();
      arg1.insert_string("something");
      NamedValue nvArg =
        argList.add_value("what", arg1, org.omg.CORBA.ARG_IN.value);

      // Create an Any object to hold the return value of the method and
      // wrap it in a NamedValue
```

Example 4-11: Client Using DII to Make Remote Method Call (continued)

```
      Any result = myORB.create_any();
      result.insert_string("dummy");
      NamedValue resultVal = myORB.create_named_value("result", result,
          org.omg.CORBA.ARG_OUT.value);

      // Get the local context from the ORB.
      // NOTE: This call does not work in Java 1.2, and returns a
      //   NOT_IMPLEMENTED exception.  To make this work in Java 1.2, simply
      //   remove this call to get_default_context(), and pass a null pointer
      //   into the _create_request() call below.  This example should work
      //   as is with any compliant Java CORBA environment, however.
      Context ctx = myORB.get_default_context();

      // Create the method request using the default context, the name of
      // the method, the NVList argument list, and the NamedValue for the
      // result.  Then invoke the method by calling invoke() on the Request.
      Request thisReq =
        objRef._create_request(ctx, "doThis", argList, resultVal);
      thisReq.invoke();

      // Get the return value from the Request object and output results.
      result = thisReq.result().value();
      System.out.println("doThis() returned: " + result.extract_string());
    }
    catch (Exception e) {
      e.printStackTrace();
    }
  }
}
```

Java IDL

Note that in most situations you will have the Java interface for the remote object available in your client along with its helper class, so you'll be able to narrow the `Object` reference to a specific type. One exception might be if you're building some kind of software development tool, and you want to provide a dynamic execution utility for the CORBA code being developed. The previous example demonstrates how a CORBA method call can be carried out at this lower level, in case you ever find it necessary to do so. And when you're trying to fix a problem with your CORBA application, it's always better to understand what's going on under the hood, so to speak.

CHAPTER 5

Java Servlets

The Java Servlet API provides a standard way to extend the functionality of any kind of server that uses a protocol based on requests and responses. Servlets are used primarily with web servers, where they provide a Java-based replacement for CGI scripts. In other words, on a web server that supports servlets (and there are many), you can use a Java servlet to create dynamic web content in much the same way you currently use a CGI script. Servlets have many advantages over CGI scripts, however. For example, servlets are persistent between invocations, which dramatically improves performance relative to CGI programs. Servlets are also portable among operating systems and among servers. Finally, servlets have access to all the APIs of the Java platform, so, for example, it is easy to create a servlet that interacts with a database, using the JDBC API.

In terms of enterprise computing, servlets are a natural fit if you are using the Web as your development platform. You can take advantage of web browsers as universally available thin clients; the web server becomes middleware that is responsible for running applications for these clients. Under this model, the user makes a request of the web server, the server invokes a servlet designed to handle the request, the servlet fulfills the request, and the result is returned to the user in the web browser. What's key here is that the servlet can use JNDI, Java IDL, and other Java Enterprise APIs to perform whatever tasks are necessary to fulfill the request.

This chapter demonstrates the basic techniques used to write servlets using Version 2.0 of the Java Servlet API. It also covers how to handle some common web-development tasks, such as cookie manipulation and session tracking, with servlets. The chapter concludes with an introduction to the new features of Version 2.1 of the Servlet API. This chapter assumes that you have some experience with web development; if you are new to web development, you may want to brush up on web basics by consulting *Webmaster in a Nutshell, 2nd Edition*, by Stephen Spainhour and Robert Eckstein (O'Reilly). For a more complete treatment of servlets, I recommend *Java Servlet Programming*, by Jason Hunter with William Crawford (O'Reilly).

The Servlet Life Cycle

When a client makes a request involving a servlet, the server loads and executes the appropriate Java classes. Those classes generate content, and the server sends the content back to the client. In most cases, the client is a web browser, the server is a web server, and the servlet returns standard HTML. From the web browser's perspective, this isn't any different from requesting a page generated by a CGI script, or, indeed, standard HTML. On the server side, however, there is one important difference: persistence.* Instead of shutting down at the end of each request, the servlet can remain loaded, ready to handle subsequent requests. Figure 5-1 shows how this all fits together.

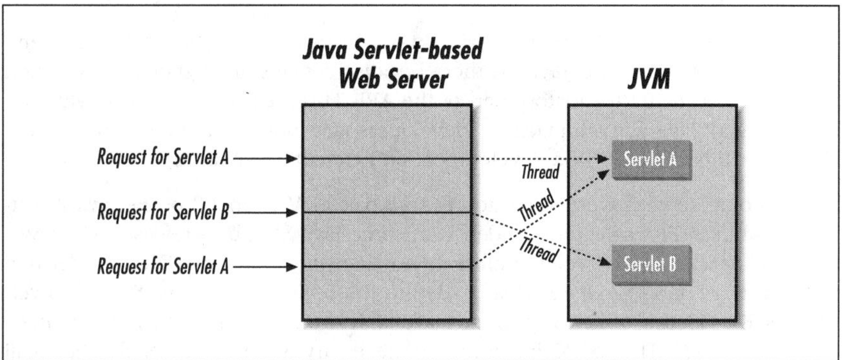

Figure 5-1: The servlet life cycle

The request-processing time for a servlet can vary, but it is typically quite fast when compared to a similar CGI program. The real advantage of a servlet, however, is that you incur most of the startup overhead only once. When a servlet loads, its `init()` method is called. You can use `init()` to create I/O intensive resources, such as database connections, for use across multiple invocations. If you have a high-traffic site, the performance benefits can be quite dramatic. Instead of putting up and tearing down a hundred thousand database connections, the servlet needs to create a connection only once. The servlet's `destroy()` method can clean up resources when the server shuts down.

Because servlets are persistent, you can actually remove a lot of filesystem and/or database accesses altogether. For example, to implement a page counter, you can simply store a number in a static variable, rather than consulting a file (or database) for every request. Using this technique, you need to read and write to the disk only occasionally to preserve state. Since a servlet remains active, it can perform other tasks when it is not servicing client requests, such as running a background processing thread (where clients connect to the servlet to view the result) or even acting as an RMI host, enabling a single servlet to handle connections from multiple types of clients. For example, if you write an order processing

---

* Note that I'm using persistent to mean "enduring between invocations," not "written to permanent storage," as it is sometimes used.

servlet, it can accept transactions from both an HTML form and an applet using RMI.

The Servlet API includes numerous methods and classes for making application development easier. Most common CGI tasks require a lot of fiddling on the programmer's part; even decoding HTML form parameters can be a chore, to say nothing of dealing with cookies and session tracking. Libraries exist to help with these tasks, but they are, of course, decidedly nonstandard. You can use the Servlet API to handle most routine tasks, thus cutting development time and keeping things consistent for multiple developers on a project.

Servlet Basics

The Servlet API consists of two packages, `javax.servlet` and `javax.servlet.http`. The `javax` is there because servlets are a standard extension to Java, rather than a mandatory part of the API. This means that while servlets are official Java, Java virtual machine developers are not required to include the classes for them in their Java development and execution environments.

At one point, servlets were slated to become part of Version 1.2 of the Java 2 platform, and the API was even included with some Java SDK beta releases. However, since the Servlet API is evolving much faster than the core Java SDK, Sun decided to keep distribution separate. This has led to the revival of the Java Servlet Development Kit (JSDK), which is currently available from Sun at *http://java.sun.com/products/servlet/*. The JSDK includes the necessary servlet classes and a small *servletrunner* application for development and testing. As of this writing, the latest available implementation is JSDK 2.1, based on Version 2.1 of the Servlet API.

The examples in this chapter were developed using Sun's Java Web Server 1.1.3, unofficially considered the reference implementation for servlets. As of this writing, a number of other products, including O'Reilly's WebSite Pro and the W3C's JigSaw, have incorporated servlet support. Various third-party vendors, including Live Software, New Atlanta, and IBM, have released add-on servlet modules for most other major web server platforms, including the Netscape server family, Apache, and Microsoft IIS. I'm not going to discuss how to load servlets on each server, since the various implementations differ in this regard. What's important is that the servlets themselves are the same for each platform.

The three core elements of the Servlet API are the `javax.servlet.Servlet` interface, the `javax.servlet.GenericServlet` class, and the `javax.servlet.http.HttpServlet` class. Normally, you create a servlet by subclassing one of the two classes, although if you are adding servlet capability to an existing object, you may find it easier to implement the interface.

The `GenericServlet` class is used for servlets that do not implement any particular communication protocol. Here's a basic servlet that demonstrates servlet structure by printing a short message:

```
import javax.servlet.*;
import java.io.*;
```

```
public class BasicServlet extends GenericServlet {

  public void service(ServletRequest req, ServletResponse resp)
    throws ServletException, IOException {

    resp.setContentType("text/plain");
    PrintWriter out = resp.getWriter();

    out.println("Hello.");
  }
}
```

BasicServlet extends the GenericServlet class and implements one method: service(). Whenever a server wants to use the servlet, it calls this service() method, passing ServletRequest and ServletResponse objects (we'll look at these in more detail shortly). The servlet tells the server what type of response to expect, gets a PrintWriter from the response object, and transmits its output.

The GenericServlet class can also implement a *filtering servlet* that takes output from an unspecified source and performs some kind of alteration. For example, a filter servlet might be used to prepend a header, scan servlet output or raw HTML files for <DATE> tags and insert the current date, or remove <BLINK> tags. A more advanced filtering servlet might insert content from a database into HTML templates. We'll talk a little more about filtering later in this chapter.

Although most servlets today work with web servers, there's no requirement for that in GenericServlet: the class implements just that, a generic servlet. As we'll see in a moment, the HttpServlet class is a subclass of GenericServlet that is designed to work with the HTTP protocol. It is entirely possible to develop other subclasses of GenericServlet that work with other server types. For example, a Java-based FTP server might use servlets to return files and directory listings or perform other tasks.

Servlets

HTTP Servlets

The HttpServlet class is an extension of GenericServlet that includes methods for handling HTTP-specific data. HttpServlet defines a number of methods, such as doGet(), doPost(), and doPut(), to handle particular types of HTTP requests (GET, POST, and so on). These methods are called by the default implementation of the service() method, which figures out what kind of request is being made and then invokes the appropriate method. Here's a simple HttpServlet:

```
import javax.servlet.*;
import javax.servlet.http.*;
import java.io.*;

public class HelloWorldServlet extends HttpServlet {

  public void doGet(HttpServletRequest req, HttpServletResponse resp)
    throws ServletException, IOException {

    resp.setContentType("text/html");
    PrintWriter out = resp.getWriter();

    out.println("<HTML>");
```

```
        out.println("<HEAD><TITLE>Have you seen this before?</TITLE></HEAD>");
        out.println("<BODY><H1>Hello, World!</H1><H6>Again.</H6></BODY></HTML>");
    }
}
```

HelloWorldServlet demonstrates many essential servlet concepts. The first thing to notice is that HelloWorldServlet extends HttpServlet–standard practice for an HTTP servlet. HelloWorldServlet defines one method, doGet(), which is called whenever anyone requests a URL that points to this servlet.* The doGet() method is actually called by the default service() method of HttpServlet. The service() method is called by the web server when a request is made of HelloWorldServlet; the method determines what kind of HTTP request is being made and dispatches the request to the appropriate doXXX() method (in this case, doGet()). doGet() is passed two objects, HttpServletRequest and HttpServletResponse, that contain information about the request and provide a mechanism for the servlet to produce output, respectively.

The doGet() method itself does three things. First, it sets the output type to "text/html", which indicates that the servlet produces standard HTML as its output. Second, it calls the getWriter() method of the HttpServletResponse parameter to get a java.io.PrintWriter that points to the client. Finally, it uses the stream to send some HTML back to the client. This isn't really a whole lot different from the BasicServlet example, but it gives us all the tools we'll need later on for more complex web applications.

If you define a doGet() method for a servlet, you may also want to override the getLastModified() method of HttpServlet. The server calls getLastModified() to find out if the content delivered by a servlet has changed. The default implementation of this method returns a negative number, which tells the server that the servlet doesn't know when its content was last updated, so the server is forced to call doGet() and return the servlet's output. If you have a servlet that changes its display data infrequently (such as a servlet that verifies uptime on several server machines once every 15 minutes), you should implement getLastModified() to allow browsers to cache responses. getLastModified() should return a long value that represents the time the content was last modified as the number of milliseconds since midnight, January 1, 1970, GMT.

A servlet should also implement getServletInfo(), which returns a string that contains information about the servlet, such as name, author, and version (just like getAppletInfo() in applets). This method is called by the web server and generally used for logging purposes.

Forms and Interaction

The problem with creating a servlet like HelloWorldServlet is that it doesn't do anything we can't already do with HTML. If we are going to bother with a servlet at all, we should do something dynamic and interactive with it. In many cases, this means processing the results of an HTML form. To make our example less

---

* In a standard Java Web Server installation, with the servlet installed in the standard *servlets* directory, this URL is *http://site:8080/servlet/HelloWorldServlet*. Note that the name of the directory (*servlets*) is unrelated to the use of "servlet" in the URL.

impersonal, let's have it greet the user by name. The HTML form that calls the servlet using a GET request might look like this:

```
<HTML>
<HEAD><TITLE>Greetings Form</TITLE></HEAD>
<BODY>
<FORM METHOD=GET ACTION="/servlet/HelloServlet">
What is your name?
<INPUT TYPE=TEXT NAME=username SIZE=20>
<INPUT TYPE=SUBMIT VALUE="Introduce Yourself">
</FORM>
</BODY>
</HTML>
```

This form submits a form variable named `username` to the URL */servlet/HelloServlet*. How does the web server know to load this particular servlet? Most servlet implementations, including the Java Web Server, allow you to place unpackaged servlets into a particular directory, and access them with a URI of */servlet/ServletName*. This is similar to the way most web servers support CGI programs.

The `HelloServlet` itself does little more than create an output stream, read the `username` form variable, and print out a nice greeting for the user. Here's the code:

```
import javax.servlet.*;
import javax.servlet.http.*;
import java.io.*;

public class HelloServlet extends HttpServlet {

  public void doGet(HttpServletRequest req, HttpServletResponse resp)
    throws ServletException, IOException {

    resp.setContentType("text/html");
    PrintWriter out = resp.getWriter();

    out.println("<HTML>");
    out.println("<HEAD><TITLE>Finally, interaction!</TITLE></HEAD>");
    out.println("<BODY><H1>Hello, " + req.getParameter("username") + "!</H1>");
    out.println("</BODY></HTML>");
  }
}
```

All we've done differently here is use the `getParameter()` method of `HttpServletRequest` to retrieve the value of a form variable.* When a server calls a servlet, it can also pass a set of request parameters. With HTTP servlets, these parameters come from the HTTP request itself, in this case in the guise of URL-encoded form variables. Note that a `GenericServlet` running in a web server also has access to these parameters using the simpler `SerlvetRequest` object. When the `HelloServlet` runs, it inserts the value of the `username` form variable into the HTML output, as shown in Figure 5-2.

* In the Java Web Server 1.1, the `getParameter()` method was deprecated in favor of `getParameterValues()`, which returns a `String` array rather than a single string. However, after an extensive write-in campaign, Sun took `getParameter()` off the deprecated list for Version 2.0 of the Servlet API, so you can safely use this method in your servlets.

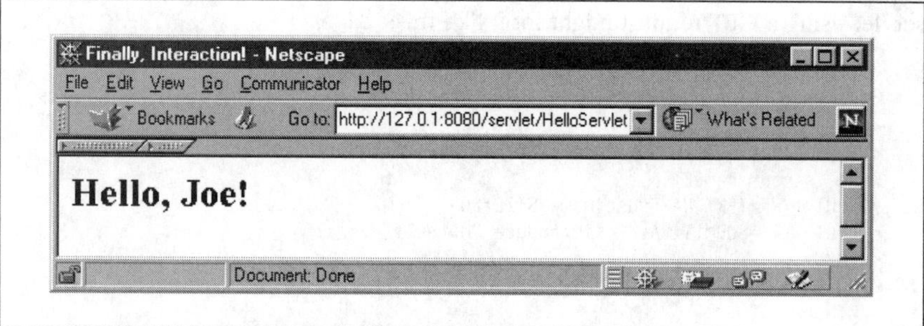

Figure 5-2: Output from HelloServlet

POST, HEAD, and Other Requests

As I mentioned before, `doGet()` is just one of a collection of enabling methods for HTTP request types. `doPost()` is the corresponding method for POST requests. The POST request is designed for posting information to the server, although in practice it is also used for long parameterized requests and larger forms, to get around limitations on the length of URLs.

If your servlet is performing database updates, charging a credit card, or doing anything that takes an explicit client action, you should make sure this activity is happening in a `doPost()` method. That's because POST requests are not *idempotent*, which means that they are not safely repeatable, and web browsers treat them specially. For example, a browser cannot bookmark or, in some cases, reload a POST request. On the other hand, GET requests are idempotent, so they can safely be bookmarked, and a browser is free to issue the request repeatedly without necessarily consulting the user. You can see why you don't want to charge a credit card in a GET method!

To create a servlet that can handle POST requests, all you have to do is override the default `doPost()` method from `HttpServlet` and implement the necessary functionality in it. If necessary, your application can implement different code in `doPost()` and `doGet()`. For instance, the `doGet()` method might display a postable data entry form that the `doPost()` method processes. `doPost()` can even call `doGet()` at the end to display the form again.

The less common HTTP request types, such as HEAD, PUT, TRACE, and DELETE, are handled by other `doXXX()` dispatch methods. A HEAD request returns HTTP headers only, PUT and DELETE allow clients to create and remove resources from the web server, and TRACE returns the request headers to the client. Since most servlet programmers don't need to worry about these requests, the `HttpServlet` class includes a default implementation of each corresponding `doXXX()` method that either informs the client that the request is unsupported or provides a minimal implementation. You can provide your own versions of these methods, but the details of implementing PUT or DELETE functionality go rather beyond our scope.

Servlet Responses

In order to do anything useful, a servlet must send a response to each request that is made of it. In the case of an HTTP servlet, the response can include three components: a status code, any number of HTTP headers, and a response body.

The `ServletResponse` and `HttpServletResponse` interfaces include all the methods needed to create and manipulate a servlet's output. We've already seen that you specify the MIME type for the data returned by a servlet using the `setContentType()` method of the response object passed into the servlet. With an HTTP servlet, the MIME type is generally "text/html," although some servlets return binary data: a servlet that loads a GIF file from a database and sends it to the web browser should set a content type of "image/gif" while a servlet that returns an Adobe Acrobat file should set it to "application/pdf".

`ServletResponse` and `HttpServletResponse` each define two methods for producing output streams, `getOutputStream()` and `getWriter()`. The former returns a `ServletOutputStream`, which can be used for textual or binary data. The latter returns a `java.io.PrintWriter` object, which is used only for textual output. The `getWriter()` method examines the content-type to determine which charset to use, so `setContentType()` should be called before `getWriter()`.

`HttpServletResponse` also includes a number of methods for handling HTTP responses. Most of these allow you to manipulate the HTTP header fields. For example, `setHeader()`, `setIntHeader()`, and `setDateHeader()` allow you to set the value of a specified HTTP header, while `containsHeader()` indicates whether a certain header has already been set. You can use either the `setStatus()` or `sendError()` method to specify the status code sent back to the server. `HttpServletResponse` defines a long list of integer constants that represent specific status codes (we'll see some of these shortly). You typically don't need to worry about setting a status code, as the default code is 200 ("OK"), meaning that the servlet sent a normal response. However, a servlet that is part of a complex application structure (such as the `file` servlet included in the Java Web Server that handles the dispatching of HTML pages) may need to use a variety of status codes. Finally, the `sendRedirect()` method allows you to issue a page redirect. Calling this method sets the `Location` header to the specified location and uses the appropriate status code for a redirect.

Servlet Requests

When a servlet is asked to handle a request, it typically needs specific information about the request so that it can process the request appropriately. We've already seen how a servlet can retrieve the value of a form variable and use that value in its output. A servlet may also need access to information about the environment in which it is running. For example, a servlet may need to find out about the actual user who is accessing the servlet, for authentication purposes.

The `ServletRequest` and `HttpServletRequest` interfaces provide access to this kind of information. When a servlet is asked to handle a request, the server passes it a request object that implements one of these interfaces. With this object, the servlet can find out about the actual request (e.g., protocol, URL, type), access parts of the raw request (e.g., headers, input stream), and get any client-specific request parameters (e.g., form variables, extra path information). For instance, the getProtocol() method returns the protocol used by the request, while getRemoteHost() returns the name of the client host. The interfaces also provide methods that let a servlet get information about the server (e.g., getServername(), getServerPort()). As we saw earlier, the getParameter() method provides access to request parameters such as form variables. There is also the getParameterValues() method, which returns an array of strings that contains all the values for a particular parameter. This array generally contains only one string, but some HTML form elements (as well as non-HTTP oriented services) do allow multiple selections or options, so the method always returns an array, even if it has a length of one.

HttpServletRequest adds a few more methods for handling HTTP-specific request data. For instance, getHeaderNames() returns an enumeration of the names of all the HTTP headers submitted with a request, while getHeader() returns a particular header value. Other methods exist to handle cookies and sessions, as we'll discuss later.

Example 5-1 shows a servlet that restricts access to users who are connecting via the HTTPS protocol, using Digest style authentication, and coming from a government site (a domain ending in *.gov*).

Example 5-1: Checking Request Information to Restrict Servlet Access

```
import javax.servlet.*;
import javax.servlet.http.*;
import java.io.*;

public class SecureRequestServlet extends HttpServlet {

  public void doGet(HttpServletRequest req, HttpServletResponse resp)
    throws ServletException, IOException {

    resp.setContentType("text/html");
    PrintWriter out = resp.getWriter();

    out.println("<HTML>");
    out.println("<HEAD><TITLE>Semi-Secure Request</TITLE></HEAD>");
    out.println("<BODY>");

    String remoteHost = req.getRemoteHost();
    String scheme = req.getScheme();
    String authType = req.getAuthType();

    if((remoteHost == null) || (scheme == null) || (authType == null)) {
      out.println("Request Information Was Not Available.");
      return;
    }

    if(scheme.equalsIgnoreCase("https") && remoteHost.endsWith(".gov")
       && authType.equals("Digest")) {
      out.println("Special, secret information.");
    }
    else {
      out.println("You are not authorized to view this data.");
    }
```

Example 5-1: Checking Request Information to Restrict Servlet Access (continued)

```
    out.println("</BODY></HTML>");
  }
}
```

Error Handling

Sometimes things just go wrong. When that happens, it's nice to have a clean way out. The Servlet API gives you two ways of to deal with errors: you can manually send an error message back to the client or you can throw a `ServletException`. The easiest way to handle an error is simply to write an error message to the servlet's output stream. This is the appropriate technique to use when the error is part of a servlet's normal operation, such as when a user forgets to fill in a required form field.

Status codes

When an error is a standard HTTP error, you should use the `sendError()` method of `HttpServletResponse` to tell the server to send a standard error status code. `HttpServletResponse` defines integer constants for all the major HTTP status codes. Table 5-1 lists the most common status codes. For example, if a servlet cannot find a file the user has requested, it can send a 404 ("File Not Found") error and let the browser display it in its usual manner. In this case, we can replace the typical `setContentType()` and `getWriter()` calls with something like this:

```
response.sendError(HttpServletResponse.SC_NOT_FOUND);
```

If you want to specify your own error message (in addition to the web server's default message for a particular error code), you can call `sendError()` with an extra `String` parameter:

```
response.sendError(HttpServletResponse.SC_NOT_FOUND,
                   "It's dark. I couldn't find anything.");
```

Table 5-1: Some Common HTTP Error Codes

Mnemonic Content	*Code*	*Default Message*	*Meaning*
`SC_OK`	200	OK	The client's request succeeded, and the server's response contains the requested data. This is the default status code.
`SC_NO_CONTENT`	204	No Content	The request succeeded, but there is no new response body to return. A servlet may find this code useful when it accepts data from a form, but wants the browser view to stay at the form. It avoids the "Document contains no data" error message.

Servlets

Table 5-1: Some Common HTTP Error Codes (continued)

Mnemonic Content	*Code*	*Default Message*	*Meaning*
SC_MOVED_ PERMANENTLY	301	Moved Permanently	The requested resource has permanently moved to a new location. Any future reference should use the new location given by the `Location` header. Most browsers automatically access the new location.
SC_MOVED_ TEMPORARILY	302	Moved Temporarily	The requested resource has temporarily moved to another location, but future references should still use the original URL to access the resource. The temporary new location is given by the `Location` header. Most browsers automatically access the new location.
SC_ UNAUTHORIZED	401	Unauthorized	The request lacked proper authorization. Used in conjunction with the `WWW-Authenticate` and `Authorization` headers.
SC_NOT_FOUND	404	Not Found	The requested resource is not available.
SC_INTERNAL_ SERVER_ERROR	500	Internal Server Error	An error occurred inside the server that prevented it from fulfilling the request.
SC_NOT_ IMPLEMENTED	501	Not Implemented	The server does not support the functionality needed to fulfill the request.
SC_SERVICE_ UNAVAILABLE	503	Service Unavailable	The server is temporarily unavailable, but service should be restored in the future. If the server knows when it will be available again, a `Retry-After` header may also be supplied.

Servlet exceptions

The Servlet API includes two `Exception` subclasses, `ServletException` and its derivative, `UnavailableException`. A servlet throws a `ServletException` to indicate a general servlet problem. When a server catches this exception, it can handle the exception however it sees fit.

UnavailableException is a bit more useful, however. When a servlet throws this exception, it is notifying the server that it is unavailable to service requests. You can throw an UnavailableException when some factor beyond your servlet's control prevents it from dealing with requests. To throw an exception that indicates permanent unavailability, use something like this:

```
throw new UnavailableException(this, "This is why you can't use the servlet.");
```

UnavailableException has a second constructor to use if the servlet is going to be temporarily unavailable. With this constructor, you specify how many seconds the servlet is going to be unavailable, as follows:

```
throw new UnavailableException(120, this, "Try back in two minutes");
```

One caveat: the servlet specification does not mandate that servers actually try again after the specified interval. If you choose to rely on this capability, you should test it first.

A file serving servlet

Example 5-2 demonstrates both of these error-handling techniques, along with another method for reading data from the server. FileServlet reads a pathname from a form parameter and returns the associated file. Note that this servlet is designed only to return HTML files. If the file cannot be found, the servlet sends the browser a 404 error. If the servlet lacks sufficient access privileges to load the file, it sends an UnavailableException instead. Keep in mind that this servlet exists as a teaching exercise: you should not deploy it on your web server. (For one thing, any security exception renders the servlet permanently unavailable, and for another, it can serve files from the root of your hard drive.)

Servlets

Example 5-2: Serving Files

```
import javax.servlet.*;
import javax.servlet.http.*;
import java.io.*;

public class FileServlet extends HttpServlet {

  public void doGet(HttpServletRequest req, HttpServletResponse resp)
    throws ServletException, IOException {

    File r;
    FileReader fr;
    BufferedReader br;
    try {
      r = new File(req.getParameter("filename"));
      fr = new FileReader(r);
      br = new BufferedReader(fr);
      if(!r.isFile()) {  // Must be a directory or something else
        resp.sendError(resp.SC_NOT_FOUND);
        return;
      }
    }
```

Example 5-2: Serving Files (continued)

```
    catch (FileNotFoundException e) {
      resp.sendError(resp.SC_NOT_FOUND);
      return;
    }
    catch (SecurityException se) { // Be unavailable permanently
      throw(new UnavailableException(this,
        "Servlet lacks appropriate privileges."));
    }

    resp.setContentType("text/html");
    PrintWriter out = resp.getWriter();
    String text;
    while( (text = br.readLine()) != null)
      out.println(text);

    br.close();
  }
}
```

Security

Servlets don't generally handle their own security arrangements. Instead, they typically rely on the capabilities of the web server to limit access to them. The security capabilities of most web servers are limited to basic on-or-off access to specific resources, controlled by username and password (or digital certificate), with possible encryption-in-transmission using SSL. Most servers are limited to basic authentication, which transmits passwords more or less in the clear, while some (including JWS) support the more advanced digest authentication protocol, which works by transmitting a hash of the user's password and a server-generated value, rather than the password itself. Both of these approaches look the same to the user; the familiar "Enter username and password" window pops up in the web browser.

The `HttpServletRequest` interface includes a pair of basic methods for retrieving standard HTTP user authentication information from the web server. If your web server is equipped to limit access, a servlet can retrieve the username with `getRemoteUser()` and the authentication method (basic, digest, or SSL) with `getAuthType()`. Consult your server documentation for details on using authentication to protect server resources.

Why are these methods useful? Consider a web application that uses the web server's authentication support to restrict access to authorized users, but needs to control access among that set of users. The username returned by `getRemoteUser()` can be used to look up specific privileges in an access control database. This is similar to what we did in Example 5-1, except access is now controlled by username, instead of hostname.

Servlet Chaining

So far, we have looked at servlets that take requests directly from the server and return their results directly to the client. Servlets were designed as a generic server extension technology, however, rather than one devoted solely to performing CGI-like functions. A servlet can just as easily take its input from another servlet, and a servlet really doesn't care very much about where its output goes.

Most web servers that implement servlets have also implemented a feature called *servlet chaining*, where the server routes a request through an administrator-defined chain of servlets. At the end of the sequence, the server sends the output to the client. Alternately, some servers can be configured to route certain MIME types through certain servlets. If a filtering servlet is configured to take all of the output with the MIME type "servlet/filterme," another servlet can produce data with that MIME type, and that data will be passed to the filtering servlet. The filtering servlet, after doing its work, can output HTML for the browser. MIME-based filtering also allows servlets to filter objects that don't come from a servlet in the first place, such as HTML files served by the web server.*

Example 5-3 demonstrates a basic servlet, derived from `HttpServlet`, that examines incoming text for a `<DATE>` tag and replaces the tag with the current date. This servlet is never called on its own, but instead after another servlet (such as, an HTML generator) has produced the actual content.

Example 5-3: Date Filtering Servlet

```
import javax.servlet.*;
import javax.servlet.http.*;
import java.io.*;
import java.util.*;

public class DateFilter extends HttpServlet {

  public void doGet(HttpServletRequest req, HttpServletResponse resp)
    throws ServletException, IOException {

    PrintWriter out = resp.getWriter();

    String contentType = req.getContentType();
    if (contentType == null)
      return; // No incoming data

    // Note that if we were using MIME filtering we would have to set this to
    // something different to avoid an infinite loop
    resp.setContentType(contentType);

    BufferedReader br = new BufferedReader(req.getReader());

    String line = null;
    Date d = new Date();
    while ((line = br.readLine()) != null) {
      int index;
      while ((index=line.indexOf("<DATE>")) >= 0)
        line = line.substring(0, index) + d + line.substring(index + 6);
      out.println(line);
    }
```

* It is interesting to note that the Java Web Server is completely servlet-based; it even uses an internal servlet to serve static HTML files. JWS users can easily implement a filtering servlet by chaining it to the end of the `file` servlet. To use servlet chaining in JWS, you must activate the feature using the administration tool.

Example 5-3: Date Filtering Servlet (continued)

```
    br.close();
  }
}
```

The DateFilter servlet works by reading each line of input, scanning for the text <DATE>, and replacing it with the current date. This example introduces the getReader() method of HttpServletRequest, which returns a PrintReader that points to the original request body. When you call getReader() in an HttpServlet, you can read the original HTTP form variables, if any. When this method is used within a filtering servlet, it provides access to the output of the previous servlet in the chain.

Custom Servlet Initialization

At the beginning of this chapter, I talked about how a servlet's persistence can be used to build more efficient web applications. This is accomplished via class variables and the init() method. When a server loads a servlet for the first time, it calls the servlet's init() method and does not make any service calls until init() has finished. In the default implementation, init() simply handles some basic housekeeping, but a servlet can override the method to perform whatever one-time tasks are required. This often means doing some sort of I/O-intensive resource creation, such as opening a database connection. You can also use the init() method to create threads that perform various ongoing tasks. For instance, a servlet that monitors the status of machines on a network might create a separate thread to periodically ping each machine. When an actual request occurs, the service methods in the servlet can use the resources created in init(). Thus, the status monitor servlet might display an HTML table with the status of the various machines. The default init() implementation is not a do-nothing method, so you should remember to always call the super.init() method as the first action in your own init() routines.*

The server passes the init() method a ServletConfig object, which can include specific servlet configuration parameters (for instance, the list of machines to monitor). ServletConfig encapsulates the servlet initialization parameters, which are accessed via the getInitParameter() and getInitParameterNames() methods. GenericServlet and HttpServlet both implement the ServletConfig interface, so these methods are always available in a servlet (one of the things the default init() implementation does is store the ServletConfig object for these methods, which is why it is important that you always call super.init()). Different web servers have different ways of setting initialization parameters, so we aren't going to discuss how to set them. Consult your server documentation for details.

Every servlet also has a destroy() method that can be overwritten. This method is called when, for whatever reason, a server unloads a servlet. You can use this method to ensure that important resources are freed, or that threads are allowed to

* Note that you no longer have to do this with Version 2.1 of the Servlet API. The specification has been changed so that you can simply override a no-argument init() method, which is called by the Generic Servlet init(ServletConfig) implementation.

finish executing unmolested. Unlike `init()`, the default implementation of `destroy()` is a do-nothing method, so you don't have to worry about invoking the superclass' `destroy()` method.

Example 5-4 shows a counter servlet that saves its state between server shutdowns. It uses the `init()` method to first try to load a default value from a servlet initialization parameter. Next the `init()` method tries to open a file named */data/counter.dat* and read an integer from it. When the servlet is shut down, the `destroy()` method creates a new *counter.dat* file with the current hit-count for the servlet.

Example 5-4: A Persistent Counter Servlet

```
import javax.servlet.*;
import javax.servlet.http.*;
import java.io.*;

public class LifeCycleServlet extends HttpServlet {

  int timesAccessed;

  public void init(ServletConfig conf) throws ServletException {

    super.init(conf);

    // Get initial value
    try {
      timesAccessed = Integer.parseInt(getInitParameter("defaultStart"));
    }
    catch(NullPointerException e) {
     timesAccessed = 0;
    }
    catch(NumberFormatException e) {
      timesAccessed = 0;
    }

    // Try loading from the disk
    try {
      File r = new File("./data/counter.dat");
      DataInputStream ds = new DataInputStream(new FileInputStream(r));
      timesAccessed = ds.readInt();
    }
    catch (FileNotFoundException e) {
      // Handle error
    }
    catch (IOException e) {
      // This should be logged
    }
    finally {
      ds.close();
    }
  }

  public void doGet(HttpServletRequest req, HttpServletResponse resp)
    throws ServletException, IOException {

    resp.setContentType("text/html");
    PrintWriter out = resp.getWriter();
```

Servlets

Example 5-4: A Persistent Counter Servlet (continued)

```
    timesAccessed++;

    out.println("<HTML>");
    out.println("<HEAD>");
    out.println("<TITLE>Life Cycle Servlet</TITLE>");
    out.println("</HEAD><BODY>");

    out.println("I have been accessed " + timesAccessed + " time[s]");
    out.println("</BODY></HTML>");
  }

  public void destroy() {

    // Write the Integer to a file
    File r = new File("./data/counter.dat");
    try {
      DataOutputStream dout = new DataOutputStream(new FileOutputStream(r));
      dout.writeInt(timesAccessed);
    }
    catch(IOException e) {
      // This should be logged
    }
    finally {
      dout.close();
    }
  }
}
```

Thread Safety

In a typical servlet scenario, only one copy of any particular servlet is loaded at any given time. Each servlet might, however, be called upon to deal with multiple requests at the same time. This means that a servlet needs to be thread-safe. If a servlet doesn't use any class variables (that is, any variables with a scope broader than the service method itself), it is generally already thread-safe. If you are using any third-party libraries or extensions, make sure that those components are also thread-safe. However, a servlet that maintains persistent resources needs to make sure that nothing untoward happens to those resources. Imagine, for example, a servlet that maintains a bank balance using an `int` in memory.* If two servlets try to access the balance at the same time, we might get this sequence of events:

> User 1 connects to the servlet to make a $100 withdrawal.
> The servlet checks the balance for User 1, finding $120.
> User 2 connects to the servlet to make a $50 withdrawal.
> The servlet checks the balance for User 2, finding $120.
> The servlet debits $100 for User 1, leaving $20.
> The servlet debits $50 for User 2, leaving -$30.
> The programmer is fired.

Obviously, this is incorrect behavior, particularly that last bit. We want the servlet to perform the necessary action for User 1, and then deal with User 2 (in this case,

---

* Hey, bear with me on this one. It's certainly more than adequate for *my* salary . . .

by giving him an insufficient funds message). We can do this by surrounding sections of code with `synchronized` blocks. While a particular synchronized block is executing, no other sections of code that are synchronized on the same object (usually the servlet or the resource being protected) can execute. For more information on thread safety and synchronization, see *Java Threads* by Scott Oaks and Henry Wong (O'Reilly).

Example 5-5 implements the ATM display for the First Bank of Java. The `doGet()` method displays the current account balance and provides a small ATM control panel for making deposits and withdrawals, as shown in Figure 5-3.* The control panel uses a POST request to send the transaction back to the servlet, which performs the appropriate action and calls `doGet()` to redisplay the ATM screen with the updated balance.

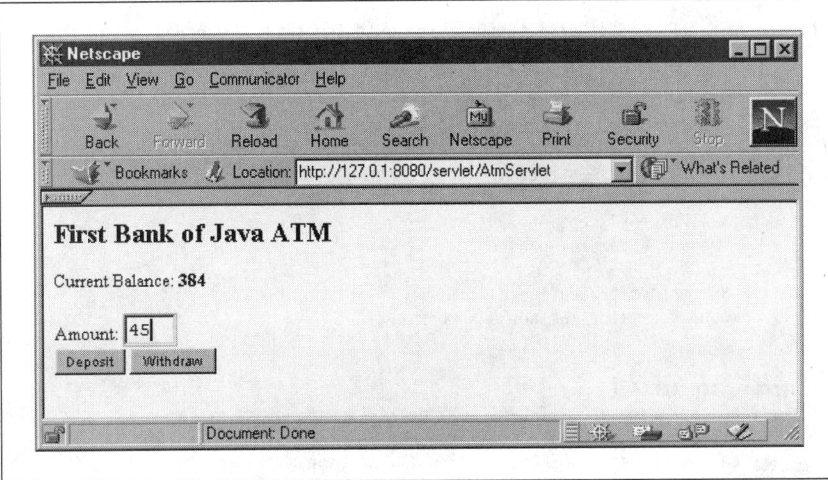

Figure 5-3: The First Bank of Java ATM display

Example 5-5: An ATM Servlet

```
import javax.servlet.*;
import javax.servlet.http.*;
import java.util.*;
import java.io.*;

public class AtmServlet extends HttpServlet {

  Account act;

  public void init(ServletConfig conf) throws ServletException {
    super.init(conf);
    act = new Account();
    act.balance = 0;
  }

  public void doGet(HttpServletRequest req, HttpServletResponse resp)
```

* Despite the fact that Java is a very large island, there's still only one account.

Example 5-5: An ATM Servlet (continued)

```
    throws ServletException, IOException {

    resp.setContentType("text/html");
    PrintWriter out = resp.getWriter();

    out.println("<HTML><BODY>");
    out.println("<H2>First Bank of Java ATM</H2>");
    out.println("Current Balance: <B>" + act.balance + "</B><BR>");
    out.println("<FORM METHOD=POST ACTION=/servlet/AtmServlet>");
    out.println("Amount: <INPUT TYPE=TEXT NAME=AMOUNT SIZE=3><BR>");
    out.println("<INPUT TYPE=SUBMIT NAME=DEPOSIT VALUE=\"Deposit\">");
    out.println("<INPUT TYPE=SUBMIT NAME=WITHDRAW VALUE=\"Withdraw\">");
    out.println("</FORM>");
    out.println("</BODY></HTML>");
  }

  public void doPost(HttpServletRequest req, HttpServletResponse resp)
    throws ServletException, IOException {

    int amt=0;

    try {
      amt = Integer.parseInt(req.getParameter("AMOUNT"));
    }
    catch (NullPointerException e) {
      // No Amount Parameter passed
    }
    catch (NumberFormatException e) {
      // Amount Parameter was not a number
    }

    synchronized(act) {
      if(req.getParameter("WITHDRAW") != null) && (amt < act.balance)
        act.balance = act.balance - amt;
      if(req.getParameter("DEPOSIT") != null) && (amt > 0)
        act.balance = act.balance + amt;
    } // end synchronized block

    doGet(req, resp);                    // Show ATM screen
  }

  public void destroy() {
    // This is where we would save the balance to a file
  }

  class Account {
    public int balance;
  }
}
```

The doPost() method alters the account balance contained within an Account object act (since Account is so simple, I've defined it as an inner class). In order to prevent multiple requests from accessing the same account at once, any code that alters act is synchronized on act. This ensures that no other code can alter act while a synchronized section is running.

The destroy() method is defined in the AtmServlet, but it contains no actual code. A real banking servlet would obviously want to write the account balance to disk before being unloaded. And if the servlet were using JDBC to store the balance in a database, it would also want to destroy all its database related objects.

A more complex servlet than `AtmServlet` might need to synchronize its entire service method, limiting the servlet to one request at a time. In these situations, it sometimes makes sense to modify the standard servlet life cycle a little bit. We can do this by implementing the `SingleThreadModel` interface. This is a tag interface that has no methods; it simply tells the server to create a pool of servlet instances, instead of a single instance of the servlet. To handle an incoming request, the server uses a servlet from the pool and only allows each copy of the servlet to serve one request at a time. Implementing this interface effectively makes a servlet thread-safe, while allowing the server to deal with more than one connection at a time. Of course, using `SingleThreadModel` does increase resource requirements and make it difficult to share data objects within a servlet.

Another use for `SingleThreadModel` is to implement simple database connection sharing. Having multiple database connections can improve performance and avoid connection overloading. Of course, for more advanced or high-traffic applications, you generally want to manage connection pooling explicitly, rather than trusting the web server to do it for you.

Server-Side Includes

Servlets are not confined to handling entire requests. Some web servers allow servlets to add small amounts of dynamic content to otherwise static HTML pages. This is similar to the server-side include functionality found in most web servers, but includes additional servlet-specific functionality. For example, let's assume that we want to use a server-side include to add a randomly selected advertisement to a page. A page that uses the advertisement servlet is written just like a normal HTML page, except that it contains one or more `<SERVLET>` tags and is saved with the *.shtml* extension. The `<SERVLET>` tag is similar to the `<APPLET>` tag, which loads an applet within a page. When a client requests a *.shtml* page, the server finds all of the `<SERVLET>` tags in the text and replaces them with the output from the appropriate servlets.

When you use a `<SERVLET>` tag, you must include a `CODE` parameter that identifies the servlet to be loaded. This can be a class name or a servlet alias set up within the server. On some servers, you can specify an optional `CODEBASE` parameter that loads the servlet code from a remote location. Any additional parameters are treated as servlet initialization parameters. Each `<SERVLET>` tag must be matched by a closing `</SERVLET>` tag. Between the opening and closing tags, you can include as many `<PARAM>` tags as necessary, where you specify `NAME` and `VALUE` attributes for each one. The servlet can then access these parameters with `getParameter()`.

Now let's look at an HTML page that actually uses a servlet with a server-side include. Here's a sample *.shtml* file:

```
<HTML>
<HEAD><TITLE>Today's News</TITLE></HEAD>
<BODY>
<H1>Headlines</H1>
<H2>Java Servlets Take Over Web!</H2>
```

```
<SERVLET CODE=AdMaker>
<PARAM NAME=pagetitle VALUE="Headlines">
</SERVLET>
</BODY>
</HTML>
```

The actual AdMaker servlet is shown in Example 5-6.

Example 5-6: An Advertising Servlet

```
import javax.servlet.*;
import javax.servlet.http.*;
import java.io.*;

public class AdMaker extends HttpServlet {

  static String[] adText = { "Al's Web Services",
                             "Bob's House of HDs",
                             "Main St. Computers" };
  int currentAd = 0;

  public void doGet(HttpServletRequest req, HttpServletResponse resp)
    throws ServletException, IOException {

    String adContent;
    PrintWriter out = resp.getWriter();
    synchronized(this) {
      adContent = adText[currentAd];
      currentAd++;
      if (currentAd >= adText.length)
        currentAd = 0;
    }
    String title = req.getParameter("pagetitle");
    if(title != null)
      out.println(title + " is brought to you by");
    else
      out.println("This page is brought to you by");
    out.println(adContent);
  }
}
```

This servlet really isn't too different from the other ones we've looked at. It accesses parameters (in this case from the <SERVLET> tag instead of a set of HTTP form values) and uses a PrintWriter to produce HTML. It does *not* set a content type or manipulate any HTTP headers, however, because that information may have been sent to the browser before the servlet begins executing.

Server-side includes can be a powerful tool, but they are not part of the standard Servlet API, and therefore some servlet implementations may not support them at all. To make matters worse, some implementations may work in a different manner (this is especially true of third-party servlet runners that plug into non-Java-aware web servers). The example here was developed and tested with Java Web Server. If you want to use server-side includes, you should read your server documentation first.

JavaServer Pages (commonly referred to as JSP) is another technology for accessing server-side Java components directly in HTML pages. The overall effect is not unlike Microsoft's Active Server Pages (ASP). As of this writing, Sun has just finalized the JSP 1.0 specification and several server vendors have announced support for it.

Cookies

Cookies spent a year or two as a little-known feature of Netscape Navigator before becoming the focus of a raging debate on electronic privacy. Ethical and moral considerations aside, cookies allow a web server to store small amounts of data on client systems. Cookies are generally used to store basic user identification or configuration information. Because a cookie's value can uniquely identify a client, cookies are often used for session tracking (although, as we'll see shortly, the Servlet API provides higher-level support for session tracking).

To create a cookie, the server (or, more precisely, a web application running on the server) includes a `Cookie` header with a specific value in an HTTP response. The browser then transmits a similar header with that value back to the server with subsequent requests, subject to certain rules. The web application can then use the cookie value to keep track of a particular user, handle session tracking, or whatever. Because cookies use a single `Cookie` header, the syntax for a cookie allows for multiple name/value pairs in the overall cookie value.

More information about the cookies is available from the original Netscape specification document at *http://home.netscape.com/newsref/std/cookie_spec.html*. The Internet Engineering Task Force is currently working on a standard cookie specification, defined in RFC-2109, available at *http://www.internic.net/rfc/rfc2109.txt*.

The Servlet API includes a class, `javax.servlet.http.Cookie`, that abstracts cookie syntax and makes it easy to work with cookies. In addition, `HttpServletResponse` provides an `addCookie())` method, and `HttpServletRequest` provides a `getCookies()` method, to aid in writing cookies to and reading cookies from the HTTP headers, respectively. To find a particular cookie, a servlet needs to read the entire collection of values and look through it:

```
Cookie[] cookies;
cookies = req.getCookies();
String userid = null;

for (int i = 0; i < cookies.length; i++)
  if (cookies[i].getName().equals("userid"))
    userid = cookies[i].getValue();
```

A cookie can be read at any time, but can be created only before any content is sent to the client. This is because cookies are sent using HTTP headers and these headers can be sent to the client before the regular content. Once any data has been written to the client, the server can flush the output and send the headers at any time, so you cannot create any new cookies safely. You must create new cookies before sending any output. Here's an example of creating a cookie:

```
String userid = createUserID();           // Create a unique ID
Cookie c = new Cookie("userid", userid);
resp.addCookie(c);                        // Add the cookie to the HTTP headers
```

Note that a web browser is only required to accept 20 cookies per site and 300 total per user, and the browser can limit each cookie's size to 4096 bytes.

Servlets

Cookies can be customized to return information only in specific circumstances. In particular, a cookie can specify a particular domain, a particular path, an age after which the cookie should be destroyed, and whether or not the cookie requires a secure (HTTPS) connection. A cookie is normally returned only to the host that specified it. For example, if a cookie is set by *server1.company.com*, it isn't returned to *server2.company.com*. We can get around this limitation by setting the domain to *.company.com* with the `setDomain()` method of `Cookie`. By the same token, a cookie is generally returned for pages only in the same directory as the servlet that created the cookie or under that directory. We can get around this limitation using `setPath()`. Here's a cookie that is returned to all pages on all top-level servers at *company.com*:

```
String userid = createUserID();   // Create a unique ID
Cookie c = new Cookie("userid", userid);
c.setDomain(".company.com");       // *.company.com, but not *.web.company.com
c.setPath("/");                    // All pages
resp.addCookie(c);                 // Add the cookie to the HTTP headers
```

Session Tracking

Very few web applications are confined to a single page, so having a mechanism for tracking users through a site can often simplify application development. The Web, however, is an inherently stateless environment. A client makes a request, the server fulfills it, and both promptly forget about each other. In the past, applications that needed to deal with a user through multiple pages (for instance, a shopping cart) had to resort to complicated dodges to hold onto state information, such as hidden fields in forms, setting and reading cookies, or rewriting URLs to contain state information.

Fortunately, Version 2.0 of the Servlet API provides classes and methods specifically designed to handle session tracking. A servlet can use the session-tracking API to delegate most of the user-tracking functions to the server. The first time a user connects to a session-enabled servlet, the servlet simply creates a `javax.servlet.http.HttpSession` object. The servlet can then bind data to this object, so subsequent requests can read the data. After a certain amount of inactive time, the session object is destroyed.

A servlet uses the `getSession()` method of `HttpServletRequest` to retrieve the current session object. This method takes a single `boolean` argument. If you pass `true`, and there is no current session object, the method creates and returns a new `HttpSession` object. If you pass `false`, the method returns `null` if there is no current session object. For example:

```
HttpSession thisUser = req.getSession(true);
```

When a new `HttpSession` is created, the server assigns a unique session ID that must somehow be associated with the client. Since clients differ in what they support, the server has a few options that vary slightly depending on the server implementation. In general, the server's first choice is to try to set a cookie on the client (which means that `getSession()` must be called before you write any other data back to the client). If cookie support is lacking, the API allows servlets to rewrite internal links to include the session ID, using the `encodeUrl()` method of

HttpServletResponse. This is optional, but recommended, particularly if your servlets share a system with other, unknown servlets that may rely on uninterrupted session tracking. However, this on-the-fly URL encoding can become a performance bottleneck because the server needs to perform additional parsing on each incoming request to determine the correct session key from the URL. (The performance hit is so significant that the Java Web Server disables URL encoding by default.)

To use URL encoding, you have to run all your internal links through encodeUrl(). Say you have a line of code like this:

```
out.println("<A HREF=\"/servlet/CheckoutServlet\">Check Out</A>");
```

You should replace it with:

```
out.print("<A HREF=\"");
out.print(resp.encodeUrl("/servlet/CheckoutServlet");
out.println("\">Check Out</A>");
```

JWS, in this case, adds an identifier beginning with $ to the end of the URL. Other servers have their own methods. Thus, with JWS, the final output looks like this:

```
<A HREF="/servlet/CheckoutServlet$FASEDAW23798ASD978">CheckOut</A>"
```

In addition to encoding your internal links, you need to use encodeRedirectUrl() to handle redirects properly. This method works in the same manner as encodeUrl(). Note that in Version 2.1 of the Servlet API, both methods have been deprecated in favor of identical methods that use the more standard "URL" in their names: encodeURL() and encodeRedirectURL().

You can access the unique session ID via the getID() method of HttpSession. This is enough for most applications, since a servlet can use some other storage mechanism (i.e., a flat file, memory, or a database) to store the unique information (e.g., hit count or shopping cart contents) associated with each session. However, the API makes it even easier to hold onto session-specific information by allowing servlets to bind objects to a session using the putValue() method of HttpSession. Once an object is bound to a session, you can use the getValue() method.

Objects bound using putValue() are available to all servlets running on the server. The system works by assigning a user-defined name to each object (the String argument); this name is used to identify objects at retrieval time. In order to avoid conflicts, the general practice is to name bound objects with names of the form *applicationname.objectname*. For example:

```
session.putValue("myservlet.hitcount", new Integer(34));
```

Now that object can be retrieved with:

```
Integer hits = (Integer)session.getValue("myservlet.hitcount");
```

Example 5-7 demonstrates a basic session-tracking application that keeps track of the number of visits to the site by a particular user. It works by storing a counter value in an HttpSession object and incrementing it as necessary. When a new session is created (as indicated by isNew(), which returns true if the session ID has not yet passed through the client and back to the server), or the counter object is not found, a new counter object is created.

Example 5-7: Counting Visits with Sessions

```
import javax.servlet.*;
import javax.servlet.http.*;
import java.io.*;

public class VisitCounterServlet extends HttpServlet {

  public void doGet(HttpServletRequest req, HttpServletResponse resp)
    throws ServletException, IOException {

    PrintWriter out = resp.getWriter();
    resp.setContentType("text/html");

    HttpSession thisUser = req.getSession(true);
    Integer visits;

    if(!thisUser.isNew()) {          //Don't check newly created sessions
      visits = (Integer)thisUser.getValue("visitcounter.visits");
      if(visits == null)
        visits = new Integer(1);
      else
        visits = new Integer(visits.intValue() + 1);
    }
    else
      visits = new Integer(1);

    // Put the new count in the session
    thisUser.putValue("visitcounter.visits", visits);

    // Finally, display the results and give them the session ID too
    out.println("<HTML><HEAD><TITLE>Visit Counter</TITLE></HEAD>");
    out.println("<BODY>You have visited this page " + visits + " time[s]");
    out.println("since your last session expired.");
    out.println("Your Session ID is " + thisUser.getId());
    out.println("</BODY></HTML>");
  }
}
```

HttpSessionBindingListener

Sometimes it is useful to know when an object is getting bound or unbound from a session object. For instance, in an application that binds a JDBC `java.sql.Connection` object to a session (something that, by the way, is ill-advised in all but very low traffic sites), it is important that the `Connection` be explicitly closed when the session is destroyed.

The `javax.servlet.http.HttpSessionBindingListener` interface handles this task. It includes two methods, `valueBound()` and `valueUnbound()`, that are called whenever the object that implements the interface is bound or unbound from a session, respectively. Each of these methods receives an `HttpSessionBindingEvent` object that provides the name of the object being bound/unbound and the session involved in the action. Here is an object that implements the `HttpSessionBindingListener` interface in order to make sure that a database connection is closed properly:

```
class ConnectionHolder implements HttpSessionBindingListener {

  java.sql.Connection dbCon;

  public ConnectionHolder(java.sql.Connection con) {
    dbCon = con;
  }

  public void valueBound(HttpSessionBindingEvent event) {
    // Do nothing
  }

  public void valueUnbound(HttpSessionBindingEvent event) {
    dbCon.close();
  }
}
```

Session Contexts

Version 2.0 of the Servlet API included the `getContext()` method of `HttpSession`, coupled with an interface named `HttpSessionContext`. Together, these allowed servlets to access other sessions running in the same context. Unfortunately, this functionality also allowed a servlet to accidentally expose all the session IDs in use on the server, meaning that an outsider with knowledge could spoof a session. To eliminate this minor security risk, the session context functionality has been deprecated in Version 2.1 of the Servlet API.

Databases and Non-HTML Content

Servlets

Most web applications need to communicate with a database, either to generate dynamic content or collect and store data from users, or both. With servlets, this communication is easily handled using the JDBC API described in Chapter 2, *JDBC*. Thanks to JDBC and the generally sensible design of the servlet life cycle, servlets are an excellent intermediary between a database and web clients.

Most of the general JDBC principles discussed in Chapter 2 apply to servlets. However, servlet developers should keep a few things in mind for optimal performance. First, JDBC `Connection` objects can be created in the servlet's `init()` method. This allows the servlet to avoid reconnecting to the database (à la CGI) with each request, saving up to a second or more on every single page request. If you anticipate high volume, you may want to create several connections and rotate between them. An excellent freeware connection-pooling system is available at *http://www.javaexchange.com*. Or, if you're using JDBC 2.0, the `javax.sql` package provides a connection-pooling mechanism. Finally, if you plan on using JDBC's transaction support, you need to create individual connections for each request or obtain exclusive use of a pooled connection.

So far, all our servlets have produced standard HTML content. Of course, this is all most servlets ever do, but it's not all that they can do. Say, for instance, that your company stores a large database of PDF documents within an Oracle database, where they can be easily accessed. Now say you want to distribute these documents on the Web. Luckily, servlets can dish out any form of content that can be defined with a MIME header. All you have to do is set the appropriate content type and use a `ServletOuputStream` if you need to transmit binary data. Example 5-8 shows how to pull an Adobe Acrobat document from an Oracle database.

Example 5-8: A Servlet That Serves PDF Files from a Database

```
import java.io.*;
import java.sql.*;
import javax.servlet.*;
import javax.servlet.http.*;

public class DBPDFReader extends HttpServlet {

  Connection con;

  public void init(ServletConfig config) throws ServletException {
    super.init(config);
    try {
      Class.forName("oracle.jdbc.driver.OracleDriver");
      con = DriverManager.getConnection("jdbc:oracle:oci7:@DBHOST",
                                        "user", "passwd");
    }
    catch (ClassNotFoundException e) {
      throw new UnavailableException(this, "Couldn't load OracleDriver");
    }
    catch (SQLException e) {
      throw new UnavailableException(this, "Couldn't get db connection");
    }
  }

  public void doGet(HttpServletRequest req, HttpServletResponse res)
    throws ServletException, IOException {

    try {
      res.setContentType("application/pdf");
      ServletOutputStream out = res.getOutputStream();

      Statement stmt = con.createStatement();
      ResultSet rs = stmt.executeQuery(
        "SELECT PDF FROM PDF WHERE PDFID = " + req.getParameter("PDFID"));

      if (rs.next()) {
        BufferedInputStream pdfData =
          new BufferedInputStream(rs.getBinaryStream("PDF"));
        byte[] buf = new byte[4 * 1024];  // 4K buffer
        int len;
        while ((len = pdfData.read(buf, 0, buf.length)) != -1) {
          out.write(buf, 0, len);
        }
      }
      else {
        res.sendError(res.SC_NOT_FOUND);
      }
    }
    catch(SQLException e) {
      // Report it
    }
  }
}
```

The Servlet API 2.1

Sun made the specification for Version 2.1 of the Servlet API available in November 1998. This version of the API includes some small "housekeeping" changes that make it more consistent and easier to use. For example, method names have been standardized to capitalize "URL", meaning `encodeUrl()` has been deprecated in favor of `encodeURL()`, and so forth. `GenericServlet` now implements `ServletContext` directly and provides a no-argument `init()` method you can override in your own servlets. The `ServletContext` interface contains two new methods, `getMajorVersion()` and `getMinorVersion()`, that can determine the latest API version supported.

In addition to these small updates (and a few others noted in Part III), Sun included a few genuinely new features. Some are fairly minor. For example, a servlet can now specify a "root cause" exception when creating a new `ServletException` object. The root cause can be read with the new `getRootCause()` method of `ServletException`. This provides somewhat more information than the old approach of creating a `ServletException` with the value returned by `getMessage()` from the exception that actually caused the problem.

Other new features, including request dispatching and shared attributes, are more significant and are discussed in the sections that follow. Note that as of this writing, few servlet engines support the new features in Version 2.1 of the Servlet API.

Request Dispatching

The new request dispatching functionality allows a servlet to delegate request handling to other components on the server. A servlet can either forward an entire request to another servlet or include bits of content from other components in its own output. In either case, this is done with a `RequestDispatcher` object that is obtained from the `ServletContext` with its new `getRequestDispatcher()` method. When you call this method, you specify the path to the servlet to which you are dispatching the request.

When you dispatch a request, you can set request attributes using the `setAttribute()` method of `ServletRequest` and read them using the `getAttribute()` method. A list of available attributes is returned by `getAttributeNames()`. All three of these methods are new in Version 2.1. Rather than taking only `String` objects (like parameters), an attribute may be any valid Java object.

`RequestDispatcher` provides two methods for dispatching requests: `forward()` and `include()`. To forward an entire request to another servlet, use the `forward()` method. When using `forward()`, the `ServletRequest` object is updated to include the new target URL. If a `ServletOutputStream` or `PrintWriter` has already been retrieved from the `ServletResponse` object, the `forward()` method throws an `IllegalStateException`.

The `include()` method of `RequestDispatcher` causes the content of the dispatchee to be included in the output of the main servlet—just like a server-side include. To see how this works, let's look at part of a servlet that does a keep-alive check on several different servers:

```
out.println("Uptime for our servers");

// Get a RequestDispatcher to the ServerMonitorServlet
RequestDispatcher d =
  getServletContext().getRequestDispatcher("/servlet/ServerMonitorServlet");

req.setAttribute("serverurl", new URL("http://www1.company.com"));
d.include(req, res);

req.setAttribute("serverurl", new URL("http://www2.company.com"));
d.include(req, res);
```

Shared Attributes

The `ServletContext` interface includes a number of new methods that support the ability for servlets to share attributes. The new `setAttribute()` method allows a servlet to set an attribute that can be shared by any other servlets that live in its `ServletContext`. The `getAttribute()` method, which previously allowed servlets to retrieve hardcoded server attributes, provides access to attribute values, while `getAttributeNames()` returns an `Enumeration` of all the shared attributes.

Shared attributes open up some exciting new possibilities. Multiple servlets within a single web application can easily share configuration information, as well as complex programmatic resources, such as a CORBA object that handles user authentication or a database connection pool.

On a related note, Version 2.1 of the Servlet API deprecates all methods related to accessing other servlets directly, due to the fact that they are inherently insecure. Thus, `getServlet()` and `getServletNames()` join the already deprecated `getServlets()`. The problem here was that `getServlet()` incorrectly allowed one servlet to call another servlet's life-cycle methods.

Resource Abstraction

Resource abstraction is a new feature that allows a servlet to access a resource on a web server, such as an HTML file, without knowing where that resource actually lives. This functionality makes it much easier to move servlets on a web server and even among web servers, such as for load-balancing purposes.

A servlet gets access to a resource using the new `getResource()` method of `ServletContext`. You specify a URI path to the resource and get back a URL object that lets you examine the requested resource. The web server controls how URI path parameters map to actual resources. Note that the resources handled by this functionality cannot be an active resource, like another servlet or a CGI script; use the `RequestDispatcher` for these kinds of resources.

Let's say we have a servlet that writes a complicated header for the content served by the page. To load the actual content, all we have to do is:

```
URL content = getServletContext().getResource("/pages/page12.html");
out.print(content.getContent());
```

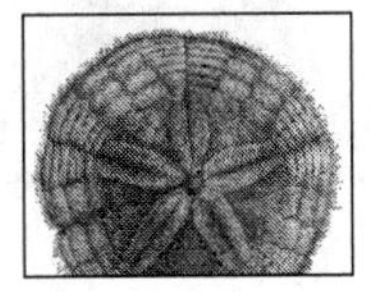

CHAPTER 6

JNDI

The Java Naming and Directory Interface (JNDI) is an API that supports accessing naming and directory services in Java programs. The purpose of a naming service is to associate names with objects and provide a way to access objects based on their names. You should be familiar with naming systems; you use them every day when you browse the filesystem on your computer or surf the Web by typing in a URL. Objects in a naming system can range from files in a filesystem and names located in Domain Name System (DNS) records, to Enterprise JavaBeans (EJB) components in an application server and user profiles in an LDAP (Lightweight Directory Access Protocol) directory. If you want to use Java to write an application such as a search utility, a network-enabled desktop, an application launcher, an address book, a network management utility, or a class browser—in short, anything that accesses objects in a naming system—JNDI is a good candidate for writing that application.

As its name implies, JNDI doesn't just deal with naming services. JNDI also encompasses directory services, which are a natural extension of naming services. The primary difference between the two is that a directory service allows the association of attributes with objects, such as an email address attribute for a user object, while a naming service does not. Thus, with a directory service, you can access the attributes of objects and search for objects based on their attributes. You can use JNDI to access directory services like LDAP and Novell Directory Services (NDS) directories.

As an enterprise programmer, you will most likely use JNDI to access Enterprise JavaBeans; the EJB specification requires that you use JNDI to locate EJB components on the network. But you can also use JNDI to find remote objects in an RMI registry on a remote server. And most enterprise Java suppliers, such as BEA WebXPress, IBM, Novell, Sun, and SCO, support JNDI access to their naming systems.

JNDI Architecture

The architecture of JNDI is somewhat like the JDBC architecture, in that both provide a standard protocol-independent API built on top of protocol-specific driver or provider implementations. This layer insulates an application from the actual data source it is using, so, for example, it doesn't matter whether the application is accessing an NDS or LDAP directory service.

The JNDI architecture includes both an application programming interface (API) and a service provider interface (SPI), as shown in Figure 6-1. A Java application uses the JNDI API to access naming and directory services, primarily through the `Context` and `DirContext` interfaces. The JNDI API is defined in the `javax.naming` and `javax.naming.directory` packages. Note that JNDI is a standard extension to the Java 2 platform; it is available at *http://java.sun.com/products/jndi/*. This chapter covers Version 1.1 of JNDI.*

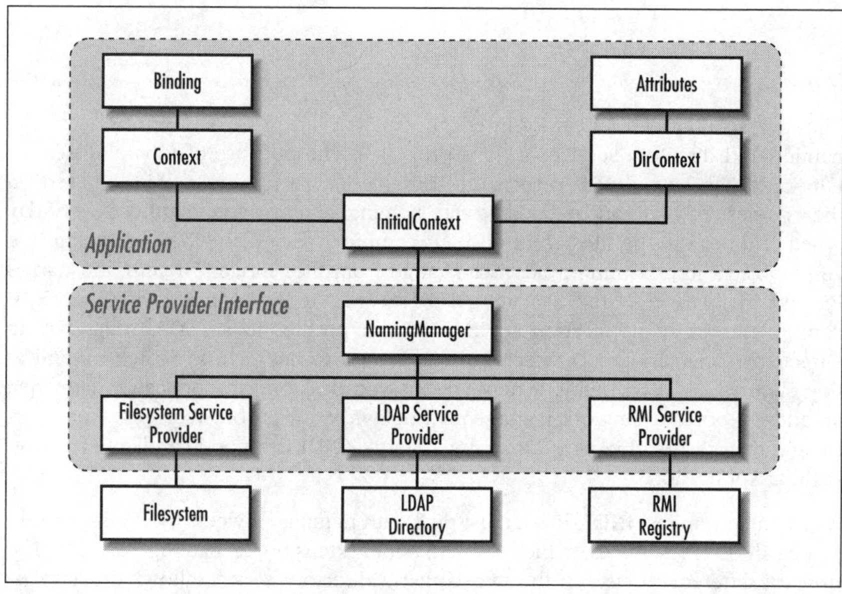

Figure 6-1: The JNDI architecture

In order for an application to actually interact with a particular naming or directory service, there must be a JNDI service provider for that service. This is where the JNDI SPI comes in. A service provider is a set of classes that implements various JNDI interfaces for a specific naming or directory service, much like a JDBC driver implements various JDBC interfaces for a particular database system. The provider can also implement other interfaces that are not part of JNDI, such as Novell's `NdsObject` interface.

* As this book went to press, Sun released a public draft of Version 1.2 of the JNDI specification. The information in this chapter is unchanged by this new version of the specification.

The classes and interfaces in the `javax.naming.spi` package are only of interest to developers who are creating service providers. For instance, the `NamingManager` class defines methods for creating `Context` objects and otherwise controlling the operation of the underlying service provider. As an application programmer, you don't have to worry about the JNDI SPI. All you have to do is make sure that you have a service provider for each naming or directory service you want to use. Sun maintains a list of available service providers on the JNDI web page listed earlier.

A JNDI Example

Before we go any further, let's take a look at a simple JNDI example. To access an object in a naming system, we need to create an initial context for the naming system, to give us an entry point into the naming system. Once we have an initial context, we can look up an object by name.

Example 6-1 demonstrates the basic JNDI tasks of getting an initial context to a naming system and looking up an object in that naming system. With slight modification, this code can be used to look up objects with any JNDI provider. So, for example, you could use `Lookup` to look up Enterprise JavaBeans or remote objects in an RMI registry and handle them however you like. All you have to change is the properties that control the naming system being accessed.

Example 6-1: Looking Up an Object in a Naming System

```
import java.util.Properties;
import javax.naming.*;

public class Lookup {
  public static void main(String[] args) {
    String name = "";
    if (args.length > 0)
      name = args[0];

    try {
      // Create a Properties object and set properties appropriately
      Properties props = new Properties();
      props.put(Context.INITIAL_CONTEXT_FACTORY,
          "com.sun.jndi.fscontext.RefFSContextFactory");
      props.put(Context.PROVIDER_URL, "file:///");

      // Create the initial context from the properties we just created
      Context initialContext = new InitialContext(props);

      // Look up the object
      Object obj = initialContext.lookup(name);
      if (name.equals(""))
        System.out.println("Looked up the initial context");
      else
        System.out.println(name + " is bound to: " + obj);
    }
    catch (NamingException nnfe) {
      System.out.println("Encountered a naming exception");
    }
  }
}
```

The first thing the Lookup application does is create a java.util.Properties object and use it to store some String values. The keys used for these values are constants defined in the javax.naming.Context class. Each constant corresponds to an underlying JNDI property name that is meant to communicate specific information about the JNDI service the application is using. Context.INITIAL_CONTEXT_FACTORY specifies the factory class that creates an initial context for the service we want to use. The class com.sun.jndi.fscontext.RefFSContextFactory is a factory class from the filesystem service provider from Sun. Context.PROVIDER_URL tells the factory class the protocol, server name, and path to use in creating an initial context. We specify the URL *file:///* to indicate the root of the local filesystem. This works on any Unix or Windows filesystem.

Once we have created the Properties object, we pass it to the javax.naming.InitialContext constructor, which returns the initial context object that is our entry point into this particular naming system. Next, we call the lookup() method on initialContext, specifying the name we want to look up. This call returns an object from the naming system, which, in this case, is a file or directory.

You can run Lookup from the command line and specify an optional name to look up. For example:

```
% java Lookup boot.ini
boot.ini is bound to: \boot.ini
```

If the name is instead a directory, the output looks a bit different:

```
% java Lookup winnt
winnt is bound to: com.sun.jndi.fscontext.RefFSContext@803adec0
```

Note that if we wanted to make Lookup more general, we might change it so that it reads its property values from a properties file. Then changing the naming system is a simple matter of editing the properties file to specify an appropriate factory object and URL. Depending on the value you use for the factory class, the object you look up could be an Enterprise JavaBeans component, a reference to a remote object, or something else.

JNDI throws naming exceptions when naming operations cannot be completed. The root naming exception, javax.naming.NamingException, is a catch all for any JNDI exception. The javax.naming package defines numerous subclasses of NamingException. A common naming exception, NameNotFoundException, is thrown when a name cannot be found, either because it doesn't exist or it is spelled incorrectly. JNDI throws a NoPermissionException when a program doesn't have sufficient rights or permissions and an OperationNotSupportedException when an application uses a JNDI method on an object that doesn't support that specific naming operation.

Introducing the Context

A naming service associates names with objects. An association between a name and an object is called a *binding*, and a set of such bindings is called a *context*. A name in a context can be bound to another context that uses the same naming conventions; the bound context is called a *subcontext*. For example, in a filesystem, a directory (such as */temp*) is a context that contains bindings between filenames and objects that the system can use to manipulate the files (often called *file handles*). If a directory contains a binding for another directory (e.g., */temp/javax*), the subdirectory is a subcontext.

JNDI represents a context in a naming system using the `javax.naming.Context` interface. This is the key interface for interacting with naming services. A `Context` knows about its set of bindings in the naming system, but little else. While you might be tempted to think of a `Context` as an exotic `java.io.File` object, you should resist making that analogy, as it will just confuse you. Unlike a `File` object, which can tell you its absolute and relative names as well as return a reference to its parent, a `Context` object can tell you only about its bindings. A `Context` cannot go up a level, tell you its absolute pathname, or even tell you its own name. When you think of a `Context`, think of an object that encapsulates its children as data and has methods that perform operations on that data, not on the `Context` itself.

Using the InitialContext Class

The `javax.naming.InitialContext` class implements the `Context` interface and serves as our entry point to a naming system. To use JNDI to access objects in a naming system, you must first create an `InitialContext`object. The `InitialContext` constructor takes a set of properties, in the form of a `java.util.Hashtable` or one of its subclasses, such as a `Properties` object. Here is how we created an `InitialContext` in the `Lookup` example:

```
Properties props = new Properties();
props.put(Context.INITIAL_CONTEXT_FACTORY,
  "com.sun.jndi.fscontext.RefFSContextFactory");
props.put(Context.PROVIDER_URL, "file:///");

// Create the initial context from the properties we just created
Context initialContext = new InitialContext(props);
```

The most fundamental property key is "java.naming.factory.initial", which corresponds to the `Context.INITIAL_CONTEXT_FACTORY` constant. The value for this property specifies the name of a factory class in a JNDI service provider. It is the job of this factory class to create an `InitialContext` that is appropriate for its service and hand the object back to us. We have to give the factory class all the information it needs to create an `InitialContext` in the form of other property values. For example, the factory class learns the protocol, server name, and path to use from the "java.naming.provider.url" property (`Context.PROVIDER_URL`).

The filesystem factory class (`com.sun.jndi.fscontext.RefFSContxtFactory`) doesn't require much in the way of information. Other factory classes can be more demanding. For example, the factory class in Sun's LDAP service provider requires the URL of the LDAP server and directory entry you want to access, a username and password, and an authentication type. Here are some properties (shown in the file format used by the `Properties` class) you might use to create an `InitialContext` with the LDAP factory class:

```
java.naming.factory.initial=com.sun.jndi.ldap.LdapCtxFactory
java.naming.provider.url=ldap://192.168.1.20/o=Planetary,c=US
java.naming.security.authentication=simple
```

```
java.naming.security.principal=cn=kris
java.naming.security.credentials=secret
```

These properties create an `InitialContext` for an organization called "Planetary" in the global X.500 namespace.

Other Naming Systems

There are many companies that support JNDI, and therefore many naming system service providers. You can find a reasonably comprehensive list of public JNDI providers from the JNDI page on the Sun web site (currently at *http://java.sun.com/products/jndi/serviceproviders.html*). You should contact the vendor of your enterprise naming system or directory for more details regarding its specialized providers. Table 6-1 lists the factory classes for some common JNDI providers.

Table 6–1: JNDI Factory Classes

Service	*Factory*
Filesystem	`com.sun.jndi.fscontext.FSContextFactory` or `com.sun.jndi.fscontext.RefFSContextFactory`
LDAPv3	`com.sun.jndi.ldap.LdapCtxFactory`
NDS	`com.novell.naming.service.nds.NdsInitialContextFactory`
NIS	`com.sun.jndi.nis.NISCtxFactory`
RMI registry	`com.sun.jndi.rmi.registry.RegistryContextFactory`

Looking Up Objects in a Context

Retrieving an object by name from a naming system or directory is called *looking up the object.* This is the job of the `lookup()` method of `Context`. Performing a lookup is analogous to getting the number of a friend from a telephone book by looking up his name. You can use JNDI to look up and retrieve an EJB component from an application server or a remote object from a remote RMI registry.

When you call `lookup()`, you specify the name of the child of the `Context` you want to find. `lookup()` returns a `java.lang.Object` that represents the child. Here's how we did it in `Lookup`:

```
Object obj = initialContext.lookup(name);
```

Calling `lookup()` retrieves an object from the underlying naming system. The JNDI service provider determines the Java representation of these objects, and we have no way of affecting the provider's decision. Depending on the naming system and the design of the provider, the object you retrieve may or may not implement `Context`. For example, if you use the Sun filesystem provider, and your current context is a directory, looking up a child that is a file returns an instance of `java.io.File`. Looking up a directory, however, returns an instance of `FSContext` or `RefFSContext`, both of which implement `Context`. As another example, say you use Novell's NDS provider, and the current context is an NDS tree. If you look up an organization, you get back an `OrganizationDirContext` that implements both `Context` and Novell's `NdsObject` interface. The bottom line is that the class you get back from `lookup()` depends on how the service provider is implemented.

JNDI leaves it up to the service provider to choose whether objects should implement `Context`. There are no strict rules about when an object should implement it, but there are some general guidelines. An object with children is a container, and the guideline for containers is that they should implement `Context`. This is because we generally perform naming operations upon these objects. For example, in the filesystem, directories can contain other objects, so the object that represents a directory should implement `Context` (which is how Sun's filesystem provider behaves). If directories don't support `Context` methods, we cannot use JNDI to look up any children of the directory.

Objects without children are leaves, and leaves may or may not implement `Context`, depending on how they are used. For example, because files have no children to look up, the methods we perform on them lie outside the naming system. The author of the Sun filesystem provider made a design choice that once we have looked up a file, we're done with JNDI. So, we can read the input stream on a file or write an output stream to it, but we cannot use JNDI to perform naming operations on the file.

The NamingShell Application

Earlier, we discussed how we might modify the `Lookup` example to make it more general, allowing us to look up Enterprise JavaBeans and remote objects. The rest of the examples in this chapter are going to be based on the `NamingShell` code shown in Example 6-2. `NamingShell` is an extensible JNDI shell that enables us to perform naming operations in any JNDI-accessible naming system. The shell provides methods for getting and setting the current object and other shell-related details, and it also keeps track of the name of the current object, something a `Context` cannot do for itself.

Once you have loaded `NamingShell`, you can use the shell to execute JNDI-related commands, just as you would use a regular shell to execute operating-system commands. I encourage you to download the code for `NamingShell` right now, so that you can experiment with it as we proceed through the rest of the chapter. `NamingShell` uses the name you type to locate a command dynamically from the filesystem. The shell has no interpreter; however, `NamingShell` expects a command to implement the `Command` interface and its `execute()` method. This means a command really interprets itself. A command throws a `CommandException` when execution fails.

As you can see, `NamingShell` itself contains very little real JNDI code. All the JNDI functionality is implemented in the various `Command` classes we create to handle particular JNDI operations. The shell simply supports the loading of commands and keeps track of various shell-related details.

Example 6-2: The NamingShell Class

```
import java.io.*;
import java.util.*;
import javax.naming.*;

class NamingShell {

  // Private variables
  private static Hashtable COMMAND_TABLE = new Hashtable();
  private static String  JNDIPROPS_FILENAME  = ".jndienv";
  private static String  PROMPT = "[no initial context]";
  private static String  VERSION = "1.0";
  private static Context CURRENT_CONTEXT, INITIAL_CONTEXT;
  private static String  CURRENT_NAME, INITIAL_NAME;
  private static boolean RUNNING = true;

  // Shell operations
  private static void exit(int status) { System.exit(status); }

  // Accessor methods
  public static Hashtable getCommands() { return COMMAND_TABLE; }
  public static Context getCurrentContext() { return CURRENT_CONTEXT; }
  public static String getCurrentName() { return CURRENT_NAME; }
  public static String getDefaultPropsFilename() { return JNDIPROPS_FILENAME; }
  public static Context getInitialContext() { return INITIAL_CONTEXT; }
  public static String getInitialName() { return INITIAL_NAME; }
  public static String getPrompt() { return PROMPT; }
  public static void setCurrentContext(Context ctx) { CURRENT_CONTEXT = ctx; }
  public static void setInitialContext(Context ctx) { INITIAL_CONTEXT = ctx; }
  public static void setInitialName(String name) { INITIAL_NAME = name; }
  public static void setPrompt(String prompt) { PROMPT = prompt; }
  public static void setCurrentName(String name) {
    CURRENT_NAME = name;
    setPrompt(name);
  }

  // Executes a preinstantiated command we are sure is already
  // present in the table
  private static void execute(Command c, Vector v) {
    if (c == null) {
      System.out.println("No command was loaded; cannot execute the command.");
      return;
    }
    try {
      c.execute(CURRENT_CONTEXT, v);
    }
    catch (CommandException ce) {
      System.out.println(ce.getMessage());
    }
  }

  // Another private method that enables us to specify a command
  // by its string name and that loads the command first
  private static void execute(String s, Vector v) {
    execute(loadCommand(s), v);
  }

  // Loads the command specified in commandName; the help command
  // relies on this method
```

Example 6-2: The NamingShell Class (continued)

```
public static Command loadCommand(String commandName) {
  // The method returns a null command unless some of its
  // internal logic assigns a new reference to it
  Command theCommand = null;

  // First see if the command is already present in the hashtable
  if (COMMAND_TABLE.containsKey(commandName)) {
    theCommand = (Command)COMMAND_TABLE.get(commandName);
    return theCommand;
  }

  try {
    // Here we use a little introspection to see if a class
    // implements Command before we instantiate it
    Class commandInterface = Class.forName("Command");
    Class commandClass = Class.forName(commandName);

    // Check to see if the class is assignable from Command
    // and if so, put the instance in the command table
    if (!(commandInterface.isAssignableFrom(commandClass)))
      System.out.println("[" + commandName + "]: Not a command");
    else {
      theCommand = (Command)commandClass.newInstance();
      COMMAND_TABLE.put(commandName, theCommand);
       return theCommand;
    }
  }
  catch (ClassNotFoundException cnfe) {
    System.out.println("[" + commandName + "]: command not found");
  }
  catch (IllegalAccessException iae) {
    System.out.println("[" + commandName + "]: illegal acces");
  }
  catch (InstantiationException ie) {
    System.out.println("["+commandName+"]: command couldn't be instantiated");
  }
  finally {
    return theCommand;          // theCommand is null if we get here
  }
}

// This method reads a line of input, gets the command and arguments
// within the line of input, and then dynamically loads the command
// from the current directory of the running shell
private static void readInput() {
  // Get the input from System.in
  BufferedReader br = new BufferedReader(new InputStreamReader(System.in));

  // Begin reading input
  try {
    while (RUNNING) {
      System.out.print(PROMPT + "% ");

      // Tokenize the line, read each token, and pass the token
      // into a convenient remaining arguments Vector that we
      // pass into the Command
      StringTokenizer tokenizer = new StringTokenizer(br.readLine());
      Vector remainingArgs = new Vector();
```

JNDI

Example 6-2: The NamingShell Class (continued)

```
        String commandToken = "";
        if (tokenizer.hasMoreTokens()) {
          commandToken = tokenizer.nextToken();
          while (tokenizer.hasMoreTokens())
            remainingArgs.addElement(tokenizer.nextToken());
        }

        // Dynamically load the class for the appropriate command
        // based upon the case-sensitive name of the first token,
        // which is the command token
        if (!(commandToken.equals("")))
          execute(commandToken, remainingArgs);
      }
    }
    catch (java.io.IOException ioe) {
      System.out.println("Caught an IO exception reading a line of input");
    }
  }
  // Constructor
  NamingShell(String[] args) {
  }

  // Main method that reads input until the user exits
  public static void main(String[] args) {
    NamingShell shell = new NamingShell(args);
    shell.readInput();
  }
}
```

The Command Interface

The `Command` interface (shown in Example 6-3) describes a standard interface for a shell command. It has an `execute()` method that contains the command logic and a `help()` method for displaying online help for the command. If `execute()` encounters a naming exception (or some other exception), it throws a `CommandException` (shown in Example 6-4), which stores the first exception as an instance variable so that the shell can display the exception appropriately.

Example 6-3: The Command Interface

```
import java.util.Vector;
import javax.naming.Context;

public interface Command {
  public void execute(Context c, Vector v)
    throws CommandException;
  public void help();
}
```

Example 6-4: The CommandException Class

```
public class CommandException extends Exception {
  Exception e; // root exception
  CommandException(Exception e, String message) {
```

Example 6-4: The CommandException Class (continued)

```
    super(message);
    this.e = e;
  }
  public Exception getRootException() {
    return e;
  }
}
```

Loading an Initial Context

As I said earlier, to use JNDI to look up an object in a naming system (or, in fact, to do anything with the naming system), you first have to create an `InitialContext` for that naming system. So, the first command we need to implement is *initctx*, for loading an initial context into `NamingShell`. Example 6-5 shows an implementation of this command.

Example 6-5: The initctx Command

```
import java.io.*;
import java.util.*;
import javax.naming.*;

public class initctx implements Command {

  public void execute(Context c, Vector v) {
    String jndiPropsFilename;
    // If no properties file is specified, use the default file;
    // otherwise use the specified file
    if (v.isEmpty())
      jndiPropsFilename = NamingShell.getDefaultPropsFilename();
    else
      jndiPropsFilename = (String)v.firstElement();

    try {
      Properties props = new Properties();
      File jndiProps = new File(jndiPropsFilename);
      props.load(new FileInputStream(jndiProps));

      NamingShell.setInitialContext(new InitialContext(props));
      NamingShell.setInitialName("/");
      NamingShell.setCurrentContext(NamingShell.getInitialContext());
      NamingShell.setCurrentName(NamingShell.getInitialName());
      System.out.print("Created initial context using ");
      System.out.println(jndiProps.getAbsolutePath());
    }
    catch (NamingException ne) {
      System.out.println("Couldn't create the initial context");
    }
    catch (FileNotFoundException fnfe) {
      System.out.print("Couldn't find properties file: ");
      System.out.println(jndiPropsFilename);
    }
    catch (IOException ioe) {
      System.out.print("Problem loading the properties file: ");
      System.out.println(jndiPropsFilename);
    }
```

JNDI

```
    catch (Exception e) {
      System.out.println("There was a problem starting the shell");
    }
  }

  public void help() { System.out.println("Usage: initctx [filename]"); }
}
```

The *initctx* command accepts an argument that specifies the name of a properties file to use in creating the `Properties` object that is passed to the `InitialContext` constructor. If no filename is specified, *initctx* looks for the default properties file specified by `NamingShell`. So, with `NamingShell`, all you have to do to use a particular naming service is create an appropriate properties file for that service.

Running the Shell

With `NamingShell` and *initctx*, we have enough functionality to actually run the shell. Before you try running the shell, make sure that the JNDI libraries (in *jndi.jar*) and any other specialized providers are specified in your classpath. Here's how we might start `NamingShell` and establish an initial context, once the classpath is set appropriately:

```
% java NamingShell
NamingShell 1.0
Type help for more information or exit to quit
[no initial context]% initctx
Created initial context using C:\temp\samples\book\.jndienv
/%
```

In this case, since we didn't specify a properties file, `NamingShell` looks for the *.jndienv* file in the current directory. For the purpose of our next few examples, let's assume that this file contains property settings that allow us to use the filesystem provider from Sun. You can change initial contexts at any time during the shell session by running *initctx* with a new filename. After you have created an initial context, you can begin performing naming operations by typing in commands. To exit the shell, simply use the *exit* command.* If you are not sure how a command works, you can get help for that command by typing:

```
/% help command
```

Listing the Children of a Context

A common JNDI operation is retrieving the list of names of an object's children. For example, an application might get the names of Enterprise JavaBeans in a Java application server to see if one is running or list the names of children of an `Ini-`

---

* The *help* and *exit* commands are implemented as separate classes, just like the JNDI-related commands. We've not going to examine the code for these commands, as they don't use JNDI. However, the code for these commands is provided in the example code that is available online (at *http://www.oreilly.com/catalog/jentnut/*).

tialContext in order to populate a Swing JTree component. You list the names of an object's children using the list() method of Context:

```
NamingEnumeration children = initialContext.list("");
```

The list() method returns a javax.naming.NamingEnumeration of javax.naming.NameClassPair objects, where each NameClassPair contains the name and class of a single child of the Context. Note that the NameClassPair is not the child itself. Its getName() method, however, enables us to learn the name of the child, while getClassName() lets us access the child's class name. The NamingEnumeration implements the java.util.Enumeration interface, so it allows us to loop through the results of calling list() using the familiar enumeration methods. JNDI actually uses NamingEnumeration as the return type of a number of naming operations; the actual objects in the enumeration vary depending on the operation.

Example 6-6 shows the implementation of a *list* command for NamingShell. Because executing list() requires a current Context, the execute() method queries the shell to determine whether one exists. If there is no current Context, the method throws an exception.

Example 6–6: The list Command

```
import java.util.Vector;
import javax.naming.*;

public class list implements Command {
  public void execute(Context c, Vector v) throws CommandException {

    String name = "";

    // An empty string is OK for a list operation as it means
    // list children of the current context.
    if (!(v.isEmpty()))
      name = (String)v.firstElement();

    // Check for current context; throw an exception if there isn't one
    if (NamingShell.getCurrentContext() == null)
      throw new CommandException(new Exception(),
        "Error: no current context.");

    // Call list() and then loop through the results, printing the names
    // and class names of the children
    try {
      NamingEnumeration enum = c.list(name);
      while (enum.hasMore()) {
        NameClassPair ncPair = (NameClassPair)enum.next();
        System.out.print(ncPair.getName() + " (type ");
        System.out.println(ncPair.getClassName() + ")");
      }
    }
    catch (NamingException e) {
      throw new CommandException(e, "Couldn't list " + name);
    }
  }

  public void help() { System.out.println("Usage: list [name]"); }
}
```

JNDI

Let's continue with our example of using NamingShell with the filesystem provider. Say that we are accessing a filesystem where we have unpacked a JAR file that contains, among others, a *javax* directory and a *naming* subdirectory. If the current Context is the *naming* directory (ignoring for a moment how we set the current Context; we'll see how to do that shortly), we can use the *list* command with the following results:

```
naming% list
AuthenticationException.class (type java.io.File)
AuthenticationNotSupportedException.class (type java.io.File)
BinaryRefAddr.class (type java.io.File)
Binding.class (type java.io.File)
CannotProceedException.class (type java.io.File)
CommunicationException.class (type java.io.File)
CompositeName.class (type java.io.File)
CompoundName.class (type java.io.File)
ConfigurationException.class (type java.io.File)
Context.class (type java.io.File)
ContextNotEmptyException.class (type java.io.File)
directory (type javax.naming.Context)
...
```

How Names Work

The list() method allows us to list the names of the children of any arbitrary child of a Context. We just saw that we can list the names of the children of a Context itself (in this case, the *naming* directory) by calling its list() method using an empty string as a parameter. Again, let's assume we have a Context object for the *naming* subdirectory under *javax*. Here's how a call to get the names of the children of this Context might look:

```
NamingEnumeration childrenOfNaming = namingContext.list("");
```

The result is a NamingEnumeration that contains NameClassPair objects representing all the children of *naming* (i.e., the classes and subpackages of javax.naming), including the *directory* directory (i.e., the javax.naming.directory subpackage).

To list the names of the children of an arbitrary child of a Context, we have to pass a name to list(). For example, we can list the children of *directory* by specifying the String "directory" as a parameter to list():

```
NamingEnumeration childrenOfDirectory = namingContext.list("directory");
```

The result here is a NamingEnumeration that contains NameClassPair objects representing all the children of *directory* (i.e., the classes of javax.naming.directory, such as DirContext).

You can also specify a name using something called a compound name. A *compound name* is composed of atomic names, like "naming" and "directory", that are separated by separator characters, which, in the case of the filesystem provider, can be either a Unix-style forward slash (/) or a Windows-style backward slash (\). Any JNDI method that takes a name as a parameter can accept a compound name.

Say we have a Context object for the *javax* directory. We can get a list of the children of *directory* as follows:

```
NamingEnumeration childrenOfDirectory = javaxContext.list("naming/directory");
```

This call returns the same NamingEnumeration we got earlier. Now consider the following call:

```
NamingEnumeration childrenOfContext = javaxContext.list("naming/Context");
```

The compound name here specifies an object that is not a Context, so it has no children. In this case, the call to list() throws a NamingException.

The separator character used in JNDI compound names varies across naming and directory services; the separator is analogous to the separator used in java.io.File. Although the Sun filesystem provider allows us to use the Unix-style forward slash and the Windows-style backward slash interchangeably, most service providers are very picky about the separator character used for that service. Unfortunately, the JNDI API does not provide a way to get the separator character programmatically the way java.io.File does. Although the javax.naming.CompoundName class reads a property called "jndi.syntax.separator" that contains the separator character, this property cannot be accessed outside the service provider. So, to find out the separator character for a particular service provider, you have to consult the documentation or some sample code for that provider.

Browsing a Naming System

So far, we know how to look up an object in a Context using lookup() and list the children of that Context with list(). Browsing is a composite operation that involves repeated calls to list() and lookup(), to see what objects are available in the naming system and to move around in those objects.

Context objects are the key to browsing. You start with a current Context and list the children of that Context to see which child you (or, more likely, the user) are interested in. Once you have selected an interesting child, you look up that child to get the actual child object. If the object implements Context, you can use this new Context object to continue browsing, by calling list() again, selecting a child, and looking up its object. If the object does not implement Context, however, you obviously cannot continue browsing down that branch of the naming system. Once you have a Context object, it is always possible to list its children and look up objects within it. So, for example, you can always use the InitialContext for a naming system to go back and start browsing at the entry point to the naming system

Example 6-7 shows an implementation of a *cd* command for NamingShell. The *cd* command changes the current context of NamingShell to the specified context; you use it in conjunction with the *list* command to browse the naming system. The name of this command comes from the Unix *cd* command for changing directories, since changing the directory on a Unix system is an analogous operation to changing the current context when NamingShell is used with the filesystem provider. To change the current context back to the initial context, use either *cd /*

or *cd* \. Note, however, that you cannot use *cd* .., as Context objects do not know about their parents, and therefore, we cannot go up the Context hierarchy.

Example 6-7: The cd Command

```
import java.util.Vector;
import javax.naming.*;

class cd implements Command {
  public void execute(Context ctx, Vector v) throws CommandException {
    if (NamingShell.getCurrentContext() == null)
      throw new CommandException(new Exception(), "No current context");
    else if (v.isEmpty())
      throw new CommandException(new Exception(), "No name specified");

    // Get args[0] and throw away the other args
    else {
      String name = (String)v.firstElement();
      try {
        if (name.equals("..")) {
          throw new CommandException(new Exception(),
            "Contexts don't know about their parents.");
        }
        else if (((name.equals("/")) || (name.equals("\\"))) {
          NamingShell.setCurrentContext(NamingShell.getInitialContext());
          NamingShell.setCurrentName(NamingShell.getInitialName());
          System.out.println("Current context now " + name);
        }
        else {
          Context c = (Context) (NamingShell.getCurrentContext()).lookup(name);
          NamingShell.setCurrentContext(c);
          NamingShell.setCurrentName(name);
          System.out.println("Current context now " + name);
        }
      }
      catch (NamingException ne) {
        throw new CommandException(ne, "Couldn't change to context " + name);
      }
      catch (ClassCastException cce) {
        throw new CommandException(cce, name + " not a Context");
      }
    }
  }

  public void help() { System.out.println("Usage: cd [name]"); }
}
```

Earlier, when we demonstrated the *list* command, I asked you to assume that the current Context for NamingShell was the *naming* subdirectory. Now we can see just how to change the current Context to that directory:

```
initctx% cd temp
Current context now temp
temp% cd javax
Current context now javax
javax% cd naming
Current context now naming
```

Of course, these commands assume we are starting from the initial context and that the *naming* directory is available in the filesystem at */temp/javax/naming*.

Listing the Bindings of a Context

The `listBindings()` method of `Context` provides an alternative means of accessing the children of a `Context`. We've seen that `list()` returns a `NamingEnumeration` of `NameValuePair` objects, where each `NameValuePair` provides access to the name and class name of a single child of the `Context`. `listBindings()` also returns a `NamingEnumeration`, but, in this case, the enumeration contains `Binding` objects. `Binding` is a subclass of `NameValuePair` that contains the actual child object, in addition to its name and class. You can use the `getObject()` method of `Binding` to get the child object.

Just as with `list()`, we can pass an empty string to `listBindings()` to return the bindings for a `Context`:

```
NamingEnumeration bindings = initialContext.listBindings("");
```

`listBindings()` is designed for situations where you need to perform some sort of operation on all the children of a `Context`, and you want to save yourself the time and trouble of looking up each child individually. Be aware, however, that `listBindings()` is potentially a very expensive operation, as it has to get each child object from the underlying naming system. If you don't need all the objects, you are better off using `list()` to get the names of the children and then just looking up the objects you need.

Creating and Destroying Contexts

With JNDI, you can create a context in a naming system using the `createSubcontext()` method of an existing `Context`. All you have to specify in this call is the name of the new subcontext. Note that `Context` does not provide a public constructor; creating a new context requires a parent `Context` (such as an `InitialContext`) whose `createSubcontext()` method we can call.

When you call `createSubcontext()`, the JNDI service provider you are using looks at the class of the `Context` whose method you are calling. Based on this class and the provider's own internal logic, the provider creates a new object of a particular class. You don't get to pick the class of this object; the provider has all the control over the class of the object it creates. (You do, however, have control over the class of object that is created when using directory services, as we'll see shortly.) The documentation for a service provider should tell you what kinds of objects `createSubcontext()` can create. Note that whatever object the provider creates, it always implements `Context`; there is no way to use JNDI to create an object that doesn't implement `Context`.

For example, if we are using the Sun filesystem provider, and our current `Context` is a directory, calling `createSubcontext()` causes the provider to create a directory, not a file. This makes sense, as a directory can have subordinates and thus implements `Context`. There is actually no way to create a file using the JNDI API and the filesystem provider; you have to drop out of JNDI to do this, as we'll see in the next section.

Example 6-8 shows the implementation of a *create* command for `NamingShell` command that demonstrates how to use `createSubcontext()`.

Example 6-8: The create Command

```
import java.util.Vector;
import javax.naming.*;

public class create implements Command {

  public void execute(Context c, Vector v) throws CommandException {

    // Check to see if we have the name we need to create a context
    if (v.isEmpty())
      throw new CommandException(new Exception(), "No name specified");

    String name = (String)v.firstElement();
    try {
      c.createSubcontext(name);
      System.out.println("Created " + name);
    }
    catch (NoPermissionException npe) {
      throw new CommandException(npe,
        "You don't have permission to create " + name + " at this context");
    }
    catch (NamingException ne) {
      throw new CommandException(ne, "Couldn't create " + name);
    }
  }

  public void help() { System.out.println("Usage: create [name]"); }
}
```

command, in conjunction with the *cd* and *list* commands we've already seen:

```
/% create test
Created test
/% cd test
Current context now test
test% create another
Created another
test% list
another (type javax.naming.Context)
```

The `destroySubcontext()` method of `Context` destroys a context, as you might expect from its name. Again, you have to specify the name of the context to be destroyed; you cannot destroy the current object by specifying an empty name. Calling the `destroySubcontext()` method on a `Context` from the Sun filesystem provider is analogous to removing a directory in the filesystem.

Example 6-9 shows the implementation of a *destroy* command for `NamingShell`. Note that it contains several `catch` statements, to handle such exceptions as insufficient permission to destroy a context, trying to destroy an object that doesn't implement the `Context` interface, and trying to destroy an object that has children.

Example 6-9: The destroy Command

```
import java.util.Vector;
import javax.naming.*;

public class destroy implements Command {
  public void execute(Context c, Vector v) throws CommandException {
```

Example 6-9: The destroy Command (continued)

```
    // Check to see if we have the name we need
    if (v.isEmpty())
      throw new CommandException(new Exception(), "No name specified");

    String name = (String)v.firstElement();

    try {
      c.destroySubcontext(name);
      System.out.println("Destroyed " + name);
    }
    catch (NameNotFoundException nnfe) {
      throw new CommandException(nnfe, "Couldn't find " + name);
    }
    catch (NotContextException nce) {
      throw new CommandException(nce,
        name + " is not a Context and couldn't be destroyed");
    }
    catch (ContextNotEmptyException cnee) {
      throw new CommandException(cnee,
        name + " is not empty and couldn't be destroyed");
    }
    catch (NamingException ne) {
      throw new CommandException(ne, name + " couldn't be destroyed");
    }
  }

  public void help() { System.out.println("Usage: destroy [name]"); }
}
```

Binding Objects

A Context stores its subordinates as a set of Binding objects. A binding is an association between an object and its name. Thus, as we've already seen, a Binding object contains an object, its name, and its class. We can add a new Binding to a Context with the bind() method. For example, here's how to add a binding for a new file object to an existing Context:

```
java.io.File newfile = java.io.File("c:\temp\newfile");
tempContext.bind("newfile", newfile);
```

Now, if we call list() on this Context, we'll see a new child named newfile. If you recall, in the previous section, I said that you have to drop out of JNDI to create a new file when using the Sun filesystem provider. The previous example shows what I meant. To create a file, we use the java.io.File constructor, which is not part of JNDI. Then, to bind the file into the naming system, we use the bind() method of Context.

If you try to bind a name to an object, and the name has already been used, the method throws a NameAlreadyBoundException. If you want to bind a new object to an existing name, use the rebind() method instead. Context also has an unbind() method you can use to remove a binding.

Accessing Directory Services

So far, we have only discussed JNDI in the context of naming services. Now it's time to turn to directory services. At its root, a directory is merely a naming service whose objects have attributes as well as names. Programming for a directory service, such as an LDAP directory, is roughly as hard as programming for a relational database.

As we've seen, a binding in JNDI is an association between a name and an object. While this association is sufficient for some naming services, a directory service needs to be able to associate more than just a name with an object. Attributes associate specialized data with an object. In JNDI, an object with attributes as well as a name is called a *directory entry*.

We've been talking about the filesystem as though it were a naming system because that is how Sun's filesystem provider implements it. But if you think about it, a filesystem is really a directory system; files and directories have attributes like permissions, user IDs, and group IDs (we just can't get at these attributes using Sun's filesystem provider).

Most of the directories you'll interact with using JNDI are based on the X.500 directory services standard. For example, both standard LDAP directories and Novell's NDS directories have been influenced by X.500. As such, it is important that you know a little bit about X.500, so that you can understand how these directories work.

X.500 Directories

X.500 is a directory services standard that was developed through a collaboration between ISO and CCITT in the late 1980s. It is the "big daddy" of most directories in use today. Like all such collaborations between standards bodies and treaty organizations, the X.500 specification has the bulk of an earthmover and is about as maneuverable. But, like an earthmover, it can really get the big jobs done.

A large contributor to X.500's bulk is its *schema*, which is the directory type system. A directory schema is a set of rules that govern the layout of the objects in the directory. The schema determines what classes of objects can reside in a directory system, what classes of children and kinds of attributes an object is permitted to have, and what classes of values those attributes can have. If you have worked with databases, be careful not to confuse a directory schema with a database schema. A database schema is the layout of tables in the database, while a directory schema is the set of rules that control the directory layout, not the layout itself.

During the mid 1990s, researchers at the University of Michigan began to examine ways of reducing the complexity of the X.500 Directory Access Protocol (DAP). These researchers came up with the "lightweight" DAP, or LDAP, which significantly slimmed down the protocol's bulk. LDAP has gathered considerable support in the industry, so that it is now considered the standard Internet directory access protocol. Netscape is in part responsible for the acceptance of LDAP, as it declared LDAP the preferred method for accessing address books incorporated into its product line and developed the Netscape Directory Server, which is the most popular general-purpose LDAP-based directory server in use today. Note that while the LDAP protocol is simpler than the X.500 protocol, an LDAP directory still uses a directory schema.

Novell's NDS is another X.500-based directory. In the early 1990s, Novell released NetWare 4.0, which included something called NetWare Directory Services (NDS), a directory that was heavily influenced by X.500. NDS provides information about various networking services, such as printing and file services. As Novell ported NDS to other non-NetWare platforms, the name of the directory morphed into Novell Directory Services, and then NDS became its official name. As further proof of the acceptance of the LDAP protocol, even Novell has declared that the LDAP protocol is the preferred directory access protocol for NDS.

JNDI supports the X.500-based notion of a directory schema. But it can just as easily support non-X.500 schemae, such as the informal schema of a filesystem. Keep in mind that what we are discussing in this section applies to all directory services, not just X.500, LDAP, or NDS directories. As with naming services, to access a particular directory service, all you need is a service provider for that service.

The DirContext Interface

`javax.naming.directory.DirContext` is JNDI's directory services interface. It extends `Context` and provides modified methods that support operations involving attributes. Like a `Context`, a `DirContext` encapsulates a set of name-to-object bindings. In addition, a `DirContext` contains a `javax.naming.directory.Attributes` object for each bound object that holds the attributes and values for that object.

The names of objects in X.500-based directories look a little different from the names we've seen so far for filesystems. If you've worked with an LDAP directory, you've probably seen names like "cn=Billy Roberts, o=Acme Products". This name is actually a compound name, while something like "o=Acme Products" is an atomic name. By convention, in an LDAP directory, the part of the name before the equals sign (e.g., "cn", "o") is stored as an attribute of the directory entry, and the rest of the name (e.g., "Billy Roberts", "Acme Products") is stored as its value. This attribute is called the *key attribute*. Table 6-2 lists some commonly used key attributes. Note that when a `DirContext` is used with an LDAP directory, it knows its name, unlike a `Context`.

Table 6-2: Common Key Attributes

Attribute	*Meaning*
"c"	A country, such as the United States or Lithuania
"o"	An organization or corporation, such as the Humane Society or Omni Consumer Products
"ou"	A division of an organization, such as the Public Relations Department or the Robotic Peace Officer Division

Table 6-2: Common Key Attributes (continued)

Attribute	*Meaning*
"cn"	The common name of an entity (often a user, where it can be a first name or a full name)
"sn"	The surname (last name) of a user

The key attribute is closely tied to the directory entry's *object class definition*, otherwise known as its type. For example, in an LDAP directory, an entry that has a key attribute of "cn" has an object class of "user", while the key attribute "o" has an object class of "organization". The schema for a directory controls the object classes that can be used in the directory. The object class of a directory entry is stored as an attribute. Note that the values used for object classes are directory-dependent, so a user entry from one directory might have a different object class than a user entry from another directory even though both have the high-level notion of a user entry.

The Attributes Interface

The `Attributes` interface represents the set of attributes for a directory entry. It has accessor methods that enable access to the entire set, as well as to specific attributes. In X.500-based directories, the name of an attribute (also called an attribute ID), such as "name", "address", or "telephonenumber", determines the type of the attribute and is called the *attribute type definition*. An attribute type definition is part of a directory's schema; the corresponding *attribute syntax definition* specifies the syntax for the attribute's value and whether it can have multiple values, among other things.

We can retrieve all the attributes of a directory entry by calling the `getAttributes()` method of `DirContext`, followed by the `getAll()` method of `Attributes`. `getAttributes()` returns an `Attributes` object. Calling the `getAll()` method of this object returns a `NamingEnumeration` of `javax.naming.directory.Attribute` objects, one for each attribute of the directory entry.

Example 6-10 shows the implementation of a *listattrs* command for `NamingShell`. This command prints the attributes of a directory entry, as well as string representations of the attribute values.

Example 6-10: The listattrs Command

```
import java.util.Vector;
import javax.naming.*;
import javax.naming.directory.*;

class listattrs implements Command {
  public void execute(Context c, Vector v) throws CommandException {

    String name = "";

    // An empty string is OK for a listattrs operation
    // as it means list attributes of the current context
    if (!(v.isEmpty()))
```

Example 6-10: The listattrs Command (continued)

```
      name = (String)v.firstElement();

    if (NamingShell.getCurrentContext() == null)
      throw new CommandException(new Exception(), "No current context");

    try {
      // Get the Attributes and then get enumeration of Attribute objects
      Attributes attrs = ((DirContext)c).getAttributes(name);
      NamingEnumeration allAttr = attrs.getAll();
      while (allAttr.hasMore()) {
        Attribute attr = (Attribute)allAttr.next();
        System.out.println("Attribute: " + attr.getID());

        // Note that this can return human-unreadable garbage
        NamingEnumeration values = attr.getAll();
        while (values.hasMore())
          System.out.println("Value: " + values.next());
      }
    }
    catch (NamingException e) {
      throw new CommandException(e, "Couldn't list attributes of " + name);
    }
    catch (ClassCastException cce) {
      throw new CommandException(cce, "Not a directory context");
    }
  }

  public void help() { System.out.println("Usage: listattrs [name]"); }
}
```

To use the *listattrs* command, you need to have access to a live directory server. To experiment with a live LDAP directory server, you might try the University of Michigan's server at *ldap://ldap.itd.umich.edu/* or Novell's test server at *ldap://nldap.com/*. Another option is to download and compile the OpenLDAP source code from *http://www.openldap.org/* and get an LDAP server running on your local network. To use the University of Michigan's LDAP server with NamingShell, you need to create a properties file that contains the following properties:

```
java.naming.factory.initial=com.sun.jndi.ldap.LdapCtxFactory
java.naming.provider.url=ldap://ldap.itd.umich.edu/
```

Make sure that the JAR file for the LDAP service provider is in the classpath of NamingShell when you use this initial context information.

Once you have NamingShell set up to use a directory server, here's how you might use the *listattrs* command:

```
o=NOVELL% listattrs cn=admin
Attribute: groupMembership
Value: cn=DEVNET SYSOP,ou=Groups,o=NOVELL
Attribute: revision
Value: 235
Attribute: uid
Value: admin
Attribute: objectClass
Value: top
Value: person
```

```
Value: organizationalPerson
Value: inetOrgPerson
Attribute: sn
Value: admin
Attribute: cn
Value: admin
```

The following code in `listattrs` retrieves the `Attributes` object of the named directory context and enumerates the individual `Attribute` objects:

```
Attributes attrs = ((DirContext)c).getAttributes(name);
NamingEnumeration allAttr = attrs.getAll();
```

Calling `getAttributes()` with the name of a directory entry returns an `Attributes` object that contains all the attributes for that entry. Another variation of `getAttributes()` allows you to pass the name of a directory entry and an array of attribute names (as `String` objects). This method returns an `Attributes` object that contains only the specified attributes. For example:

```
String[] attrIDs = {"name", "telephonenumber"};
Attributes partialAttrs = dirContext.getAttributes(name, attrIDs);
```

In `listattrs`, we used the `getAll()` method of `Attributes` to return an enumeration of `Attribute` objects. The `Attributes` interface also provides a `getIDs()` method that returns an enumeration of just the attribute names (or IDs) for the directory entry. If you know the attribute you want, you can specify the attribute name in a call to the `get()` method, which returns a single `Attribute` object. For example:

```
Attribute addr = attrs.get("address");
```

The Attribute Interface

The `Attribute` interface represents a single directory attribute. We've already seen this interface in the *listattrs* command, where we used it to print the names and values of all the attributes of a directory context.

An attribute can have a single value or multiple values, as specified in the schema for the directory. For example, a "name" attribute might have a single value (e.g., "Billy"), while a "telephonenumber" attribute might have multiple values (e.g., "800 555 1212" and "303 444 6633").

JNDI provides several methods for working with values in an attribute. For instance, we can get one or more values, add or remove a single value, remove all values, and determine if a particular value is present.

The `get()` method of `Attribute` returns a single attribute value as a `java.lang.Object`. If the attribute has only a single value, `get()` returns that value. If the attribute has multiple values, the service provider determines the value that is returned. The following code shows how to get a single value from an attribute:

```
DirContext user ... ;              // Created somewhere else in the program
Attributes attrs = user.getAttributes("");
Attribute attr  = attrs.get("telephonenumber");
Object onePhoneNumber = attr.get();
```

The getAll() method returns multiple attribute values as a NamingEnumeration of objects, as we saw in listattrs. Here's how to print all values stored in an attribute:

```
Attribute attr  = attrs.get("telephonenumber");
NamingEnumeration phoneNumbers = attr.getAll();
while (phoneNumbers.hasMore())
  System.out.println(phoneNumbers.next());
```

The add() method of Attribute enables us to add another value to an attribute:

```
Attribute attr = attrs.get("telephonenumber");
attr.add("520 765 4321");        // Add a new number
```

If we try to add a value to an attribute that doesn't support multiple values, the method does not throw an exception. The attribute simply does not accept the new value. By the same token, you can use the remove() method to remove a value from an attribute.

```
Attribute attr = attrs.get("telephonenumber");
attr.remove("303 444 6633");       // Remove the old number
```

To remove all the values from an attribute, you can call the clear() method. Note that none of these method calls actually affect the directory entry; they simply modify the local Attribute object. To make a permanent change, you have to call the modifyAttributes() method of DirContext and provide it with a modified Attribute object, as discussed in the next section.

The contains() method lets you determine whether an attribute has a certain value, while size() returns the number of values the attribute has:

```
Attribute attr = attrs.get("telephonenumber");
boolean itsThere = attr.contains("800 555 1212");  // Check for certain value
int valuesItHas = attr.size();  // Check how many values it has
```

Modifying Directory Entries

Modifying the attribute values of a directory entry involves using the modifyAttributes() method of DirContext. One variant of this method takes the name of a directory entry, a modification type, and an Attributes object that contains modified Attribute objects, while another variant takes a name and an array of javax.naming.directory.ModificationItem objects. A ModificationItem encapsulates a modified Attribute object and a modification type.

The only part of this operation that warrants much explanation is the creation of modified Attribute objects. The javax.naming.directory.BasicAttributes and javax.naming.directory.BasicAttribute classes implement the Attributes and Attribute interfaces, respectively. These are the classes you'll typically use to create modified attribute values.

For example, let's say we want to remove the phone number "303 444 6633" from a user entry's "telephonenumber" attribute and replace it with the new number "520 765 4321." In the following code, we create two BasicAttributes objects, newNumber and oldNumber, and use them in calls to modifyAttributes():

```
DirContext user ... ;       // Created somewhere else in the program

BasicAttribute newAttr = new BasicAttribute();
newAttr.add("telephonenumber", "520 765 4321");
BasicAttributes newNumber = new BasicAttributes();
newNumber.put(newAttr);

BasicAttributes oldNumber =
  new BasicAttributes("telephonenumber", "303 444 6633");

user.modifyAttributes("", DirContext.REMOVE_ATTRIBUTE, oldNumber);
user.modifyAttributes("", DirContext.ADD_ATTRIBUTE, newNumber);
```

In this code, we use two different techniques to create `BasicAttributes` objects. For `newNumber`, we first create a new `BasicAttribute` and add a "telephonenumber" attribute to it. Then we create a new `BasicAttributes` object and put the `BasicAttribute` in it. With `oldNumber`, we use the convenience constructor of `BasicAttributes` to accomplish the same task in one line of code.

Now we use the two `BasicAttributes` objects in two calls to `modifyAttributes()`, one to remove the old number and one to add the new. `DirContext` defines three constants we can use to specify the type of modification we are doing: `ADD_ATTRIBUTES`, `REMOVE_ATTRIBUTES`, and`REPLACE_ATTRIBUTES`. With any of these types, `modifyAttributes()` uses the ID of each `Attribute` object to determine which attribute to modify by adding, removing, or replacing attribute values. The net result of our two calls is that the old number is replaced with the new number. Of course, we could have done this with one call to `modifyAttributes()` if we had used the `REPLACE_ATTRIBUTES` modification type.

The following code shows how to make the same change using the variant of `modifyAttributes()` that takes an array of `ModificationItem` objects:

```
ModificationItem[] mods = new ModificationItem[2];
mods[0] = new ModificationItem(DirContext.REMOVE_ATTRIBUTE,
  new BasicAttribute("telephonenumber", "303 444 6633"));
mods[1] = new ModificationItem(DirContext.ADD_ATTRIBUTE,
  new BasicAttribute("telephonenumber", "520 765 4321"));
user.modifyAttributes("", mods);
```

Again, this change could also have been done with a single `ModificationItem`, using `REPLACE_ATTRIBUTES`.

Note that the examples here do not reflect any particular directory. In order to change a "telephonenumber" attribute value for a particular directory, you need to consult the schema of that directory for the appropriate attribute type and syntax definitions.

Note also that we have only discussed modifying existing attribute values, not adding new attributes altogether. The reason is that adding new attribute IDs requires modifying the schema, or type system, of a directory. JNDI supports schema access and modification, but the details on how to do so are beyond the scope of this chapter.

Creating Directory Entries

So far, we have been accessing directory entries that are already present in the directory. Now it's time to learn how to create directory entries of our own, using the createSubcontext() method of DirContext. As we discussed earlier, when you create a subcontext of a Context object, the service provider controls the type of object that is created. With a DirContext, this is not the case; you actually have complete control over the type of object you create with createSubcontext() (within the constraints of the directory schema, of course).

As I noted earlier, the object class definition determines the type of a directory entry, and the entry stores its object class as an attribute. So, in order to create a directory entry, we must pass the object class attribute and some other attributes into the parent entry's createSubcontext() method.

Most directories require that you specify attributes for at least the object class definition (e.g., "objectclass=") and key attribute (e.g., common name, "cn=") of a directory entry. Often directories require that you specify more attributes than just these. The minimum set of attributes necessary for creating a directory entry are called the *mandatory attributes*. They are mandatory because if you do not specify them, createSubcontext() throws an InvalidAttributesException. Other attributes that are not required, but that add more useful data to the entry, are called *extended attributes*.

Say we have a reference to a DirContext called orgUnit (where this directory entry lives in an LDAP v3 directory), and we want to create a user entry that is a child of orgUnit to represent the network user Billy Roberts. Here's how we can create a user entry for Billy:*

```
DirContext orgUnit = ... ;      // Created somewhere else in the program

BasicAttributes mandatory = new BasicAttributes("cn", "Billy");
BasicAttribute objectclass = new BasicAttribute("objectclass", "user");
BasicAttribute surname = new BasicAttribute("surname", "Roberts");
mandatory.put(objectclass);
mandatory.put(surname);

orgUnit.createSubcontext("cn=Billy", mandatory);
```

Note that the createSubcontext() method of DirContext resembles the createSubcontext() method of Context; the only difference is the addition of an Attributes parameter. In this example, we create a BasicAttributes object and put three attributes in it. While all the attribute values here are String objects (because that's what an LDAP directory requires), the JNDI API allows you to specify any kind of object as an attribute value.

In this example, orgUnit represents an organizational unit, under which Billy Roberts' newly created user entry resides. In an LDAP directory, an organizational unit is an object class definition that represents a division of a company, and a user is an object class definition that represents a person who uses network

* Note that I didn't implement a "create directory entry" command for NamingShell because most public-access LDAP servers don't allow you to create new entries.

resources. It is natural that a division of a company can contain a person, but it doesn't necessarily work in the opposite direction; it doesn't make sense that a user can contain an organizational unit. The LDAP schema dictates these rules and also specifies the values we can use for the "objectclass" attribute (which is where "user" came from in the example code).

When you are creating your own directory entries, be sure to consult the schema for the directory you are using. If you attempt to create a type of entry that cannot reside under a particular `DirContext`, or you specify an incorrect value for the "objectclass" attribute, `createSubcontext()` throws an exception.

Searching a Directory

One of the most useful features a directory service can offer is the ability to search its entries for ones that have attribute values that meet certain criteria. JNDI supports this kind of searching in directory systems, which means you can implement search functionality in your JNDI applications. `DirContext` provides a number of different `search()` methods that allow you to specify what you are searching for and let you control how the search operates.

Search Criteria

There are two ways to specify what you are searching for. The simpler technique is to create a set of attributes that serve as the search criteria. In this case, you can either set an attribute value, meaning that an entry must have that attribute value to match or leave the value empty, so that all entries that have the attribute match, no matter what the value.

The more flexible way to specify search criteria is with a search filter string. A search filter allows you to express search criteria using LDAP search syntax, specified in RFC-2254. Note that this syntax works with all JNDI providers, not just LDAP; it's the JNDI standard for searching all kinds of directories. The search filter is a `String` that takes the following general form:

```
(attribute operator value)
```

You can use an asterisk (*) to represent a wildcard. For example, here's how to search for all entries in an LDAP directory:

```
(objectclass=*)
```

A search for all users takes the form of:

```
(objectclass=user)
```

You can also use the wildcard character to represent completion, just like in a Unix shell or a DOS prompt. For example, here's a filter for searching for all users whose first names start with "k":

```
(cn=k*)
```

You can use operators other than equals (=), as in:

```
(revision<24)
```

You can also combine search filters with operators such as AND (&) and OR (|). The way to do this is to wrap the entire expression in parentheses:

```
(&(objectclass=computer)(cn=Billy))
```

Finally, you can nest search expressions:

```
(&(|(objectclass=computer)(objectclass=user))(cn=Billy)))
```

Obviously, the attributes you specify in a search depend on the directory service you are searching.

Search Results

Regardless of how you specify the search criteria, the `search()` method you call returns a `NamingEnumeration` of `SearchResult` objects. There is a `SearchResult` for each directory entry that matches the search criteria. `SearchResult` is a direct subclass of `Binding` that stores a set of `Attributes` along with the usual name, class name, and object. (As we'll see shortly, the object in a `SearchResult` may be `null`, depending on the `SearchControls` you set.) Since a search operation returns a `NamingEnumeration`, you must cast the object that the enumeration returns from the `next()` method to a `SearchResult` object. Once you have done that, you can retrieve attributes with the `getAttributes()` method and use methods inherited from `Binding` (and `NameClassPair`) to get other information about the matching entry.

Search Controls

The `search()` methods that take a `SearchControls` object allow you to control how a search operates. You can set the scope of a search, whether the search should return objects, and the maximum amount of time the search should take, among other things. The easiest way to create a `SearchControls` object is to use the default constructor and then call various `set()` methods to set particular search properties.

For example, the `setSearchScope()` method controls where the search should look for matching directory entries. Most of the time, you set the scope of a `SearchControls` object to search an entire subtree, but you can also limit the search to an object or its children. Table 6-3 lists the available search scopes.

Table 6-3: SearchControls Search Scopes

Scope	*Meaning*
`OBJECT_SCOPE`	Searches only the object itself
`ONELEVEL_SCOPE`	Searches only the children of the search target
`SUBTREE_SCOPE`	Searches the entire subtree

The `setReturningObjFlag()` method determines whether the results of a search contain references to the actual directory entries or only the names and class names of the entries. The default behavior is not to return the actual entries, meaning that calling getObject() on a SearchResult returns null.

The SearchControls object also allows you to specify other aspects of the behavior of a search:

- The number of milliseconds to wait for the directory to return the search results (by default, a search can take as long as it takes)
- The number of entries that can be returned from the search (by default, as many as are present)
- Whether to follow links to finish the search (no by default)
- What attributes if any to return (all by default)

In general, the default behavior is typically what you want for these parameters.

A Search Command

Now that we've discussed how the various search() methods work, let's look at a real example. Example 6-11 shows the implementation of a *search* command for NamingShell. This example uses the search() method that takes the name of the context to be searched, a search filter that describes the search criteria, and a SearchControls object.

Example 6–11: The search Command

```
import java.util.Vector;
import javax.naming.*;
import javax.naming.directory.*;

class search implements Command {
  public void execute(Context c, Vector v) throws CommandException {

    if (NamingShell.getCurrentContext() == null)
      throw new CommandException(new Exception(), "No current context");
    else if (v.isEmpty())
      throw new CommandException(new Exception(), "No filter specified");
    String filter = (String)v.firstElement();
    try {
      SearchControls cons = new SearchControls();
      cons.setSearchScope(SearchControls.SUBTREE_SCOPE);
      NamingEnumeration results = ((DirContext)c).search("", filter, cons);
      while (results.hasMore()) {
        SearchResult result = (SearchResult)results.next();
        System.out.println(result.getName());
      }
    }
    catch (InvalidSearchFilterException isfe) {
      throw new CommandException(isfe,
      "The filter [" + filter + "] is invalid");
    }
    catch (NamingException e) {
      throw new CommandException(e, "The search for " + filter + " failed");
    }
    catch (ClassCastException cce) {
      throw new CommandException(cce, "Not a directory context");
```

Example 6-11: The search Command (continued)

```
    }
  }

  public void help() { System.out.println("Usage: search filter"); }
}
```

The *search* command always starts searching in the current context, so you need to move to the appropriate location in the directory service using *cd* before you use *search*. *search* requires you to specify a search filter as its first argument. Note that you cannot use any spaces in the filter, or the filter will be parsed as multiple arguments and therefore not work. Here's how we might use the *search* command:

```
o=Novell% search (&(objectclass=person)(cn=a*))
cn=admin
cn=admin,ou=cook1,ou=user
cn=admin,ou=fj,ou=user
cn=admin,ou=Stanford,ou=user
cn=admin,ou=Ed Reed,ou=user
cn=admin,ou=antimony,ou=user
cn=admin,ou=keaves,ou=user
cn=admin,ou=acme,ou=user
cn=admin,ou=nld,ou=user
cn=admin,ou=wibble,ou=user
cn=admin,ou=xxx,ou=user
cn=admin,ou=piet,ou=user
cn=admin,ou=adamtest1,ou=user
cn=admin,ou=novell,ou=user
...
```

JNDI

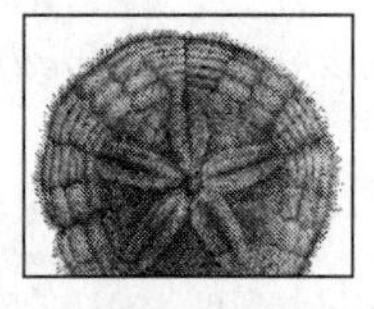

CHAPTER 7

Enterprise JavaBeans

The introduction of RMI and JavaBeans to the core Java APIs brought a standard distributed object framework and a component model to Java. The Enterprise JavaBeans (EJB) architecture builds on these foundations to provide a standard *distributed component model.*

So, you may ask, how are EJB* components different from regular distributed objects built using RMI or local (nondistributed) components defined using the JavaBeans component model? Well, they aren't, really. An EJB component is an RMI object, in the sense that it's exported as a remote object using RMI. And an EJB component is also a JavaBeans component, since it has properties that can be introspected, and it uses the JavaBeans conventions for defining accessor methods for its properties. An EJB is much more than the sum of these parts, however. The EJB architecture provides a framework in which the enterprise bean developer can easily take advantage of transaction processing, security, persistence, and resource-pooling facilities provided by an EJB environment. These facilities don't come free, of course. You need to understand how they work and what rules your EJB object needs to follow in order to participate in these services.

Enterprise JavaBeans are useful in any situation where regular distributed objects are useful. They excel, however, in situations that take advantage of the component nature of EJB objects and the other services that EJB objects can provide with relative ease, such as transaction processing and persistence. A good example is an online banking application. A user sitting at home wants to connect to all her financial accounts, no matter where and with whom they may live, and see them tied together into one convenient interface. The EJB component architecture allows the various financial institutions to export user accounts as different implementations of a common `Account` interface, just as we would do with other distributed object APIs. But since these remote `Account` objects are also JavaBeans

* For the sake of space on the page, strain on your eyes, and my time on the keyboard, I'm going to abbreviate "Enterprise JavaBeans" as "EJB" throughout most of this chapter. I hope you don't mind.

components, the client-side financial application can introspect on the `Account` objects to determine specialized public properties that certain accounts may have, so they can be shown to the client along with the common account properties. Also, the `Account` objects can be made into transactional EJB objects, which allows the client to perform a number of account operations within a single transaction, then either commit them all or roll them back. This can be a critical feature in financial applications, especially if you need to ensure that a supporting transfer can be executed before a withdrawal request is submitted. The transactional support in EJB ensures that if an error occurs during the transfer and an exception is raised, the entire transaction can be rolled back, and the client-side application can inform you of the reason.

The EJB component model insulates applications and beans (for the most part) from the details of the component services included in the specification. A benefit of this separation is the ability to deploy the same enterprise bean under different conditions, as needed by specific applications. The parameters used to control a bean's transactional nature, persistence, resource pooling, and security management are specified in separate *deployment descriptors*, not embedded in the bean implementation or the client application. So, when a bean is deployed in a distributed application, the properties of the deployment environment (client load levels, database configuration, etc.) can be accounted for and reflected in the settings of the bean's deployment options.

The EJB API is a standard extension to Java, available in the `javax.ejb` package and its subpackages. You have to explicitly install this extension API in order to write code against the EJB interfaces. You can find the latest version of the API at *http://www.javasoft.com/products/ejb/*. You should also note that EJB is just a specification for how distributed components should work within the Java environment. In order to actually create and use EJB objects, you need to install an EJB-enabled server.

Note that this chapter provides a basic introduction to Enterprise JavaBeans. For more complete coverage, see *Enterprise JavaBeans* by Richard Monson-Haefel (O'Reilly).

A Note on Evolving Standards

The information and code examples in this chapter are based on Version 1.0 of the Enterprise JavaBeans specification, released in March 1998. The code examples have been tested in two different EJB servers for compatibility: Weblogic/BEA's Tengah server Version 3.1.2 and the 0.4 Version of the free reference EJB server provided by the good folks at EJBHome (*http://ejbhome.iona.com*).

At the time of this writing, Sun has released a public draft of Version 1.1 of the EJB specification and has plans for a 2.0 version, to be released at a later date. The information in this chapter is largely unchanged by the incremental 1.1 update, but some details on the changes in 1.1 are described at the end of the chapter. It's unclear how much of the material in this chapter will be applicable to EJB 2.0.

EJB Roles

In Chapter 3, *Remote Method Invocation*, I described two fundamental roles in the RMI environment: the client of the remote object, and the object itself, which acts as a kind of server or service provider. These two roles exist in the EJB environment as well, but EJB adds a third role, called the *container provider*. The container provider is responsible for implementing all the extra services for an EJB object that I mentioned earlier: transaction processing, security, object persistence, and resource pooling. If you're familiar with CORBA, you can think of the EJB container as being roughly equivalent to the ORB in CORBA, with a few of the CORBA services thrown in as well. In EJB, however, the container is strictly a server-side entity. The client doesn't need its own container to use EJB objects, but an EJB object needs to have a container in order to be exported for remote use. Figure 7-1 shows a conceptual diagram of how the three EJB roles interact with each other.

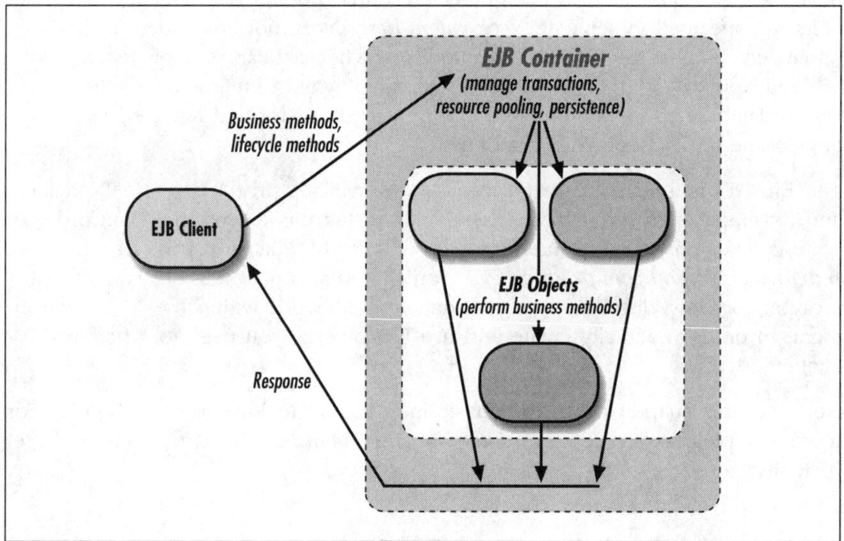

Figure 7-1: The basic roles in an EJB environment

The EJB Client

An EJB client uses remote EJB objects to access data, perform tasks, and generally get things done. In the EJB environment, the first action a client performs is to find the home interface for a type of EJB object that it wants to use. This home interface is a kind of object factory, used to create new instances of the EJB type, look up existing instances (only when using entity EJB objects, discussed later), and delete EJB objects. This is a bit different from RMI, where the client first has to get a direct handle to an existing RMI object. In many RMI applications, however, this first RMI object is a kind of object factory that creates other RMI object references. So, in a sense, the use of home interfaces in EJB is just formalizing the role of factory objects in distributed component applications.

EJB home interfaces are located by clients using JNDI (see Chapter 6, *JNDI*, for more information). An EJB server publishes the home interface for a particular EJB object under a particular name in a JNDI namespace. The EJB client needs to specify the JNDI server and the name that the EJB home interface is stored under in order to start things off. The following code shows a simple EJB client that uses remote `Person` beans:

```
import javax.ejb.*;
import javax.naming.*;
import java.rmi.*;
import java.util.Properties;

public class PersonClient {
  public static void main(String[] args) {
    String name = args[0];

    try {
      // Get a JNDI context for our EJB server (EJBHome, in this case)
      Properties p = new Properties();
      p.put(Context.INITIAL_CONTEXT_FACTORY,
            "com.ejbhome.naming.spi.rmi.RMIInitCtxFactory");
      // Add URL, host or port options, if needed...;
      Context context = new InitialContext(p);

      // Get the home interface for Person beans
      PersonHome pHome =
        (PersonHome)context.lookup("People");

      // Create a named person
      Person person = pHome.create(name);

      // Use the remote stub interface to access the person's data
      . . .
    }
    catch (NoSuchPersonException nspe) {
      System.out.println("Invalid person: " + name);
    }
    catch (Exception e) {
      System.out.println("Error while creating/using person.");
    }
  }
}
```

We'll examine the details of this client a bit later in the chapter, but the example shows the fundamental steps an EJB client performs:

- Get a JNDI context from the EJB server.
- Use this context to look up a home interface for the bean you want to use.
- Use this home interface to create (or find) a bean.
- Call methods on the bean.

The Enterprise JavaBeans Object

If you develop your own EJB object, you need to provide three Java interfaces/classes in order to fully describe your EJB object to an EJB container:

- A home interface
- A remote interface
- An enterprise bean implementation

The remote interface and the object implementation are similar to the corresponding RMI interfaces. A client issues method requests through a stub derived from the remote interface and eventually these requests make their way to the corresponding bean instance on the server. The home interface is a new twist: it acts as a bean factory, providing a way for a client to create, locate, and destroy EJB objects that it uses. With the home interface in the picture, the remote interface acts as the interface the client uses to interact with EJB objects, and the implementation is where the object itself does its thing.

Here is an example home interface for the `Person` bean used in the previous example:

```
import javax.ejb.*;
import java.rmi.RemoteException;
import java.util.Hashtable;
import java.util.Enumeration;

public interface PersonHome extends EJBHome {
  // Create a new (nameless) person
  public Person create() throws RemoteException;

  // Create a named person.
  // Throws an exception if the person can't be found.
  public Person create(String name)
    throws RemoteException, NoSuchPersonException;

  // Lookup a Person by name (the "primary key")
  public Person findByPrimaryKey(PersonPK key)
    throws RemoteException, FinderException;

  // Lookup people with a given string in their name.
  public Enumeration findByPartialName(String fragment)
    throws RemoteException, FinderException;
}
```

This home interface includes methods to create `Person` beans and to find them if they already exist on the server. The remote interface for our `Person` bean is shown here:

```
import javax.ejb.*;
import java.rmi.Remote;
import java.rmi.RemoteException;

public interface Person extends Remote, EJBObject {
  public String getName() throws RemoteException;
  public void setName(String name) throws RemoteException;
}
```

This interface shows the business methods that are available to clients. When a client gets a reference to a bean through the `PersonHome` interface, it is given a stub that implements the `Person` interface.

The EJB object implementation needs to implement all the business methods in the remote interface, plus some methods used by the container to tell it about various events in its lifetime. The EJB object does not need to implement the remote interface, which is another new twist compared to RMI, where the server object always implements the remote interface. In EJB, the container arranges for method calls on the remote interface to be transferred to the EJB object. You just need to ensure that the EJB object has methods that match the signatures of the methods in the remote interface. We'll see an example of EJB object implementation a bit later.

Various pieces of these Java classes (home, remote, and implementation) are provided for the sake of the client, to allow a client to create EJB objects and call remote methods on them. Other pieces are provided for the EJB container, to allow it to notify the EJB object about transaction- and persistence-related events, for example.

In addition to the interfaces that describe the EJB object type, an EJB object also provides *deployment descriptors* to its containers. The deployment descriptors tell the container the name to use for registering the bean's home interface in JNDI, how to manage transactions for the bean, the access rights that remote identities are given to invoke methods on the EJB, and how persistence of the EJB objects should be handled. The container does all the heavy lifting with regard to providing these services, but the EJB object has to tell the container how it would prefer to have these services managed.

There are two fundamental types of Enterprise JavaBeans: *session* beans and *entity* beans.* A session bean is accessed by a single client at a time and is nonpersistent. It lives for a specific period of time (a session), and then gets removed by the server. An entity bean, on the other hand, represents a data entity stored in persistent storage (e.g., a database or filesystem). It can be accessed by multiple clients concurrently and is persistent beyond a client session or the lifetime of the EJB server.

To illustrate the difference between session and entity beans, suppose you're building an online banking system using EJB components. An automated bank teller, which reports on account balances and executes deposits and withdrawals on specified accounts, could be implemented as a session bean. A single client uses the teller bean to perform services on bank accounts that are maintained in some separate persistent store (the bank's database). A EJB object that directly represents a bank account, however, should be an entity bean. Multiple clients can access the account to perform transactions, and the state of the account entity should be persistent across the lifetime of the online banking server.

* In Version 1.0 of the EJB specification, support for entity beans is optional in compliant EJB servers.

The EJB Container

Most readers need to be familiar only with EJB containers from the perspective of an EJB client or an EJB object. For example, a Java application server that you might use to deploy an EJB-based application provides an implementation of the EJB container role. EJB-enabled application servers, with their own EJB containers and deployment tools, are available from Weblogic/BEA, Bluestone, IBM, Netscape, and Art Technology Group, among others.

The EJB container represents the value-added features of EJB over standard remote objects built using RMI or CORBA. The EJB container manages the details of transactional processing, resource pooling, and data persistence for you, which reduces the burden on client applications and EJB objects and allows them to deal with just the business at hand.

An EJB application server can contain multiple EJB containers, each managing multiple EJB objects. In this chapter, I'll refer to EJB servers and EJB containers somewhat interchangeably, depending on the context. In general, though, the container is strictly the runtime elements that interact directly with your EJB objects to provide client proxy services and notifications, while the server is the other glue outside the core EJB standard that integrates the EJB containers into a larger application management structure of some kind.

An EJB container is the heart of an EJB environment, in the same way an ORB is the heart of a CORBA environment. The container registers EJB objects for remote access, manages transactions between clients and EJB objects, provides access control over specific methods on the EJB, and manages the creation, pooling, and destruction of enterprise beans. The container also registers the home interface for each type of bean under a given name in a JNDI namespace, allowing remote clients to find the home interfaces and use them to create enterprise beans.

Once you provide the EJB container with the home and remote interfaces and the implementation class for your bean, along with a deployment descriptor, the container is responsible for generating the various classes that connect these components, as shown in Figure 7-2. The home and remote interfaces you provide are RMI `Remote` interfaces; the container generates both the client stubs and the server-side implementation for these interfaces. When a client looks up a bean's home interface through JNDI, it receives an instance of the home stub class. All methods invoked on this stub are remotely invoked, via RMI, on the corresponding home implementation object on the EJB server. Similarly, if the client creates or finds any beans through the home stub, the client receives remote object stubs, and methods invoked on the stubs are passed through RMI to corresponding implementation objects on the server. These remote objects are linked, through the EJB container, to a corresponding enterprise bean object, which is an instance of your bean-implementation class. Optionally, the EJB container may also generate a container-specific subclass of your bean implementation (e.g., if it wants to augment some of your bean methods to facilitate synchronization with the container).

The container receives client requests to create, look up, and/or remove beans. It either handles them itself or passes the requests to corresponding methods on the EJB object. Once the client obtains a reference to a remote interface for an EJB object, the container intercedes in remote method calls on the bean, to provide the

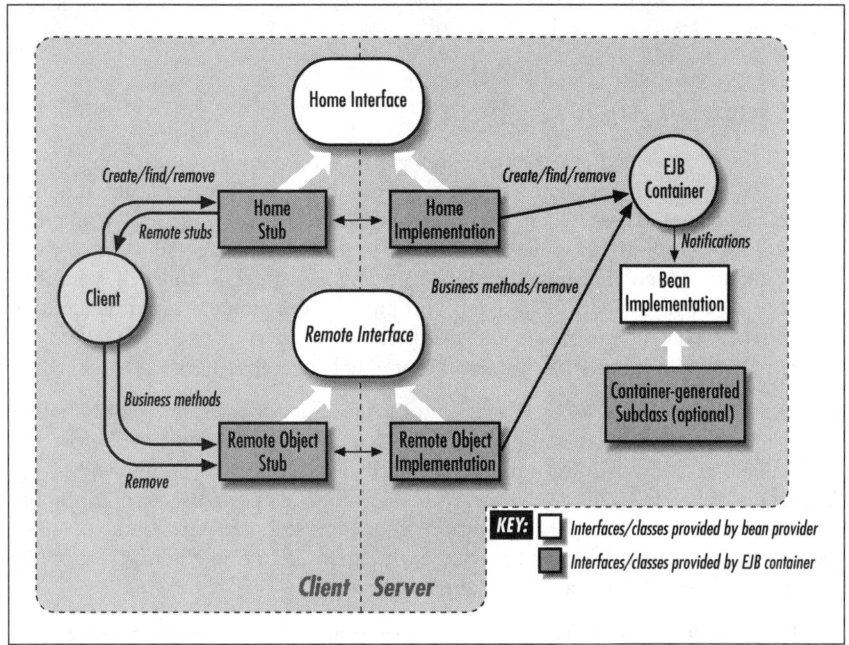

Figure 7-2: Relationship of bean-provider classes and container-generated classes

bean with required transaction management and security measures. The container also provides support for persistence of enterprise beans, either by storing/loading the bean state itself or by notifying the bean that it needs to store or reload its state from persistent storage.

A container can maintain multiple EJB objects and object types during its lifetime. The container has some freedom to manage resources on the server for performance or other reasons. For example, a container can choose to temporarily serialize a bean and store it to the server filesystem or some other persistent store; this is called *passivating* a bean. The EJB object is notified of this and given a chance to release any shared resources or transient data that shouldn't be serialized. The bean is also notified after it is activated again, to allow it to restore any transient state or reopen shared resources.

An EJB container can make any EJB object type available for remote use. When you deploy an EJB object within an EJB server, you can specify how the container should manage the bean during runtime, in terms of transaction management, resource pooling, access control, and data persistence. This is done using deployment descriptors, which contain parameter settings for these various options. These settings can be customized for each deployment of an EJB object. You might purchase an EJB object from a vendor and deploy it on your EJB server with a particular set of container management options, while someone else who purchased the same bean can deploy it with a different set of deployment options. We discuss the details of the runtime options available in deployment descriptors and how to use them later in this chapter, when we talk about deploying EJB components.

Transaction Management

One of the value-added features that Enterprise JavaBeans provides over regular remote objects is semiautomated transaction management. I'll periodically mention transaction-related issues when we look at creating, deploying, and using EJB objects, so this section introduces some basic transaction-management concepts. If you're not interested in using the transaction-management features of your EJB server, you can safely skip this section and jump to the material on implementing EJB object. If you plan to make JDBC calls from within your bean, however, you should note the information in the section on database transactions.

Transactions break up a series of interactions into units of work that can be either committed if they are successfully executed or rolled back at any time before the transaction is committed. If a transaction is rolled back, all parties involved in the transaction are responsible for restoring their state to its pretransaction condition. Transaction support is especially important in a distributed environment, since agents may lose network contact with each other or one agent may die while engaged in a series of interactions with another agent.

The EJB container is the principal player in the area of transaction management, since it is responsible for either generating transactions around client interactions with the bean, or detecting client-requested transactions and then notifying the EJB objects about transaction boundaries (start and end). The Enterprise JavaBeans architecture relies on the Java Transaction API (JTA) for transaction support. The JTA represents a transaction with the `javax.transaction.UserTransaction` interface.* Complete coverage of the JTA and the concepts of transaction-based processing are beyond the scope of this chapter, but a few words of overview here should be enough for you to get an understanding of how this can be a valuable feature of Enterprise JavaBeans. In addition, the JTA interfaces and classes are documented in Part III.

A client or an EJB object can declare a new transaction by creating a `UserTransaction` object. The transaction is started by calling the `begin()` method on the transaction object, and ended by calling either the `commit()` method (for a successful completion) or the `rollback()` method (to abort the transaction and revert to the state before the transaction began). The following code shows the (now cliché) example of a banking transaction in an EJB context:

```
// Get the JNDI context, and use it to get the Account home interface
Context ctx = new InitialContext(props);
AccountHome acctHome = (AccountHome)ctx.lookup("Accounts");
```

* Note that shortly after the EJB 1.0 specification was released, the name of the (then beta) JTA was changed, so that `javax.jts.UserTransaction` became `javax.transaction.UserTransaction`. I'm using the new class name here, but keep in mind that you might see the old package names in the EJB 1.0 documentation from Sun.

```
// Get two accounts
Account savings = acctHome.findByNameAndType("Jim Farley", "savings");
Account checking = acctHome.findByNameAndType("Jim Farley", "checking");

// Get a transaction object, using a JNDI lookup on the EJB context
javax.transaction.UserTransaction xaction =
    (UserTransaction)ctx.lookup("javax.transaction.UserTransaction");

// Perform a transaction
xaction.begin();
try {
  savings.deposit(1500.0);
  checking.transfer(savings, 750.0);
  xaction.commit();
}
// If anything goes wrong, roll back the work we've done.
catch (Exception e) {
  xaction.rollback();
}
```

This code might be seen in a client application using an EJB server for banking services. In this case, the client is using the transaction to ensure that both the deposit to savings and the transfer to checking are committed only if both operations are successful. If either one fails, the `rollback()` method is called on the transaction to ensure that any changes are undone. An EJB object might use similar procedures if it is managing its own transactions, the only difference being that the bean would be able to use its `EJBContext` to get a transaction from its container:

```
xaction = myContext.getUserTransaction();
```

The use of the `EJBContext` in enterprise beans is covered later in the chapter.

In the context of an Enterprise JavaBeans component, transaction boundaries can be defined by the client of the EJB object, the container, or the EJB object itself. In all cases, the EJB container decides how to handle the transaction context whenever a remote method is invoked on an EJB object. During a bean's lifetime, the container decides whether to execute the bean's business methods within the client's transaction or within a transaction that the container defines, or to allow the bean to manage its own transaction boundaries. When it is deployed, a bean can choose one of the following transaction-support attributes:

`TX_NOT_SUPPORTED`
: The bean cannot support transactions, so its methods must be called without a transaction context. If the client has initiated a transaction, it is suspended by the container before the bean's method is invoked. After the method completes, the container resumes the client's transaction.

`TX_SUPPORTS`
: The bean supports transactions if requested. If the client calls a method on the bean, while within a transaction, the client's transaction context is passed to the bean as part of the bean's `EJBContext`.

TX_REQUIRED
: The bean requires that all method requests be executed within a transaction context. If the client is already in a transaction of its own, the transaction context is passed on to the bean in its EJBContext. If not, the container creates a new transaction before calling the bean's method and commits the transaction when the bean's method finishes, but before the method results are returned to the client.

TX_REQUIRES_NEW
: The bean requires that all remote method requests be executed within a new transaction. The container automatically starts a new transaction before calling a remote method on the bean, and commits the transaction when the method finishes, but before the results are returned to the client. If the client calls a remote method while within a transaction, the client's transaction is suspended by the container before executing the bean's method within the new transaction and resumed after the new transaction is committed.

TX_MANDATORY
: The bean must be run within the context of a client-initiated transaction. If the client calls a remote method on the bean without starting a transaction first, the container throws a `javax.jts.TransactionRequired Exception`.

TX_BEAN_MANAGED
: The bean manages all its own transaction boundaries and does not execute within the client's transactions. If the client calls a remote method on the bean from within a client-generated transaction, the client transaction is suspended for the duration of the execution of the remote method. The bean's business methods are run within a transaction only if the bean explicitly creates one (the container does not automatically generate a transaction for each method call). The bean's methods run within the transaction until it is ended by the bean, and the container ensures that the transaction context is provided in the bean's EJBContext as long as the transaction is open.

Making the EJB Server Aware of Database Transactions

In order for an EJB server to properly implement the various transaction levels listed previously, it needs to be aware of JDBC connections and database transactions that you make from within your enterprise bean. This is key to the EJB server's ability to provide your beans with semiautomatic transaction management. While your bean methods are executing within a given transaction context, the EJB server needs to ensure all database transactions that you make are held pending the commit or rollback of the transaction. If the transaction is committed, the pending database updates are committed to their respective data sources. If the transaction is rolled back, the pending database updates are rolled back as well.

To allow the EJB server to do this, your enterprise bean typically needs to acquire JDBC connections in a manner specified by your EJB server. Unfortunately, the EJB 1.0 specification does not provide a standard method for acquiring database connections from an EJB container. Until this oversight in the EJB specification is amended, EJB server vendors have to provide their own methods for an EJB object to get connections that are monitored by the EJB container. Most EJB vendors provide a way to define a pool of JDBC connections and a means for requesting connections from this pool at runtime. BEA's WebLogic server, for example, allows you to specify a connection pool in a server property file and then use a JDBC URL to pull connections from this pool at runtime. An example properties entry might look like this:

```
weblogic.jdbc.connectionPool.myPool=\
  url=jdbc:weblogic:oracle,\
  driver=weblogic.jdbc.oci.Driver,\
  loginDelaySecs=1,\
  initialCapacity=5,\
  maxCapacity=10,\
  capacityIncrement=1,\
  props=user=jsmith;password=foobar;server=main
```

This line of the properties file asks the server to create a connection pool named `myPool` with the specified JDBC driver and connection properties. The server reads this information from the properties file on startup and creates the pool, and then your EJB object can ask for connections from the pool using a specific JDBC URL:

```
Connection conn = DriverManager.getConnection("jdbc:weblogic:jts:myPool");
```

This allows the WebLogic server to issue your bean a JDBC connection that is controlled by the server. However, there is currently no consensus among EJB providers concerning support for this method of providing JDBC connections to EJB objects and clients. Before using JDBC code in your enterprise beans, make sure to consult your EJB server documentation to see specifically how it provides JDBC connection management.

Transaction Isolation Levels

Normally, you would expect multiple transactions originating from multiple client requests on your bean to be effectively serialized. In other words, if multiple client transactional requests are made of your bean, the end effect of satisfying all these requests by timesharing the bean between each client/transaction should be the same as if each request were serialized at the boundaries of each transaction. The ANSI SQL standard defines three ways in which this transaction isolation rule can be violated:

Dirty reads
: If transaction A updates a record in the database, followed by transaction B reading the record, then transaction A performs a rollback on its update operation, the result is that transaction B has read an invalid state of the record.

Nonrepeatable reads
: If transaction A reads a record, followed by transaction B updating the same record, then transaction A reads the same record a second time, transaction A has read two different values for the same record.

Phantom reads
: If transaction A performs a query on the database with a particular search criteria (`WHERE` clause), followed by transaction B creating new records that sat-

isfy the search criteria, followed by transaction A repeating its query, transaction A sees new, phantom records in the results of the second query.

When you deploy your enterprise bean within an EJB container, you can specify what level of transaction isolation you want it to enforce for you, using one of the following isolation levels:

`TRANSACTION_READ_UNCOMMITTED`
: All the defined isolation violations are allowed.

`TRANSACTION_READ_COMMITTED`
: Dirty reads are prevented, but nonrepeatable reads and phantom reads are allowed.

`TRANSACTION_REPEATABLE_READ`
: Only phantom reads are allowed.

`TRANSACTION_SERIALIZABLE`
: All the defined isolation violations are prevented, making concurrent transactions effectively serialized.

These levels can be applied to an entire bean or to individual methods on the bean. If you don't specify one of these isolation levels, the EJB server typically uses the default isolation level dictated by the database being used for persistent storage. For more information on these isolation levels and their meaning, consult the JDBC specification or the ODBC specification. Chapter 2, *JDBC*, also briefly discusses database isolation levels. I mention them here just so that you are aware that they exist and can seek out more information if the details of transaction isolation are important for your enterprise beans.

Implementing a Basic EJB Object

Now it's time to start talking about actually implementing an Enterprise JavaBeans component. No matter whether you are creating an entity bean or a session bean, there are three Java interfaces/classes you need to provide:

Home interface
: The home interface is accessed directly by clients and used to create and/or find EJB objects of a specific type.

Remote bean interface
: The remote interface for the bean is also used directly by clients. When a client creates or finds an EJB object through a home interface, it is given a reference to a stub that implements the remote interface for the bean. The remote interface defines the methods the EJB object exports to remote clients.

Bean implementation
: The EJB object implementation itself must implement all the remote methods defined in its remote interface, provide methods that correspond to the methods on its home interface for creating and/or finding the bean, and also implement the methods used by the EJB container to manage the bean.

To demonstrate the various components that make up an Enterprise JavaBeans object, we'll look at a simple example: a profile server. The profile server is a stateless session bean that provides profile information for named users. This profile information consists of name/value pairs that might represent preferences in an application, historical usage patterns, etc. You might see a profile server running behind an online information service, allowing users to personalize the content and appearance of the site when they enter. After we've gone through this general example of writing a bean, we'll look more closely at the differences between implementing session beans and entity beans.

Table 7-1 shows how the methods of the home interface, the remote interface, and the bean implementation are related to each other.

Table 7-1: Related Methods

Home Interface Method	*Remote Interface Method*	*EJB Object Method*
`remote-type create(args) throws CreateException, RemoteException;`	N/A	`public void ejbCreate(args);` // Session beans `public primary-key-type ejbCreate(args);` // Entity beans
`remote-type` or `Enumeration findBymethod(args) throws FinderException, RemoteException;` // Entity beans only	N/A	`public primary-key-type` or `Enumeration ejbFindBymethod(args);` // Entity beans only
`public void remove();`	`public void remove();`	`public void ejbRemove();`
N/A	Business method (must throw `RemoteException`)	Business method, same signature (throwing `RemoteException` is optional)

Home Interface

The client needs a way to create a local reference to a profile server, so we have to provide a home interface for our bean, as shown in Example 7-1. This home interface provides a single `create()` method that takes no arguments and returns the bean's remote interface type, `ProfileServer`.

Example 7-1: Home Interface for the Profile Server Bean

```
import javax.ejb.*;
import java.rmi.RemoteException;

public interface ProfileServerHome extends EJBHome {
  public ProfileServer create() throws CreateException, RemoteException;
}
```

The home interface for an EJB object extends the `javax.ejb.EJBHome` interface. The home interface is also an RMI remote interface, since `EJBHome` extends `java.rmi.Remote`. The home interface can contain multiple `create()` methods that

Enterprise JavaBeans

take various initialization arguments for the bean to be created. The `create()` method returns a reference to our bean's remote interface (`ProfileServer`, in this case).

As shown in Table 7-1, for each `create()` method on the home interface, the EJB object implementation must have a matching `ejbCreate()` method that takes the same arguments. The `create()` method on the home interface has to declare that it throws `java.rmi.RemoteException`, since the home interface is an RMI remote interface. It also has to throw `javax.ejb.CreateException`, in case some error occurs during the EJB creation process (as opposed to some general RMI-related problem). If the corresponding `ejbCreate()` method on the bean implementation throws any other exceptions, the `create()` method has to include these in its `throws` clause as well. In this example, the bean's `ejbCreate()` method doesn't throw any exceptions, so we don't need to add any additional exceptions here.

Home interfaces for entity beans can also include finder methods, used to find existing persistent entity beans that were previously created. We'll discuss them in detail a bit later, when we talk about entity beans.

Remote Interface

You usually start putting together an EJB by defining its remote interface. This interface contains declarations of the methods that are available to remote clients, so it really points to the heart of the EJB object. The remote interface for our `ProfileServer` is shown in Example 7-2. A remote EJB interface must extend the `javax.ejb.EJBObject` interface. `EJBObject` in turn extends the `java.rmi.Remote` interface, which makes the EJB remote interface an RMI remote interface as well.

Example 7-2: Remote Interface for the Profile Server Bean

```
import javax.ejb.*;
import java.rmi.RemoteException;
import java.rmi.Remote;

public interface ProfileServer extends EJBObject {
  public Profile getProfile(String name)
    throws NoSuchPersonException, RemoteException;
}
```

The `ProfileServer` interface defines a single remote method, `getProfile()`, that accepts a username as its only argument. It returns a `Profile` object, containing the profile information for the person named. If the person's profile cannot be found on the server, a `NoSuchPersonException` is thrown. This is an application-specific exception whose implementation isn't shown here. Since the `ProfileServer` interface is an RMI remote interface, its methods must throw `RemoteException` in case some RMI communication problem occurs during a method call. Also, the arguments and return values for the methods have to be `Serializable`, and/or they need to be exportable RMI objects themselves. Our `getProfile()` method returns a `Profile` object, which we'll implement as an RMI-exportable object. The remote interface for `Profile` is shown in Example 7-3. The interface has only two remote methods, one to set profile entry values and one to get those values. Note: the implementation of the `Profile` remote interface isn't shown in this chapter.

Example 7-3: RMI Remote Interface for a Profile Object

```
import java.rmi.Remote;
import java.rmi.RemoteException;

public interface Profile extends Remote {
  public String getProfileEntry(String name) throws RemoteException;
  public void setProfileEntry(String name, String value)
    throws RemoteException;
}
```

When you deploy your EJB object, you can specify who is allowed to call each method on your bean through the remote interface. In this case, we might want only certain clients to be able to query for user profiles, so we might want to limit access to the `getProfile()` method on our `ProfileServer` bean. We discuss the access control features of bean deployment descriptors later in the chapter.

The Bean Implementation

Now that we have a home interface that lets clients create EJB references and a remote interface that describes the EJB methods, we need to actually implement the EJB object itself. Our `ProfileServerBean` is shown in Example 7-4. If you are familiar with RMI, this should look like an RMI server object, with some extra methods included. These extra methods are the hooks the EJB container uses to manage the bean as a component. At the end of the class is the implementation of the `getProfile()` method from the remote interface. The `ejbCreate()` method is also included here, to match the `create()` method on the home interface.

Example 7-4: The ProfileServerBean Implementation

```
import javax.ejb.*;
import java.rmi.RemoteException;

public class ProfileServerBean implements SessionBean {
  private SessionContext mContext = null;

  // Session bean methods
  public void ejbPassivate() {
    System.out.println("ProfileServerBean passivated.");
  }

  public void ejbActivate() {
    System.out.println("ProfileServerBean activated.");
  }

  public void ejbCreate() {
    System.out.println("ProfileServerBean created.");
  }

  public void ejbRemove() {
    System.out.println("ProfileServerBean removed.");
  }

 // Get session context from container
  public void setSessionContext(SessionContext context) {
    System.out.println("ProfileServerBean context set.");
    mContext = context;
```

Example 7-4: The ProfileServerBean Implementation (continued)

```
  }

 // Business methods
  public Profile getProfile(String name) throws NoSuchPersonException {
    // Here, we just create a ProfileImpl and return it.
    ProfileImpl profile = null;
    try {
      profile = new ProfileImpl(name);
    }
    catch (RemoteException re) {
      System.out.println("Failed creating profile for " + name);
      re.printStackTrace();
      throw new NoSuchPersonException();
    }

    return profile;
  }
}
```

The class for an EJB object must implement the `javax.ejb.EnterpriseBean` interface. This is usually done indirectly, through either the `javax.ejb.SessionBean` interface or the `javax.ejb.EntityBean` interface. In our example, we're defining a session bean, so the `ProfileServerBean` class implements the `SessionBean` interface.

The EJB class must be declared as `public`, to allow the container to introspect the class when generating the classes that hook the bean to the container and to allow the container to invoke methods on the bean directly where necessary. The bean class can optionally implement the bean's remote interface, but this isn't strictly required. In our case, we haven't implemented the bean's remote `ProfileServer` interface in the `ProfileServerBean` class. When the EJB server generates the classes that bridge the bean to the container, it also provides a class that implements the remote interface and acts as a proxy to the EJB class itself.*

In fact, for practical reasons, you probably don't want your EJB implementation to implement the remote interface for your bean. The remote interface has to extend the `EJBObject` interface, which includes a set of abstract methods that clients can use to retrieve the bean's home interface, get the primary key for entity beans, etc. When you deploy your bean, you'll use tools provided by the EJB container tools to generate stub and skeleton classes for the remote interface that implement these methods from `EJBObject`. If you implement the remote interface with your bean implementation class, you have to provide implementations for the `EJBObject` methods as well.

All Enterprise JavaBean objects, whether they are session beans or entity beans, must implement the following methods:

---

* Depending on the server implementation and how it chooses to generate these classes, it may be useful for you to provide an EJB class that directly implements the remote interface, since it might eliminate one level of method indirection. This is server-dependent, however, so there's no guarantee that this will help (or hurt).

`public void ejbActivate()`
: Called by the container when the bean has been deserialized from passive storage on the server. Allows the bean to reclaim any resources freed during passivation (e.g., file handles, network connections) or restore any other state not explicitly saved when the bean was serialized.

`public void ejbPassivate()`
: Called by the container just before the bean is to be serialized and stored in passive storage (e.g., disk, database) on the server. Allows the bean to release any non-serializable resources (e.g., open files, network connections).

`public void ejbCreate(. . .)`
: Called after the client invokes one of the `create()` methods on the bean's home interface. The bean and its home interface usually provide at least one `create()/ejbCreate()` pair to allow the client to create new beans. Session beans are required to provide at least one create method, but create methods are optional on entity beans, since entity beans can also be acquired using finder methods. The container creates the bean object using one of its standard constructors and might create several beans of the same type at server startup to act as a pool for future client requests. The `ejbCreate()` method indicates that a client is ready to use the bean; the arguments indicate the identity or starting state of the bean. For entity beans, the return type of an `ejbCreate()` method should be the bean's primary key type (see the later section "Implementing Entity Beans" for more details).

`public void ejbRemove()`
: Called by the container just before the bean is to be removed from the container and made eligible for garbage collection. The container may call this when all remote and local references to the bean have been removed.

These methods are used by the bean's container to notify the bean of various changes in its runtime state. In our example, the `ProfileServerBean` doesn't need to perform any actions in these methods, so they are included as empty methods that simply print messages to standard output, indicating that they have been called.

Implementing Session Beans

Now that we've seen a simple bean example, let's move on and talk about the specifics of implementing session beans (we'll get to entity beans after that). A session bean is much like a regular remote object, with the added benefit of being a JavaBeans component. The session bean serves as a remote extension of the client, running on a remote EJB server. Usually, a session bean is used by a single client, and the state data maintained by the session bean is owned by this client. The client acquires a reference to a session bean, and asks it to perform services by calling methods on the bean. These method calls might retrieve or update data in a remote database, filter data to be returned to the client, or update the session-related state information (if any) that the client is maintaining with the bean.

A session bean doesn't live beyond the lifetime of its server. If your client has a reference to a session bean, and the server restarts, that session bean reference is no longer valid. You can reacquire a session bean of the same type from the same server, but it's not guaranteed to be in the same state as the bean you had before the server restart. An EJB container also has the option of destroying a session bean after some timeout period while the bean is in an inactive state on the server (i.e., if there are no client references to the session bean for a period that exceeds the session timeout for the bean).

Stateful session beans can optionally receive notification of transaction boundaries from the EJB container. The container notifies the bean when a new client transaction is beginning and when the client transaction has either been completed or rolled back. If the session bean receives a rollback notification, it should manually reset its state information.

Session beans implement the `javax.ejb.SessionBean` interface. This interface extends the `javax.ejb.EnterpriseBean` interface and specifies `ejbActivate()`, `ejbPassivate()`, `ejbRemove()`, and `setSessionContext()` methods.

In addition to the standard EJB object methods mentioned in the previous section, a session bean also needs to implement a `setSessionContext()` method, as specified in the `SessionBean` interface. The container calls this method on the session bean just after the bean has been created, passing in a `javax.ejb.SessionContext` object that represents the runtime context for the bean. The session context is valid for the life of the bean. The session bean can use the `SessionContext` to get a reference to the remote object associated with the bean, by calling the `getEJBObject()` method on the context object. Since the bean is not required to implement the remote interface for the bean, this object may be different from the bean itself, and may implement a class generated by the server based on the remote interface, the home interface, and the bean implementation you provided. More about that later, when we talk about deploying EJB objects.

The `SessionContext` that the container passes to a session bean is also an `EJBContext`, which is a general representation for runtime context information, regardless of whether the bean is an entity or session bean. Among other things, the `EJBContext` has accessors that allow the bean to get a reference to its home interface (`getEJBHome()`), a list of environment properties used to deploy the bean (`getEnvironment()`), and the identity of the client that is currently executing a transaction with the bean (`getCallerIdentity()`).

Stateless Versus Stateful Session Beans

Session beans can be either stateful or stateless. A *stateless* session bean does not maintain state across method calls. If a client makes a series of remote method calls and/or transactions with the stateless bean, the bean is in the same state at the start of each method call or transaction. Our `ProfileServerBean` is such a bean. Stateless session beans of the same type can be considered identical to each other, and can be pooled and reused by multiple clients. A stateless session bean can be used concurrently by multiple remote clients without fear of conflicting with each other, since there is no shared state data that can be corrupted. Stateless beans don't need to be passivated since they have no state that needs to be restored when they're reactivated. The container simply destroys any stateless session beans it feels are no longer needed.

A *stateful* session bean, on the other hand, does maintain state that can be accessed and changed directly by the client's interactions with the bean. A stateful session bean is generally not intended to be accessed by more than a single remote client; the state of the stateful session bean along with its remote methods act as an extension of the client that created the bean.

To illustrate the difference between stateless and stateful session beans, let's take our `ProfileServerBean` and convert it to a stateful session bean. The `ProfileServerBean` is stateless because all it does is accept requests for user profiles and return the profiles directly to the client as RMI object references. The client then interacts with the `Profile` object directly, and the `Profile` manages the state of the interaction, in the form of the values of the profile entries. If the profile were a stateful enterprise bean itself, we wouldn't need the `ProfileServer` at all.

Example 7-5 shows the remote interface for a stateful `Profile` bean. It's similar to the remote interface for the RMI-based `Profile` we used in the stateless `ProfileServerBean` example. It has `setEntry()` and `getEntry()` methods that access entries using their names. The `Profile` bean also has accessors for the name of its user.

Example 7-5: Remote Interface for the Stateful Session Bean

```
import javax.ejb.*;
import java.rmi.Remote;
import java.rmi.RemoteException;

public interface Profile extends EJBObject {
  public String getName() throws RemoteException;
  public void setName(String name) throws RemoteException;
  public String getEntry(String key) throws RemoteException;
  public void setEntry(String key, String value) throws RemoteException;
}
```

The implementation of the stateful `ProfileBean` is shown in Example 7-6. It has the requisite implementations for the bean methods needed by the container and includes two `ejbCreate()` methods: one with no arguments that creates an unnamed profile and another that takes the name of the user of the profile. The corresponding `create()` methods on the `ProfileHome` interface are shown in Example 7-7. The state of this stateful session bean is maintained in a `String` field that holds the profile user's name and a `Properties` object that keeps the profile entries. The principal design difference between the `ProfileBean` and the stateless `ProfileServerBean` is the state information stored on the `ProfileBean` in its data members. The get/set accessors from the remote `Profile` interface are implemented here as operations on these fields.

Example 7-6: Implementation of the Stateful Session Bean

```
import javax.ejb.*;
import java.rmi.RemoteException;
import java.util.Properties;

public class ProfileBean implements SessionBean {
  // Name of the person owning the profile
  private String mName = "";
  // Entries in the profile (name/value pairs)
  private Properties mEntries = new Properties();
```

Example 7-6: Implementation of the Stateful Session Bean (continued)

```
  // Store session context
  private SessionContext mContext = null;

  // Session bean methods
  public void ejbActivate() {
    System.out.println("ProfileBean activated.");
  }

  public void ejbRemove() {
    System.out.println("ProfileBean removed.");
  }

  public void ejbPassivate() {
    System.out.println("ProfileBean passivated.");
  }

  public void setSessionContext(SessionContext context) {
    System.out.println("ProfileBean context set.");
    mContext = context;
  }

  public void ejbCreate() {
    System.out.println("Nameless ProfileBean created.");
  }

  public void ejbCreate(String name) throws NoSuchPersonException {
    mName = name;
    System.out.println("ProfileBean created for " + mName + ".");
  }

  // Business methods
  public String getName() {
    return mName;
  }

  public void setName(String name) {
    mName = name;
  }

  public String getEntry(String key) {
    return mEntries.getProperty(key);
  }

  public void setEntry(String key, String value) {
    mEntries.put(key, value);
  }
}
```

Example 7-7: Home Interface for the Stateful Session Bean

```
import javax.ejb.*;
import java.rmi.RemoteException;

public interface ProfileHome extends EJBHome {
  public Profile create() throws RemoteException, CreateException;
  public Profile create(String name) throws RemoteException, CreateException;
}
```

This stateful bean is used by clients to maintain a set of application-specific profile entries for a named user. Here is an example client scenario:

```
// Get the Profile bean's home interface
ProfileHome pHome = ...
// Create a profile for a person
System.out.println("Creating profile for " + name);
Profile profile = pHome.create(name);
// Get/set some entries in the profile
System.out.println("Setting profile entries for " + name);
profile.setEntry("favoriteColor", "blue");
profile.setEntry("language", "German");
System.out.println("Getting profile entries for " + name);
System.out.println("\tFavorite color: " +
  profile.getEntry("favoriteColor"));
System.out.println("\tLanguage: " + profile.getEntry("language"));
```

After getting the home interface for the `ProfileBean`, the client creates a profile for a named user, sets the values for some profile entries, and gets them back again.

An EJB container must be told at deployment time whether a session bean is stateful or stateless. The container uses this information to determine how to handle pooling of the session beans and whether to passivate the bean or not, among other things. Since stateless beans can be used by any client, the container pools stateless beans and doles them out to clients as needed. If new stateless beans are needed, the container creates them, and when they aren't needed (e.g., the rate of client requests decreases), they are simply destroyed. In order to allow the container to fill its pool, any stateless session bean must provide a single `create()` method with no arguments. Stateless beans implement only the no-argument creation method, since they have no client state that could be affected by arguments. An additional restriction on stateless beans is that they cannot participate in transaction synchronization and cannot implement the `SessionSynchronization` interface, which is described in the next section.

Optional Transaction Support

Since session beans don't typically represent persistent shared data, and stateful session beans can only be accessed by a single client at a time, user transaction boundaries may not be important to such a bean. If, however, the session bean is managing database data for the user, it may want to know about the beginning and ending of user transactions, so that it can cache data at the start and commit its database updates at the end. For this reason, the EJB specification allows session beans to optionally implement the `javax.ejb.SessionSynchronization` interface. By implementing this interface, the session bean indicates that it wants the container to notify it about the beginning and end of transactions.

In this case, the bean must implement the three methods declared on the interface: `afterBegins()`, `beforeCompletion()`, and `afterCompletion()`. The container calls the bean's `afterBegin()` method just after a new transaction begins. This lets the bean allocate any resources it might need during the transaction and cache database data, for example. Just before the transaction completes, the container calls the bean's `beforeCompletion()` method. In this method, the bean can release any resources or cached data it may have initialized during the transaction. The `afterCompletion()` method is called just after the transaction has completed. The container passes in a `boolean` value that is `true` if the transaction was committed and `false` if the transaction was rolled back. The bean can use this notification to deal with rollbacks, for example, allowing the bean to undo any changes made during the transaction.

Implementing Entity Beans

An entity bean represents data that is stored in a database or some other persistent storage. Entity beans are persistent across client sessions and the lifetime of the server. Each entity bean of a given type has a unique identity that can look up the same bean from multiple clients. No matter when or where you get a reference to an entity bean with a given identity, the bean should reflect the current state of the persistent data it represents. Multiple clients can access an entity bean at the same time. The EJB container manages these concurrent transactions for the entity bean, ensuring that client transactions are properly isolated from each other. Note that support for entity beans is not strictly required by the EJB 1.0 specification. This has been changed in the EJB 1.1 specification, which makes entity bean support mandatory in EJB-compliant application servers.

An entity bean can be passivated by its container, but the meaning of being passivated is slightly different. A container passivates an entity bean (calling its `ejbPassivate()` method in the process) when it wants to disassociate the bean from the persistent data entity it has been representing. After being passivated, the bean may be put into the container's pool of entity beans to associate with another client-requested entity or it may be removed from the server altogether.

At a fundamental level, entity beans are implemented similarly to session beans. You need to provide a home interface, a remote interface, and a bean implementation. An entity bean, however, requires some additional methods in its home interface and bean implementation, to support the management of its persistent state and to allow clients to look up the entity bean from persistent storage. Entity beans must also provide a class that serves as its primary key, or index, into its persistent storage.

There are two ways persistent storage for an entity bean can be managed: by the EJB container or by the bean itself. In the first case, called a *container-managed* entity bean, the bean leaves the database calls to the container. The deployment tools provided with the EJB server are responsible for generating these database calls in the classes it uses to deploy your bean. In the second case, called *bean-managed* entity beans, you provide the database calls for managing your bean's persistent storage as part of your bean implementation.

If you can rely on the EJB container to handle your entity bean's persistence, this can be a huge benefit, since it saves you from having to add JDBC code to your beans. But the automated persistence support in EJB is limited, and there are times when you'll need to manage persistence directly in your bean implementation. We discuss the pros and cons of each of these scenarios a bit later in this section.

Primary Keys

If you develop an entity bean, you must provide the EJB container with a class that serves as the primary key for the bean. A primary key includes all of the information needed to uniquely identify an item in persistent storage. The primary key for a person's records in a database, for example, might be a first and last name, or a social security number (for U.S. citizens), or some other identification number. If you're developing an EJB object that represents a bank account, you might make the primary key an object that holds the account number, which is a unique identifier for an `Account` object. An EJB container typically creates unique identifiers for all session and entity beans, so that it can internally track individual beans. The primary key used for entity beans is a more public unique identifier, in that clients can see the primary key for an entity bean, and the primary key is used directly by the bean implementation to load/update its state from persistent storage.

If we were to develop an entity-bean version of our `ProfileBean` (which we'll do shortly), the primary key class might look something like the following:

```
public class ProfilePK implements java.io.Serializable {
  public String mName;
  public ProfilePK() {
    mName = null;
  }
  public ProfilePK(String name) {
    mName = name;
  }
}
```

Since there is a one-to-one correspondence between named users and their profiles, we just use the name of the user as our primary key for an entity `ProfileBean`.

The primary key class for an entity bean must be derived from `java.io.Serializable`. If any of the persistence of the entity bean is container-managed, the primary key class must also obey the following:

- It must be a public class.
- It must have a default constructor (one with no arguments) that is public.
- All its data members must be public.
- All of the names of the data members on the class must be names of container-managed data members on the entity bean.

Enterprise JavaBeans

The primary key for our `ProfileBean` is really just a wrapper around a `String` field that holds a name. We've done this to support the option of using container-managed persistence for the bean. We have to use the `ProfilePK` class as the primary key, not just a `String`, because the EJB container needs to be able to introspect on the primary key and match its fields with the corresponding fields on the bean class.

Finder Methods

Since entity beans are persistent and can be accessed by multiple clients, clients have to be able to find them as well as create them. To this end, an entity bean's home interface can provide `findXXX()` methods, and the bean implementation has to have corresponding `ejbFindXXX()` methods that take the same arguments and have the same return types. The `findXXX()` methods on the home interface can have any name, as long as the method name begins with `find`. A bank account bean, for example, might define a `findByName()` method that accepts a string that is the name of the person whose accounts are desired.

Each `findXXX()` method on the home interface must return either an instance of the bean's remote interface or a collection of these objects. In the EJB 1.0 specification, only `Enumeration` objects can return collections of entity beans, but the EJB 1.1 specification allows EJB implementations to also use Java 2 `Collection` types as return types for `findXXX()` methods. In our bank account example, the `findByName()` method can return multiple accounts (e.g., if a person has both checking and savings accounts), so it should be declared as returning an `Enumeration`.

The home interface for an entity-based `ProfileBean` is shown in Example 7-8. It provides two finder methods: `findByPrimaryKey()` finds a profile by its primary key (which encapsulates the user's name), and `findByEntryValue()` finds profiles that have a particular attribute value set. The first finder method returns a single `Profile` object, since there is only a single `Profile` for each user. The second finder method returns a collection of `Profile` objects (as an `Enumeration`), as multiple user profiles might have a given attribute value. The `findByPrimaryKey()` method is a standard finder method defined by the EJB specification; its only argument is always the primary key type for the entity bean.

Example 7-8: Home Interface for an Entity ProfileBean

```
import javax.ejb.*;
import java.rmi.RemoteException;

public interface ProfileHome extends EJBHome {
  public Profile create() throws CreateException, RemoteException;
  public Profile create(String name)
    throws RemoteException, DuplicateProfileException;

  public Profile findByPrimaryKey(ProfilePK key)
    throws RemoteException, FinderException;
  public Enumeration findByEntryValue(String key, String value)
    throws RemoteException, FinderException;
}
```

A client can use the `findXXX()` methods on the home interface to determine if a bean (or beans) with a given identity already exists in persistent storage. If a `findXXX()` method finds an appropriate bean (or beans), a single primary key (or set of keys) is initialized to represent the unique identity of the bean(s) that matched the client query, and these key(s) are returned to the client. If the identified bean cannot be found in persistent storage, a `javax.ejb.FinderException` is thrown. All `findXXX()` methods on the bean's home interface must declare that they can throw `FinderException` and `RemoteException` (since the method is an RMI remote method).

The EJB container intercepts the client's invocation of the finder method and invokes the corresponding `ejbFindXXX()` method on an instance of the entity bean on the server. An entity bean of the appropriate type is pulled from the container's pool and its `ejbFindXXX()` method is called with the client's arguments. The `ejbFindXXX()` method on the bean should do the necessary queries to persistent storage to determine if the requested data exists there, then create primary key instances and initialize them with the results of the query. The primary key objects are the return value of the `ejbFindXXX()` method. The EJB container is responsible for taking the key(s) returned by the `ejbFindXXX()` method and converting them to remote objects, whose stubs are returned to the client that invoked the finder method.

It's important to note that the entity bean that executes the `ejbFindXXX()` method doesn't necessarily represent the entities being looked up by the client. The container uses the bean to call the method, takes the primary key or keys returned, and then uses them to either create new beans or reinitialize existing beans.

An entity bean implementation must at a minimum provide an `ejbFindByPrimaryKey()` method that accepts a primary key object as its argument. The implementation must also provide additional `findXXX()` methods to match any other `ejbfindXXX()` methods on the home interface. Each `ejbFind` method must have the same arguments and return types as the corresponding `find` method.

Entity Bean Implementation

I've already mentioned a few additional requirements on entity bean implementations, but here is a list of all the additional methods an entity bean either must implement or has the option to implement:

`public` *`priKeyType`* `ejbFindByPrimaryKey(`*`priKeyType`*`) throws FinderException`
: The only required finder method on an entity bean. Both the argument and the return type must be the bean's primary key type.

`public void ejbPostCreate()`
: If needed, an entity bean can optionally provide an `ejbPostCreate()` method for each `ejbCreate()` method it provides, taking the same arguments. The container calls the `ejbPostCreate()` method after the bean's `ejbCreate()` method has been called and after the container has initialized the transaction context for the bean.

`public void ejbLoad()`
: Called by the container to cause the bean instance to load its state from persistent storage. The container can call this bean method any time after the bean has been created, to do an initial load from persistent storage or to refresh the bean's state from the database.

`public void ejbStore()`
: Called by the container to cause the bean to write its current runtime state to persistent storage. This method can be called any time after a bean is created.

`public void setEntityContext(EntityContext ctx)`
: The container calls this method after a new instance of the bean has been constructed, but before any of its `ejbCreate()` methods are called. The bean is responsible for storing the context object.

`public void unsetEntityContext(EntityContext ctx)`
: The container calls this method before the entity bean is destroyed.

Most of these methods, like `ejbLoad()` and `ejbStore()`, are invoked by the EJB container to notify the bean about persistent store management.

In addition to these entity-specific methods on bean implementations, the semantics of some of the other standard methods are slightly different for entity beans. Each `ejbCreate()` method, for example, should not only assign any state data passed in as variables, but also create a record in persistent storage for the new entity bean. The signatures of `ejbCreate()` methods on entity beans can be different too. For an entity bean that manages its own persistence (a bean-managed entity bean), the `ejbCreate()` methods return the primary key type for the bean. For a container-managed entity bean, the `ejbCreate()` methods return `void`, the same as for session beans. The `ejbRemove()` method is called by the container when the bean is to be removed from the server. The bean should also remove its state from the persistent storage in its `ejbRemove()` implementation, since a request by a client to `remove()` an entity bean is really a request to remove the record from persistent storage as well.

A persistent ProfileBean

The major drawback in our stateful session `ProfileBean` is that the profile data it represents isn't persistent. A profile is created by a client and updated through remote method calls, but once the `ProfileBean` is removed by the server or the server crashes/restarts, the accumulated profile data is lost. What we really want is a bean whose state is persistent stored in a relational database or some other persistent storage, that can be reloaded at a later time, when the user reenters a profiled application. An entity EJB object provides this functionality, and an EJB container that supports entity beans provides your bean with facilities that make it easier to manage persistent state. It's also possible to have the container manage the persistence of the bean for you, if that's desired.

Let's look at the implementation for the entity bean version of our `ProfileBean`, shown in Example 7-9. We've already seen the home interface and remote interface for this entity bean in earlier examples. The purpose of the bean is the same as our stateful session version: it represents a profile for a named application user, maintaining a list of name/value pairs for various attributes and options. The difference is that this `ProfileBean` represents a profile entity that exists as data in persistent storage (a database, in this case). The most obvious differences in the actual code are the JDBC calls peppered throughout the class, where the bean manages its persistent data. There are a few extra methods defined as well. Most of them are required by the EJB specification for entity beans and a few are utility methods used by the JDBC code to connect to the database and make updates.

Example 7-9: An Entity ProfileBean with Bean-Managed Persistence

```
import javax.ejb.*;
import java.rmi.RemoteException;
import java.util.Properties;
import java.util.Enumeration;
import java.util.Vector;
import java.sql.*;

public class ProfileBean implements EntityBean {
  // Entries in the profile (name/value pairs)
  public Properties mEntries;

  // Store context (nonpersistent)
  private transient EntityContext mContext = null;

  // Entity bean methods

  // During activation, create our entry lookup table
  public void ejbActivate() {
    mEntries = new Properties();
    System.out.println("ProfileBean activated.");
  }

   // Load bean from persistent store. In this case, we're managing the dbase
   // storage, so we store our profile entries as independent records in a
   // separate "PROFILE_ENTRY" table.
  public void ejbLoad() throws RemoteException {
    try {
      // Get primary key from context, use it to load our data
      ProfilePK key = (ProfilePK)mContext.getPrimaryKey();
      loadFromDB(key);
    }
    catch (Exception e) {
      System.out.println("Failed to load ProfileBean: ");
      e.printStackTrace();
      throw new RemoteException("ejbLoad failed: ", e);
    }
    System.out.println("ProfileBean load finished.");
  }

  protected void loadFromDB(ProfilePK key) throws FinderException {
    boolean found = false;
    try {
      // Get a connection and select our profile record
      Connection conn = newConnection();
      Statement s = conn.createStatement();
      s.executeQuery("select name from profile where name = '" + key.mName +
                     "'");
      ResultSet rs = s.getResultSet();
      if (rs.next()) {
        found = true;
        // We found a profile record, so look up the entries
        s.executeQuery("select key, value from profile_entry where name = '"
                       + key.mName + "'");
        rs = s.getResultSet();
        while (rs.next()) {
          String pKey = rs.getString(1);
          String pValue = rs.getString(2);
          mEntries.put(pKey, pValue);
```

Enterprise JavaBeans

```
      }
    }
  }
  catch (SQLException e) {
    throw new FinderException("Failed to load profile entries from DB: " +
                              e.toString());
  }
  finally { try { s.close(); conn.close(); }
  if (!found) {
    // No profile record found, throw a FinderException
    throw new FinderException("No profile found for " + key.mName);
  }
}

// Get connection (BEA/WebLogic-specific version)
private Connection newConnection() throws SQLException {
  // Make sure that the JDBC driver is loaded
  try {
    Class.forName("weblogic.jdbc.oci.Driver");
  }
  catch (ClassNotFoundException cnfe) {
    System.out.println("Failed to load JDBC drivers.");
  }
  // Get the connection from the pool that we specified in the
  // WebLogic server properties file
  return DriverManager.getConnection("jdbc:weblogic:jts:myPool");
}

// Store bean to persistent store. Properties are stored as records in the
// PROFILE_ENTRY table.
public void ejbStore() throws RemoteException {
  // Get our primary key from our context
  ProfilePK key = (ProfilePK)mContext.getPrimaryKey();
  try {
    Connection conn = newConnection();
    // Clear out old profile entries
    Statement s = conn.createStatement();
    s.executeUpdate("delete from PROFILE_ENTRY where name = '" + key.mName
                    + "'");
    Enumeration pKeys = mEntries.propertyNames();
    // Add each entry to the PROFILE_ENTRY table
    while (pKeys.hasMoreElements()) {
      String pKey = (String)pKeys.nextElement();
      String pValue = mEntries.getProperty(pKey);
      s.executeUpdate("insert into PROFILE_ENTRY (name,key,value) values "
                      + "('" + key.mName + "', '" + pKey + "', '"
                      + pValue + "')");
    }
    // Close the statement and the connection, just to be tidy...
    s.close();
    conn.close();
  }
  catch (Exception e) {
    // Store operation failed, toss a RemoteException
    throw new RemoteException("ejbStore failed: ", e);
  }
  System.out.println("ProfileBean store finished.");
}
```

Example 7-9: An Entity ProfileBean with Bean-Managed Persistence (continued)

```
// Remove this named profile from the database
public void ejbRemove() {
  // Get this profile's name
  ProfilePK key = (ProfilePK)mContext.getPrimaryKey();
  try {
    Connection conn = newConnection();
    // Clear out any profile entries
    Statement s = conn.createStatement();
    s.executeUpdate("delete from profile_entry where name = '" + key.mName
                    + "'");
    // Clear out the profile itself
    s.executeUpdate("delete from profile where name = '" + key.mName
                    + "'");

    s.close();
    conn.close();
    System.out.println("ProfileBean removed.");
  }
  catch (SQLException se) {
    System.out.println("Error removing profile for " + key.mName);
    se.printStackTrace();
  }
}

// When we're passivated, release our entries.
public void ejbPassivate() {
  mEntries = null;
  System.out.println("ProfileBean passivated.");
}

// Get context from container
public void setEntityContext(EntityContext context) {
  mContext = context;
  System.out.println("ProfileBean context set.");
}

// Container is removing our context...
public void unsetEntityContext() throws RemoteException {
  mContext = null;
  System.out.println("ProfileBean context unset.");
}

// Since we're managing persistence here in the bean, we need to
// implement the finder methods
public ProfilePK ejbFindByPrimaryKey(ProfilePK key)
  throws FinderException, RemoteException {
  loadFromDB(key);
  return key;
}

public Enumeration ejbFindByEntryValue(String key, String value)
  throws RemoteException, FinderException {
  Vector userList = new Vector();
  // Get a new connection from the EJB server
  try {
    Connection conn = newConnection();
    Statement s = conn.createStatement();
    // Issue a query for matching profile entries, grabbing just the name
```

```
      s.executeQuery("select distinct(name) from profile_entry where " +
                     " key = '" + key + "' and value = '" + value + "'");
      // Convert the results in primary keys and return an enumeration
      ResultSet results = s.getResultSet();
      while (results.next()) {
        String name = results.getString(1);
        userList.addElement(new ProfilePK(name));
      }
    }
    catch (SQLException se) {
      // Failed to do database lookup
      throw new FinderException();
    }
    return userList.elements();
  }

  // Create method (corresponds to each create() method on the
  // home interface, ProfileHome).  Nothing to initialize in this case
  public ProfilePK ejbCreate() {
    System.out.println("Nameless ProfileBean created.");
    return new ProfilePK();
  }

  // Create method with name of profile owner.
  public ProfilePK ejbCreate(String name) throws DuplicateProfileException {
    try {
      Connection conn = newConnection();
      Statement s = conn.createStatement();
      s.executeUpdate("insert into profile (name) values ('" + name + "')");
      s.close();
      conn.close();
    }
    catch (SQLException se) {
      System.out.println("Error creating profile, assuming duplicate.");
      throw new DuplicateProfileException("SQL error creating profile for " +
                                          name + ": " + se.toString());
    }

    System.out.println("ProfileBean created for " + name + ".");
    return new ProfilePK(name);
  }

  // Post-creation notification.  Nothing to do here, but we need
  // to provide an implementation.
  public void ejbPostCreate() {
    System.out.println("ProfileBean post-create called.");
  }

  // Post-creation notification.  Nothing to do here, what we need
  // to provide an implementation.
  public void ejbPostCreate(String name) {
    System.out.println("ProfileBean post-create called for " + name + ".");
  }

  // Business methods
  public String getName() {
    ProfilePK key = (ProfilePK)mContext.getPrimaryKey();
    return key.mName;
```

```
  }

  public String getEntry(String key) {
    return mEntries.getProperty(key);
  }

  public void setEntry(String key, String value) {
    mEntries.put(key, value);
  }
}
```

The structure of the entity `ProfileBean` is similar to the stateful session bean version in Example 7-6. A `Properties` object holds the profile entries for the user, and the `getEntry()` and `setEntry()` remote method implementations access this `Properties` object for the client. You might notice that there is no data member on the entity `ProfileBean` to hold the name of the user. We can do this here because we're not using the EJB container to manage the bean's persistence for us, so we're relying on the fact that the name is found in the primary key object, and the primary key is stored for us in the `EntityContext` the container gives us through the `setEntityContext()` method. If we were using container-managed persistence, however, we'd have to have a field on the bean for the name, so that the container would know how to set it. The `getName()` remote method on `ProfileBean` shows how we retrieve the username for the profile using the `getPrimaryKey()` method on the `EntityContext`.

We've also removed the `setName()` remote method from the entity `ProfileBean`, since we don't want to allow the client to change the name of an existing, active entity bean. The `Profile` remote interface for this bean, not shown here, is similar to the `Profile` interface in Example 7-5, but does not have a `setName()` method. Since the `Profile` is now a persistent entity bean and the name is the primary key, or identifying attribute, of the bean, the name of the bean can only be set when the bean is created. While the entity bean is active, it is associated with a profile entity for a specific user, and the client can only read the name associated with the profile.

In the `ProfileBean` code, you'll notice many of the EJB-required methods, including `ejbActivate()`, `ejbPassivate()`, `ejbCreate()`, and `ejbRemove()`. The `ejbActivate()` and `ejbPassivate()` methods handle the movement of the bean out of and into the EJB server's entity bean pool, respectively.

The `ejbCreate()` methods on the `ProfileBean` create a new profile entity in the database. There is a matching `ejbCreate()` method for each `create()` method on our `ProfileHome` interface from Example 7-8. The EJB container is responsible for intercepting the generated primary key object, converting it to a remote `Profile` object, and returning a remote `Profile` stub to the client that called the `create()` method on the `ProfileHome` interface. The `ejbRemove()` method on our `ProfileBean` deletes all the records for this profile entity from the database.

The `ProfileBean` also contains methods specific to entity beans. For each `ejbCreate()` method, it has a corresponding `ejbPostCreate()` method, which is called by the container after the `ejbCreate()` method has returned, and the container has initialized the bean's transaction context. There's nothing more for us to do in our

ProfileBean at this point, so we just print a message to standard output in each ejbPostCreate() method.

There is an ejbFindXXX() method in our entity ProfileBean that corresponds to each findXXX() method in ProfileHome. The ejbFindByPrimaryKey() method simply takes the primary key passed in as an argument and attempts to load the data for the entity from the database. If successful, it returns the primary key back to the container, where it is converted to a remote Profile object to be returned to the client. Note that it's not necessary for us to actually load all the profile data here in the finder method; we need to verify only that the named entity exists in the database and either return the primary key to signal success or throw an exception. The container takes the returned primary key and assigns it to one of the beans in its pool (possibly the same one it called the finder method on, but not necessarily). Since we already have the loadFromDB() method used in ejbLoad(), it is a simple matter to reuse it here in the finder method. If the performance hit for loading the profile data twice is too great, we'd have to rewrite the finder method to simply check the PROFILE table for a record matching the name in the primary key.

The ejbFindByEntryValue() method takes a key and value String arguments and attempts to find any and all profile entities with a matching key/value pair in the PROFILE_ENTRY table. Each name that has such a record is converted to a primary key object and returned to the container in an Enumeration. The container converts each primary key object into a remote Profile object and returns the set to the client. If we encounter a database problem along the way, we throw a FinderException.

The Entity Context

The EJB container provides context information to an entity bean in the form of an EntityContext object. The container sets this object using the bean's setEntityContext() method and removes it when the bean is being removed by calling the bean's unsetEntityContext() method. Like SessionContext, EntityContext provides the bean with access to its corresponding remotely exported object through the getEJBObject() method. The EntityContext, in addition, gives an entity bean access to its primary key through getPrimaryKey(). The declared return type of this method is Object, but the object returned is of the bean's primary key type. Note that the data accessed through the EntityContext might be changed by the EJB container during the bean's lifetime, as explained in the next section. For this reason, you shouldn't store the EJB remote object reference or primary key in data variables in the bean object, since they might not be valid for the entire lifetime of the bean. Our entity ProfileBean, for example, stores the EntityContext reference in an instance variable, where it can access the context data as needed during its lifetime.

Life Cycle of an Entity Bean

Before the first client asks for an entity bean by calling a create() or findXXX() method on its home interface, an EJB container might decide to create a pool of entity beans to handle client requests for beans. This potentially reduces the amount of time it takes for a client to receive a entity bean remote reference after it makes a request for an entity bean. To add a bean to its pool, the container creates an instance of your bean implementation class and sets its context using the `setEntityContext()` method. At this point, the entity bean hasn't been associated with a particular data entity, so it doesn't have a corresponding remote object.

When a client calls a `create()` method on the bean's home interface, the container picks a bean out of the pool and calls its corresponding `ejbCreate()` method. If the `ejbCreate()` method is successful, it returns one or more primary key objects to the container. For each primary key, the container picks an entity bean out of its pool to be assigned to the entity represented by the key. Next, the container assigns the bean's identity by setting the properties in its `EntityContext` object (e.g., its primary key and remote object values). If the bean has an `ejbPostCreate()` method, that gets called after the bean's entity identity has been set. The `ejbCreate()` method should create the entity in persistent storage, if the bean is managing its own persistence.

Alternately, the client might call a `findXXX()` method on the home interface. The container picks one of the pooled entity beans and calls the corresponding `ejbFindXXX()` method on it. If the finder method finds one or more matching entities in persistent storage, the container uses pooled entity beans to represent these entities. It picks entity beans out of the pool and calls their `ejbActivate()` methods. Before calling `ejbActivate()`, the container sets the bean's context by assigning the corresponding primary key and remote object reference in its context.

After an entity bean has been activated (either by being created through one of its `ejbCreate()` methods or by being found and having its `ejbActivate()` method called), it is associated with a specific entity in persistent storage, and with a specific remote object that has been exported to a remote client or clients. At any point after this, the container can call the bean's `ejbLoad()` or `ejbStore()` method to force the bean to read or write its state from/to persistent storage. The bean's business methods can also be invoked by clients when it is in this state.

At some point, the container may decide to put the bean back into its internal pool. This might happen after all remote references to the bean have been released or after a certain period of inactivity with the bean. The container might also do this as a reaction to client loading issues (e.g., time-sharing pooled beans between client requests). When the container wants to remove the association between the bean and the remote object, but doesn't want the object's state removed from persistent store, it calls the bean's `ejbPassivate()` method. The bean can release any resources it allocated while in the active state, but it doesn't have to update persistent storage for the entity it represents, as this was done the last time its `ejbStore()` method was invoked by the container.

The bean can also lose its association with an entity when the client decides to remove the entity. The client does this either by calling a `remove()` method on the bean's home interface or calling the `remove()` method directly on an EJB object. When one of these things happens, the container calls the bean's `ejbRemove()` method, and the bean should delete the data in persistent storage pertaining to the entity it represents. After the `ejbRemove()` method completes, the container puts the bean back into its internal pool.

Handles on Entity Beans

Every bean's remote interface extends the `EJBObject` interface. This interface allows the client to obtain a serializable handle on the enterprise bean. This handle is a persistent reference to the bean that can be serialized and then stored in local storage on the bean or emailed as an attachment to other users, for example. Later, a client can deserialize the handle object and continue interacting with the bean it references. The handle contains all of the information needed to reestablish a remote reference to the enterprise bean it represents. Since this is only useful for beans that are still valid when the handle is reconstituted, it is usually only applicable to entity beans.

The handle for a bean can be obtained using the `getHandle()` method on a remote bean object reference:

```
Profile profile = ...;
Handle pHandle = profile.getHandle();
```

`getHandle()` returns a `javax.ejb.Handle` object. The `Handle` interface itself does not extend `java.io.Serializable`, but any class that implements it is required by the EJB specification to extend `Serializable`. Typically, the `Handle` implementation is provided by the EJB container, which enforces this restriction. So you can always assume that the `Handle` for an EJB object can be stored in serialized format, if needed:

```
ObjectOutputStream oout = ...;
oout.writeObject(pHandle);
```

Later, you can read the object back from its serialized state and obtain a reference to the remote bean object, using the `getEJBObject()` method on the handle:

```
ObjectInputStream oin = ...;
Handle pHandleIn = (Handle)oin.readObject();
Profile profileIn = (Profile)pHandleIn.getEJBObject();
profileIn.getEntry("favoriteColor");
```

Container-Managed Persistence

In our entity-based `ProfileBean`, shown in Example 7-9, the persistent state of the profile entity is managed by the bean itself. There's JDBC code in the `ProfileBean` implementation that loads, stores, and removes the entity's database entries. This is called *bean-managed persistence*: the EJB container calls the appropriate methods on your entity bean, but your bean implementation is responsible for connecting to the database and making all of the necessary queries and updates to reflect the life cycle of the data entity.

As I mentioned earlier, the EJB specification provides another option: *container-managed persistence*. In this case, you define data members on your entity bean implementation that hold the state of the entity and tell the EJB container how to map these data members to persistent storage. If the persistent storage is a database, you tell the container which columns in which tables hold the various data members of your entity. With container-managed persistence, the container is responsible for loading, updating, and removing the entity data from persistent storage, based on the mapping you provide. The container also implements all the finder methods required by the bean's home interface.

If you want to take advantage of container-managed persistence, you have to indicate this to the EJB container when you deploy the bean. You also provide the data mapping at deployment time. To see this in action, let's use a simple entity bean that represents a person using just a first and last name:

```
import javax.ejb.*;
import java.rmi.RemoteException;
import jen.ejb.NoSuchPersonException;
import java.util.Properties;

public class PersonBean implements EntityBean {
  // First name of person
  public String mFirstName = "";
  // Last name
  public String mLastName = "";

  // Store context (nonpersistent)
  private transient EntityContext mContext = null;

  // No need for us to activate anything in this bean, but we need to
  // provide an implementation.
  public void ejbActivate() {
    System.out.println("ProfileBean activated.");
  }

  // Load bean from persistent store. Container is doing this for us, so
  // nothing to do here.
  public void ejbLoad() throws RemoteException {}

  // Store bean to persistent store.  Container is doing this, so nothing
  // to do here, either.
  public void ejbStore() throws RemoteException {}

  // Nothing to do on a remove.
  public void ejbRemove() {}

  // No state to store on passivation (it's all in persistenct storage).
  public void ejbPassivate() {}

  // Get context from container.
  public void setEntityContext(EntityContext context) {
    mContext = context;
  }

  // Container is removing our context.
  public void unsetEntityContext() throws RemoteException {
    mContext = null;
  }

  // Create method (corresponds to each create() method on the
  // home interface).  Nothing to initialize in this case.
  public void ejbCreate() {
    System.out.println("Nameless PersonBean created.");
  }

  // Postcreation notification.  Nothing to do here, but we need
  // to provide an implementation.
```

```
    public void ejbPostCreate() {
      System.out.println("PersonBean post-create called.");
    }

    // Create method with name of person.
    public void ejbCreate(String fname, String lname)
      throws NoSuchPersonException {
      mFirstName = fname;
      mLastName = lname;
    }

    // Postcreation notification.  Nothing to do here, but we need
    // to provide an implementation.
    public void ejbPostCreate(String fname, String lname) {}

    // Business methods
    public String getFirstName() {
      return mFirstName;
    }

    public String getLastName() {
      return mLastName;
    }
  }
```

We're going to focus on the bean implementation here; I leave it to you to sort out the home and remote interfaces for this bean. The `PersonBean` has two data members, representing the first and last name of the person. In comparison to our entity `ProfileBean` from earlier, this bean is much simpler, since the `ejbRemove()`, `ejbLoad()`, and `ejbStore()` methods are empty. We're going to let the container handle the loading and storing of the bean's data and the removal of any entities from the database, so we don't need to do anything about these operations in our bean implementation.

In order for an EJB container to manage the persistence of this bean, we need to tell it what data members should be stored persistently and where to store them in the database. We'll see some examples of container-managed data mappings in the section on deploying enterprise beans, but to give you a sense of how this works, here's the relevant section from a deployment descriptor file for BEA's WebLogic EJB server:

```
...
(persistentStoreProperties
  persistentStoreType    jdbc
  (jdbc
    tableName             PERSON
                    . . .
    (attributeMap
      mFirstName          FIRST_NAME
      mLastName           LAST_NAME
    )
  )
)
...
containerManagedFields    [mFirstName mLastName]
primaryKeyClassName       PersonPK
...
```

In this part of the bean's deployment descriptor, we're telling the container that the mFirstName and mLastName members of the PersonBean are stored persistently, and that they should be stored in the FIRST_NAME and LAST_NAME columns of the PERSON table. We also have to tell the container which JDBC connection pool to use to connect to the database, but I've omitted those details for now.

We also need to tell the container the primary key class for our entity bean. In this case, it's the PersonPK class, which looks like this:

```
public class PersonPK implements java.io.Serializable {
  public String mFirstName;
  public String mLastName;

  public PersonPK() {
    mFirstName = null;
    mLastName = null;
  }
  public PersonPK(String fname, String lname) {
    mFirstName = fname;
    mLastName = lname;
  }
}
```

Since we're using container-managed persistence, the primary key class for our bean has to include members that match the corresponding members on the bean class. This allows the bean to map the key fields to bean fields automatically and to generate the default finder methods for the bean.

If you choose container-managed persistence for your bean, the EJB container generates all the ejbFindXXX() methods required for the finder methods on the home interface. It automatically generates an ejbFindByPrimaryKey() method, based on the data-mapping information you provide at deployment time. For any other ejbFindXXX() methods, you need to provide the container with a recipe for implementing the methods. The EJB 1.0 specification doesn't provide a standard format for specifying these additional finder methods for your bean, nor does it provide a means for you to specify some of the finder methods yourself in the bean implementation and leave the rest for the EJB container to implement. Some EJB providers allow you to provide code segments at deployment time for the finder methods, while other providers define a descriptive scripting language that allows you to describe the logic of the method implementation to the EJB container. In either case, the container takes this information and creates implementations for the finder methods. These finder methods are located within one of the support classes it generates, usually in a generated subclass of your home interface.

As an example, suppose we want to have a finder method for our PersonBean class called findFreds() that finds all the people whose first name starts with "Fred." BEA's WebLogic server specifies a syntax for describing the logic of a finder method in the bean's deployment descriptor file. The segment of the descriptor that describes this finder method for a WebLogic server might look like this:

```
(finderDescriptors
  "findFreds()" "(like mFirstName Fred%)"
)
```

If you are implementing an entity bean with many complicated finder methods, or if you are concerned with your bean being easily portable between EJB server providers, you may want to shy away from container-managed persistence and stick with managing the persistent data yourself. With some EJB providers, you may find that the format they provide for describing finder methods is too limited for your purposes. And deploying the bean in different EJB servers means porting the descriptions of your finder methods from server to server, which defeats the purpose of writing to a distributed component standard.

If your EJB object is using container-managed persistence, the container is handling the loading and storing of persistent data. You still can provide `ejbLoad()` and `ejbStore()` methods on your bean implementation, however. The `ejbLoad()` method is called just after the container has loaded the specified data fields from persistent storage into your data members, and `ejbStore()` is called just before the container writes your data members to persistent storage. If there is any conversion or bookkeeping you need to handle, you can do that in these methods.

Container-managed beans also rely on the container to create and remove the entities they represent from persistent storage. The bean can still provide `ejbCreate()` and `ejbRemove()` methods, however. The appropriate creation method is called just before the container creates the required records for the new entity in the database. The bean can use these methods to initialize any data members the container accesses while creating the records. The container also invokes the bean's `ejbRemove()` method just before the container removes the necessary records from persistent storage. This lets you do any cleanup before the entity is removed.

Handling complex data structures

Each EJB container is limited to some degree in the way that data on your bean implementation can be mapped into persistent data fields. There is no standard format defined for the data mapping the container supports, so it's possible a particular EJB provider won't support whatever complicated mapping you require for your bean. For the most part, however, you can expect EJB providers to limit the format to a single persistent data field being mapped to a single data member on your bean implementation. If the data structures on your bean are too complicated for you to provide an explicit mapping to persistent data fields, you have to decide how to deal with this.

In our entity `ProfileBean` example, we've stored the profile entries in a `Properties` object. We don't know at deployment time how many entries there will be, so we can't enumerate a mapping to database fields. We really want each entry in the `Properties` object to be stored in the `PROFILE_ENTRY` table in our database, along with the name of the owner of the entry, which is exactly how we implemented our bean-managed implementation in Example 7-9.

One option is to give up on container-managed persistence and manage it yourself in the bean implementation. Another is to make each entry in the profile its own bean and store the entries in a list on the profile bean. This would probably turn out to be too expensive in terms of interactions with the container and memory, however. Each entry in the profile would need to be managed separately by the container, with all of the relevant lifecycle notifications.

Another option is to serialize your data structures into individual data members on your bean and allow the container to read/write the serialized bytes to database fields as binary data. In our entity ProfileBean example, rather than using the PROFILE and PROFILE_ENTRY tables we used in the bean-managed version, we can define a single table to hold the name of the profile owner, along with the serialized bytecodes for the Properties object that represents the profile entries. We can then use the ejbStore() method on our bean to convert the Properties object to an array of bytes:

```
public void ejbStore() throws RemoteException {
  try {
    ByteArrayOutputStream byteOut = new ByteArrayOutputStream();
    ObjectOutputStream objOut = new ObjectOutputStream(byteOut);
    objOut.writeObject(mEntries);
    mEntriesBytes = byteOut.toByteArray();
  }
  catch (Exception e) {
    throw new RemoteException("ejbStore failed: ", e);
  }
}
```

After the container calls our ejbStore() method, it can write the mEntriesBytes data member on our bean to a raw data field in the database (e.g., a LONG BINARY field in a SQL database). On the reading end, we can use the ejbLoad() method to convert the bytes loaded by the container to the mEntriesBytes data member into a Properties object:

```
public void ejbLoad() throws RemoteException {
  try {
    ByteArrayInputStream byteIn = new ByteArrayInputStream(mEntriesBytes);
    ObjectInputStream objIn = new ObjectInputStream(byteIn);
    mEntries = (Properties)objIn.readObject();
  }
  catch (Exception e) {
    throw new RemoteException("ejbLoad failed: ", e);
  }
}
```

This workaround allows us to deploy our entity ProfileBean with container-managed persistence, but it makes our database records unusable for other, non-Java applications. There's no way, for example, to check on a user's profile entries using a simple SQL query.

Deploying an Enterprise JavaBeans Object

Once you've written the home and remote interfaces and the implementation of your enterprise bean, you need to deploy your beans in an EJB container, which involves the following steps:

1. Specifying the various deployment options for your bean, using the deployment tools provided by the EJB container. These options include transaction support options, access control settings, and data mappings (for container-managed entity beans).

2. Using the container-provided tools to create a serialized deployment descriptor, which bundles up your deployment options into a single serialized object.

3. Generating the container-specific classes, as shown in Figure 7-2.

4. Optionally packaging your enterprise beans into an EJB-JAR file.

As shown in Figure 7-2, the EJB container generates a set of classes that deploy your EJB object. It's up to the EJB container to provide a tool or tools for generating these classes. Some may be command-line tools that accept some sort of properties file that tells the EJB container about your bean, while others may be GUI tools that let you control the deployment options of your bean using a visual interface. Regardless of the deployment/generation tool your EJB application server provides, it needs to be told the fully qualified names for the home and remote interfaces for your EJB object and for the bean implementation class. It also needs to be told how to deploy your bean, in terms of transaction support, client access to features of your bean, and management of the persistent data (if any) associated with your bean. The baseline information and options needed for deploying your enterprise bean are as follows:

Bean implementation class and interfaces
: The fully qualified names of your bean implementation class and the home and remote interfaces for your bean.

Bean type
: Is the bean a session or entity bean? If it is a session bean, is it stateful or stateless? If it is an entity bean, is its persistence bean-managed or container-managed?

JNDI name for home interface
: The name under which the home interface for the bean is exported through JNDI by the server. Clients use this name to look up the home interface.

Transaction support attribute
: The level of transaction support required by the bean. Specify one of the values described earlier in the chapter.

Transaction isolation level
: The level of transaction isolation required by the bean. Specify one of the values described earlier in the chapter.

Access control attributes
: Which remote identities should have access to the methods on your bean? What identity should your bean assume when it accesses resources (a database, other EJB objects, etc.)?

Session time-out (session beans only)
: The maximum lifetime for a session bean.

Database/member mapping (container-managed entity beans only)
: The data members on your bean that need to be stored persistently and their corresponding database fields.

Reentrant flag (entity beans only)

Is your bean implementation reentrant (i.e., can the bean's methods make loopback calls to themselves, directly or through other bean methods)? This property is always `false` for session beans.

Primary key class (entity beans only)

The fully qualified name of the class that serves as the primary key for your entity bean.

Environment variables

Miscellaneous environment properties, either EJB server-specific or bean-specific, that are provided to the bean in its `EJBContext`.

Some EJB containers may expand on this baseline list to include properties they need for extended services they may provide or additional controls they provide to supplement the basic EJB deployment options.

All these deployment properties are represented as publicly accessible properties on the `DeploymentDescriptor`, `SessionDescriptor`, and `EntityDescriptor` classes in the `javax.ejb.deployment` package. If you want to create an EJB-JAR package for your bean, the EJB server tools typically allow you to bundle your deployment options into an instance of either the `SessionDescriptor` or `EntityDescriptor` class and serialize the object to a file to be included in the EJB-JAR file as the bean's *deployment descriptor*. See the later section "Packaging Enterprise Beans" for more details.

At the time of this writing, the released EJB specification doesn't include a standard format for deployment descriptor files. The EJB 1.1 public draft includes an XML-based deployment descriptor schema, but until the 1.1 specification is released and this standard deployment descriptor file format is widely supported, you need to deal with the vendor-specific formats currently provided by each EJB server. Currently, the only way to provide a portable deployment descriptor for your enterprise bean is to do the work of the server deployment tools yourself. To do this, you have to write some Java code that creates an instance of the appropriate `DeploymentDescriptor` subclass, fills in the properties on this object, and then serializes the descriptor object to a file. If you need to do this, refer to Chapter 20 for details on `DeploymentDescriptor` and its subclasses. For the examples that follow, however, I'm going to show snippets of deployment descriptor files for a particular EJB server, BEA's WebLogic application server.

Container-Managed Data Mapping

If you are deploying an entity bean with container-managed persistence, you need to tell the EJB container which fields on your bean implementation are persistent and how to map them to persistent storage. For example, suppose we are deploying our entity `ProfileBean`, using container-managed persistence. Let's assume that we've made the modifications to our bean implementation we discussed in the section "Container-Managed Persistence." In other words, we've created a table called `PROFILE_BYTES` with a single `LONG BINARY` column named `DATA` to hold our serialized `Properties` object. Now we simply have to tell the container that the `mEntriesBytes` member on our modified `ProfileBean` is mapped to the `DATA` column on the PROFILE_BYTES table, with an entry in a textual deployment options file like this example shown for BEA WebLogic server:

```
(persistentStoreProperties
  persistentStoreType    jdbc
  (jdbc
    tableName            PROFILE_BYTES
      ...
      (attributeMap
        mName            NAME
        mEntriesBytes    DATA
    )
  )
)
...
containerManagedFields  [mName mEntriesBytes]
```

Based on these mappings, the EJB container generates all of the necessary JDBC calls in its generated classes.

Access-Control Deployment Attributes

There are precious few details in the EJB 1.0 specification about support for security in EJB containers, but there is a construct provided for you to specify certain access control levels at deployment time.

Essentially, the EJB server should provide some means for mapping a client-provided identity (in the form of a java.security.Identity object) to a named user or role on the EJB server itself. Then you, the bean provider, can specify which users and/or roles can access each method on your bean. The EJB server allows you to specify access control levels in some server-specific way (ideally, using the same deployment tools as the other deployment attributes). There should be a way to specify access for the entire bean, as well as for individual methods. Any method without an access-control entry assumes the access level of the bean as a default. So, for the various versions of our ProfileBean, we might want to allow anyone to get profile entries off of the bean, but only allow profile administrators (users or applications) to set profile entries. We might do this by specifying access-control entries such as:

```
(accessControlEntries
  DEFAULT                        [everyone]
  "setEntry(String, String)" [profileAdmin]
)
```

This allows any user who identifies himself as *profileAdmin* to invoke the setEntry() method on the ProfileBean, while all other remote methods on the bean are accessible to everyone.

As a step towards standardizing the specification of client identities to the EJB server, there is a proposal being considered by various EJB providers that involves the use of a reserved JNDI name entry to hold the client's identity. The client would provide an Identity object to the EJB server as the value of the Context.PROVIDER_IDENTITY property, passed in when the client creates its initial JNDI naming context from the server. This issue should be settled in an upcoming update to the EJB specification.

In addition to specifying client access rules for your bean, you need to specify to the EJB server what identity your bean should assume when it accesses controlled resources, such as other EJB objects and databases. This is done using two deployment properties: run-as-mode and run-as-identity. The *run-as-mode* property indicates whether the bean should assume the identity of the client that invoked it (`CLIENT_IDENTITY`), the identity of some system-defined account (`SYSTEM_IDENTITY`), or the identity of some other specific user account (`SPECIFIED_IDENTITY`). The `SYSTEM_IDENTITY` option causes the EJB server to use a platform-specific privileged account. A server may use the *root* account on Unix systems or the Administrator account on Windows NT systems, for example. Some EJB servers may use the account that runs the server when the `SYSTEM_IDENTITY` is specified. The *run-as-identity* property is used when run-as-mode is set to `SPECIFIED_IDENTITY`. The identity given in the run-as-identity property is the identity the bean assumes when accessing system resources and other beans.

The run-as-mode and run-as-identity attributes are settable at the bean level or at the individual method level, in the same way client access levels are applied. If you set these attributes for specific methods on your bean, that means you want those methods to be executed using the specified identity for access-control purposes. There are some restrictions imposed by the EJB specification, however. Within a single transaction, all methods invoked on your bean must be run with the same identity. If a client transaction attempts to execute methods you've deployed with different access-control identities, the server throws an RMI `RemoteException` to the client. If your bean is a stateful session bean, all methods executed during a session lifetime must be the same. If a client attempts, within the same session, to execute methods on your bean that have different access-control identities associated with them, the EJB server throws an RMI `RemoteException`.

Generating the Container Classes and Deployment Descriptor

Once you've specified all the deployment options for your bean, the container provides a utility for converting these deployment properties to a serialized deployment descriptor. This deployment descriptor is a serialized instance of either the `EntityDescriptor` or `SessionDescriptor` class from the `javax.ejb.deployment` package. The container tools store all the deployment options you specified into an instance of one of these classes, depending on what type of bean you're deploying, and serialize the object to a file you specify, one for each type of bean that you are deploying. You can then use these deployment descriptors to package your enterprise beans into EJB-JAR files, as described a bit later.

In addition to the deployment descriptor, you also need to use the EJB container's tools to generate the container-specific classes that deploy your bean, as shown in Figure 7-2. In order to generate these classes, the container tools need to take into account your deployment options. If you're deploying an entity bean, for example, the tool needs to know whether the bean uses container-managed persistence or not, so that the tool knows whether it needs to include JDBC code for the bean in its generated classes. The container tools typically allow you to specify where to generate the deployment classes.

Once you have your compiled interfaces and bean implementation class, the deployment descriptor, and the container-generated classes for your bean, you're ready to package your bean in an EJB-JAR file.

Packaging Enterprise JavaBeans

EJB-JAR files are the standard packaging format for Enterprise JavaBeans. They are normal Java archive (JAR) files, created using the standard *jar* utility, but they contain specific files that provide all the information needed for an EJB container to deploy the beans that are contained in the EJB-JAR file. An EJB-JAR file can contain one or many beans.

An EJB-JAR file contains three components:

- The class files for each bean, including their home and remote interfaces, and the bean implementations.
- A deployment descriptor, in the form of a serialized instance of either the `EntityDescriptor` or `SessionDescriptor` classes from the `javax.ejb.deployment` package.
- A manifest file, located in the file *META-INF/MANIFEST.MF* within the JAR file, with a section for each bean that names its deployment descriptor within the JAR file.

The manifest file is a simple text file, with sections delimited by blank lines. Each section has name/value pairs. The name starts the line, followed by a colon, followed by the value. EJB-JAR files define two tags: "Name" and "Enterprise-Bean". The Name line specifies the serialized deployment descriptor for an enterprise bean, while Enterprise-Bean marks the section as relevant to the EJB server and always has a value of "True". Here's a typical manifest file that might be used for an EJB-JAR file that contains a few of our bean examples:

```
Name: jen/ejb/stateless/ProfileServerBeanDD.ser
Enterprise-Bean: True

Name: jen/ejb/entity/beanManaged/ProfileBeanDD.ser
Enterprise-Bean: True
```

This manifest file describes two enterprise beans. The EJB-JAR file that contains this manifest must contain the two serialized deployment descriptors named in the manifest file, all class files specified in the deployment descriptors for the beans, and all container-generated classes for deploying the bean.

An EJB-JAR file contains everything an EJB container needs to deploy your bean. The container reads the manifest file and, for each bean specified, loads the serialized deployment descriptor and checks its parameters. The container looks in the JAR file for the class files needed for the bean and deploys the bean using the additional parameters specified in the deployment descriptors.

Some EJB container/server providers include a utility to facilitate the creation of EJB-JAR files from your bean classes. It's a simple matter, however, to create one using the standard *jar* utility provided with nearly every Java SDK implementation. Assuming that you have created a manifest file, such as the one shown earlier, in a file named ProfileManifest.txt, you can create an EJB-JAR file for the previous two beans with the following command:

```
% jar cmf ProfileManifest.txt ProfileBeans.jar\
jen/ejb/stateless jen/ejb/entity/beanManaged
```

This command creates an EJB-JAR file named *ProfileBeans.jar* in the current directory. The *jar* utility automatically places the manifest file in the proper location in the JAR file for you. Note that we're assuming that the subdirectories we've included in the JAR file contain both the class files we need and the serialized deployment decriptors mentioned in the manifest file.

Using an Enterprise JavaBeans Object

So far, we've seen how to write an enterprise bean and how to deploy it through an EJB container. Now let's look at how you use an enterprise bean as a client.

Finding Home Interfaces Through JNDI

Once an enterprise bean is deployed within an EJB container, the home interface for the bean has been exported under a particular name using JNDI. As a client, you need to know how to connect to the JNDI context of the remote EJB server, and you need to know the name for the bean home interface you're interested in. A typical way to connect to the JNDI naming context is to specify the initial context factory for JNDI and create a new naming context through it (for more details, see Chapter 6):

```
Hashtable props = new Hashtable();
// Specify the context factory for our EJB server
props.put(Context.INITIAL_CONTEXT_FACTORY,
          "my.ejb.server.context.factory");
// Specify the URL for the context provider, if any
props.put(Context.PROVIDER_URL, "my.server.jndi.url");
// Trying looking up the context
javax.naming.Context ctx = null;
try {
  ctx = new javax.naming.InitialContext(props);
}
catch (NamingException ne) {
  System.out.println("Failed to create JNDI context from EJB server");
}
```

In this example client, we make a Hashtable that contains two standard JNDI properties, the INITIAL_CONTEXT_FACTORY and PROVIDER_URL properties. These property names are String constants defined on the javax.naming.Context interface, whose values are "java.naming.factory.initial" and "java.naming.provider.url", respectively. You can use the explicit string values if you prefer, but the constant values are provided by the Context interface as a convenience, since they're a bit easier to remember. The value of INITIAL_CONTEXT_FACTORY is the class name for a context factory, provided by your JNDI provider (the EJB server, in this case), and PROVIDER_URL is a URL used to connect remotely to the JNDI server running within the EJB server. The proper values for both of these items should be provided by your EJB application server provider.

You can also specify the security principal under which you want to interact with the EJB/JNDI server, by including the Context.SECURITY_PRINCIPAL property in the call to create your naming context. This property value should be a java.security.Identity object that represents the identity of your client:

```
Hashtable props = new Hashtable();
// Initialized other connection properties...
java.security.Identity id = . . .;
props.put(Context.SECURITY_PRINCIPAL, id);
javax.naming.Context ctx = new javax.naming.InitialContext(props);
...
```

Some EJB server providers use this identity in determining access to bean features, as specified in the bean deployment descriptors. The EJB 1.0 specification doesn't provide a standard for providing this identity, however, so check the documentation on your EJB server for specific details. For more details on accessing remote JNDI servers, see Chapter 6.

Now that we have a JNDI naming context from the EJB server, we can look up the home interface for the bean we're interested in:

```
ProfileHome pHome = null;
try {
  pHome =
    (ProfileHome)ctx.lookup("jen.ejb.entity.beanManaged.ProfileHome");
}
catch (NamingException ne) {
  System.out.println("Failed to lookup home for ProfileBean.");
}
```

In this case, we've assumed that the bean provider has deployed its home interface on the EJB server under the name "jen.ejb.entity.beanManaged.ProfileHome". With the home interface stub, our client can now create or find beans located on the server.

Creating/Finding Beans

The home interface for the bean contains methods that allow a client to create new beans or find existing beans (for entity beans). Continuing our example client, assuming we're using our entity ProfileBean from Example 7-9 and its corresponding home interface, we can create a new ProfileBean and get a stub reference to it as follows:

```
Profile profile = null;
try {
  profile = pHome.create("Kaitlyn");
}
catch (DuplicatePersonException dpe) {
  System.out.println("Profile already exists for Kaitlyn.");
}
catch (RemoteException re) {
  System.out.println("Remote exception while creating profile.");
}
```

Here we're trying to create a new profile for someone named "Kaitlyn". We're using the create() method defined on our ProfileHome interface, which we've declared to throw RemoteException and our own DuplicatePersonException. In the client, we catch each of these exceptions and print a corresponding error message if it occurs.

Now, if we thought a profile already existed for Kaitlyn, we could try finding it in persistent storage first, using one of the finder methods on our home interface:

```
try {
  profile = pHome.findByPrimaryKey(new ProfilePK("Kaitlyn"));
}
catch (FinderException fe) {
  System.out.println("No profile found for Kaitlyn.");
}
catch (RemoteException re) {
  System.out.println("Remote exception while finding profile.");
}
```

If we weren't sure whether a profile for Kaitlyn had been created or not, we could try finding it first, using the code above, then create one if needed:

```
if (profile == null) {
  // Create profile as before ...
}
```

Using Client-Side Transactions

I mentioned before that you can specify at deployment time how your bean handles transactions, using one of the transaction attributes we already discussed. On the client-side, you can use the Java Transaction API (JTA) to create your own transaction boundaries. These transactions are taken into account, along with the bean's transaction-handling attributes, by the EJB container, to determine which transaction context to put the bean into for each remote method call your client makes. Again, a complete description of the JTA is beyond the scope of this chapter, but it's useful to take a quick look at how to create your own client transactions.

Continuing the example client we've been working with in this section, we've already found the home interface for the ProfileBean and created/found a Profile for Kaitlyn. Now we want to make some changes to Kaitlyn's profile, but we want to make sure that all our changes are made before we commit them. To do this, we create our own "javax.transaction.UserTransaction"* and either commit it or roll it back, depending on whether we get an exception while setting the profile entries:


```
javax.transaction.UserTransaction xact =
  (UserTransaction)jndiCtx.lookup("javax.transaction.UserTransaction");

xact.begin();
try {
  profile.setEntry("username", "kschmitz");
```

* Note that shortly after the EJB 1.0 specification was released, the name of the (then beta) JTA was changed, so that javax.jts.UserTransaction became javax.transaction.UserTransaction. I'm using the new class name here, but keep in mind that you might see the old package names in the EJB 1.0 documentation from Sun.

```
    profile.setEntry("password", "foobar");
    profile.setEntry("interestGroups", "dogs:cartoons:napping");
    xact.commit();
  }
  catch (RemoteException re) {
    xact.rollback();
  }
```

We acquire the transaction from whatever transaction provider we're using on the client side. Here, we assume that we've retrieved a "JNDI context" from the EJB server and use it to look up an instance of "javax.transaction.UserTransaction" that the EJB server provides. When we use this transaction object, the EJB server can manage the transaction around calls to enterprise bean methods. We begin the transaction before starting our profile update. We make our updates to Kaitlyn's profile, and, if successful, we commit the transaction. If we get an exception from the EJB server along the way, we rollback our changes by calling `rollback()` on the transaction.

If the ProfileBean was deployed with a transaction attribute of `TX_SUPPORTS`, `TX_REQUIRED`, or `TX_MANDATORY`, the EJB container should execute the bean methods within our client transaction context. The corresponding database updates are committed to the database when we `commit()` our transaction or rolled back if we `rollback()` our transaction. The bean does not need to know anything about the transaction boundaries, even if it is managing its own persistence. The EJB container manages the association between the client-specified transaction boundaries and the JDBC transactions initiated by the bean implementation.

Changes in EJB 1.1 Specification

Shortly before publication of this book, Sun released a public draft of Version 1.1 of the EJB specification. In this incremental release, Sun tightened up a few areas, changed its scheme for deployment descriptors, and made various other updates to the specification. The major updates are described below, followed by a short laundry list of the more significant changes.

XML-Based Deployment Descriptors

In EJB 1.1, the `javax.ejb.deployment` package is deprecated, and deployment descriptors for enterprise beans are composed using XML, instead of serialized `DeploymentDescriptor` objects. In the XML DTD defined in EJB 1.1, there's a clear separation of information regarding the structure of the enterprise bean(s) from information regarding the use of the beans in a particular application. The structural information for an enterprise bean includes components such as its various classes, environment variables the bean recognizes, and the container-managed fields (for entity bean). Application-specific information includes, for example, values for environment variables, the various client roles that are used for controlling access to beans, and permission settings for these various roles.

Similar to the deployment descriptors defined in EJB 1.0, these XML-based deployment descriptors are intended to include only structural information when a bean provider ships a collection of enterprise beans to application developers, and both structural information and application-specific information when an application provider ships an EJB-based application to an application deployer. The separation of these two types of information in the XML deployment descriptor makes this process more straightforward than under EJB 1.0.

The XML deployment descriptor for a set of enterprise beans can be provided separately or as part of an EJB-JAR file. In an EJB-JAR file, the deployment descriptor must be in the file *META-INF/ejb-jar.xml*.

Entity Beans Required

In EJB 1.0, support for entity beans was optional for compliant EJB servers. In EJB 1.1, all compliant servers must provide support for entity beans.

Home Handles

EJB 1.1 adds a new `HomeHandle` interface and a `getHomeHandle()` method on the `EJBHome` interface. A `HomeHandle` is a serializable reference to a home interface for an enterprise bean, analogous to the `Handle` interface, which represents a serializable reference to an EJB object. This allows a client to get a handle for a home interface and serialize it to some persistent storage, like a filesystem or database. The serialized `HomeHandle` can be deserialized later (in the same or another Java VM) and used to acquire a reference to the same home interface.

Detailed Programming Restrictions for Bean Implementations

EJB 1.1 lists detailed restrictions on what an enterprise bean implementation should avoid in its business methods in order to be portable across different EJB servers. These include rules against using sockets, creating class loaders, and including writable static fields on EJB implementation classes.

Assorted Other Changes

In addition to changes already listed, the following are some of the more significant updates introduced in the EJB 1.1 specification:

- Finder methods on entity beans can now return `java.util.Collection` types from Version 1.2 of the Java 2 platform.
- Entity bean primary keys can now be `java.lang.String` objects.
- All `ejbCreate()` methods on entity beans, including those with container-managed persistence, must now return the bean's primary key type. Previously, container-managed entity beans had `ejbCreate()` methods that returned `null`, and bean-managed beans returned their primary key type. With this change, a container-managed bean can implement `ejbCreate()` methods that return `null`, and this bean can optionally be subclassed to define a bean-managed bean that returns an actual primary key.

- All EJB clients should use the `narrow()` method on the `javax.rmi.PortableRemoteObject` interface in order to cast remote and home object interfaces for enterprise beans. This guarantees that clients will be compatible with EJB servers that use RMI-IIOP for exporting enterprise beans.

PART II

Enterprise Reference

Part II contains reference material on two enterprise-related technologies, SQL and IDL, and on the tools provided with Sun's Java Development Kit for RMI and Java IDL.

Chapter 8, *SQL Reference*
Chapter 9, *RMI Tools*
Chapter 10, *IDL Reference*
Chapter 11, *CORBA Services Reference*
Chapter 12, *Java IDL Tools*

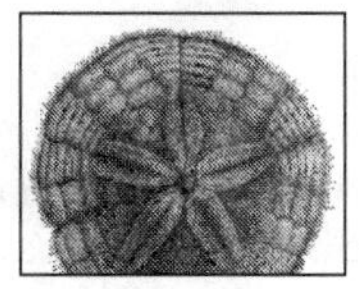

CHAPTER 8

SQL Reference

There are dozens of different database management systems on the market today, from nearly as many vendors. Developing applications that are more or less database independent requires a standardized interface to the underlying data. Since the early 1980s, this interface has been SQL, a sophisticated database manipulation language.*

Unlike Java, SQL is a declarative language. It allows users to specify particular actions on the database and retrieve the results of those actions. It specifies a set of standardized data types and standard error messages, but it lacks procedural constructs. There are no conditionals or loops standard in SQL.

There are several versions of the SQL standard. SQL-86 and SQL-89 have been superceded by SQL-92, which is supported by most database vendors, although there are a number of platform-specific variations. Many databases also include additional data types, operators, and functions beyond those specified in the SQL-92 standard. In addition, there are three levels of SQL-92 conformance: entry-level, intermediate, and full. Many products support only the entry-level SQL-92 standard, leaving out some advanced features. JDBC drivers are supposed to provide entry-level functionality and, for the most part, they do.

This chapter presents a brief introduction to the structure of a relational database system and a quick reference to the most commonly used SQL commands. The complete set of SQL commands is simply too large to cover here: even a concise SQL reference can run to several hundred pages. I have endeavored to provide the information that most client-side programmers need. For a complete introduction to most aspects of SQL, I highly recommend *SQL Clearly Explained* by Jan Harrington (AP Professional).

* The acronym expands out to either Structured Query Language (based on the original IBM acronym from the 1970s) or Standard Query Language (which has been more popular in recent years). Perhaps because of this confusion, most people just say SQL, pronounced either see-quell or ess-cue-ell.

Relational Databases

Data storage and retrieval are two of the biggest tasks facing most enterprise applications. There are lots of ways to store data on a disk, but for large-scale applications a relational database management system (RDBMS) is far and away the most popular choice.

Data in an RDBMS is organized into tables, where these tables contain rows and columns. You can think of an individual table as a spreadsheet with a little more organization: column data types are fixed and there may be rules governing the formatting of each column. This alone is enough for a database system (plain DBMS). A relational database system has one other key attribute: individual tables can be *related* based on some common data. Figure 8-1 shows three tables in a relational structure. The `CUSTOMERS` table is related to the `ORDERS` table based on the `CUSTOMER_ID` field, and the `ORDERS` table is related to the `ITEMS` table based on the `ORDER_ID` field. SQL provides a standardized means of accessing the data in tables and working with the relationships between tables.

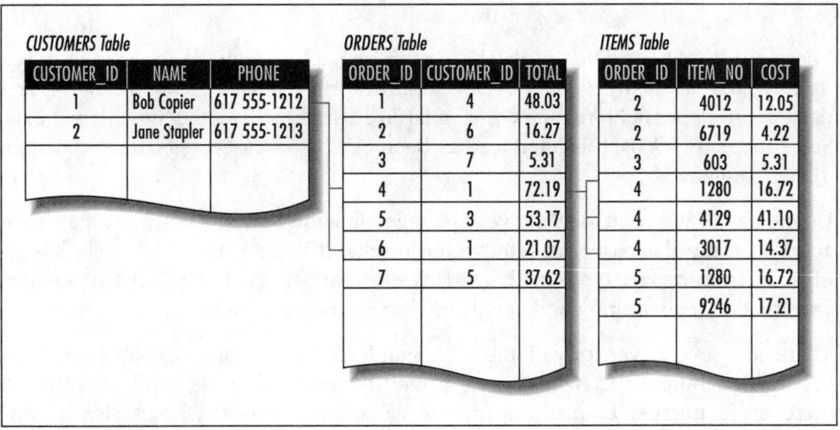

Figure 8-1: Three related tables

The highest-level organizational concept in an RDBMS system is a *cluster*.* A cluster contains one or more *catalogs*, which are usually the highest-level object a programmer ever has to deal with. A catalog contains a group of schemas. A schema contains a group of tables and other objects and is generally assigned to a particular application or user account. Generally, the database administrator is responsible for dealing with clusters and catalogs. Most users work within a particular schema.

To reference a table within a particular schema, separate the schema name and the table name with a dot:

* The naming comes from the older SQL standards, where a cluster represented physical storage space. This is no longer the case, but the name persists.

```
schema_name.table_name
```

To reference a particular column within a particular schema:

```
schema_name.table_name.column_name
```

To set a particular schema as the default, use the SET SCHEMA SQL statement:

```
SET SCHEMA schema_name
```

When you log into a database, you are generally assigned a default schema. When accessing tables within the default schema, you may omit the schema name.

When creating new objects, the names you assign to them must be unique within the schema. SQL-92 allows names up to 128 characters, including letters, numbers, and the underscore (_) character.

Data Types

Each column in a table has a particular data type associated with it. SQL-92 defines a fairly broad set of data types. Different RDBMS packages provide extensions to these basic types, for multimedia data, Java objects, and so on. Oracle's NUMBER data type, for instance, allows database designers to specify the exact precision of integer and floating point data types. The basic SQL-92 types are listed in Table 8-1. The names in parentheses are SQL-92 specified alternates for the main type names.

Table 8-1: SQL-92 Data Types

SQL Data Type	*Description*
INTEGER (INT)	A signed integer value. The number of bits represented is implementation-dependent.
SMALLINT	A smaller signed integer value, used when storage or memory is at a premium. Generally 8 bits, but implementation-dependent.
NUMERIC	A signed fixed-precision decimal. When creating a NUMERIC, you must specify the total length of the number (including the decimal point) and the number of decimal places. NUMERIC(8, 4) allows three digits, a decimal point, and four more digits.
DECIMAL	Defined the same way as a NUMERIC, but may store additional precision (more decimal places).
REAL	A single-precision floating-point value. Range and accuracy are implementation-dependent.
DOUBLE PRECISION (DOUBLE)	A double-precision floating-point value. Range and accuracy are implementation dependent, but are equal to or better than a REAL.

Table 8-1: SQL-92 Data Types (continued)

SQL Data Type	*Description*
`BIT`	A fixed number (one or more) of bits. A length specifier (`BIT(`*`n`*`)`) is optional. The default size is 1 bit.
`BIT VARYING`	Storage for up to n bits (`BIT VARYING (`*`n`*`)`). Many databases have alternate implementations of this data type, such as Oracle's `VARBINARY`.
`DATE`	A date value (day, month, and year).
`TIME`	A time value. Precision is implementation-dependent.
`TIMESTAMP`	A date and time.
`CHARACTER (CHAR)`	A fixed-length character string. Specified as `CHAR(`*`n`*`)`. Unused characters are padded with blanks. The default size is 1.
`CHARACTER VARYING (VARCHAR)`	A variable length string, up to size *n*. Specified as `VARCHAR(`*`n`*`)`.
`INTERVAL`	A date or time interval. Not directly supported by JDBC.

Note that the data types given here are not the same as those in Table 2-1 in Chapter 2, *JDBC*. When mapping between SQL types and Java types, a JDBC driver matches the physical data type (either SQL-92 or database-specific) and the closest Java type. For example, calling the `getType()` method of `ResultSet` on a `BIT VARYING` field generally returns a `Types.LONGVARBINARY` value. This translation allows most JDBC programs to switch between different databases without losing functionality. Also, many databases implement additional types: the `FLOAT` type is so common that many people think it is required by the specification.

Schema Manipulation Commands

SQL includes two broad classes of commands. The first are schema manipulation commands, which allow the creation, modification, and deletion of high-level database objects such as tables. This section describes these commands. I've provided a syntax summary for each command. In case you aren't familiar with the style, items in square brackets are optional or not always required, while items in curly braces are either always required or required within the context of some optional item. A vertical bar (`|`) indicates a choice, while an ellipsis indicates that an entry may be repeated any number of times. Items in all uppercase are part of the SQL statement, while items in lowercase constant width italic represent names and values that you supply when using the statement.

CREATE TABLE

As its name says, the CREATE TABLE command creates a table. Here's the syntax:

```
CREATE [ [ GLOBAL | LOCAL ] TEMPORARY ] TABLE table_name
 ( { column_name { data_type | domain_name } [ column_size ]
      [ column_constraint ... ] ... }
    [ DEFAULT default_value ], ...
    [ table_constraint ], ...
    [ ON COMMIT { DELETE | PRESERVE } ROWS ] )
```

Here's a simple example:

```
CREATE TABLE BOOKS
 (
   TITLE VARCHAR (25) PRIMARY KEY,
   AUTHOR VARCHAR(25) NOT NULL DEFAULT 'Unknown',
   EDITION INTEGER,
   PRICE NUMBER(6,2)
 )
```

The PRIMARY KEY and NOT NULL identifiers are column constraints. The NOT NULL constraint prevents any entry in a column being set to null. Here, it's combined it with a default value. PRIMARY KEY identifies the column that's used as the primary key (or main unique identifier) for the table. If a table has a primary key column (it doesn't have to), there can be only one such column, no row has a null value in the primary key column, and no two rows have the same primary key.

A table constraint affects every row in the table. UNIQUE is a common example:

```
CREATE TABLE BOOKS
 (
   TITLE VARCHAR (25),
   AUTHOR VARCHAR(25),
   EDITION INTEGER,
   PRICE NUMBER(6,2),
   UNIQUE
 )
```

Used as a table constraint, UNIQUE indicates that each row in the table must have a unique combination of values. You can also specify particular columns that must form a unique combination:

```
UNIQUE(TITLE, AUTHOR, EDITION)
```

This mandates only unique title/author/edition combinations. Note that UNIQUE can also be used as a column constraint.

We can use PRIMARY KEY as a table constraint to specify more than one column as the primary key:

```
CREATE TABLE BOOKS
 (
   TITLE VARCHAR (25) NOT NULL,
   AUTHOR VARCHAR(25) NOT NULL,
   EDITION INTEGER NOT NULL,
   PRICE NUMBER(6,2),
   PRIMARY KEY (TITLE, AUTHOR, EDITION)
 )
```

Since entry-level SQL-92 requires that primary keys remain not `null`, we use `NOT NULL` column constraints on the primary key columns in this case.

ALTER TABLE

The `ALTER TABLE` command allows you to modify the structure of an existing table. Here's the syntax:

```
ALTER TABLE table_name
   { ADD [COLUMN] column_name definition }
   { ALTER [COLUMN] column_name definition
      { SET DEFAULT default_value } | { DROP DEFAULT } }
   { DROP [COLUMN] COLUMN_NAME [ RESTRICT | CASCADE ] }
   { ADD table_constraint_definition }
   { DROP constraint_name  [ RESTRICT | CASCADE] }
```

Note that the modifications you can make are somewhat limited. While you can add and remove columns (subject to the requirements of any constraints that may have been placed on the table), you cannot reorder columns. To perform major changes, you generally need to create a new table and move the existing data from the old table to the new table.

Here's a statement that adds two columns to a table:

```
ALTER TABLE BOOKS
 ADD PUBLISHED_DATE DATE,
 ADD PUBLISHER CHAR (30) NOT NULL
```

Note that the ability to specify multiple operations in an `ALTER TABLE` command is not part of the SQL specification, although most databases support this functionality.

Here's how to change the type of a column:*

```
ALTER TABLE BOOKS
 MODIFY PUBLISHER VARCHAR (25)
```

When this statement runs, the database attempts to convert all existing data into the new format. If this is impossible, the modification fails. In the previous example, if any record has a publisher entry of more than 30 characters, the statement might fail (exact behavior depends on the implementation). If you are converting from a character field to, say, an integer field, the whole `ALTER TABLE` command might fail entirely. At the minimum, such a change requires that all entries contain a valid string representation of an integer.

To allow `null` values in the `PUBLISHER` column, use `MODIFY`:

```
ALTER TABLE BOOKS
 MODIFY PUBLISHER NULL
```

To remove the `PUBLISHER` column entirely, use `DROP`:

---

* If you look back at the syntax for `ALTER TABLE`, you'll see that the official syntax for this kind of operation is `ALTER`, although most databases use `MODIFY` instead.

```
ALTER TABLE BOOKS
 DROP PUBLISHER
```

The ALTER TABLE command is not required for entry-level SQL-92 conformance. Due to its extreme usefulness, however, it is supported by most DBMS packages, although it often varies from the standard. More esoteric features, such as the RENAME command, are not supported by most packages. In general, it is not safe to count on anything beyond the basic ADD, DROP, and MODIFY (ALTER) commands.

DROP

The DROP command allows you to permanently delete an object within the database. For example, to drop the BOOKS table, execute this statement:

```
DROP TABLE BOOKS
```

DROP also can delete other database objects, such as indexes, views, and domains:

```
DROP INDEX index_name
DROP VIEW view_name
DROP DOMAIN domain_name
```

Once something has been dropped, it is usually gone for good—certainly once the current transaction has been committed, but often before.

Data Manipulation Commands

Empty tables aren't very useful, and, even once they've been populated with data, we need some way of getting that data back out. The SQL data manipulation commands allow you to read data from a table and to create, update, and remove existing data.

SELECT

The SELECT statement is the most important statement in SQL and also the most complex. It allows you to retrieve data from a table or a set of tables. Here's the syntax:

```
SELECT [ DISTINCT ]
   { summary_function, ... }
   | { data_manipulation_expression, ... }
   | { column_name, ... }
FROM
   { { table_name [ AS correlation_name ] }
   | { subquery [ AS correlation_name ] }
   | joined_tables}
[ WHERE predicate ]
[ GROUP BY column_name, ... [ HAVING group_selection_predicate ] ]
[ { UNION | INTERSECT | EXCEPT } [ ALL ]
     [ CORRESPONDING [ BY (column_name, ...] ]
      select_statement | { TABLE table_name }
                        | table_value_constructor ]
[ ORDER BY {{output_column [ ASC | DESC ]}, ...}
           | {{positive_integer [ ASC | DESC ]}, ...}]
```

The simplest possible SELECT, one that displays all columns of all rows of a single table, looks like this:

```
SELECT * FROM BOOKS
```

If this statement is executed in a command-line SQL interpreter, the output might look like this:

```
TITLE                 | AUTHOR           | EDITION | PRICE
----------------------+------------------+---------+-------
Me                    | Garrison Keillor |       1 | 24.99
Bleak House           | Charles Dickens  |      57 |  8.99
A Tale Of Two Cities  | Charles Dickens  |     312 |  4.99
```

To sort the output by title, we can add an ORDER BY clause to the statement:

```
SELECT * FROM BOOKS ORDER BY TITLE
```

Now the output is:

```
TITLE                 | AUTHOR           | EDITION | PRICE
----------------------+------------------+---------+-------
A Tale Of Two Cities  | Charles Dickens  |     312 |  4.99
Bleak House           | Charles Dickens  |      57 |  8.99
Me                    | Garrison Keillor |       1 | 24.99
```

To select just the TITLE and AUTHOR columns:

```
SELECT TITLE, AUTHOR FROM BOOKS
```

To select a subset of records, use the WHERE clause:

```
SELECT * FROM BOOKS WHERE PRICE < 10.0
```

This returns the Charles Dickens books, but not the Garrison Keillor book. You can have multiple criteria:

```
SELECT * FROM BOOKS WHERE PRICE < 10.0 OR EDITION = 1
```

This returns all three books. If we had specified a price less than 10 and an edition equal to 1, we wouldn't have received any records back. The various predicates you can use are listed in Table 8-2. Note that not all of the more esoteric ones (such as LIKE) are supported by all databases.

Table 8-2: SQL Predicates

Operator	*Meaning*
=	Equals
<	Less than
>	Greater than
<=	Less than or equal to
>=	Greater than or equal to
!= or <>	Not equal to (some implementations may only support one of these)
LIKE	Wildcard match

Table 8-2: SQL Predicates (continued)

Operator	*Meaning*
IS NULL	Checks for a null value
IN	Checks to see if a value is contained within a set
BETWEEN	Checks to see if a date value is between two other date values

The final four predicates in the table can be used with the NOT modifier (e.g., NOT LIKE, IS NOT NULL, etc.).

String comparisons

The = operator can generally be used for exact string comparisons. The LIKE operator allows wildcard searches using two wildcard characters: % to match any number of characters and _ to match at most one character. Here's a query that selects all records that have a LAST_NAME that contains the letters "for":

```
SELECT LAST_NAME FROM CUSTOMERS WHERE LAST_NAME LIKE'%for%'
```

This matches last names like Buford, Crawford, and Trefor, but may not match Fordham, since most databases implement LIKE in a case-sensitive manner (Microsoft Access is a notable exception to this rule). Case-insensitive searches generally require a single-case version of the column or the use of a case-adjusting function (we'll discuss functions later in this chapter).

Subqueries and joins

The IN predicate allows you to check whether a value appears in another set of values. The simplest way to use this feature is in a SQL statement like this:

```
SELECT * FROM BOOKS WHERE PRICE IN (5.95, 4.95, 7.95)
```

This is simply another form for:

```
SELECT * FROM BOOKS WHERE PRICE = 5.95 OR PRICE = 4.95 OR PRICE = 7.95
```

But we can do something more interesting with IN. Let's assume that we have a table, called PRICES, that holds all the prices we want to search on. In this case, we can generate the set of values using another query, as follows:

```
SELECT * FROM BOOKS WHERE PRICE IN
  SELECT PRICE FROM PRICES
```

Note that we didn't put parentheses around the second SELECT statement: use parentheses only when you are specifying the entire list manually.

Subqueries like this are useful, but they still restrict the output columns to those of a single table.

Rather than using subqueries, two tables are normally connected via a join. A *join* allows a query to include references to multiple tables and to restrict the output based on the relations between those tables. The basic join is an *equi-join* (or inner join): data in two tables is linked based on a shared value. An order-tracking database might include a CUSTOMERS table and an ORDERS table. The CUSTOMERS table has a customer identifier (CUSTOMER_ID) as its primary key. The orders table also has a CUSTOMER_ID column, although not as a primary key, since there may be more than one order per customer (see Figure 8-1 for a graphical representation of these tables). Here's the SQL to combine the two tables based on the CUSTOMER_ID column:

```
SELECT * FROM CUSTOMERS, ORDERS WHERE ORDERS.CUSTOMER_ID =
   CUSTOMERS.CUSTOMER_ID
```

Since it's an equi-join, it works just as well the other way around:

```
SELECT * FROM CUSTOMERS, ORDERS WHERE CUSTOMERS.CUSTOMER_ID =
   ORDERS.CUSTOMER_ID
```

In SQL-92, there is a JOIN operator that performs the same operation with a slightly different syntax:*

```
SELECT CUSTOMERS.CUSTOMER_ID, CUSTOMERS.NAME, ORDERS.ORDER_ID, ORDERS.TOTAL
  FROM CUSTOMERS INNER JOIN ORDERS ON CUSTOMERS.CUSTOMER_ID = ORDERS.CUSTOMER_ID
```

This example indicates the specific columns to return. Using the data shown in Figure 8-1, the output of this query might look like this:

```
CUSTOMER_ID | NAME         | ORDER_ID | TOTAL
------------+--------------+----------+--------
          1 | Bob Copier |          4 | 72.19
          1 | Bob Copier |          6 | 21.07
```

Note that some databases require you to use INNER JOIN instead of JOIN, while others allow just JOIN because inner joins are the default join.

To join on more than one table, use multiple JOIN statements. Here we add an ITEMS table that includes the ORDER_ID from the ORDERS table:

```
SELECT * FROM ITEMS JOIN ORDERS JOIN CUSTOMERS
```

This query joins the CUSTOMERS and ORDERS tables based on CUSTOMER_ID, and the ORDERS and ITEMS tables based on ORDER_ID. The join is performed from left to right, so this three-table join goes from the largest table to the smallest table.

As useful as the JOIN keyword is, it is not required for entry-level SQL-92 implementations, so here's a three-column join using the syntax we started with:

```
SELECT CUSTOMERS.CUSTOMER_ID, CUSTOMERS.NAME, ORDERS.ORDER_ID, ORDER.TOTAL,
  ITEMS.ITEM_NO, ITEMS.COST FROM CUSTOMERS, ORDERS, ITEMS
  WHERE ORDERS.CUSTOMER_ID = CUSTOMERS.CUSTOMER_ID
  AND ITEMS.ORDER_ID = ORDERS.ORDER_ID
```

* Note that some databases allow you to use JOIN without the ON clause. In this case, the join operates on columns that have the same name.

Again, using the data shown in Figure 8-1, the output from this query might look as follows:

```
CUSTOMER_ID | NAME        | ORDER_ID | TOTAL | ITEM_NO | COST
------------+-------------+----------+-------+---------+-------
          1 | Bob Copier  |        4 | 72.19 |    1280 | 16.72
          1 | Bob Copier  |        4 | 72.19 |    4129 | 41.10
          1 | Bob Copier  |        4 | 72.19 |    3017 | 14.37
```

So far, all we've talked about is equi-joins, or inner joins. There are also outer joins, which do not require a matching key in both tables. An *outer join* includes all the records from one table and any records from another table that match the primary key of the first table. If there are no corresponding records in the second table, those columns are simply left blank in the result. Outer joins are divided into left outer and right outer joins: in a left join, the primary key table is on the left, and in a right join, it is on the right. Here's the syntax for a LEFT JOIN (or LEFT OUTER JOIN) on CUSTOMERS and ORDERS:

```
SELECT CUSTOMERS.CUSTOMER_ID, CUSTOMERS.NAME, ORDERS.ORDER_ID, ORDERS.TOTAL
  FROM CUSTOMERS LEFT JOIN ORDERS ON CUSTOMERS.CUSTOMER_ID = ORDERS.CUSTOMER_ID
```

This includes all the customer records and order records for all the customers that have them. Here's some possible output using the data shown in Figure 8-1:

```
CUSTOMER_ID | NAME          | ORDER_ID | TOTAL
------------+---------------+----------+--------
          1 | Bob Copier    |        4 | 72.19
          1 | Bob Copier    |        6 | 21.07
          2 | John Stapler  |          |
```

If we were to do a RIGHT JOIN on CUSTOMERS and ORDERS, the result would be the same as an inner join, since there are no records in ORDERS that don't have a match in CUSTOMERS.

Groups

The GROUP BY clause allows you to collapse multiple records into groups with a common field. For instance, to select all the records in the BOOKS table grouped by AUTHOR:

```
SELECT AUTHOR FROM BOOKS GROUP BY AUTHOR
```

This returns one row for each distinct author in the table. This query is not really that useful though, since we can do the same thing with the DISTINCT keyword (SELECT DISTINCT). However, we can use an aggregate function on each of the groups to do something more useful:

```
SELECT AUTHOR, COUNT(*) FROM BOOKS GROUP BY AUTHOR
```

This query returns two columns: the author and the number of books by that author in the table. Here's the output, based on the BOOKS table we used earlier:

```
AUTHOR           | COUNT(*)
-----------------+----------
Charles Dickens  |        2
Garrison Keillor |        1
```

We'll talk more about aggregate functions later in this chapter.

INSERT

The INSERT statement loads data into a table. Here's the syntax:

```
INSERT INTO table_name
   [ (column_name, ...) ]
   subquery | { VALUES (val1, val2,...) } | DEFAULT VALUES
```

To load static data, simply specify the table and the actual data:

```
INSERT INTO CUSTOMERS VALUES (3, 'Tom Fax', '617 555-1214')
```

This statement inserts the values 3, "Tom Fax", and "617 555-1214" into the first three fields of a new row in the CUSTOMERS table. If there are more than three fields in the CUSTOMERS table, this statement fails. If you don't want to insert into every column, you can specify the columns you want to insert into:

```
INSERT INTO CUSTOMERS (CUSTOMER_ID, NAME) VALUES (3, 'Tom Fax')
```

Note, however, that this kind of statement can fail if we do not provide a value for a field that is specified as NOT NULL.

To add more than one row at a time and to add data from other tables, we can specify a subquery rather than a set of specific values. To fill the JUNKMAIL table with values from the CUSTOMERS and ADDRESSES tables, run this query:

```
INSERT INTO JUNKMAIL (NAME, ADDR, CITY, STATE, ZIP)
  SELECT NAME, ADDR, CITY, STATE, ZIP FROM CUSTOMERS JOIN ADDRESSES
```

The database first performs a join on CUSTOMERS and ADDRESSES. It matches on the CUSTOMER_ID field and outputs the NAME field from CUSTOMERS and the other fields from ADDRESSES. The rows from the join are then inserted into the JUNKMAIL table, which can now be used to fill our mailboxes with catalogs.

UPDATE

The UPDATE statement modifies data in one or more existing rows. It consists of one or more SET statements and an optional WHERE clause. If the WHERE clause is not present, the operation is performed on every row in the table. Here's the syntax:

```
UPDATE table_name
   SET { column_name = { value | NULL | DEFAULT }, ...}
   [ { WHERE predicate }
     | { WHERE CURRENT OF cursor_name } ]
```

Here's an example that updates a few fields:

```
UPDATE ADDRESSES
   SET ADDR = '1282 Country Club Drive', STATE='CA' WHERE CUSTOMER_ID
   = 432
```

This statement sets the ADDR and STATE fields of the ADDRESSES table to particular values on all records where CUSTOMER_ID equals 432. Sometimes we do want to run an UPDATE on all records. Here's an example that makes sure all the STATE fields are in uppercase:

```
UPDATE ADDRESSES SET STATE = UPPER(STATE)
```

Note how we can use a field from the table itself in the SET statement.

The WHERE CURRENT OF clause allows you to update the row at the current cursor location in a multiple-table row. This is not something that JDBC programmers need to concern themselves with, although it can be of interest to an underlying JDBC 2.0 driver.

DELETE

DELETE is very simple: it removes rows from a table. Here's the syntax:

```
DELETE FROM table_name
   [ { WHERE predicate }
   | { WHERE CURRENT OF cursor_name } ]
```

To delete all the rows in ORDERS:

```
DELETE FROM ORDERS
```

To delete a specific record:

```
DELETE FROM ORDERS WHERE ORDER_ID = 32
```

Once a row has been deleted, there is no way to recover it.

Functions

SQL is not a procedural language, but it does provide some data transformation capabilities. In addition to the string concatenation operator (||), the SQL-92 specification defines two sets of functions: aggregate functions and value functions.

Aggregate Functions

In the section on the SELECT statement, we saw an aggregate function used to count the number of records within a group. In the main, this is what aggregate functions do: they act on all the records of query, counting rows, averaging fields, and so forth. For example, here's how to count the number of rows returned by a SELECT statement:

```
SELECT COUNT(*) FROM CUSTOMERS
```

Instead of returning each row of the CUSTOMERS table, this query returns a single-column, single-row result that contains the number of records in CUSTOMERS.

The other aggregate functions are AVG, SUM, MAX, and MIN. Unlike COUNT, which works on either a single column or all columns, the other functions work only on a single column. AVG and SUM can be applied against numerical data types only (integers, reals, etc.), while MAX and MIN work with any data type. Here are some examples:

```
SELECT MIN(AGE) FROM GUESTS
SELECT MAX(NAME) FROM GUESTS
SELECT AVG(AGE), SUM(AGE) FROM GUESTS
```

Value Functions

Value functions work on particular column values and return modified data. Some of them also generate values from system information.

Date/time functions

There are three date and time functions that retrieve the current date, current time, and current timestamp, respectively, from the database:

```
CURRENT_DATE
CURRENT_TIME[(precision)]
CURRENT_TIMESTAMP[(precision)]
```

`CURRENT_TIME` and `CURRENT_TIMESTAMP` accept an optional precision level, which specifies the decimal fractions of a second to be included in the time portion of the value. The current time zone is used with all these functions.

Here's how you might use these functions in a query:

```
SELECT * FROM ORDERS WHERE ORDER_DATE = CURRENT_DATE
INSERT INTO VISITORS (VISIT_TS) VALUES (CURRENT_TIMESTAMP)
```

Some databases have platform-specific commands that duplicate this functionality (these commands often predate SQL-92). Oracle's `SYSDATE` is one example. Note that these functions are not required for entry-level SQL-92.

String manipulation functions

The concatenation operator, `||`, has been around since before the SQL-92 standard. It allows you to concatenate multiple column values and string literals. Say we have a table that contains `FIRST_NAME` and `LAST_NAME` fields, and we want to display them in a "last, first" form. Here's a SQL statement that returns a single column that does just that:

```
SELECT LAST_NAME || ', ' || FIRST_NAME FROM CUSTOMERS
```

In addition, the SQL-92 standard defines a number of other functions that can be used in SQL statements. `UPPER` and `LOWER` convert a column into uppercase or lowercase, respectively:

```
SELECT UPPER(LAST_NAME) FROM CUSTOMERS
SELECT LOWER(FIRST_NAME) FROM CUSTOMERS
```

These functions can also be used in `WHERE` predicates, for example, to produce a case-insensitive search:

```
SELECT * FROM CUSTOMERS WHERE UPPER(FIRST_NAME) LIKE 'WILL%'
```

Most databases support `UPPER` and `LOWER`, but they are only required for full SQL-92 conformance, not entry-level conformance.

The TRIM function removes characters from one or both ends of a string:

```
TRIM ([ [ LEADING | TRAILING | BOTH ] [ character ] FROM ] string )
```

Calling TRIM on a string trims leading and trailing whitespace. Here's how to trim just leading blanks:

```
SELECT TRIM(LEADING ' ' FROM FIRST_NAME) FROM CUSTOMERS
```

And here's how to trim all "-" characters from both sides of a string:

```
SELECT TRIM(BOTH '-' FROM FIRST_NAME) FROM CUSTOMERS
```

Like UPPER and LOWER, TRIM is only required for full SQL-92 conformance, although it is supported by most database implementations.

The SUBSTRING command extracts a given number of characters from a larger string. It is defined as:

```
SUBSTRING (source_string FROM start_pos FOR number_of_characters)
```

For example, to get each customer's initials, we might use the following query:

```
SELECT SUBSTRING (FIRST_NAME FROM 1 FOR 1), SUBSTRING(LAST_NAME FROM 1 FOR 1)
```

SUBSTRING is only required for intermediate level SQL-92 conformance.

Return Codes

The SQL-92 standard defines a set of SQLSTATE return codes. SQLSTATE is defined as a five-character string, where the leftmost two characters define the error class, and the remaining three characters define the error subclass. Some database vendors may extend these return codes; classes beginning with the numbers 5 through 9 and letters I through Z are reserved for such implementation-specific extensions. The SQLSTATE code for a particular JDBC action can be retrieved via the getSQLState() method of SQLException. Table 8-3 lists the SQLSTATE return codes defined in SQL-92.

Table 8-3: SQL-92 SQLSTATE Return Codes

Class	*Class Definition*	*Subclass*	*Subclass Definition*
00	Successful completion	000	None
01	Warning	000	None
		001	Cursor operation conflict
		002	Disconnect error
		003	Null value eliminated in set function
		004	String data, right truncation
		005	Insufficient item descriptor areas
		006	Privilege not revoked

Table 8–3: SQL-92 SQLSTATE Return Codes (continued)

Class	*Class Definition*	*Subclass*	*Subclass Definition*
		007	Privilege not granted
		008	Implicit zero-bit padding
		009	Search expression too long for information schema
		00A	Query expression too long for information schema
02	No data	000	None
07	Dynamic SQL error	000	None
		001	Using clause doesn't match dynamic parameters
		002	Using clause doesn't match target specifications
		003	Cursor specification can't be executed
		004	Using clause required for dynamic parameters
		005	Prepared statement not a cursor specification
		006	Restricted data type attribute violation
		007	Using clause required for result fields
		008	Invalid descriptor count
		009	Invalid descriptor index
08	Connection Exception	000	None
		001	SQL-client unable to establish SQL-connection
		002	Connection name in use
		003	Connection doesn't exist
		004	SQL-server rejected establishment of SQL-connection
		006	Connection failure
		007	Transaction resolution unknown
0A	Feature not supported	000	None
		001	Multiple server transactions
21	Cardinality violation	000	None

Table 8-3: SQL-92 SQLSTATE Return Codes (continued)

Class	*Class Definition*	*Subclass*	*Subclass Definition*
22	Data exception	000	None
		001	String data, right truncation
		002	Null value, no indicator
		003	Numeric value out of range
		005	Error in assignment
		007	Invalid date-time format
		008	Date-time field overflow
		009	Invalid time zone displacement value
		011	Substring error
		012	Division by zero
		015	Internal field overflow
		018	Invalid character value for cast
		019	Invalid escape character
		021	Character not in repertoire
		022	Indicator overflow
		023	Invalid parameter value
		024	Unterminated C string
		025	Invalid escape sequence
		026	String data, length mismatch
		027	Trim error
23	Integrity constraint violation	000	None
24	Invalid cursor state	000	None
25	Invalid transaction state	000	None
26	Invalid SQL statement name	000	None
27	Triggered data change violation	000	None
28	Invalid authorization specification	000	None
2A	Syntax error or access rule violation in direct SQL statement	000	None
2B	Dependent privilege descriptors still exist	000	None
2C	Invalid character set name	000	None

Table 8–3: SQL-92 SQLSTATE Return Codes (continued)

Class	*Class Definition*	*Subclass*	*Subclass Definition*
2D	Invalid transaction termination	000	None
2E	Invalid connection name	000	None
33	Invalid SQL descriptor name	000	None
34	Invalid cursor name	000	None
35	Invalid condition number	000	None
37	Syntax error or access rule violation in dynamic SQL statement	000	None
3C	Ambiguous cursor name	000	None
3F	Invalid schema name	000	None
40	Transaction rollback	000	None
		001	Serialization failure
		002	Integrity constraint violation
		003	Statement completion unknown
42	Syntax error or access rule violation	000	None
44	With check option violation	000	None

CHAPTER 9

RMI Tools

rmic — JDK 1.1 and later

The Java RMI Compiler

Synopsis

rmic [*options*] *fully-qualified-classnames*

Description

The *rmic* compiler generates the stub and skeleton classes for remote objects you've written. Once you've compiled your remote objects using a standard Java compiler, like *javac*, you need to run *rmic*, specifying the classnames of your remote implementation classes using their full package names.

As an example, suppose you defined an interface named utils.remote.TimeServer that extends java.rmi.Remote, and wrote an implementation of this interface named utils.remote.TimeServerImpl. After compiling both with a Java compiler, you would run *rmic*, specifying utils.remote.TimeServerImpl as the class name argument.

Running *rmic* generates a skeleton class for each remote object type named *xxx_Skel*, where the *xxx* is the name of the remote interface. The skeleton is responsible for receiving client requests on a server object and dispatching these requests to the actual remote object. A stub class, named *xxx_Stub*, is also generated. The stub class is used for client references to the remote object. When a client gets a reference to a remote object, it receives an instance of the stub class, which forwards any method requests to the server object over the network. In our example, the stub and skeleton classes would be called utils.remote.TimeServer_Stub and utils.remote.TimeServer_Skel, respectively.

Both the stub class and the skeleton class implement the same remote interface as your remote object implementation, so they can be typecast to the remote interface.

Options

-classpath *pathlist*

Provides the classpath *rmic* uses to find any required classes, overriding the environment CLASSPATH or the default classpath. The directories in the list are separated by colons on Unix environments, by semicolons in Windows environments.

-d *path*
: The destination directory where the compiler should write the generated class files. If a -d option is given, the package of the generated classes places the stubs and skeletons in their proper subdirectories in the given destination. If the directories don't exist, *rmic* creates them for you. If no -d option is given, the stubs and skeletons are still generated to fall within the same package as the remote implementation, but the class files are placed in the current directory.

-depend
: Forces the compiler to attempt to recompile interdependent classes whose class files are out of date with each other. Without this option, the compiler attempts to recompile only class files explicitly referenced in the command-line options.

-g
: Includes debugging information in the generated stub and skeleton classes, for use with Java debuggers.

-J
: Passes the option immediately following the -J to the Java interpreter. There should be no spaces between the -J and the option to be passed to the interpreter.

-keep
-keepgenerated
: Keeps the Java source files for the stub and skeleton classes generated by the compiler. The Java files are written to the same directory as the class files, with or without a -d option specified. Without the -keepgenerated option, the Java source files are removed after the stub and skeleton classes are generated.

-nowarn
: Instructs the *rmic* compiler to eliminate warning messages from its output. Only errors encountered during compilation are reported.

-vcompat
: Creates a stub and skeleton classes that are compatible with both JDK 1.1 and the Java 2 SDK 1.2 versions of RMI. This option is enabled by default and does not need to be specified.

-verbose
: Prints verbose messages as compilation takes place, including which class is being compiled and class files that are loaded during compilation.

-v1.1
: Creates stub and skeleton classes that are compatible with the JDK 1.1 version of RMI. These classes may not run in a Java 2 runtime environment.

-v1.2
: Creates stub and skeleton classes that are compatible with the Java 1.2 (Java 2) version of RMI. These classes may not run in a Java 1.1 runtime environment.

Environment

CLASSPATH
: An ordered list of directories, ZIP files, and/or JAR files that the *rmic* compiler should use to look for classes. This list is separated by colons on Unix environments, semicolons on Windows environments. The list is searched in order for a given class when it is encountered during compilation. The compiler automatically appends the system classpath to the CLASSPATH, if it is specified. If the CLASSPATH is not set in the environment, the compiler uses the

current directory and the system classpath as its classpath. The CLASSPATH environment variable is overridden by the -classpath option to *rmic*.

rmiregistry — JDK 1.1 and later

The Java RMI Object Registry

Synopsis

```
rmiregistry [ port ]
```

Description

The *rmiregistry* command starts a remote object naming registry on the current host. The RMI registry binds remote objects to names, so that remote clients can request object references by name, using a URL-like syntax, and use the object references to invoke methods.

Internally, the *rmiregistry* command uses the java.rmi.registry.LocateRegistry class to instantiate a registry object. If no port is provided, the default port for the registry is 1099. Typically, the registry is run in the background on a server and remains running for the lifetime of the objects that it contains. If the registry crashes, and the registry is running in a separate Java VM from the actual remote objects, the remote objects are still available over RMI, and any remote references to these objects that existed before the crash are still valid. But all the name bindings the objects had in the registry are lost and need to be recreated after a new registry is started.

Environment

CLASSPATH
: An ordered list of directories, ZIP files, and/or JAR files that the *rmiregistry* command should use to look for classes. This list is separated by colons on Unix environments, semicolons on Windows environments. The list is searched in order for a given class when it is encountered during execution. The registry automatically appends the system classpath to the CLASSPATH, if it is specified. If the CLASSPATH is not set in the environment, the daemon uses the current directory and the system classpath as its classpath.

See Also

java.rmi.registry.LocateRegistry, java.rmi.Naming.

rmid — Java2 SDK 1.2 and later

The RMI Activation Daemon

Synopsis

```
rmid [ options ]
```

Description

The *rmid* command starts an RMI activation daemon on the local host. The activation daemon services all requests to register activatable objects and is responsible for activating objects due to client requests to invoke methods on them.

If no port option is given, the activation daemon runs on a default port of 1098. Internally, the activation daemon creates a java.rmi.activation.Activator and its own RMI naming registry (listening to port 1098). The daemon binds a java.rmi.activation.ActivationSystem object to the name "java.rmi.activation.ActivationSystem" in its internal registry.

Options

-C*cmdlineOption*
: Uses the given option as a command-line option to the Java VM for each activation group started by the daemon. This can pass default properties to the VM, for example, or set its memory limits to some default value. The Java interpreter option should immediately follow the -C option, with no spaces.

-log *path*
: Uses the given directory for any logging or temporary files needed by the activation daemon. If this option is not specified, the daemon writes its log files to a new directory named *log* in the current directory.

-port *portnum*
: Uses this port for the internal registry started by the activation daemon. If this option is not given, the daemon's internal naming registry runs by default on port 1098 of the local host. If you want the activation daemon's registry to listen to the default registry port, you can start the daemon with this command (Unix version):

```
$ rmid -port 1099 &
```

-stop
: Stop any activation daemon currently running on the specified port, or the default port if none is specified.

Environment

CLASSPATH
: An ordered list of directories, ZIP files, and/or JAR files that the *rmid* daemon should use to look for classes. This list is separated by colons on Unix environments, semicolons on Windows environments. The list is searched in order for a given class when it is encountered during execution. The daemon automatically appends the system classpath to the CLASSPATH, if it is specified. If the CLASSPATH is not set in the environment, the daemon uses the current directory and the system classpath as its classpath.

See Also

rmic, java.rmi.activation.Activator

serialver — JDK 1.1 and later

The RMI Serial Version Utility

Synopsis

```
serialver [ options ] fully-qualified-classnames
```

Description

The *serialver* utility generates a serial version ID you can use to mark a given class definition to track its versions as it evolves. The utility returns a static int member declaration you can paste into your Java class definition. In other words, this command:

```
% serialver AccountImpl
```

generates output something like:

```
AccountImpl: static final long serialVersionUID = 37849129093280989384L;
```

If versioning of your remote object classes becomes a problem for clients, this utility can tag a class with a version ID that can be checked to see if the proper version is being exported by your server for a given client, or if its local version is out of date. Serial version IDs are used by Java object serialization to uniquely identify class definitions.

Options

-show
Uses the graphical version of the tool, which displays a GUI interface that allows you to type in a fully qualified classname and press a button to see the serial version ID generated.

Environment

CLASSPATH
An ordered list of directories, ZIP files, and/or JAR files that the *serialver* utility should use to look for classes. This list is separated by colons on Unix environments, semicolons on Windows environments. The list is searched in order for a given class when it is encountered during execution. The utility automatically appends the system classpath to the CLASSPATH, if it is specified. If the CLASSPATH is not set in the environment, the utility uses the current directory and the system classpath as its classpath.

CHAPTER 10

IDL Reference

This chapter serves as a quick reference for CORBA's language-independent Interface Definition Language (IDL). It also provides a summary of the Java mapping of IDL (i.e., how IDL interface definitions are mapped by an IDL-to-Java compiler into equivalent Java interfaces). For a complete, definitive reference on IDL and the Java mapping of IDL, consult the IDL specification issued by the OMG ("IDL Syntax and Semantics," Chapter 3 of *The Common Object Request Broker: Architecture and Specification*, published by the OMG and available at *www.omg.org*).

Since this reference combines an IDL reference with an overview of the Java mapping of IDL, I'll be using a combination of IDL and Java examples throughout. In order to make it clear which language is being used in each example, I've stolen a convention from the CORBA standards documents, where a comment preceding the example code indicates the language that is in use.

IDL, as the name implies, is a language for defining object interfaces. IDL is language-neutral, so interfaces defined in IDL can be converted to objects implemented in any language with an IDL mapping. One way to think of the role IDL plays is to imagine that you already have a set of interacting objects defined and then think of IDL as a way to export a subset of those interfaces so that they can be accessed by remote entities. Any member variables or operations you define in the IDL interfaces are visible and accessible by remote entities, providing they can obtain a reference to instances of these interfaces (see Chapter 4, *Java IDL*, for more details on the use of CORBA objects). If you proceed this way, the definitions of the variables and operations on the IDL interfaces have to match those on the actual implementations you are exporting, according to the rules of the IDL mapping to the language they are written in.

Of course, this is not the typical way that you use IDL in practice.* You usually want to do an abstract design of a distributed application and its set of objects first, define the IDL interfaces for the objects that need to be used remotely, then compile these IDL interfaces into language-specific interfaces. The next step is to write implementations of the interfaces in whatever programming language you are using. You are free to add additional operations and member variables to your language-specific implementations, but these features won't be accessible remotely unless you add them to the corresponding IDL interface.

There are five high-level entities you can define in an IDL specification:

- Modules, which act as namespaces
- Interfaces to objects (with their operations and data attributes)
- Data types
- Constants
- Exceptions

These high-level entities are listed here in roughly hierarchical order. Modules contain other modules, interfaces, data types, constants, and exceptions. Interfaces contain data types, constants, and exceptions that are specific to that interface, along with the operations and attributes for the interface. We'll look at the IDL syntax that defines each of these, and, in each case, we'll see how the IDL is mapped into equivalent Java code. Before we do that, though, we need to cover some of the basics of IDL: keywords, identifiers, comments, and various types of literals.

IDL Keywords

Table 10-1 lists the reserved keywords in IDL. These keywords are case-sensitive, and they cannot be used as identifiers in any IDL constructs.

Table 10–1: IDL Reserved Keywords

`any`	`default`	`in`	`oneway`	`struct`	`wchar`
`attribute`	`double`	`inout`	`out`	`switch`	`wstring`
`boolean`	`enum`	`interface`	`raises`	`TRUE`	
`case`	`exception`	`long`	`readonly`	`typedef`	
`char`	`FALSE`	`module`	`sequence`	`unsigned`	
`const`	`fixed`	`Object`	`short`	`union`	
`context`	`float`	`octet`	`string`	`void`	

* One notable exception is the task of wrapping legacy code with a CORBA frontend, but even here you normally use middleware objects to interface directly with the legacy code.

Identifiers

Identifiers name various IDL constructs, like modules, interfaces, and constants. In IDL, an identifier has to follow these rules:

- It contains alphanumeric characters from the ISO Latin-1* character set (e.g., a–z, A–Z, 0–9, plus various characters with accents, graves, tildes, etc.), and the underscore character (_).
- It can be of any length, and all characters in an identifier are significant.
- The first character must be an alphabetic character.
- Identifiers are case-insensitive, in the sense that two identifiers that differ only by case are considered a name collision and cause an IDL compiler error. This rule stems from the fact that IDL needs to be mappable into many implementation languages, some of which are case-insensitive.
- Identifiers must be spelled and capitalized consistently throughout an IDL file.
- All IDL identifiers share the same namespace, so interfaces, modules, user-defined types, etc. within the same scope must have unique identifiers. An interface named `List` and a module named `List` within the same scope cause a name collision and an IDL compiler error. See the section "Naming Scopes" for more details.

Mapping Identifiers to Java

An IDL-to-Java compiler attempts to map all IDL identifiers unchanged into equivalent Java identifiers.

An exception is the case where a mapped identifier conflicts with an identifier created automatically by the IDL compiler. IDL interfaces, for example, when they are mapped to Java, have two additional Java interfaces created for them, named with the original interface name, with `Helper` and `Holder` appended (see Chapter 4 for details on the purpose of these generated interfaces). So, an interface named `List` is mapped into a Java interface named `List`, and also causes the creation of Java interfaces named `ListHelper` and `ListHolder`. If there is another identifier in the IDL file you've named `ListHelper` or `ListHolder`, its mapped Java identifier has an underscore prepended to it (e.g., `_ListHelper`, `_ListHolder`) to avoid a conflict with the generated interface names. In general, identifiers automatically generated by the IDL compiler have precedence over other identifiers declared explicitly in the IDL file.

The other exception to the general rule of directly mapping IDL identifiers to Java identifiers is with a mapping that conflicts with a Java keyword. In this case, the mapped Java identifier has an underscore prepended to it. If, for example, you declared a constant named `package` (not a reserved keyword in IDL), it is mapped to a Java variable named `_package`.

---

* ISO Latin-1 refers to the standard ISO 8859-1. You can find a listing of the character set in the HTML 3.2 standard, at *http://www.w3.org/TR/REC-html32.html*.

Comments

Comments in IDL follow the format of C, C++, and Java comments. A block comment starts with the character sequence /* and ends with the character sequence */. A line comment begins with the character sequence //, and ends at the end of the line on which it begins.

Mapping Comments to Java

There are no rules for mapping IDL comments to Java. Many IDL-to-Java compilers simply drop comments from IDL files during the conversion to Java, since in many cases the comments refer to the IDL code and may not be totally relevant in the generated Java code.

Basic Data Types

IDL supports the basic data types shown in Table 10-2. In the same table, I've shown the Java type that each is mapped to according to the standard IDL-to-Java mapping. Note that there isn't a standard mapping defined for the `fixed` and `long double` IDL types. These data types were added to the IDL syntax relatively recently, and the IDL Java mapping hasn't been updated to include these as of this writing. Another important thing to note is that Java doesn't support unsigned types, such as `unsigned short`. So the IDL `short` and `unsigned short` types are both mapped to the Java `short` data type. You should be aware of this when writing implementations of IDL-generated Java interfaces, since it is up to you to either ensure that their values remain positive or deal with the fact that their values may be set to negative values.

Table 10-2: IDL Basic Data Types, Sizes, and Java Mappings

IDL Type Specifier	*Required Size*	*Java Data Type*
`short`	16 bits	`short`
`long`	32 bits	`int`
`long long`	64 bits	`long`
`unsigned short`	16 bits	`short`
`unsigned long`	32 bits	`int`
`unsigned long long`	64 bits	`long`
`char`	8 bits	`char`
`wchar`	Implementation-dependent	`char`
`string`	Unlimited	`java.lang.String`
`string`<*`size`*>	*`size`* `chars`	`java.lang.String`
`wstring`	Unlimited	`java.lang.String`
`wstring`<*`size`*>	*`size`* `wchars`	`java.lang.String`
`boolean`	Implementation-dependent	`boolean`

Table 10-2: IDL Basic Data Types, Sizes, and Java Mappings (continued)

IDL Type Specifier	*Required Size*	*Java Data Type*
`octet`	8 bits	`byte`
`any`		
`float`	IEEE single-precision	`float`
`double`	IEEE double-precision	`double`
`long double`	IEEE double-extended	Not defined
`fixed`	31 decimal digits	Not defined

Strings and Characters

There are two character types included in IDL: `char` and `wchar`. A `char` represents an 8-bit character from a single-byte character set, such as ASCII. A `wchar` represents a wide character from any character set, including multibyte character sets like Kanji. The size of a `wchar` is implementation-specific.

I've included the IDL `string` and `wstring` data types in this table as well, although technically they should be considered constructed data types (arrays of a basic data type, characters). Since they're so frequently used, it's useful to have them together with all of the IDL basic data types.

A `string` is the equivalent of an array of `char` values, and a `wstring` is an array of `wchar` values. In each case, there are two ways to specify a string type: with or without a size specification, in angle brackets following the type name. If you provide a size specification in your IDL declaration (e.g., `string<10> name`), the language mapping is responsible for enforcing the size limits of the string. If you don't provide a size specification, the string is allowed to grow to any size, limited only by the implementation language.

If support for a multibyte character set is important for your application, it's best to declare all your character and string data as `wchar` and `wstring` values. This way you'll be sure to get multibyte support in languages that support it.

Mapping strings and characters to Java

In the IDL-to-Java mapping, both `char` and `wchar` are mapped to the Java `char` type, and both `string` and `wstring` are mapped to the `java.lang.String` class. In Java, the `char` type represents a two-byte Unicode character and can therefore support multibyte character sets by default.

When marshalling and unmarshalling data items during remote method calls, the ORB is responsible for performing bounds checks on the data members being set. If a value exceeds the limits declared for the string member in the IDL specification of the interface, an `org.omg.CORBA.MARSHAL` exception is thrown.

Constants and Literals

Literals are explicit values inserted into IDL code. Sometimes a literal is used to specify a default value for an interface attribute or to declare the value for a constant. Literals can be boolean (`TRUE` or `FALSE`), numeric (integer, floating point, or fixed point), or character-based (a single character or a string).

Literals are most often used in IDL to initialize the values of constants. Constants are named variables that are restricted from being modified after being initialized. In IDL, a constant is declared using the syntax:

```
// IDL
const type identifier = value;
```

where *`type`* is any valid basic data type or declared interface type, *`identifier`* is any valid IDL identifier, and *`value`* is any IDL expression that evaluates to a literal value. The initialization expression can be a simple literal or a complex expression combining multiple literals using logical or mathematical operators. You can declare a few useful numeric constants as follows, for example:

```
// IDL
const float half = 1 / 2;
const float quarter = 1 / 4;
```

Most of the operators present in C/C++, such as addition (+), subtraction (-), multiplication (*), division (/), and the logical and bitwise operators (`|`, `&`, `^`, `||`, `&&`, etc.) are supported by IDL.

Mapping Constants to Java

If an IDL constant is declared within an interface definition, the constant is mapped to a `public final static` member on the corresponding Java interface.

If the IDL constant is declared outside an interface definition, a Java interface is created to hold the constant value as a `public static final` value. The generated interface has the same name as the IDL identifier given to the constant, and the static class member has the name `value`. Consider the following IDL constant declaration:

```
// IDL
const float PI = 3.14159;
interface GeometricOperators {
        ...
```

This causes the generation of the following Java interface:

```
// Java
public final class PI {
    public static final float value = (float) (3.14159D);
}
```

In your Java code, you can reference the constant value using `PI.value`.

Boolean Literals

There are two boolean literals (naturally) in IDL. They are specified using the keywords `TRUE` and `FALSE`. Their IDL type is `boolean`. In Java, they are mapped to the `boolean` values `true` and `false`.

Numeric Literals

Integer literals, floating-point literals, and fixed-point literals comprise numeric literals in IDL.

Integer literals

An integer value in IDL can be declared in decimal, octal, or hexadecimal notation. Any sequence of digits that does not start with a zero is considered a decimal integer value. If the sequence is all digits but starts with a zero, it's assumed to be an octal value. If the literal starts with `0X` or `0x`, it's taken to be a hexadecimal value.

Floating-point literals

A floating-point literal is a decimal integer, optionally followed by a decimal point and a fractional component, and/or by the letter `e` or `E` followed by an exponent expressed as a decimal integer. Either the fractional component (with the decimal point) or the exponent (with the `e` or `E`) must be present for the literal to be interpreted as a floating-point value and not an integer. Similarly, either the initial integer component or the decimal point must be present. So, for example, these are valid floating-point literals:

```
2.34
0.314159e1
3E19
.0003413
```

Fixed-point literals

A fixed-point literal consists of a decimal integer, optionally followed by a decimal point and fractional component (expressed as a decimal value), followed by the letter `d` or `D`. Either the integer component or the fractional component must be present. The decimal point is optional. The trailing `d` or `D` must be present in order for the literal to be interpreted as a fixed-point value. The following are all valid fixed-point literals:

```
1.50d
.025d
1.333D
12d
```

IDL Reference

Mapping numeric literals to Java

Numeric literals are mapped by taking into account the context in which they are used. Typically, a literal initializes a constant, so the declared type of the constant has to be checked to determine whether the literal is valid for the type and how it should be mapped to a Java literal. For example, these two similar IDL constant declarations:

```
// IDL
const short largeVal = 2e5;
const float largeFloatVal = 2e5;
```

are mapped by Sun's *idltojava* compiler to these Java declarations:

```
// Java
public static final short largeVal = (short) (2e5D);
public static final float largeFloatVal = (float) (2e5D);
```

Sun's *idltojava* compiler doesn't do any type checking on the IDL literal before converting it to its Java form and inserting it into the cast operation shown previously. So it is possible for the *idltojava* compiler to generate invalid Java code. For example:

```
// IDL
const float literalTest = TRUE;
```

is converted without warning by *idltojava* to:

```
// Java
public static final float literalTest = (float)(true);
```

Character Literals

A character literal is a character specification enclosed in single quotes (e.g., 'a'). Character literals can be specified using only elements of the ISO 8859-1 character set. Some characters need to be specified with a sequence of more than one character. These include characters that are nonprintable and the single- and double-quote characters that delimit string and character literals. These characters are specified with escape sequences, which start with a backslash character (\). Table 10-3 lists the escape sequences supported by IDL and the nonprintable characters they represent.

Table 10-3: IDL Escape Sequences

Escape Sequence	*Meaning*
\a	Alert
\\	Backslash
\b	Backspace
\r	Carriage return
\"	Double quote
\f	Form feed
\x## (e.g., \x4e)	Hexadecimal number

Table 10-3: IDL Escape Sequences (continued)

Escape Sequence	*Meaning*
\n	Newline
\### (e.g.,)	Octal number
\?	Question mark
\'	Single quote
\t	Tab
\v	Vertical tab

Character literals, including the escape sequences listed in Table 10-3, are converted unchanged into Java literals.

String Literals

A string literal is a sequence of characters delimited by double quote (") characters. If two string literals are adjacent to each other in an IDL file, they are concatenated. So, in this example:

```
// IDL
const string acctHolder = "Jim" "Farley";
```

the generated Java code is:*

```
// Java
public static final String acctHolder = "Jim Farley";
```

If you want to use the double-quote character in a string literal, you have to use its escape sequence (see Table 10-3).

Naming Scopes

Each IDL file you create defines a namespace or naming scope for identifiers you declare within that file. This namespace is further subdivided into nested scopes whenever you declare a new module, interface, structure, union, or exception in your IDL file. You can think of the naming scope within an IDL file as a sort of naming directory. By default, you start at the root of the directory, and each time you open a declaration of one of these items, you start a new subdirectory of the naming directory, named after the identifier you use for the item.

You can specify a scope using the `::` delimiter, which is analogous to the / or \ delimiter in file directories. The root scope for the IDL file is represented as `::` by itself, and nested scopes are specified by adding their names, such as `::utils::math::MatrixOps`. The names in a scope name can refer to any identifiers that might exist in each scope. In this example, `utils` and `math` might refer to modules (the `math` module is declared within the `utils` module), and `MatrixOps`

* There appears to be an error in Sun's *idltojava* compiler (with the version released as of this writing, at least) that causes it to raise a syntax error when it encounters adjacent string literals. The IDL specification dictates the behavior as described here, though.

might refer to an interface declared within the math module. The intermediate elements in a scoped name must refer to one of the IDL elements that define their own scopes, but the final element in a scoped name can refer to any item with its own identifier, including constants, data members on interfaces, etc.

Within any particular scope in the naming scope of an IDL file (including the root scope), *all* identifiers within that scope must be unique. Separate nested scopes off of one parent scope can have identical identifiers declared within them and can share identifiers with their parent scope as well, but two identifiers at the same level within a scope can't be the same. As as example, the following is legal in an IDL file:

```
// IDL
module utils {
        interface math {
                const float PI = 3.14159;
        };
        interface baking {
                const string PI = "apple";
        };
};
```

The two definitions of PI (::utils::math::PI and ::utils::baking::PI) do not conflict, since they each have distinct absolute scoped names within the IDL file. You cannot, however, declare a constant named math within the utils module, since its fully scoped name is ::utils::math, which conflicts with the name of the math interface.

Scoped names that begin with :: are absolute names, and are relative to the root file scope of the IDL file. Names that don't start with :: are relative to the local scope in which they appear. So we can add two new constants to our math interface that use scoped names to reference our versions of PI:

```
// IDL
module utils {
        interface math {
                const float PI = 3.14159;
                const float PIsquared = PI * PI;
                const string PIOfTheDay = ::utils::baking::PI;
        };
        interface baking {
                const string PI = "apple";
        };
};
```

The reference to PI in the definition of the PIsquared constant is relative to the ::utils::math scope, so it refers to the float constant. The reference to PI in the PIOfTheDay definition is absolute and references the string definition of PI in the baking interface.

User-Defined Data Types

In addition to the basic data types already described, IDL supports user-defined data types, which are aggregations of these basic types. These complex data types include arrays, sequences, enumerations, and constructed data types you define yourself using structs and unions. We'll go over each in detail in this section.

A complex data type is used in IDL by first giving it a type name, then using the type name wherever you would use a basic data- or interface-type name (e.g., declaring attributes, method arguments). There are a few ways a name is assigned to a complex data type:

- With structures, unions, and enumerations, the name is included in the declaration of the data type.
- A `typedef` can be used to assign a name to a specific type (basic or complex).

Before we go on to see how complex data types are declared in IDL, let's take a look at how a `typedef` assigns a type name to a complex data type.

Typedefs

A `typedef` associates a name with another data type. Here is the syntax of an IDL `typedef`:

```
typedef type identifier
```

The *`type`* can be any basic IDL data type, a user-defined data structure (structure, union, or enumeration), an IDL interface type, or a sequence. The *`identifier`* can be a simple IDL identifier, or it can include dimension specifications for an array. So the following are all valid `typedef` statements:

```
// IDL
typedef short myShort;
typedef long longArray[2][2];
typedef PrintServer pserver;
```

After declaring these `typedefs` in your IDL file, you can use `myShort`, `longArray`, and `pserver` as type names when declaring method arguments, return values, or interface attributes.

Mapping typedefs to Java

If an IDL `typedef` refers to a basic IDL type, the Java equivalent to that type is used wherever the `typedef` identifier is used. So our `myShort` `typedef` in the previous section is replaced by the Java type `short` wherever it's used.

Any `typedefs` that refer to user-defined types are replaced by the mapped Java class or interface for the target IDL type. If the type used in an IDL `typedef` is itself a `typedef`, its target type is found, and so on, until a final user-defined type or basic IDL type is found. Consider this example:

```
// IDL
struct LinkedList {
        any item;
        any next;
};
```

```
typedef LinkedList DefList;
typedef DefList MyList;
```

Wherever either DefList or MyList appears in the IDL file, it is mapped to the Java class generated for the LinkedList type, since they both refer (directly or indirectly) to that type.

Arrays

Arrays can only be declared within the context of a typedef. Once you've assigned the array type to a type name using the typedef, you can use the new type name to declare array members on interfaces. IDL doesn't provide a way to initialize array values, so you cannot declare array constants in IDL, since constants have to be initialized in their declaration.

To declare an array, simply add dimensions in brackets to a variable identifier. For example, to define a two-dimensional array of short values:

```
// IDL
typedef short short2x2Array[2][2];
```

IDL requires that you explicitly specify each dimension of the array, in order to support mappings to languages that have a similar requirement.

Mapping arrays to Java

Arrays are mapped into Java as arrays (naturally). So, if we use the short2x2Array type defined above in an IDL interface:

```
// IDL
interface MatrixOps {
        attribute short2x2Array identity2D;
        ...
```

the corresponding Java code looks like so:

```
// Java
public interface MatrixOps {
        short[][] identity2D();
        void identity2D(short[][] arg);
        ...
```

We'll look more at how interface attributes are mapped to Java later, but you can infer from this that the short IDL array is mapped to a short array in Java. The attribute is mapped to get() and set() methods for that attribute. Since Java doesn't allow array type specifiers to include dimensions, our declaration that the identity2D attribute be a 2-by-2 array has been lost in the mapping. It's up to you to provide an implementation of this interface that enforces the intended dimensions of the array within the Java interface.

In addition to mapping the array type to equivalent type specifiers, each array typedef in IDL causes the generation of corresponding helper and holder classes in Java. The type name specified in the IDL typedef is used as the prefix for the xxxHelper and xxxHolder class names. So our short2x2Array type has short2x2ArrayHelper and short2x2ArrayHolder classes generated for it. The helper class provides the static methods that read and write the array type over CORBA I/O streams, when the array type is used as a method argument or return type. These methods enforce the array dimensions that you dictate in your IDL `typedef`; if the array is not of the correct type when being marshalled, the `write()` method throws an `org.omg.CORBA.MARSHAL` exception. The holder class is used whenever you use your array type as an `inout` or `out` method argument. For more details on the purposes of helper and holder classes, see Chapter 4.

Sequences

An IDL sequence is a one-dimensional array. To declare a sequence, you need to declare the type of the elements in the sequence, and optionally the maximum size of the sequence:

```
// IDL
typedef sequence<long, 2> longVector;
typedef sequence<short> unboundedShortVector;
typedef sequence<sequence<float, 2> > coordVector;
```

Like arrays, sequences have to be declared within a `typedef` and then the new type name can be used for typing attributes, method arguments, and return values. Note that the elements in a sequence can themselves be a sequence. Also notice that if you don't provide a bound for a sequence of sequences, you need to put a space between the two > brackets, so that they aren't parsed as a >> operator.

Mapping sequences to Java

Sequences are mapped to Java almost identically to arrays. A sequence of a given IDL type becomes a Java array of the equivalent Java type, sequences of sequences become two-dimensional arrays, etc. A holder and helper class are generated for each sequence `typedef` as well, using the type name specified in the `typedef`. The `write()` method on the helper class enforces any size bounds you specify on the sequence, throwing an `org.omg.CORBA.MARSHAL` exception if they don't match.

Structs

A fixed data structure is declared using the `struct` construct in IDL. A `struct` is declared using the following syntax:

```
// IDL
struct type-name {
        data-member;
        data-member;
        ...
};
```

The type name is any valid identifier in IDL. Each data member is specified using a type specification and an identifier that references the member (similar to attributes on an interface, described under "Attributes" in section "Interface Declarations"). You can use basic data types, arrays, sequences, and any other `typedefs` as types for members of a struct. You can declare a recursive structure (a structure that includes members of its own type) by using a sequence declaration:

```
// IDL
struct LispStringList {
        string car;
        sequence<LispStringList> cdr;
};
```

Mapping structs to Java

An IDL struct is mapped to a public final Java class with the same name as the struct. Each member of the struct is mapped to a public instance member on the Java class. The Java class includes a default constructor that leaves the member variables uninitialized and a constructor that accepts a value for each member. Our example struct above is mapped to the following Java class:

```
// Java
public final class LispStringList {
        // instance variables
        public String car;
        public LispStringList[] cdr;
        // constructors
        public LispStringList() { }
        public LispStringList(String __car, LispStringList[] __cdr) {
                car = __car;
                cdr = __cdr;
        }
}
```

Each struct also has a Java holder class generated for it, which marshalls the data type when it's used as an inout or out method argument or as a method return value.

Enumerations

An enumeration in IDL declares an ordered list of identifiers, whose values are assigned in ascending order according to their order in the enumeration. An enumeration is given a type name so that the elements of the enumeration can be referenced. The syntax for declaring an IDL enumeration is:

```
// IDL
enum type-name { element-name, element-name, ... };
```

The elements in the enumeration are guaranteed to be assigned actual values so that the comparison operators in the implementation language recognize the order of the elements as specified in the enum declaration. In other words, the first element is less than the second, the second is less than the third, etc. An example enum declaration follows:

```
// IDL
enum ErrorCode { BadValue, DimensionError, Overflow, Underflow };
```

Mapping enumerations to Java

Each enumerated type you declare in IDL is mapped to a `public final` Java class of the same name as the enumeration. The class holds a single `private int` instance member called `value`. A single `private` constructor is generated for the class, which takes an `int` argument that initializes the `value` member.

For each element of the enumeration, two components are added to the Java class: a `static final int` data member and a `static` instance of the generated Java class. The static data member generated for each element is given a value that enforces the order of the elements in the enumeration, and the static class instance generated for each element is initialized with this same value. The static class instance is given the same name as the element in the enumeration, and the static data member is given the element's name prepended with an underscore. These two representations for each element of the enumeration let you reference the element value using either a corresponding `int` value or the generated Java class type. If the enumerated type is used as a method argument or return value in an IDL interface, your Java implementation has to use the object versions of the elements.

Our example enumeration generates a Java class like the following:

```
// Java
public final class ErrorCode {
        public static final int _BadValue = 0,
                _DimensionError = 1,
                _Overflow = 2,
                _Underflow = 3;
        public static final ErrorCode BadValue = new ErrorCode(_BadValue);
        public static final ErrorCode DimensionError = new
     ErrorCode(_DimensionError);
        public static final ErrorCode Overflow = new ErrorCode(_Overflow);
        public static final ErrorCode Underflow = new ErrorCode(_Underflow);
        public int value() {
                return _value;
        }
        public static final ErrorCode from_int(int i) throws
     org.omg.CORBA.BAD_PARAM {
                switch (i) {
                        case _BadValue:
                                return BadValue;
                        case _DimensionError:
                                return DimensionError;
                        case _Overflow:
                                return Overflow;
                        case _Underflow:
                                return Underflow;
                        default:
                                throw new org.omg.CORBA.BAD_PARAM();
                }
        }
        private ErrorCode(int _value){
                this._value = _value;
        }
        private int _value;
}
```

So we can refer to the elements in the enumeration in our Java code using any of the following forms:

```
// Java
int error1 = ErrorCode._BadValue;
ErrorCode error2 = ErrorCode.Overflow;
int error2Val = error2.value();
```

Each enumerated type also has a holder class generated for it that is used whenever the enumerated type is used in IDL as an `out` or `inout` method argument. Although not strictly required by the IDL Java mapping defined by the OMG, an enumerated type might also have a helper class generated for it.

Unions

IDL unions are similar in nature to discriminated unions in C and C++. A single tag field, or *discriminator*, determines the data element held by the union. Depending on the value of the discriminator field, a particular instance of the union type may hold a different data member. The union is declared using a `switch` statement to declare the various possible formats, or branches, of the union structure:

```
// IDL
union type-name switch (discriminator-type) {
        case tag-value:
                [data-element;]
        case tag-value:
                [data-element;]
        . . .
        [default:]
                data-element;
};
```

The discriminator for the union is declared using only the type for the discriminator (no identifier is given to the discriminator, since there is only a single discriminator per union type). The type for the discriminator must be an integer, character, boolean, or enumerated type (`string`, `struct`, `union`, `array`, and `sequence` are not allowed).

Each branch in the `switch` defines a data element that represents the value of the union if its discriminator is a given value. Each data member identifier in a union `switch` has to be unique. Multiple cases can be mapped to the same data element by listing them sequentially within the `switch`. A single optional `default` case can be given for any values not given their own cases. Consider the following union:

```
// IDL
typedef Coord2d sequence<long, 2>;
typedef Coord3d sequence<long, 3>;
union MultiCoord switch (short) {
        case 1:
                long pos;
        case 2:
                Coord2d val2d;
        case 3:
        default:
                Coord3d val3d;
};
```

This declares a type named MultiCoord that represents a one-, two-, or three-dimensional coordinate, depending on the value of its discriminator value. The default is for the coordinate to be three-dimensional, so the case for a discriminator value of 3 is the same as the default case. Since a union can have only a single data member per case, we have to use typedef types for the coordinate values. Depending on the discriminator value, the union contains either a simple integer position, a Coord2D type that is declared as a sequence of two integer values, or a Coord3D type that is a sequence of three integer values.

If the discriminator value is given a value not listed in a case, the union consists of the data member in the default case, if present. If there is no default case, the union has only its discriminator value and no data members.

Mapping unions to Java

Each IDL union is mapped to a public final Java class of the same name as the union identifier. The class contains a single, default constructor. The class has some kind of data member for maintaining the value of the union discriminator (the details of which are not dictated by the IDL-to-Java mapping) and a discriminator() method for accessing it as a short value. The standard also doesn't specify how data members for the union are implemented in the Java class. Each branch you specify in the IDL union is mapped to an accessor method and modifier method for that branch, and these methods are named after the identifier given to the data member in the branch. If you use one of the modifier methods to set that branch of the union type, the discriminator is automatically set to the corresponding value. If you attempt to access the value from a branch, and the union is not set to that branch, an org.omg.CORBA.BAD_OPERATION exception is thrown. The return value types and method arguments for the discriminator() method and the case accessor/modifier methods are determined based on the standard type conversion rules for mapping IDL to Java.

Our MultiCoord union example is mapped to the following Java class by Sun's *idltojava* compiler:

```
// Java
public final class MultiCoord {
        // instance variables
        private boolean __initialized;
        private short __discriminator;
        private java.lang.Object __value;
        private short _default = 4;
        // constructor
        public MultiCoord() {
                __initialized = false;
                __value = null;
        }
        // discriminator accessor
        public short discriminator() throws org.omg.CORBA.BAD_OPERATION {
                if (!__initialized) {
                        throw new org.omg.CORBA.BAD_OPERATION();
                }
                return __discriminator;
        }
        // branch constructors and get and set accessors
```

```
        public int pos() throws org.omg.CORBA.BAD_OPERATION {
                if (!__initialized) {
                        throw new org.omg.CORBA.BAD_OPERATION();
                }
                switch (__discriminator) {
                        case (short) (1L):
                                break;
                        default:
                                throw new org.omg.CORBA.BAD_OPERATION();
                }
                return ((org.omg.CORBA.IntHolder) __value).value;
        }
        public void pos(int value) {
                __initialized = true;
                __discriminator = (short) (1L);
                __value = new org.omg.CORBA.IntHolder(value);
        }
        public int[] val2d() throws org.omg.CORBA.BAD_OPERATION {
                if (!__initialized) {
                        throw new org.omg.CORBA.BAD_OPERATION();
                }
                switch (__discriminator) {
                        case (short) (2L):
                                break;
                        default:
                                throw new org.omg.CORBA.BAD_OPERATION();
                }
                return (int[]) __value;
        }
        public void val2d(int[] value) {
                __initialized = true;
                __discriminator = (short) (2L);
                __value = value;
        }
        public int[] val3d() throws org.omg.CORBA.BAD_OPERATION {
                if (!__initialized) {
                        throw new org.omg.CORBA.BAD_OPERATION();
                }
                switch (__discriminator) {
                        default:
                                break;
                        case (short) (1L):
                        case (short) (2L):
                                throw new org.omg.CORBA.BAD_OPERATION();
                }
                return (int[]) __value;
        }
        public void val3d(int[] value) {
                __initialized = true;
                __discriminator = (short) (3L);
                __value = value;
        }
}
```

Notice that Sun's *idltojava* compiler implements the data branches in the union using a single `java.lang.Object` data member, which references an object of the appropriate type when the union is put into a particular branch.

In this case, the default case and the third case share the same branch, so no accessor or modifier method is generated for the default case. If we have a default case that is separate from all other explicit cases in the union (i.e., has its own branch), an accessor and modifier method are generated for its branch as well. If two explicit cases are mapped to the same branch in the switch, the Java modifier method generated for that branch sets the discriminator value to the value of the first case included for that branch. In these cases, another modifier method, which takes a second argument that is the value for the discriminator, is also generated. As an example, if we want to use a `Coord2D` for both 1D and 2D coordinates, we can modify our IDL union to have both case 1 and 2 use the same branch:

```
typedef sequence<long, 2> Coord2d;
typedef sequence<long, 3> Coord3d;
union MultiCoord switch (short) {
 case 1:
 case 2:
   Coord2d val2d;
 case 3:
   Coord3d val3d;
 default:
   Coord3d valDef;
};
```

In this situation, the generated Java has an additional method included for the `val2d` branch:

```
public void val2d(int discrim, int[] value) { ... }
```

This allows you to set the union to that branch and also specify which discriminator is intended. This can be useful in some cases, such as our modified `MultiCoord` example, where the value of the discriminator determines the usage for the object.*

If no explicit `default` case is given in the union and if the listed cases do not completely cover the possible values for the discriminator, the generated Java class includes a single method named `default()` that takes no arguments and returns a `void`. This serves as the modifier for the default case, setting the union discriminator to some unused value.

The union class also has a holder class generated for it. Although not specified in the standard mapping, it might also have a helper class generated, but you shouldn't depend on the helper class being present in the generated Java.

Exceptions

You can define exceptions in IDL that signal errors or other unusual circumstances that may occur during a remote method call. Exceptions are declared with a unique name and an optional set of data attributes:

```
// IDL
exception identifier { data-member; data-member; ...};
```

---

* The current version of Sun's *idltojava* compiler, which originally shipped with the beta 2 of JDK 1.2, violates this part of the standard and does not generate the extra modifier method for multicase branches.

Each data member on the exception type is simply a type specification followed by a unique identifier for the data member. The data provides the caller with additional information about what went wrong during the remote method call.

Using our geometric examples from earlier, we might define an exception that is thrown when a `MultiCoord` with unexpected dimensions is passed into a method:

```
// IDL
exception BadDimension {
        short expected;
        short passed;
};
```

A server object that raises one of these exceptions can set these data values, and the client making the request can read these values and interpret what went wrong.

Exceptions can be declared within any module or interface scope in your IDL file.

Standard Exceptions

In addition to user-defined exceptions, there is a set of standard exceptions defined within the CORBA module. These standard exceptions can be raised by any method, even though they are not listed explicitly in the method definition. These exceptions can be referenced in IDL using the `CORBA::` scope (e.g., `CORBA::BAD_PARAM`). The standard CORBA exceptions are listed in Table 10-4. Every standard CORBA exception includes two data members: an `unsigned long` minor error code that can further specify the type of error that occurred, and a `completion_status enum` that can be either `COMPLETED_YES`, `COMPLETED_NO`, or `COMPLETED_MAYBE`. These status values indicate that before the exception was raised, the method was either completed, never initiated, or in an unknown state, respectively. A more complete description of the standard exceptions (in their Java form) can be found in Chapter 28, *The org.omg.CORBA Package*.

Table 10-4: Standard CORBA Exceptions

Exception Name	*Meaning*
`BAD_CONTEXT`	Failure while accessing the context object.
`BAD_INV_ORDER`	Some methods were called out of their expected order.
`BAD_OPERATION`	An invalid method was called.
`BAD_PARAM`	An invalid argument was passed into a method.
`BAD_TYPECODE`	A bad typecode was used.
`COMM_FAILURE`	A communication failure occurred.
`DATA_CONVERSION`	Error while converting data.
`FREE_MEM`	Failed to free some memory.
`IMP_LIMIT`	Some implementation limit was exceeded.
`INITIALIZE`	The ORB initialization failed.

Table 10-4: Standard CORBA Exceptions (continued)

Exception Name	*Meaning*
`INTERNAL`	An internal ORB error occurred.
`INTF_REPOS`	Error attempting to access interface repository.
`INV_FLAG`	An invalid flag was given.
`INV_IDENT`	Invalid identifier syntax was encountered.
`INV_OBJREF`	An invalid object reference was encountered.
`INVALID_TRANSACTION`	An invalid transaction was used.
`MARSHAL`	An error occurred while marshalling method arguments or results.
`NO_IMPLEMENT`	The implementation for the method is not available.
`NO_MEMORY`	Failed to allocate dynamic memory needed to execute the request.
`NO_PERMISSION`	Not allowed to execute the method.
`NO_RESOURCES`	There were insufficient resources for the request.
`NO_RESPONSE`	No response received for request.
`OBJ_ADAPTER`	The object adapter encountered an error.
`OBJECT_NOT_EXIST`	The referenced object does not exist on the server.
`PERSIST_STORE`	An error occurred while accessing persistent storage.
`TRANSACTION_REQUIRED`	An operation requiring a transaction was called without one.
`TRANSACTION_ROLLEDBACK`	A transactional operation didn't complete because its transaction was rolled back.
`TRANSIENT`	A transient error occurred, but the method can be tried again.
`UNKNOWN`	An error occurred that the ORB could not interpret.

Mapping Exceptions to Java

Standard exceptions are mapped to exception classes in `org.omg.CORBA` that extend the `org.omg.CORBA.SystemException` class. User-defined exceptions are mapped to `public final` Java classes that extend `org.omg.CORBA.UserException`, which is derived directly from `java.lang.Exception`. Otherwise, the exception is mapped to Java the same way as a `struct`, as described earlier. Each data member is mapped to a `public` data member of the corresponding type, and a set of constructors are defined for the exception class.

Module Declarations

A module is a name-scoping construct in IDL. It is similar to a package in Java, or LISP or a namespace in C++. A module is declared with the `module` keyword, followed by an identifier for the module, and then the body of the module, enclosed in braces:

```
// IDL
module identifier { ... };
```

Modules can contain IDL interface definitions, constants, or user-defined types such as `typedefs`, `structs`, unions, and enumerations.

Mapping Modules to Java

Modules in IDL are mapped to packages in Java, and nested modules are mapped to subpackages, with the innermost module being mapped to the rightmost subpackage. Consider the following interfaces and modules defined in IDL:

```
// IDL
module util{
        interface MatrixOps { . . . };

        module dbase {
                interface Query { . . . };
        };
};
```

The generated Java code includes an interface named `MatrixOps`, starting with this `package` statement:

```
// Java
package util;
```

and another interface named `Query`, with this `package` statement:

```
// Java
package util.dbase;
```

Interface Declarations

An IDL interface is just a collection of data attributes and methods that define the semantics of the interface. Declaring an interface is another way to create a new data type in IDL, but unlike structs and unions, an interface can have both data members and methods that can be called on objects of its type. An interface is also a name-scoping construct, similar to a module. You can declare an IDL interface and simply include a set of constants you want associated with that interface name. In this case, you have to specify the interface scope in order to refer to the constants from within other scopes.

An interface consists of the following elements:

```
// IDL
interface identifier [: inheritance-spec] {
        interface-body
};
```

The interface identifier can be any valid IDL identifier. The body of the interface can contain any of the following constructs:

- A user-defined type (struct, union, typedef, enum)
- A constant declaration
- An interface-specific exception declaration
- Data attributes
- Methods or operations

We've already seen the syntax for the first three items in earlier sections of this IDL overview. They become part of an interface simply by being declared within the braces of the body of the interface. In the next few sections, we'll see how to define interface attributes and methods, and then we'll look at how inheritance of IDL interfaces works.

Attributes

Attributes are data members that belong to an interface. To readers familiar with JavaBeans, declaring an attribute on an interface is roughly analogous to adding a property to a JavaBeans component. An attribute in an IDL interface indicates that the interface provides some way to read and (in most cases) write the attribute value.

The syntax for declaring an attribute within an interface body is:

```
// IDL
[readonly] attribute type identifier [, identifier, ...];
```

The attribute is signified by the `attribute` keyword, followed by a type specification for the attribute and an identifier name. You can declare multiple attributes of the same type by providing their identifiers in a comma-delimited list after the type specifier:

```
// IDL
attribute short coord_x, coord_y, coord_z;
```

The type specifier can be any valid type, including IDL basic types, other interfaces, and user-defined types previously defined or declared in a `typedef`. For example:

```
// IDL
enum ErrorCode { BadValue, DimensionError, Overflow, Underflow };

interface AttrTest {
  struct coord {
    short x;
    short y;
  };
```

```
    attribute ErrorCode lastError;
    readonly attribute coord COG;
    attribute string name;
};
```

The optional readonly keyword can precede the attribute declaration. This indicates that the attribute can be read only externally and not directly written. This typically means that the value of this attribute is set only as a side effect of some other method(s). In our example, the COG attribute may represent the center-of-gravity of some geometric object, and we'll only want that to be recomputed as the result of other methods that change the geometry of the object.

Methods

>Methods (or operations, to use the IDL vernacular) provide a way for remote clients to interact with the objects defined by an interface. A method declaration in IDL is composed of an identifier for the method, the type of data returned by the method, and a list of parameters that the method accepts. An IDL method can also (optionally) be declared to use specific call semantics, to possibly raise certain exceptions during its execution, and to accept certain context variables from the client environment.

The syntax of a method declaration within an IDL interface is:

```
// IDL
[call-semantics] return-type identifier ([param, param, ...])
  [exception-clause] [context-clause];
```

The only required elements in a method declaration are the method identifier and the return type, so an example of the simplest form of method declaration is:

```
// IDL
boolean doSomething();
```

This method simply returns a boolean flag when it is complete. It doesn't accept any arguments, uses the default call semantics, raises no nonstandard exceptions, and accepts no context variables from the client environment.

The return type for an IDL method can be any valid type, including user-defined types such as structs and other interfaces. If a method doesn't return any data, the return type should be declared as void.

The identifier for a method is a valid IDL identifier. In IDL, two methods in the same interface cannot have the same identifier (i.e., there is no method overloading, as there is in C++ and Java).

Parameters

The parameters for a method on an interface are declared within the parentheses following the method identifier and are separated by commas. The syntax for an individual method parameter is:

```
arg-direction arg-type identifier
```

The identifier is any valid IDL identifier, and the parameter type is any valid IDL type, including user-defined types.

The direction specification indicates whether the parameter is passed into the server, returned from the server, or both. The direction specification can have one of three values: `in`, `out`, or `inout`. An parameter tagged as `in` is only passed from the client to the server object. An parameter tagged as `out` is not taken from the client, but its value is set by the server and returned if the method returns successfully. An `inout` parameter is passed in both directions; the data from the client is passed to the server, and the server may modify the data and have the updates returned back to the client if the method returns successfully.

Here's a modified method declaration for `doSomething()` that specifies some parameters:

```
boolean doSomething(in string whatToDo, inout string whatToDoItTo);
```

The first parameter tells the server object what to do, so it is input-only. The second parameter is the thing to be acted upon, so it is declared as `inout` to allow the modified object to be passed back to the client.

If a method raises an exception during its execution, the values of any `out` or `inout` parameters to the method are undefined. They may or may not have been modified by the method before the exception was raised, and execution was halted.

Exceptions

If a method on an interface can raise any exceptions during its execution, you have to declare this in IDL by adding a clause to the method declaration that lists all the exceptions that can be raised by the method. This is similar to the `throws` clause on Java methods. The syntax for the `raises` clause looks like:

```
// IDL
raises (exception-type, exception-type, ...)
```

Every exception you list in this clause has to be defined earlier in the IDL file.

Every method that you declare on an IDL interface can potentially throw one of the standard ORB exceptions we mentioned earlier (see Table 10-4). You cannot list these standard exceptions in the `raises` clause for your methods.

As an example, let's specify a `BadDirective` exception for our `doSomething()` method, which is raised if the client passes in a string directive the server object doesn't understand. We can modify the method declaration to look like the this:

```
// IDL
boolean doSomething(in string whatToDo, inout string whatToDoItTo)
        raises (BadDirective);
```

Again, we must have declared the `BadDirective` exception and any data it contains earlier in the IDL file.

Context values

IDL supports the concept of a client context, which can contain name/value pairs that describe the client's environment in some way. You might have an authenticated username stored in the client's context, for example. The name of a context value is a string, and its value is an Any object. The interface to the context is provided by the IDL Context interface, and a mapping of this interface must be provided in any language-specific binding of the CORBA standard.

You can add a context clause to your method declarations that indicates which client context variables should be propagated to the server when the method is invoked. The server object can then query these context variables during the execution of the method. The syntax for adding a context clause to your method declaration is:

```
// IDL
context (var-name, var-name, ...)
```

Each *var-name* is a string literal that names the context variable to be propagated to the server when the method is called.

Suppose that when we invoke our doSomething() method, we want to be able to log who is making the request. We can look for a username variable in the client context and assume it is the authenticated identity of the client. We can specify that this context variable should be included in the method call by adding a context clause to our method declaration:

```
// IDL
boolean doSomething(in string whatToDo, inout string whatToDoItTo)
        raises (BadDirective) context ("username");
```

A Java client might use this method like so:

```
// Java
// Get the context
Context ctx = ORB.get_default_context();

// Add a username to the context
Any username = new Any();
username.insert_string("JimF");
ctx.set_one_value("username", username);

// Call the remote method
obj.doSomething("anything", "entity");
```

Since we declared the doSomething() method to include the username context variable in its invocations, this variable appears in the server's context and can be queried during execution of the method.*

You might wonder when this context feature should be used, as opposed to just adding a method argument to the method declaration. I could have just as easily added another string argument to my declaration for the doSomething() method:

* Sun's implementation of the Java IDL binding (including its *idltojava* compiler) does not support context variables. The Context interface is available in the Java IDL API, but context clauses on IDL methods are not represented in the generated Java code, and no context data is transferred to the server.

```
boolean doSomething(in string whatToDo, inout string whatToDoItTo,
        in string username) raises BadDirective;
```

One argument for using context variables is to make things easier on the client when certain data for a method is optional. Rather than including an explicit argument and forcing the user to add a nil value of some kind to the method call (`null` in Java, for example), you can make the optional data a context variable, and the user can choose to set it or not. In most cases, though, you'll find that context variables are used rarely, if at all.

Call semantics

If you don't specify any call semantics at the start of your method declaration, the default semantics is "at-most-once." This means that if a method call returns with no exceptions, the method was called a single time on the server object. If an exception is raised, the method was called at most once (the exception occurred either before the method was invoked, or during execution of the method).

You can choose to use alternate call semantics for your method by including a call attribute at the start of your method declaration. In the current CORBA standard, only a single alternative, called "best-effort" semantics, is available. In this case, whether the method call returns successfully or not, there's no guarantee that the method was actually invoked on the server object. The difference between the default semantics and "best-effort" semantics is roughly equivalent to the difference between TCP and UDP IP network connections and their handling of data packets.

You specify best-effort call semantics by adding the keyword `oneway` to the start of your method declaration:

```
// IDL
oneway void tryToDoSomething(in whatToDo);
```

If you specify that a method is `oneway`, the return type of the method has to be `void`, and it can't have any `out` or `inout` arguments. The method is effectively called asynchronously, so the client can't synchronously receive return data from the server object.

Interface Inheritance

You can inherit attributes and methods from another IDL interface by deriving your interface from it. The syntax for declaring the inheritance of an interface in its header is:

```
interface identifier : parent-interface, parent-interface, ... {
```

The parent interfaces can be any pre-defined interfaces, in the same module as this interface or in different modules. If the parent interfaces are from other modules, you need to use the `::` scope specifier to identify them.

Method and attribute inheritance

A derived interface inherits all the attributes and methods from its parent interfaces. Although IDL allows for multiple inheritance, it's illegal to have two inherited attributes or methods with the same identifier. You also can't declare an attribute or method within your interface with the same name as an inherited attribute or method (i.e., you cannot *overload* a method or attribute). Say you have two interfaces declared as follows:

```
// IDL
interface A {
        boolean f(int float x);
};

interface B {
        void f();
};
```

You cannot define a new interface that derives from both these interfaces, since the definition of the method `f()` would be ambiguous. Note that, unlike C++ and Java, IDL only uses the name for the method as its unique identifier, and not the entire method signature. This rule is a result of IDL's multilanguage support, since some languages may be similarly limited.

Constant, type, and exception inheritance

A derived interface also inherits any constants, user-defined types, and exceptions defined in its parent interfaces. They can be referred to in the derived interface as if they had been defined within the interface. For example, say we define the following base interface:

```
// IDL
interface Server {
        exception ServiceInterrupted {};
        boolean doSomething(in string what) raises (ServiceInterrupted);
};
```

We can use the `ServiceInterrupted` exception defined within the `Server` interface in another interface by naming its scope:

```
// IDL
interface PrintServer {
        boolean printSomething(in string what)
                raises (Server::ServiceInterrupted);
};
```

Alternately, we can derive the `PrintServer` from the `Server` interface, and then the exception can be used as if it existed in the `PrintServer` scope:

```
// IDL
interface PrintServer : Server {
  boolean printSomething(in string what) raises (ServiceInterrupted);
};
```

It is legal to define a constant, type, or exception in a derived interface that uses the same name as one of these things in its parent interface. If you do this, though, you need to refer to them unambiguously in your interface declaration, using fully scoped names if necessary. If you declare your own ServiceInterrupted exception in the PrintServer interface, for example, you need to provide a scope for the exception in the raises clause, in order for the IDL compiler to know which version you're referring to:

```
// IDL
interface PrintServer : Server {
        exception ServiceInterrupted { string printerName; };
        boolean printSomething(in string what)
                raises (PrintServer::ServiceInterrupted);
```

If you don't, the IDL compiler throws back an error about ServiceInterrupted being ambiguous.

IDL early binding

It's important to realize that IDL does early binding of constants, user-defined types, and exceptions as it compiles your IDL. This means that the definition of a constant, type, or exception is bound to a particular reference within an interface as it's encountered in your IDL file, not after all definitions have been examined. Consider the following IDL definitions:

```
// IDL
struct Coord {
        short x;
        short y;
};

interface GeometricObj {
        attribute Coord cog;
};

interface GeometricObj3D : GeometricObj {
        struct Coord {
                short x;
                short y;
                short z;
        };
        attribute Coord cog3D;
};
```

The cog attribute in the GeometricObj interface is off the global Coord type (with x and y members only), since at the time the cog attribute is encountered in the IDL file, this is the binding definition for Coord. The GeometricObj3D interface inherits this attribute with this type. However, the cog3D attribute declared in the GeometricObj3D interface is of the GeometricObj3D::Coord type (with x, y, and z members), since at that point, the Coord struct within the GeometricObj3D scope has been defined and is the default reference of the relative Coord type used in the cog3D declaration.

Mapping Interfaces to Java

As you might expect, each interface you define in IDL is mapped to a public interface in Java. Helper and holder class are also generated for each interface; the names of these interfaces are generated using the identifier of the IDL interface, with Helper and Holder appended to it.

The Java interface extends the org.omg.CORBA.Object interface. Any inheritance specification you provide in your IDL interface is mapped directly to interface inheritance in Java, using extends clauses. So our earlier GeometricObj3D example that inherits from GeometricObj is mapped into a Java interface that begins:

```
// Java
public interface GeometricObj3D
    extends org.omg.CORBA.Object, GeometricObj { ...
```

Helper and holder classes

The helper class generated for an interface includes a static narrow() method that allows you to safely cast a CORBA Object reference to a reference of the interface type. If the Object isn't of the expected type, an org.omg.CORBA.BAD_PARAM exception is thrown. The helper class also includes other static methods that let you read or write objects of the interface type over I/O streams and insert/extract an object of this type from an Any value.

The holder class is used whenever the interface is used as the type for an out or inout method parameter. The holder class is responsible for marshalling the contents of the object to the server object for the method call (for inout arguments), and then unmarshalling the (possibly updated) return value. The holder class has a constructor defined that lets you wrap the holder around an existing instance of the original interface, and it has a public value member that lets you access the object argument both before and after the method call.

See Chapter 4 for more details on helper and holder classes.

Attributes

Each attribute you declare on the IDL interface is mapped to two accessor methods, with the same name as the attribute. So an attribute declared within an IDL interface as follows:

```
// IDL
attribute string name;
```

is mapped to these two methods on the corresponding Java interface:

```
// Java
String name();
void name(String n);
```

If you include the readonly tag in your IDL attribute declaration, the Java interface has only the read accessor method, not the update accessor.

Methods

Methods declared on your IDL interface are mapped one-to-one to methods on the Java interface. The return values and any in parameters are mapped directly to their corresponding types in Java. Any out or inout parameters in the IDL method are mapped to their holder classes in the Java method. This includes basic IDL types, which have their own holder classes defined for them in the standard Java mapping. So this IDL method:

```
// IDL
boolean setPrintServer(in PrintServer server,
         out PrintServer previousServer,
         out long requestsHandled);
```

is mapped to the following Java method on the corresponding interface:

```
// Java
boolean setPrintServer(PrintServer server,
         PrintServerHolder previousServer,
         IntHolder requestsHandled);
```

Note that the last argument is declared a `long` in IDL, which is mapped to `int` in Java, so the `IntHolder` class is used in the mapped Java method.

To use this method, we have to create holder objects for the output parameters, then check their values after the method call:

```
// Java
PrintServer newServer = . . .;
PrintServerHolder prevHolder = new PrintServerHolder();
IntHolder numReqHolder = new IntHolder();
xxx.setPrintServer(newServer, prevHolder, numReqHolder);
int numReq = numReqHolder.value;
PrintServer prevServer = prevHolder.value;
```

We don't need to initialize the contents of the holders, since they are being used for `out` parameters. If they were used for `inout` parameters, we'd either have to initialize their contents at construction time or set their `value` members directly.

If there is a `raises` clause on your IDL method declaration, it is mapped to an equivalent `throws` clause on the Java method. The context clause and call semantics (`oneway`) on an IDL method declaration affect only the implementation of the generated Java method, not its signature.

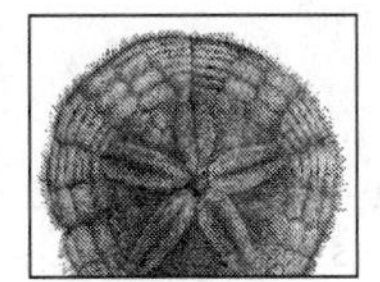

CHAPTER 11

CORBA Services Reference

The CORBA standard includes a rich set of object services. These services can be optionally offered by a CORBA provider as part of its CORBA-compliant environment. Most vendors include a Naming Service, since it is the principal means for finding CORBA objects. The other services, such as Security and Event Services, are not required by all users, so they are often provided as optional add-ons.

This quick reference for the CORBA services is just that: a quick reference, not a comprehensive one. While it is important for you to understand what the various CORBA services can offer, it is beyond the scope of this book to provide a complete reference for all 15 of them. I've provided a short overview of each service, along with a few of its particulars, such as its principal interfaces and other services that it depends upon. If any of the services seem like a viable solution for your needs in a CORBA environment, you can get full details on the specification for the services from the OMG (*CORBA Services: Common Object Services Specification*, published by the OMG and available at *www.omg.org*).

Generally speaking, each of the CORBA services defines a standard, ordered, explicit way of doing something. You may be able to do this activity in another way using only the core CORBA interfaces, but whatever technique you use will be nonstandard, ad hoc, and implicit. As an example, you might construct a means whereby your object is automatically notified of a change in another, possibly remote, object, just using standard CORBA constructs. The Event Service provides a standardized set of interfaces for defining these notification channels, so that outside agents can participate as well. When you are deciding between developing a custom approach or using a CORBA service, you should consider the level at which you need to depend on this service, your need for interoperability with other agents in this area, and the costs involved.

Naming Service

The Naming Service is the most commonly used service in CORBA, since it provides the principal way for clients to find objects on the network. Remote object references can be bound to names within the Naming Service, and clients can access these object references over the network by asking for them by name from the Naming Service. There are more details on the Naming Service available in Chapter 4, *Java IDL*.

The principal interface in the Naming Service is the `NamingContext`. It represents a directory or subdirectory of named objects. This interface can bind, look up, and unbind objects and subcontexts within the naming directory. The names of objects within a `NamingContext` are composed of `NameComponent` arrays. Browsing through the contents of a `NamingContext` can be done with a `BindingIterator`.

Security Service

The CORBA Security Service provides the tools you need to secure a distributed application. It supports the authentication of remote users of object services, access controls for key objects and services in the system, auditing functions, the ability to establish secure communications channels between clients and object services, and nonrepudiated events. Note that encryption functions (i.e., algorithms for encrypting data and generating digital signatures) are not included in the Security Service specification. The Security Service is a higher-level security framework that needs to use cryptography in its implementation, but this use is not spelled out in the specification. Implementors are free to use whatever lower-level cryptographic APIs suit their needs, as long as their use supports the higher-level specifications of the Security Service.

The Security Service framework layers security measures on top of the basic ORB object-to-object model defined in the core CORBA architecture. Security measures are taken on either end of a secure communication. Access control is defined down to the level of individual methods on objects, and access rights can be delegated by one authenticated object to another.

The `PrincipleAuthenticator` interface authenticates identities. A `Credentials` object is assigned to each user; it describes the user's security profile, including access rights, authenticated identities, etc. The `Current` object provides details about the security features in effect in the current execution context. There are also extensions to the `org.omg.CORBA.Object` interface, to support such actions as querying the `Credentials` of an `Object`.

Event Service

The Event Service provides a flexible framework for asynchronous interaction between distributed objects. The asynchronous method invocation facility provided by the Dynamic Invocation Interface is a very basic form of the services the Event Service provides. These kinds of asynchronous communications can be useful in situations where *notification*, rather than *interaction*, is needed. You may want your client to be notified when data in a dynamically updated database is modified, for example. The Event Service provides a framework for setting up these communications channels.

Agents engaged in event services are distinguished as event consumers or event suppliers. In both cases, the agents can engage either in push or pull event communications. These four cases are represented by the `PushConsumer`, `PullConsumer`, `PushSupplier`, and `PullSupplier` interfaces. Event communications take place over `EventChannel` objects, to which consumers and suppliers of events are connected.

CORBA Services

Persistent Object Service

This service provides a common framework for CORBA objects to interact with various underlying persistence engines (relational databases, object databases, etc.) for the purpose of either accessing the persistent state of other objects or storing their own state persistently. In a sense, the Persistent Object Service can be thought of as middleware between CORBA objects and database protocols being defined by the Object Data Management Group (ODMG).

Persistence can be managed at either the object level or the data-member level. Typically, an object is allowed to control its own persistent state, but, if necessary, a client of an object can control particular elements of the object's persistent state.

The definers of the Persistent Object Service seemed to have a penchant for acronyms. A persistent object is represented by the `PO` interface. Each `PO` has a `PID`, which is a unique identifier for its persistent data. Methods on a `PO` allow you to load and store its state to persistent storage. Internally, a `PO` uses the persistent object manager interface, `POM`. Interfaces to specific data storage services are provided by persistent data services, represented as `PDS` objects.

The Persistent Object Service service depends on both the Externalization Service, for converting objects into a format suitable for persistent storage media, and the Life Cycle Service, for creating, moving, and deleting objects.

Life Cycle Service

This service defines a standard protocol by which clients of distributed objects can cause the creation, copying, movement, and deletion of remote objects. The service is defined around the concept of object *factories*, which are responsible for creating objects of specific types.

All objects participating in the Life Cycle Service implement the `LifeCycleObject` interface. There is no specific interface defined for object factories, but they can be located using the `FactoryFinder` interface.

Some of the interfaces in this service reference Naming Service interfaces. Also, when dealing with connected graphs of objects, the Relationship Service structures are referenced.

Concurrency Control Service

The Concurrency Control Service defines a framework for managing concurrent access to remote objects from multiple clients. It is analogous to the multithreading support present in some programming languages, such as C++ and Java, but in a distributed context. The Concurrency Control Service provides facilities for interfacing with the Transaction Service to allow transactional clients to participate in concurrent access to resources from within transaction contexts.

The Concurrency Control Service uses a model based on locks that are acquired by clients for defined resources. Locks can be of different types (read, write, etc.), and different locking models can be specified, such as multiple-possession, two-phase locks, etc. Clients that attempt to acquire a lock on a resource and are refused because of conflicts with existing locks are queued on a first-come, first-serve basis.

Resources are implicitly represented by the `LockSet` interface, which request and relinquish locks on resources. The `TransactionalLockSet` is an equivalent interface for transactional clients. Lock sets are created using the `LockSetFactory` interface.

The transaction-related interfaces in this service depend on Transaction Service interfaces.

Externalization Service

This service defines the means for converting objects into a form suitable for export over general media, such as network streams or disk storage, and then reconstituting this data back into object references, potentially in a different ORB and/or process. The service allows for pluggable data formats for externalized objects, but a standard serialized format for objects is provided, to ensure that a baseline protocol can be shared among users of the service.

The Externalization Service uses a `Stream` object for externalizing and internalizing objects. A `StreamFactory` creates `Stream` objects. Specific sources or destinations for streams can be supported by subclasses of the `StreamFactory` (e.g., `FileStreamFactory`). Objects that are to be externalized must extend the `Streamable` interface.

This service uses the Life Cycle Service to create and destroy `Stream` and `StreamFactory` objects. The Relationship Service manages the externalization of graphs of related objects.

Relationship Service

This service allows for the explicit definition of relationships among objects. Relationships are defined in terms of type, roles within the relationship, and the cardinality of each role. An object fulfills a role when it participates in a relationship. You can define an agent/proxy relationship, for example, in which a single object fulfills the agent role and multiple objects serve as proxies for that agent.

The `Relationship` and `Role` interfaces are at the heart of the service. `RelationshipFactory` and `RoleFactory` objects create `Relationship` and `Role` objects, respectively. A `RelationshipIterator` can iterate through the relationships a given object plays roles in. In addition to these generic relationship interfaces, the service also provides several specific relationship types, in their own modules. Object graphs can be created using the interfaces in the `CosGraphs` module, containment relationships can be created using the `CosContainment` module, and reference relationships are defined using the `CosReference` module.

Transaction Service

Transactions are best defined using the tried-and-true ACID characteristics, which are familiar to database researchers. ACID refers to units of work that are:

Atomic
: Any and all actions carried out as part of the transaction are committed when the transaction is committed or undone/cancelled if the transaction is cancelled (rolled back).

Consistent
: The actions within a transaction produce results that are consistent.

Isolated
: Transactions do not see each other's effects until they are committed. If a transaction is rolled back, its effects are not seen by other contexts.

Durable
: If a transaction completes successfully, its effects are made permanent.

The Transaction Service defines interfaces that allow distributed objects to create and engage in transactional interactions. A transactional interaction can involve a series of remote method calls. If a significant error is encountered along the way, the transaction can be rolled back, and the effects of all previous method calls are undone, as if the transaction never started in the first place. When a transactional client starts a transaction and then makes remote method calls, its transaction context is propagated along with the requests. Only transactional objects (i.e., objects whose internal actions and side effects should be undone by a rollback of the transaction and who participate in the Transaction Service protocol) heed the transaction context information.

An important item to note about the Transaction Service, and about transaction APIs in general, is that they principally provide a framework for the notification and management of transaction boundaries, but no facilities to ease the rollback of transactions. The application objects still need to do the hard work of undoing any work that was done during a transaction if it gets rolled back. In other words, the Transaction Service tells you when to do it, but not how.

Transactions are usually managed using the `Current` interface, which starts and ends transactions. Transactions can be directly manipulated using the `Control` interface, which contains a `Terminator` that ends the transaction with either a commit or rollback, and a `Coordinator` that checks for relationships between transactions. `Resource` objects can be registered as participating in transactions, which allows them to be notified of transaction boundaries (commit, rollback).

The Transaction Service depends on both the Concurrency Control Service, for its locking services, and the Persistent Object Service, to support the durability (persistence) of transaction effects on objects.

Query Service

The Query Service provides a general object query mechanism for distributed objects. With this service, collections of objects can be searched to generate subcollections, or subsets of objects within a collection can be deleted or updated through a query. The facilities defined in the Query Service can be mapped to, but are not limited to, persistent storage facilities, such as relational or object databases.

Collections of objects are represented by `Collection` objects, which are created using a `CollectionFactory`. You iterate through a `Collection` of objects using an `Iterator`. `QueryEvaluator` objects issue a `Query` against a given `Collection`. The result of evaluating a `Query` can be of any type, but typically it is a `Collection` of some kind. A `QueryManager` is a type of `QueryEvaluator` that allows you to create queries.

Licensing Service

The Licensing Service is a protocol for controlled access to objects and services under a licensing model. Conceptually, you can think of it as an extension of the Security Service, with some additional access semantics having to do with consumable and expirable access. A license gives a user certain limited rights to use a particular remote object or set of objects.

In the License Service model, a client makes a request for a licensed service from a service provider, giving the provider some proof of ownership of a license. The provider then turns to a license manager to acquire a license service, which it uses to verify the existence of a license and check its policy against the proposed usage. The producer can then ask to be notified of license expiration during its use, or it can poll the license service for changes in the license state.

The `LicenseServiceManager` provides access to license services specific to certain producers. The `ProducerSpecificLicenseService` provides a producer with the methods needed to check on license validity, and start and end license usage sessions.

The License Service depends on the Security Service for license verification and secure communications and on the Event Service for asynchonous notification of license events to producers. Some implementations may also use the Relationship, Property, and Query Services.

Property Service

This service defines name/value pairs that can be assigned to objects, without being explicitly defined or required by their IDL interfaces. Properties can represent any application-specific attributes that can tag objects for various purposes.

The Property Service provides interfaces for defining, initializing, and iterating through sets of properties, but it does not specify how properties are associated with objects, as this is an implementation detail.

A set of properties is represented by the `PropertySet` interface, which allows you to create, modify, or delete properties in the set. A property is represented as a string name and an `Any` value. A subclass of `PropertySet`, `PropertySetDef`, allows you to query for metadata about the properties (e.g., whether each is read/write or read-only). A `PropertiesIterator` can be used to iterate through the contents of a set, and a `PropertySetFactory` allows you to create new `PropertySet` objects.

Time Service

This service gives programs the ability to acquire an accurate value for the current time and an estimate of the error of the value provided. The Time Service uses a Universal Time Coordinated time representation to report time values. This representation uses time intervals of 100 nanoseconds, starting on midnight, October 15, 1582. The time reported is always relative to the Greenwich Mean Time (GMT).

The Time Service also provides facilities for generating time-based events, using timers and alarms, and for the ordering and linear positioning of events in time.

An implementation of the Time Service is responsible for communicating with an accurate time source, such as a Cesium clock or radio time broadcasts, for determining its time and error estimates.

Time is reported from a `TimeService` object in the form of `UTO` objects, which stand for universal time objects. Time intervals are given in the form of `TIO` objects, or time interval objects. A timer event is represented by a `TimerEventT` structure that includes the time the event triggered and any data that was specified to be delivered with the event. A timer event is indirectly created through the `TimerEventService` by registering a consumer for the event, which returns a `TimerEventHandler` object that can set the trigger time for the event, set the data to be delivered with the event, or cancel the event.

The timer event portion of the Time Service depends on an Event Service being available.

Trading Service

This service is analogous to a market-trading context, in which agents make buy offers for items they want (bids) and sell offers for items that they have (asks), and the trading system is responsible for matching the bids and asks to execute trades. In the Trading Service, objects describe the services that they can offer to the system, and clients issue a description of the desired properties of an object. The Trading Service then matches object services with clients seeking these services.

Buyers, or importers, of services use a `Lookup` interface to advertise their needs, while sellers, or exporters, of services use a `Register` interface to advertise the properties of their services. If an importer receives multiple hits on a query issued through the `Lookup` interface, it is given an `OfferIterator` to iterate through the offers for any that it wants to accept. An `Admin` interface queries for all outstanding offers and queries and controls parameters related to how the two are matched.

Collection Service

The Collection Service supports the grouping of objects into various types of collections, such as sets, queues, and sequences. The service also includes representations for iterators of these collections and for operations to be performed to elements of a collection.

The `Collection` interface is the root of a large family of subclasses that define specific types of collections, such as `Set`, `Heap`, `Stack`, `Queue`, `SortedSet`, etc. There are also factory classes for these that allow you to create collections of each type. Similarly, the `Iterator` interface is the root of the hierarchy of iterator types, such as `EqualityIterator` and `SequentialIterator`. The `Operations` interface is provided as a base class for any operation a user may perform on a collection.

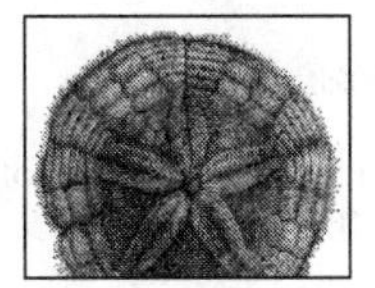

CHAPTER 12

Java IDL Tools

idltojava — Java 2 SDK 1.2 and later

The Java IDL Compiler

Synopsis

```
idltojava [ options ] IDLfiles
```

Description

The *idltojava* compiler generates Java source files from IDL interface, module, and type descriptions. The compiler ostensibly follows the standard IDL Java mapping defined by the OMG. Note that according to the standard mapping, a single IDL construct may result in several Java constructs being generated. A single IDL interface, for example, generates five Java source files.

The *idltojava* compiler performs a preprocessing stage during compilation, much like a C or C++ compiler. The preprocessor accepts #define, #undefine, #include, and #pragma directives for preprocessing. Some of the compiler options are related to this preprocessing stage. The #pragma directives that *idltojava* accepts are:

#pragma prefix *repos_prefix*
: Prepend the given prefix name to any repository names. Note that Java IDL does not support the CORBA Interface Repository, so the usefulness of this option is questionable.

#pragma javaPackage *rootPackage*
: Place all packages generated from the IDL file within the given root package.

Note that #pragma directives must appear at the beginning of the IDL file.

Options

-D*symbol*=*value*
: Define the named symbol with the given value during preprocessing of the IDL file. This command, for example:

```
% idltojava -DmaxArray=10 myFile.idl
```

causes the preprocessor to have the symbol maxArray defined as specified during preprocessing of the IDL file *myFile.idl.*

-f*flag-name*
-fno-*flag-name*

This option turns on and off execution flags for the compiler. The option with just the flag name turns on the named flag, and the option with no- followed by the flag name turns off the named flag. There is no space after the -f in both cases.

The possible flags are listed in the following table:

Flag name	*Default*	*Description*
caseless	off	Compile the IDL without considering case when comparing identifiers.
client	on	Generate client-side Java stubs for the IDL entities encountered.
cpp	on	Run a C/C++ preprocessor over the IDL files before compilation. An error is reported and compilation stops if the preprocessor is not found. Affected by the CPP and CPPARGS environment variables described in the next section, or uses the defaults if none given.
list-flags	off	Print the value of all the flags used for compilation.
list-options	off	Print a list of the command-line options used for compilation.
map-included-files	off	Generate Java code for any IDL files included by #include directives.
portable	on	Generate portable stub and skeleton Java classes (e.g., code that uses the CORBA portability layer provided in the org.omg.CORBA.portable package).
server	on	Generate server-side Java skeletons for the IDL entities encountered.
tie	off	Generate xxxTie and xxxOperations classes for each server skeleton, thus making them eligible for use in delegation-based operation.
verbose	off	Print extensive messages on the compilation procedure.
version	off	Print the version number and timestamp for the *idltojava* compiler in use.
write-files	on	Write the generated Java source files to the destination directory. If this flag is off, the compiler is acting as simply an IDL syntax checker.

-I*path* The given path should be used to search for files specified in #include directives found in the IDL file. There is no space between the -I and the path.

-j *path* The given path should be used as the destination for the generated Java source files. If a Java class is mapped to a Java package, the compiler creates subdirectories in the given destination automatically to store the Java files. There is a space between the -j and the path.

-U*symbol* The named symbol should be undefined when the compiler starts preprocessing the IDL files. There is no space between the -U and the symbol name.

Environment

CPP The full path to a C/C++ pre-processor to use when the cpp flag is on during compilation. If this variable is not set in the environment, the *idltojava* compiler uses a default of */usr/ccs/lib/cpp* on Solaris and the Microsoft Visual C++ preprocessor on Windows systems.

CPPARGS A list of arguments to be passed to the preprocessor.

Bugs

As of this writing, Sun still has not released a final version of *idltojava* to correspond to the final Java IDL API included in the Java SDK 1.2. The current available version is the early-access version, which has the following notable bugs:

- Adjacent string literals cause a syntax error, instead of being concatenated as defined in the IDL specification.
- A special modifier method, accepting a discriminator value, is not generated in the Java code for IDL unions with multicase branches.
- Any context clauses on IDL method declarations are ignored silently.

tnameserv — Java 2 SDK 1.2 and later

The Java IDL Naming Service Daemon

Synopsis

```
tnameserv [ options ]
```

Description

The *tnameserv* daemon is the CORBA Naming Service daemon provided with Java IDL. The Naming Service allows remote CORBA objects to be bound to names with the naming directory of the service. Remote clients can connect to the Naming Service through standard CORBA APIs and ask for references to these objects by name or browse through the objects bound to names in the directory.

The daemon should be run in the background. The *tnameserv* implementation of the Naming Service is a nonpersistent one (i.e., bindings created and stored in the naming context are only valid during the lifetime of the *tnameserv* daemon).

Options

-ORBInitialPort *portnum*

Listen to the specified port for client requests on the Naming Service. The default port is 900. This option corresponds to the Java property org.omg.CORBA.ORBInitialPort.

PART III

API Quick Reference

Part III is the real heart of this book: quick-reference material for the Java Enterprise APIs. Please read the following section, "How To Use This Quick Reference," to learn how to get the most out of this material.

Chapter 13, *The java.rmi Package*
Chapter 14, *The java.rmi.activation Package*
Chapter 15, *The java.rmi.dgc Package*
Chapter 16, *The java.rmi.registry Package*
Chapter 17, *The java.rmi.server Package*
Chapter 18, *The java.sql Package*
Chapter 19, *The javax.ejb Package*
Chapter 20, *The javax.ejb.deployment Package*
Chapter 21, *The javax.jms Package*
Chapter 22, *The javax.naming Package*
Chapter 23, *The javax.naming.directory Package*
Chapter 24, *The javax.naming.spi Package*
Chapter 25, *The javax.servlet Package*
Chapter 26, *The javax.servlet.http Package*
Chapter 27, *The javax.sql Package*
Chapter 28, *The javax.transaction Package*
Chapter 29, *The javax.transaction.xa Package*
Chapter 30, *The org.omg.CORBA Package*
Chapter 31, *The org.omg.CORBA.DynAnyPackage Package*
Chapter 32, *The org.omg.CORBA.ORBPackage Package*
Chapter 33, *The org.omg.CORBA.portable Package*
Chapter 34, *The org.omg.CORBA.TypeCodePackage Package*
Chapter 35, *The org.omg.CosNaming Package*
Chapter 36, *The org.omg.CosNaming.NamingContextPackage Package*
Chapter 37, *Class, Method, and Field Index*

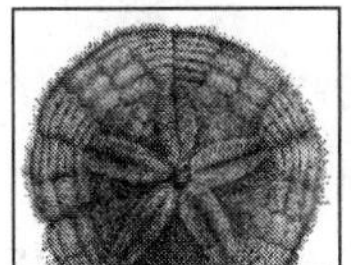

How to Use This Quick Reference

The quick-reference section that follows packs a lot of information into a small space. This introduction explains how to get the most out of that information. It describes how the quick reference is organized and how to read the individual entries.

Finding a Quick-Reference Entry

The quick reference is organized into chapters, one per package. Each chapter begins with an overview of the package and includes a hierarchy diagram for the classes and interfaces in the package. Following this overview are quick-reference entries for all the classes and interfaces in the package.

Entries are organized alphabetically by class *and* package name, so that related classes are grouped near each other. Thus, in order to find an entry for a particular class, you must also know the name of the package that contains that class. Usually, the package name is obvious from the context, and you should have no trouble looking up the quick-reference entry you want. Use the chapter tabs and the "dictionary-style" headers, which are located at the upper outside corner of each page, to help you find packages and classes.

Occasionally, you may need to look up a class for which you do not already know the package. In this case, refer to Chapter 37, *Class, Method, and Field Index*. This index allows you to look up a class by class name and find the package it is part of. (The index also allows you to look up a method or field name and find the class or classes define it.)

Reading a Quick-Reference Entry

Each quick-reference entry contains quite a bit of information. The sections that follow describe the structure of a quick-reference entry, explaining what information is available, where it is found, and what it means. While reading the following descriptions, you will find it helpful to flip through the reference section itself to find examples of the features being described.

Class Name, Package Name, Availability, and Flags

Each quick-reference entry begins with a four-part title that specifies the name, package, and availability of the class, and may also specify various additional flags that describe the class. The class name appears in bold at the upper left of the title. The package name appears, in smaller print, in the lower- left, below the class name.

The upper-right portion of the title indicates the availability of the class; it specifies the earliest release that contained the class. If a class was introduced in Java 1.1, for example, this portion of the title reads "Java 1.1". If the class was introduced in Version 1.2 of the Java 2 platform, the availability reads "Java 1.2," for simplicity's sake. If the class is part of a standard extension, this portion of the title specifies the name (or acronym) of the standard extension and the earliest version in which the class appeared. For example, the availability might read "Servlets 2.0" or "JNDI 1.1." The availability section of the title is also indicates whether a class has been deprecated, and, if so, in what release. For example, it might read "Java 1.1; Deprecated in Java 1.2."

In the lower-right corner of the title you may find a list of flags that describe the class. The possible flags and their meanings are as follows:

checked
: The class is a checked exception, which means that it extends java.lang.Exception, but not java.lang.RuntimeException. In other words, it must be declared in the throws clause of any method that may throw it.

cloneable
: The class, or a superclass, implements java.lang.Cloneable.

collection
: The class, or a superclass, implements java.util.Collection or java.util.Map.

comparable
: The class, or a superclass, implements java.lang.Comparable.

error
: The class extends java.lang.Error.

event
: The class extends java.util.EventObject.

event adapter
: The class, or a superclass, implements java.util.EventListener, and the class name ends with "Adapter."

event listener
: The class, or a superclass, implements java.util.EventListener.

layout manager
: The class, or a superclass, implements java.awt.LayoutManager.

PJ1.1
: The class or interface is part of the Personal Java 1.1 platform.

PJ1.1(mod)
: The class or interface is supported, in modified form, by the Personal Java 1.1 platform.

PJ1.1(opt)
: The class or interface is an optional part of the Personal Java 1.1 platform. Support for the class is implementation-dependent.

remote
: The class, or a superclass, implements java.rmi.Remote.

runnable
: The class, or a superclass, implements java.lang.Runnable.

serializable
: The class, or a superclass, implements java.io.Serializable and may be serialized.

unchecked
: The class is an unchecked exception, which means it extends java.lang.RuntimeException and, therefore, does not need to be declared in the throws clause of a method that may throw it.

Description

The title of each quick-reference entry is followed by a short description of the most important features of the class or interface. This description may be anywhere from a couple of sentences to several paragraphs long.

Synopsis

The most important part of every quick-reference entry is the *class synopsis*, which follows the title and description. The synopsis for a class looks a lot like the source code for the class, except that the method bodies are omitted, and some additional annotations are added. If you know Java syntax, you can read the class synopsis.

The first line of the synopsis contains information about the class itself. It begins with a list of class modifiers, such as public, abstract, and final. These modifiers are followed by the class or interface keyword and then by the name of the class. The class name may be followed by an extends clause that specifies the superclass and an implements clause that specifies any interfaces the class implements.

The class definition line is followed by a list of the fields and methods the class defines. Once again, if you understand basic Java syntax, you should have no trouble making sense of these lines. The listing for each member includes the modifiers, type, and name of the member. For methods, the synopsis also includes the type and name of each method parameter and an optional throws clause that lists the exceptions the method can throw. The member names are in boldface, so that it is easy to scan the list of members looking for the one you want. The names of method parameters are in italics to indicate that they are not to be used literally. The member listings are printed on alternating gray and white backgrounds to keep them visually separate.

Member availability and flags

Each member listing is a single line that defines the API for that member. These listings use Java syntax, so their meaning is immediately clear to any Java programmer. There is some auxiliary information associated with each member synopsis, however, that requires explanation.

Recall that each quick-reference entry begins with a title section that includes the release in which the class was first defined. When a member is introduced into a class after the initial release of the class, the version in which the member was introduced appears, in small print, to the left of the member synopsis. For example, if a class was first introduced in Java 1.1, but had a new method added in Version 1.2 of Java 2, the title contains the string "Java 1.1," and the listing for the new member is preceded by the number "1.2." Furthermore, if a member has been deprecated, that fact is indicated with a hash mark (#) to the left of the member synopsis.

The area to the right of the member synopsis displays a variety of flags that provide additional information about the member. Some of these flags indicate additional specification details that do not appear in the member API itself. Other flags contain implementation-specific information. This information can be quite useful in understanding the class and in debugging your code, but be aware that it may differ between implementations. The implementation-specific flags displayed in this book are based on Sun's implementation of Java for Microsoft Windows.

The following flags may be displayed to the right of a member synopsis:

native
: An implementation-specific flag that indicates that a method is implemented in native code. Although native is a Java keyword and can appear in method signatures, it is part of the method implementation, not part of its specification. Therefore, this information is included with the member flags, rather than as part of the member listing. This flag is useful as a hint about the expected performance of a method.

synchronized
: An implementation-specific flag that indicates a method implementation is declared synchronized, meaning that it obtains a lock on the object or class before executing. Like the native keyword, the synchronized keyword is part of the method implementation, not part of the specification, so it appears as a

flag, not in the method synopsis itself. This flag is a useful hint that the method is probably implemented in a thread-safe manner.

Whether or not a method is thread-safe is part of the method specification, and this information *should* appear (although it often does not) in the method documentation. There are a number of different ways to make a method thread-safe, however, and declaring the method with the synchronized keyword is only one possible implementation. In other words, a method that does not bear the synchronized flag can still be thread-safe.

Overrides:
Indicates that a method overrides a method in one of its superclasses. The flag is followed by the name of the superclass that the method overrides. This is a specification detail, not an implementation detail. As we'll see in the next section, overriding methods are usually grouped together in their own section of the class synopsis. The Overrides: flag is used only when an overriding method is not grouped in that way.

Implements:
Indicates that a method implements a method in an interface. The flag is followed by the name of the interface that is implemented. This is a specification detail, not an implementation detail. As we'll see in the next section, methods that implement an interface are usually grouped into a special section of the class synopsis. The Implements: flag is used only for methods that are not grouped in this way.

empty
Indicates that the implementation of the method has an empty body. This can be a hint to the programmer that the method may need to be overridden in a subclass.

constant
An implementation flag that indicates a method has a trivial implementation. Only methods with a void return type can be truly empty. Any method declared to return a value must have at least a return statement. The "constant" flag indicates the method implementation is empty except for a return statement that returns a constant value. Such a method might have a body like return null; or return false;. Like the "empty" flag, this flag indicates that a method may need to be overridden.

default:
This flag is used with property accessor methods that read the value of a property (i.e., methods whose names begins with "get" and take no arguments). The flag is followed by the default value of the property. Strictly speaking, default property values are a specification detail. In practice, however, these defaults are not always documented, and care should be taken, because the default values may change between implementations.

Not all property accessors have a "default:" flag. A default value is determined by dynamically loading the class in question, instantiating it using a no-argument constructor, and then calling the method to find what it returns. This technique can be used only on classes that can be dynamically loaded and instantiated and that have no-argument constructors, so default values are shown for those classes only. Furthermore, note that when a class is instantiated using a different constructor, the default values for its properties may be different.

bound
: This flag is used with property accessor methods for bound properties of JavaBeans components. The presence of this flag means that calling the method generates a `java.beans.PropertyChangeEvent`. This is a specification detail, but it is sometimes not documented. Information about bound properties is obtained from the `BeanInfo` object for the class.

constrained
: Indicates that a JavaBeans component property is constrained. In other words, the method may throw a `java.beans.PropertyVetoException`. This is a specification detail, not an implementation detail.

expert
: Indicates that the `BeanInfo` object for this class specifies this method is intended for use by experts only. This hint is intended for visual programming tools, but users of this book may find the hint useful as well.

hidden
: Indicates that the `BeanInfo` object for this class specifies this method is for internal use only. This is a hint that visual programming tools should hide the property or event from the programmer. This book does not hide these methods, of course, but this flag indicates you should probably avoid using the method.

preferred
: Indicates that the `BeanInfo` object for this class specifies that this method is an accessor for a default or preferred property or event. This is a hint to visual programming tools to display the property or event in a prominent way, and it may also be a useful hint to readers of this book.

=
: For `static final` fields, this flag is followed by the constant value of the field. Only constants of primitive and `String` types and constants with the value `null` are displayed. Some constant values are specification details, while others are implementation details. The reason that symbolic constants are defined, however, is so you can write code that does not rely directly upon the constant value. Use this flag to help you understand the class, but do not rely upon the constant values in your own programs.

Functional grouping of members

Within a class synopsis, the members are not listed in strict alphabetical order. Instead, they are broken into functional groups and listed alphabetically within each group. Constructors, methods, fields, and inner classes are listed separately. Instance methods are kept separate from static (class) methods. Constants are separated from nonconstant fields; public members are listed separately from protected members. Grouping members by category breaks a class down into smaller, more comprehensible segments, making the class easier to understand. This grouping also makes it easier for you to find a desired member.

Functional groups are separated from each other in a class synopsis with Java comments, such as "// Public Constructors", "// Inner Classes", and "// Methods Implementing Servlet". The various functional categories are as follows (in the order in which they appear in a class synopsis):

Constructors
: Displays the constructors for the class. Public constructors and protected constructors are displayed separately in subgroupings. If a class defines no constructor at all, the Java compiler adds a default no-argument constructor that is displayed here. If a class defines only private constructors, it cannot be instantiated, and a special, empty grouping entitled "No Constructor" indicates this fact. Constructors are listed first because the first thing you do with most classes is instantiate them by calling a constructor.

Constants
: Displays all constants (i.e., fields that are declared static and final) defined by the class. Public and protected constants are displayed in separate subgroups. Constants are listed here, near the top of the class synopsis, because constant values are often used throughout the class as legal values for method parameters and return values.

Inner Classes
: Groups all inner classes and interfaces defined by the class or interface. For each inner class, there is a single-line synopsis. Each inner class also has its own quick-reference entry that includes a full class synopsis for the inner class. Like constants, inner classes are listed near the top of the class synopsis because they are often used by other members of the class.

Static Methods
: Lists the static methods (class methods) of the class, broken down into subgroups for public static methods and protected static methods.

Event Listener Registration Methods
: Lists the public instance methods that register and deregister event listener objects with the class. The names of these methods begin with the words "add" and "remove" and end in "Listener." These methods are always passed a java.util.EventListener object, and are typically defined in pairs, so the pairs are listed together. The methods are listed alphabetically by event name, rather than by method name.

Public Instance Methods
: Contains all public instance methods that are not grouped elsewhere.

Implementing Methods
: Groups the methods that implement the same interface. There is one subgroup for each interface implemented by the class. Methods defined by the same interface are almost always related to each other, so this is a useful functional grouping of methods.

Overriding Methods
: Groups the methods that override methods of a superclass broken into subgroups by superclass. This is typically a useful grouping, because it helps to make it clear how a class modifies the default behavior of its superclasses. In

practice, it is also often true that methods that override the same superclass are functionally related to each other.

Protected Instance Methods
Contains all protected instance methods that are not grouped elsewhere.

Fields
Lists all nonconstant fields of the class, breaking them down into subgroups for public and protected static fields, and public and protected instance fields. Many classes do not define any publicly accessible fields. For those that do, many object-oriented programmers prefer not to use those fields directly, but instead to use accessor methods when such methods are available.

Deprecated Members
Deprecated methods and deprecated fields are grouped at the very bottom of the class synopsis. Use of these members is strongly discouraged.

Class Hierarchy

For any class or interface that has a nontrivial class hierarchy, the class synopsis is followed by a "Hierarchy" section. This section lists all superclasses of the class, as well as any interfaces implemented by those superclasses. It may also list any interfaces extended by an interface. In the hierarchy listing, arrows indicate superclass to subclass relationships, while the interfaces implemented by a class follow the class name in parentheses. For example, the following hierarchy indicates that `javax.servlet.ServletException` extends `Exception`, which extends `Throwable` (which implements `Serializable`), which extends `Object`:

```
Object→Throwable(Serializable)→Exception→ServletException
```

If a class has subclasses, the "Hierarchy" section is followed by a "Subclasses" section that lists those subclasses. If an interface has implementations, the "Hierarchy" section is followed by an "Implementations" section that lists those implementations. While the "Hierarchy" section shows ancestors of the class, the "Subclasses" or "Implementations" section shows descendants.

Cross References

The class hierarchy section of a quick-reference entry is followed by a number of optional "cross reference" sections that indicate other, related classes and methods that may be of interest. These sections are:

Passed To
This section lists all methods and constructors that are passed an object of this type as an argument. This is useful when you have an object of a given type and want to figure out what you can do with it.

Returned By
This section lists all methods (but not constructors) that return an object of this type. This is useful when you know that you want to work with an object of this type, but don't know how to obtain one.

Thrown By

For checked exception classes, this section lists all methods and constructors that throw exceptions of this type. This material helps you figure out when a given exception or error may be thrown. Note, however, that this section is based on the exception types listed in the throws clauses of methods and constructors. Subclasses of RuntimeException and Error do not have to be listed in throws clauses, so it is not possible to generate a complete cross reference of methods that throw these types of unchecked exceptions.

Type Of

This section lists all of the fields and constants that are of this type, which can help you figure out how to obtain an object of this type.

A Note About Class Names

Throughout the quick reference, you'll notice that classes are sometimes referred to by class name alone and at other times referred to by class name and package name. If package names were always used, the class synopses would become long and hard to read. On the other hand, if package names were never used, it would sometimes be difficult to know what class was being referred to. The rules for including or omitting the package name are complex. They can be summarized approximately as follows, however:

- If the class name alone is ambiguous, the package name is always used.
- If the class is part of java.lang or java.io, the package name is omitted.
- If the class being referred to is part of the current package (and has a quick-ref entry in the current chapter), the package name is omitted. The package name is also omitted if the class being referred to is part of a package that contains the current package. And it is sometimes omitted if the class being referred to is part of a subpackage of the current package.

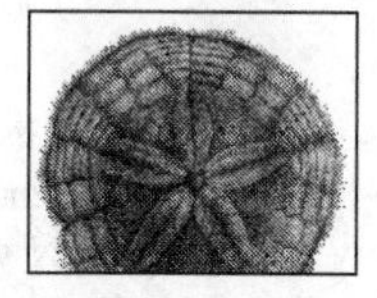

CHAPTER 13

The java.rmi Package

The java.rmi package is the main RMI package; it contains the principle objects used in RMI clients and servers. Figure 13-1 shows the class hierarchy for this package.

The Remote interface and the Naming class define and locate RMI objects over the network. The RMISecurityManager class provides additional security semantics required for RMI interactions. The MarshalledObject class is used during remote method calls for certain method arguments. In addition, this core package contains a number of basic RMI exception types used during remote object lookups and remote method calls.

AccessException — Java 1.1

java.rmi — *serializable checked PJ1.1(opt)*

This subclass of RemoteException is thrown when you attempt to perform an improper operation on a Naming or Registry object. A registry allows only local requests to bind, rebind, or unbind objects, so an attempt to call one of these methods on a remote registry results in an AccessException being thrown.

```
public class AccessException extends RemoteException {
// Public Constructors
   public AccessException(String s);
   public AccessException(String s, Exception ex);
}
```

Hierarchy: Object→ Throwable(Serializable)→ Exception→ IOException→ RemoteException→ AccessException

Thrown By: java.rmi.registry.Registry.{bind(), list(), lookup(), rebind(), unbind()}

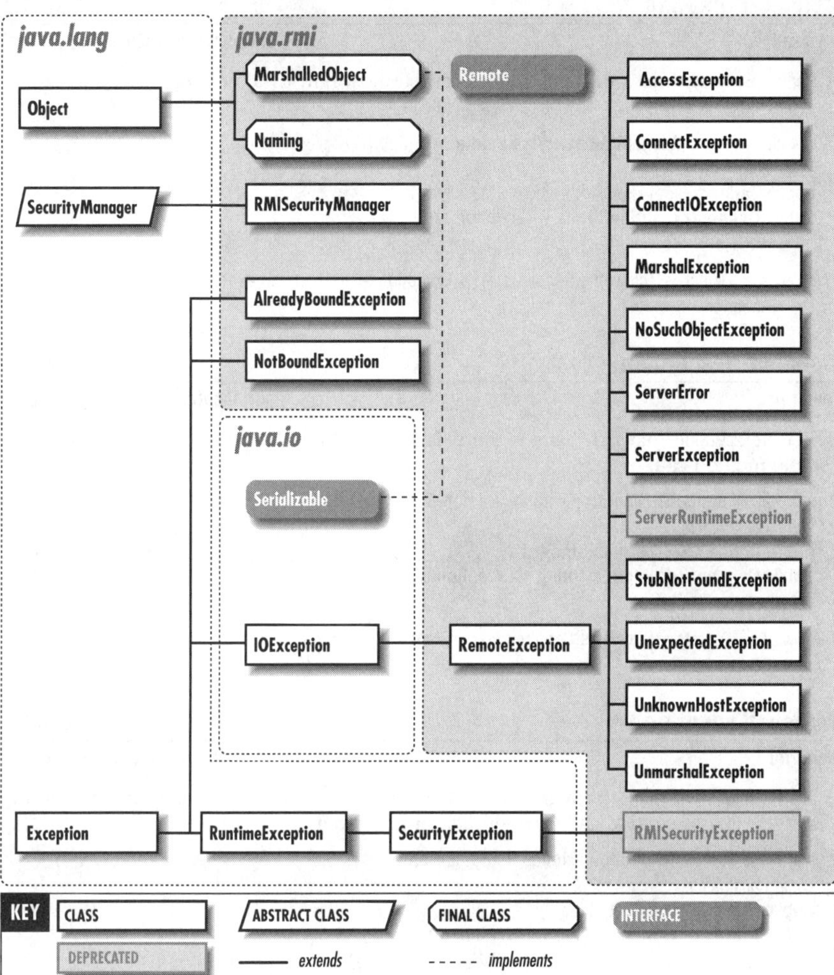

Figure 13-1: The java.rmi package

AlreadyBoundException — Java 1.1

java.rmi — *serializable checked PJ1.1(opt)*

An exception that's thrown when an attempt is made to bind an object to a name that is already bound.

```
public class AlreadyBoundException extends Exception {
// Public Constructors
    public AlreadyBoundException();
    public AlreadyBoundException(String s);
}
```

Hierarchy: Object→ Throwable(Serializable)→ Exception→ AlreadyBoundException

Thrown By: Naming.bind(), java.rmi.registry.Registry.bind()

ConnectException **Java 1.1**

java.rmi ***serializable checked PJ1.1(opt)***

A RemoteException that's thrown when a remote host refuses to connect during a remote method call.

```
public class ConnectException extends RemoteException {
// Public Constructors
   public ConnectException(String s);
   public ConnectException(String s, Exception ex);
}
```

Hierarchy: Object→ Throwable(Serializable)→ Exception→ IOException→ RemoteException→ ConnectException

ConnectIOException **Java 1.1**

java.rmi ***serializable checked PJ1.1(opt)***

A RemoteException that's thrown if there is an I/O error while attempting to make a remote method call.

```
public class ConnectIOException extends RemoteException {
// Public Constructors
   public ConnectIOException(String s);
   public ConnectIOException(String s, Exception ex);
}
```

Hierarchy: Object→ Throwable(Serializable)→ Exception→ IOException→ RemoteException→ ConnectIOException

MarshalException **Java 1.1**

java.rmi ***serializable checked PJ1.1(opt)***

A RemoteException that's thrown if an I/O error occurs while attempting to marshal any part of a remote method call (header data or method arguments).

```
public class MarshalException extends RemoteException {
// Public Constructors
   public MarshalException(String s);
   public MarshalException(String s, Exception ex);
}
```

Hierarchy: Object→ Throwable(Serializable)→ Exception→ IOException→ RemoteException→ MarshalException

MarshalledObject **Java 1.2**

java.rmi ***serializable***

A MarshalledObject represents an object that has been serialized and marshalled according to the RMI specification. If the original object was a remote object reference, the MarshalledObject contains a serialized stub for the object. Otherwise, the object is serialized and tagged with a codebase URL that can be used on the receiving end to find the class definition for the object, if needed.

The MarshalledObject constructor allows you to serialize an existing object into marshalled form. The get() method returns a copy of the serialized object it contains. You can also compare the equality of the serialized objects of two MarshalledObject objects.

MarshalledObject objects are used primarily by the RMI activation API, to allow for the passing of initialization parameters for activated objects in a standard way, for example.

```
public final class MarshalledObject implements Serializable {
// Public Constructors
    public MarshalledObject(Object obj) throws IOException;
// Public Instance Methods
    public Object get() throws IOException, ClassNotFoundException;
// Public methods overriding Object
    public boolean equals(Object obj);
    public int hashCode();
}
```

Hierarchy: Object→ MarshalledObject(Serializable)

Passed To: java.rmi.activation.Activatable.{Activatable(), exportObject()}, java.rmi.activation.ActivationDesc.ActivationDesc(), java.rmi.activation.ActivationGroup.activeObject(), java.rmi.activation.ActivationGroupDesc.ActivationGroupDesc(), java.rmi.activation.ActivationMonitor.activeObject()

Returned By: java.rmi.activation.ActivationDesc.getData(), java.rmi.activation.ActivationGroup.newInstance(), java.rmi.activation.ActivationGroup_Stub.newInstance(), java.rmi.activation.ActivationGroupDesc.getData(), java.rmi.activation.ActivationInstantiator.newInstance(), java.rmi.activation.Activator.activate()

Naming — Java 1.1

java.rmi — *PJ1.1(opt)*

This is the primary application interface to the naming service within the RMI registry. You can get references to remote objects with the lookup() method. To bind local object implementations to names within the local registry, use the bind() and rebind() methods. Locally bound objects can be removed from the name registry using unbind(). To obtain all of the names for objects currently stored in the registry, use the list() method.

Each name argument to the methods on the Naming interface takes the form of a URL (e.g., *rmi://remoteHost:port/objName*). If you are referencing a local object and the object is exported to the default registry port, the URL can simply take the form of the object's name in the local registry, (e.g., *objName*). This is possible because the *rmi:* protocol is assumed if it isn't present in the URL and the default host is the local host.

Note that while the lookup() method can reference any remote RMI registry, the bind(), rebind(), and unbind() methods can only be called on the local registry. Attempting to call these methods against a remote registry results in an AccessException being thrown.

```
public final class Naming {
// No Constructor
// Public Class Methods
    public static void bind(String name, Remote obj) throws AlreadyBoundException,
        java.net.MalformedURLException, RemoteException;
    public static String[ ] list(String name) throws RemoteException, java.net.MalformedURLException;
    public static Remote lookup(String name) throws NotBoundException,
        java.net.MalformedURLException, RemoteException;
    public static void rebind(String name, Remote obj) throws RemoteException,
        java.net.MalformedURLException;
    public static void unbind(String name) throws RemoteException, NotBoundException,
        java.net.MalformedURLException;
}
```

java.rmi

NoSuchObjectException — Java 1.1

java.rmi — *serializable checked PJ1.1(opt)*

This subclass of RemoteException is thrown when you attempt to invoke a method on a remote object that is no longer available.

```
public class NoSuchObjectException extends RemoteException {
// Public Constructors
   public NoSuchObjectException(String s);
}
```

Hierarchy: Object→ Throwable(Serializable)→ Exception→ IOException→ RemoteException→ NoSuchObjectException

Thrown By: java.rmi.activation.Activatable.unexportObject(), java.rmi.server.RemoteObject.toStub(), java.rmi.server.UnicastRemoteObject.unexportObject()

NotBoundException — Java 1.1

java.rmi — *serializable checked PJ1.1(opt)*

An exception that is thrown by a Naming instance when a lookup is attempted using a name with no object bound to it.

```
public class NotBoundException extends Exception {
// Public Constructors
   public NotBoundException();
   public NotBoundException(String s);
}
```

Hierarchy: Object→ Throwable(Serializable)→ Exception→ NotBoundException

Thrown By: Naming.{lookup(), unbind()}, java.rmi.registry.Registry.{lookup(), unbind()}

Remote — Java 1.1

java.rmi — *remote PJ1.1(opt)*

Every remote object must implement the Remote interface. In addition, any methods you want to be remotely callable must be defined within an interface that extends the Remote interface. This is a place-holder interface that identifies all remote objects, but doesn't define any methods of its own.

```
public abstract interface Remote {
}
```

Implementations: java.rmi.activation.ActivationGroup_Stub, java.rmi.activation.ActivationInstantiator, java.rmi.activation.ActivationMonitor, java.rmi.activation.ActivationSystem, java.rmi.activation.Activator, java.rmi.dgc.DGC, java.rmi.registry.Registry, java.rmi.server.RemoteObject, javax.ejb.EJBHome, javax.ejb.EJBObject

Passed To: Naming.{bind(), rebind()}, java.rmi.activation.Activatable.{exportObject(), unexportObject()}, java.rmi.activation.ActivationGroup.activeObject(), java.rmi.registry.Registry.{bind(), rebind()}, java.rmi.server.RemoteObject.toStub(), java.rmi.server.RemoteRef.invoke(), java.rmi.server.ServerRef.exportObject(), java.rmi.server.Skeleton.dispatch(), java.rmi.server.UnicastRemoteObject.{exportObject(), unexportObject()}

Returned By: Naming.lookup(), java.rmi.activation.Activatable.{exportObject(), register()}, java.rmi.activation.ActivationID.activate(), java.rmi.registry.Registry.lookup(), java.rmi.server.RemoteObject.toStub(), java.rmi.server.UnicastRemoteObject.exportObject()

RemoteException — Java 1.1

java.rmi — *serializable checked PJ1.1(opt)*

This subclass of IOException is thrown when an error occurs during any remote object operation. The RemoteException includes a Throwable data member that represents the nested exception that caused the RemoteException to be thrown. For example, if an exception occurs on the server while executing a remote method, the client receives a RemoteException (in the form of a ServerException, one of its subclasses) with its Throwable data member initialized to the server-side exception that caused the client-side RemoteException to be delivered.

```
public class RemoteException extends IOException {
// Public Constructors
   public RemoteException();
   public RemoteException(String s);
   public RemoteException(String s, Throwable ex);
// Public methods overriding Throwable
   public String getMessage();                                    default:null
1.2 public void printStackTrace();
1.2 public void printStackTrace(PrintStream ps);
1.2 public void printStackTrace(PrintWriter pw);
// Public Instance Fields
   public Throwable detail;
}
```

Hierarchy: Object→ Throwable(Serializable)→ Exception→ IOException→ RemoteException

Subclasses: AccessException, java.rmi.ConnectException, ConnectIOException, MarshalException, NoSuchObjectException, ServerError, ServerException, ServerRuntimeException, StubNotFoundException, UnexpectedException, java.rmi.UnknownHostException, UnmarshalException, java.rmi.activation.ActivateFailedException, java.rmi.server.ExportException, java.rmi.server.SkeletonMismatchException, java.rmi.server.SkeletonNotFoundException, javax.transaction.InvalidTransactionException, javax.transaction.TransactionRequiredException, javax.transaction.TransactionRolledbackException

Thrown By: Too many methods to list.

RMISecurityException — Java 1.1; Deprecated in Java 1.2

java.rmi — *serializable unchecked PJ1.1(opt)*

A SecurityException thrown by the RMISecurityManager when a security violation is detected during a remote operation.

```
public class RMISecurityException extends SecurityException {
// Public Constructors
#  public RMISecurityException(String name);
#  public RMISecurityException(String name, String arg);
}
```

Hierarchy: Object→ Throwable(Serializable)→ Exception→ RuntimeException→ SecurityException→ RMISecurityException

RMISecurityManager class — Java 1.1

java.rmi — *PJ1.1(opt)*

The RMISecurityManager enforces the security policy for classes that are loaded as stubs for remote objects, by overriding all relevant access-check methods from the SecurityManager. By default, stub objects are only allowed to perform class definition and class access operations. If you don't set the local security manager as RMISecurityManager (using the System.setSecurityManager() method), stub classes are only loadable from the local filesystem. Applets engaging in RMI calls do not need to use the RMISecurityManager, since the security manager provided by the browser does the necessary access control on loading remote classes, etc.

You don't normally need to interact with the RMISecurityManager directly within your application code, except to set it as the system security manager before starting your RMI code.

```
public class RMISecurityManager extends SecurityManager {
// Public Constructors
   public RMISecurityManager();
}
```

Hierarchy: Object→ SecurityManager→ RMISecurityManager

ServerError class **Java 1.1**

java.rmi ***serializable checked PJ1.1(opt)***

A nonrecoverable error that occurs while a server is executing a remote method. The nested Throwable data member (inherited from RemoteException) contains the server-side exception that generated the error.

```
public class ServerError extends RemoteException {
// Public Constructors
   public ServerError(String s, Error err);
}
```

Hierarchy: Object→ Throwable(Serializable)→ Exception→ IOException→ RemoteException→ ServerError

ServerException **Java 1.1**

java.rmi ***serializable checked PJ1.1(opt)***

This exception is thrown if a RemoteException is thrown while the server object is executing a remote method.

```
public class ServerException extends RemoteException {
// Public Constructors
   public ServerException(String s);
   public ServerException(String s, Exception ex);
}
```

Hierarchy: Object→ Throwable(Serializable)→ Exception→ IOException→ RemoteException→ ServerException

ServerRuntimeException **Java 1.1; Deprecated in Java 1.2**

java.rmi ***serializable checked PJ1.1(opt)***

An exception that occurs if a RuntimeException is thrown while a server object is executing a remote method. The nested Throwable data member (inherited from RemoteException) contains the server-side runtime exception that generated the exception.

```
public class ServerRuntimeException extends RemoteException {
// Public Constructors
#  public ServerRuntimeException(String s, Exception ex);
}
```

Hierarchy: Object→ Throwable(Serializable)→ Exception→ IOException→ RemoteException→ ServerRuntimeException

StubNotFoundException — Java 1.1

java.rmi — ***serializable checked PJ1.1(opt)***

This exception can occur either when an object is being exported to participate in remote RMI calls or during a remote method call. During export on the server, this exception is thrown if the stub class for the object cannot be found or used for some reason (e.g., the stub class isn't in the CLASSPATH of the server process or the stub class can't be instantiated). During a remote method call, the client can receive this exception if the remote object hasn't been exported completely or correctly.

```
public class StubNotFoundException extends RemoteException {
// Public Constructors
   public StubNotFoundException(String s);
   public StubNotFoundException(String s, Exception ex);
}
```

Hierarchy: Object→ Throwable(Serializable)→ Exception→ IOException→ RemoteException→ StubNotFoundException

UnexpectedException — Java 1.1

java.rmi — ***serializable checked PJ1.1(opt)***

An UnexpectedException is thrown if an exception that isn't specified on a remote method's signature is encountered during the return from a remote method call. The unexpected exception can occur on the server or on the client. The nested Throwable object (inherited from RemoteException) contains the actual exception that occurred.

```
public class UnexpectedException extends RemoteException {
// Public Constructors
   public UnexpectedException(String s);
   public UnexpectedException(String s, Exception ex);
}
```

Hierarchy: Object→ Throwable(Serializable)→ Exception→ IOException→ RemoteException→ UnexpectedException

UnknownHostException — Java 1.1

java.rmi — ***serializable checked PJ1.1(opt)***

This RemoteException is thrown if the host specified during a Naming lookup cannot be found.

```
public class UnknownHostException extends RemoteException {
// Public Constructors
   public UnknownHostException(String s);
   public UnknownHostException(String s, Exception ex);
}
```

Hierarchy: Object→ Throwable(Serializable)→ Exception→ IOException→ RemoteException→ UnknownHostException

Thrown By: java.rmi.registry.RegistryHandler.registryStub()

UnmarshalException — Java 1.1

java.rmi — ***serializable checked PJ1.1(opt)***

This RemoteException is thrown if an error occurs while unmarshalling the return value from a remote method call. The source of the error could be an I/O error while sending the header or the value of the return from the server to the client, or the fact that the class of the return object is not found.

```
public class UnmarshalException extends RemoteException {
// Public Constructors
   public UnmarshalException(String s);
   public UnmarshalException(String s, Exception ex);
}
```

Hierarchy: Object→ Throwable(Serializable)→ Exception→ IOException→ RemoteException→ UnmarshalException

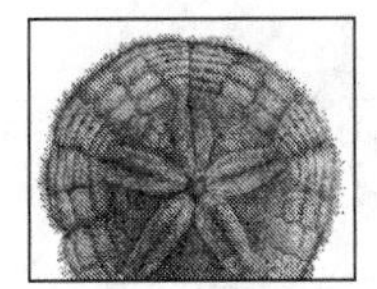

CHAPTER 14

The java.rmi.activation Package

The java.rmi.activation package contains the interfaces, classes, and exceptions that represent the RMI activation system, introduced in Java 2. This RMI service allows you to define remote objects that are not instantiated on the server until a client request triggers their activation. The activation system provides the means to specify how a remote object is activated and how activated objects are grouped into Java VMs. The activation also supports persistent remote references, or in other words, references to remote objects that can persist beyond the lifetime of an individual server object. Figure 14-1 shows the class hierarchy for this package.

Activatable — Java 1.2

java.rmi.activation — *serializable remote*

This abstract subclass of java.rmi.server.RemoteServer represents a server object that is persistent and activatable. This is in contrast to a java.rmi.server.UnicastRemoteObject, which represents a server object that is only available during the lifetime of the server process. Both UnicastRemoteObject objects and Activatable objects support only point-to-point communication, however.

The Activatable class provides a set of constructors and a corresponding set of static exportObject() methods that can be used to register and export server objects, either pre-instantiated or not. The exportObject() methods are provided for server objects that choose not to extend the Activatable class. Other static methods are the register() method, which can be used to register an activatable object without instantiating it, the unexportObject() method, which removes the specified object from the RMI runtime system, the unregister() method, which removes the activation registration for the given ActivationID, and the inactive() method, which tells the activation system that the object associated with the given ActivationID should be inactivated. The getID() method is an instance method that allows you to get the ActivationID for a server object.

```
public abstract class Activatable extends java.rmi.server.RemoteServer {
// Protected Constructors
   protected Activatable(ActivationID id, int port) throws RemoteException;
   protected Activatable(ActivationID id, int port, java.rmi.server.RMIClientSocketFactory csf,
```

java.rmi.activation

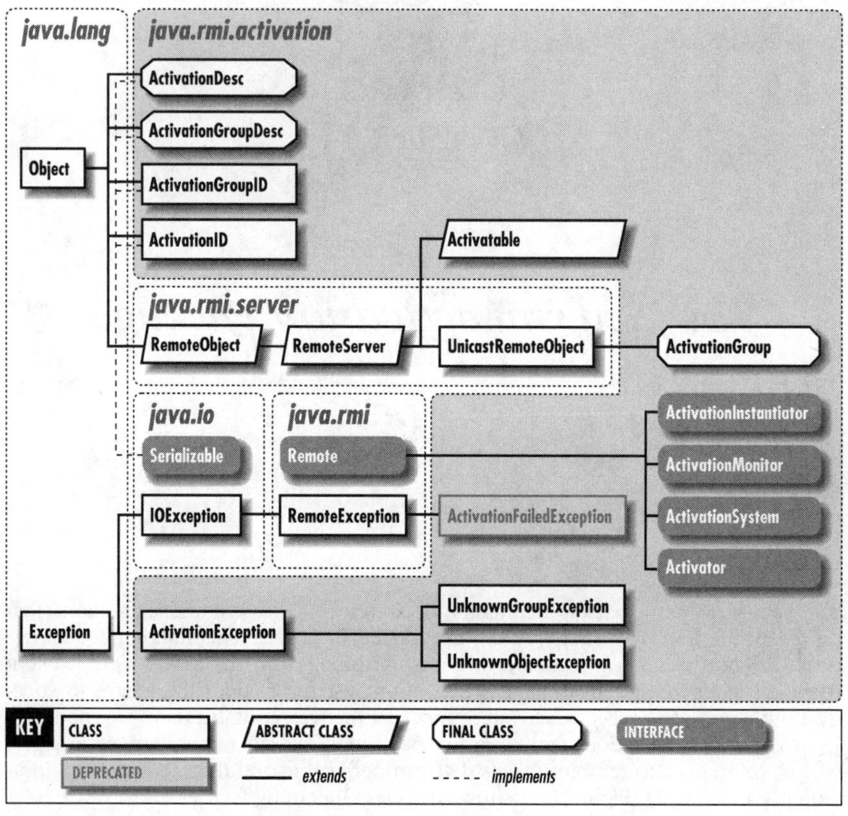

Figure 14-1: The java.rmi.activation package

```
java.rmi.server.RMIServerSocketFactory ssf) throws RemoteException;
    protected Activatable(String location, MarshalledObject data, boolean restart, int port)
        throws ActivationException, RemoteException;
    protected Activatable(String location, MarshalledObject data, boolean restart, int port,
                          java.rmi.server.RMIClientSocketFactory csf, java.rmi.server.RMIServerSocketFactory ssf)
        throws ActivationException, RemoteException;
// Public Class Methods
    public static Remote exportObject(Remote obj, ActivationID id, int port) throws RemoteException;
    public static ActivationID exportObject(Remote obj, String location, MarshalledObject data, boolean restart,
                                            int port) throws ActivationException, RemoteException;
    public static Remote exportObject(Remote obj, ActivationID id, int port,
                                      java.rmi.server.RMIClientSocketFactory csf,
                                      java.rmi.server.RMIServerSocketFactory ssf) throws RemoteException;
    public static ActivationID exportObject(Remote obj, String location, MarshalledObject data, boolean restart,
                                            int port, java.rmi.server.RMIClientSocketFactory csf,
                                            java.rmi.server.RMIServerSocketFactory ssf)
        throws ActivationException, RemoteException;
    public static boolean inactive(ActivationID id) throws UnknownObjectException, ActivationException,
        RemoteException;
    public static Remote register(ActivationDesc desc) throws UnknownGroupException,
        ActivationException, RemoteException;
```

```
    public static boolean unexportObject(Remote obj, boolean force) throws NoSuchObjectException;
    public static void unregister(ActivationID id) throws UnknownObjectException, ActivationException,
        RemoteException;
// Protected Instance Methods
    protected ActivationID getID();
}
```

Hierarchy: Object→ java.rmi.server.RemoteObject(Remote, Serializable)→ java.rmi.server.RemoteServer→ Activatable

ActivateFailedException — Java 1.2

java.rmi.activation — *serializable checked*

This subclass of RemoteException is thrown to a client when a remote method call fails because the object could not be activated.

```
public class ActivateFailedException extends RemoteException {
// Public Constructors
    public ActivateFailedException(String s);
    public ActivateFailedException(String s, Exception ex);
}
```

Hierarchy: Object→ Throwable(Serializable)→ Exception→ IOException→ RemoteException→ ActivateFailedException

ActivationDesc — Java 1.2

java.rmi.activation — *serializable*

An ActivationDesc represents a description for how a remote object should be activated. It contains an activation group ID for the object, the class name for the object to be instantiated, a codebase that can be used to load the class description, if necessary, and a MarshalledObject that contains object-specific initialization data. Once an ActivationDesc has been created, it can be used to register an object for activation using the Activatable.register() method.

```
public final class ActivationDesc implements Serializable {
// Public Constructors
    public ActivationDesc(String className, String location, MarshalledObject data)
        throws ActivationException;
    public ActivationDesc(ActivationGroupID groupID, String className, String location, MarshalledObject data);
    public ActivationDesc(String className, String location, MarshalledObject data, boolean restart)
        throws ActivationException;
    public ActivationDesc(ActivationGroupID groupID, String className, String location, MarshalledObject data,
                          boolean restart);
// Public Instance Methods
    public String getClassName();
    public MarshalledObject getData();
    public ActivationGroupID getGroupID();
    public String getLocation();
    public boolean getRestartMode();
// Public methods overriding Object
    public boolean equals(Object obj);
    public int hashCode();
}
```

Hierarchy: Object→ ActivationDesc(Serializable)

Passed To: Activatable.register(), ActivationGroup.newInstance(), ActivationGroup_Stub.newInstance(), ActivationInstantiator.newInstance(), ActivationSystem.{registerObject(), setActivationDesc()}

Returned By: ActivationSystem.{getActivationDesc(), setActivationDesc()}

ActivationException — Java 1.2

java.rmi.activation — *serializable checked*

This is a base class used for all nonremote, activation-related exceptions (i.e., exceptions thrown between components of the activation system or by the local activation system to clients invoking its methods).

```
public class ActivationException extends Exception {
// Public Constructors
   public ActivationException();
   public ActivationException(String s);
   public ActivationException(String s, Throwable ex);
// Public methods overriding Throwable
   public String getMessage();                                   default:null
   public void printStackTrace();
   public void printStackTrace(PrintWriter pw);
   public void printStackTrace(PrintStream ps);
// Public Instance Fields
   public Throwable detail;
}
```

Hierarchy: Object→ Throwable(Serializable)→ Exception→ ActivationException

Subclasses: UnknownGroupException, UnknownObjectException

Thrown By: Too many methods to list.

ActivationGroup — Java 1.2

java.rmi.activation — *serializable remote*

An ActivationGroup represents a group of activatable objects that are meant to run within the same Java VM. The ActivationGroup serves as a go-between for the ActivationMonitor and the activatable objects, forwarding messages about the active state of objects in its group. The activeObject() methods forward a message to the activation system about a newly activated object in the group, while the inactiveObject() method does the same for deactivated objects.

You can explicitly create your own ActivationGroup using the createGroup() method. If you don't specify a group ID when you create an ActivationDesc for an activatable object, it is assigned to a default group. When you create an ActivationGroup, you provide an ActivationGroupDesc object that describes how the group is to be created (e.g, from what class the group object should be constructed, or what Properties should be set for the group).

The ActivationGroup class is abstract, so you must provide a concrete implementation in order to create groups. In addition to satisfying the interface defined in ActivationGroup, the subclass must also provide a constructor that takes an ActivationGroupID and a MarshalledObject as arguments. This constructor is invoked by the createGroup() method. A concrete subclass of ActivationGroup must also implement the newInstance() method inherited from ActivationInstantiator.

```
public abstract class ActivationGroup extends java.rmi.server.UnicastRemoteObject
      implements ActivationInstantiator {
// Protected Constructors
   protected ActivationGroup(ActivationGroupID groupID) throws RemoteException;
// Public Class Methods
```

```
    public static ActivationGroup createGroup(ActivationGroupID id,                     synchronized
                                              ActivationGroupDesc desc, long incarnation)
        throws ActivationException;
    public static ActivationGroupID currentGroupID();                                   synchronized
    public static ActivationSystem getSystem() throws ActivationException;              synchronized
    public static void setSystem(ActivationSystem system) throws ActivationException;   synchronized
// Public Instance Methods
    public abstract void activeObject(ActivationID id, Remote obj) throws ActivationException,
        UnknownObjectException, RemoteException;
    public boolean inactiveObject(ActivationID id) throws ActivationException, UnknownObjectException,
        RemoteException;
// Methods implementing ActivationInstantiator
    public abstract MarshalledObject newInstance(ActivationID id, ActivationDesc desc)
        throws ActivationException, RemoteException;
// Protected Instance Methods
    protected void activeObject(ActivationID id, MarshalledObject mobj) throws ActivationException,
        UnknownObjectException, RemoteException;
    protected void inactiveGroup() throws UnknownGroupException, RemoteException;
}
```

Hierarchy: Object→ java.rmi.server.RemoteObject(Remote, Serializable)→ java.rmi.server.RemoteServer→ java.rmi.server.UnicastRemoteObject→ ActivationGroup(ActivationInstantiator(Remote))

Returned By: ActivationGroup.createGroup()

ActivationGroupDesc — Java 1.2

java.rmi.activation — *serializable*

An ActivationGroupDesc contains the information to create a new activation group. It includes the class that should construct the group object, a codebase that can find the class description, if necessary, and a MarshalledObject containing any additional initialization information required by the group. In addition, each constructor allows you to specify a Properties list that overrides any default runtime properties in the Java VM for the group and a CommandEnvironment object that allows you to customize the Java executable that starts the group's VM and its command-line arguments.

```
public final class ActivationGroupDesc implements Serializable {
// Public Constructors
    public ActivationGroupDesc(java.util.Properties overrides,
                               ActivationGroupDesc.CommandEnvironment cmd);
    public ActivationGroupDesc(String className, String location, MarshalledObject data,
                               java.util.Properties overrides, ActivationGroupDesc.CommandEnvironment cmd);
// Inner Classes
    public static class CommandEnvironment implements Serializable;
// Public Instance Methods
    public String getClassName();
    public ActivationGroupDesc.CommandEnvironment getCommandEnvironment();
    public MarshalledObject getData();
    public String getLocation();
    public java.util.Properties getPropertyOverrides();
// Public methods overriding Object
    public boolean equals(Object obj);
    public int hashCode();
}
```

Hierarchy: Object→ ActivationGroupDesc(Serializable)

Passed To: ActivationGroup.createGroup(), ActivationSystem.{registerGroup(), setActivationGroupDesc()}

Returned By: ActivationSystem.{getActivationGroupDesc(), setActivationGroupDesc()}

ActivationGroupDesc.CommandEnvironment — Java 1.2

java.rmi.activation — *serializable*

This inner class of ActivationGroupDesc specifies customized startup parameters for the Java VM for an activation group. It contains a command path, which specifies where to find the Java executable to be run, and an array of command-line arguments for the Java executable.

```
public static class ActivationGroupDesc.CommandEnvironment implements Serializable {
// Public Constructors
   public CommandEnvironment(String cmdpath, String[ ] argv);
// Public Instance Methods
   public String[ ] getCommandOptions();
   public String getCommandPath();
// Public methods overriding Object
   public boolean equals(Object obj);
   public int hashCode();
}
```

Hierarchy: Object→ ActivationGroupDesc.CommandEnvironment(Serializable)

Passed To: ActivationGroupDesc.ActivationGroupDesc()

Returned By: ActivationGroupDesc.getCommandEnvironment()

ActivationGroupID — Java 1.2

java.rmi.activation — *serializable*

An ActivationGroupID uniquely identifies a group within the activation system. The ActivationGroup can also use its ActivationGroupID to query for its ActivationSystem, if needed. An ActivationGroupID is generated for a new group by the ActivationSystem.registerGroup() method.

```
public class ActivationGroupID implements Serializable {
// Public Constructors
   public ActivationGroupID(ActivationSystem system);
// Public Instance Methods
   public ActivationSystem getSystem();
// Public methods overriding Object
   public boolean equals(Object obj);
   public int hashCode();
}
```

Hierarchy: Object→ ActivationGroupID(Serializable)

Passed To: ActivationDesc.ActivationDesc(), ActivationGroup.{ActivationGroup(), createGroup()}, ActivationMonitor.inactiveGroup(), ActivationSystem.{activeGroup(), getActivationGroupDesc(), setActivationGroupDesc(), unregisterGroup()}

Returned By: ActivationDesc.getGroupID(), ActivationGroup.currentGroupID(), ActivationSystem.registerGroup()

ActivationID — Java 1.2

java.rmi.activation — *serializable*

An ActivationID uniquely identifies an activatable object within the activation system. It also contains an opaque reference to the Activator responsible for activating the object, which it uses when its activate() method is invoked. An ActivationID is generated for an activatable object by registering it using the Activatable.register() method (the stub returned by this method is initialized with the ActivationID) or by using one of the Activatable.exportObject() methods.

```
public class ActivationID implements Serializable {
// Public Constructors
   public ActivationID(Activator activator);
// Public Instance Methods
   public Remote activate(boolean force) throws ActivationException, UnknownObjectException,
       RemoteException;
// Public methods overriding Object
   public boolean equals(Object obj);
   public int hashCode();
}
```

Hierarchy: Object→ ActivationID(Serializable)

Passed To: Activatable.{Activatable(), exportObject(), inactive(), unregister()}, ActivationGroup.{activeObject(), inactiveObject(), newInstance()}, ActivationGroup_Stub.newInstance(), ActivationInstantiator.newInstance(), ActivationMonitor.{activeObject(), inactiveObject()}, ActivationSystem.{getActivationDesc(), setActivationDesc(), unregisterObject()}, Activator.activate()

Returned By: Activatable.{exportObject(), getID()}, ActivationSystem.registerObject()

ActivationInstantiator — Java 1.2

java.rmi.activation — *remote*

This interface represents an object that is responsible for activating objects, using its newInstance() method. The arguments to the method provide the ActivationID for the object within the activation system and the ActivationDesc provided for the object when it was registered, which includes the information needed to activate the object. The ActivationGroup class implements this interface; concrete subclasses of ActivationGroup must provide an implementation of the newInstance() method.

```
public abstract interface ActivationInstantiator extends Remote {
// Public Instance Methods
   public abstract MarshalledObject newInstance(ActivationID id, ActivationDesc desc)
       throws ActivationException, RemoteException;
}
```

Hierarchy: (ActivationInstantiator(Remote))

Implementations: ActivationGroup, ActivationGroup_Stub

Passed To: ActivationSystem.activeGroup()

ActivationMonitor — Java 1.2

java.rmi.activation — *remote*

An ActivationMonitor monitors a single activation group. It must be notified by the group when objects within the group become active or inactive or when the group as a whole becomes inactive. This lets the ActivationMonitor know when an object needs to be (re)activated, for example.

```
public abstract interface ActivationMonitor extends Remote {
// Public Instance Methods
   public abstract void activeObject(ActivationID id, MarshalledObject obj)
       throws UnknownObjectException, RemoteException;
   public abstract void inactiveGroup(ActivationGroupID id, long incarnation)
       throws UnknownGroupException, RemoteException;
```

```
    public abstract void inactiveObject(ActivationID id) throws UnknownObjectException,
        RemoteException;
}
```

Hierarchy: (ActivationMonitor(Remote))

Returned By: ActivationSystem.activeGroup()

ActivationSystem — Java 1.2

java.rmi.activation — *remote*

The ActivationSystem is the backbone of the activation runtime. It interacts with Activator objects to activate objects and groups and ActivationMonitor objects to determine when such activations are necessary. The ActivationSystem handling a particular Java VM can be obtained using the static ActivationGroup.getSystem() method.

The methods on the ActivationSystem are largely used by other classes in the activation package to implement various functions. The Activatable.register() method, for example, registers the activatable object by calling the registerObject() method on the ActivationSystem.

```
public abstract interface ActivationSystem extends Remote {
// Public Constants
    public static final int SYSTEM_PORT;                                        =1098
// Public Instance Methods
    public abstract ActivationMonitor activeGroup(ActivationGroupID id, ActivationInstantiator group,
                                                  long incarnation) throws UnknownGroupException,
        ActivationException, RemoteException;
    public abstract ActivationDesc getActivationDesc(ActivationID id) throws ActivationException,
        UnknownObjectException, RemoteException;
    public abstract ActivationGroupDesc getActivationGroupDesc(ActivationGroupID id)
        throws ActivationException, UnknownGroupException, RemoteException;
    public abstract ActivationGroupID registerGroup(ActivationGroupDesc desc)
        throws ActivationException, RemoteException;
    public abstract ActivationID registerObject(ActivationDesc desc) throws ActivationException,
        UnknownGroupException, RemoteException;
    public abstract ActivationDesc setActivationDesc(ActivationID id, ActivationDesc desc)
        throws ActivationException, UnknownObjectException, UnknownGroupException;
    public abstract ActivationGroupDesc setActivationGroupDesc(ActivationGroupID id,
                                                               ActivationGroupDesc desc)
        throws ActivationException, UnknownGroupException, RemoteException;
    public abstract void shutdown() throws RemoteException;
    public abstract void unregisterGroup(ActivationGroupID id) throws ActivationException,
        UnknownGroupException, RemoteException;
    public abstract void unregisterObject(ActivationID id) throws ActivationException,
        UnknownObjectException, RemoteException;
}
```

Hierarchy: (ActivationSystem(Remote))

Passed To: ActivationGroup.setSystem(), ActivationGroupID.ActivationGroupID()

Returned By: ActivationGroup.getSystem(), ActivationGroupID.getSystem()

Activator — Java 1.2

java.rmi.activation — *remote*

An Activator is responsible for activating remote objects and their groups. Its only method, activate(), triggers the activation system protocol. The activator first finds the ActivationDesc matching the given ActivationID and checks the activation information contained in it. If the target group for the object is not active, the Activator starts its Java VM and activates the group object itself. Finally, the Activator tells the group to (re)create the object by calling the newInstance() method on the group.

```
public abstract interface Activator extends Remote {
// Public Instance Methods
   public abstract MarshalledObject activate(ActivationID id, boolean force) throws ActivationException,
       UnknownObjectException, RemoteException;
}
```

Hierarchy: (Activator(Remote))

Passed To: ActivationID.ActivationID()

UnknownGroupException — Java 1.2

java.rmi.activation — ***serializable checked***

This exception is thrown if an unregistered ActivationGroupID is used, either directly as a method argument or indirectly within an ActivationDesc.

```
public class UnknownGroupException extends ActivationException {
// Public Constructors
   public UnknownGroupException(String s);
}
```

Hierarchy: Object→ Throwable(Serializable)→ Exception→ ActivationException→ UnknownGroupException

Thrown By: Activatable.register(), ActivationGroup.inactiveGroup(), ActivationMonitor.inactiveGroup(), ActivationSystem.{activeGroup(), getActivationGroupDesc(), registerObject(), setActivationDesc(), setActivationGroupDesc(), unregisterGroup()}

UnknownObjectException — Java 1.2

java.rmi.activation — ***serializable checked***

This exception is thrown if an invalid ActivationID is passed as a method argument (e.g., the ID was not generated by the current ActivationSystem).

```
public class UnknownObjectException extends ActivationException {
// Public Constructors
   public UnknownObjectException(String s);
}
```

Hierarchy: Object→ Throwable(Serializable)→ Exception→ ActivationException→ UnknownObjectException

Thrown By: Activatable.{inactive(), unregister()}, ActivationGroup.{activeObject(), inactiveObject()}, ActivationID.activate(), ActivationMonitor.{activeObject(), inactiveObject()}, ActivationSystem.{getActivationDesc(), setActivationDesc(), unregisterObject()}, Activator.activate()

CHAPTER 15

The java.rmi.dgc Package

The java.rmi.dgc package contains an interface and two classes that support distributed garbage collection in RMI. Distributed garbage collection is normally handled automatically by the RMI system, so most applications do not need to use this package. Figure 15-1 shows the class hierarchy for this package.

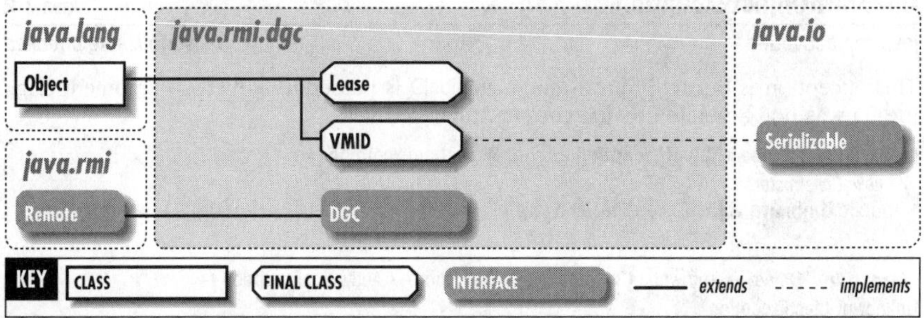

Figure 15–1: The java.dgc.activation package

DGC **Java 1.1**

java.rmi.dgc *remote PJ1.1(opt)*

This interface provides an abstraction for the server side of distributed garbage collection, using the notion of dirty and clean calls.

```
public abstract interface DGC extends Remote {
// Public Instance Methods
   public abstract void clean(java.rmi.server.ObjID[ ] ids, long sequenceNum, VMID vmid, boolean strong)
        throws RemoteException;
   public abstract Lease dirty(java.rmi.server.ObjID[ ] ids, long sequenceNum, Lease lease)
        throws RemoteException;
}
```

Hierarchy: (DGC(Remote))

Lease **Java 1.1**

java.rmi.dgc *serializable PJ1.1(opt)*

This class encapsulates a unique virtual machine identifier and a lease duration that manages garbage collection of distributed objects.

```
public final class Lease implements Serializable {
// Public Constructors
   public Lease(VMID id, long duration);
// Public Instance Methods
   public long getValue();
   public VMID getVMID();
}
```

Hierarchy: Object→ Lease(Serializable)

Passed To: DGC.dirty()

Returned By: DGC.dirty()

VMID **Java 1.1**

java.rmi.dgc *serializable PJ1.1(opt)*

This class represents a virtual machine identifier that is unique across all Java virtual machines.

```
public final class VMID implements Serializable {
// Public Constructors
   public VMID();
// Public Class Methods
   public static boolean isUnique();                                    constant
// Public methods overriding Object
   public boolean equals(Object obj);
   public int hashCode();
   public String toString();
}
```

Hierarchy: Object→ VMID(Serializable)

Passed To: DGC.clean(), Lease.Lease()

Returned By: Lease.getVMID()

CHAPTER 16

The java.rmi.registry Package

The java.rmi.registry package contains classes that provide an interface and an implementation for the various elements of the RMI object naming registry. Figure 16-1 shows the class hierarchy for this package.

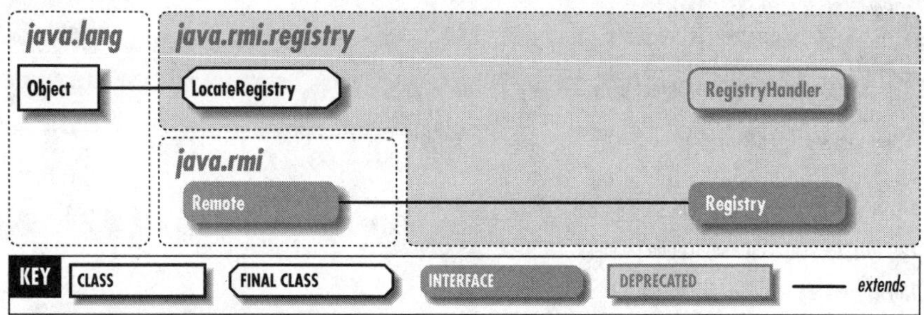

Figure 16–1: The java.rmi.registry package

LocateRegistry — Java 1.1

java.rmi.registry — *PJ1.1(opt)*

This class provides a low-level interface to an RMI registry service, residing either on the local host or on a remote server. On an object lookup, the Naming service parses the host and port from the remote object URL and uses methods of LocateRegistry to connect to the remote registry. The various getRegistry() methods provide the means to get a reference to the local registry or a stub to a remote registry running on a given host and port. The createRegistry() methods create a registry running on the local host on the given port number. The second form of the createRegistry() method allows you to specify custom socket factories the registry uses when it communicates with clients and server objects.

```
public final class LocateRegistry {
// No Constructor
// Public Class Methods
   public static Registry createRegistry(int port) throws RemoteException;
1.2 public static Registry createRegistry(int port, java.rmi.server.RMIClientSocketFactory csf,
                                   java.rmi.server.RMIServerSocketFactory ssf) throws RemoteException;
   public static Registry getRegistry() throws RemoteException;
   public static Registry getRegistry(String host) throws RemoteException;
   public static Registry getRegistry(int port) throws RemoteException;
   public static Registry getRegistry(String host, int port) throws RemoteException;
1.2 public static Registry getRegistry(String host, int port, java.rmi.server.RMIClientSocketFactory csf)
       throws RemoteException;
}
```

Registry **Java 1.1**

java.rmi.registry *remote PJ1.1(opt)*

The Registry is an interface to the RMI object registry that runs on every node in a distributed RMI system. While the Naming interface can look up objects stored in any registry on the network, a Registry operates on a single registry on a single host. URL object names are passed into methods on the Naming service, which finds the right Registry stub using the LocateRegistry class, and then calls the lookup() method on the remote (or local) Registry to get a stub for the remote object. A similar sequence of calls takes place with the local Registry when bind(), rebind(), or unbind() are called on the Naming interface.

The Registry stores objects under unique names. An object is assigned to a name in the Registry using its bind() method. The object assigned to a particular name can be changed using the rebind() method. Objects are removed from the Registry using the unbind() method. The lookup() method finds objects by name in the Registry, while the list() method gets a list of the names of all objects currently in the Registry.

```
public abstract interface Registry extends Remote {
// Public Constants
   public static final int REGISTRY_PORT;                                        =1099
// Public Instance Methods
   public abstract void bind(String name, Remote obj) throws RemoteException, AlreadyBoundException,
       AccessException;
   public abstract String[ ] list() throws RemoteException, AccessException;
   public abstract Remote lookup(String name) throws RemoteException, NotBoundException,
       AccessException;
   public abstract void rebind(String name, Remote obj) throws RemoteException, AccessException;
   public abstract void unbind(String name) throws RemoteException, NotBoundException,
       AccessException;
}
```

Hierarchy: (Registry(Remote))

Returned By: LocateRegistry.{createRegistry(), getRegistry()}, RegistryHandler.{registryImpl(), registryStub()}

RegistryHandler **Java 1.1; Deprecated in Java 1.2**

java.rmi.registry *PJ1.1(opt)*

This interface is mainly of interest to implementors of RMI registry services. It defines the interface to the internal registry-handling implementation.

```
public abstract interface RegistryHandler {
// Deprecated Public Methods
#   public abstract Registry registryImpl(int port) throws RemoteException;
#   public abstract Registry registryStub(String host, int port) throws RemoteException,
        java.rmi.UnknownHostException;
}
```

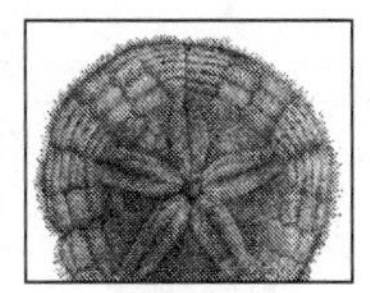

CHAPTER 17

The java.rmi.server Package

The java.rmi.server package contains the classes that develop server implementations of remote objects. Figure 17-1 shows the class hierarchy for this package.

The RemoteServer class in this package acts as the base class for all RMI server objects. A single subclass of RemoteServer, UnicastRemoteObject, is provided in this package. It implements a nonpersistent, point-to-point object communication scheme. Other subclasses of RemoteServer could be written to implement multicast object communication, replicated objects, etc.

This package also contains several Exception subclasses relevant to the server implementation of a remote object.

ExportException — Java 1.1

java.rmi.server — *serializable checked PJ1.1(opt)*

This RemoteException is thrown if an attempt is made to export a remote object on a port already in use.

```
public class ExportException extends RemoteException {
// Public Constructors
   public ExportException(String s);
   public ExportException(String s, Exception ex);
}
```

Hierarchy: Object→ Throwable(Serializable)→ Exception→ IOException→ RemoteException→ ExportException

Subclasses: SocketSecurityException

LoaderHandler — Java 1.1; Deprecated in Java 1.2

java.rmi.server — *PJ1.1(opt)*

This defines the interface to the internal handler used by the RMIClassLoader to load classes over the network.

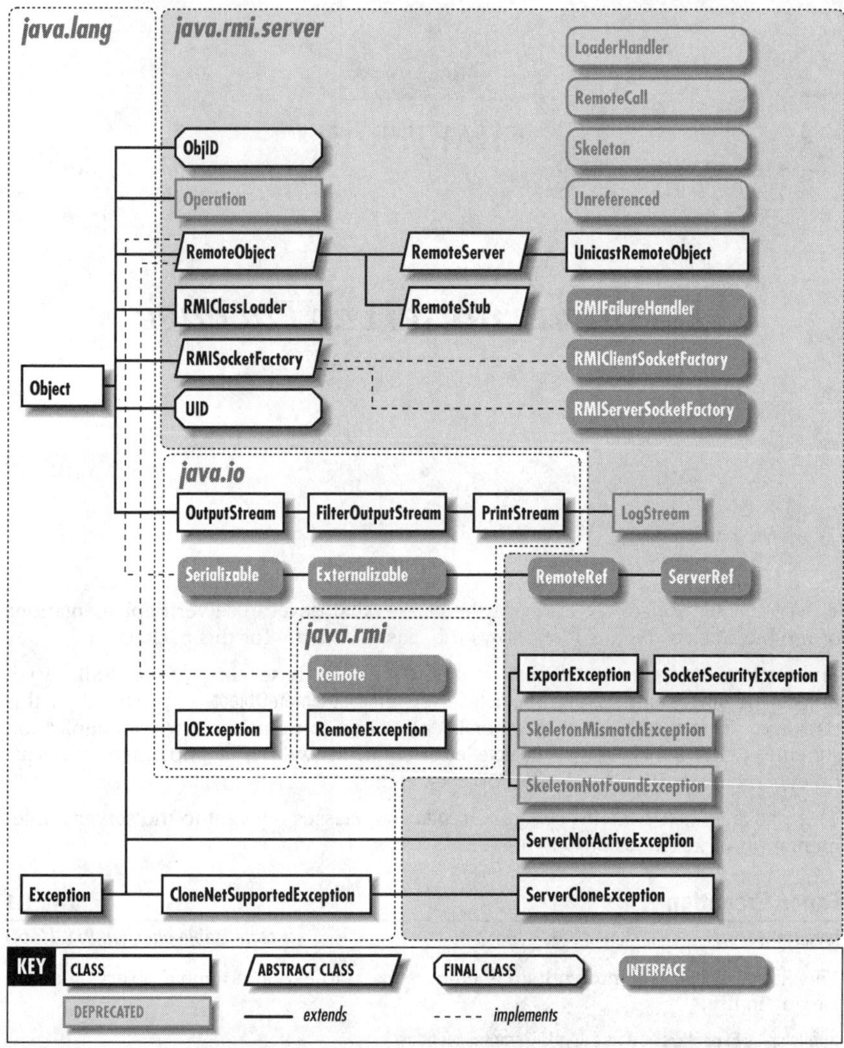

Figure 17-1: The java.rmi.server package

```
public abstract interface LoaderHandler {
// Public Constants
   public static final String packagePrefix;                                ="sun.rmi.server"
// Deprecated Public Methods
#  public abstract Object getSecurityContext(ClassLoader loader);
#  public abstract Class loadClass(String name) throws java.net.MalformedURLException,
       ClassNotFoundException;
#  public abstract Class loadClass(java.net.URL codebase, String name)
       throws java.net.MalformedURLException, ClassNotFoundException;
}
```

LogStream — Java 1.1; Deprecated in Java 1.2

java.rmi.server — *PJ1.1(opt)*

This class provides the server with an output stream to an error log. A LogStream cannot be created directly by an application. Instead, a handle on a LogStream is obtained by calling the static log() method with the name of the desired log. If the named log doesn't exist, the default log is returned. The default PrintStream creates new LogStream objects can be retrieved through the getDefaultStream() method and set using the setDefaultStream() method.

```
public class LogStream extends PrintStream {
// No Constructor
// Public Constants
   public static final int BRIEF;                                         =10
   public static final int SILENT;                                         =0
   public static final int VERBOSE;                                       =20
// Deprecated Public Methods
#  public static PrintStream getDefaultStream();                  synchronized
#  public java.io.OutputStream getOutputStream();                 synchronized
#  public static LogStream log(String name);
#  public static int parseLevel(String s);
#  public static void setDefaultStream(PrintStream newDefault);  synchronized
#  public void setOutputStream(java.io.OutputStream out);        synchronized
#  public String toString();                                 Overrides:Object
#  public void write(int b);                            Overrides:PrintStream
#  public void write(byte[ ] b, int off, int len);      Overrides:PrintStream
}
```

Hierarchy: Object→ java.io.OutputStream→ FilterOutputStream→ PrintStream→ LogStream

Returned By: LogStream.log()

ObjID — Java 1.1

java.rmi.server — *serializable PJ1.1(opt)*

An ObjID is used on an object server to uniquely identify exported remote objects. It is used in an RMI server during distributed garbage collection.

The equals() method is overridden from Object to return true only if the objects identified by the two ObjID values are equal. The ObjID class also has read() and write() methods that marshal and unmarshal an ObjID from I/O streams.

```
public final class ObjID implements Serializable {
// Public Constructors
   public ObjID();
   public ObjID(int num);
// Public Constants
1.2 public static final int ACTIVATOR_ID;                                  =1
   public static final int DGC_ID;                                         =2
   public static final int REGISTRY_ID;                                    =0
// Public Class Methods
   public static ObjID read(ObjectInput in) throws IOException;
// Public Instance Methods
   public void write(ObjectOutput out) throws IOException;
// Public methods overriding Object
   public boolean equals(Object obj);
   public int hashCode();
   public String toString();
}
```

Hierarchy: Object→ ObjID(Serializable)

Passed To: java.rmi.dgc.DGC.{clean(), dirty()}

Returned By: ObjID.read()

Operation — Java 1.1; Deprecated in Java 1.2

java.rmi.server — *PJ1.1(opt)*

An Operation contains a description of a method on a remote object. This class is used only in the stub classes generated by the *rmic* compiler. The Java 2 *rmic* compiler no longer uses the Operation class, so it is deprecated, but still present in the Java 2 SDK 1.2 to support RMI stubs generated by the JDK 1.1 *rmic* compiler.

```
public class Operation {
// Public Constructors
#  public Operation(String op);
// Deprecated Public Methods
#  public String getOperation();
#  public String toString();                                    Overrides:Object
}
```

Passed To: RemoteRef.newCall()

Returned By: Skeleton.getOperations()

RemoteCall — Java 1.1; Deprecated in Java 1.2

java.rmi.server — *PJ1.1(opt)*

RemoteCall is the interface used by stubs and skeletons to perform remote method calls. The getInputStream() and getOutputStream() methods return streams that can marshal arguments, or return values and then unmarshal them on the other end of the method call.

```
public abstract interface RemoteCall {
// Deprecated Public Methods
#  public abstract void done() throws IOException;
#  public abstract void executeCall() throws Exception;
#  public abstract ObjectInput getInputStream() throws IOException;
#  public abstract ObjectOutput getOutputStream() throws IOException;
#  public abstract ObjectOutput getResultStream(boolean success) throws IOException,
       StreamCorruptedException;
#  public abstract void releaseInputStream() throws IOException;
#  public abstract void releaseOutputStream() throws IOException;
}
```

Passed To: RemoteRef.{done(), invoke()}, Skeleton.dispatch()

Returned By: RemoteRef.newCall()

RemoteObject — Java 1.1

java.rmi.server — *serializable remote PJ1.1(opt)*

The RemoteObject class reimplements key Object methods for remote objects. It also maintains a RemoteRef object, which is a handle to the actual remote object. The equals() implementation returns true only if the two referenced remote objects are equal. The hashCode() method is implemented so that every remote stub that refers to the same remote object has the same hash code.

```
public abstract class RemoteObject implements Remote, Serializable {
// Protected Constructors
```

```
   protected RemoteObject();
   protected RemoteObject(RemoteRef newref);
// Public Class Methods
1.2 public static Remote toStub(Remote obj) throws NoSuchObjectException;
// Public Instance Methods
1.2 public RemoteRef getRef();
// Public methods overriding Object
   public boolean equals(Object obj);
   public int hashCode();
   public String toString();
// Protected Instance Fields
   protected transient RemoteRef ref;
}
```

Hierarchy: Object→ RemoteObject(Remote, Serializable)

Subclasses: RemoteServer, RemoteStub

Passed To: RemoteRef.newCall()

RemoteRef **Java 1.1**

java.rmi.server ***serializable PJ1.1(opt)***

A RemoteRef is a handle on the object that implements a remote object reference. Each RemoteObject contains a RemoteRef that acts as its interface to the actual remote object it represents. Normally, you don't need to interact directly with RemoteRef objects from your application code. Rather, application code interacts with RemoteObject objects, which use their internal RemoteRef objects to perform remote method invocations.

The newCall() method creates a call object for invoking a remote method on the referenced object. The invoke() method actually executes a remote-method invocation. If a remote method returns successfully, the done() method is called to clean up the connection to the remote object.

The remoteEquals(), remoteHashCode(), and remoteToString() methods on RemoteRef are used by RemoteObject to implement the remote versions of the equals(), hashCode(), and toString() methods.

```
public abstract interface RemoteRef extends Externalizable {
// Public Constants
   public static final String packagePrefix;                    ="sun.rmi.server"
1.2 public static final long serialVersionUID;               =3632638527362204081
// Public Instance Methods
   public abstract String getRefClass(ObjectOutput out);
1.2 public abstract Object invoke(Remote obj, java.lang.reflect.Method method, Object[ ] params, long opnum)
       throws Exception;
   public abstract boolean remoteEquals(RemoteRef obj);
   public abstract int remoteHashCode();
   public abstract String remoteToString();
// Deprecated Public Methods
#  public abstract void done(RemoteCall call) throws RemoteException;
#  public abstract void invoke(RemoteCall call) throws Exception;
#  public abstract RemoteCall newCall(RemoteObject obj, Operation[ ] op, int opnum, long hash)
       throws RemoteException;
}
```

Hierarchy: (RemoteRef(Externalizable(Serializable)))

Implementations: ServerRef

Passed To: java.rmi.activation.ActivationGroup_Stub.ActivationGroup_Stub(), RemoteObject.RemoteObject(), RemoteRef.remoteEquals(), RemoteServer.RemoteServer(), RemoteStub.{RemoteStub(), setRef()}

Returned By: RemoteObject.getRef()

Type Of: RemoteObject.ref

RemoteServer — Java 1.1

java.rmi.server — ***serializable remote PJ1.1(opt)***

This class acts as an abstract base class for all remote object server implementations. The intent is for subclasses to implement the semantics of the remote object (e.g., multicast remote objects, replicated objects). As of JDK 1.1 and later, the only concrete subclass provided is UnicastRemoteObject, which implements a nonreplicated remote object. The java.activation.Activatable class is a new abstract subclass in Java 2 that represents a server object that is persistent and activatable.

The getClientHost() method returns the name of the host for the client being served in the current thread. The getLog() and setLog() methods access the call log for a RemoteServer.

```
public abstract class RemoteServer extends RemoteObject {
// Protected Constructors
   protected RemoteServer();
   protected RemoteServer(RemoteRef ref);
// Public Class Methods
   public static String getClientHost() throws ServerNotActiveException;
   public static PrintStream getLog();
   public static void setLog(java.io.OutputStream out);
}
```

Hierarchy: Object→ RemoteObject(Remote, Serializable)→ RemoteServer

Subclasses: java.rmi.activation.Activatable, UnicastRemoteObject

RemoteStub — Java 1.1

java.rmi.server — ***serializable remote PJ1.1(opt)***

All client stub classes generated by the *rmic* compiler are derived from this abstract class. A client receives a RemoteStub when it successfully looks up a remote object through the RMI registry. A client stub serves as a client interface to the remote object it references, converting method calls on its interface to remote method invocations on the remote object implementation.

```
public abstract class RemoteStub extends RemoteObject {
// Protected Constructors
   protected RemoteStub();
   protected RemoteStub(RemoteRef ref);
// Deprecated Protected Methods
#  protected static void setRef(RemoteStub stub, RemoteRef ref);
}
```

Hierarchy: Object→ RemoteObject(Remote, Serializable)→ RemoteStub

Subclasses: java.rmi.activation.ActivationGroup_Stub

Passed To: RemoteStub.setRef()

Returned By: ServerRef.exportObject(), UnicastRemoteObject.exportObject()

RMIClassLoader **Java 1.1**

java.rmi.server *PJ1.1(opt)*

This class loads classes over the network using URLs. The class has two loadClass() methods, one for loading a class from a given (absolute) URL and another for loading a class from a given (relative) URL, starting at a particular codebase.

```
public class RMIClassLoader {
// No Constructor
// Public Class Methods
1.2 public static String getClassAnnotation(Class cl);
    public static Class loadClass(java.net.URL codebase, String name)
        throws java.net.MalformedURLException, ClassNotFoundException;
1.2 public static Class loadClass(String codebase, String name) throws java.net.MalformedURLException,
        ClassNotFoundException;
// Deprecated Public Methods
#   public static Object getSecurityContext(ClassLoader loader);
#   public static Class loadClass(String name) throws java.net.MalformedURLException,
        ClassNotFoundException;
}
```

RMIClientSocketFactory **Java 1.2**

java.rmi.server

This interface represents a source for client sockets that is used by the RMI internals to make client connections during RMI calls. It is possible to provide a custom socket factory to be used with a particular remote object, by using the appropriate constructors on the UnicastRemoteObject or Activatable classes, or, with a particular registry, by using the appropriate LocateRegistry.createRegistry() method. This can be useful in situations where a firewall lies between the client and the server object or remote registry, and specialized sockets are needed to negotiate the firewall protocol.

The RMIClientSocketFactory associated with a remote object is used by any remote stub references to establish connections with the server object.

```
public abstract interface RMIClientSocketFactory {
// Public Instance Methods
    public abstract java.net.Socket createSocket(String host, int port) throws IOException;
}
```

Implementations: RMISocketFactory

Passed To: java.rmi.activation.Activatable.{Activatable(), exportObject()}, java.rmi.registry.LocateRegistry.{createRegistry(), getRegistry()}, UnicastRemoteObject.{exportObject(), UnicastRemoteObject()}

RMIFailureHandler **Java 1.1**

java.rmi.server *PJ1.1(opt)*

The failure() method on the current RMIFailureHandler is called when the RMI communication system fails to create a Socket or ServerSocket. The current handler is set using the setFailureHandler() method on RMISocketFactory. The failure() method returns a boolean value that indicates whether the RMI system should retry the socket connection.

```
public abstract interface RMIFailureHandler {
// Public Instance Methods
    public abstract boolean failure(Exception ex);
}
```

Passed To: RMISocketFactory.setFailureHandler()

Returned By: RMISocketFactory.getFailureHandler()

RMIServerSocketFactory — Java 1.2

java.rmi.server

This interface represents a source for server sockets that is used by the RMI internals to make client connections during RMI calls. It is possible to provide a custom socket factory to be used with a particular remote object, by using the appropriate constructors on the UnicastRemoteObject or Activatable classes, or, with a particular registry, by using the appropriate LocateRegistry.createRegistry() method. This can be useful in situations where a firewall lies between the client and the server object or the remote registry, and specialized sockets are needed to negotiate the firewall protocol.

The RMIServerSocketFactory creates ServerSocket objects that are used by remote objects to accept client connections.

```
public abstract interface RMIServerSocketFactory {
// Public Instance Methods
   public abstract java.net.ServerSocket createServerSocket(int port) throws IOException;
}
```

Implementations: RMISocketFactory

Passed To: java.rmi.activation.Activatable.{Activatable(), exportObject()}, java.rmi.registry.LocateRegistry.createRegistry(), UnicastRemoteObject.{exportObject(), UnicastRemoteObject()}

RMISocketFactory — Java 1.1

java.rmi.server — *PJ1.1(opt)*

This abstract class provides an interface for the RMI internals to use to create sockets for both client and server communications. It implements both the RMIClientSocketFactory and the RMIServerSocketFactory interfaces, so it can create either Socket objects for clients or ServerSocket objects for servers. The factory maintains a RMIFailureHandler to deal with failures encountered while attempting to create sockets. If an error is encountered while creating a socket, the failure() method on the current RMIFailureHandler is called. If the return value is true, the RMISocketFactory attempts the socket creation again; otherwise the factory gives up and throws an IOException.

Client sockets are created using the createSocket() method (inherited from RMIClientSocketFactory), while server sockets are created using the createServerSocket() method (inherited from RMIServerSocketFactory). The current RMISocketFactory for the runtime system can be accessed using the static getSocketFactory() and setSocketFactory() methods. The RMIFailureHandler for the current factory is accessed using the getFailureHandler() and setFailureHandler() methods.

```
public abstract class RMISocketFactory implements RMIClientSocketFactory, RMIServerSocketFactory {
// Public Constructors
   public RMISocketFactory();
// Public Class Methods
1.2 public static RMISocketFactory getDefaultSocketFactory();                          synchronized
   public static RMIFailureHandler getFailureHandler();                                synchronized
   public static RMISocketFactory getSocketFactory();                                  synchronized
   public static void setFailureHandler(RMIFailureHandler fh);                         synchronized
   public static void setSocketFactory(RMISocketFactory fac) throws IOException;       synchronized
// Methods implementing RMIClientSocketFactory
   public abstract java.net.Socket createSocket(String host, int port) throws IOException;
```

```
// Methods implementing RMIServerSocketFactory
   public abstract java.net.ServerSocket createServerSocket(int port) throws IOException;
}
```

Hierarchy: Object→ RMISocketFactory(RMIClientSocketFactory, RMIServerSocketFactory)

Passed To: RMISocketFactory.setSocketFactory()

Returned By: RMISocketFactory.{getDefaultSocketFactory(), getSocketFactory()}

ServerCloneException — Java 1.1

java.rmi.server — *serializable checked PJ1.1(opt)*

This exception is thrown if an attempt to clone a RemoteServer object fails while the clone is being exported. The nested exception is the RemoteException that was thrown during the cloning operation.

```
public class ServerCloneException extends CloneNotSupportedException {
// Public Constructors
   public ServerCloneException(String s);
   public ServerCloneException(String s, Exception ex);
// Public methods overriding Throwable
   public String getMessage();
1.2 public void printStackTrace();
1.2 public void printStackTrace(PrintStream ps);
1.2 public void printStackTrace(PrintWriter pw);
// Public Instance Fields
   public Exception detail;
}
```

Hierarchy: Object→ Throwable(Serializable)→ Exception→ CloneNotSupportedException→ ServerCloneException

ServerNotActiveException — Java 1.1

java.rmi.server — *serializable checked PJ1.1(opt)*

This exception is thrown if the getClientHost() method is called on a RemoteServer when the server isn't handling a remote method call.

```
public class ServerNotActiveException extends Exception {
// Public Constructors
   public ServerNotActiveException();
   public ServerNotActiveException(String s);
}
```

Hierarchy: Object→ Throwable(Serializable)→ Exception→ ServerNotActiveException

Thrown By: RemoteServer.getClientHost(), ServerRef.getClientHost()

ServerRef — Java 1.1

java.rmi.server — *serializable PJ1.1(opt)*

This is an interface to the server-side implementation of a remote object. The getClientHost() method returns the name of the host whose remote method call is currently being serviced by the object implementation. If the server object is not servicing a remote method call when getClientHost() is called, a ServerNotActiveException is thrown. Using the data provided, the exportObject() method either creates or finds a client stub for the given object implementation.

```
public abstract interface ServerRef extends RemoteRef {
// Public Constants
1.2 public static final long serialVersionUID;                =-4557750989390278438
// Public Instance Methods
   public abstract RemoteStub exportObject(Remote obj, Object data) throws RemoteException;
   public abstract String getClientHost() throws ServerNotActiveException;
}
```

Hierarchy: (ServerRef(RemoteRef(Externalizable(Serializable))))

Skeleton — Java 1.1; Deprecated in Java 1.2

java.rmi.server — *PJ1.1(opt)*

Server-side skeleton classes generated by the *rmic* compiler implement the Skeleton interface. The dispatch() method invokes a method on the server object, and getOperations() returns an array of Operation objects that represent the methods available on the server object.

The Skeleton interface is used in classes generated by the *rmic* compiler in JDK 1.1. The Java 2 SDK 1.2 *rmic* compiler doesn't use the Skeleton interface for its skeleton classes, so it has been deprecated as of Java 2.

```
public abstract interface Skeleton {
// Deprecated Public Methods
#  public abstract void dispatch(Remote obj, RemoteCall theCall, int opnum, long hash) throws Exception;
#  public abstract Operation[ ] getOperations();
}
```

SkeletonMismatchException — Java 1.1; Deprecated in Java 1.2

java.rmi.server — *serializable checked PJ1.1(opt)*

This RemoteException is thrown during a remote method call if a mismatch is detected on the server between the hash code of the client stub and the hash code of the server implementation. It is usually received by the client wrapped in a ServerException.

```
public class SkeletonMismatchException extends RemoteException {
// Public Constructors
#  public SkeletonMismatchException(String s);
}
```

Hierarchy: Object→ Throwable(Serializable)→ Exception→ IOException→ RemoteException→ SkeletonMismatchException

SkeletonNotFoundException — Java 1.1; Deprecated in Java 1.2

java.rmi.server — *serializable checked PJ1.1(opt)*

This RemoteException is thrown during the export of a remote object, if the corresponding skeleton class for the object either cannot be found or loaded for some reason.

```
public class SkeletonNotFoundException extends RemoteException {
// Public Constructors
   public SkeletonNotFoundException(String s);
   public SkeletonNotFoundException(String s, Exception ex);
}
```

Hierarchy: Object→ Throwable(Serializable)→ Exception→ IOException→ RemoteException→ SkeletonNotFoundException

SocketSecurityException — Java 1.1

java.rmi.server — *serializable checked PJ1.1(opt)*

This exception is a subclass of ExportException that is thrown if a socket security violation is encountered while attempting to export a remote object. An example would be an attempt to export an object on an illegal port.

```
public class SocketSecurityException extends ExportException {
// Public Constructors
   public SocketSecurityException(String s);
   public SocketSecurityException(String s, Exception ex);
}
```

Hierarchy: Object→ Throwable(Serializable)→ Exception→ IOException→ RemoteException→ ExportException→ SocketSecurityException

UID — Java 1.1

java.rmi.server — *serializable PJ1.1(opt)*

A UID is an identifier that is unique with respect to a particular host. UID objects are used internally by RMI's distributed garbage collector and are generally not dealt with directly in application code.

```
public final class UID implements Serializable {
// Public Constructors
   public UID();
   public UID(short num);
// Public Class Methods
   public static UID read(DataInput in) throws IOException;
// Public Instance Methods
   public void write(DataOutput out) throws IOException;
// Public methods overriding Object
   public boolean equals(Object obj);
   public int hashCode();
   public String toString();
}
```

Hierarchy: Object→ UID(Serializable)

Returned By: UID.read()

UnicastRemoteObject — Java 1.1

java.rmi.server — *serializable remote PJ1.1(opt)*

This class represents a nonreplicated remote object, or in other words, an object that lives as a singular implementation on a server, with a point-to-point connection to each client through reference stubs. This remote server class does not implement persistence, so client references to the object are valid only during the lifetime of the object.

```
public class UnicastRemoteObject extends RemoteServer {
// Protected Constructors
    protected UnicastRemoteObject() throws RemoteException;
1.2 protected UnicastRemoteObject(int port) throws RemoteException;
1.2 protected UnicastRemoteObject(int port, RMIClientSocketFactory csf, RMIServerSocketFactory ssf)
        throws RemoteException;
// Public Class Methods
    public static RemoteStub exportObject(Remote obj) throws RemoteException;
1.2 public static Remote exportObject(Remote obj, int port) throws RemoteException;
1.2 public static Remote exportObject(Remote obj, int port, RMIClientSocketFactory csf,
                                      RMIServerSocketFactory ssf) throws RemoteException;
```

```
1.2 public static boolean unexportObject(Remote obj, boolean force) throws NoSuchObjectException;
// Public methods overriding Object
   public Object clone() throws CloneNotSupportedException;
}
```

Hierarchy: Object→ RemoteObject(Remote, Serializable)→ RemoteServer→ UnicastRemoteObject

Subclasses: java.rmi.activation.ActivationGroup

Unreferenced — Java 1.1

java.rmi.server — *PJ1.1(opt)*

If a server object implements this interface, the unreferenced() method is called by the RMI runtime system when the last client reference to a remote object is dropped. A remote object shouldn't be garbage collected until all its remote and local references are gone. So the unreferenced() method isn't a trigger for an object to be finalized, but rather a chance for the remote object to respond appropriately when its client reference count goes to zero. The unreferenced object could, for example, start a timer countdown to move the object to persistent storage after a given idle time with respect to remote clients.

```
public abstract interface Unreferenced {
// Public Instance Methods
   public abstract void unreferenced();
}
```

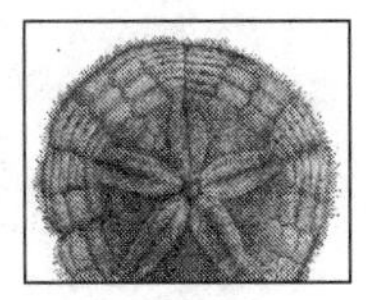

CHAPTER 18

The java.sql Package

The java.sql package contains the entire JDBC API that sends SQL (Structured Query Language) statements to relational databases and retrieves the results of executing those SQL statements. Figure 18-1 shows the class hierarchy of this package. The JDBC 1.0 API became part of the core Java API in Java 1.1. The JDBC 2.0 API supports a variety of new features and is part of the Java 2 platform.

The Driver interface represents a specific JDBC implementation for a particular database system. Connection represents a connection to a database. The Statement, PreparedStatement, and CallableStatement interfaces support the execution of various kinds of SQL statements. ResultSet is a set of results returned by the database in response to a SQL query. The ResultSetMetaData interface provides metadata about a result set, while DatabaseMetaData provides metadata about the database as a whole.

Array — Java 1.2

java.sql

Provides an interface to SQL ARRAY objects. Each getArray() method returns a standard Java array of objects of the type returned by getBaseType(). Two getArray() methods support a java.util.Map parameter that can customize the SQL-type-to-Java-object mapping. The contents of the array can also be returned as a ResultSet using the various getResultSet() methods.

```
public abstract interface Array {
// Public Instance Methods
   public abstract Object getArray() throws SQLException;
   public abstract Object getArray(java.util.Map map) throws SQLException;
   public abstract Object getArray(long index, int count) throws SQLException;
   public abstract Object getArray(long index, int count, java.util.Map map) throws SQLException;
   public abstract int getBaseType() throws SQLException;
   public abstract String getBaseTypeName() throws SQLException;
   public abstract ResultSet getResultSet() throws SQLException;
   public abstract ResultSet getResultSet(java.util.Map map) throws SQLException;
   public abstract ResultSet getResultSet(long index, int count) throws SQLException;
```

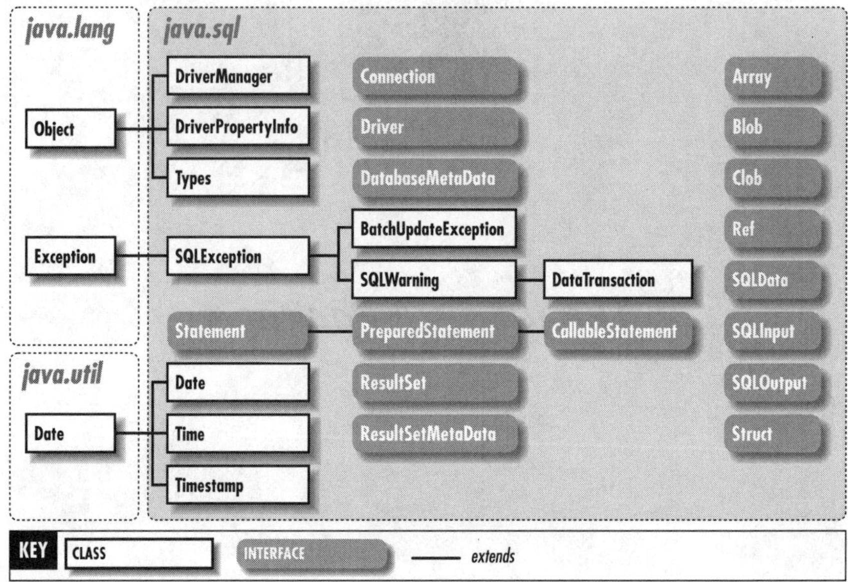

Figure 18-1: The java.sql Package

```
    public abstract ResultSet getResultSet(long index, int count, java.util.Map map) throws SQLException;
}
```

Passed To: PreparedStatement.setArray(), SQLOutput.writeArray(), javax.sql.RowSet.setArray()

Returned By: CallableStatement.getArray(), ResultSet.getArray(), SQLInput.readArray()

BatchUpdateException — Java 1.2

java.sql — *serializable checked*

This exception, which is a subclass of SQLException, is thrown when a batch update operation fails. The exception includes a method, getUpdateCounts(), that returns an array of int values, where the values correspond to the update counts for the successful update operations in the batch.

```
public class BatchUpdateException extends SQLException {
// Public Constructors
    public BatchUpdateException();
    public BatchUpdateException(int[ ] updateCounts);
    public BatchUpdateException(String reason, int[ ] updateCounts);
    public BatchUpdateException(String reason, String SQLState, int[ ] updateCounts);
    public BatchUpdateException(String reason, String SQLState, int vendorCode, int[ ] updateCounts);
// Public Instance Methods
    public int[ ] getUpdateCounts();                                    default:null
}
```

Hierarchy: Object→ Throwable(Serializable)→ Exception→ SQLException→ BatchUpdateException

Blob — Java 1.2

java.sql

The Blob interface encapsulates a SQL BLOB field. The interface actually contains a pointer to the BLOB within the database, rather than the complete (and potentially very large) object. Data can be retrieved via a java.io.InputStream returned by getInputStream() or as an array of bytes returned by getBytes(). The length() method returns the number of bytes in the BLOB. The position() methods scan the contents of the Blob for a particular content sequence, represented by either another Blob object or a byte array. (The position() methods do not provide the current read-index within the BLOB).

```
public abstract interface Blob {
// Public Instance Methods
   public abstract java.io.InputStream getBinaryStream() throws SQLException;
   public abstract byte[ ] getBytes(long pos, int length) throws SQLException;
   public abstract long length() throws SQLException;
   public abstract long position(byte[ ] pattern, long start) throws SQLException;
   public abstract long position(Blob pattern, long start) throws SQLException;
}
```

Passed To: Blob.position(), PreparedStatement.setBlob(), SQLOutput.writeBlob(), javax.sql.RowSet.setBlob()

Returned By: CallableStatement.getBlob(), ResultSet.getBlob(), SQLInput.readBlob()

CallableStatement — Java 1.1

java.sql — *PJ1.1(opt)*

The CallableStatement interface allows programs to access SQL stored procedures within the database. You create a CallableStatement with the prepareCall() method of Connection. Question-mark characters (?) are used as placeholders for input and output values in the syntax that calls stored procedures:

```
{? = call procedure_name[(?[,?...])]}
{call procedure_name[(?[,?...])]}
```

Parameters are numbered sequentially starting from 1. Input parameters are set with the same setXXX() methods as in a PreparedStatement. Output parameters must be registered using the registerOutParameter() methods, and may be retrieved after the statement executes using the getXXX() methods, which are identical to those in ResultSet. To execute a statement, you call execute(), which is inherited from PreparedStatement.

```
public abstract interface CallableStatement extends PreparedStatement {
// Public Instance Methods
1.2 public abstract java.sql.Array getArray(int i) throws SQLException;
1.2 public abstract java.math.BigDecimal getBigDecimal(int parameterIndex) throws SQLException;
1.2 public abstract Blob getBlob(int i) throws SQLException;
    public abstract boolean getBoolean(int parameterIndex) throws SQLException;
    public abstract byte getByte(int parameterIndex) throws SQLException;
    public abstract byte[ ] getBytes(int parameterIndex) throws SQLException;
1.2 public abstract Clob getClob(int i) throws SQLException;
    public abstract java.sql.Date getDate(int parameterIndex) throws SQLException;
1.2 public abstract java.sql.Date getDate(int parameterIndex, java.util.Calendar cal) throws SQLException;
    public abstract double getDouble(int parameterIndex) throws SQLException;
    public abstract float getFloat(int parameterIndex) throws SQLException;
    public abstract int getInt(int parameterIndex) throws SQLException;
    public abstract long getLong(int parameterIndex) throws SQLException;
    public abstract Object getObject(int parameterIndex) throws SQLException;
1.2 public abstract Object getObject(int i, java.util.Map map) throws SQLException;
1.2 public abstract Ref getRef(int i) throws SQLException;
```

```
   public abstract short getShort(int parameterIndex) throws SQLException;
   public abstract String getString(int parameterIndex) throws SQLException;
   public abstract Time getTime(int parameterIndex) throws SQLException;
1.2 public abstract Time getTime(int parameterIndex, java.util.Calendar cal) throws SQLException;
   public abstract Timestamp getTimestamp(int parameterIndex) throws SQLException;
1.2 public abstract Timestamp getTimestamp(int parameterIndex, java.util.Calendar cal)
       throws SQLException;
   public abstract void registerOutParameter(int parameterIndex, int sqlType) throws SQLException;
1.2 public abstract void registerOutParameter(int paramIndex, int sqlType, String typeName)
       throws SQLException;
   public abstract void registerOutParameter(int parameterIndex, int sqlType, int scale)
       throws SQLException;
   public abstract boolean wasNull() throws SQLException;
// Deprecated Public Methods
#  public abstract java.math.BigDecimal getBigDecimal(int parameterIndex, int scale)
       throws SQLException;
}
```

Hierarchy: (CallableStatement(PreparedStatement(Statement)))

Returned By: java.sql.Connection.prepareCall()

Clob — Java 1.2

java.sql

The Clob interface encapsulates a SQL CLOB field. The interface actually contains a pointer to the CLOB within the database, rather than the complete character string. Data is retrieved via getAsciiStream(), which returns an InputStream, or via getCharacterStream(), which returns a Reader. The getSubString() method returns a specific substring within the CLOB, while the position() methods search the CLOB for a pattern and return the index of the pattern's first appearance.

```
public abstract interface Clob {
// Public Instance Methods
   public abstract java.io.InputStream getAsciiStream() throws SQLException;
   public abstract Reader getCharacterStream() throws SQLException;
   public abstract String getSubString(long pos, int length) throws SQLException;
   public abstract long length() throws SQLException;
   public abstract long position(Clob searchstr, long start) throws SQLException;
   public abstract long position(String searchstr, long start) throws SQLException;
}
```

Passed To: Clob.position(), PreparedStatement.setClob(), SQLOutput.writeClob(), javax.sql.RowSet.setClob()

Returned By: CallableStatement.getClob(), ResultSet.getClob(), SQLInput.readClob()

Connection — Java 1.1

java.sql — *PJ1.1(opt)*

The Connection interface represents an individual database connection. The object includes factory methods for Statement, PreparedStatement, and CallableStatement objects and a number of transaction control methods (setAutoCommit(), commit(), rollback(), getAutoCommit(), setTransactionIsolation(), and getTransactionIsolation()). Other methods provide information about the database. The most important of these is getMetaData(), which returns a DatabaseMetaData object. The getWarnings() method returns any warnings pending for this connection.

Connection objects are created with the static DriverManager.getConnection() method.

```
public abstract interface Connection {
// Public Constants
   public static final int TRANSACTION_NONE;                                                          =0
   public static final int TRANSACTION_READ_COMMITTED;                                                =2
   public static final int TRANSACTION_READ_UNCOMMITTED;                                              =1
   public static final int TRANSACTION_REPEATABLE_READ;                                               =4
   public static final int TRANSACTION_SERIALIZABLE;                                                  =8
// Public Instance Methods
   public abstract void clearWarnings() throws SQLException;
   public abstract void close() throws SQLException;
   public abstract void commit() throws SQLException;
   public abstract Statement createStatement() throws SQLException;
1.2 public abstract Statement createStatement(int resultSetType, int resultSetConcurrency)
       throws SQLException;
   public abstract boolean getAutoCommit() throws SQLException;
   public abstract String getCatalog() throws SQLException;
   public abstract DatabaseMetaData getMetaData() throws SQLException;
   public abstract int getTransactionIsolation() throws SQLException;
1.2 public abstract java.util.Map getTypeMap() throws SQLException;
   public abstract SQLWarning getWarnings() throws SQLException;
   public abstract boolean isClosed() throws SQLException;
   public abstract boolean isReadOnly() throws SQLException;
   public abstract String nativeSQL(String sql) throws SQLException;
   public abstract CallableStatement prepareCall(String sql) throws SQLException;
1.2 public abstract CallableStatement prepareCall(String sql, int resultSetType, int resultSetConcurrency)
       throws SQLException;
   public abstract PreparedStatement prepareStatement(String sql) throws SQLException;
1.2 public abstract PreparedStatement prepareStatement(String sql, int resultSetType,
                                                      int resultSetConcurrency) throws SQLException;
   public abstract void rollback() throws SQLException;
   public abstract void setAutoCommit(boolean autoCommit) throws SQLException;
   public abstract void setCatalog(String catalog) throws SQLException;
   public abstract void setReadOnly(boolean readOnly) throws SQLException;
   public abstract void setTransactionIsolation(int level) throws SQLException;
1.2 public abstract void setTypeMap(java.util.Map map) throws SQLException;
}
```

Returned By: DatabaseMetaData.getConnection(), Driver.connect(), DriverManager.getConnection(), Statement.getConnection(), javax.sql.DataSource.getConnection(), javax.sql.PooledConnection.getConnection(), javax.sql.RowSetInternal.getConnection()

DatabaseMetaData — Java 1.1

java.sql — *PJ1.1(opt)*

The getMetaData() method of the Connection interface returns a DatabaseMetaData object that encapsulates nonconnection-dependent information about the underlying database. A number of methods return ResultSet objects that should be treated like any other ResultSet.

DatabaseMetaData methods that accept String parameters with names ending in "Pattern" allow for simple wildcard searching. These methods treat the % character as matching any number of characters and the _ character as matching any single character. If these parameters are set to null, pattern matching is not performed.

```
public abstract interface DatabaseMetaData {
// Public Constants
   public static final int bestRowNotPseudo;                                                          =1
   public static final int bestRowPseudo;                                                             =2
```

```
public static final int bestRowSession;                                    =2
public static final int bestRowTemporary;                                  =0
public static final int bestRowTransaction;                                =1
public static final int bestRowUnknown;                                    =0
public static final int columnNoNulls;                                     =0
public static final int columnNullable;                                    =1
public static final int columnNullableUnknown;                             =2
public static final int importedKeyCascade;                                =0
public static final int importedKeyInitiallyDeferred;                      =5
public static final int importedKeyInitiallyImmediate;                     =6
public static final int importedKeyNoAction;                               =3
public static final int importedKeyNotDeferrable;                          =7
public static final int importedKeyRestrict;                               =1
public static final int importedKeySetDefault;                             =4
public static final int importedKeySetNull;                                =2
public static final int procedureColumnIn;                                 =1
public static final int procedureColumnInOut;                              =2
public static final int procedureColumnOut;                                =4
public static final int procedureColumnResult;                             =3
public static final int procedureColumnReturn;                             =5
public static final int procedureColumnUnknown;                            =0
public static final int procedureNoNulls;                                  =0
public static final int procedureNoResult;                                 =1
public static final int procedureNullable;                                 =1
public static final int procedureNullableUnknown;                          =2
public static final int procedureResultUnknown;                            =0
public static final int procedureReturnsResult;                            =2
public static final short tableIndexClustered;                             =1
public static final short tableIndexHashed;                                =2
public static final short tableIndexOther;                                 =3
public static final short tableIndexStatistic;                             =0
public static final int typeNoNulls;                                       =0
public static final int typeNullable;                                      =1
public static final int typeNullableUnknown;                               =2
public static final int typePredBasic;                                     =2
public static final int typePredChar;                                      =1
public static final int typePredNone;                                      =0
public static final int typeSearchable;                                    =3
public static final int versionColumnNotPseudo;                            =1
public static final int versionColumnPseudo;                               =2
public static final int versionColumnUnknown;                              =0
// Public Instance Methods
public abstract boolean allProceduresAreCallable() throws SQLException;
public abstract boolean allTablesAreSelectable() throws SQLException;
public abstract boolean dataDefinitionCausesTransactionCommit() throws SQLException;
public abstract boolean dataDefinitionIgnoredInTransactions() throws SQLException;
1.2 public abstract boolean deletesAreDetected(int type) throws SQLException;
public abstract boolean doesMaxRowSizeIncludeBlobs() throws SQLException;
public abstract ResultSet getBestRowIdentifier(String catalog, String schema, String table, int scope,
                                               boolean nullable) throws SQLException;
public abstract ResultSet getCatalogs() throws SQLException;
public abstract String getCatalogSeparator() throws SQLException;
public abstract String getCatalogTerm() throws SQLException;
public abstract ResultSet getColumnPrivileges(String catalog, String schema, String table,
                                              String columnNamePattern) throws SQLException;
public abstract ResultSet getColumns(String catalog, String schemaPattern, String tableNamePattern,
                                     String columnNamePattern) throws SQLException;
1.2 public abstract java.sql.Connection getConnection() throws SQLException;
```

```
public abstract ResultSet getCrossReference(String primaryCatalog, String primarySchema,
                                            String primaryTable, String foreignCatalog,
                                            String foreignSchema, String foreignTable)
    throws SQLException;
public abstract String getDatabaseProductName() throws SQLException;
public abstract String getDatabaseProductVersion() throws SQLException;
public abstract int getDefaultTransactionIsolation() throws SQLException;
public abstract int getDriverMajorVersion();
public abstract int getDriverMinorVersion();
public abstract String getDriverName() throws SQLException;
public abstract String getDriverVersion() throws SQLException;
public abstract ResultSet getExportedKeys(String catalog, String schema, String table)
    throws SQLException;
public abstract String getExtraNameCharacters() throws SQLException;
public abstract String getIdentifierQuoteString() throws SQLException;
public abstract ResultSet getImportedKeys(String catalog, String schema, String table)
    throws SQLException;
public abstract ResultSet getIndexInfo(String catalog, String schema, String table, boolean unique,
                                       boolean approximate) throws SQLException;
public abstract int getMaxBinaryLiteralLength() throws SQLException;
public abstract int getMaxCatalogNameLength() throws SQLException;
public abstract int getMaxCharLiteralLength() throws SQLException;
public abstract int getMaxColumnNameLength() throws SQLException;
public abstract int getMaxColumnsInGroupBy() throws SQLException;
public abstract int getMaxColumnsInIndex() throws SQLException;
public abstract int getMaxColumnsInOrderBy() throws SQLException;
public abstract int getMaxColumnsInSelect() throws SQLException;
public abstract int getMaxColumnsInTable() throws SQLException;
public abstract int getMaxConnections() throws SQLException;
public abstract int getMaxCursorNameLength() throws SQLException;
public abstract int getMaxIndexLength() throws SQLException;
public abstract int getMaxProcedureNameLength() throws SQLException;
public abstract int getMaxRowSize() throws SQLException;
public abstract int getMaxSchemaNameLength() throws SQLException;
public abstract int getMaxStatementLength() throws SQLException;
public abstract int getMaxStatements() throws SQLException;
public abstract int getMaxTableNameLength() throws SQLException;
public abstract int getMaxTablesInSelect() throws SQLException;
public abstract int getMaxUserNameLength() throws SQLException;
public abstract String getNumericFunctions() throws SQLException;
public abstract ResultSet getPrimaryKeys(String catalog, String schema, String table)
    throws SQLException;
public abstract ResultSet getProcedureColumns(String catalog, String schemaPattern,
                                              String procedureNamePattern, String columnNamePattern)
    throws SQLException;
public abstract ResultSet getProcedures(String catalog, String schemaPattern,
                                        String procedureNamePattern) throws SQLException;
public abstract String getProcedureTerm() throws SQLException;
public abstract ResultSet getSchemas() throws SQLException;
public abstract String getSchemaTerm() throws SQLException;
public abstract String getSearchStringEscape() throws SQLException;
public abstract String getSQLKeywords() throws SQLException;
public abstract String getStringFunctions() throws SQLException;
public abstract String getSystemFunctions() throws SQLException;
public abstract ResultSet getTablePrivileges(String catalog, String schemaPattern,
                                             String tableNamePattern) throws SQLException;
public abstract ResultSet getTables(String catalog, String schemaPattern, String tableNamePattern,
                                    String[] types) throws SQLException;
```

```
    public abstract ResultSet getTableTypes() throws SQLException;
    public abstract String getTimeDateFunctions() throws SQLException;
    public abstract ResultSet getTypeInfo() throws SQLException;
1.2 public abstract ResultSet getUDTs(String catalog, String schemaPattern, String typeNamePattern, int[ ] types)
        throws SQLException;
    public abstract String getURL() throws SQLException;
    public abstract String getUserName() throws SQLException;
    public abstract ResultSet getVersionColumns(String catalog, String schema, String table)
        throws SQLException;
1.2 public abstract boolean insertsAreDetected(int type) throws SQLException;
    public abstract boolean isCatalogAtStart() throws SQLException;
    public abstract boolean isReadOnly() throws SQLException;
    public abstract boolean nullPlusNonNullIsNull() throws SQLException;
    public abstract boolean nullsAreSortedAtEnd() throws SQLException;
    public abstract boolean nullsAreSortedAtStart() throws SQLException;
    public abstract boolean nullsAreSortedHigh() throws SQLException;
    public abstract boolean nullsAreSortedLow() throws SQLException;
1.2 public abstract boolean othersDeletesAreVisible(int type) throws SQLException;
1.2 public abstract boolean othersInsertsAreVisible(int type) throws SQLException;
1.2 public abstract boolean othersUpdatesAreVisible(int type) throws SQLException;
1.2 public abstract boolean ownDeletesAreVisible(int type) throws SQLException;
1.2 public abstract boolean ownInsertsAreVisible(int type) throws SQLException;
1.2 public abstract boolean ownUpdatesAreVisible(int type) throws SQLException;
    public abstract boolean storesLowerCaseIdentifiers() throws SQLException;
    public abstract boolean storesLowerCaseQuotedIdentifiers() throws SQLException;
    public abstract boolean storesMixedCaseIdentifiers() throws SQLException;
    public abstract boolean storesMixedCaseQuotedIdentifiers() throws SQLException;
    public abstract boolean storesUpperCaseIdentifiers() throws SQLException;
    public abstract boolean storesUpperCaseQuotedIdentifiers() throws SQLException;
    public abstract boolean supportsAlterTableWithAddColumn() throws SQLException;
    public abstract boolean supportsAlterTableWithDropColumn() throws SQLException;
    public abstract boolean supportsANSI92EntryLevelSQL() throws SQLException;
    public abstract boolean supportsANSI92FullSQL() throws SQLException;
    public abstract boolean supportsANSI92IntermediateSQL() throws SQLException;
1.2 public abstract boolean supportsBatchUpdates() throws SQLException;
    public abstract boolean supportsCatalogsInDataManipulation() throws SQLException;
    public abstract boolean supportsCatalogsInIndexDefinitions() throws SQLException;
    public abstract boolean supportsCatalogsInPrivilegeDefinitions() throws SQLException;
    public abstract boolean supportsCatalogsInProcedureCalls() throws SQLException;
    public abstract boolean supportsCatalogsInTableDefinitions() throws SQLException;
    public abstract boolean supportsColumnAliasing() throws SQLException;
    public abstract boolean supportsConvert() throws SQLException;
    public abstract boolean supportsConvert(int fromType, int toType) throws SQLException;
    public abstract boolean supportsCoreSQLGrammar() throws SQLException;
    public abstract boolean supportsCorrelatedSubqueries() throws SQLException;
    public abstract boolean supportsDataDefinitionAndDataManipulationTransactions() throws
        SQLException;
    public abstract boolean supportsDataManipulationTransactionsOnly() throws SQLException;
    public abstract boolean supportsDifferentTableCorrelationNames() throws SQLException;
    public abstract boolean supportsExpressionsInOrderBy() throws SQLException;
    public abstract boolean supportsExtendedSQLGrammar() throws SQLException;
    public abstract boolean supportsFullOuterJoins() throws SQLException;
    public abstract boolean supportsGroupBy() throws SQLException;
    public abstract boolean supportsGroupByBeyondSelect() throws SQLException;
    public abstract boolean supportsGroupByUnrelated() throws SQLException;
    public abstract boolean supportsIntegrityEnhancementFacility() throws SQLException;
    public abstract boolean supportsLikeEscapeClause() throws SQLException;
    public abstract boolean supportsLimitedOuterJoins() throws SQLException;
```

```
    public abstract boolean supportsMinimumSQLGrammar() throws SQLException;
    public abstract boolean supportsMixedCaseIdentifiers() throws SQLException;
    public abstract boolean supportsMixedCaseQuotedIdentifiers() throws SQLException;
    public abstract boolean supportsMultipleResultSets() throws SQLException;
    public abstract boolean supportsMultipleTransactions() throws SQLException;
    public abstract boolean supportsNonNullableColumns() throws SQLException;
    public abstract boolean supportsOpenCursorsAcrossCommit() throws SQLException;
    public abstract boolean supportsOpenCursorsAcrossRollback() throws SQLException;
    public abstract boolean supportsOpenStatementsAcrossCommit() throws SQLException;
    public abstract boolean supportsOpenStatementsAcrossRollback() throws SQLException;
    public abstract boolean supportsOrderByUnrelated() throws SQLException;
    public abstract boolean supportsOuterJoins() throws SQLException;
    public abstract boolean supportsPositionedDelete() throws SQLException;
    public abstract boolean supportsPositionedUpdate() throws SQLException;
1.2 public abstract boolean supportsResultSetConcurrency(int type, int concurrency)
        throws SQLException;
1.2 public abstract boolean supportsResultSetType(int type) throws SQLException;
    public abstract boolean supportsSchemasInDataManipulation() throws SQLException;
    public abstract boolean supportsSchemasInIndexDefinitions() throws SQLException;
    public abstract boolean supportsSchemasInPrivilegeDefinitions() throws SQLException;
    public abstract boolean supportsSchemasInProcedureCalls() throws SQLException;
    public abstract boolean supportsSchemasInTableDefinitions() throws SQLException;
    public abstract boolean supportsSelectForUpdate() throws SQLException;
    public abstract boolean supportsStoredProcedures() throws SQLException;
    public abstract boolean supportsSubqueriesInComparisons() throws SQLException;
    public abstract boolean supportsSubqueriesInExists() throws SQLException;
    public abstract boolean supportsSubqueriesInIns() throws SQLException;
    public abstract boolean supportsSubqueriesInQuantifieds() throws SQLException;
    public abstract boolean supportsTableCorrelationNames() throws SQLException;
    public abstract boolean supportsTransactionIsolationLevel(int level) throws SQLException;
    public abstract boolean supportsTransactions() throws SQLException;
    public abstract boolean supportsUnion() throws SQLException;
    public abstract boolean supportsUnionAll() throws SQLException;
1.2 public abstract boolean updatesAreDetected(int type) throws SQLException;
    public abstract boolean usesLocalFilePerTable() throws SQLException;
    public abstract boolean usesLocalFiles() throws SQLException;
}
```

Returned By: java.sql.Connection.getMetaData()

DataTruncation — Java 1.1

java.sql — *serializable checked PJ1.1(opt)*

This subclass of SQLWarning is a special warning used when JDBC unexpectedly truncates a data value. It is chained as a warning on read operations and thrown as an exception on write operations.

```
public class DataTruncation extends SQLWarning {
// Public Constructors
    public DataTruncation(int index, boolean parameter, boolean read, int dataSize, int transferSize);
// Public Instance Methods
    public int getDataSize();
    public int getIndex();
    public boolean getParameter();
    public boolean getRead();
    public int getTransferSize();
}
```

Hierarchy: Object→ Throwable(Serializable)→ Exception→ SQLException→ SQLWarning→ DataTruncation

Date **Java 1.1**

java.sql ***cloneable serializable comparable PJ1.1(opt)***

A wrapper around the java.util.Date class that adjusts the time value (milliseconds since January 1, 1970 0:00:00 GMT) to conform to the SQL DATE specification. The DATE type only deals with the day, month, and year, so the hours, minutes, seconds, and milliseconds are set to 00:00:00.00 in the current time zone. The Date class also includes a static valueOf() method that decodes the JDBC Date escape syntax *yyyy-mm-dd* into a Date value.

```
public class Date extends java.util.Date {
// Public Constructors
   public Date(long date);
#  public Date(int year, int month, int day);
// Public Class Methods
   public static java.sql.Date valueOf(String s);
// Public methods overriding Date
   public void setTime(long date);
   public String toString();
// Deprecated Public Methods
#  public int getHours();                         Overrides:Date
#  public int getMinutes();                       Overrides:Date
#  public int getSeconds();                       Overrides:Date
#  public void setHours(int i);                   Overrides:Date
#  public void setMinutes(int i);                 Overrides:Date
#  public void setSeconds(int i);                 Overrides:Date
}
```

Hierarchy: Object→ java.util.Date(Serializable, Cloneable, Comparable)→ java.sql.Date

Passed To: PreparedStatement.setDate(), ResultSet.updateDate(), SQLOutput.writeDate(), javax.sql.RowSet.setDate()

Returned By: CallableStatement.getDate(), java.sql.Date.valueOf(), ResultSet.getDate(), SQLInput.readDate()

Driver **Java 1.1**

java.sql ***PJ1.1(opt)***

Every JDBC driver must implement the Driver interface. Most programmers never need to deal with this interface, except when using the DriverManager.registerDriver() method, which is generally not recommended. The better way to register a driver is to load the driver by calling Class.forName() on the driver class, which automatically registers the driver as well.

```
public abstract interface Driver {
// Public Instance Methods
   public abstract boolean acceptsURL(String url) throws SQLException;
   public abstract java.sql.Connection connect(String url, java.util.Properties info) throws SQLException;
   public abstract int getMajorVersion();
   public abstract int getMinorVersion();
   public abstract DriverPropertyInfo[ ] getPropertyInfo(String url, java.util.Properties info)
       throws SQLException;
   public abstract boolean jdbcCompliant();
}
```

Passed To: DriverManager.{deregisterDriver(), registerDriver()}

Returned By: DriverManager.getDriver()

DriverManager — Java 1.1

java.sql — *PJ1.1(opt)*

The DriverManager class is responsible for loading JDBC drivers and creating Connection objects. It starts by loading all the drivers specified in the jdbc.drivers system property. Individual drivers can also be loaded by calling Class.forName() with the driver class name.

Programs use the static DriverManager.getConnection() method to create individual database connections. The driver manager creates the Connection using the appropriate driver, based on the JDBC URL specified in the call to getConnection().

```
public class DriverManager {
// No Constructor
// Public Class Methods
    public static void deregisterDriver(Driver driver) throws SQLException;                    synchronized
    public static java.sql.Connection getConnection(String url) throws SQLException;           synchronized
    public static java.sql.Connection getConnection(String url, java.util.Properties info)     synchronized
        throws SQLException;
    public static java.sql.Connection getConnection(String url, String user, String password)  synchronized
        throws SQLException;
    public static Driver getDriver(String url) throws SQLException;                            synchronized
    public static java.util.Enumeration getDrivers();                                          synchronized
    public static int getLoginTimeout();
1.2 public static PrintWriter getLogWriter();
    public static void println(String message);                                                synchronized
    public static void registerDriver(Driver driver) throws SQLException;                      synchronized
    public static void setLoginTimeout(int seconds);
1.2 public static void setLogWriter(PrintWriter out);                                          synchronized
// Deprecated Public Methods
#   public static PrintStream getLogStream();
#   public static void setLogStream(PrintStream out);                                          synchronized
}
```

DriverPropertyInfo — Java 1.1

java.sql — *PJ1.1(opt)*

The DriverPropertyInfo class contains the properties required to create a new database connection using a particular driver. It is returned by the getDriverProperties() method of Driver. This class is useful only for programmers who need to interact directly with the driver in a dynamic manner.

```
public class DriverPropertyInfo {
// Public Constructors
    public DriverPropertyInfo(String name, String value);
// Public Instance Fields
    public String[ ] choices;
    public String description;
    public String name;
    public boolean required;
    public String value;
}
```

Returned By: Driver.getPropertyInfo()

PreparedStatement — Java 1.1

java.sql — *PJ1.1(opt)*

The PreparedStatement interface allows programs to precompile SQL statements for increased performance. You obtain a PreparedStatement object with the prepareStatement() method of Connection. Parameters in the statement are denoted by ? characters in the SQL string and indexed from 1 to *n*. Individual parameter values are set using the setXXX() methods, while the clearParameters() method clears all the parameters. Note that some JDBC drivers do not implement setObject() properly when dealing with null field types. Once all parameters have been set, the statement is executed using execute(), executeQuery(), or executeUpdate(). Unlike with the Statement object, the execution methods take no parameters.

```
public abstract interface PreparedStatement extends Statement {
// Public Instance Methods
1.2 public abstract void addBatch() throws SQLException;
    public abstract void clearParameters() throws SQLException;
    public abstract boolean execute() throws SQLException;
    public abstract ResultSet executeQuery() throws SQLException;
    public abstract int executeUpdate() throws SQLException;
1.2 public abstract ResultSetMetaData getMetaData() throws SQLException;
1.2 public abstract void setArray(int i, java.sql.Array x) throws SQLException;
    public abstract void setAsciiStream(int parameterIndex, java.io.InputStream x, int length)
        throws SQLException;
    public abstract void setBigDecimal(int parameterIndex, java.math.BigDecimal x) throws SQLException;
    public abstract void setBinaryStream(int parameterIndex, java.io.InputStream x, int length)
        throws SQLException;
1.2 public abstract void setBlob(int i, Blob x) throws SQLException;
    public abstract void setBoolean(int parameterIndex, boolean x) throws SQLException;
    public abstract void setByte(int parameterIndex, byte x) throws SQLException;
    public abstract void setBytes(int parameterIndex, byte[ ] x) throws SQLException;
1.2 public abstract void setCharacterStream(int parameterIndex, Reader reader, int length)
        throws SQLException;
1.2 public abstract void setClob(int i, Clob x) throws SQLException;
    public abstract void setDate(int parameterIndex, java.sql.Date x) throws SQLException;
1.2 public abstract void setDate(int parameterIndex, java.sql.Date x, java.util.Calendar cal)
        throws SQLException;
    public abstract void setDouble(int parameterIndex, double x) throws SQLException;
    public abstract void setFloat(int parameterIndex, float x) throws SQLException;
    public abstract void setInt(int parameterIndex, int x) throws SQLException;
    public abstract void setLong(int parameterIndex, long x) throws SQLException;
    public abstract void setNull(int parameterIndex, int sqlType) throws SQLException;
1.2 public abstract void setNull(int paramIndex, int sqlType, String typeName) throws SQLException;
    public abstract void setObject(int parameterIndex, Object x) throws SQLException;
    public abstract void setObject(int parameterIndex, Object x, int targetSqlType) throws SQLException;
    public abstract void setObject(int parameterIndex, Object x, int targetSqlType, int scale)
        throws SQLException;
1.2 public abstract void setRef(int i, Ref x) throws SQLException;
    public abstract void setShort(int parameterIndex, short x) throws SQLException;
    public abstract void setString(int parameterIndex, String x) throws SQLException;
    public abstract void setTime(int parameterIndex, Time x) throws SQLException;
1.2 public abstract void setTime(int parameterIndex, Time x, java.util.Calendar cal) throws SQLException;
    public abstract void setTimestamp(int parameterIndex, Timestamp x) throws SQLException;
1.2 public abstract void setTimestamp(int parameterIndex, Timestamp x, java.util.Calendar cal)
        throws SQLException;
```

```
// Deprecated Public Methods
#  public abstract void setUnicodeStream(int parameterIndex, java.io.InputStream x, int length)
       throws SQLException;
}
```

Hierarchy: (PreparedStatement(Statement))

Implementations: CallableStatement

Returned By: java.sql.Connection.prepareStatement()

Ref — Java 1.2

java.sql

The Ref interface provides a pointer to a structured data type within the database. The getBaseType() method returns the name of the underlying type.

```
public abstract interface Ref {
// Public Instance Methods
   public abstract String getBaseTypeName() throws SQLException;
}
```

Passed To: PreparedStatement.setRef(), SQLOutput.writeRef(), javax.sql.RowSet.setRef()

Returned By: CallableStatement.getRef(), ResultSet.getRef(), SQLInput.readRef()

ResultSet — Java 1.1

java.sql — *PJ1.1(opt)*

The ResultSet interface represents a database result set, allowing programs to access the data in the result set. ResultSet objects are usually generated by the execute(), executeUpdate(), and executeQuery() methods of Statement and PreparedStatement. They are also returned by certain metadata methods.

The JDBC 1.0 ResultSet allows you to scroll navigate through the data once from beginning to end, iterating through rows using the next() method and retrieving individual fields using the getXXX() methods. The getMetaData() method returns a ResultSetMetaData object that describes the structure of the underlying data.

JDBC 2.0 introduces a number of new features: complete scrolling capabilities (the previous(), first(), last(), and related methods), direct updating of data via the updateXXX() methods, and insertion of new data rows using the insertRow() method. Since there are relatively few JDBC 2.0-compliant drivers (currently available as of this book's print date), you may want to avoid the JDBC 2.0 methods for the time being.

```
public abstract interface ResultSet {
// Public Constants
1.2 public static final int CONCUR_READ_ONLY;                         =1007
1.2 public static final int CONCUR_UPDATABLE;                         =1008
1.2 public static final int FETCH_FORWARD;                            =1000
1.2 public static final int FETCH_REVERSE;                            =1001
1.2 public static final int FETCH_UNKNOWN;                            =1002
1.2 public static final int TYPE_FORWARD_ONLY;                        =1003
1.2 public static final int TYPE_SCROLL_INSENSITIVE;                  =1004
1.2 public static final int TYPE_SCROLL_SENSITIVE;                    =1005
// Public Instance Methods
1.2 public abstract boolean absolute(int row) throws SQLException;
1.2 public abstract void afterLast() throws SQLException;
1.2 public abstract void beforeFirst() throws SQLException;
1.2 public abstract void cancelRowUpdates() throws SQLException;
```

```
    public abstract void clearWarnings( ) throws SQLException;
    public abstract void close( ) throws SQLException;
1.2 public abstract void deleteRow( ) throws SQLException;
    public abstract int findColumn(String columnName) throws SQLException;
1.2 public abstract boolean first( ) throws SQLException;
1.2 public abstract java.sql.Array getArray(String colName) throws SQLException;
1.2 public abstract java.sql.Array getArray(int i) throws SQLException;
    public abstract java.io.InputStream getAsciiStream(String columnName) throws SQLException;
    public abstract java.io.InputStream getAsciiStream(int columnIndex) throws SQLException;
1.2 public abstract java.math.BigDecimal getBigDecimal(String columnName) throws SQLException;
1.2 public abstract java.math.BigDecimal getBigDecimal(int columnIndex) throws SQLException;
    public abstract java.io.InputStream getBinaryStream(String columnName) throws SQLException;
    public abstract java.io.InputStream getBinaryStream(int columnIndex) throws SQLException;
1.2 public abstract Blob getBlob(String colName) throws SQLException;
1.2 public abstract Blob getBlob(int i) throws SQLException;
    public abstract boolean getBoolean(String columnName) throws SQLException;
    public abstract boolean getBoolean(int columnIndex) throws SQLException;
    public abstract byte getByte(String columnName) throws SQLException;
    public abstract byte getByte(int columnIndex) throws SQLException;
    public abstract byte[ ] getBytes(String columnName) throws SQLException;
    public abstract byte[ ] getBytes(int columnIndex) throws SQLException;
1.2 public abstract Reader getCharacterStream(String columnName) throws SQLException;
1.2 public abstract Reader getCharacterStream(int columnIndex) throws SQLException;
1.2 public abstract Clob getClob(String colName) throws SQLException;
1.2 public abstract Clob getClob(int i) throws SQLException;
1.2 public abstract int getConcurrency( ) throws SQLException;
    public abstract String getCursorName( ) throws SQLException;
    public abstract java.sql.Date getDate(String columnName) throws SQLException;
    public abstract java.sql.Date getDate(int columnIndex) throws SQLException;
1.2 public abstract java.sql.Date getDate(String columnName, java.util.Calendar cal) throws SQLException;
1.2 public abstract java.sql.Date getDate(int columnIndex, java.util.Calendar cal) throws SQLException;
    public abstract double getDouble(String columnName) throws SQLException;
    public abstract double getDouble(int columnIndex) throws SQLException;
1.2 public abstract int getFetchDirection( ) throws SQLException;
1.2 public abstract int getFetchSize( ) throws SQLException;
    public abstract float getFloat(String columnName) throws SQLException;
    public abstract float getFloat(int columnIndex) throws SQLException;
    public abstract int getInt(String columnName) throws SQLException;
    public abstract int getInt(int columnIndex) throws SQLException;
    public abstract long getLong(String columnName) throws SQLException;
    public abstract long getLong(int columnIndex) throws SQLException;
    public abstract ResultSetMetaData getMetaData( ) throws SQLException;
    public abstract Object getObject(String columnName) throws SQLException;
    public abstract Object getObject(int columnIndex) throws SQLException;
1.2 public abstract Object getObject(String colName, java.util.Map map) throws SQLException;
1.2 public abstract Object getObject(int i, java.util.Map map) throws SQLException;
1.2 public abstract Ref getRef(String colName) throws SQLException;
1.2 public abstract Ref getRef(int i) throws SQLException;
1.2 public abstract int getRow( ) throws SQLException;
    public abstract short getShort(String columnName) throws SQLException;
    public abstract short getShort(int columnIndex) throws SQLException;
1.2 public abstract Statement getStatement( ) throws SQLException;
    public abstract String getString(String columnName) throws SQLException;
    public abstract String getString(int columnIndex) throws SQLException;
    public abstract Time getTime(String columnName) throws SQLException;
    public abstract Time getTime(int columnIndex) throws SQLException;
1.2 public abstract Time getTime(String columnName, java.util.Calendar cal) throws SQLException;
1.2 public abstract Time getTime(int columnIndex, java.util.Calendar cal) throws SQLException;
```

```
    public abstract Timestamp getTimestamp(String columnName) throws SQLException;
    public abstract Timestamp getTimestamp(int columnIndex) throws SQLException;
1.2 public abstract Timestamp getTimestamp(String columnName, java.util.Calendar cal)
        throws SQLException;
1.2 public abstract Timestamp getTimestamp(int columnIndex, java.util.Calendar cal) throws SQLException;
1.2 public abstract int getType() throws SQLException;
    public abstract SQLWarning getWarnings() throws SQLException;
1.2 public abstract void insertRow() throws SQLException;
1.2 public abstract boolean isAfterLast() throws SQLException;
1.2 public abstract boolean isBeforeFirst() throws SQLException;
1.2 public abstract boolean isFirst() throws SQLException;
1.2 public abstract boolean isLast() throws SQLException;
1.2 public abstract boolean last() throws SQLException;
1.2 public abstract void moveToCurrentRow() throws SQLException;
1.2 public abstract void moveToInsertRow() throws SQLException;
    public abstract boolean next() throws SQLException;
1.2 public abstract boolean previous() throws SQLException;
1.2 public abstract void refreshRow() throws SQLException;
1.2 public abstract boolean relative(int rows) throws SQLException;
1.2 public abstract boolean rowDeleted() throws SQLException;
1.2 public abstract boolean rowInserted() throws SQLException;
1.2 public abstract boolean rowUpdated() throws SQLException;
1.2 public abstract void setFetchDirection(int direction) throws SQLException;
1.2 public abstract void setFetchSize(int rows) throws SQLException;
1.2 public abstract void updateAsciiStream(String columnName, java.io.InputStream x, int length)
        throws SQLException;
1.2 public abstract void updateAsciiStream(int columnIndex, java.io.InputStream x, int length)
        throws SQLException;
1.2 public abstract void updateBigDecimal(String columnName, java.math.BigDecimal x)
        throws SQLException;
1.2 public abstract void updateBigDecimal(int columnIndex, java.math.BigDecimal x) throws SQLException;
1.2 public abstract void updateBinaryStream(String columnName, java.io.InputStream x, int length)
        throws SQLException;
1.2 public abstract void updateBinaryStream(int columnIndex, java.io.InputStream x, int length)
        throws SQLException;
1.2 public abstract void updateBoolean(String columnName, boolean x) throws SQLException;
1.2 public abstract void updateBoolean(int columnIndex, boolean x) throws SQLException;
1.2 public abstract void updateByte(String columnName, byte x) throws SQLException;
1.2 public abstract void updateByte(int columnIndex, byte x) throws SQLException;
1.2 public abstract void updateBytes(String columnName, byte[ ] x) throws SQLException;
1.2 public abstract void updateBytes(int columnIndex, byte[ ] x) throws SQLException;
1.2 public abstract void updateCharacterStream(String columnName, Reader reader, int length)
        throws SQLException;
1.2 public abstract void updateCharacterStream(int columnIndex, Reader x, int length)
        throws SQLException;
1.2 public abstract void updateDate(String columnName, java.sql.Date x) throws SQLException;
1.2 public abstract void updateDate(int columnIndex, java.sql.Date x) throws SQLException;
1.2 public abstract void updateDouble(String columnName, double x) throws SQLException;
1.2 public abstract void updateDouble(int columnIndex, double x) throws SQLException;
1.2 public abstract void updateFloat(String columnName, float x) throws SQLException;
1.2 public abstract void updateFloat(int columnIndex, float x) throws SQLException;
1.2 public abstract void updateInt(String columnName, int x) throws SQLException;
1.2 public abstract void updateInt(int columnIndex, int x) throws SQLException;
1.2 public abstract void updateLong(String columnName, long x) throws SQLException;
1.2 public abstract void updateLong(int columnIndex, long x) throws SQLException;
1.2 public abstract void updateNull(String columnName) throws SQLException;
1.2 public abstract void updateNull(int columnIndex) throws SQLException;
1.2 public abstract void updateObject(String columnName, Object x) throws SQLException;
```

```
1.2 public abstract void updateObject(int columnIndex, Object x) throws SQLException;
1.2 public abstract void updateObject(String columnName, Object x, int scale) throws SQLException;
1.2 public abstract void updateObject(int columnIndex, Object x, int scale) throws SQLException;
1.2 public abstract void updateRow() throws SQLException;
1.2 public abstract void updateShort(String columnName, short x) throws SQLException;
1.2 public abstract void updateShort(int columnIndex, short x) throws SQLException;
1.2 public abstract void updateString(String columnName, String x) throws SQLException;
1.2 public abstract void updateString(int columnIndex, String x) throws SQLException;
1.2 public abstract void updateTime(String columnName, Time x) throws SQLException;
1.2 public abstract void updateTime(int columnIndex, Time x) throws SQLException;
1.2 public abstract void updateTimestamp(String columnName, Timestamp x) throws SQLException;
1.2 public abstract void updateTimestamp(int columnIndex, Timestamp x) throws SQLException;
    public abstract boolean wasNull() throws SQLException;
// Deprecated Public Methods
#   public abstract java.math.BigDecimal getBigDecimal(String columnName, int scale)
        throws SQLException;
#   public abstract java.math.BigDecimal getBigDecimal(int columnIndex, int scale) throws SQLException;
#   public abstract java.io.InputStream getUnicodeStream(String columnName) throws SQLException;
#   public abstract java.io.InputStream getUnicodeStream(int columnIndex) throws SQLException;
}
```

Implementations: javax.sql.RowSet

Returned By: Too many methods to list.

ResultSetMetaData — Java 1.1

java.sql — *PJ1.1(opt)*

This interface provides metainformation about the data underlying a particular ResultSet. In particular, you can get information about the columns of the ResultSet with getColumnCount(), getColumnLabel(), and getColumnTypeName().

```
public abstract interface ResultSetMetaData {
// Public Constants
    public static final int columnNoNulls;                                    =0
    public static final int columnNullable;                                   =1
    public static final int columnNullableUnknown;                            =2
// Public Instance Methods
    public abstract String getCatalogName(int column) throws SQLException;
1.2 public abstract String getColumnClassName(int column) throws SQLException;
    public abstract int getColumnCount() throws SQLException;
    public abstract int getColumnDisplaySize(int column) throws SQLException;
    public abstract String getColumnLabel(int column) throws SQLException;
    public abstract String getColumnName(int column) throws SQLException;
    public abstract int getColumnType(int column) throws SQLException;
    public abstract String getColumnTypeName(int column) throws SQLException;
    public abstract int getPrecision(int column) throws SQLException;
    public abstract int getScale(int column) throws SQLException;
    public abstract String getSchemaName(int column) throws SQLException;
    public abstract String getTableName(int column) throws SQLException;
    public abstract boolean isAutoIncrement(int column) throws SQLException;
    public abstract boolean isCaseSensitive(int column) throws SQLException;
    public abstract boolean isCurrency(int column) throws SQLException;
    public abstract boolean isDefinitelyWritable(int column) throws SQLException;
    public abstract int isNullable(int column) throws SQLException;
    public abstract boolean isReadOnly(int column) throws SQLException;
    public abstract boolean isSearchable(int column) throws SQLException;
    public abstract boolean isSigned(int column) throws SQLException;
```

```
    public abstract boolean isWritable(int column) throws SQLException;
}
```

Implementations: javax.sql.RowSetMetaData

Returned By: PreparedStatement.getMetaData(), ResultSet.getMetaData()

SQLData — Java 1.2

java.sql

Allows custom mapping of user-defined SQL types. This interface is generally implemented by a development tool or driver vendor and is never called by the programmer directly.

```
public abstract interface SQLData {
// Public Instance Methods
    public abstract String getSQLTypeName() throws SQLException;
    public abstract void readSQL(SQLInput stream, String typeName) throws SQLException;
    public abstract void writeSQL(SQLOutput stream) throws SQLException;
}
```

Passed To: SQLOutput.writeObject()

SQLException — Java 1.1

java.sql — *serializable checked PJ1.1(opt)*

A SQLException object is thrown by any JDBC method that encounters an error. SQLException extends the java.lang.Exception class and adds a vendor-specific error code and an XOPEN SQL state code. SQLException objects can be chained together. The next exception in the chain is retrieved via getNextException(), which returns null if there are no more exceptions available. The setNextException() method adds an exception to the end of the chain.

```
public class SQLException extends Exception {
// Public Constructors
    public SQLException();
    public SQLException(String reason);
    public SQLException(String reason, String SQLState);
    public SQLException(String reason, String SQLState, int vendorCode);
// Public Instance Methods
    public int getErrorCode();                                   default:0
    public SQLException getNextException();                      default:null
    public String getSQLState();                                 default:null
    public void setNextException(SQLException ex);               synchronized
}
```

Hierarchy: Object→ Throwable(Serializable)→ Exception→ SQLException

Subclasses: BatchUpdateException, SQLWarning

Passed To: SQLException.setNextException(), javax.sql.ConnectionEvent.ConnectionEvent()

Returned By: SQLException.getNextException(), javax.sql.ConnectionEvent.getSQLException()

Thrown By: Too many methods to list.

SQLInput — Java 1.2

java.sql

Represents an input stream for a user-defined SQL type. SQLInput is used by the driver and is never called by the programmer directly.

```
public abstract interface SQLInput {
// Public Instance Methods
   public abstract java.sql.Array readArray() throws SQLException;
   public abstract java.io.InputStream readAsciiStream() throws SQLException;
   public abstract java.math.BigDecimal readBigDecimal() throws SQLException;
   public abstract java.io.InputStream readBinaryStream() throws SQLException;
   public abstract Blob readBlob() throws SQLException;
   public abstract boolean readBoolean() throws SQLException;
   public abstract byte readByte() throws SQLException;
   public abstract byte[ ] readBytes() throws SQLException;
   public abstract Reader readCharacterStream() throws SQLException;
   public abstract Clob readClob() throws SQLException;
   public abstract java.sql.Date readDate() throws SQLException;
   public abstract double readDouble() throws SQLException;
   public abstract float readFloat() throws SQLException;
   public abstract int readInt() throws SQLException;
   public abstract long readLong() throws SQLException;
   public abstract Object readObject() throws SQLException;
   public abstract Ref readRef() throws SQLException;
   public abstract short readShort() throws SQLException;
   public abstract String readString() throws SQLException;
   public abstract Time readTime() throws SQLException;
   public abstract Timestamp readTimestamp() throws SQLException;
   public abstract boolean wasNull() throws SQLException;
}
```

Passed To: SQLData.readSQL()

SQLOutput — Java 1.2

java.sql

Represents an output stream for a user-defined SQL type. SQLOutput is used by the driver and is never called by the programmer directly.

```
public abstract interface SQLOutput {
// Public Instance Methods
   public abstract void writeArray(java.sql.Array x) throws SQLException;
   public abstract void writeAsciiStream(java.io.InputStream x) throws SQLException;
   public abstract void writeBigDecimal(java.math.BigDecimal x) throws SQLException;
   public abstract void writeBinaryStream(java.io.InputStream x) throws SQLException;
   public abstract void writeBlob(Blob x) throws SQLException;
   public abstract void writeBoolean(boolean x) throws SQLException;
   public abstract void writeByte(byte x) throws SQLException;
   public abstract void writeBytes(byte[ ] x) throws SQLException;
   public abstract void writeCharacterStream(Reader x) throws SQLException;
   public abstract void writeClob(Clob x) throws SQLException;
   public abstract void writeDate(java.sql.Date x) throws SQLException;
   public abstract void writeDouble(double x) throws SQLException;
   public abstract void writeFloat(float x) throws SQLException;
   public abstract void writeInt(int x) throws SQLException;
   public abstract void writeLong(long x) throws SQLException;
   public abstract void writeObject(SQLData x) throws SQLException;
   public abstract void writeRef(Ref x) throws SQLException;
   public abstract void writeShort(short x) throws SQLException;
   public abstract void writeString(String x) throws SQLException;
   public abstract void writeStruct(Struct x) throws SQLException;
   public abstract void writeTime(Time x) throws SQLException;
```

```
    public abstract void writeTimestamp(Timestamp x) throws SQLException;
}
```

Passed To: SQLData.writeSQL()

SQLWarning — Java 1.1

java.sql — *serializable checked PJ1.1(opt)*

Represents a nonfatal warning condition. Warnings are silently chained to the object whose method produced them. You can retrieve warnings with the getWarnings() method implemented by most JDBC classes.

```
public class SQLWarning extends SQLException {
// Public Constructors
    public SQLWarning();
    public SQLWarning(String reason);
    public SQLWarning(String reason, String SQLstate);
    public SQLWarning(String reason, String SQLstate, int vendorCode);
// Public Instance Methods
    public SQLWarning getNextWarning();                         default:null
    public void setNextWarning(SQLWarning w);
}
```

Hierarchy: Object→ Throwable(Serializable)→ Exception→ SQLException→ SQLWarning

Subclasses: DataTruncation

Passed To: SQLWarning.setNextWarning()

Returned By: java.sql.Connection.getWarnings(), ResultSet.getWarnings(), SQLWarning.getNextWarning(), Statement.getWarnings()

Statement — Java 1.1

java.sql — *PJ1.1(opt)*

The Statement interface executes SQL statements. Statement objects are returned by the createStatement() method of Connection. The execute(), executeUpdate(), and executeQuery() methods each take a Stringparameter that contains a SQL statement. execute() returns a boolean value that indicates whether a ResultSet is available. The ResultSet can then be retrieved with getResultSet(). executeUpdate() returns an update count and is used for INSERT, UPDATE, DELETE, and other data manipulation statements. executeQuery() is used for SELECTstatements, so it returns a ResultSet. There can be only one ResultSet active per query; the current ResultSet is closed when a new SQL statement of any kind is executed.

```
public abstract interface Statement {
// Public Instance Methods
1.2 public abstract void addBatch(String sql) throws SQLException;
    public abstract void cancel() throws SQLException;
1.2 public abstract void clearBatch() throws SQLException;
    public abstract void clearWarnings() throws SQLException;
    public abstract void close() throws SQLException;
    public abstract boolean execute(String sql) throws SQLException;
1.2 public abstract int[ ] executeBatch() throws SQLException;
    public abstract ResultSet executeQuery(String sql) throws SQLException;
    public abstract int executeUpdate(String sql) throws SQLException;
1.2 public abstract java.sql.Connection getConnection() throws SQLException;
1.2 public abstract int getFetchDirection() throws SQLException;
1.2 public abstract int getFetchSize() throws SQLException;
```

```
   public abstract int getMaxFieldSize() throws SQLException;
   public abstract int getMaxRows() throws SQLException;
   public abstract boolean getMoreResults() throws SQLException;
   public abstract int getQueryTimeout() throws SQLException;
   public abstract ResultSet getResultSet() throws SQLException;
1.2 public abstract int getResultSetConcurrency() throws SQLException;
1.2 public abstract int getResultSetType() throws SQLException;
   public abstract int getUpdateCount() throws SQLException;
   public abstract SQLWarning getWarnings() throws SQLException;
   public abstract void setCursorName(String name) throws SQLException;
   public abstract void setEscapeProcessing(boolean enable) throws SQLException;
1.2 public abstract void setFetchDirection(int direction) throws SQLException;
1.2 public abstract void setFetchSize(int rows) throws SQLException;
   public abstract void setMaxFieldSize(int max) throws SQLException;
   public abstract void setMaxRows(int max) throws SQLException;
   public abstract void setQueryTimeout(int seconds) throws SQLException;
}
```

Implementations: PreparedStatement

Returned By: java.sql.Connection.createStatement(), ResultSet.getStatement()

Struct — Java 1.2

java.sql

The Struct interface provides a mapping for an SQL structured type. The getAttributes() method returns an array of objects representing each attribute in the structured type. Custom type maps can be specified by including a java.util.Map attribute.

```
public abstract interface Struct {
// Public Instance Methods
   public abstract Object[ ] getAttributes() throws SQLException;
   public abstract Object[ ] getAttributes(java.util.Map map) throws SQLException;
   public abstract String getSQLTypeName() throws SQLException;
}
```

Passed To: SQLOutput.writeStruct()

Time — Java 1.1

java.sql — *cloneable serializable comparable PJ1.1(opt)*

A wrapper around the java.util.Date class that adjusts the time value (milliseconds since January 1, 1970 0:00:00 GMT) to conform to the SQL TIME specification. The TIME type only deals with the time of day, so the date components are set to January 1, 1970 and should not be altered. The Time class also includes a static valueOf() method that decodes the JDBC Time escape syntax *hh:mm:ss* into a Time value.

```
public class Time extends java.util.Date {
// Public Constructors
   public Time(long time);
   public Time(int hour, int minute, int second);
// Public Class Methods
   public static Time valueOf(String s);
// Public methods overriding Date
   public void setTime(long time);
   public String toString();
// Deprecated Public Methods
#  public int getDate();                                          Overrides:Date
```

```
# public int getDay();                                          Overrides:Date
# public int getMonth();                                        Overrides:Date
# public int getYear();                                         Overrides:Date
# public void setDate(int i);                                   Overrides:Date
# public void setMonth(int i);                                  Overrides:Date
# public void setYear(int i);                                   Overrides:Date
}
```

Hierarchy: Object→ java.util.Date(Serializable, Cloneable, Comparable)→ Time

Passed To: PreparedStatement.setTime(), ResultSet.updateTime(), SQLOutput.writeTime(), javax.sql.RowSet.setTime()

Returned By: CallableStatement.getTime(), ResultSet.getTime(), SQLInput.readTime(), Time.valueOf()

Timestamp **Java 1.1**

java.sql ***cloneable serializable comparable PJ1.1(opt)***

Extends the java.util.Date class to function as an SQL TIMESTAMP value by adding a nanoseconds component. The getTime() method returns the time in milliseconds since January 1, 1970 00:00:00 GMT to the latest integral second. To include fractional seconds, divide the value returned by getNanos() by 1 million and add this to the result returned by getTime(). This allows accurate comparisons with java.util.Date objects. The valueOf() method parses a String in the format *yyyy-mm-dd hh:mm:ss.fffffffff* into a Timestamp.

```
public class Timestamp extends java.util.Date {
// Public Constructors
   public Timestamp(long time);
#  public Timestamp(int year, int month, int date, int hour, int minute, int second, int nano);
// Public Class Methods
   public static Timestamp valueOf(String s);
// Public Instance Methods
   public boolean after(Timestamp ts);
   public boolean before(Timestamp ts);
   public boolean equals(Timestamp ts);
   public int getNanos();
   public void setNanos(int n);
// Public methods overriding Date
1.2 public boolean equals(Object ts);
   public String toString();
}
```

Hierarchy: Object→ java.util.Date(Serializable, Cloneable, Comparable)→ Timestamp

Passed To: PreparedStatement.setTimestamp(), ResultSet.updateTimestamp(), SQLOutput.writeTimestamp(), Timestamp.{after(), before(), equals()}, javax.sql.RowSet.setTimestamp()

Returned By: CallableStatement.getTimestamp(), ResultSet.getTimestamp(), SQLInput.readTimestamp(), Timestamp.valueOf()

Types **Java 1.1**

java.sql ***PJ1.1(opt)***

The Types class defines a set of integer constants that represent SQL data types. The type names and constant values are the ones specified in the XOPEN specification.

```
public class Types {
// No Constructor
```

```
// Public Constants
1.2 public static final int ARRAY;                                  =2003
    public static final int BIGINT;                                 =-5
    public static final int BINARY;                                 =-2
    public static final int BIT;                                    =-7
1.2 public static final int BLOB;                                   =2004
    public static final int CHAR;                                   =1
1.2 public static final int CLOB;                                   =2005
    public static final int DATE;                                   =91
    public static final int DECIMAL;                                =3
1.2 public static final int DISTINCT;                               =2001
    public static final int DOUBLE;                                 =8
    public static final int FLOAT;                                  =6
    public static final int INTEGER;                                =4
1.2 public static final int JAVA_OBJECT;                            =2000
    public static final int LONGVARBINARY;                          =-4
    public static final int LONGVARCHAR;                            =-1
    public static final int NULL;                                   =0
    public static final int NUMERIC;                                =2
    public static final int OTHER;                                  =1111
    public static final int REAL;                                   =7
1.2 public static final int REF;                                    =2006
    public static final int SMALLINT;                               =5
1.2 public static final int STRUCT;                                 =2002
    public static final int TIME;                                   =92
    public static final int TIMESTAMP;                              =93
    public static final int TINYINT;                                =-6
    public static final int VARBINARY;                              =-3
    public static final int VARCHAR;                                =12
}
```

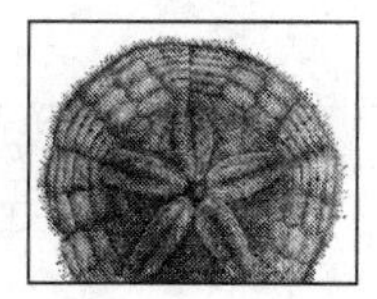

CHAPTER 19

The javax.ejb Package

The javax.ejb package is the primary package in the Enterprise JavaBeans API. It contains interfaces for all the key entities you need to create and use EJB objects. It also contains a number of EJB-specific exceptions. Figure 19-1 shows the class hierarchy of this package.

There are no concrete implementations provided for any of the interfaces in the javax.ejb package. EJB providers build their own implementations based on the EJB specification and provide them in their EJB-enabled servers. You should, however, build EJB server objects and clients strictly using the standard interfaces defined in this package, in order to keep your code compatible with any standard EJB server.

CreateException — EJB 1.0

javax.ejb — *serializable checked*

This exception must be thrown by all create() methods declared in an Enterprise JavaBeans object's home interface. It is thrown if an error occurs during the process of creating the bean, as opposed to a communications error with the server before or after the bean is created.

```
public class CreateException extends Exception {
// Public Constructors
   public CreateException();
   public CreateException(String message);
}
```

Hierarchy: Object→ Throwable(Serializable)→ Exception→ CreateException

Subclasses: DuplicateKeyException

DuplicateKeyException — EJB 1.0

javax.ejb — *serializable checked*

This extension of CreateException is thrown if a client attempts to create an entity bean using a primary key that matches the key of an existing entity bean of the same type.

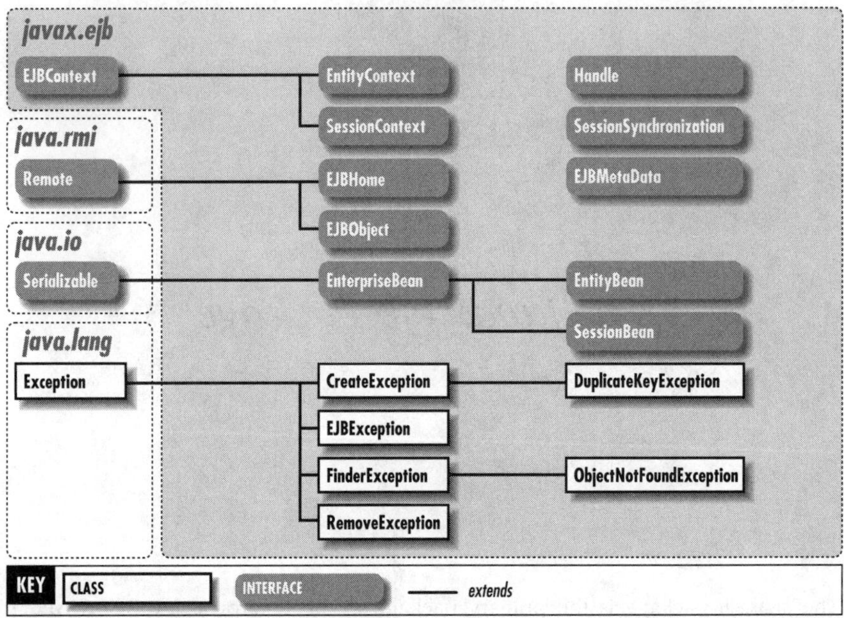

Figure 19-1: The javax.ejb package

```
public class DuplicateKeyException extends CreateException {
// Public Constructors
   public DuplicateKeyException();
   public DuplicateKeyException(String message);
}
```

Hierarchy: Object→ Throwable(Serializable)→ Exception→ CreateException→ DuplicateKeyException

EJBContext **EJB 1.0**

javax.ejb

The EJBContext interface is the base interface for context objects provided to EJB objects by their containers. EJBContext represents runtime context information the EJB object can use during method calls to check on environment variables, query the identity of the caller, etc.

The getCallerIdentity() and isCallerInRole() methods are provided to allow the EJB object to check on the identity of the caller, if it is known. The getEnvironment() method provides a Properties list with any environment variables the EJB container exports to its EJB objects. The getEJBHome() method returns an instance of the EJB object's home interface, which allows the EJB object to query about its own type, implementing classes, etc.

The rest of the EJBContext methods are related to transaction support. The getUserTransaction() method is the EJB object's access to the container-provided implementation of the javax.transaction.UserTransaction interface. The getRollbackOnly() method tells the EJB object if it is operating within a transaction that has been rolled back, and the setRollbackOnly() method sets the current enclosing transaction, if any, to be rolled back.

```
public interface EJBContext {
// Public Instance Methods
   public abstract java.security.Identity getCallerIdentity();
   public abstract EJBHome getEJBHome();
   public abstract java.util.Properties getEnvironment();
   public abstract boolean getRollbackOnly();
   public abstract javax.jts.UserTransaction getUserTransaction() throws java.lang.IllegalStateException;
   public abstract boolean isCallerInRole(java.security.Identity role);
   public abstract void setRollbackOnly();
}
```

Implementations: EntityContext, SessionContext

EJBException — EJB 1.0

javax.ejb — *serializable checked*

Thrown by an Enterprise JavaBeans implementation when it encounters an error during the execution of a client-invoked business method or a container-invoked notification method. The container receives the exception (since it serves as a proxy for all client interactions with the bean) and is responsible for converting the EJBException to an appropriate subclass of java.rmi.RemoteException to be returned to the client.

If the EJB object was operating within a container-defined transaction context when the exception was thrown, the container does a rollback on the transaction before throwing the RemoteException to the client. If the bean was operating within a client-defined transaction context, the container marks the transaction for rollback and throws a javax.transaction.TransactionRolledbackException (a subclass of RemoteException) to the client, to indicate that it should give up on its transaction.

```
public class EJBException extends Exception {
// Public Constructors
   public EJBException();
   public EJBException(Exception ex);
   public EJBException(String message);
// Public Instance Methods
   public Exception getCausedByException();                                default:null
}
```

Hierarchy: Object→ Throwable(Serializable)→ Exception→ EJBException

EJBHome — EJB 1.0

javax.ejb — *remote*

The EJBHome interface is the base interface for all home interfaces for Enterprise JavaBeans. If you develop an Enterprise JavaBeans object, you have to provide a home interface for it that extends this interface. The home interface allows clients to create beans of the corresponding type and to find them, if it is an entity bean. When you extend the EJBHome interface to create a home interface for your EJB object type, you must specify any create or finder methods for the bean you intend to provide for the client. The EJBHome interface provides two remove() methods that let a client remove its reference to a bean from the container and a getEJBMetaData() method that returns an EJBMetaData instance for the EJB object's type.

```
public interface EJBHome extends java.rmi.Remote {
// Public Instance Methods
   public abstract EJBMetaData getEJBMetaData() throws java.rmi.RemoteException;
   public abstract void remove(Object primaryKey) throws java.rmi.RemoteException, RemoveException;
```

```
    public abstract void remove(Handle handle) throws java.rmi.RemoteException, RemoveException;
}
```

Hierarchy: (EJBHome(java.rmi.Remote))

Returned By: EJBContext.getEJBHome(), EJBMetaData.getEJBHome(), EJBObject.getEJBHome()

EJBMetaData — EJB 1.0

javax.ejb

This interface provides metadata on a particular type of Enterprise JavaBeans object. It allows you to query for the bean type's home interface, the Class for its home interface, the Class of its primary key (for entity beans only), the Class for its remote interface, and whether the bean is a session bean or an entity bean. This metadata might be used by EJB development tools to introspect on additional aspects of EJB classes that cannot be obtained from the Object introspection methods. Any implementation of this interface is required to be serializable and must be valid for use over RMI.

```
public interface EJBMetaData {
// Public Instance Methods
    public abstract EJBHome getEJBHome();
    public abstract Class getHomeInterfaceClass();
    public abstract Class getPrimaryKeyClass();
    public abstract Class getRemoteInterfaceClass();
    public abstract boolean isSession();
}
```

Returned By: EJBHome.getEJBMetaData()

EJBObject — EJB 1.0

javax.ejb — *remote*

This interface is the base interface for all remote interfaces for Enterprise JavaBeans. When a client acquires a remote reference to an EJB object, it is given an instance of the EJBObject interface as a stub. If you develop an Enterprise JavaBeans object, you must provide a remote interface for it by extending the EJBObject interface. In the remote interface for your EJB object type, you specify the business methods on your bean that are accessible by remote clients.

The EJBObject interface provides methods that allow a client to query the bean's home interface, get a portable handle for the remote bean, get the primary key for the bean (if it is an entity bean), compare the bean for equality with another bean, and remove the client's reference to the bean.

```
public interface EJBObject extends java.rmi.Remote {
// Public Instance Methods
    public abstract EJBHome getEJBHome() throws java.rmi.RemoteException;
    public abstract Handle getHandle() throws java.rmi.RemoteException;
    public abstract Object getPrimaryKey() throws java.rmi.RemoteException;
    public abstract boolean isIdentical(EJBObject obj) throws java.rmi.RemoteException;
    public abstract void remove() throws java.rmi.RemoteException, RemoveException;
}
```

Hierarchy: (EJBObject(java.rmi.Remote))

Passed To: EJBObject.isIdentical()

Returned By: EntityContext.getEJBObject(), Handle.getEJBObject(), SessionContext.getEJBObject()

EnterpriseBean **EJB 1.0**

javax.ejb *serializable*

This interface is the base interface for all Enterprise JavaBeans implementations. If you develop an Enterprise JavaBeans object, your bean implementation must extend this interface, usually by extending one of the derived interfaces, SessionBean or EntityBean. The EnterpriseBean interface is a marker interface only and does not define any methods.

```
public interface EnterpriseBean extends Serializable {
}
```

Hierarchy: (EnterpriseBean(Serializable))

Implementations: EntityBean, SessionBean

EntityBean **EJB 1.0**

javax.ejb *serializable*

This interface is the base interface for all entity EJB objects. The methods defined on the EntityBean interface are used by EJB containers to notify the entity bean about entity-specific events, such as the need to (re)load its state from persistent storage.

The ejbActivate() and ejbPassivate() methods are called on the bean by the container when the bean is associated and disassociated with a specific entity, respectively. The ejbLoad() and ejbStore() methods are called when the entity bean needs to read and write its persistent state, respectively. The ejbRemove() method is called when the entity associated with this bean should be removed from persistent storage. When the container sets the entity bean's context, it calls the setEntityContext() method. The container removes the association with a given context by calling the unsetEntityContext() method.

```
public interface EntityBean extends EnterpriseBean {
// Public Instance Methods
   public abstract void ejbActivate() throws java.rmi.RemoteException;
   public abstract void ejbLoad() throws java.rmi.RemoteException;
   public abstract void ejbPassivate() throws java.rmi.RemoteException;
   public abstract void ejbRemove() throws java.rmi.RemoteException, RemoveException;
   public abstract void ejbStore() throws java.rmi.RemoteException;
   public abstract void setEntityContext(EntityContext ctx) throws java.rmi.RemoteException;
   public abstract void unsetEntityContext() throws java.rmi.RemoteException;
}
```

Hierarchy: (EntityBean(EnterpriseBean(Serializable)))

EntityContext **EJB 1.0**

javax.ejb

This extension of the EJBContext interface represents runtime context information for an entity bean. In addition to the context provided by the EJBContext methods, EntityContext allows the entity bean to query for its primary key and a remote reference to itself.

```
public interface EntityContext extends EJBContext {
// Public Instance Methods
   public abstract EJBObject getEJBObject() throws java.lang.IllegalStateException;
   public abstract Object getPrimaryKey() throws java.lang.IllegalStateException;
}
```

Hierarchy: (EntityContext(EJBContext))

Passed To: EntityBean.setEntityContext()

FinderException — EJB 1.0

javax.ejb — *serializable checked*

This exception must be thrown by any finder methods declared on an entity bean's home interface. It is thrown if an error occurred while the server attempted to find the requested entity or entities.

```
public class FinderException extends Exception {
// Public Constructors
   public FinderException();
   public FinderException(String message);
}
```

Hierarchy: Object→ Throwable(Serializable)→ Exception→ FinderException

Subclasses: ObjectNotFoundException

Handle — EJB 1.0

javax.ejb

A Handle represents a portable reference to a remote EJB object, in that it can be serialized, passed across Java VM boundaries, and then used to reconstitute a remote reference to the same EJB object from which it was acquired. You acquire a handle for an EJB object using the getHandle() method on its remote EJBObject.

The Handle interface acts as a base interface for EJB type-specific handle classes, which are typically generated for you by container deployment tools. Its only method is getEJBObject(), which returns a remote reference to the EJB object that it represents.

```
public interface Handle {
// Public Instance Methods
   public abstract EJBObject getEJBObject() throws java.rmi.RemoteException;
}
```

Passed To: EJBHome.remove()

Returned By: EJBObject.getHandle()

ObjectNotFoundException — EJB 1.0

javax.ejb — *serializable checked*

This subclass of FinderException is thrown by finder methods that are declared to return a single entity bean, when the requested entity can't be found in the server's persistent storage.

```
public class ObjectNotFoundException extends FinderException {
// Public Constructors
   public ObjectNotFoundException();
   public ObjectNotFoundException(String message);
}
```

Hierarchy: Object→ Throwable(Serializable)→ Exception→ FinderException→ ObjectNotFoundException

RemoveException — EJB 1.0

javax.ejb — *serializable checked*

Thrown by the remove methods on an EJB home interface, when an attempt to remove a bean from its container is rejected or fails at either the container or the EJB object level.

```
public class RemoveException extends Exception {
// Public Constructors
   public RemoveException();
   public RemoveException(String message);
}
```

Hierarchy: Object→ Throwable(Serializable)→ Exception→ RemoveException

Thrown By: EJBHome.remove(), EJBObject.remove(), EntityBean.ejbRemove()

SessionBean — EJB 1.0

javax.ejb — *serializable*

This is the base interface for all session Enterprise JavaBeans implementations. The methods on this interface are used by the EJB container to notify the bean about certain events.

The ejbActivate() and ejbPassivate() methods are invoked by the container when the bean leaves/enters (respectively) a passive state in the container. After the ejbPassivate() method completes, the container should be able to serialize the bean object and store it to disk or some other persistent storage, if the container chooses. During the ejbActivate() method, the bean can restore any data or resources it released when it was passivated. The container calls ejbRemove() on the bean just before the bean is destroyed. The container sets the bean's context by calling its setSessionContext() method. The session bean keeps the same context throughout its lifetime, so there is no corresponding unset method, as there is for EntityBean.

```
public interface SessionBean extends EnterpriseBean {
// Public Instance Methods
   public abstract void ejbActivate() throws java.rmi.RemoteException;
   public abstract void ejbPassivate() throws java.rmi.RemoteException;
   public abstract void ejbRemove() throws java.rmi.RemoteException;
   public abstract void setSessionContext(SessionContext ctx) throws java.rmi.RemoteException;
}
```

Hierarchy: (SessionBean(EnterpriseBean(Serializable)))

SessionContext — EJB 1.0

javax.ejb

This extension of the EJBContext interface represents runtime context information for a session bean. In addition to the context provided by the EJBContex methods, SessionContext allows the session bean to query for a remote reference to itself.

```
public interface SessionContext extends EJBContext {
// Public Instance Methods
   public abstract EJBObject getEJBObject() throws java.lang.IllegalStateException;
}
```

Hierarchy: (SessionContext(EJBContext))

Passed To: SessionBean.setSessionContext()

SessionSynchronization — EJB 1.0

javax.ejb

Session beans are not required to be transactional, but if you want your session bean to be notified of transaction boundaries, you can have your bean implementation class extend the SessionSynchronization interface. The EJB container invokes the methods on this interface to notify your bean about the start and end of transactions.

The afterBegin() is called when a new transaction has started. Any business methods invoked on the bean between this point and a subsequent call to its beforeCompletion() method execute within the context of this transaction. The beforeCompletion() method is called on the bean when a transaction is about to end. The afterCompletion() method is called after the transaction has ended, and the boolean argument tells the bean whether the transaction was committed successfully (true) or rolled back (false).

```
public interface SessionSynchronization {
// Public Instance Methods
   public abstract void afterBegin() throws java.rmi.RemoteException;
   public abstract void afterCompletion(boolean committed) throws java.rmi.RemoteException;
   public abstract void beforeCompletion() throws java.rmi.RemoteException;
}
```

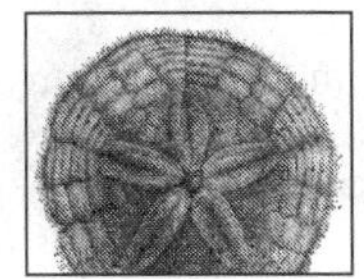

CHAPTER 20

The javax.ejb.deployment Package

The javax.ejb.deployment package defines classes used by EJB containers to encapsulate information about EJB objects. An EJB container should provide a tool that creates an instance of the EntityDescriptor or SessionDescriptor class for a bean, initializes its fields, and then serializes that initialized instance. Then, when the bean is deployed into the EJB container, the container reads the serialized deployment descriptor class and its properties to obtain configuration information for the bean. Figure 20-1 shows the class hierarchy of this package.

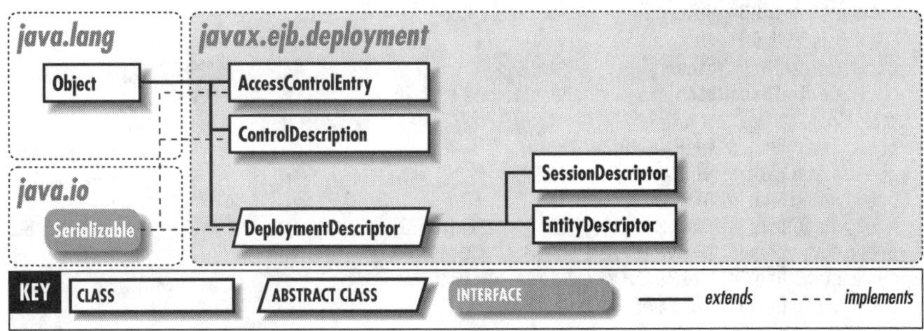

Figure 20–1: The javax.ejb.deployment package class hierarchy

AccessControlEntry — EJB 1.0

javax.ejb.deployment — *serializable*

This is a serializable class that represents a security-related entry within a bean deployment descriptor. Each AccessControlEntry included within a DeploymentDescriptor specifies a list of identities, in the form of java.security.Identity objects, that should have access to a particular method on a bean. If there is no method set for the entry, the entry is considered the default access control entry for the entire bean, listing which identities should have access to the bean. Any method on a bean without its own AccessControlEntry object uses the default entry for access control.

```
public class AccessControlEntry implements Serializable {
// Public Constructors
   public AccessControlEntry();
   public AccessControlEntry(java.lang.reflect.Method method);
   public AccessControlEntry(java.lang.reflect.Method method, java.security.Identity[ ] identities);
// Public Instance Methods
   public java.security.Identity[ ] getAllowedIdentities();                    default:null
   public java.security.Identity getAllowedIdentities(int index);
   public java.lang.reflect.Method getMethod();                                default:null
   public void setAllowedIdentities(java.security.Identity[ ] values);
   public void setAllowedIdentities(int index, java.security.Identity value);
   public void setMethod(java.lang.reflect.Method value);
}
```

Hierarchy: Object→ AccessControlEntry(Serializable)

Passed To: DeploymentDescriptor.setAccessControlEntries()

Returned By: DeploymentDescriptor.getAccessControlEntries()

ControlDescriptor **EJB 1.0**

javax.ejb.deployment ***serializable***

A ControlDescriptor is a component of a DeploymentDescriptor that specifies how a container should manage the transaction and security features for a specific method on a bean. If no method is specified in the ControlDescriptor, the features apply by default to all methods on the bean, unless a method has its own ControlDescriptor.

The methods on the ControlDescriptor let you specify the transaction isolation level (using the constant TRANSACTION_XXX members of the class), the identity under which to run the method, the run-as mode (CLIENT_IDENTITY, SPECIFIED_IDENTITY, or SYSTEM_IDENTITY), and how transactions should be managed for the method (using the TX_XXX constants).

```
public class ControlDescriptor implements Serializable {
// Public Constructors
   public ControlDescriptor();
   public ControlDescriptor(java.lang.reflect.Method method);
// Public Constants
   public static final int CLIENT_IDENTITY;                                    =0
   public static final int SPECIFIED_IDENTITY;                                 =1
   public static final int SYSTEM_IDENTITY;                                    =2
   public static final int TRANSACTION_READ_COMMITTED;                         =2
   public static final int TRANSACTION_READ_UNCOMMITTED;                       =1
   public static final int TRANSACTION_REPEATABLE_READ;                        =4
   public static final int TRANSACTION_SERIALIZABLE;                           =8
   public static final int TX_BEAN_MANAGED;                                    =1
   public static final int TX_MANDATORY;                                       =5
   public static final int TX_NOT_SUPPORTED;                                   =0
   public static final int TX_REQUIRED;                                        =2
   public static final int TX_REQUIRES_NEW;                                    =4
   public static final int TX_SUPPORTS;                                        =3
// Public Instance Methods
   public int getIsolationLevel();                                             default:2
   public java.lang.reflect.Method getMethod();                                default:null
   public java.security.Identity getRunAsIdentity();                           default:null
   public int getRunAsMode();                                                  default:1
   public int getTransactionAttribute();                                       default:3
```

```
    public void setIsolationLevel(int value);
    public void setMethod(java.lang.reflect.Method value);
    public void setRunAsIdentity(java.security.Identity value);
    public void setRunAsMode(int value);
    public void setTransactionAttribute(int value);
}
```

Hierarchy: Object→ ControlDescriptor(Serializable)

Passed To: DeploymentDescriptor.setControlDescriptors()

Returned By: DeploymentDescriptor.getControlDescriptors()

DeploymentDescriptor — EJB 1.0

javax.ejb.deployment — *serializable*

DeploymentDescriptor is a serializable class that contains all the parameters that tell an EJB container how to deploy and manage a bean. A serialized DeploymentDescriptor object is packaged with the relevant classes for an EJB object when it is deployed within an EJB container. The container deserializes the DeploymentDescriptor object and reads the deployment information from it.

This abstract base class defines deployment properties that apply to any type of bean; the SessionDescriptor and EntityDescriptor subclasses define additional properties specific to deploying session beans and entity beans.

The DeploymentDescriptor provides access to a list of AccessControlEntry objects that specify the access levels for the methods on the bean, as well as a list of ControlDescriptor objects that specify how transactions and security features should be handled for specific methods on the bean. The descriptor also contains the class names for the bean implementation class, its home interface, and its remote interface, as well as a boolean flag that indicates whether the bean is reentrant.

```
public abstract class DeploymentDescriptor implements Serializable {
// Public Constructors
    public DeploymentDescriptor();
// Public Instance Methods
    public AccessControlEntry[ ] getAccessControlEntries();
    public AccessControlEntry getAccessControlEntries(int index);
    public javax.naming.Name getBeanHomeName();
    public ControlDescriptor[ ] getControlDescriptors();
    public ControlDescriptor getControlDescriptors(int index);
    public String getEnterpriseBeanClassName();
    public java.util.Properties getEnvironmentProperties();
    public String getHomeInterfaceClassName();
    public boolean getReentrant();
    public String getRemoteInterfaceClassName();
    public boolean isReentrant();
    public void setAccessControlEntries(AccessControlEntry[ ] values);
    public void setAccessControlEntries(int index, AccessControlEntry value);
    public void setBeanHomeName(javax.naming.Name value);
    public void setControlDescriptors(ControlDescriptor[ ] value);
    public void setControlDescriptors(int index, ControlDescriptor value);
    public void setEnterpriseBeanClassName(String value);
    public void setEnvironmentProperties(java.util.Properties value);
    public void setHomeInterfaceClassName(String value);
    public void setReentrant(boolean value);
    public void setRemoteInterfaceClassName(String value);
```

```
// Protected Instance Fields
    protected int versionNumber;
}
```

Hierarchy: Object→ DeploymentDescriptor(Serializable)

Subclasses: EntityDescriptor, SessionDescriptor

EntityDescriptor — EJB 1.0

javax.ejb.deployment — ***serializable***

This extension of DeploymentDescriptor adds deployment properties specific to entity beans. It contains a list of bean properties whose persistence should be managed by the container, as well as the name of the bean's primary key class.

```
public class EntityDescriptor extends DeploymentDescriptor {
// Public Constructors
    public EntityDescriptor();
// Public Instance Methods
    public java.lang.reflect.Field[ ] getContainerManagedFields();                default:null
    public java.lang.reflect.Field getContainerManagedFields(int index);
    public String getPrimaryKeyClassName();                                        default:""
    public void setContainerManagedFields(java.lang.reflect.Field[ ] values);
    public void setContainerManagedFields(int index, java.lang.reflect.Field value);
    public void setPrimaryKeyClassName(String value);
}
```

Hierarchy: Object→ DeploymentDescriptor(Serializable)→ EntityDescriptor

SessionDescriptor — EJB 1.0

javax.ejb.deployment — ***serializable***

This extension of DeploymentDescriptor class adds deployment properties specific to session beans. Included are the bean's timeout period and whether it's stateful or stateless.

```
public class SessionDescriptor extends DeploymentDescriptor {
// Public Constructors
    public SessionDescriptor();
// Public Constants
    public static final int STATEFUL_SESSION;                                      =1
    public static final int STATELESS_SESSION;                                     =0
// Public Instance Methods
    public int getSessionTimeout();                                                default:0
    public int getStateManagementType();                                           default:1
    public void setSessionTimeout(int value);
    public void setStateManagementType(int value);
}
```

Hierarchy: Object→ DeploymentDescriptor(Serializable)→ SessionDescriptor

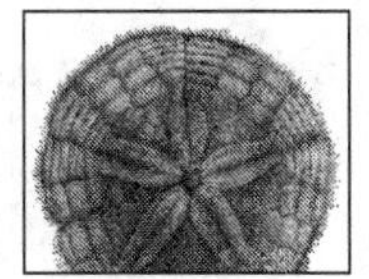

CHAPTER 21

The javax.jms Package

javax.jms

The javax.jms package implements the Java Message Service (JMS), which provides an API for message-based communication between separate Java processes. Message-based communication is asynchronous; a message addressed to a recipient or group is sent, and the recipient receives and acts on the message at some later time. This is different from other network-based communication between clients, like RMI, where the sender of a message waits for a response before continuing.

In the JMS model, clients of a message service send and receive messages through a provider that is responsible for delivering messages. JMS 1.0 provides two models for messaging among clients: *point-to-point* and *publish/subscribe*. In *point-to-point messaging*, a message is created by one client and addressed for a single remote recipient. The provider is handed the message and delivers it to the one recipient targeted by the message. This model revolves around message queues: a message sender queues outgoing messages for delivery and a message recipient queues incoming messages for handling. The interfaces provided in the javax.jms package for point-to-point messaging have "Queue" as their prefix (QueueConnection, QueueSession, etc.). In *publish/subscribe messaging*, a hierarchical content tree is established. Clients publish messages to specific nodes or topics in the tree, and these messages are delivered to any clients that have subscribed to these nodes. Interfaces related to publish/subscribe messaging have "Topic" as their prefix (TopicConnection, TopicSession, etc.). Point-to-point messaging is analogous to typical email messaging; publish/subscribe messaging works like Internet newsgroups.

In a typical scenario, a JMS client gets a reference to a ConnectionFactory from the JMS provider (usually through a JNDI lookup). The ConnectionFactory creates a Connection to the provider. With the Connection, a client can create Session objects to send and receive messages. Within a single Session, messages are sent and received in a serial order. Once the client has a Session, it can send and receive Message objects composed of a header, optional properties, and a body. Different types of Message objects can hold different contents in their body (e.g., text, binary data, name/value pairs).

Figure 21-1 shows the interfaces in the javax.jms package, while Figure 21-2 shows the classes and exceptions.

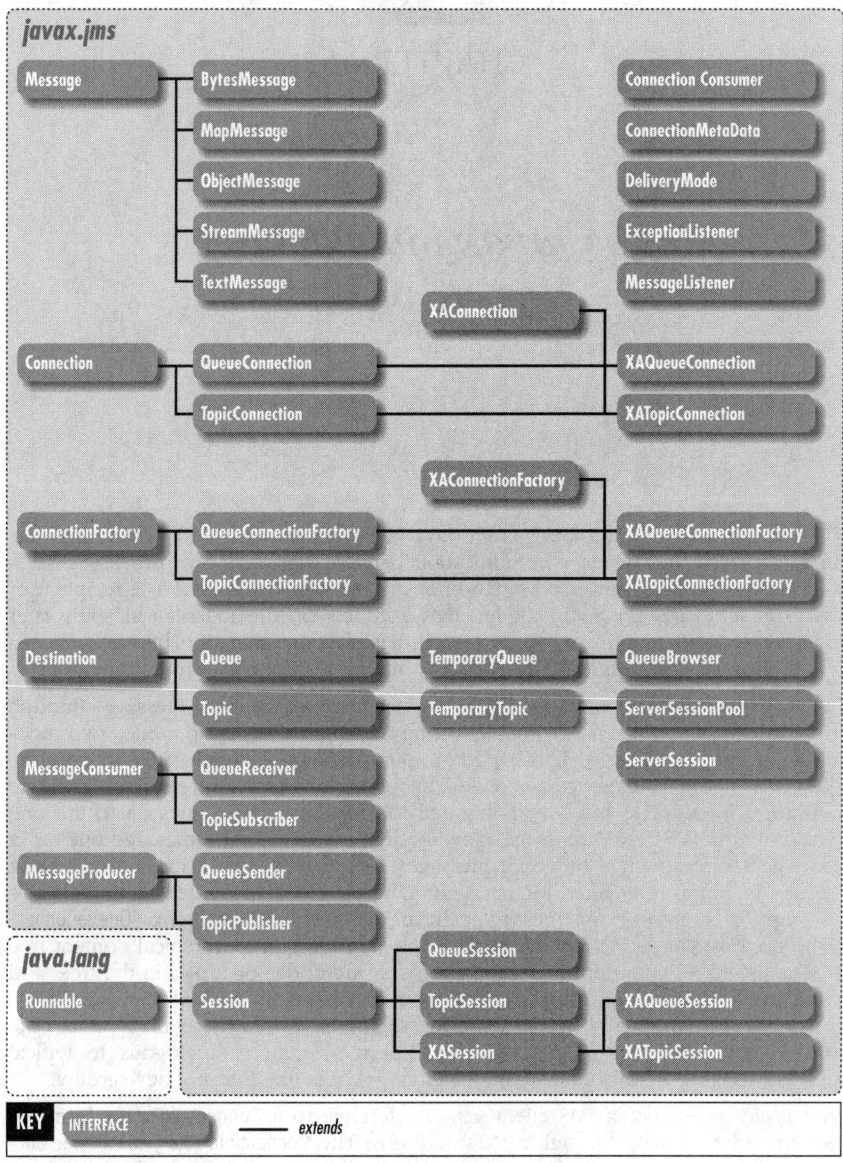

Figure 21-1: The interfaces of the javax.jms package

BytesMessage **JMS 1.0**

javax.jms

A BytesMessage is a Message that contains an uninterpreted stream of bytes as its body. This is typically used to wrap an existing (non-JMS) message format so that it can be

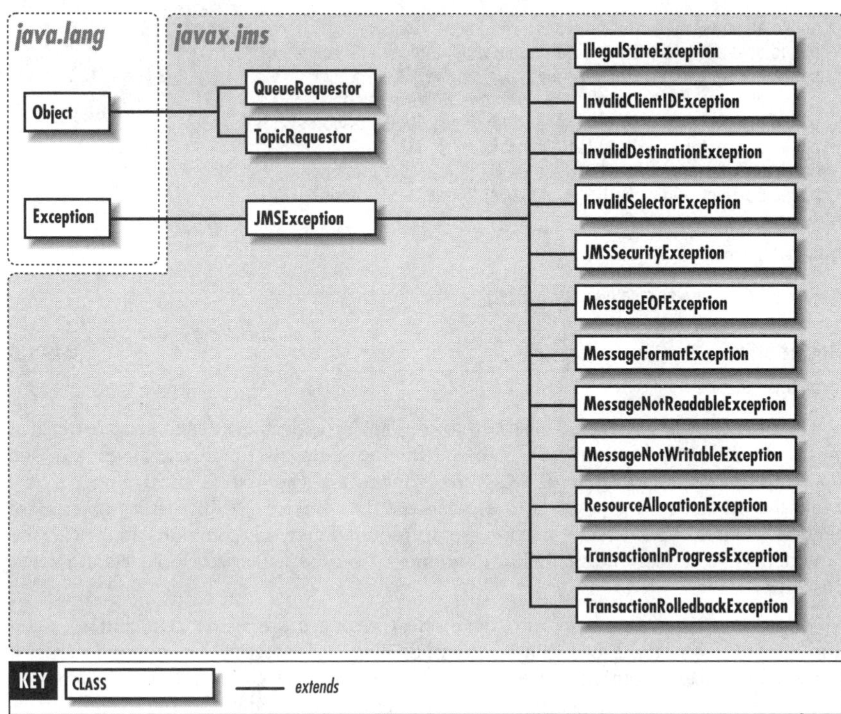

Figure 21-2: The classes and exceptions of the javax.jms package

delivered over JMS. Data is written to the message's binary body using its writeXXX() methods and read using its readXXX() methods. Once a BytesMessage has been created (using a series of write calls), the reset() method can put the message into read-only mode. Until this is done, the message is in write-only mode, and the contents cannot be read.

```
public interface BytesMessage extends Message {
// Public Instance Methods
   public abstract boolean readBoolean() throws JMSException;
   public abstract byte readByte() throws JMSException;
   public abstract int readBytes(byte[ ] value) throws JMSException;
   public abstract int readBytes(byte[ ] value, int length) throws JMSException;
   public abstract char readChar() throws JMSException;
   public abstract double readDouble() throws JMSException;
   public abstract float readFloat() throws JMSException;
   public abstract int readInt() throws JMSException;
   public abstract long readLong() throws JMSException;
   public abstract short readShort() throws JMSException;
   public abstract int readUnsignedByte() throws JMSException;
   public abstract int readUnsignedShort() throws JMSException;
   public abstract String readUTF() throws JMSException;
   public abstract void reset() throws JMSException;
   public abstract void writeBoolean(boolean value) throws JMSException;
   public abstract void writeByte(byte value) throws JMSException;
   public abstract void writeBytes(byte[ ] value) throws JMSException;
   public abstract void writeBytes(byte[ ] value, int offset, int length) throws JMSException;
```

```
    public abstract void writeChar(char value) throws JMSException;
    public abstract void writeDouble(double value) throws JMSException;
    public abstract void writeFloat(float value) throws JMSException;
    public abstract void writeInt(int value) throws JMSException;
    public abstract void writeLong(long value) throws JMSException;
    public abstract void writeObject(Object value) throws JMSException;
    public abstract void writeShort(short value) throws JMSException;
    public abstract void writeUTF(String value) throws JMSException;
}
```

Hierarchy: (BytesMessage(Message))

Returned By: Session.createBytesMessage()

Connection — JMS 1.0

javax.jms

A JMS client needs to have a Connection to the JMS provider in order to send or receive messages. The javax.jms.Connection interface for messaging is roughly analogous to the java.sql.Connection interface in JDBC—one connects a client to a messaging service, while the other connects a client to a persistent data service. JMS Connection objects are generally expensive to create, because setup requires network communication with the provider. Thus, a client normally has only one, or very few, Connection objects to its JMS provider.

A Connection can either be in running mode (messages are being sent and received through the connection), or it can be stopped. When a Connection is in stopped mode, it can send messages, but not receive them. A newly created Connection is in stopped mode so that you can finish setting up your client (e.g., creating Session objects; creating MessageConsumer and/or MessageProducer objects). A Connection can be started and stopped using stop() and start() multiple times, if necessary. When you're done with a Connection, you should free up its resources by calling its close() method.

A Connection object creates sessions for message exchanges. The methods for creating sessions are defined by extensions of the Connection interface (QueueConnection and TopicConnection).

```
public interface Connection {
// Public Instance Methods
    public abstract void close() throws JMSException;
    public abstract String getClientID() throws JMSException;
    public abstract ConnectionMetaData getMetaData() throws JMSException;
    public abstract void setClientID(String clientID) throws JMSException;
    public abstract void setExceptionListener(ExceptionListener listener) throws JMSException;
    public abstract void start() throws JMSException;
    public abstract void stop() throws JMSException;
}
```

Implementations: QueueConnection, TopicConnection

ConnectionConsumer — JMS 1.0

javax.jms

A ConnectionConsumer is used in situations where messages need to be read concurrently by multiple agents within the same process (e.g., within an application server running multiple message-based applications). The ConnectionConsumer delivers messages to one or more Session objects that are associated with MessageListener objects for individual clients. It contains a reference to a ServerSessionPool that accesses the Session objects concurrently reading messages. ConnectionConsumer is typically used by an application server to provide a message-handling service for client applications; applications normally don't need to use the interface directly.

```
public interface ConnectionConsumer {
// Public Instance Methods
   public abstract void close() throws JMSException;
   public abstract ServerSessionPool getServerSessionPool() throws JMSException;
}
```

Returned By: QueueConnection.createConnectionConsumer(), TopicConnection.{createConnectionConsumer(), createDurableConnectionConsumer()}

ConnectionFactory — JMS 1.0

javax.jms

A messaging client uses a ConnectionFactory to get a Connection object to a message provider. A ConnectionFactory is usually acquired through a JNDI lookup. The ConnectionFactory interface doesn't define methods for creating Connection objects; these methods are provided by extensions to this interface (e.g., QueueConnectionFactory, TopicConnectionFactory).

```
public interface ConnectionFactory {
}
```

Implementations: QueueConnectionFactory, TopicConnectionFactory

ConnectionMetaData — JMS 1.0

javax.jms

The Connection.getMetaData() method returns a ConnectionMetaData object that holds information about the JMS connection, including the version of JMS being used by the provider and version information about the provider itself.

```
public interface ConnectionMetaData {
// Public Instance Methods
   public abstract int getJMSMajorVersion() throws JMSException;
   public abstract int getJMSMinorVersion() throws JMSException;
   public abstract String getJMSProviderName() throws JMSException;
   public abstract String getJMSVersion() throws JMSException;
   public abstract int getProviderMajorVersion() throws JMSException;
   public abstract int getProviderMinorVersion() throws JMSException;
   public abstract String getProviderVersion() throws JMSException;
}
```

Returned By: javax.jms.Connection.getMetaData()

DeliveryMode — JMS 1.0

javax.jms

This interface defines constants that represent delivery modes a JMS provider can support. NON_PERSISTENT delivery implies that a significant failure by the provider before a message can be delivered causes the message to be lost. PERSISTENT delivery mode implies that the provider stores messages to persistent storage, so that the messages survive a crash by the provider. A message sender specifies the delivery mode for a Message in its header, using the Message.setJMSDeliveryMode() method, and the provider is responsible for honoring the delivery mode.

```
public interface DeliveryMode {
// Public Constants
```

javax.jms

```
    public static final int NON_PERSISTENT;                                    =1
    public static final int PERSISTENT;                                        =2
}
```

Destination **JMS 1.0**

javax.jms

A Destination represents a delivery address for a message. This interface is simply a marker interface, without any methods or members, since JMS does not attempt to define an addressing syntax. An implementor of a JMS provider needs to provide implementations of this interface that define its message-addressing syntax. Destination objects might be published by a JMS provider using JNDI. In this case, a JMS client needs to assemble the name of the queue in the syntax expected by the provider and then do a JNDI lookup to get a reference to the Destination.

```
public interface Destination {
}
```

Implementations: Queue, Topic

Passed To: Message.{setJMSDestination(), setJMSReplyTo()}

Returned By: Message.{getJMSDestination(), getJMSReplyTo()}

ExceptionListener **JMS 1.0**

javax.jms

An ExceptionListener gets asynchronous notification of errors that occur with a Connection to a JMS provider. If a client registers an ExceptionListener with a Connection using the Connection.setExceptionListener() method, the provider calls the onException() method on the ExceptionListener when any error occurs, passing it the exception that describes the error.

```
public interface ExceptionListener {
// Public Instance Methods
    public abstract void onException(JMSException exception);
}
```

Passed To: javax.jms.Connection.setExceptionListener()

IllegalStateException **JMS 1.0**

javax.jms *serializable checked*

Thrown if a request is made of a provider at a time when the request cannot be satisfied.

```
public class IllegalStateException extends JMSException {
// Public Constructors
    public IllegalStateException(String reason);
    public IllegalStateException(String reason, String errorCode);
}
```

Hierarchy: Object→ Throwable(Serializable)→ Exception→ JMSException→ IllegalStateException

InvalidClientIDException **JMS 1.0**

javax.jms *serializable checked*

Thrown by the Connection.setClientID() method when an invalid client ID is given.

```
public class InvalidClientIDException extends JMSException {
// Public Constructors
   public InvalidClientIDException(String reason);
   public InvalidClientIDException(String reason, String errorCode);
}
```

Hierarchy: Object→ Throwable(Serializable)→ Exception→ JMSException→ InvalidClientIDException

InvalidDestinationException — JMS 1.0

javax.jms — *serializable checked*

Thrown when the provider encounters a destination it cannot understand or is no longer accessible by the provider (e.g., a topic has been removed from a publish/subscribe context, or a queue associated with a user account has been removed because the account has been closed).

```
public class InvalidDestinationException extends JMSException {
// Public Constructors
   public InvalidDestinationException(String reason);
   public InvalidDestinationException(String reason, String errorCode);
}
```

Hierarchy: Object→ Throwable(Serializable)→ Exception→ JMSException→ InvalidDestinationException

InvalidSelectorException — JMS 1.0

javax.jms — *serializable checked*

Thrown when a malformed selector is given to a provider (e.g., as part of a MessageSelector).

```
public class InvalidSelectorException extends JMSException {
// Public Constructors
   public InvalidSelectorException(String reason);
   public InvalidSelectorException(String reason, String errorCode);
}
```

Hierarchy: Object→ Throwable(Serializable)→ Exception→ JMSException→ InvalidSelectorException

JMSException — JMS 1.0

javax.jms — *serializable checked*

This is the base class for all JMS-related exceptions. It provides a provider-specific error code and a nested exception that is the source of the error.

```
public class JMSException extends Exception {
// Public Constructors
   public JMSException(String reason);
   public JMSException(String reason, String errorCode);
// Public Instance Methods
   public String getErrorCode();
   public Exception getLinkedException();
   public void setLinkedException(Exception ex);                synchronized
}
```

Hierarchy: Object→ Throwable(Serializable)→ Exception→ JMSException

Subclasses: javax.jms.IllegalStateException, InvalidClientIDException, InvalidDestinationException, InvalidSelectorException, JMSSecurityException, MessageEOFException, MessageFormatException, MessageNotReadableException, MessageNotWriteableException, ResourceAllocationException, TransactionInProgressException, TransactionRolledBackException

Passed To: ExceptionListener.onException()

Thrown By: Too many methods to list.

JMSSecurityException **JMS 1.0**

javax.jms *serializable checked*

Thrown by a provider when a request cannot be satisfied for security reasons (e.g., a client-provided name/password fails authentication).

```
public class JMSSecurityException extends JMSException {
// Public Constructors
   public JMSSecurityException(String reason);
   public JMSSecurityException(String reason, String errorCode);
}
```

Hierarchy: Object→ Throwable(Serializable)→ Exception→ JMSException→ JMSSecurityException

MapMessage **JMS 1.0**

javax.jms

A MapMessage has a set of name/value pairs as its message body. The name of a property is a String, and the value is a Java primitive type. There are getXXX() and setXXX() methods for each primitive type, plus getObject() and setObject() methods for situations where the type of the value is not known until runtime. If a property is set to a value of a certain type, it has to be read back using a get method appropriate for that type, according to this table:

If written as:	*Can be read as:* boolean	byte	char	short	int	long	float	double	String	byte[]
boolean	X								X	
byte		X		X	X	X			X	
char			X						X	
short				X	X	X			X	
int					X	X			X	
long						X			X	
float							X	X	X	
double								X	X	
String	X	X	X	X	X	X	X	X	X	
byte[]										X

If a value is read using an inappropriate get method, a MessageFormatException is thrown. The getMapNames() methods returns an Enumeration of names for the values in the MapMessage. A client that receives a MapMessage can read only the contents of the message until it calls clearBody() on the message. If a client tries to write values to the message before this, a MessageNotWriteableException is thrown.

```
public interface MapMessage extends Message {
// Public Instance Methods
   public abstract boolean getBoolean(String name) throws JMSException;
   public abstract byte getByte(String name) throws JMSException;
   public abstract byte[ ] getBytes(String name) throws JMSException;
```

```
public abstract char getChar(String name) throws JMSException;
public abstract double getDouble(String name) throws JMSException;
public abstract float getFloat(String name) throws JMSException;
public abstract int getInt(String name) throws JMSException;
public abstract long getLong(String name) throws JMSException;
public abstract java.util.Enumeration getMapNames( ) throws JMSException;
public abstract Object getObject(String name) throws JMSException;
public abstract short getShort(String name) throws JMSException;
public abstract String getString(String name) throws JMSException;
public abstract boolean itemExists(String name) throws JMSException;
public abstract void setBoolean(String name, boolean value) throws JMSException;
public abstract void setByte(String name, byte value) throws JMSException;
public abstract void setBytes(String name, byte[ ] value) throws JMSException;
public abstract void setBytes(String name, byte[ ] value, int offset, int length) throws JMSException;
public abstract void setChar(String name, char value) throws JMSException;
public abstract void setDouble(String name, double value) throws JMSException;
public abstract void setFloat(String name, float value) throws JMSException;
public abstract void setInt(String name, int value) throws JMSException;
public abstract void setLong(String name, long value) throws JMSException;
public abstract void setObject(String name, Object value) throws JMSException;
public abstract void setShort(String name, short value) throws JMSException;
public abstract void setString(String name, String value) throws JMSException;
}
```

Hierarchy: (MapMessage(Message))

Returned By: Session.createMapMessage()

Message — JMS 1.0

javax.jms

The Message interface is the base interface for all messages in JMS. A Message is composed of a set of predefined header fields, an optional set of application-specific properties, and a body that contains the content of the message. A set and get method are provided for each header field supported by a JMS message. The possible header fields include:

JMSCorrelationID
: A String that identifies another message (e.g., original message for a response) with which this message is related. The ID value is dictated by either the JMS provider or the application.

JMSDeliveryMode
: One of the static values of the DeliveryMode interface.

JMSDestination
: The target of this message, as a Destination object.

JMSExpiration
: The time (in milliseconds since the epoch) when the message will expire. Each client specifies a time-to-live for the messages they send, so this header field is automatically set at send time to the current time plus the client's time-to-live.

JMSMessageID
: A unique String identifier for this message. The provider sets this field automatically when a message is sent.

JMSPriority
A value from 0 to 9 (9 is highest) that indicates the urgency of the message. JMS providers are supposed to attempt to deliver messages with a priority from 5 to 9 before attempting to deliver lower-priority messages.

JMSRedelivered
An indicator that the message was delivered to the client earlier but no acknowledgment was received.

JMSReplyTo
A Destination where the receiver can send a reply to the message.

JMSTimestamp
The time (in milliseconds since the epoch) at which a message was given to a JMS provider for sending.

JMSType
A String that indicates the type of the message. There are no standard values for a message's type; they can be provider- or application-specific.

Properties with names prefixed by "JMSX" are reserved for use by the JMS standard.

Properties can be added to a message using the setXXXProperty() methods and read using the getXXXProperty() methods. If a property is written with a value of a given type, it needs to be read from the message according to the following table:

If written as:	*Can be read as:* boolean	byte	short	int	long	float	double	String
boolean	X							X
byte		X	X	X	X			X
short			X	X	X			X
int				X	X			X
long					X			X
float						X	X	X
double							X	X
String	X	X	X	X	X	X	X	X

If in invalid get method is used for a property, a MessageFormatException is thrown.

```
public interface Message {
// Public Constants
   public static final int DEFAULT_DELIVERY_MODE;                    =-1
   public static final int DEFAULT_PRIORITY;                         =-1
   public static final int DEFAULT_TIME_TO_LIVE;                     =-1
// Public Instance Methods
   public abstract void acknowledge() throws JMSException;
   public abstract void clearBody() throws JMSException;
   public abstract void clearProperties() throws JMSException;
   public abstract boolean getBooleanProperty(String name) throws JMSException;
   public abstract byte getByteProperty(String name) throws JMSException;
   public abstract double getDoubleProperty(String name) throws JMSException;
   public abstract float getFloatProperty(String name) throws JMSException;
   public abstract int getIntProperty(String name) throws JMSException;
   public abstract String getJMSCorrelationID() throws JMSException;
   public abstract byte[ ] getJMSCorrelationIDAsBytes() throws JMSException;
   public abstract int getJMSDeliveryMode() throws JMSException;
```

```
    public abstract Destination getJMSDestination() throws JMSException;
    public abstract long getJMSExpiration() throws JMSException;
    public abstract String getJMSMessageID() throws JMSException;
    public abstract int getJMSPriority() throws JMSException;
    public abstract boolean getJMSRedelivered() throws JMSException;
    public abstract Destination getJMSReplyTo() throws JMSException;
    public abstract long getJMSTimestamp() throws JMSException;
    public abstract String getJMSType() throws JMSException;
    public abstract long getLongProperty(String name) throws JMSException;
    public abstract Object getObjectProperty(String name) throws JMSException;
    public abstract java.util.Enumeration getPropertyNames() throws JMSException;
    public abstract short getShortProperty(String name) throws JMSException;
    public abstract String getStringProperty(String name) throws JMSException;
    public abstract boolean propertyExists(String name) throws JMSException;
    public abstract void setBooleanProperty(String name, boolean value) throws JMSException;
    public abstract void setByteProperty(String name, byte value) throws JMSException;
    public abstract void setDoubleProperty(String name, double value) throws JMSException;
    public abstract void setFloatProperty(String name, float value) throws JMSException;
    public abstract void setIntProperty(String name, int value) throws JMSException;
    public abstract void setJMSCorrelationID(String correlationID) throws JMSException;
    public abstract void setJMSCorrelationIDAsBytes(byte[ ] correlationID) throws JMSException;
    public abstract void setJMSDeliveryMode(int deliveryMode) throws JMSException;
    public abstract void setJMSDestination(Destination destination) throws JMSException;
    public abstract void setJMSExpiration(long expiration) throws JMSException;
    public abstract void setJMSMessageID(String id) throws JMSException;
    public abstract void setJMSPriority(int priority) throws JMSException;
    public abstract void setJMSRedelivered(boolean redelivered) throws JMSException;
    public abstract void setJMSReplyTo(Destination replyTo) throws JMSException;
    public abstract void setJMSTimestamp(long timestamp) throws JMSException;
    public abstract void setJMSType(String type) throws JMSException;
    public abstract void setLongProperty(String name, long value) throws JMSException;
    public abstract void setObjectProperty(String name, Object value) throws JMSException;
    public abstract void setShortProperty(String name, short value) throws JMSException;
    public abstract void setStringProperty(String name, String value) throws JMSException;
}
```

Implementations: BytesMessage, MapMessage, ObjectMessage, StreamMessage, TextMessage

Passed To: MessageListener.onMessage(), QueueRequestor.request(), QueueSender.send(), TopicPublisher.publish(), TopicRequestor.request()

Returned By: MessageConsumer.{receive(), receiveNoWait()}, QueueRequestor.request(), Session.createMessage(), TopicRequestor.request()

MessageConsumer — JMS 1.0

javax.jms

A JMS client uses a MessageConsumer to receive messages. A client creates a message consumer by specifying a Destination from which to receive messages and an optional message selector that filters messages according to their header fields and property values. The methods for creating MessageConsumer objects are defined in subinterfaces of the Connection interface.

A message selector is a filter string whose syntax is based on the SQL92 conditional expression syntax. See the JMS specification for more details on the syntax of message selectors.

A client can use a MessageConsumer synchronously by polling it with its receive methods or asynchronously by registering a MessageListener with the consumer. When a message arrives that matches the sending Destination and the message selector, the onMessage() method on the registered listener is called.

A MessageConsumer should be freed by calling its close() method, to free up any resources allocated for it by the provider.

```
public interface MessageConsumer {
// Public Instance Methods
   public abstract void close() throws JMSException;
   public abstract MessageListener getMessageListener() throws JMSException;
   public abstract String getMessageSelector() throws JMSException;
   public abstract Message receive() throws JMSException;
   public abstract Message receive(long timeOut) throws JMSException;
   public abstract Message receiveNoWait() throws JMSException;
   public abstract void setMessageListener(MessageListener listener) throws JMSException;
}
```

Implementations: QueueReceiver, TopicSubscriber

MessageEOFException — JMS 1.0

javax.jms — *serializable checked*

Thrown if the end of a StreamMessage or BytesMessage is reached before it is expected.

```
public class MessageEOFException extends JMSException {
// Public Constructors
   public MessageEOFException(String reason);
   public MessageEOFException(String reason, String errorCode);
}
```

Hierarchy: Object→ Throwable(Serializable)→ Exception→ JMSException→ MessageEOFException

MessageFormatException — JMS 1.0

javax.jms — *serializable checked*

Thrown when an attempt is made to read data from a message as the wrong data type or to write data to a message in a type it does not support.

```
public class MessageFormatException extends JMSException {
// Public Constructors
   public MessageFormatException(String reason);
   public MessageFormatException(String reason, String errorCode);
}
```

Hierarchy: Object→ Throwable(Serializable)→ Exception→ JMSException→ MessageFormatException

MessageListener — JMS 1.0

javax.jms

A MessageListener is registered by a client with a MessageConsumer, to allow the client to asynchronously receive messages. When the consumer receives a message, the listener's onMessage() method is invoked. The consumer waits until the onMessage() method is complete before delivering the next message.

```
public interface MessageListener {
// Public Instance Methods
   public abstract void onMessage(Message message);
}
```

Passed To: MessageConsumer.setMessageListener(), Session.setMessageListener()

Returned By: MessageConsumer.getMessageListener(), Session.getMessageListener()

MessageNotReadableException — JMS 1.0

javax.jms — *serializable checked*

Thrown if a client attempts to read data from a write-only message (e.g., a StreamMessage whose contents have not yet been reset).

```
public class MessageNotReadableException extends JMSException {
// Public Constructors
   public MessageNotReadableException(String reason);
   public MessageNotReadableException(String reason, String errorCode);
}
```

Hierarchy: Object→ Throwable(Serializable)→ Exception→ JMSException→ MessageNotReadableException

MessageNotWriteableException — JMS 1.0

javax.jms — *serializable checked*

Thrown when an attempt is made to write data to a read-only message (e.g., a received MapMessage that has not yet had its clearBody() method called).

```
public class MessageNotWriteableException extends JMSException {
// Public Constructors
   public MessageNotWriteableException(String reason);
   public MessageNotWriteableException(String reason, String errorCode);
}
```

Hierarchy: Object→ Throwable(Serializable)→ Exception→ JMSException→ MessageNotWriteableException

MessageProducer — JMS 1.0

javax.jms

A client uses a MessageProducer to send messages. A MessageProducer can be tied to a specific Destination, and any messages sent through the producer are addressed to the Destination specified when it was created. If a Destination is not specified when a MessageProducer is created, a Destination has to provide for each message sent. Methods to create MessageProducer objects are provided by subinterfaces of the Session interface (e.g., TopicSession, QueueSession).

A MessageProducer has a default delivery mode, priority, and time-to-live for messages it sends. There are get and set methods for these default properties. If these properties are specified on a message, they override the defaults of the MessageProducer.

```
public interface MessageProducer {
// Public Instance Methods
   public abstract void close() throws JMSException;
   public abstract int getDeliveryMode() throws JMSException;
   public abstract boolean getDisableMessageID() throws JMSException;
   public abstract boolean getDisableMessageTimestamp() throws JMSException;
   public abstract int getPriority() throws JMSException;
   public abstract int getTimeToLive() throws JMSException;
   public abstract void setDeliveryMode(int deliveryMode) throws JMSException;
   public abstract void setDisableMessageID(boolean value) throws JMSException;
   public abstract void setDisableMessageTimestamp(boolean value) throws JMSException;
```

```
    public abstract void setPriority(int deliveryMode) throws JMSException;
    public abstract void setTimeToLive(int timeToLive) throws JMSException;
}
```

Implementations: QueueSender, TopicPublisher

ObjectMessage **JMS 1.0**

javax.jms

This is a message that contains a single serialized Java object as its body. Only a Serializable object can be used as the body of an ObjectMessage. When an ObjectMessage is received, it is read-only until the clearBody() method is called on it.

```
public interface ObjectMessage extends Message {
// Public Instance Methods
    public abstract Serializable getObject() throws JMSException;
    public abstract void setObject(Serializable object) throws JMSException;
}
```

Hierarchy: (ObjectMessage(Message))

Returned By: Session.createObjectMessage()

Queue **JMS 1.0**

javax.jms

A Queue is a Destination specific to point-to-point messaging. The Queue has a String name whose syntax is dictated by the provider. Queue objects are created using the createQueue() method on a QueueSession.

```
public interface Queue extends Destination {
// Public Instance Methods
    public abstract String getQueueName() throws JMSException;
    public abstract String toString();
}
```

Hierarchy: (Queue(Destination))

Implementations: TemporaryQueue

Passed To: QueueConnection.createConnectionConsumer(), QueueRequestor.QueueRequestor(), QueueSender.send(), QueueSession.{createBrowser(), createReceiver(), createSender()}

Returned By: QueueBrowser.getQueue(), QueueReceiver.getQueue(), QueueSender.getQueue(), QueueSession.createQueue()

QueueBrowser **JMS 1.0**

javax.jms

A QueueBrowser peeks at the contents of a message queue without actually removing messages. A QueueBrowser has an optional message selector that can filter the messages checked for on the queue. QueueBrowser objects are created using the createBrowser() methods on QueueSession.

```
public interface QueueBrowser {
// Public Instance Methods
    public abstract void close() throws JMSException;
    public abstract java.util.Enumeration getEnumeration() throws JMSException;
    public abstract String getMessageSelector() throws JMSException;
```

```
    public abstract Queue getQueue() throws JMSException;
}
```

Returned By: QueueSession.createBrowser()

QueueConnection JMS 1.0

javax.jms

A QueueConnection is a Connection specific to a point-to-point messaging provider. The QueueConnection allows clients to create QueueSession objects using the createQueueSession() method.

```
public interface QueueConnection extends javax.jms.Connection {
// Public Instance Methods
    public abstract ConnectionConsumer createConnectionConsumer(Queue queue,
                                                                String messageSelector,
                                                                ServerSessionPool sessionPool, int maxMessages)
        throws JMSException;
    public abstract QueueSession createQueueSession(boolean transacted, int acknowledgeMode)
        throws JMSException;
}
```

Hierarchy: (QueueConnection(javax.jms.Connection))

Implementations: XAQueueConnection

Returned By: QueueConnectionFactory.createQueueConnection()

QueueConnectionFactory JMS 1.0

javax.jms

A QueueConnectionFactory is exported by point-to-point providers to allow clients to create QueueConnection objects to the provider. The default createQueueConnection() method creates a connection under the default user identity of the client JVM, while the other constructor accepts a name and password that authenticates the connection request.

```
public interface QueueConnectionFactory extends ConnectionFactory {
// Public Instance Methods
    public abstract QueueConnection createQueueConnection() throws JMSException;
    public abstract QueueConnection createQueueConnection(String userName, String password)
        throws JMSException;
}
```

Hierarchy: (QueueConnectionFactory(ConnectionFactory))

Implementations: XAQueueConnectionFactory

QueueReceiver JMS 1.0

javax.jms

A QueueReceiver is a MessageConsumer specific to point-to-point messaging. The getQueue() method returns the Queue associated with the receiver. QueueReceiver objects are created using the createReceiver() methods on QueueSession.

```
public interface QueueReceiver extends MessageConsumer {
// Public Instance Methods
    public abstract Queue getQueue() throws JMSException;
}
```

javax.jms

Hierarchy: (QueueReceiver(MessageConsumer))

Returned By: QueueSession.createReceiver()

QueueRequestor — JMS 1.0

javax.jms

QueueRequestor is a utility class provided for situations in which a client wants to send a message to a specific destination and wait for a response. A QueueRequestor is constructed with a QueueSession and a destination Queue, and then its request() method is called with the Message to be sent. The QueueRequestor sets the reply-to destination on the message to a temporary Queue that it creates. It sends the message and waits for a response. The response Message is the return value of the request() method.

```
public class QueueRequestor {
// Public Constructors
   public QueueRequestor(QueueSession session, Queue queue) throws JMSException;
// Public Instance Methods
   public void close() throws JMSException;
   public Message request(Message message) throws JMSException;
}
```

QueueSender — JMS 1.0

javax.jms

A QueueSender is a MessageProducer that sends messages in a point-to-point context. QueueSender objects are created using the createQueue() method on QueueSession, specifying a default Queue as the target of messages. A client can override the default message target by using one of the send() methods on the QueueSender that accepts a target Queue. If a send() method is called without a target Queue, and the QueueSender does not have a default target Queue defined (e.g., it was created with a null target Queue), an InvalidDestinationException is thrown.

```
public interface QueueSender extends MessageProducer {
// Public Instance Methods
   public abstract Queue getQueue() throws JMSException;
   public abstract void send(Message message) throws JMSException;
   public abstract void send(Queue queue, Message message) throws JMSException;
   public abstract void send(Message message, int deliveryMode, int priority, long timeToLive)
       throws JMSException;
   public abstract void send(Queue queue, Message message, int deliveryMode, int priority, long timeToLive)
       throws JMSException;
}
```

Hierarchy: (QueueSender(MessageProducer))

Returned By: QueueSession.createSender()

QueueSession — JMS 1.0

javax.jms — *runnable*

The QueueSession is a Session specific to a point-to-point messaging context. It provides methods for creating point-to-point message consumers (QueueReceiver), producers (QueueSender), and destinations (Queue), as well as utilities objects such as QueueBrowser and TemporaryQueue.

```
public interface QueueSession extends Session {
// Public Instance Methods
```

```
    public abstract QueueBrowser createBrowser(Queue queue) throws JMSException;
    public abstract QueueBrowser createBrowser(Queue queue, String messageSelector)
        throws JMSException;
    public abstract Queue createQueue(String queueName) throws JMSException;
    public abstract QueueReceiver createReceiver(Queue queue) throws JMSException;
    public abstract QueueReceiver createReceiver(Queue queue, String messageSelector)
        throws JMSException;
    public abstract QueueSender createSender(Queue queue) throws JMSException;
    public abstract TemporaryQueue createTemporaryQueue( ) throws JMSException;
}
```

Hierarchy: (QueueSession(Session(Runnable)))

Passed To: QueueRequestor.QueueRequestor()

Returned By: QueueConnection.createQueueSession(), XAQueueSession.getQueueSession()

ResourceAllocationException **JMS 1.0**

javax.jms ***serializable checked***

Thrown when a request is made of a provider, and it cannot be completed due to resource issues.

```
public class ResourceAllocationException extends JMSException {
// Public Constructors
    public ResourceAllocationException(String reason);
    public ResourceAllocationException(String reason, String errorCode);
}
```

Hierarchy: Object→ Throwable(Serializable)→ Exception→ JMSException→ ResourceAllocationException

ServerSession **JMS 1.0**

javax.jms

A ServerSession is used by an application server when it needs to separate Session objects to individual threads, for concurrent access to and handling of flows of messages. The ServerSession represents a JMS Session tied to a thread. A ConnectionConsumer keeps a pool of ServerSession objects, which it handles messages as they arrive. The ConnectionConsumer assigns one or more messages to the Session contained in the ServerSession, and then calls the ServerSession's start() method. The ServerSession calls start() on the Thread for the Session, which eventually calls the run() method of the Session (Session implements the java.lang.Runnable interface).

```
public interface ServerSession {
// Public Instance Methods
    public abstract Session getSession( ) throws JMSException;
    public abstract void start( ) throws JMSException;
}
```

Returned By: ServerSessionPool.getServerSession()

ServerSessionPool **JMS 1.0**

javax.jms

A ConnectionConsumer uses a ServerSessionPool to manage a pool of ServerSession objects. The ServerSessionPool can manage the pool any way it likes and can block if the pool is exhausted.

```
public interface ServerSessionPool {
// Public Instance Methods
   public abstract ServerSession getServerSession() throws JMSException;
}
```

Passed To: QueueConnection.createConnectionConsumer(), TopicConnection.{createConnectionConsumer(), createDurableConnectionConsumer()}

Returned By: ConnectionConsumer.getServerSessionPool()

Session — JMS 1.0

javax.jms — *runnable*

A Session provides a client with the means for creating messages, message producers, and message consumers. Extensions of Session create type-specific versions of these objects (e.g., QueueSender and TopicPublisher).

Within a Session, messages are sent and received in a serial order. The Session interface also provides facilities for JMS providers that chose to provide transactional support in their Session implementations. A transaction is started when the Session is created. In a messaging context, a transaction consists of a series of message transmissions and receipts. Committing a messaging transaction (by calling commit() on the corresponding Session) causes all pending transmissions to be sent and all pending receipts to be finalized and acknowledged. If a transaction is aborted (by calling the rollback() method on the Session), the outgoing messages are destroyed, and incoming messages are cancelled. A new transaction is started as soon as the current one is committed or rolled back.

```
public interface Session extends Runnable {
// Public Constants
   public static final int AUTO_ACKNOWLEDGE;                    =1
   public static final int CLIENT_ACKNOWLEDGE;                  =2
   public static final int DUPS_OK_ACKNOWLEDGE;                 =3
// Public Instance Methods
   public abstract void close() throws JMSException;
   public abstract void commit() throws JMSException;
   public abstract BytesMessage createBytesMessage() throws JMSException;
   public abstract MapMessage createMapMessage() throws JMSException;
   public abstract Message createMessage() throws JMSException;
   public abstract ObjectMessage createObjectMessage() throws JMSException;
   public abstract ObjectMessage createObjectMessage(Serializable object) throws JMSException;
   public abstract StreamMessage createStreamMessage() throws JMSException;
   public abstract TextMessage createTextMessage() throws JMSException;
   public abstract TextMessage createTextMessage(StringBuffer stringBuffer) throws JMSException;
   public abstract MessageListener getMessageListener() throws JMSException;
   public abstract boolean getTransacted() throws JMSException;
   public abstract void recover() throws JMSException;
   public abstract void rollback() throws JMSException;
   public abstract void setMessageListener(MessageListener listener) throws JMSException;
}
```

Hierarchy: (Session(Runnable))

Implementations: QueueSession, TopicSession, XASession

Returned By: ServerSession.getSession()

StreamMessage — JMS 1.0

javax.jms

A StreamMessage is a Message whose body consists of a stream of serialized Java primitive data items. It is similar in many ways to a BytesMessage, except that the contents of a StreamMessage are read in the same order they are written by the sender. Otherwise, StreamMessage has a similar set of read/write methods and similar rules about how certain data types are read from the message as BytesMessage.

```
public interface StreamMessage extends Message {
// Public Instance Methods
   public abstract boolean readBoolean() throws JMSException;
   public abstract byte readByte() throws JMSException;
   public abstract int readBytes(byte[ ] value) throws JMSException;
   public abstract char readChar() throws JMSException;
   public abstract double readDouble() throws JMSException;
   public abstract float readFloat() throws JMSException;
   public abstract int readInt() throws JMSException;
   public abstract long readLong() throws JMSException;
   public abstract Object readObject() throws JMSException;
   public abstract short readShort() throws JMSException;
   public abstract String readString() throws JMSException;
   public abstract void reset() throws JMSException;
   public abstract void writeBoolean(boolean value) throws JMSException;
   public abstract void writeByte(byte value) throws JMSException;
   public abstract void writeBytes(byte[ ] value) throws JMSException;
   public abstract void writeBytes(byte[ ] value, int offset, int length) throws JMSException;
   public abstract void writeChar(char value) throws JMSException;
   public abstract void writeDouble(double value) throws JMSException;
   public abstract void writeFloat(float value) throws JMSException;
   public abstract void writeInt(int value) throws JMSException;
   public abstract void writeLong(long value) throws JMSException;
   public abstract void writeObject(Object value) throws JMSException;
   public abstract void writeShort(short value) throws JMSException;
   public abstract void writeString(String value) throws JMSException;
}
```

Hierarchy: (StreamMessage(Message))

Returned By: Session.createStreamMessage()

TemporaryQueue — JMS 1.0

javax.jms

A TemporaryQueue is a Queue used internally by a QueueConnection.

```
public interface TemporaryQueue extends Queue {
// Public Instance Methods
   public abstract void delete() throws JMSException;
}
```

Hierarchy: (TemporaryQueue(Queue(Destination)))

Returned By: QueueSession.createTemporaryQueue()

TemporaryTopic — JMS 1.0

javax.jms

A TemporaryTopic is a Topic used internally by a TopicConnection.

```
public interface TemporaryTopic extends Topic {
// Public Instance Methods
   public abstract void delete() throws JMSException;
}
```

Hierarchy: (TemporaryTopic(Topic(Destination)))

Returned By: TopicSession.createTemporaryTopic()

TextMessage — JMS 1.0

javax.jms

A TextMessage is a Message whose body is a String. The contents of the message can be retrieved using the getText() method. The text of the message might be simple ASCII, or it could be structured according to a syntax like HTML or XML.

```
public interface TextMessage extends Message {
// Public Instance Methods
   public abstract String getText() throws JMSException;
   public abstract void setText(String string) throws JMSException;
}
```

Hierarchy: (TextMessage(Message))

Returned By: Session.createTextMessage()

Topic — JMS 1.0

javax.jms

A Topic is an address for a message in a publish/subscribe context. The Topic interface simply defines a String name for the topic. Providers define how topics are defined and grouped into a hierarchy.

```
public interface Topic extends Destination {
// Public Instance Methods
   public abstract String getTopicName() throws JMSException;
   public abstract String toString();
}
```

Hierarchy: (Topic(Destination))

Implementations: TemporaryTopic

Passed To: TopicConnection.{createConnectionConsumer(), createDurableConnectionConsumer()}, TopicPublisher.publish(), TopicRequestor.TopicRequestor(), TopicSession.{createDurableSubscriber(), createPublisher(), createSubscriber()}

Returned By: TopicPublisher.getTopic(), TopicSession.createTopic(), TopicSubscriber.getTopic()

TopicConnection — JMS 1.0

javax.jms

A TopicConnection is a Connection to a publish/subscribe-based JMS provider. It provides methods for creating TopicSession objects, as well as ConnectionConsumer objects.

```
public interface TopicConnection extends javax.jms.Connection {
// Public Instance Methods
   public abstract ConnectionConsumer createConnectionConsumer(Topic topic, String messageSelector,
                                                  ServerSessionPool sessionPool, int maxMessages)
      throws JMSException;
```

```
   public abstract ConnectionConsumer createDurableConnectionConsumer(Topic topic,
                                                                      String messageSelector,
                                                                      ServerSessionPool sessionPool, int maxMessages)
       throws JMSException;
   public abstract TopicSession createTopicSession(boolean transacted, int acknowledgeMode)
       throws JMSException;
}
```

Hierarchy: (TopicConnection(javax.jms.Connection))

Implementations: XATopicConnection

Returned By: TopicConnectionFactory.createTopicConnection()

TopicConnectionFactory — JMS 1.0

javax.jms

A TopicConnectionFactory is exported by publish/subscribe providers to allow clients to create TopicConnection objects to the provider. The default createTopicConnection() method creates a connection under the default user identity of the client JVM, while the other constructor accepts a name and password that authenticates the connection request.

```
public interface TopicConnectionFactory extends ConnectionFactory {
// Public Instance Methods
   public abstract TopicConnection createTopicConnection() throws JMSException;
   public abstract TopicConnection createTopicConnection(String userName, String password)
       throws JMSException;
}
```

Hierarchy: (TopicConnectionFactory(ConnectionFactory))

Implementations: XATopicConnectionFactory

TopicPublisher — JMS 1.0

javax.jms

A TopicPublisher is a MessageProducer specific to a publish/subscribe context. TopicPublisher objects are created using the createPublisher() method on a TopicSession. A TopicPublisher is created with a Topic under which it publishes messages. A client can override the default Topic using one of the publish() methods that accepts a Topic as an argument along with the Message to be sent. Sending a Message without a Topic (i.e., the TopicPublisher was created with a null Topic, and the Message was sent without specifying a Topic) causes an InvalidDestinationException to be thrown.

```
public interface TopicPublisher extends MessageProducer {
// Public Instance Methods
   public abstract Topic getTopic() throws JMSException;
   public abstract void publish(Message message) throws JMSException;
   public abstract void publish(Topic topic, Message message) throws JMSException;
   public abstract void publish(Message message, int deliveryMode, int priority, long timeToLive)
       throws JMSException;
   public abstract void publish(Topic topic, Message message, int deliveryMode, int priority, long timeToLive)
       throws JMSException;
}
```

Hierarchy: (TopicPublisher(MessageProducer))

Returned By: TopicSession.createPublisher()

TopicRequestor **JMS 1.0**

javax.jms

TopicRequestor is a utility class provided for situations where a client wants to send a message to a specific Topic and wait for a response. The TopicRequestor is constructed with a TopicSession and a destination Topic, and then its request() method is called with the Message to be sent. The TopicRequestor sets the reply-to destination on the message to a temporary Topic it creates. It sends the message and waits for a response. The response Message is the return value of the request() method.

```
public class TopicRequestor {
// Public Constructors
   public TopicRequestor(TopicSession session, Topic topic) throws JMSException;
// Public Instance Methods
   public void close() throws JMSException;
   public Message request(Message message) throws JMSException;
}
```

TopicSession **JMS 1.0**

javax.jms *runnable*

A TopicSession is a Session specific to a publish/subscribe context. It provides methods for creating publish/subscribe message consumers (TopicSubscriber), message producers (TopicPublisher), and message destinations (Topic). It also has methods for creating utilities objects such as TemporaryTopic.

```
public interface TopicSession extends Session {
// Public Instance Methods
   public abstract TopicSubscriber createDurableSubscriber(Topic topic, String name)
      throws JMSException;
   public abstract TopicSubscriber createDurableSubscriber(Topic topic, String name,
                                                           String messageSelector, boolean noLocal)
      throws JMSException;
   public abstract TopicPublisher createPublisher(Topic topic) throws JMSException;
   public abstract TopicSubscriber createSubscriber(Topic topic) throws JMSException;
   public abstract TopicSubscriber createSubscriber(Topic topic, String messageSelector, boolean noLocal)
      throws JMSException;
   public abstract TemporaryTopic createTemporaryTopic() throws JMSException;
   public abstract Topic createTopic(String topicName) throws JMSException;
   public abstract void unsubscribe(String name) throws JMSException;
}
```

Hierarchy: (TopicSession(Session(Runnable)))

Passed To: TopicRequestor.TopicRequestor()

Returned By: TopicConnection.createTopicSession(), XATopicSession.getTopicSession()

TopicSubscriber **JMS 1.0**

javax.jms

A TopicSubscriber is a MessageConsumer specific to a publish/subscribe context. TopicSubscriber objects are created using the createSubscriber() and createDurableSubscriber() methods on the TopicSession. A TopicSubscriber is created with a Topic to subscribe to and can optionally be created with a message selector that filters the messages received by the subscriber. If a client is both publishing and subscribing to the same Topic, the no-local attribute on the TopicSubscriber specifies whether to filter out messages published by the same connection.

If a TopicSubscriber is created as durable (using createDurableSubscriber() on the TopicSession), the provider collects messages for this subscriber even when the subscriber is inactive. The provider keeps these messages until the subscriber receives them, or until they expire according to the sender's time-to-live header attribute. In order for the client to retrieve the messages collected under a durable TopicSubscriber after it has reactivated itself, it has to create a new TopicSubscriber under the same Topic with the same client ID.

```
public interface TopicSubscriber extends MessageConsumer {
// Public Instance Methods
   public abstract boolean getNoLocal() throws JMSException;
   public abstract Topic getTopic() throws JMSException;
}
```

Hierarchy: (TopicSubscriber(MessageConsumer))

Returned By: TopicSession.{createDurableSubscriber(), createSubscriber()}

TransactionInProgressException — JMS 1.0

javax.jms — *serializable checked*

Thrown if an invalid request is made during a transactional session (e.g., attempting to commit() a session while a message is still being sent).

```
public class TransactionInProgressException extends JMSException {
// Public Constructors
   public TransactionInProgressException(String reason);
   public TransactionInProgressException(String reason, String errorCode);
}
```

Hierarchy: Object→ Throwable(Serializable)→ Exception→ JMSException→ TransactionInProgressException

TransactionRolledBackException — JMS 1.0

javax.jms — *serializable checked*

Thrown by the Session.commit() method if the transaction needs to be rolled back because of some internal error.

```
public class TransactionRolledBackException extends JMSException {
// Public Constructors
   public TransactionRolledBackException(String reason);
   public TransactionRolledBackException(String reason, String errorCode);
}
```

Hierarchy: Object→ Throwable(Serializable)→ Exception→ JMSException→ TransactionRolledBackException

XAConnection — JMS 1.0

javax.jms

This interface represents a Connection to a provider that supports transactional messaging, according to the X/Open XA protocol for transactional processing. Subinterfaces of XAConnection generate transactional sessions in the form of XASession objects.

```
public interface XAConnection {
}
```

Implementations: XAQueueConnection, XATopicConnection

XAConnectionFactory — JMS 1.0

javax.jms

A transactional JMS provider exports an XAConnectionFactory for clients to use to create XAConnection objects. Clients typically find a provider's XAConnectionFactory using a JNDI lookup.

```
public interface XAConnectionFactory {
}
```

Implementations: XAQueueConnectionFactory, XATopicConnectionFactory

XAQueueConnection — JMS 1.0

javax.jms

An XAQueueConnection is a Connection to a transactional provider of point-to-point messaging. It extends the QueueConnection interface with a createXAQueueSession() method, which creates a transactional XAQueueSession.

```
public interface XAQueueConnection extends javax.jms.XAConnection, QueueConnection {
// Public Instance Methods
   public abstract XAQueueSession createXAQueueSession() throws JMSException;
}
```

Hierarchy: (XAQueueConnection(javax.jms.XAConnection, QueueConnection(javax.jms.Connection)))

Returned By: XAQueueConnectionFactory.createXAQueueConnection()

XAQueueConnectionFactory — JMS 1.0

javax.jms

An XAQueueConnectionFactory is a QueueConnectionFactory that creates XAQueueConnection objects to a transactional point-to-point JMS provider.

```
public interface XAQueueConnectionFactory extends XAConnectionFactory, QueueConnectionFactory {
// Public Instance Methods
   public abstract XAQueueConnection createXAQueueConnection() throws JMSException;
   public abstract XAQueueConnection createXAQueueConnection(String userName, String password)
       throws JMSException;
}
```

Hierarchy: (XAQueueConnectionFactory(XAConnectionFactory, QueueConnectionFactory(ConnectionFactory)))

XAQueueSession — JMS 1.0

javax.jms — *runnable*

An XAQueueSession is a wrapper around a QueueSession. It represents a transactional session with a JMS point-to-point provider.

```
public interface XAQueueSession extends XASession {
// Public Instance Methods
   public abstract QueueSession getQueueSession() throws JMSException;
}
```

Hierarchy: (XAQueueSession(XASession(Session(Runnable))))

Returned By: XAQueueConnection.createXAQueueSession()

XASession — JMS 1.0

javax.jms — *runnable*

An XASession is a Session with a provider that supports transactional messaging according to the X/Open XA protocol for transactional processing. The XASession contains a javax.transaction.xa.XAResource object that represents the association of the Session with a transaction context.

```
public interface XASession extends Session {
// Public Instance Methods
   public abstract javax.transaction.xa.XAResource getXAResource();
}
```

Hierarchy: (XASession(Session(Runnable)))

Implementations: XAQueueSession, XATopicSession

XATopicConnection — JMS 1.0

javax.jms

An XATopicConnection represents a Connection to a transactional provider of publish/subscribe messaging. It extends the TopicConnection interface with a createXATopicSession() method, which creates a transactional XATopicSession.

```
public interface XATopicConnection extends javax.jms.XAConnection, TopicConnection {
// Public Instance Methods
   public abstract XATopicSession createXATopicSession() throws JMSException;
}
```

Hierarchy: (XATopicConnection(javax.jms.XAConnection, TopicConnection(javax.jms.Connection)))

Returned By: XATopicConnectionFactory.createXATopicConnection()

XATopicConnectionFactory — JMS 1.0

javax.jms

An XATopicConnectionFactory is a TopicConnectionFactory that creates XATopicConnection objects to a transactional publish/subscribe JMS provider.

```
public interface XATopicConnectionFactory extends XAConnectionFactory, TopicConnectionFactory {
// Public Instance Methods
   public abstract XATopicConnection createXATopicConnection() throws JMSException;
   public abstract XATopicConnection createXATopicConnection(String userName, String password)
      throws JMSException;
}
```

Hierarchy: (XATopicConnectionFactory(XAConnectionFactory, TopicConnectionFactory(ConnectionFactory)))

XATopicSession — JMS 1.0

javax.jms — *runnable*

An XATopicSession is a wrapper around a TopicSession. It represents a transactional session with a JMS publish/subscribe provider.

```
public interface XATopicSession extends XASession {
// Public Instance Methods
   public abstract TopicSession getTopicSession() throws JMSException;
}
```

Hierarchy: (XATopicSession(XASession(Session(Runnable))))

Returned By: XATopicConnection.createXATopicSession()

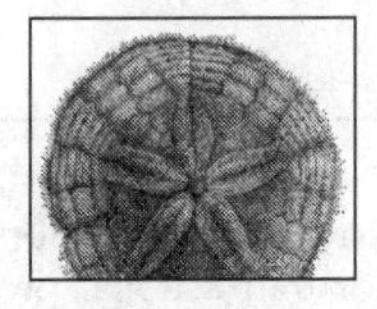

CHAPTER 22

The javax.naming Package

The javax.naming package contains the core interfaces, classes, and exceptions for performing naming operations with JNDI. Context represents named objects in a naming system, while InitialContext provides an entry point into a naming system. Binding is the association between a name and an object in a naming system. NamingException is the root of a large collection of naming exceptions defined by JNDI. Figure 22-1 shows the classes and interfaces of the javax.naming package, while Figure 22-2 shows the exception hierarchy.

AuthenticationException — JNDI 1.1

javax.naming — *serializable checked*

Thrown when JNDI encounters an error authenticating to the naming system, such as when a bad username or password is used.

```
public class AuthenticationException extends NamingSecurityException {
// Public Constructors
   public AuthenticationException();
   public AuthenticationException(String explanation);
}
```

Hierarchy: Object→ Throwable(Serializable)→ Exception→ NamingException→ NamingSecurityException→ AuthenticationException

AuthenticationNotSupportedException — JNDI 1.1

javax.naming — *serializable checked*

Thrown when the requested type of authentication is not supported.

```
public class AuthenticationNotSupportedException extends NamingSecurityException {
// Public Constructors
   public AuthenticationNotSupportedException();
   public AuthenticationNotSupportedException(String explanation);
}
```

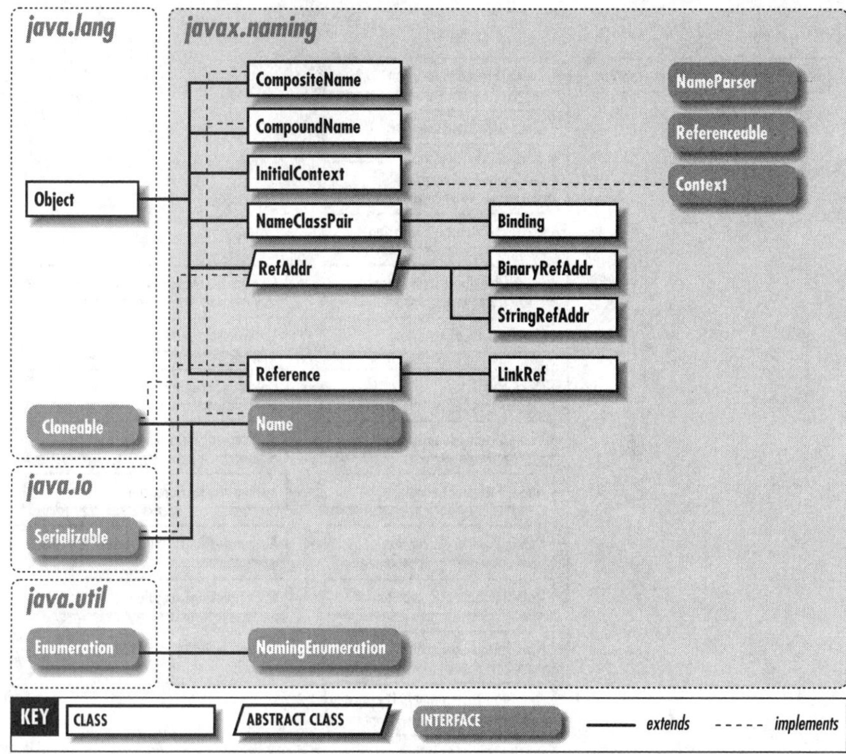

Figure 22-1: The classes and interfaces of the javax.naming package

Hierarchy: Object→ Throwable(Serializable)→ Exception→ NamingException→ NamingSecurityException→ AuthenticationNotSupportedException

BinaryRefAddr — JNDI 1.1

javax.naming — *serializable*

A concrete subclass of RefAddr that provides a binary representation of a communications endpoint, such as an IP address.

```
public class BinaryRefAddr extends RefAddr {
// Public Constructors
    public BinaryRefAddr(String addrType, byte[ ] src);
    public BinaryRefAddr(String addrType, byte[ ] src, int offset, int count);
// Public methods overriding RefAddr
    public boolean equals(Object obj);
    public Object getContent( );
    public int hashCode( );
    public String toString( );
}
```

Hierarchy: Object→ RefAddr(Serializable)→ BinaryRefAddr

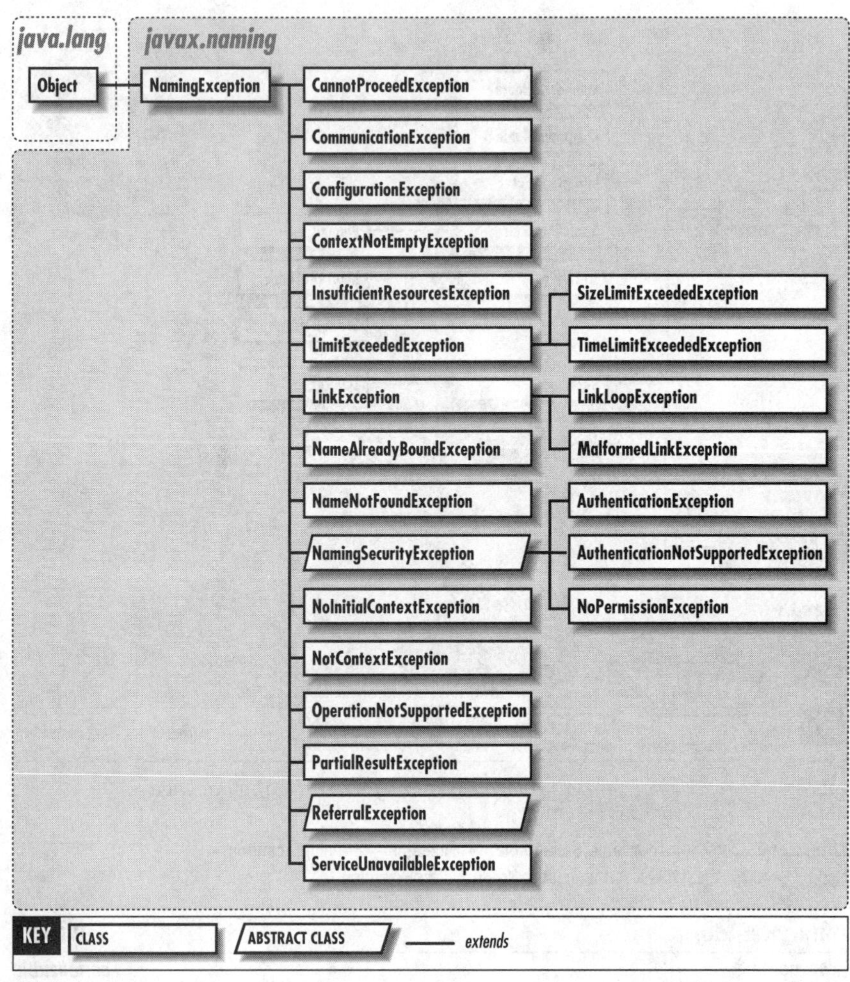

Figure 22-2: The exception hierarchy of the javax.naming package

Binding — JNDI 1.1

javax.naming — *serializable*

This class represents the association between a name and an object. The listBindings() method of Context returns a NamingEnumeration of Binding objects.

```
public class Binding extends NameClassPair {
// Public Constructors
   public Binding(String name, Object obj);
   public Binding(String name, String className, Object obj);
   public Binding(String name, Object obj, boolean isRelative);
   public Binding(String name, String className, Object obj, boolean isRelative);
// Public Instance Methods
   public Object getObject();
   public void setObject(Object obj);
```

```
// Public methods overriding NameClassPair
   public String getClassName();
   public String toString();
}
```

Hierarchy: Object→ NameClassPair(Serializable)→ javax.naming.Binding

Subclasses: javax.naming.directory.SearchResult

CannotProceedException — JNDI 1.1

javax.naming — *serializable checked*

Thrown when a service provider cannot further resolve a name, such as when a component of a name resides in another service provider.

```
public class CannotProceedException extends NamingException {
// Public Constructors
   public CannotProceedException();
   public CannotProceedException(String explanation);
// Public Instance Methods
   public Name getAltName();                                        default:null
   public javax.naming.Context getAltNameCtx();                     default:null
   public java.util.Hashtable getEnvironment();                     default:null
   public Name getRemainingNewName();                               default:null
   public void setAltName(Name altName);
   public void setAltNameCtx(javax.naming.Context altNameCtx);
   public void setEnvironment(java.util.Hashtable environment);
   public void setRemainingNewName(Name newName);
// Protected Instance Fields
   protected Name altName;
   protected javax.naming.Context altNameCtx;
   protected java.util.Hashtable environment;
   protected Name remainingNewName;
}
```

Hierarchy: Object→ Throwable(Serializable)→ Exception→ NamingException→ CannotProceedException

Passed To: javax.naming.spi.DirectoryManager.getContinuationDirContext(), javax.naming.spi.NamingManager.getContinuationContext()

CommunicationException — JNDI 1.1

javax.naming — *serializable checked*

Thrown when a JNDI method is unable to communicate with the naming service for some reason.

```
public class CommunicationException extends NamingException {
// Public Constructors
   public CommunicationException();
   public CommunicationException(String explanation);
}
```

Hierarchy: Object→ Throwable(Serializable)→ Exception→ NamingException→ CommunicationException

CompositeName — JNDI 1.1

javax.naming — *cloneable serializable*

This class represents a sequence of names that span multiple namespaces. Each component of a CompositeName is a String name. The CompositeName does not know to which naming system each name component belongs. JNDI uses the forward slash character ("/") to separate constituent name components.

```
public class CompositeName implements Name {
// Public Constructors
   public CompositeName();
   public CompositeName(String n) throws InvalidNameException;
// Protected Constructors
   protected CompositeName(java.util.Enumeration comps);
// Methods implementing Name
   public Name add(String comp) throws InvalidNameException;
   public Name add(int posn, String comp) throws InvalidNameException;
   public Name addAll(Name suffix) throws InvalidNameException;
   public Name addAll(int posn, Name n) throws InvalidNameException;
   public Object clone();
   public int compareTo(Object obj);
   public boolean endsWith(Name n);
   public String get(int posn);
   public java.util.Enumeration getAll();
   public Name getPrefix(int posn);
   public Name getSuffix(int posn);
   public boolean isEmpty();                                    default:true
   public Object remove(int posn) throws InvalidNameException;
   public int size();
   public boolean startsWith(Name n);
// Public methods overriding Object
   public boolean equals(Object obj);
   public int hashCode();
   public String toString();
}
```

Hierarchy: Object→ CompositeName(Name(Cloneable, Serializable))

CompoundName — JNDI 1.1

javax.naming — ***cloneable serializable***

This class represents a name that is made up of atomic names from a single name space.

```
public class CompoundName implements Name {
// Public Constructors
   public CompoundName(String n, java.util.Properties syntax) throws InvalidNameException;
// Protected Constructors
   protected CompoundName(java.util.Enumeration comps, java.util.Properties syntax);
// Methods implementing Name
   public Name add(String comp) throws InvalidNameException;
   public Name add(int posn, String comp) throws InvalidNameException;
   public Name addAll(Name suffix) throws InvalidNameException;
   public Name addAll(int posn, Name n) throws InvalidNameException;
   public Object clone();
   public int compareTo(Object obj);
   public boolean endsWith(Name n);
   public String get(int posn);
   public java.util.Enumeration getAll();
   public Name getPrefix(int posn);
   public Name getSuffix(int posn);
   public boolean isEmpty();
   public Object remove(int posn) throws InvalidNameException;
   public int size();
```

```
    public boolean startsWith(Name n);
// Public methods overriding Object
    public boolean equals(Object obj);
    public int hashCode();
    public String toString();
// Protected Instance Fields
    protected transient NameImpl impl;
    protected transient java.util.Properties mySyntax;
}
```

Hierarchy: Object→ CompoundName(Name(Cloneable, Serializable))

ConfigurationException — JNDI 1.1

javax.naming — *serializable checked*

Thrown when JNDI has experienced a configuration problem, such as a missing environment property or a misconfigured security protocol.

```
public class ConfigurationException extends NamingException {
// Public Constructors
    public ConfigurationException();
    public ConfigurationException(String explanation);
}
```

Hierarchy: Object→ Throwable(Serializable)→ Exception→ NamingException→ ConfigurationException

Context — JNDI 1.1

javax.naming

This interface represents an object in a naming system. A Context keeps track of a set of name-to-object bindings for its subordinates in the naming system, so it defines methods to examine and update these bindings. The lookup() method looks up a subordinate object, while list() and listBindings() provide access to all of the subordinates.

A Context only knows about its subordinates, not about itself or what is above it in the naming system. Thus, there are no methods to get the name of a Context or move up in the naming hierarchy.

```
public abstract interface Context {
// Public Constants
    public static final String AUTHORITATIVE;                 ="java.naming.authoritative"
    public static final String BATCHSIZE;                     ="java.naming.batchsize"
    public static final String DNS_URL;                       ="java.naming.dns.url"
    public static final String INITIAL_CONTEXT_FACTORY;       ="java.naming.factory.initial"
    public static final String LANGUAGE;                      ="java.naming.language"
    public static final String OBJECT_FACTORIES;              ="java.naming.factory.object"
    public static final String PROVIDER_URL;                  ="java.naming.provider.url"
    public static final String REFERRAL;                      ="java.naming.referral"
    public static final String SECURITY_AUTHENTICATION;       ="java.naming.security.authentication"
    public static final String SECURITY_CREDENTIALS;          ="java.naming.security.credentials"
    public static final String SECURITY_PRINCIPAL;            ="java.naming.security.principal"
    public static final String SECURITY_PROTOCOL;             ="java.naming.security.protocol"
    public static final String URL_PKG_PREFIXES;              ="java.naming.factory.url.pkgs"
// Public Instance Methods
    public abstract Object addToEnvironment(String propName, Object propVal) throws NamingException;
    public abstract void bind(Name name, Object obj) throws NamingException;
    public abstract void bind(String name, Object obj) throws NamingException;
    public abstract void close() throws NamingException;
```

javax.naming

```
    public abstract Name composeName(Name name, Name prefix) throws NamingException;
    public abstract String composeName(String name, String prefix) throws NamingException;
    public abstract javax.naming.Context createSubcontext(Name name) throws NamingException;
    public abstract javax.naming.Context createSubcontext(String name) throws NamingException;
    public abstract void destroySubcontext(Name name) throws NamingException;
    public abstract void destroySubcontext(String name) throws NamingException;
    public abstract java.util.Hashtable getEnvironment() throws NamingException;
    public abstract NameParser getNameParser(Name name) throws NamingException;
    public abstract NameParser getNameParser(String name) throws NamingException;
    public abstract NamingEnumeration list(Name name) throws NamingException;
    public abstract NamingEnumeration list(String name) throws NamingException;
    public abstract NamingEnumeration listBindings(Name name) throws NamingException;
    public abstract NamingEnumeration listBindings(String name) throws NamingException;
    public abstract Object lookup(Name name) throws NamingException;
    public abstract Object lookup(String name) throws NamingException;
    public abstract Object lookupLink(Name name) throws NamingException;
    public abstract Object lookupLink(String name) throws NamingException;
    public abstract void rebind(Name name, Object obj) throws NamingException;
    public abstract void rebind(String name, Object obj) throws NamingException;
    public abstract Object removeFromEnvironment(String propName) throws NamingException;
    public abstract void rename(Name oldName, Name newName) throws NamingException;
    public abstract void rename(String oldName, String newName) throws NamingException;
    public abstract void unbind(Name name) throws NamingException;
    public abstract void unbind(String name) throws NamingException;
}
```

Implementations: InitialContext, javax.naming.directory.DirContext

Passed To: CannotProceedException.setAltNameCtx(), javax.naming.spi.NamingManager.getObjectInstance(), javax.naming.spi.ObjectFactory.getObjectInstance()

Returned By: CannotProceedException.getAltNameCtx(), javax.naming.Context.createSubcontext(), InitialContext.{createSubcontext(), getDefaultInitCtx(), getURLOrDefaultInitCtx()}, ReferralException.getReferralContext(), javax.naming.spi.InitialContextFactory.getInitialContext(), javax.naming.spi.NamingManager.{getContinuationContext(), getInitialContext(), getURLContext()}

Type Of: CannotProceedException.altNameCtx, InitialContext.defaultInitCtx

ContextNotEmptyException — JNDI 1.1

javax.naming — ***serializable checked***

Thrown when the destroySubcontext() method is called to destroy a Context that is not empty.

```
public class ContextNotEmptyException extends NamingException {
// Public Constructors
    public ContextNotEmptyException();
    public ContextNotEmptyException(String explanation);
}
```

Hierarchy: Object→ Throwable(Serializable)→ Exception→ NamingException→ ContextNotEmptyException

InitialContext — JNDI 1.1

javax.naming

This class represents the starting point for accessing a naming system. Typically, you set the value of the java.naming.factory.initial property (represented by the constant Context.INITIAL_CONTEXT_FACTORY) to the fully qualified package name of a factory class in a JNDI service provider. This factory class creates an InitialContext that is appropriate for the naming system you are using.

```
public class InitialContext implements javax.naming.Context {
// Public Constructors
   public InitialContext() throws NamingException;
   public InitialContext(java.util.Hashtable environment) throws NamingException;
// Methods implementing Context
   public Object addToEnvironment(String propName, Object propVal) throws NamingException;
   public void bind(String name, Object obj) throws NamingException;
   public void bind(Name name, Object obj) throws NamingException;
   public void close() throws NamingException;
   public String composeName(String name, String prefix) throws NamingException;
   public Name composeName(Name name, Name prefix) throws NamingException;
   public javax.naming.Context createSubcontext(String name) throws NamingException;
   public javax.naming.Context createSubcontext(Name name) throws NamingException;
   public void destroySubcontext(Name name) throws NamingException;
   public void destroySubcontext(String name) throws NamingException;
   public java.util.Hashtable getEnvironment() throws NamingException;
   public NameParser getNameParser(String name) throws NamingException;
   public NameParser getNameParser(Name name) throws NamingException;
   public NamingEnumeration list(Name name) throws NamingException;
   public NamingEnumeration list(String name) throws NamingException;
   public NamingEnumeration listBindings(Name name) throws NamingException;
   public NamingEnumeration listBindings(String name) throws NamingException;
   public Object lookup(Name name) throws NamingException;
   public Object lookup(String name) throws NamingException;
   public Object lookupLink(Name name) throws NamingException;
   public Object lookupLink(String name) throws NamingException;
   public void rebind(Name name, Object obj) throws NamingException;
   public void rebind(String name, Object obj) throws NamingException;
   public Object removeFromEnvironment(String propName) throws NamingException;
   public void rename(Name oldName, Name newName) throws NamingException;
   public void rename(String oldName, String newName) throws NamingException;
   public void unbind(Name name) throws NamingException;
   public void unbind(String name) throws NamingException;
// Protected Instance Methods
   protected javax.naming.Context getDefaultInitCtx() throws NamingException;
   protected javax.naming.Context getURLOrDefaultInitCtx(Name name) throws NamingException;
   protected javax.naming.Context getURLOrDefaultInitCtx(String name) throws NamingException;
// Protected Instance Fields
   protected javax.naming.Context defaultInitCtx;
   protected boolean gotDefault;
   protected java.util.Hashtable myProps;
}
```

Hierarchy: Object→ InitialContext(javax.naming.Context)

Subclasses: javax.naming.directory.InitialDirContext

InsufficientResourcesException — JNDI 1.1

javax.naming — *serializable checked*

Thrown when there are insufficient system resources, such as memory or disk space, to perform an operation.

```
public class InsufficientResourcesException extends NamingException {
// Public Constructors
   public InsufficientResourcesException();
```

javax.naming

```
    public InsufficientResourcesException(String explanation);
}
```

Hierarchy: Object→ Throwable(Serializable)→ Exception→ NamingException→ InsufficientResourcesException

InterruptedNamingException — JNDI 1.1

javax.naming — *serializable checked*

Thrown when a naming operation has been interrupted.

```
public class InterruptedNamingException extends NamingException {
// Public Constructors
    public InterruptedNamingException();
    public InterruptedNamingException(String explanation);
}
```

Hierarchy: Object→ Throwable(Serializable)→ Exception→ NamingException→ InterruptedNamingException

InvalidNameException — JNDI 1.1

javax.naming — *serializable checked*

Thrown when a specified name violates the syntax of a particular naming system.

```
public class InvalidNameException extends NamingException {
// Public Constructors
    public InvalidNameException();
    public InvalidNameException(String explanation);
}
```

Hierarchy: Object→ Throwable(Serializable)→ Exception→ NamingException→ InvalidNameException

Thrown By: CompositeName.{add(), addAll(), CompositeName(), remove()}, CompoundName.{add(), addAll(), CompoundName(), remove()}, Name.{add(), addAll(), remove()}

LimitExceededException — JNDI 1.1

javax.naming — *serializable checked*

Thrown when a method fails because it has exceeded a user- or system-specified limit.

```
public class LimitExceededException extends NamingException {
// Public Constructors
    public LimitExceededException();
    public LimitExceededException(String explanation);
}
```

Hierarchy: Object→ Throwable(Serializable)→ Exception→ NamingException→ LimitExceededException

Subclasses: SizeLimitExceededException, TimeLimitExceededException

LinkException — JNDI 1.1

javax.naming — *serializable checked*

Thrown when a method cannot resolve a link.

```
public class LinkException extends NamingException {
// Public Constructors
    public LinkException();
    public LinkException(String explanation);
```

```
// Public Instance Methods
   public String getLinkExplanation();                                      default:null
   public Name getLinkRemainingName();                                      default:null
   public Name getLinkResolvedName();                                       default:null
   public Object getLinkResolvedObj();                                      default:null
   public void setLinkExplanation(String msg);
   public void setLinkRemainingName(Name name);
   public void setLinkResolvedName(Name name);
   public void setLinkResolvedObj(Object obj);
// Public methods overriding NamingException
   public String toString();
   public String toString(boolean detail);
// Protected Instance Fields
   protected String linkExplanation;
   protected Name linkRemainingName;
   protected Name linkResolvedName;
   protected Object linkResolvedObj;
}
```

Hierarchy: Object→ Throwable(Serializable)→ Exception→ NamingException→ LinkException

Subclasses: LinkLoopException, MalformedLinkException

LinkLoopException — JNDI 1.1

javax.naming — *serializable checked*

Thrown when a loop is detected when resolving a link or when JNDI has reached a limit on link counts.

```
public class LinkLoopException extends LinkException {
// Public Constructors
   public LinkLoopException();
   public LinkLoopException(String explanation);
}
```

Hierarchy: Object→ Throwable(Serializable)→ Exception→ NamingException→ LinkException→ LinkLoopException

LinkRef — JNDI 1.1

javax.naming — *cloneable serializable*

LinkRef is a subclass of Reference that contains a name, called the *link name*, that is bound to an atomic name in a context.

```
public class LinkRef extends javax.naming.Reference {
// Public Constructors
   public LinkRef(String linkName);
   public LinkRef(Name linkName);
// Public Instance Methods
   public String getLinkName() throws NamingException;
}
```

Hierarchy: Object→ javax.naming.Reference(Cloneable, Serializable)→ LinkRef

MalformedLinkException — JNDI 1.1

javax.naming — *serializable checked*

Thrown when a link name is improperly constructed.

```
public class MalformedLinkException extends LinkException {
// Public Constructors
   public MalformedLinkException();
   public MalformedLinkException(String explanation);
}
```

Hierarchy: Object→ Throwable(Serializable)→ Exception→ NamingException→ LinkException→ MalformedLinkException

Name **JNDI 1.1**

javax.naming ***cloneable serializable***

This interface represents the name of an object in a naming system. A Name can be either a compound name or a composite name. This interface is used primarily by developers who are writing JNDI service providers, not by JNDI application developers. As an application developer, you can use String objects instead of Name objects to specify names in Context and javax.naming.directory.DirContext method calls.

```
public abstract interface Name extends Cloneable, Serializable {
// Public Instance Methods
   public abstract Name add(String comp) throws InvalidNameException;
   public abstract Name add(int posn, String comp) throws InvalidNameException;
   public abstract Name addAll(Name suffix) throws InvalidNameException;
   public abstract Name addAll(int posn, Name n) throws InvalidNameException;
   public abstract Object clone();
   public abstract int compareTo(Object obj);
   public abstract boolean endsWith(Name n);
   public abstract String get(int posn);
   public abstract java.util.Enumeration getAll();
   public abstract Name getPrefix(int posn);
   public abstract Name getSuffix(int posn);
   public abstract boolean isEmpty();
   public abstract Object remove(int posn) throws InvalidNameException;
   public abstract int size();
   public abstract boolean startsWith(Name n);
}
```

Hierarchy: (Name(Cloneable, Serializable))

Implementations: CompositeName, CompoundName

Passed To: Too many methods to list.

Returned By: Too many methods to list.

Type Of: CannotProceedException.{altName, remainingNewName}, LinkException.{linkRemainingName, linkResolvedName}, NamingException.{remainingName, resolvedName}, javax.naming.spi.ResolveResult.remainingName

NameAlreadyBoundException **JNDI 1.1**

javax.naming ***serializable checked***

Thrown when a binding operation fails because the name is already bound.

```
public class NameAlreadyBoundException extends NamingException {
// Public Constructors
   public NameAlreadyBoundException();
   public NameAlreadyBoundException(String explanation);
}
```

Hierarchy: Object→ Throwable(Serializable)→ Exception→ NamingException→ NameAlreadyBoundException

NameClassPair — JNDI 1.1

javax.naming — *serializable*

This class represents the name and class of an object bound to a Context. The list() method of Context returns an NamingEnumeration of NameClassPair objects. Note that NameClassPair does not represent the object itself; that is the job of its subclass Binding.

```
public class NameClassPair implements Serializable {
// Public Constructors
   public NameClassPair(String name, String className);
   public NameClassPair(String name, String className, boolean isRelative);
// Public Instance Methods
   public String getClassName();
   public String getName();
   public boolean isRelative();
   public void setClassName(String name);
   public void setName(String name);
   public void setRelative(boolean r);
// Public methods overriding Object
   public String toString();
}
```

Hierarchy: Object→ NameClassPair(Serializable)

Subclasses: javax.naming.Binding

NameNotFoundException — JNDI 1.1

javax.naming — *serializable checked*

Thrown when a component of a name cannot be resolved because it is not bound.

```
public class NameNotFoundException extends NamingException {
// Public Constructors
   public NameNotFoundException();
   public NameNotFoundException(String explanation);
}
```

Hierarchy: Object→ Throwable(Serializable)→ Exception→ NamingException→ NameNotFoundException

NameParser — JNDI 1.1

javax.naming

This interface is for parsing names from a hierarchical namespace. A NameParser knows the syntactic information, such as left-to-right orientation and the name separator, needed to parse names.

```
public abstract interface NameParser {
// Public Instance Methods
   public abstract Name parse(String name) throws NamingException;
}
```

Returned By: javax.naming.Context.getNameParser(), InitialContext.getNameParser()

NamingEnumeration — JNDI 1.1

javax.naming

This interface represents a list of items returned from a JNDI operation. It extends java.util.Enumeration, so a NamingEnumeration can be treated as a normal enumeration.

```
public abstract interface NamingEnumeration extends java.util.Enumeration {
// Public Instance Methods
   public abstract boolean hasMore() throws NamingException;
   public abstract Object next() throws NamingException;
}
```

Hierarchy: (NamingEnumeration(java.util.Enumeration))

Returned By: Too many methods to list.

NamingException — JNDI 1.1

javax.naming — *serializable checked*

The base class of all exceptions thrown by Context and javax.naming.directory.DirContext methods. NamingException can include information about where the operation failed, such as the portion of a name that has been resolved and the portion that remains to be resolved. A NamingException can also include a root cause exception, which is the exception object that caused the naming exception to be thrown.

```
public class NamingException extends Exception {
// Public Constructors
   public NamingException();
   public NamingException(String explanation);
// Public Instance Methods
   public void appendRemainingComponent(String name);
   public void appendRemainingName(Name name);
   public String getExplanation();                                    default:null
   public Name getRemainingName();                                    default:null
   public Name getResolvedName();                                     default:null
   public Object getResolvedObj();                                    default:null
   public Throwable getRootCause();                                   default:null
   public void setRemainingName(Name name);
   public void setResolvedName(Name name);
   public void setResolvedObj(Object obj);
   public void setRootCause(Throwable e);
   public String toString(boolean detail);
// Public methods overriding Throwable
   public String toString();
// Protected Instance Fields
   protected Name remainingName;
   protected Name resolvedName;
   protected Object resolvedObj;
   protected Throwable rootException;
}
```

Hierarchy: Object→ Throwable(Serializable)→ Exception→ NamingException

Subclasses: Too many classes to list.

Thrown By: Too many methods to list.

NamingSecurityException — JNDI 1.1

javax.naming — *serializable checked*

The abstract superclass of all security-related naming exceptions.

```
public abstract class NamingSecurityException extends NamingException {
// Public Constructors
   public NamingSecurityException();
   public NamingSecurityException(String explanation);
}
```

Hierarchy: Object→ Throwable(Serializable)→ Exception→ NamingException→ NamingSecurityException

Subclasses: AuthenticationException, AuthenticationNotSupportedException, NoPermissionException

NoInitialContextException — JNDI 1.1

javax.naming — *serializable checked*

Thrown when JNDI cannot create an initial context.

```
public class NoInitialContextException extends NamingException {
// Public Constructors
   public NoInitialContextException();
   public NoInitialContextException(String explanation);
}
```

Hierarchy: Object→ Throwable(Serializable)→ Exception→ NamingException→ NoInitialContextException

NoPermissionException — JNDI 1.1

javax.naming — *serializable checked*

Thrown when there is an attempt to perform an operation that is forbidden by the underlying naming system due to insufficient privileges.

```
public class NoPermissionException extends NamingSecurityException {
// Public Constructors
   public NoPermissionException();
   public NoPermissionException(String explanation);
}
```

Hierarchy: Object→ Throwable(Serializable)→ Exception→ NamingException→ NamingSecurityException→ NoPermissionException

NotContextException — JNDI 1.1

javax.naming — *serializable checked*

Thrown when there is an attempt to perform a Context-related operation on an object that is not a Context.

```
public class NotContextException extends NamingException {
// Public Constructors
   public NotContextException();
   public NotContextException(String explanation);
}
```

Hierarchy: Object→ Throwable(Serializable)→ Exception→ NamingException→ NotContextException

OperationNotSupportedException **JNDI 1.1**

javax.naming *serializable checked*

Thrown when the provider's implementation of Context does not support a method that has been invoked (e.g., trying to list the subordinates of a leaf object like a print job that by definition cannot have any children).

```
public class OperationNotSupportedException extends NamingException {
// Public Constructors
   public OperationNotSupportedException();
   public OperationNotSupportedException(String explanation);
}
```

Hierarchy: Object→ Throwable(Serializable)→ Exception→ NamingException→ OperationNotSupportedException

PartialResultException **JNDI 1.1**

javax.naming *serializable checked*

Thrown when an operation cannot be completed and has returned only a partial result (e.g., returning only a partial list of subordinates).

```
public class PartialResultException extends NamingException {
// Public Constructors
   public PartialResultException();
   public PartialResultException(String explanation);
}
```

Hierarchy: Object→ Throwable(Serializable)→ Exception→ NamingException→ PartialResultException

RefAddr **JNDI 1.1**

javax.naming *serializable*

This abstract class represents the address of a communications end point. It is used by Reference to represent the communication mechanism and address of a reference. Concrete implementations support addresses such as URLs, DNS names, and IP addresses.

```
public abstract class RefAddr implements Serializable {
// Protected Constructors
   protected RefAddr(String addrType);
// Public Instance Methods
   public abstract Object getContent();
   public String getType();
// Public methods overriding Object
   public boolean equals(Object obj);
   public int hashCode();
   public String toString();
// Protected Instance Fields
   protected String addrType;
}
```

Hierarchy: Object→ RefAddr(Serializable)

Subclasses: BinaryRefAddr, StringRefAddr

Passed To: javax.naming.Reference.{add(), Reference()}

Returned By: javax.naming.Reference.get()

Reference **JNDI 1.1**

javax.naming ***cloneable serializable***

This class represents an object external to a naming system that is referred to by an object in the naming system. A Reference contains an address for retrieving the object from its naming system. The address is a communications end point that enables JNDI to contact the object. The address can be any concrete subclass of RefAddr, such as a StringRefAddr for representing a URL or DNS name. A Reference also contains the class name of the referenced object.

```
public class Reference implements Cloneable, Serializable {
// Public Constructors
   public Reference(String className);
   public Reference(String className, RefAddr addr);
   public Reference(String className, String factory, String factoryLocation);
   public Reference(String className, RefAddr addr, String factory, String factoryLocation);
// Public Instance Methods
   public void add(RefAddr addr);
   public void add(int posn, RefAddr addr);
   public void clear();
   public RefAddr get(String addrType);
   public RefAddr get(int posn);
   public java.util.Enumeration getAll();
   public String getClassName();
   public String getFactoryClassLocation();
   public String getFactoryClassName();
   public Object remove(int posn);
   public int size();
// Public methods overriding Object
   public Object clone();
   public boolean equals(Object obj);
   public int hashCode();
   public String toString();
// Protected Instance Fields
   protected java.util.Vector addrs;
   protected String classFactory;
   protected String classFactoryLocation;
   protected String className;
}
```

Hierarchy: Object→ javax.naming.Reference(Cloneable, Serializable)

Subclasses: LinkRef

Returned By: Referenceable.getReference()

Referenceable **JNDI 1.1**

javax.naming

This interface is implemented by an object that can provide a reference to itself in the form of a Reference object.

```
public abstract interface Referenceable {
// Public Instance Methods
   public abstract javax.naming.Reference getReference() throws NamingException;
}
```

ReferralException **JNDI 1.1**

javax.naming ***serializable checked***

Thrown when a referral cannot be continued, such as when more information is required. Note that this is an abstract class.

```
public abstract class ReferralException extends NamingException {
// Protected Constructors
   protected ReferralException();
   protected ReferralException(String explanation);
// Public Instance Methods
   public abstract javax.naming.Context getReferralContext() throws NamingException;
   public abstract Object getReferralInfo();
   public abstract boolean skipReferral();
}
```

Hierarchy: Object→ Throwable(Serializable)→ Exception→ NamingException→ ReferralException

ServiceUnavailableException **JNDI 1.1**

javax.naming ***serializable checked***

Thrown when the name service is not available for some reason.

```
public class ServiceUnavailableException extends NamingException {
// Public Constructors
   public ServiceUnavailableException();
   public ServiceUnavailableException(String explanation);
}
```

Hierarchy: Object→ Throwable(Serializable)→ Exception→ NamingException→ ServiceUnavailableException

SizeLimitExceededException **JNDI 1.1**

javax.naming ***serializable checked***

Thrown when a method produces a result that exceeds a size limit.

```
public class SizeLimitExceededException extends LimitExceededException {
// Public Constructors
   public SizeLimitExceededException();
   public SizeLimitExceededException(String explanation);
}
```

Hierarchy: Object→ Throwable(Serializable)→ Exception→ NamingException→ LimitExceededException→ SizeLimitExceededException

StringRefAddr **JNDI 1.1**

javax.naming ***serializable***

A concrete subclass of RefAddr that provides a string form of the address of a communications end point.

```
public class StringRefAddr extends RefAddr {
// Public Constructors
   public StringRefAddr(String addrType, String addr);
// Public methods overriding RefAddr
   public Object getContent();
}
```

Hierarchy: Object→ RefAddr(Serializable)→ StringRefAddr

TimeLimitExceededException **JNDI 1.1**

javax.naming *serializable checked*

Thrown when a method does not finish within a certain time limit.

```
public class TimeLimitExceededException extends LimitExceededException {
// Public Constructors
   public TimeLimitExceededException();
   public TimeLimitExceededException(String explanation);
}
```

Hierarchy: Object→ Throwable(Serializable)→ Exception→ NamingException→ LimitExceededException→ TimeLimitExceededException

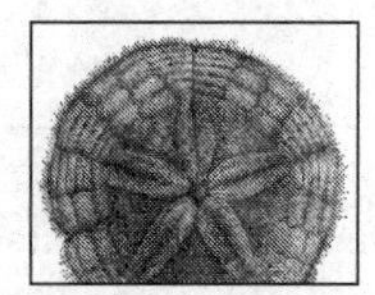

CHAPTER 23

The javax.naming.directory Package

The javax.naming.directory package contains the core interfaces, classes, and exceptions for performing directory operations with JNDI. DirContext defines the interface to directory services, while Attribute represents an attribute that is associated with a directory entry. Figure 23-1 shows the hierarchy of this package.

Attribute — JNDI 1.1

javax.naming.directory — ***cloneable serializable***

This interface represents an attribute associated with a directory entry. The directory schema determines the classes of attributes that a directory entry with a certain object class definition is permitted to have. The class of a particular attribute is called the *attribute type definition.* The name of an attribute, called the *attribute ID*, is determined by the attribute type definition and has a String representation that refers to that particular attribute. Each attribute can have zero or more values of a particular class. The class of values an attribute is permitted to have is called the *attribute syntax definition.*

The directory schema, and therefore the attribute type and syntax definitions, depend on the underlying directory your JNDI application is using. You can use getAttributeDefinition() to determine the type definition for a particular attribute and getAttributeSyntaxDefinition() to determine the attribute syntax definition.

The get() method returns a single attribute value as a java.lang.Object, while getAll() returns multiple attribute values as a javax.naming.NamingEnumeration of objects. If the attribute has only a single value, get() returns that value. If the attribute has multiple values, the service provider determines the value that is returned.

Updates performed on Attribute do not affect the directory entry. To modify the directory entry, you must call the modifyAttributes() method of DirContext with an Attributes object that contains a modified Attribute.

```
public abstract interface Attribute extends Cloneable, Serializable {
// Public Instance Methods
   public abstract boolean add(Object attrVal);
   public abstract void clear();
```

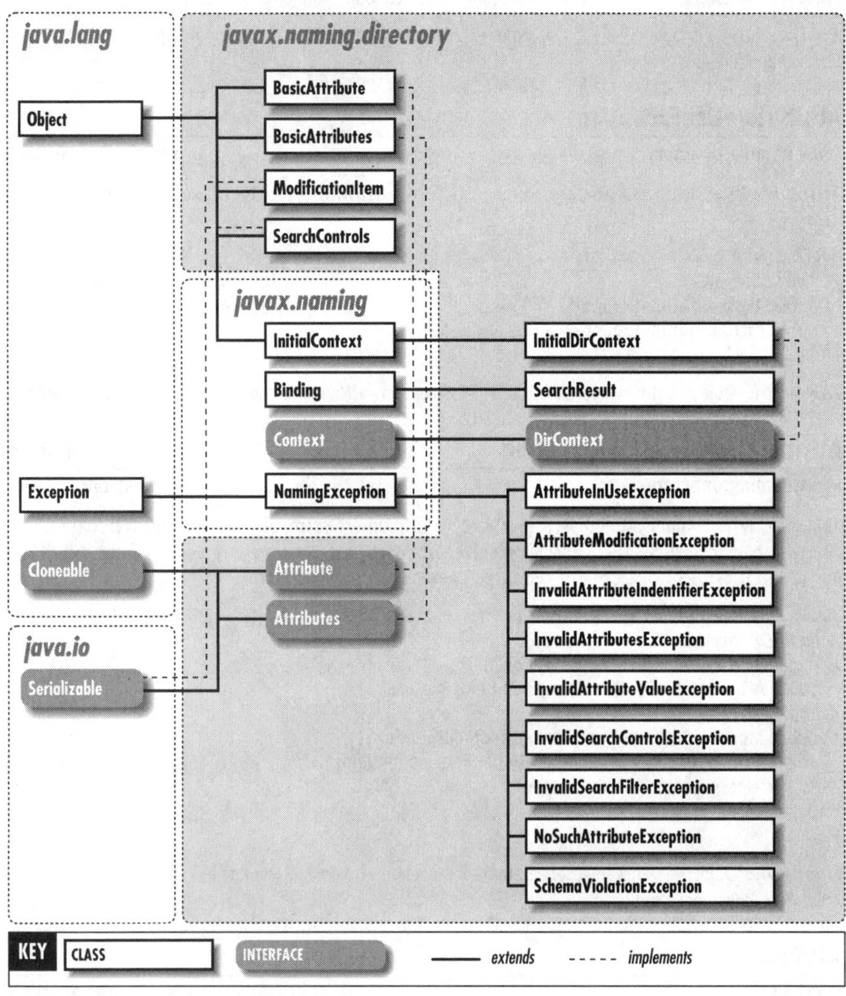

Figure 23-1: The javax.naming.directory package


```
    public abstract Object clone();
    public abstract boolean contains(Object attrVal);
    public abstract Object get() throws NamingException;
    public abstract NamingEnumeration getAll() throws NamingException;
    public abstract DirContext getAttributeDefinition() throws NamingException;
    public abstract DirContext getAttributeSyntaxDefinition() throws NamingException;
    public abstract String getID();
    public abstract boolean remove(Object attrval);
    public abstract int size();
}
```

Hierarchy: (Attribute(Cloneable, Serializable))

Implementations: BasicAttribute

Passed To: Attributes.put(), BasicAttributes.put(), ModificationItem.ModificationItem()

Returned By: Attributes.{get(), put(), remove()}, BasicAttributes.{get(), put(), remove()}, ModificationItem.getAttribute()

AttributeInUseException — JNDI 1.1

javax.naming.directory — *serializable checked*

Thrown when there is an attempt to add an attribute already present in the directory entry.

```
public class AttributeInUseException extends NamingException {
// Public Constructors
   public AttributeInUseException();
   public AttributeInUseException(String explanation);
}
```

Hierarchy: Object→ Throwable(Serializable)→ Exception→ NamingException→ AttributeInUseException

AttributeModificationException — JNDI 1.1

javax.naming.directory — *serializable checked*

Thrown when modifyAttributes() method of DirContext cannot be executed because the operation contradicts the directory schema. You can retrieve an array of modification items JNDI could not perform using getUnexecutedModifications().

```
public class AttributeModificationException extends NamingException {
// Public Constructors
   public AttributeModificationException();
   public AttributeModificationException(String explanation);
// Public Instance Methods
   public ModificationItem[ ] getUnexecutedModifications();                default:null
   public void setUnexecutedModifications(ModificationItem[ ] e);
// Public methods overriding NamingException
   public String toString();
}
```

Hierarchy: Object→ Throwable(Serializable)→ Exception→ NamingException→ AttributeModificationException

Attributes — JNDI 1.1

javax.naming.directory — *cloneable serializable*

This interface represents a collection of attributes associated with a directory entry. Individual attributes are unordered, and the Attributes object can have zero or more attributes. The getAll() method returns an enumeration of Attribute objects, while getIDs() returns an enumeration of just the attribute names (or IDs) for the directory entry. If you know the attribute you want, you can specify the attribute name in a call to the get() method, which returns a single Attribute object.

An Attributes object can be case-sensitive or insensitive. In an LDAP or NDS directory, a case-insensitive attribute corresponds to "case ignore string." This means when searching for a particular attribute or comparing two attributes, case sensitivity can affect the results.

Updates performed on an Attributes object do not affect the directory entry. To modify the directory entry, you must call the modifyAttributes() method of DirContext using the updated Attributes object.

When creating a set of attributes for use in an application, you typically use a BasicAttributes object.

```
public abstract interface Attributes extends Cloneable, Serializable {
// Public Instance Methods
   public abstract Object clone();
   public abstract Attribute get(String attrID);
   public abstract NamingEnumeration getAll();
   public abstract NamingEnumeration getIDs();
   public abstract boolean isCaseIgnored();
   public abstract Attribute put(Attribute attr);
   public abstract Attribute put(String attrID, Object val);
   public abstract Attribute remove(String attrID);
   public abstract int size();
}
```

Hierarchy: (Attributes(Cloneable, Serializable))

Implementations: BasicAttributes

Passed To: Too many methods to list.

Returned By: DirContext.getAttributes(), InitialDirContext.getAttributes(), SearchResult.getAttributes()

BasicAttribute — JNDI 1.1

javax.naming.directory — ***cloneable serializable***

This class is a basic implementation of the Attribute interface. BasicAttribute has a convenience constructor that enables you to create the object with attribute data by using a string that represents the attribute ID and a java.lang.Object that represents the attribute value. This constructor is equivalent to creating a BasicAttribute object with the attribute ID as a parameter and then calling the add() method.

```
public class BasicAttribute implements Attribute {
// Public Constructors
   public BasicAttribute(String id);
   public BasicAttribute(String id, Object value);
// Methods implementing Attribute
   public boolean add(Object attrVal);
   public void clear();
   public Object clone();
   public boolean contains(Object attrVal);
   public Object get() throws NamingException;
   public NamingEnumeration getAll() throws NamingException;
   public DirContext getAttributeDefinition() throws NamingException;
   public DirContext getAttributeSyntaxDefinition() throws NamingException;
   public String getID();
   public boolean remove(Object attrval);
   public int size();
// Public methods overriding Object
   public boolean equals(Object obj);
   public int hashCode();
   public String toString();
// Protected Instance Fields
   protected String attrID;
   protected transient java.util.Vector values;
}
```

Hierarchy: Object→ BasicAttribute(Attribute(Cloneable, Serializable))

BasicAttributes **JNDI 1.1**

javax.naming.directory ***cloneable serializable***

This class is a basic implementation of the Attributes interface. BasicAttributes has a convenience constructor that enables you to create the set of attributes with attribute data by using a string that represents an attribute ID, and a java.lang.Object that represents an attribute value. This constructor is equivalent to creating a BasicAttributes object with an empty constructor and then calling the two-argument put() method.

You can construct a BasicAttributes object as case-sensitive or insensitive. In an LDAP or NDS directory, a case-insensitive attribute corresponds to "case ignore string."

```
public class BasicAttributes implements Attributes {
// Public Constructors
   public BasicAttributes();
   public BasicAttributes(boolean ignoreCase);
   public BasicAttributes(String attrID, Object val);
   public BasicAttributes(String attrID, Object val, boolean ignoreCase);
// Methods implementing Attributes
   public Object clone();
   public Attribute get(String attrID);
   public NamingEnumeration getAll();
   public NamingEnumeration getIDs();
   public boolean isCaseIgnored();                                    default:false
   public Attribute put(Attribute attr);
   public Attribute put(String attrID, Object val);
   public Attribute remove(String attrID);
   public int size();
// Public methods overriding Object
   public String toString();
}
```

Hierarchy: Object→ BasicAttributes(Attributes(Cloneable, Serializable))

DirContext **JNDI 1.1**

javax.naming.directory

This interface provides a Java representation of a directory entry and is a subclass of javax.naming.Context. The practical difference between a Context and a DirContext is the association of attributes with a DirContext and the consequent methods for retrieving and modifying attribute data.

The directory schema determines the classes of directory entries that can be present in a directory. You can access the directory schema using getSchema(). The class of a directory entry is its object class definition. You can access the object class definition using the getSchemaClassDefinition() method. Most directory providers distribute documents that describe their directory schemae. Consult your directory service provider for a schema definition.

The getAttributes() method returns an Attributes object that contains either all the attributes of an entry or just those attributes specified in a String array. createSubcontext() creates a new directory entry, while modifyAttributes() changes attributes values. The various search() methods allow you to search directory entries, using optional search filters and SearchControls objects.

```
public abstract interface DirContext extends javax.naming.Context {
// Public Constants
   public static final int ADD_ATTRIBUTE;                             =1
   public static final int REMOVE_ATTRIBUTE;                          =3
```

```
    public static final int REPLACE_ATTRIBUTE;                                                              =2
// Public Instance Methods
    public abstract void bind(Name name, Object obj, Attributes attrs) throws NamingException;
    public abstract void bind(String name, Object obj, Attributes attrs) throws NamingException;
    public abstract DirContext createSubcontext(Name name, Attributes attrs) throws NamingException;
    public abstract DirContext createSubcontext(String name, Attributes attrs) throws NamingException;
    public abstract Attributes getAttributes(Name name) throws NamingException;
    public abstract Attributes getAttributes(String name) throws NamingException;
    public abstract Attributes getAttributes(Name name, String[ ] attrIds) throws NamingException;
    public abstract Attributes getAttributes(String name, String[ ] attrIds) throws NamingException;
    public abstract DirContext getSchema(Name name) throws NamingException;
    public abstract DirContext getSchema(String name) throws NamingException;
    public abstract DirContext getSchemaClassDefinition(Name name) throws NamingException;
    public abstract DirContext getSchemaClassDefinition(String name) throws NamingException;
    public abstract void modifyAttributes(String name, ModificationItem[ ] mods)
        throws NamingException;
    public abstract void modifyAttributes(Name name, ModificationItem[ ] mods) throws NamingException;
    public abstract void modifyAttributes(Name name, int mod_op, Attributes attrs)
        throws NamingException;
    public abstract void modifyAttributes(String name, int mod_op, Attributes attrs) throws NamingException;
    public abstract void rebind(Name name, Object obj, Attributes attrs) throws NamingException;
    public abstract void rebind(String name, Object obj, Attributes attrs) throws NamingException;
    public abstract NamingEnumeration search(String name, Attributes matchingAttributes)
        throws NamingException;
    public abstract NamingEnumeration search(Name name, Attributes matchingAttributes)
        throws NamingException;
    public abstract NamingEnumeration search(String name, String filter, SearchControls cons)
        throws NamingException;
    public abstract NamingEnumeration search(Name name, Attributes matchingAttributes,
                                             String[ ] attributesToReturn) throws NamingException;
    public abstract NamingEnumeration search(Name name, String filter, SearchControls cons)
        throws NamingException;
    public abstract NamingEnumeration search(String name, Attributes matchingAttributes,
                                             String[ ] attributesToReturn) throws NamingException;
    public abstract NamingEnumeration search(String name, String filterExpr, Object[ ] filterArgs,
                                             SearchControls cons) throws NamingException;
    public abstract NamingEnumeration search(Name name, String filterExpr, Object[ ] filterArgs,
                                             SearchControls cons) throws NamingException;
}
```

Hierarchy: (DirContext(javax.naming.Context))

Implementations: InitialDirContext

Returned By: Attribute.{getAttributeDefinition(), getAttributeSyntaxDefinition()}, BasicAttribute.{getAttributeDefinition(), getAttributeSyntaxDefinition()}, DirContext.{createSubcontext(), getSchema(), getSchemaClassDefinition()}, InitialDirContext.{createSubcontext(), getSchema(), getSchemaClassDefinition()}, javax.naming.spi.DirectoryManager.getContinuationDirContext()

InitialDirContext — JNDI 1.1

javax.naming.directory

This class represents the starting context for performing directory operations and is a subclass of javax.naming.InitialContext. Use this class when your application must perform directory operations on an initial context.

```
public class InitialDirContext extends InitialContext implements DirContext {
// Public Constructors
```

```
   public InitialDirContext() throws NamingException;
   public InitialDirContext(java.util.Hashtable environment) throws NamingException;
// Methods implementing DirContext
   public void bind(String name, Object obj, Attributes attrs) throws NamingException;
   public void bind(Name name, Object obj, Attributes attrs) throws NamingException;
   public DirContext createSubcontext(String name, Attributes attrs) throws NamingException;
   public DirContext createSubcontext(Name name, Attributes attrs) throws NamingException;
   public Attributes getAttributes(String name) throws NamingException;
   public Attributes getAttributes(Name name) throws NamingException;
   public Attributes getAttributes(Name name, String[ ] attrIds) throws NamingException;
   public Attributes getAttributes(String name, String[ ] attrIds) throws NamingException;
   public DirContext getSchema(String name) throws NamingException;
   public DirContext getSchema(Name name) throws NamingException;
   public DirContext getSchemaClassDefinition(String name) throws NamingException;
   public DirContext getSchemaClassDefinition(Name name) throws NamingException;
   public void modifyAttributes(Name name, ModificationItem[ ] mods) throws NamingException;
   public void modifyAttributes(String name, ModificationItem[ ] mods) throws NamingException;
   public void modifyAttributes(String name, int mod_op, Attributes attrs) throws NamingException;
   public void modifyAttributes(Name name, int mod_op, Attributes attrs) throws NamingException;
   public void rebind(Name name, Object obj, Attributes attrs) throws NamingException;
   public void rebind(String name, Object obj, Attributes attrs) throws NamingException;
   public NamingEnumeration search(String name, Attributes matchingAttributes) throws NamingException;
   public NamingEnumeration search(Name name, Attributes matchingAttributes) throws NamingException;
   public NamingEnumeration search(Name name, String filter, SearchControls cons)
      throws NamingException;
   public NamingEnumeration search(Name name, Attributes matchingAttributes, String[ ] attributesToReturn)
      throws NamingException;
   public NamingEnumeration search(String name, String filter, SearchControls cons)
      throws NamingException;
   public NamingEnumeration search(String name, Attributes matchingAttributes, String[ ] attributesToReturn)
      throws NamingException;
   public NamingEnumeration search(String name, String filterExpr, Object[ ] filterArgs, SearchControls cons)
      throws NamingException;
   public NamingEnumeration search(Name name, String filterExpr, Object[ ] filterArgs, SearchControls cons)
      throws NamingException;
}
```

Hierarchy: Object→ InitialContext(javax.naming.Context)→ InitialDirContext(DirContext(javax.naming.Context))

InvalidAttributeIdentifierException — JNDI 1.1

javax.naming.directory — *serializable checked*

Thrown when there is an attempt to create an attribute with an attribute ID that doesn't exist in the directory's schema.

```
public class InvalidAttributeIdentifierException extends NamingException {
// Public Constructors
   public InvalidAttributeIdentifierException();
   public InvalidAttributeIdentifierException(String explanation);
}
```

Hierarchy: Object→ Throwable(Serializable)→ Exception→ NamingException→ InvalidAttributeIdentifierException

InvalidAttributesException — JNDI 1.1

javax.naming.directory — *serializable checked*

Thrown when an add or modification operation has specified an inappropriate attribute type for the object class specified by the directory's schema.

```
public class InvalidAttributesException extends NamingException {
// Public Constructors
   public InvalidAttributesException();
   public InvalidAttributesException(String explanation);
}
```

Hierarchy: Object→ Throwable(Serializable)→ Exception→ NamingException→ InvalidAttributesException

InvalidAttributeValueException — JNDI 1.1

javax.naming.directory — *serializable checked*

Thrown when an add or modification operation has specified an inappropriate value for the attribute type specified by the directory's schema.

```
public class InvalidAttributeValueException extends NamingException {
// Public Constructors
   public InvalidAttributeValueException();
   public InvalidAttributeValueException(String explanation);
}
```

Hierarchy: Object→ Throwable(Serializable)→ Exception→ NamingException→ InvalidAttributeValueException

InvalidSearchControlsException — JNDI 1.1

javax.naming.directory — *serializable checked*

Thrown when a SearchControls object is invalid.

```
public class InvalidSearchControlsException extends NamingException {
// Public Constructors
   public InvalidSearchControlsException();
   public InvalidSearchControlsException(String msg);
}
```

Hierarchy: Object→ Throwable(Serializable)→ Exception→ NamingException→ InvalidSearchControlsException

InvalidSearchFilterException — JNDI 1.1

javax.naming.directory — *serializable checked*

Thrown when a search filter is invalid.

```
public class InvalidSearchFilterException extends NamingException {
// Public Constructors
   public InvalidSearchFilterException();
   public InvalidSearchFilterException(String msg);
}
```

Hierarchy: Object→ Throwable(Serializable)→ Exception→ NamingException→ InvalidSearchFilterException

ModificationItem — JNDI 1.1

javax.naming.directory — *serializable*

This class encapsulates an attribute that is to be modified and a code that determines the type of modification being performed.

```
public class ModificationItem implements Serializable {
// Public Constructors
    public ModificationItem(int mod_op, Attribute attr);
// Public Instance Methods
    public Attribute getAttribute();
    public int getModificationOp();
// Public methods overriding Object
    public String toString();
}
```

Hierarchy: Object→ ModificationItem(Serializable)

Passed To: AttributeModificationException.setUnexecutedModifications(), DirContext.modifyAttributes(), InitialDirContext.modifyAttributes()

Returned By: AttributeModificationException.getUnexecutedModifications()

NoSuchAttributeException — JNDI 1.1

javax.naming.directory — *serializable checked*

Thrown when a method attempts to access a nonexistent attribute.

```
public class NoSuchAttributeException extends NamingException {
// Public Constructors
    public NoSuchAttributeException();
    public NoSuchAttributeException(String explanation);
}
```

Hierarchy: Object→ Throwable(Serializable)→ Exception→ NamingException→ NoSuchAttributeException

SchemaViolationException — JNDI 1.1

javax.naming.directory — *serializable checked*

Thrown when a method violates schema rules.

```
public class SchemaViolationException extends NamingException {
// Public Constructors
    public SchemaViolationException();
    public SchemaViolationException(String explanation);
}
```

Hierarchy: Object→ Throwable(Serializable)→ Exception→ NamingException→ SchemaViolationException

SearchControls — JNDI 1.1

javax.naming.directory — *serializable*

This class represents the information needed to control the behavior of the search() method of DirContext. Contains information that determines the scope of search, the maximum number of results returned by a search, the maximum amount of time permitted to return search results, and other data you can use to fine-tune the behavior of search operations.

```
public class SearchControls implements Serializable {
// Public Constructors
    public SearchControls();
    public SearchControls(int scope, long countlim, int timelim, String[ ] attrs, boolean retobj, boolean deref);
// Public Constants
```

```
    public static final int OBJECT_SCOPE;                                          =0
    public static final int ONELEVEL_SCOPE;                                        =1
    public static final int SUBTREE_SCOPE;                                         =2
// Public Instance Methods
    public long getCountLimit();                                            default:0
    public boolean getDerefLinkFlag();                                  default:false
    public String[ ] getReturningAttributes();                           default:null
    public boolean getReturningObjFlag();                               default:false
    public int getSearchScope();                                            default:1
    public int getTimeLimit();                                              default:0
    public void setCountLimit(long limit);
    public void setDerefLinkFlag(boolean on);
    public void setReturningAttributes(String[ ] attrs);
    public void setReturningObjFlag(boolean on);
    public void setSearchScope(int scope);
    public void setTimeLimit(int ms);
}
```

Hierarchy: Object→ SearchControls(Serializable)

Passed To: DirContext.search(), InitialDirContext.search()

SearchResult — JNDI 1.1

javax.naming.directory — *serializable*

This class represents a result of performing a search() method on a DirContext. It is a subclass of javax.naming.Binding. You can perform directory operations on a SearchResult without first having to look up the object in the directory. Each search() method actually returns an NamingEnumeration of SearchResults objects.

```
public class SearchResult extends javax.naming.Binding {
// Public Constructors
    public SearchResult(String name, Object obj, Attributes attrs);
    public SearchResult(String name, String className, Object obj, Attributes attrs);
    public SearchResult(String name, Object obj, Attributes attrs, boolean isRelative);
    public SearchResult(String name, String className, Object obj, Attributes attrs, boolean isRelative);
// Public Instance Methods
    public Attributes getAttributes();
    public void setAttributes(Attributes attrs);
// Public methods overriding Binding
    public String toString();
}
```

Hierarchy: Object→ NameClassPair(Serializable)→ javax.naming.Binding→ SearchResult

CHAPTER 24

The javax.naming.spi Package

The javax.naming.spi package defines the service provider interface (SPI) for JNDI. Only system programmers who are developing JNDI providers need to use this package; JNDI application programmers can ignore it. The classes and interfaces in this package allow JNDI service providers to be plugged in underneath the JNDI API. Figure 24-1 shows the hierarchy of this package.

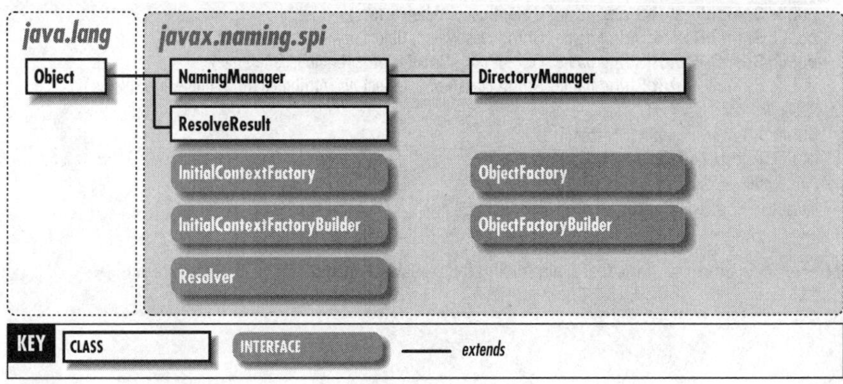

Figure 24-1: The javax.naming.spi package

DirectoryManager JNDI 1.1

javax.naming.spi

DirectoryManager is a subclass of NamingManager that contains a method for creating javax.naming.directory.DirContext objects.

```
public class DirectoryManager extends NamingManager {
// No Constructor
```

```
// Public Class Methods
   public static javax.naming.directory.DirContext getContinuationDirContext(
                                                        CannotProceedException cpe)
        throws NamingException;
}
```

Hierarchy: Object→ NamingManager→ DirectoryManager

InitialContextFactory — JNDI 1.1

javax.naming.spi

This interface represents a factory that creates an initial context for a naming or directory service. The initial context serves as the entry point into the service. A JNDI service provider always includes an InitialContextFactory that can be used as the value of the java.naming.factory.initial property

```
public abstract interface InitialContextFactory {
// Public Instance Methods
   public abstract javax.naming.Context getInitialContext(java.util.Hashtable environment)
        throws NamingException;
}
```

Returned By: InitialContextFactoryBuilder.createInitialContextFactory()

InitialContextFactoryBuilder — JNDI 1.1

javax.naming.spi

This interface represents a builder that creates initial context factories. A program can override the default initial context factory builder by calling NamingManager.setInitialContextFactoryBuilder() and specifying a new builder. Such a builder must implement this interface.

```
public abstract interface InitialContextFactoryBuilder {
// Public Instance Methods
   public abstract InitialContextFactory createInitialContextFactory(java.util.Hashtable environment)
        throws NamingException;
}
```

Passed To: NamingManager.setInitialContextFactoryBuilder()

NamingManager — JNDI 1.1

javax.naming.spi

The NamingManager class contains methods for creating javax.naming.Context objects and otherwise controlling the operation of the underlying service provider.

```
public class NamingManager {
// No Constructor
// Public Class Methods
   public static javax.naming.Context getContinuationContext(CannotProceedException cpe)
        throws NamingException;
   public static javax.naming.Context getInitialContext(java.util.Hashtable environment)
        throws NamingException;
   public static Object getObjectInstance(Object refInfo, Name name, javax.naming.Context nameCtx,
                                          java.util.Hashtable environment) throws Exception;
   public static javax.naming.Context getURLContext(String scheme, java.util.Hashtable environment)
        throws NamingException;
   public static boolean hasInitialContextFactoryBuilder();                       synchronized
```

```
    public static void setInitialContextFactoryBuilder(InitialContextFactoryBuilder builder)    synchronized
        throws NamingException;
    public static void setObjectFactoryBuilder(ObjectFactoryBuilder builder)                    synchronized
        throws NamingException;
}
```

Subclasses: DirectoryManager

ObjectFactory — JNDI 1.1

javax.naming.spi

This interface represents a factory for creating objects. JNDI supports the dynamic loading of object implementations with object factories. For example, say you have a naming system that binds file objects to names in the namespace. If the filesystem service provider binds filenames to Reference objects, a Reference object can create a file object through an object factory. This means that a call to lookup() a filename (in the appropriate Context) returns an actual file object the programmer can manipulate as necessary. An ObjectFactory is responsible for creating objects of a specific type.

```
public abstract interface ObjectFactory {
// Public Instance Methods
    public abstract Object getObjectInstance(Object obj, Name name, javax.naming.Context nameCtx,
                                             java.util.Hashtable environment) throws Exception;
}
```

Returned By: ObjectFactoryBuilder.createObjectFactory()

ObjectFactoryBuilder — JNDI 1.1

javax.naming.spi

This interface represents a builder that creates object factories. A program can override the default object factory builder by calling NamingManager.setObjectFactoryBuilder() and specifying a new builder. Such a builder must implement this interface.

```
public abstract interface ObjectFactoryBuilder {
// Public Instance Methods
    public abstract ObjectFactory createObjectFactory(Object obj, java.util.Hashtable info)
        throws NamingException;
}
```

Passed To: NamingManager.setObjectFactoryBuilder()

Resolver — JNDI 1.1

javax.naming.spi

The Resolver interface contains methods that are implemented by objects that can act as intermediate contexts for naming resolution purposes.

```
public abstract interface Resolver {
// Public Instance Methods
   public abstract ResolveResult resolveToClass(Name name, Class contextType) throws NamingException;
   public abstract ResolveResult resolveToClass(String name, Class contextType) throws NamingException;
}
```

ResolveResult **JNDI 1.1**

javax.naming.spi

This class represents the result of resolving a name.

```
public class ResolveResult {
// Public Constructors
   public ResolveResult(Object robj, Name rname);
   public ResolveResult(Object robj, String rcomp);
// Protected Constructors
   protected ResolveResult();
// Public Instance Methods
   public void appendRemainingComponent(String name);
   public void appendRemainingName(Name name);
   public Name getRemainingName();
   public Object getResolvedObj();
   public void setRemainingName(Name name);
   public void setResolvedObj(Object obj);
// Protected Instance Fields
   protected Name remainingName;
   protected Object resolvedObj;
}
```

Returned By: Resolver.resolveToClass()

CHAPTER 25

The javax.servlet Package

The javax.servlet package is the core of the Servlet API. It contains the classes necessary for a standard, protocol-independent servlet. Every servlet must implement the Servlet interface in one form or another. The abstract GenericServlet class provides the framework for developing basic servlets. The package also includes a variety of utility classes that communicate with the server and the client. Figure 25-1 shows the class hierarchy of this package.

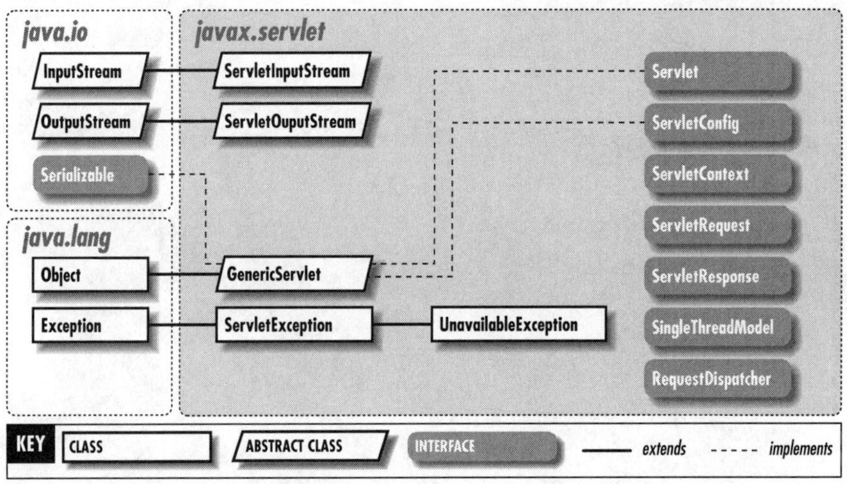

Figure 25-1: The javax.servlet package

GenericServlet — Servlets 1.0

javax.servlet — *serializable*

The GenericServlet class provides a basic implementation of the Servlet and ServletConfig interfaces. If you are creating a protocol-independent servlet, you probably want to subclass this class rather than implement the Servlet interface directly. Note that the service() method is declared as abstract; this is the only method you have to override to implement a generic servlet.

GenericServlet includes basic implementations of the init() and destroy() methods, which perform basic setup and cleanup tasks, respectively. The init() method that takes a ServletConfig object stores that object for later use. This means that if you override the method and fail to call the super.init(ServletConfig) method, you won't be able to use the ServletConfig methods later. In Version 2.1 of the Servlet API, you can override a no-argument version of init() that is dispatched by the default init(ServletConfig) method of GenericServlet.

```
public abstract class GenericServlet implements Servlet, ServletConfig, Serializable {
// Public Constructors
   public GenericServlet();
// Public Instance Methods
2.1 public void init() throws ServletException;                                    empty
   public void log(String msg);
2.1 public void log(String message, Throwable t);
// Methods implementing Servlet
   public void destroy();
   public ServletConfig getServletConfig();
   public String getServletInfo();
   public void init(ServletConfig config) throws ServletException;
   public abstract void service(ServletRequest req, ServletResponse res) throws ServletException,
       IOException;
// Methods implementing ServletConfig
   public String getInitParameter(String name);
   public java.util.Enumeration getInitParameterNames();
   public ServletContext getServletContext();
}
```

Hierarchy: Object→ GenericServlet(Servlet, ServletConfig, Serializable)

Subclasses: javax.servlet.http.HttpServlet

RequestDispatcher — Servlets 2.1

javax.servlet

RequestDispatcher allows a servlet to delegate some or all of the processing of a request to another resource on the web server. A RequestDispatcher object is retrieved by calling the getRequestDispatcher() method on the ServletContext object. The forward() method passes a request on to another servlet for processing, while the include() method includes the output of another servlet in the output of the current servlet.

```
public interface RequestDispatcher {
// Public Instance Methods
   public abstract void forward(ServletRequest request, ServletResponse response)
       throws ServletException, IOException;
   public abstract void include(ServletRequest request, ServletResponse response)
       throws ServletException, IOException;
}
```

Returned By: ServletContext.getRequestDispatcher()

Servlet — Servlets 1.0

javax.servlet

The Servlet interface defines the basic structure of a servlet. All servlets implement this interface, either directly or by subclassing a class that does. The interface declares the basic servlet functionality: initializing a servlet, handling client requests, and destroying a servlet.

init() is called when the servlet is first initialized. Since init() creates resources the servlet can reuse, it is guaranteed to finish executing before the servlet handles any client requests. The server calls the service() method for each client request. The servlet interacts with the client via ServletRequest and ServletResponse objects passed to service(). destroy() is called to clean up resources (such as database connections) or save state when the server shuts down. The getServletInfo() method should return a String that describes a servlet, and the getServletConfig() method should return the ServletConfig object that was passed to the init() method.

```
public interface Servlet {
// Public Instance Methods
   public abstract void destroy();
   public abstract ServletConfig getServletConfig();
   public abstract String getServletInfo();
   public abstract void init(ServletConfig config) throws ServletException;
   public abstract void service(ServletRequest req, ServletResponse res) throws ServletException,
       IOException;
}
```

Implementations: GenericServlet

Passed To: UnavailableException.UnavailableException()

Returned By: ServletContext.getServlet(), UnavailableException.getServlet()

ServletConfig — Servlets 1.0

javax.servlet

A ServletConfig object passes configuration information from the server to a servlet. ServletConfig supports initialization parameters (also known simply as init parameters) defined by the server administrator for a particular servlet. These parameters are accessed via the getInitParameter() and getInitParameterNames() methods. ServletConfig also includes a ServletContext object, accessible via getServletContext(), for direct interaction with the server.

```
public interface ServletConfig {
// Public Instance Methods
   public abstract String getInitParameter(String name);
   public abstract java.util.Enumeration getInitParameterNames();
   public abstract ServletContext getServletContext();
}
```

Implementations: GenericServlet

Passed To: GenericServlet.init(), Servlet.init()

Returned By: GenericServlet.getServletConfig(), Servlet.getServletConfig()

ServletContext **Servlets 1.0**

javax.servlet

ServletContext defines methods that allow a servlet to interact with the host server. This includes reading server-specific attributes, finding information about particular files located on the server, and writing to the server log files. If there are several virtual servers running, each one may return a different ServletContext.

Servlets can also use ServletContext to interact with other servlets loaded on the same server. In Version 1.0 of the Servlet API, this was done via the getServlets() method. In Version 2.0, getServlets() was deprecated in favor of getServlet() and getServletNames(). In Version 2.1, getServlet() and getServletNames() were both deprecated in favor of the new setAttribute() and getAttribute() methods.

```
public interface ServletContext {
// Public Instance Methods
    public abstract Object getAttribute(String name);
2.1 public abstract java.util.Enumeration getAttributeNames();
2.1 public abstract ServletContext getContext(String uripath);
2.1 public abstract int getMajorVersion();
    public abstract String getMimeType(String file);
2.1 public abstract int getMinorVersion();
    public abstract String getRealPath(String path);
2.1 public abstract RequestDispatcher getRequestDispatcher(String urlpath);
2.1 public abstract java.net.URL getResource(String path) throws java.net.MalformedURLException;
2.1 public abstract java.io.InputStream getResourceAsStream(String path);
    public abstract String getServerInfo();
    public abstract void log(String msg);
2.1 public abstract void log(String message, Throwable throwable);
2.1 public abstract void removeAttribute(String name);
2.1 public abstract void setAttribute(String name, Object object);
// Deprecated Public Methods
#   public abstract Servlet getServlet(String name) throws ServletException;
2.0# public abstract java.util.Enumeration getServletNames();
#   public abstract java.util.Enumeration getServlets();
2.0# public abstract void log(Exception exception, String msg);
}
```

Returned By: GenericServlet.getServletContext(), ServletConfig.getServletContext(), ServletContext.getContext()

ServletException **Servlets 1.0**

javax.servlet *serializable checked*

A generic Exception class used for basic servlet errors. In version 2.1, a servlet can specify a Throwable root cause for this exception (using the constructors that accept Throwable parameters). The root cause can be retrieved with the getRootCause() method.

```
public class ServletException extends Exception {
// Public Constructors
2.0 public ServletException();
2.1 public ServletException(Throwable rootCause);
    public ServletException(String message);
2.1 public ServletException(String message, Throwable rootCause);
// Public Instance Methods
2.1 public Throwable getRootCause();                                  default:null
}
```

javax.servlet

Hierarchy: Object→ Throwable(Serializable)→ Exception→ ServletException

Subclasses: UnavailableException

Thrown By: GenericServlet.{init(), service()}, RequestDispatcher.{forward(), include()}, Servlet.{init(), service()}, ServletContext.getServlet(), javax.servlet.http.HttpServlet.{doDelete(), doGet(), doOptions(), doPost(), doPut(), doTrace(), service()}

ServletInputStream — Servlets 1.0

javax.servlet

ServletInputStream provides an input stream for reading data from a client request. A servlet can get a ServletInputStream by calling the getInputStream() method of ServletRequest. While ServletInputStream does contain a readLine() method for reading textual data one line at a time, this functionality was taken over by BufferedReader objects and the getReader() method of ServletRequest in Version 2.0 of the Servlet API. Thus, ServletInputStream should be used only to read binary data, generally in the context of a filtering servlet.

```
public abstract class ServletInputStream extends java.io.InputStream {
// Protected Constructors
   protected ServletInputStream();
// Public Instance Methods
   public int readLine(byte [ ] b, int off, int len) throws IOException;
}
```

Hierarchy: Object→ java.io.InputStream→ ServletInputStream

Passed To: javax.servlet.http.HttpUtils.parsePostData()

Returned By: ServletRequest.getInputStream()

ServletOutputStream — Servlets 1.0

javax.servlet

ServletOutputStream provides an output stream for sending binary data back to a client. A servlet can get a ServletOutputStream by calling the getOutputStream() method of ServletResponse. ServletOutputStream was the only available output method in Version 1.0 of the Servlet API. For text and HTML output, it has been supplanted by PrintWriter objects produced by the getWriter() method of ServletResponse. The various print() and println() methods should therefore be regarded as legacies.

```
public abstract class ServletOutputStream extends java.io.OutputStream {
// Protected Constructors
   protected ServletOutputStream();
// Public Instance Methods
   public void print(long l) throws IOException;
   public void print(float f) throws IOException;
   public void print(double d) throws IOException;
   public void print(int i) throws IOException;
   public void print(String s) throws IOException;
   public void print(boolean b) throws IOException;
   public void print(char c) throws IOException;
   public void println() throws IOException;
   public void println(long l) throws IOException;
   public void println(float f) throws IOException;
   public void println(double d) throws IOException;
   public void println(int i) throws IOException;
   public void println(String s) throws IOException;
   public void println(boolean b) throws IOException;
```

```
    public void println(char c) throws IOException;
}
```

Hierarchy: Object→ java.io.OutputStream→ ServletOutputStream

Returned By: ServletResponse.getOutputStream()

ServletRequest — Servlets 1.0

javax.servlet

A ServletRequest object encapsulates information about a client request. The server passes a ServletRequest object to the service() method of a servlet. ServletRequest provides access to request parameters, such as form values or other request-specific parameters. These are accessed using the getParameterNames(), getParameter(), and getParameterValues() methods. Raw request data can be read by the getReader() method (for textual data) and the getInputStream() method (for binary data). The getContentType(), getContentLength(), and getCharacterEncoding() methods can help retrieve this information. Other methods provide information about the client (getRemoteAddr(), getRemoteHost()), the request itself (getScheme(), getProtocol()), and the server (getServerName(), getServerPort()). Version 2.1 also adds the getAttribute() and setAttribute() methods, which are generally used with the new RequestDispatcher interface.

```
public interface ServletRequest {
// Public Instance Methods
    public abstract Object getAttribute(String name);
2.1 public abstract java.util.Enumeration getAttributeNames();
2.0 public abstract String getCharacterEncoding();
    public abstract int getContentLength();
    public abstract String getContentType();
    public abstract ServletInputStream getInputStream() throws IOException;
    public abstract String getParameter(String name);
    public abstract java.util.Enumeration getParameterNames();
    public abstract String[ ] getParameterValues(String name);
    public abstract String getProtocol();
2.0 public abstract BufferedReader getReader() throws IOException;
    public abstract String getRemoteAddr();
    public abstract String getRemoteHost();
    public abstract String getScheme();
    public abstract String getServerName();
    public abstract int getServerPort();
2.1 public abstract void setAttribute(String key, Object o);
// Deprecated Public Methods
#   public abstract String getRealPath(String path);
}
```

Implementations: javax.servlet.http.HttpServletRequest

Passed To: GenericServlet.service(), RequestDispatcher.{forward(), include()}, Servlet.service(), javax.servlet.http.HttpServlet.service()

ServletResponse — Servlets 1.0

javax.servlet

The ServletResponse object sends MIME-encoded data back to the client. The interface defines a getOutputStream() method that returns a ServletOutputStream for sending binary data and a getWriter() method that returns a PrintWriter for sending textual data. The setContentType() and setContentLength() methods can explicitly set the content type and content length (often necessary for keep-alive connections and other tasks). If you call setContentType(), you should do so before you call getWriter(), as getWriter() consults the content type to determine which charset to use.

```
public interface ServletResponse {
// Public Instance Methods
2.0 public abstract String getCharacterEncoding();
    public abstract ServletOutputStream getOutputStream() throws IOException;
2.0 public abstract PrintWriter getWriter() throws IOException;
    public abstract void setContentLength(int len);
    public abstract void setContentType(String type);
}
```

Implementations: javax.servlet.http.HttpServletResponse

Passed To: GenericServlet.service(), RequestDispatcher.{forward(), include()}, Servlet.service(), javax.servlet.http.HttpServlet.service()

SingleThreadModel **Servlets 2.0**

javax.servlet

SingleThreadModel is a tag interface that tells the server to create a pool of servlet instances to serve individual requests. In this case, the server ensures that each instance of the servlet handles only one service request at a time. SingleThreadModel provides easy thread safety, but imposes performance penalties.

```
public interface SingleThreadModel {
}
```

UnavailableException **Servlets 1.0**

javax.servlet ***serializable checked***

An UnavailableException indicates that a servlet is unable to handle client requests, either temporarily or permanently. To specify temporary unavailability, use the three-argument constructor and specify the duration of the servlet's downtime. If a servlet specifies temporary unavailability, the server may (but is not required to) attempt to reload the servlet after the specified interval.

```
public class UnavailableException extends ServletException {
// Public Constructors
    public UnavailableException(Servlet servlet, String msg);
    public UnavailableException(int seconds, Servlet servlet, String msg);
// Public Instance Methods
    public Servlet getServlet();
    public int getUnavailableSeconds();
    public boolean isPermanent();
}
```

Hierarchy: Object→ Throwable(Serializable)→ Exception→ ServletException→ UnavailableException

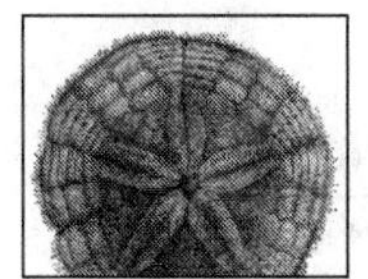

CHAPTER 26

The javax.servlet.http Package

The javax.servlet.http package supports the development of servlets that use the HTTP protocol. The classes in this package extend the basic servlet functionality to support various HTTP specific features, including request and response headers, different request methods, and cookies. The abstract HttpServlet class extends javax.servlet.GenericServlet and serves as the base class for HTTP servlets. HttpServletRequest and HttpServletResponse allow additional interaction with the client. Finally, since the HTTP protocol is inherently stateless, the package also includes HttpSession and some related classes to support session tracking. Figure 26-1 shows the class hierarchy of this package.

Cookie — Servlets 2.0

javax.servlet.http — *cloneable*

The Cookie class provides servlets with an easy way to read, create, and manipulate HTTP-style cookies. Cookies provide a way to store a small amount of information on the client and are typically used for session tracking or storing user-configuration information. The getCookies() method of HttpServletRequest returns an array of Cookie objects. To set a new cookie on the client, a servlet creates a new Cookie object and uses the addCookie() method of HttpServletResponse. This must be done before sending any other content, since cookies are created within the HTTP header stream. The various methods of the Cookie class allow a servlet to set and get various attributes of a Cookie object, such as its path and domain.

```
public class Cookie implements Cloneable {
// Public Constructors
   public Cookie(String name, String value);
// Public Instance Methods
   public String getComment();
   public String getDomain();
   public int getMaxAge();
   public String getName();
   public String getPath();
   public boolean getSecure();
```

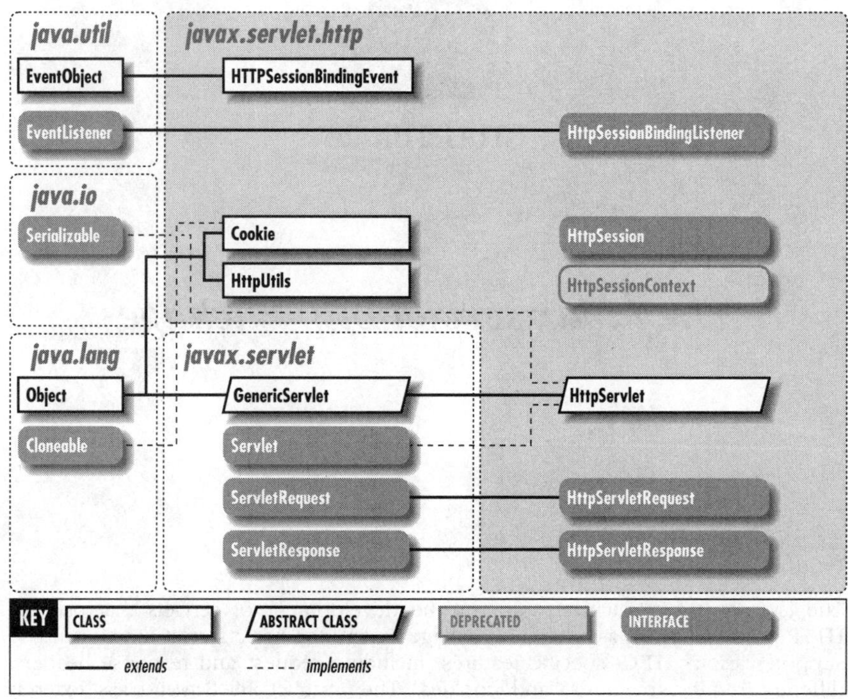

Figure 26-1: The javax.servlet.http package

```
    public String getValue();
    public int getVersion();
    public void setComment(String purpose);
    public void setDomain(String pattern);
    public void setMaxAge(int expiry);
    public void setPath(String uri);
    public void setSecure(boolean flag);
    public void setValue(String newValue);
    public void setVersion(int v);
// Public methods overriding Object
    public Object clone();
}
```

Hierarchy: Object→ Cookie(Cloneable)

Passed To: HttpServletResponse.addCookie()

Returned By: HttpServletRequest.getCookies()

HttpServlet — Servlets 1.0

javax.servlet.http — ***serializable***

The abstract HttpServlet class serves as a framework for servlets that generate content for the World Wide Web using the HTTP protocol. Rather than overriding the service() method, you should override one or more of the method-specific request handlers (doGet(), doPost(), doPut(), etc.). The default service() implementation dispatches incoming requests to the appropriate methods, and so should not be overridden. The default implementations of doGet(), doPost(), doDelete(), and doPut() all return an HTTP BAD_REQUEST error, so if you want to handle one of these kinds of requests, you must override the appropriate method.

A web server calls getLastModified() in response to conditional GET requests. The default implementation returns -1. If you know when the output of your servlet last changed, you can return that time, specified in milliseconds since midnight, January 1, 1970 GMT, instead. This allows web browsers to cache your servlet's response.

```
public abstract class HttpServlet extends GenericServlet implements Serializable {
// Public Constructors
    public HttpServlet();
// Public methods overriding GenericServlet
    public void service(ServletRequest req, ServletResponse res) throws ServletException, IOException;
// Protected Instance Methods
2.0 protected void doDelete(HttpServletRequest req, HttpServletResponse resp) throws ServletException,
        IOException;
    protected void doGet(HttpServletRequest req, HttpServletResponse resp) throws ServletException,
        IOException;
2.0 protected void doOptions(HttpServletRequest req, HttpServletResponse resp) throws ServletException,
        IOException;
    protected void doPost(HttpServletRequest req, HttpServletResponse resp) throws ServletException,
        IOException;
2.0 protected void doPut(HttpServletRequest req, HttpServletResponse resp) throws ServletException,
        IOException;
2.0 protected void doTrace(HttpServletRequest req, HttpServletResponse resp) throws ServletException,
        IOException;
    protected long getLastModified(HttpServletRequest req);
    protected void service(HttpServletRequest req, HttpServletResponse resp) throws ServletException,
        IOException;
}
```

Hierarchy: Object→ GenericServlet(Servlet, ServletConfig, Serializable)→ HttpServlet(Serializable)

HttpServletRequest — Servlets 1.0

javax.servlet.http

HttpServletRequest extends javax.servlet.ServletRequest and provides a number of methods that make it easy to access specific information related to an HTTP request. This includes methods for directly accessing HTTP headers: getHeader(), getIntHeader(), getDateHeader(), and getHeaderNames(). Other methods return various information about the request, including getMethod(), which returns the request method (GET, POST, etc), getPathInfo(), which returns any extra path information attached to the request, getPathTranslated(), which translates the extra path information into a filesystem path, and getServletPath(), which returns the URI pointing to the current servlet, minus any extra path information. The interface also includes the getCookies() method for retrieving cookie data and getSession() for accessing the current HttpSession object.

```
public interface HttpServletRequest extends ServletRequest {
// Public Instance Methods
    public abstract String getAuthType();
2.0 public abstract Cookie[ ] getCookies();
    public abstract long getDateHeader(String name);
    public abstract String getHeader(String name);
    public abstract java.util.Enumeration getHeaderNames();
    public abstract int getIntHeader(String name);
    public abstract String getMethod();
    public abstract String getPathInfo();
```

```
   public abstract String getPathTranslated();
   public abstract String getQueryString();
   public abstract String getRemoteUser();
2.0 public abstract String getRequestedSessionId();
   public abstract String getRequestURI();
   public abstract String getServletPath();
2.1 public abstract HttpSession getSession();
2.0 public abstract HttpSession getSession(boolean create);
2.0 public abstract boolean isRequestedSessionIdFromCookie();
2.1 public abstract boolean isRequestedSessionIdFromURL();
2.0 public abstract boolean isRequestedSessionIdValid();
// Deprecated Public Methods
2.0# public abstract boolean isRequestedSessionIdFromUrl();
}
```

Hierarchy: (HttpServletRequest(ServletRequest))

Passed To: HttpServlet.{doDelete(), doGet(), doOptions(), doPost(), doPut(), doTrace(), getLastModified(), service()}, HttpUtils.getRequestURL()

HttpServletResponse — Servlets 1.0

javax.servlet.http

HttpServletResponse extends javax.servlet.ServletResponse and provides additional methods for HTTP-specific actions and a set of HTTP response code constants. The containsHeader(), setHeader(), setDateHeader(), and setIntHeader() methods allow servlets to set and update specific HTTP response headers. The addCookie() method writes a cookie, represented by a Cookie object, to the client. The sendError() and setStatus() methods allow servlets to set specific HTTP result codes, along with an optional customized error message. The encodeUrl() and encodeRedirectUrl() methods (deprecated in 2.1 in favor of encodeURL() and encodeRedirectURL()) methods support session tracking without the use of cookies. The sendRedirect() method handles an HTTP page redirect.

```
public interface HttpServletResponse extends ServletResponse {
// Public Constants
   public static final int SC_ACCEPTED;                                  =202
   public static final int SC_BAD_GATEWAY;                               =502
   public static final int SC_BAD_REQUEST;                               =400
2.0 public static final int SC_CONFLICT;                                 =409
2.0 public static final int SC_CONTINUE;                                 =100
   public static final int SC_CREATED;                                   =201
   public static final int SC_FORBIDDEN;                                 =403
2.0 public static final int SC_GATEWAY_TIMEOUT;                          =504
2.0 public static final int SC_GONE;                                     =410
2.0 public static final int SC_HTTP_VERSION_NOT_SUPPORTED;               =505
   public static final int SC_INTERNAL_SERVER_ERROR;                     =500
2.0 public static final int SC_LENGTH_REQUIRED;                          =411
2.0 public static final int SC_METHOD_NOT_ALLOWED;                       =405
   public static final int SC_MOVED_PERMANENTLY;                         =301
   public static final int SC_MOVED_TEMPORARILY;                         =302
2.0 public static final int SC_MULTIPLE_CHOICES;                         =300
   public static final int SC_NO_CONTENT;                                =204
2.0 public static final int SC_NON_AUTHORITATIVE_INFORMATION;            =203
2.0 public static final int SC_NOT_ACCEPTABLE;                           =406
   public static final int SC_NOT_FOUND;                                 =404
   public static final int SC_NOT_IMPLEMENTED;                           =501
   public static final int SC_NOT_MODIFIED;                              =304
   public static final int SC_OK;                                        =200
```

```
2.0 public static final int SC_PARTIAL_CONTENT;                              =206
2.0 public static final int SC_PAYMENT_REQUIRED;                             =402
2.0 public static final int SC_PRECONDITION_FAILED;                          =412
2.0 public static final int SC_PROXY_AUTHENTICATION_REQUIRED;                =407
2.0 public static final int SC_REQUEST_ENTITY_TOO_LARGE;                     =413
2.0 public static final int SC_REQUEST_TIMEOUT;                              =408
2.0 public static final int SC_REQUEST_URI_TOO_LONG;                         =414
2.0 public static final int SC_RESET_CONTENT;                                =205
2.0 public static final int SC_SEE_OTHER;                                    =303
    public static final int SC_SERVICE_UNAVAILABLE;                          =503
2.0 public static final int SC_SWITCHING_PROTOCOLS;                          =101
    public static final int SC_UNAUTHORIZED;                                 =401
2.0 public static final int SC_UNSUPPORTED_MEDIA_TYPE;                       =415
2.0 public static final int SC_USE_PROXY;                                    =305
// Public Instance Methods
2.0 public abstract void addCookie(Cookie cookie);
    public abstract boolean containsHeader(String name);
2.1 public abstract String encodeRedirectURL(String url);
2.1 public abstract String encodeURL(String url);
    public abstract void sendError(int sc) throws IOException;
    public abstract void sendError(int sc, String msg) throws IOException;
    public abstract void sendRedirect(String location) throws IOException;
    public abstract void setDateHeader(String name, long date);
    public abstract void setHeader(String name, String value);
    public abstract void setIntHeader(String name, int value);
    public abstract void setStatus(int sc);
// Deprecated Public Methods
2.0# public abstract String encodeRedirectUrl(String url);
2.0# public abstract String encodeUrl(String url);
#   public abstract void setStatus(int sc, String sm);
}
```

Hierarchy: (HttpServletResponse(ServletResponse))

Passed To: HttpServlet.{doDelete(), doGet(), doOptions(), doPost(), doPut(), doTrace(), service()}

HttpSession — Servlets 2.0

javax.servlet.http

The HttpSession interface is the core of the session tracking functionality introduced in Version 2.0 of the Servlet API. A servlet obtains an HttpSession objects from the getSession() method of HttpServletRequest. The putValue() and removeValue() methods bind Java objects to a particular session. When possible, bound objects should be (but do not need to be) serializable. getValueNames() returns a String array that contains the names of all objects bound to the session.

```
public interface HttpSession {
// Public Instance Methods
    public abstract long getCreationTime();
    public abstract String getId();
    public abstract long getLastAccessedTime();
2.1 public abstract int getMaxInactiveInterval();
    public abstract Object getValue(String name);
    public abstract String[ ] getValueNames( );
    public abstract void invalidate( );
    public abstract boolean isNew( );
    public abstract void putValue(String name, Object value);
    public abstract void removeValue(String name);
```

```
2.1 public abstract void setMaxInactiveInterval(int interval);
// Deprecated Public Methods
#   public abstract HttpSessionContext getSessionContext();
}
```

Passed To: HttpSessionBindingEvent.HttpSessionBindingEvent()

Returned By: HttpServletRequest.getSession(), HttpSessionBindingEvent.getSession(), HttpSessionContext.getSession()

HttpSessionBindingEvent — Servlets 2.0

javax.servlet.http — ***serializable event***

An HttpSessionBindingEvent is passed to the appropriate method of an HttpSessionBindingListener when an object is bound to or unbound from an HttpSession. The getName() method returns the name to which the bound object has been assigned, and the getSession() method provides a reference to the session the object is being bound to.

```
public class HttpSessionBindingEvent extends java.util.EventObject {
// Public Constructors
    public HttpSessionBindingEvent(HttpSession session, String name);
// Public Instance Methods
    public String getName();
    public HttpSession getSession();
}
```

Hierarchy: Object→ java.util.EventObject(Serializable)→ HttpSessionBindingEvent

Passed To: HttpSessionBindingListener.{valueBound(), valueUnbound()}

HttpSessionBindingListener — Servlets 2.0

javax.servlet.http — ***event listener***

An object that implements HttpSessionBindingListener is notified with calls to valueBound() and valueUnbound() when it is bound to and unbound from an HttpSession, respectively. The valueUnbound() method is also called when a session is deleted for inactivity or at server shutdown.

```
public interface HttpSessionBindingListener extends java.util.EventListener {
// Public Instance Methods
    public abstract void valueBound(HttpSessionBindingEvent event);
    public abstract void valueUnbound(HttpSessionBindingEvent event);
}
```

Hierarchy: (HttpSessionBindingListener(java.util.EventListener))

HttpSessionContext — Servlets 2.0; Deprecated in Servlets 2.1

javax.servlet.http

HttpSessionContext provides access to all of the currently active sessions on the server. Note that this class is deprecated as of Version 2.1 of the Servlet API, due to a minor security risk whereby a servlet could expose all the session IDs in use on the server.

```
public interface HttpSessionContext {
// Deprecated Public Methods
#   public abstract java.util.Enumeration getIds();
#   public abstract HttpSession getSession(String sessionId);
}
```

Returned By: HttpSession.getSessionContext()

HttpUtils **Servlets 1.0**

javax.servlet.http

The HttpUtils class contains three static methods that perform useful HTTP-related tasks. getRequestURL() forms a functional approximation of the original request URL, including scheme, server name, server port, extra path information, and query string, based on an HttpServletRequest object. The parsePostData() and parseQueryString() methods parse URL-encoded form variables from an InputStream or a String. In most cases, a servlet should use the getParameter(), getParameterValues(), and getParameterNames() methods of HttpServletRequest instead.

```
public class HttpUtils {
// Public Constructors
   public HttpUtils();
// Public Class Methods
   public static StringBuffer getRequestURL(HttpServletRequest req);
   public static java.util.Hashtable parsePostData(int len, ServletInputStream in);
   public static java.util.Hashtable parseQueryString(String s);
}
```

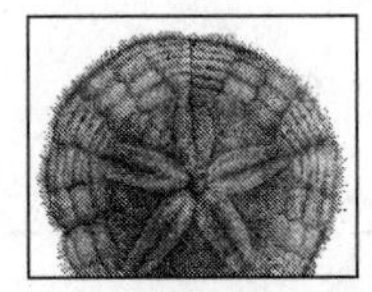

CHAPTER 27

The javax.sql Package

The javax.sql package contains the JDBC 2.0 Standard Extension API. The classes and interfaces in this package provide new functionality, such as connection pooling, that do not fall under the scope of the original JDBC API and can therefore be safely packaged separately. The DataSource interface serves as a factory for Connectionobjects; DataSource objects can be registered with a JNDI server, making it possible to get the name of a database from a name service. PooledConnectionsupports connection pooling, which allows an application to handle multiple database connections in a fairly transparent manner. RowSet extends the ResultSetinterface to a JavaBeans component that can be manipulated at design time and used with non-SQL data sources. Figure 27-1 shows the class hierarchy of the javax.sql package.

ConnectionEvent — JDBC 2.0 Extension

javax.sql — *serializable event*

Provides information about a pooled connection when an event occurs on the connection. If the event is an error event, ConnectionEvent includes the SQLException that is about to be thrown to the application.

```
public class ConnectionEvent extends java.util.EventObject {
// Public Constructors
   public ConnectionEvent(PooledConnection con);
   public ConnectionEvent(PooledConnection con, java.sql.SQLException ex);
// Public Instance Methods
   public java.sql.SQLException getSQLException();
}
```

Hierarchy: Object→ java.util.EventObject(Serializable)→ ConnectionEvent

Passed To: ConnectionEventListener.{connectionClosed(), connectionErrorOccurred()}

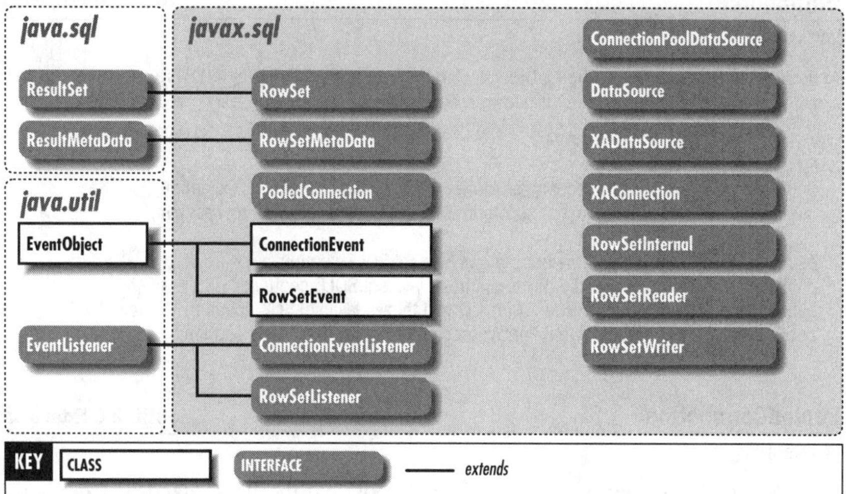

Figure 27-1: The javax.sql package

ConnectionEventListener — JDBC 2.0 Extension

javax.sql — *event listener*

An object that implements ConnectionEventListener registers to receive event notifications from PooledConnection objects. The connectionClosed() method is called when the close() method of the PooledConnection object is called, while the connectionErrorOccurred() method is called immediately before an SQLException is thrown to indicate a fatal error condition (one that renders the connection unusable in the future).

```
public abstract interface ConnectionEventListener extends java.util.EventListener {
// Public Instance Methods
   public abstract void connectionClosed(ConnectionEvent event);
   public abstract void connectionErrorOccurred(ConnectionEvent event);
}
```

Hierarchy: (ConnectionEventListener(java.util.EventListener))

Passed To: PooledConnection.{addConnectionEventListener(), removeConnectionEventListener()}

ConnectionPoolDataSource — JDBC 2.0 Extension

javax.sql

A factory for PooledConnection objects. Can be registered with a JNDI service or used standalone (for example, in a servlet).

```
public abstract interface ConnectionPoolDataSource {
// Public Instance Methods
   public abstract int getLoginTimeout() throws java.sql.SQLException;
   public abstract PrintWriter getLogWriter() throws java.sql.SQLException;
   public abstract PooledConnection getPooledConnection() throws java.sql.SQLException;
   public abstract PooledConnection getPooledConnection(String user, String password)
      throws java.sql.SQLException;
   public abstract void setLoginTimeout(int seconds) throws java.sql.SQLException;
   public abstract void setLogWriter(PrintWriter out) throws java.sql.SQLException;
}
```

DataSource — JDBC 2.0 Extension

javax.sql

A factory for java.sql.Connection objects. Can be registered with a JNDI service, so that an application can get the name of a database from a name service.

```
public abstract interface DataSource {
// Public Instance Methods
   public abstract java.sql.Connection getConnection() throws java.sql.SQLException;
   public abstract java.sql.Connection getConnection(String username, String password)
       throws java.sql.SQLException;
   public abstract int getLoginTimeout() throws java.sql.SQLException;
   public abstract PrintWriter getLogWriter() throws java.sql.SQLException;
   public abstract void setLoginTimeout(int seconds) throws java.sql.SQLException;
   public abstract void setLogWriter(PrintWriter out) throws java.sql.SQLException;
}
```

PooledConnection — JDBC 2.0 Extension

javax.sql

PooledConnection provides an application-level hook into the JDBC Standard Extension's connection pooling functionality. Call getConnection() to retrieve a standard java.sql.Connection object for database access from the connection pool. Use close() to return this connection to the pool.

```
public abstract interface PooledConnection {
// Event Registration Methods (by event name)
   public abstract void addConnectionEventListener(ConnectionEventListener listener);
   public abstract void removeConnectionEventListener(ConnectionEventListener listener);
// Public Instance Methods
   public abstract void close() throws java.sql.SQLException;
   public abstract java.sql.Connection getConnection() throws java.sql.SQLException;
}
```

Implementations: javax.sql.XAConnection

Passed To: ConnectionEvent.ConnectionEvent()

Returned By: ConnectionPoolDataSource.getPooledConnection()

RowSet — JDBC 2.0 Extension

javax.sql

RowSet extends the java.sql.ResultSet interface so that RowSet objects are JavaBeans components and can be manipulated by visual programming tools. A RowSet can be implemented on top of any JDBC-compliant ResultSet. The setCommand() method specifies what data the row set should contain (for a database generated set, this might be an SQL statement).

```
public abstract interface RowSet extends java.sql.ResultSet {
// Event Registration Methods (by event name)
   public abstract void addRowSetListener(RowSetListener listener);
   public abstract void removeRowSetListener(RowSetListener listener);
// Public Instance Methods
   public abstract void clearParameters() throws java.sql.SQLException;
   public abstract void execute() throws java.sql.SQLException;
   public abstract String getCommand();
   public abstract String getDataSourceName();
   public abstract boolean getEscapeProcessing() throws java.sql.SQLException;
```

```
public abstract int getMaxFieldSize() throws java.sql.SQLException;
public abstract int getMaxRows() throws java.sql.SQLException;
public abstract String getPassword();
public abstract int getQueryTimeout() throws java.sql.SQLException;
public abstract int getTransactionIsolation();
public abstract java.util.Map getTypeMap() throws java.sql.SQLException;
public abstract String getUrl() throws java.sql.SQLException;
public abstract String getUsername();
public abstract boolean isReadOnly();
public abstract void setArray(int i, java.sql.Array x) throws java.sql.SQLException;
public abstract void setAsciiStream(int parameterIndex, java.io.InputStream x, int length)
    throws java.sql.SQLException;
public abstract void setBigDecimal(int parameterIndex, java.math.BigDecimal x)
    throws java.sql.SQLException;
public abstract void setBinaryStream(int parameterIndex, java.io.InputStream x, int length)
    throws java.sql.SQLException;
public abstract void setBlob(int i, java.sql.Blob x) throws java.sql.SQLException;
public abstract void setBoolean(int parameterIndex, boolean x) throws java.sql.SQLException;
public abstract void setByte(int parameterIndex, byte x) throws java.sql.SQLException;
public abstract void setBytes(int parameterIndex, byte[ ] x) throws java.sql.SQLException;
public abstract void setCharacterStream(int parameterIndex, Reader reader, int length)
    throws java.sql.SQLException;
public abstract void setClob(int i, java.sql.Clob x) throws java.sql.SQLException;
public abstract void setCommand(String cmd) throws java.sql.SQLException;
public abstract void setConcurrency(int concurrency) throws java.sql.SQLException;
public abstract void setDataSourceName(String name) throws java.sql.SQLException;
public abstract void setDate(int parameterIndex, java.sql.Date x) throws java.sql.SQLException;
public abstract void setDate(int parameterIndex, java.sql.Date x, java.util.Calendar cal)
    throws java.sql.SQLException;
public abstract void setDouble(int parameterIndex, double x) throws java.sql.SQLException;
public abstract void setEscapeProcessing(boolean enable) throws java.sql.SQLException;
public abstract void setFloat(int parameterIndex, float x) throws java.sql.SQLException;
public abstract void setInt(int parameterIndex, int x) throws java.sql.SQLException;
public abstract void setLong(int parameterIndex, long x) throws java.sql.SQLException;
public abstract void setMaxFieldSize(int max) throws java.sql.SQLException;
public abstract void setMaxRows(int max) throws java.sql.SQLException;
public abstract void setNull(int parameterIndex, int sqlType) throws java.sql.SQLException;
public abstract void setNull(int paramIndex, int sqlType, String typeName) throws java.sql.SQLException;
public abstract void setObject(int parameterIndex, Object x) throws java.sql.SQLException;
public abstract void setObject(int parameterIndex, Object x, int targetSqlType)
    throws java.sql.SQLException;
public abstract void setObject(int parameterIndex, Object x, int targetSqlType, int scale)
    throws java.sql.SQLException;
public abstract void setPassword(String password) throws java.sql.SQLException;
public abstract void setQueryTimeout(int seconds) throws java.sql.SQLException;
public abstract void setReadOnly(boolean value) throws java.sql.SQLException;
public abstract void setRef(int i, java.sql.Ref x) throws java.sql.SQLException;
public abstract void setShort(int parameterIndex, short x) throws java.sql.SQLException;
public abstract void setString(int parameterIndex, String x) throws java.sql.SQLException;
public abstract void setTime(int parameterIndex, java.sql.Time x) throws java.sql.SQLException;
public abstract void setTime(int parameterIndex, java.sql.Time x, java.util.Calendar cal)
    throws java.sql.SQLException;
public abstract void setTimestamp(int parameterIndex, java.sql.Timestamp x)
    throws java.sql.SQLException;
public abstract void setTimestamp(int parameterIndex, java.sql.Timestamp x, java.util.Calendar cal)
    throws java.sql.SQLException;
public abstract void setTransactionIsolation(int level) throws java.sql.SQLException;
public abstract void setType(int type) throws java.sql.SQLException;
```

```
    public abstract void setTypeMap(java.util.Map map) throws java.sql.SQLException;
    public abstract void setUrl(String url) throws java.sql.SQLException;
    public abstract void setUsername(String name) throws java.sql.SQLException;
}
```

Hierarchy: (RowSet(java.sql.ResultSet))

Passed To: RowSetEvent.RowSetEvent()

RowSetEvent — JDBC 2.0 Extension

javax.sql — *serializable event*

Generated when an important event, such as a change in a column's value, occurs within a RowSet.

```
public class RowSetEvent extends java.util.EventObject {
// Public Constructors
    public RowSetEvent(RowSet source);
}
```

Hierarchy: Object→ java.util.EventObject(Serializable)→ RowSetEvent

Passed To: RowSetListener.{cursorMoved(), rowChanged(), rowSetChanged()}

RowSetInternal — JDBC 2.0 Extension

javax.sql

Implemented by a RowSet object that wishes to support the reader/writer row-loading paradigm. Contains additional methods used by RowSetReader and RowSetWriter.

```
public abstract interface RowSetInternal {
// Public Instance Methods
    public abstract java.sql.Connection getConnection() throws java.sql.SQLException;
    public abstract java.sql.ResultSet getOriginal() throws java.sql.SQLException;
    public abstract java.sql.ResultSet getOriginalRow() throws java.sql.SQLException;
    public abstract Object[ ] getParams() throws java.sql.SQLException;
    public abstract void setMetaData(RowSetMetaData md) throws java.sql.SQLException;
}
```

Passed To: RowSetReader.readData(), RowSetWriter.writeData()

RowSetListener — JDBC 2.0 Extension

javax.sql — *event listener*

Implemented by an object that wishes to be informed of events generated by a RowSet.

```
public abstract interface RowSetListener extends java.util.EventListener {
// Public Instance Methods
    public abstract void cursorMoved(RowSetEvent event);
    public abstract void rowChanged(RowSetEvent event);
    public abstract void rowSetChanged(RowSetEvent event);
}
```

Hierarchy: (RowSetListener(java.util.EventListener))

Passed To: RowSet.{addRowSetListener(), removeRowSetListener()}

RowSetMetaData — JDBC 2.0 Extension

javax.sql

Extends java.sql.ResultSetMetaData to support the functionality of RowSet objects.

```
public abstract interface RowSetMetaData extends java.sql.ResultSetMetaData {
// Public Instance Methods
   public abstract void setAutoIncrement(int columnIndex, boolean property)
        throws java.sql.SQLException;
   public abstract void setCaseSensitive(int columnIndex, boolean property) throws java.sql.SQLException;
   public abstract void setCatalogName(int columnIndex, String catalogName)
        throws java.sql.SQLException;
   public abstract void setColumnCount(int columnCount) throws java.sql.SQLException;
   public abstract void setColumnDisplaySize(int columnIndex, int size) throws java.sql.SQLException;
   public abstract void setColumnLabel(int columnIndex, String label) throws java.sql.SQLException;
   public abstract void setColumnName(int columnIndex, String columnName)
        throws java.sql.SQLException;
   public abstract void setColumnType(int columnIndex, int SQLType) throws java.sql.SQLException;
   public abstract void setColumnTypeName(int columnIndex, String typeName)
        throws java.sql.SQLException;
   public abstract void setCurrency(int columnIndex, boolean property) throws java.sql.SQLException;
   public abstract void setNullable(int columnIndex, int property) throws java.sql.SQLException;
   public abstract void setPrecision(int columnIndex, int precision) throws java.sql.SQLException;
   public abstract void setScale(int columnIndex, int scale) throws java.sql.SQLException;
   public abstract void setSchemaName(int columnIndex, String schemaName)
        throws java.sql.SQLException;
   public abstract void setSearchable(int columnIndex, boolean property) throws java.sql.SQLException;
   public abstract void setSigned(int columnIndex, boolean property) throws java.sql.SQLException;
   public abstract void setTableName(int columnIndex, String tableName) throws java.sql.SQLException;
}
```

Hierarchy: (RowSetMetaData(java.sql.ResultSetMetaData))

Passed To: RowSetInternal.setMetaData()

RowSetReader — JDBC 2.0 Extension

javax.sql

Loads data into a RowSet that implements RowSetInternal. The extensions to ResultSet introduced in JDBC 2.0 insert data.

```
public abstract interface RowSetReader {
// Public Instance Methods
   public abstract void readData(RowSetInternal caller) throws java.sql.SQLException;
}
```

RowSetWriter — JDBC 2.0 Extension

javax.sql

Writes data from a RowSet that implements RowSetInternal. The data from the RowSet can be written back to a data source (not necessarily a database).

```
public abstract interface RowSetWriter {
// Public Instance Methods
   public abstract boolean writeData(RowSetInternal caller) throws java.sql.SQLException;
}
```

XAConnection — JDBC 2.0 Extension

javax.sql

An extended version of PooledConnection that can be used in a distributed transaction environment, using the Java Transaction API (in the javax.transaction package).

```
public abstract interface XAConnection extends PooledConnection {
// Public Instance Methods
   public abstract javax.transaction.xa.XAResource getXAResource() throws java.sql.SQLException;
}
```

Hierarchy: (XAConnection(PooledConnection))

Returned By: XADataSource.getXAConnection()

XADataSource — JDBC 2.0 Extension

javax.sql

A factory for XAConnection objects.

```
public abstract interface XADataSource {
// Public Instance Methods
   public abstract int getLoginTimeout() throws java.sql.SQLException;
   public abstract PrintWriter getLogWriter() throws java.sql.SQLException;
   public abstract javax.sql.XAConnection getXAConnection() throws java.sql.SQLException;
   public abstract javax.sql.XAConnection getXAConnection(String user, String password)
         throws java.sql.SQLException;
   public abstract void setLoginTimeout(int seconds) throws java.sql.SQLException;
   public abstract void setLogWriter(PrintWriter out) throws java.sql.SQLException;
}
```

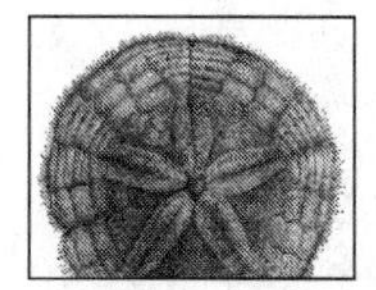

CHAPTER 28

The javax.transaction Package

The javax.transaction package is the main package in the Java Transaction API (JTA). The JTA defines the interfaces needed to interact with a transaction manager. A transaction manager sits in between an application and some shared resource, such as a relational database or a messaging service, and ensures that transactional interactions between the two are handled correctly. An application server interacts directly with the transaction manager on behalf of client applications. An application server uses the TransactionManager interface and Transaction objects, while a client application acquires UserTransaction objects through the application server. Figure 28-1 shows the class hierarchy for the javax.transaction package.

HeuristicCommitException — JTA 1.0

javax.transaction — *serializable checked*

Thrown when an attempt is made to roll back a resource whose updates have been committed due to a heuristic decision (e.g., a resource lost contact with the transaction manager and decided to commit after one phase of a two-phase commit).

```
public class HeuristicCommitException extends Exception {
// Public Constructors
   public HeuristicCommitException();
   public HeuristicCommitException(String msg);
}
```

Hierarchy: Object→ Throwable(Serializable)→ Exception→ HeuristicCommitException

HeuristicMixedException — JTA 1.0

javax.transaction — *serializable checked*

Thrown by the commit() methods on Transaction and UserTransaction to indicate that some updates were rolled back due to a heuristic decision (e.g., some resources involved in a transaction lost contact with the transaction manager and decided to rollback, but some others had already committed).

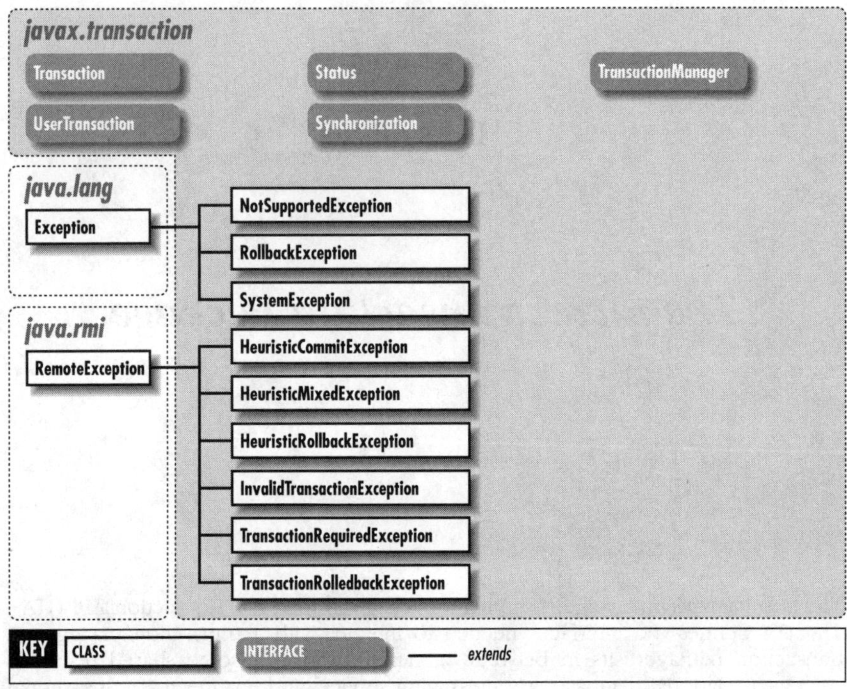

Figure 28-1: The javax.transaction package

```
public class HeuristicMixedException extends Exception {
// Public Constructors
   public HeuristicMixedException();
   public HeuristicMixedException(String msg);
}
```

Hierarchy: Object→ Throwable(Serializable)→ Exception→ HeuristicMixedException

Thrown By: Transaction.commit(), TransactionManager.commit(), UserTransaction.commit()

HeuristicRollbackException — JTA 1.0

javax.transaction — *serializable checked*

Thrown by the commit() methods on Transaction and UserTransaction to indicate that the transaction has been rolled back due to a heuristic decision (e.g., the resource lost contact with the transaction manager and decided to abort the transaction).

```
public class HeuristicRollbackException extends Exception {
// Public Constructors
   public HeuristicRollbackException();
   public HeuristicRollbackException(String msg);
}
```

Hierarchy: Object→ Throwable(Serializable)→ Exception→ HeuristicRollbackException

Thrown By: Transaction.commit(), TransactionManager.commit(), UserTransaction.commit()

InvalidTransactionException — JTA 1.0

javax.transaction — *serializable checked*

Thrown when an attempt is made to operate on a transaction that is in an invalid state.

```
public class InvalidTransactionException extends java.rmi.RemoteException {
// Public Constructors
   public InvalidTransactionException();
   public InvalidTransactionException(String msg);
}
```

Hierarchy: Object→ Throwable(Serializable)→ Exception→ IOException→ java.rmi.RemoteException→ InvalidTransactionException

Thrown By: TransactionManager.resume()

NotSupportedException — JTA 1.0

javax.transaction — *serializable checked*

Thrown when a request is made for an unsupported operation. Typically thrown by the transaction manager when an attempt is made to create a nested exception and these are not supported by the transaction manager.

```
public class NotSupportedException extends Exception {
// Public Constructors
   public NotSupportedException();
   public NotSupportedException(String msg);
}
```

Hierarchy: Object→ Throwable(Serializable)→ Exception→ NotSupportedException

Thrown By: TransactionManager.begin(), UserTransaction.begin()

RollbackException — JTA 1.0

javax.transaction — *serializable checked*

Thrown when an invalid operation is requested on a transaction that has either rolled back or been marked for rollback-only (e.g., calling TransactionManager.enlistResource() on such a transaction).

```
public class RollbackException extends Exception {
// Public Constructors
   public RollbackException();
   public RollbackException(String msg);
}
```

Hierarchy: Object→ Throwable(Serializable)→ Exception→ RollbackException

Thrown By: Transaction.{commit(), enlistResource(), registerSynchronization()}, TransactionManager.commit(), UserTransaction.commit()

Status — JTA 1.0

javax.transaction

This interface simply serves to hold static integer status codes for transactions. The Transaction.getStatus() method can query the status of a transaction, and these codes indicate the meaning of the returned value.

```
public abstract interface Status {
// Public Constants
   public static final int STATUS_ACTIVE;                                    =0
   public static final int STATUS_COMMITTED;                                 =3
   public static final int STATUS_COMMITTING;                                =8
   public static final int STATUS_MARKED_ROLLBACK;                           =1
   public static final int STATUS_NO_TRANSACTION;                            =6
   public static final int STATUS_PREPARED;                                  =2
   public static final int STATUS_PREPARING;                                 =7
   public static final int STATUS_ROLLEDBACK;                                =4
   public static final int STATUS_ROLLING_BACK;                              =9
   public static final int STATUS_UNKNOWN;                                   =5
}
```

Synchronization — JTA 1.0

javax.transaction

A Synchronization object gets notification of the end of a transaction. The Synchronization interface must be implemented by a concrete application class, which can then request callbacks from the transaction manager. The Synchronization object is registered with an active transaction by calling the Transaction.registerSynchronization() method, passing in the Synchronization object. An exception is thrown if the transaction is not active or has already been marked for rollback. Before the transaction manager starts the commit on the transaction, it calls the beforeCompletion() method on any registered Synchronization objects. After the transaction completes, the transaction manager calls the afterCompletion() method.

```
public abstract interface Synchronization {
// Public Instance Methods
   public abstract void afterCompletion(int status);
   public abstract void beforeCompletion();
}
```

Passed To: Transaction.registerSynchronization()

SystemException — JTA 1.0

javax.transaction — *serializable checked*

Thrown by the transaction manager when a significant error occurs that effectively disables the manager.

```
public class SystemException extends Exception {
// Public Constructors
   public SystemException();
   public SystemException(String s);
   public SystemException(int errcode);
// Public Instance Fields
   public int errorCode;
}
```

Hierarchy: Object→ Throwable(Serializable)→ Exception→ SystemException

Thrown By: Transaction.{commit(), delistResource(), enlistResource(), getStatus(), registerSynchronization(), rollback(), setRollbackOnly()}, TransactionManager.{begin(), commit(), getStatus(), getTransaction(), resume(), rollback(), setRollbackOnly(), setTransactionTimeout(), suspend()}, UserTransaction.{begin(), commit(), getStatus(), rollback(), setRollbackOnly(), setTransactionTimeout()}

Transaction **JTA 1.0**

javax.transaction

A Transaction represents a global transaction managed by the transaction manager. When the TransactionManager interface is used directly (e.g., by an application server) to create and control transactions, Transaction objects represent the transactions created. The TransactionManager.getTransaction() method gets the transaction associated with the current thread. With the Transaction object, the caller can commit() or rollback() the Transaction, enlist or remove resources from the transaction, and get the status of the Transaction. The setRollbackOnly() method flags the Transaction so that it can be only rolled back, not committed. The registerSynchronization() method registers a Synchronization callback object with the Transaction.


```
public abstract interface Transaction {
// Public Instance Methods
   public abstract void commit() throws RollbackException, HeuristicMixedException,
       HeuristicRollbackException, SecurityException;
   public abstract boolean delistResource(javax.transaction.xa.XAResource xaRes, int flag)
       throws java.lang.IllegalStateException, javax.transaction.SystemException;
   public abstract boolean enlistResource(javax.transaction.xa.XAResource xaRes)
       throws RollbackException, java.lang.IllegalStateException, javax.transaction.SystemException;
   public abstract int getStatus() throws javax.transaction.SystemException;
   public abstract void registerSynchronization(Synchronization sync) throws RollbackException,
       java.lang.IllegalStateException, javax.transaction.SystemException;
   public abstract void rollback() throws java.lang.IllegalStateException,
       javax.transaction.SystemException;
   public abstract void setRollbackOnly() throws java.lang.IllegalStateException,
       javax.transaction.SystemException;
}
```

Passed To: TransactionManager.resume()

Returned By: TransactionManager.{getTransaction(), suspend()}

TransactionManager **JTA 1.0**

javax.transaction

The TransactionManager interface is used by a transactional application server, such as an EJB server, to create and manage transactions on behalf of client applications. The application server can use the TransactionManager interface to create new transactions for the current thread, suspend and resume the current transaction, and commit or rollback the transaction. The setTransactionTimeout() method sets the timeout (in seconds) for any subsequent transactions started through the TransactionManager.

```
public abstract interface TransactionManager {
// Public Instance Methods
   public abstract void begin() throws NotSupportedException, javax.transaction.SystemException;
   public abstract void commit() throws RollbackException, HeuristicMixedException,
       HeuristicRollbackException, SecurityException;
   public abstract int getStatus() throws javax.transaction.SystemException;
   public abstract Transaction getTransaction() throws javax.transaction.SystemException;
   public abstract void resume(Transaction tobj) throws InvalidTransactionException,
       java.lang.IllegalStateException, javax.transaction.SystemException;
   public abstract void rollback() throws java.lang.IllegalStateException, SecurityException,
       javax.transaction.SystemException;
   public abstract void setRollbackOnly() throws java.lang.IllegalStateException,
       javax.transaction.SystemException;
   public abstract void setTransactionTimeout(int seconds) throws javax.transaction.SystemException;
```

```
    public abstract Transaction suspend() throws javax.transaction.SystemException;
}
```

TransactionRequiredException JTA 1.0

javax.transaction *serializable checked*

Thrown when a transaction-related operation is requested, but there is no active transaction.

```
public class TransactionRequiredException extends java.rmi.RemoteException {
// Public Constructors
    public TransactionRequiredException();
    public TransactionRequiredException(String msg);
}
```

Hierarchy: Object→ Throwable(Serializable)→ Exception→ IOException→ java.rmi.RemoteException→ TransactionRequiredException

TransactionRolledbackException JTA 1.0

javax.transaction *serializable checked*

Thrown when an operation requested on a particular transaction is irrelevant because the transaction has been rolled back.

```
public class TransactionRolledbackException extends java.rmi.RemoteException {
// Public Constructors
    public TransactionRolledbackException();
    public TransactionRolledbackException(String msg);
}
```

Hierarchy: Object→ Throwable(Serializable)→ Exception→ IOException→ java.rmi.RemoteException→ TransactionRolledbackException

UserTransaction JTA 1.0

javax.transaction

UserTransaction is the interface used by client applications to manage transactions. Typically, a transactional application server publishes a UserTransaction through JNDI, so a client gets a reference to the UserTransaction using a lookup on the JNDI Context. The client can use the UserTransaction to begin() a new transaction in the current thread. If there is already an active transaction in the current thread and the transaction manager does not support nested transactions, a NotSupportedException is thrown. The client can either commit() or rollback() the current transaction when it is complete. The setRollbackOnly() method flags the current transaction so that it can be only rolled back. The setTransactionTimeout() method sets the timeout, in seconds, of any subsequent transactions started through the transaction manager.

```
public abstract interface UserTransaction {
// Public Instance Methods
    public abstract void begin() throws NotSupportedException, javax.transaction.SystemException;
    public abstract void commit() throws RollbackException, HeuristicMixedException,
        HeuristicRollbackException, SecurityException;
    public abstract int getStatus() throws javax.transaction.SystemException;
    public abstract void rollback() throws java.lang.IllegalStateException, SecurityException,
        javax.transaction.SystemException;
```

```
    public abstract void setRollbackOnly() throws java.lang.IllegalStateException,
        javax.transaction.SystemException;
    public abstract void setTransactionTimeout(int seconds) throws javax.transaction.SystemException;
}
```

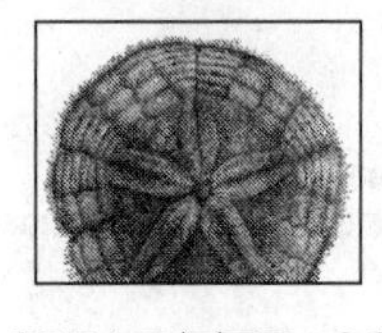

CHAPTER 29

The javax.transaction.xa Package

The javax.transaction.xa package represents a Java mapping of certain elements of the X/Open XA interface specification. The XA interface defines a standard two-way communication protocol between a transaction manager and a resource manager, such as a relational database, so that they can engage in distributed transactional processing. These interfaces are used internally by the JTA to implement its transaction management services. Normally, you shouldn't have to use these interfaces directly in application code. Figure 29-1 shows the class hierarchy of the package.

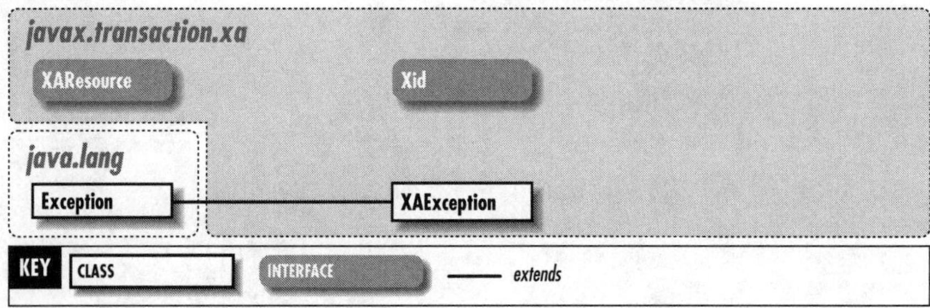

Figure 29–1: The javax.transaction.xa package

XAException — JTA 1.0

javax.transaction.xa — *serializable checked*

Thrown by a resource manager when an error occurs while handling a request from the transaction manager. The static error codes allow the transaction manager to determine the cause of the error.

```
public class XAException extends Exception {
// Public Constructors
```

```
   public XAException();
   public XAException(String s);
   public XAException(int errcode);
// Public Constants
   public static final int XA_HEURCOM;                    =7
   public static final int XA_HEURHAZ;                    =8
   public static final int XA_HEURMIX;                    =5
   public static final int XA_HEURRB;                     =6
   public static final int XA_NOMIGRATE;                  =9
   public static final int XA_RBBASE;                     =100
   public static final int XA_RBCOMMFAIL;                 =101
   public static final int XA_RBDEADLOCK;                 =102
   public static final int XA_RBEND;                      =107
   public static final int XA_RBINTEGRITY;                =103
   public static final int XA_RBOTHER;                    =104
   public static final int XA_RBPROTO;                    =105
   public static final int XA_RBROLLBACK;                 =100
   public static final int XA_RBTIMEOUT;                  =106
   public static final int XA_RBTRANSIENT;                =107
   public static final int XA_RDONLY;                     =3
   public static final int XA_RETRY;                      =4
   public static final int XAER_ASYNC;                    =-2
   public static final int XAER_DUPID;                    =-8
   public static final int XAER_INVAL;                    =-5
   public static final int XAER_NOTA;                     =-4
   public static final int XAER_OUTSIDE;                  =-9
   public static final int XAER_PROTO;                    =-6
   public static final int XAER_RMERR;                    =-3
   public static final int XAER_RMFAIL;                   =-7
// Public Instance Fields
   public int errorCode;
}
```

Hierarchy: Object→ Throwable(Serializable)→ Exception→ XAException

Thrown By: XAResource.{commit(), end(), forget(), getTransactionTimeout(), isSameRM(), prepare(), recover(), rollback(), setTransactionTimeout(), start()}

XAResource — JTA 1.0

javax.transaction.xa

The XAResource interface is implemented by shared resources that want to engage in distributed transactions. A single resource manager (e.g., a database server or message service) can export multiple transactional resources (database connections, sessions with a message service), represented as XAResource objects. The transaction manager uses the XAResource interface to associate a resource with a transaction using the start() method, to ask the resource to commit() or rollback() any work done while it was associated with a transaction, and finally to end() the association with a transaction. Other methods on XAResource manage the association of the resource with the transaction context.

```
public abstract interface XAResource {
// Public Constants
   public static final int TMENDRSCAN;                    =8388608
   public static final int TMFAIL;                        =536870912
   public static final int TMJOIN;                        =2097152
   public static final int TMNOFLAGS;                     =0
   public static final int TMONEPHASE;                    =1073741824
   public static final int TMRESUME;                      =134217728
```

```
    public static final int TMSTARTRSCAN;                                    =16777216
    public static final int TMSUCCESS;                                       =67108864
    public static final int TMSUSPEND;                                       =33554432
    public static final int XA_OK;                                                  =0
    public static final int XA_RDONLY;                                              =3
// Public Instance Methods
    public abstract void commit(Xid xid, boolean onePhase) throws XAException;
    public abstract void end(Xid xid, int flags) throws XAException;
    public abstract void forget(Xid xid) throws XAException;
    public abstract int getTransactionTimeout() throws XAException;
    public abstract boolean isSameRM(XAResource xares) throws XAException;
    public abstract int prepare(Xid xid) throws XAException;
    public abstract Xid[ ] recover(int flag) throws XAException;
    public abstract void rollback(Xid xid) throws XAException;
    public abstract boolean setTransactionTimeout(int seconds) throws XAException;
    public abstract void start(Xid xid, int flags) throws XAException;
}
```

Passed To: Transaction.{delistResource(), enlistResource()}, XAResource.isSameRM()

Returned By: javax.jms.XASession.getXAResource(), javax.sql.XAConnection.getXAResource()

Xid — JTA 1.0

javax.transaction.xa

An Xid is an identifier for a transaction. This interface is used by transaction managers and resource managers as the representation for transactions. The methods on the interface allow these two entities to query for specific components of the transaction identifier.

```
public abstract interface Xid {
// Public Constants
    public static final int MAXBQUALSIZE;                                          =64
    public static final int MAXGTRIDSIZE;                                          =64
// Public Instance Methods
    public abstract byte[ ] getBranchQualifier();
    public abstract int getFormatId();
    public abstract byte[ ] getGlobalTransactionId();
}
```

Passed To: XAResource.{commit(), end(), forget(), prepare(), rollback(), start()}

Returned By: XAResource.recover()

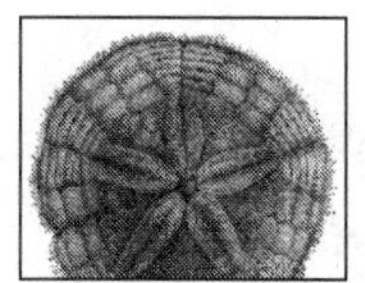

CHAPTER 30

The org.omg.CORBA Package

The org.omg.CORBA package contains the bulk of the Java classes in the Java IDL API. The classes in this package represent the mapping between Java and the CORBA module defined in IDL in the CORBA standard. That means this package includes the bulk of the interfaces, constants, etc., that make up CORBA. Key classes in this package are the ORB class, which is a Java implementation of an ORB, and the Object interface, which serves as the root class for all CORBA objects. Figure 30-1 shows the hierarchy of interfaces defined in org.omg.CORBA, Figure 30-2 shows the class hierarchy, and Figure 30-3 shows the exceptions.

Any — Java 1.2

org.omg.CORBA — *serializable*

A wrapper for any IDL type, whether user-defined or a basic type. You can access the TypeCode for the contents of an Any object using the type() methods. Use the extract_XXX() and insert_XXX() methods to get to the data itself.

An Any object is the value in a NamedValue object. Any objects are used often in the Dynamic Invocation Interface, to compose arguments to method requests.

```
public abstract class Any implements org.omg.CORBA.portable.IDLEntity {
// Public Constructors
   public Any();
// Public Instance Methods
   public abstract org.omg.CORBA.portable.InputStream create_input_stream();
   public abstract org.omg.CORBA.portable.OutputStream create_output_stream();
   public abstract boolean equal(Any a);
   public abstract Any extract_any() throws BAD_OPERATION;
   public abstract boolean extract_boolean() throws BAD_OPERATION;
   public abstract char extract_char() throws BAD_OPERATION;
   public abstract double extract_double() throws BAD_OPERATION;
   public java.math.BigDecimal extract_fixed();
   public abstract float extract_float() throws BAD_OPERATION;
   public abstract int extract_long() throws BAD_OPERATION;
   public abstract long extract_longlong() throws BAD_OPERATION;
```

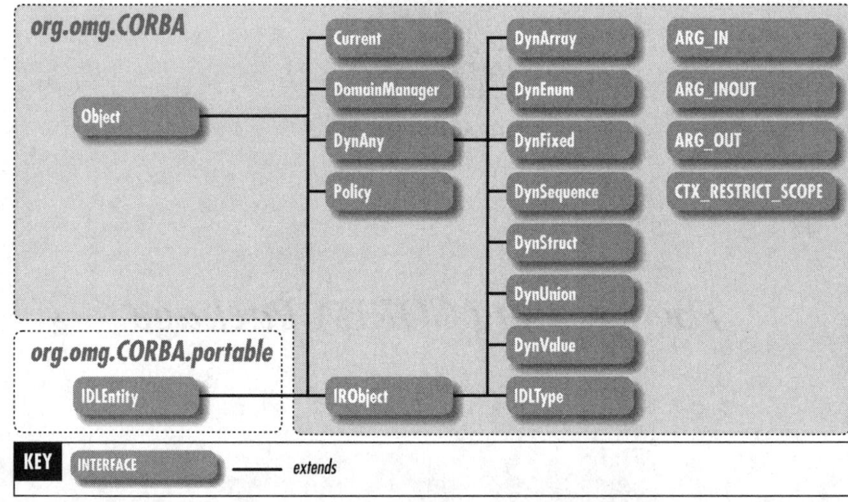

Figure 30-1: The interfaces in the org.omg.CORBA package

```
public abstract org.omg.CORBA.Object extract_Object() throws BAD_OPERATION;
public abstract byte extract_octet() throws BAD_OPERATION;
public abstract short extract_short() throws BAD_OPERATION;
public abstract String extract_string() throws BAD_OPERATION;
public abstract TypeCode extract_TypeCode() throws BAD_OPERATION;
public abstract int extract_ulong() throws BAD_OPERATION;
public abstract long extract_ulonglong() throws BAD_OPERATION;
public abstract short extract_ushort() throws BAD_OPERATION;
public Serializable extract_Value() throws BAD_OPERATION;
public abstract char extract_wchar() throws BAD_OPERATION;
public abstract String extract_wstring() throws BAD_OPERATION;
public abstract void insert_any(Any a);
public abstract void insert_boolean(boolean b);
public abstract void insert_char(char c) throws DATA_CONVERSION;
public abstract void insert_double(double d);
public void insert_fixed(java.math.BigDecimal value);
public void insert_fixed(java.math.BigDecimal value, TypeCode type);
public abstract void insert_float(float f);
public abstract void insert_long(int l);
public abstract void insert_longlong(long l);
public abstract void insert_Object(org.omg.CORBA.Object o);
public abstract void insert_Object(org.omg.CORBA.Object o, TypeCode t) throws BAD_OPERATION;
public abstract void insert_octet(byte b);
public abstract void insert_short(short s);
public abstract void insert_Streamable(org.omg.CORBA.portable.Streamable s);
public abstract void insert_string(String s) throws DATA_CONVERSION, MARSHAL;
public abstract void insert_TypeCode(TypeCode t);
public abstract void insert_ulong(int l);
public abstract void insert_ulonglong(long l);
public abstract void insert_ushort(short s);
public void insert_Value(Serializable v);
public void insert_Value(Serializable v, TypeCode t) throws MARSHAL;
public abstract void insert_wchar(char c);
public abstract void insert_wstring(String s) throws MARSHAL;
public abstract void read_value(org.omg.CORBA.portable.InputStream is, TypeCode t)
```

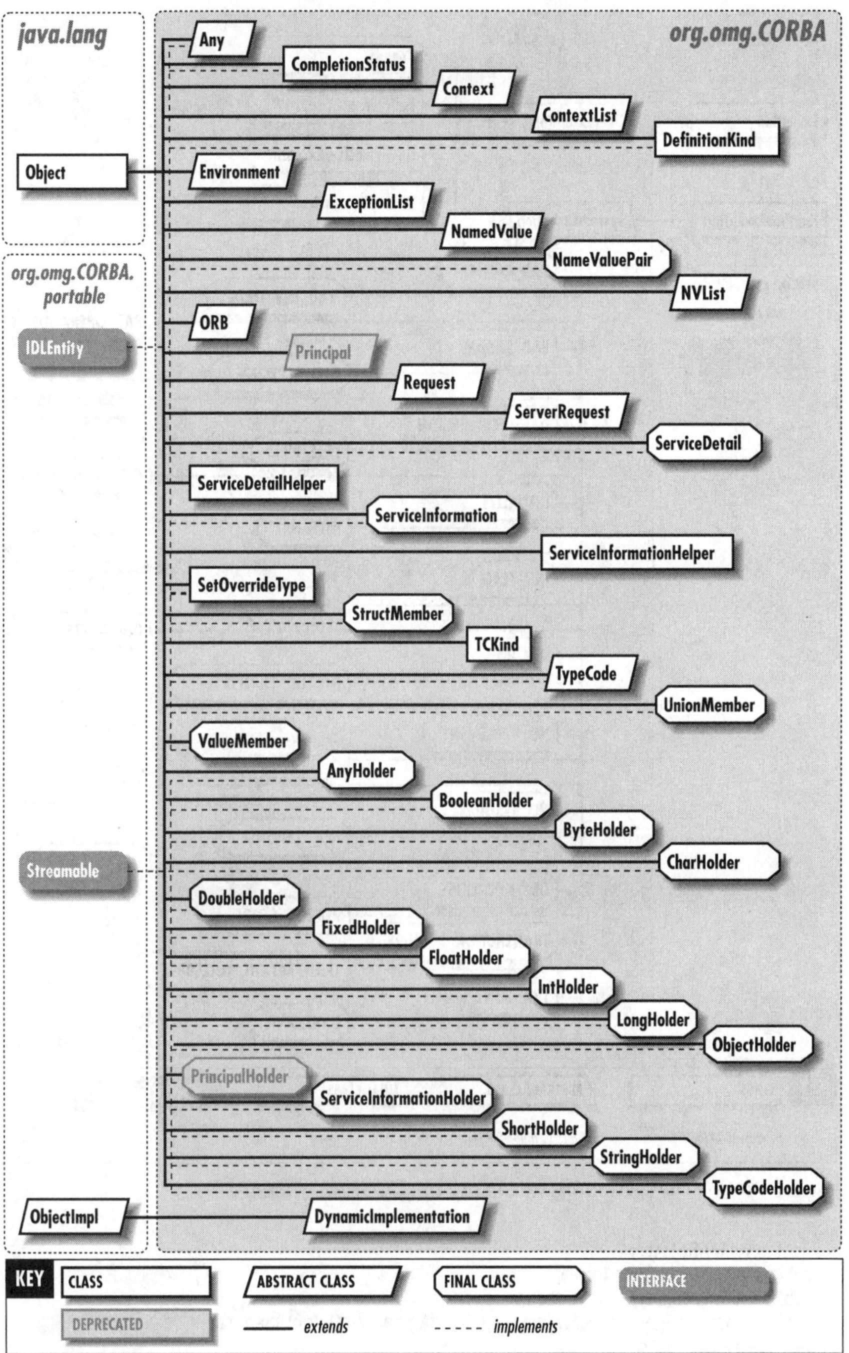

Figure 30-2: The classes in the org.omg.CORBA package

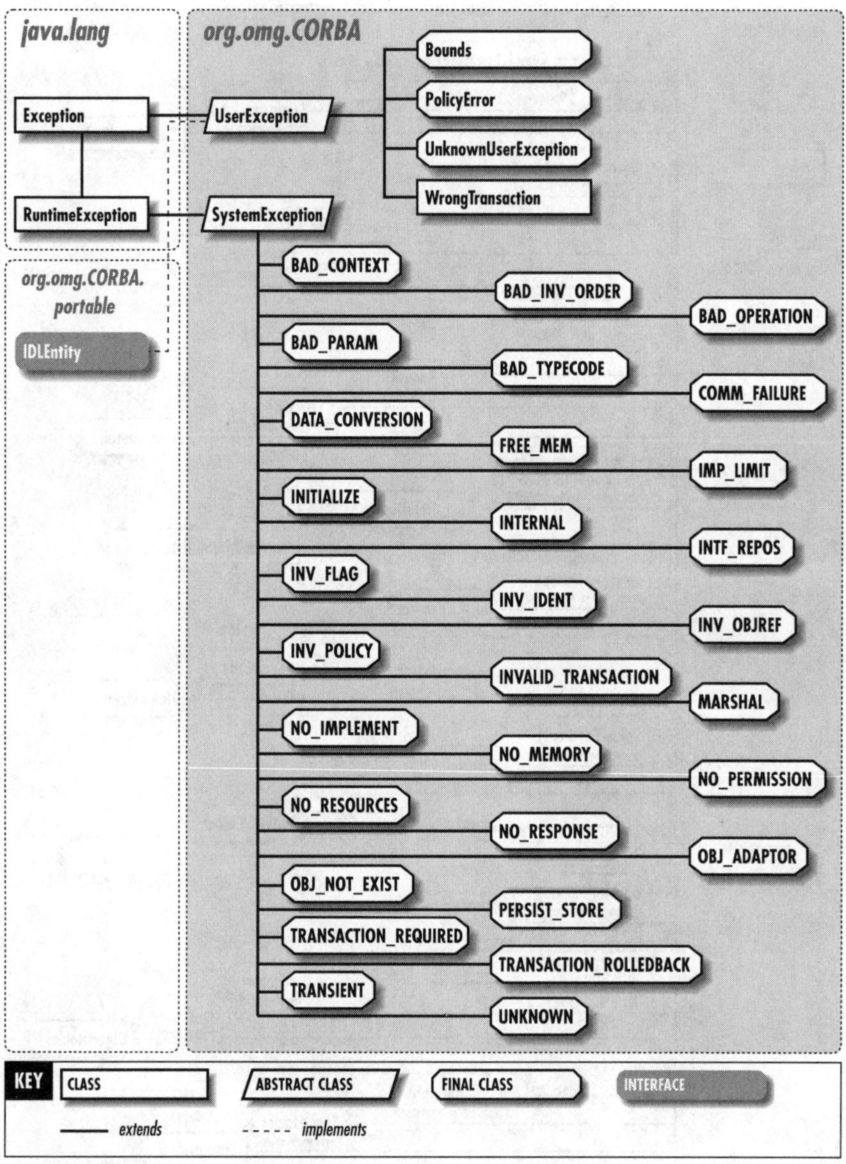

Figure 30-3: The exceptions in the org.omg.CORBA package

```
        throws MARSHAL;
    public abstract TypeCode type();
    public abstract void type(TypeCode t);
    public abstract void write_value(org.omg.CORBA.portable.OutputStream os);
// Deprecated Public Methods
#   public abstract org.omg.CORBA.Principal extract_Principal() throws BAD_OPERATION;
```

```
#   public abstract void insert_Principal(org.omg.CORBA.Principal p);
}
```

Hierarchy: Object→ Any(org.omg.CORBA.portable.IDLEntity(Serializable))

Passed To: Too many methods to list.

Returned By: Any.extract_any(), DynAny.{get_any(), to_any()}, DynArray.get_elements(), DynSequence.get_elements(), NamedValue.value(), ORB.create_any(), Request.{add_in_arg(), add_inout_arg(), add_named_in_arg(), add_named_inout_arg(), add_named_out_arg(), add_out_arg(), return_value()}, TypeCode.member_label(), org.omg.CORBA.portable.InputStream.read_any()

Type Of: AnyHolder.value, NameValuePair.value, UnionMember.label, UnknownUserException.except

AnyHolder — Java 1.2

org.omg.CORBA

The holder class for Any objects. The AnyHolder class is used primarily to wrap out and inout arguments to methods when composing Dynamic Invocation Interface requests.

```
public final class AnyHolder implements org.omg.CORBA.portable.Streamable {
// Public Constructors
   public AnyHolder();
   public AnyHolder(Any initial);
// Methods implementing Streamable
   public void _read(org.omg.CORBA.portable.InputStream input);
   public TypeCode _type();
   public void _write(org.omg.CORBA.portable.OutputStream output);
// Public Instance Fields
   public Any value;
}
```

Hierarchy: Object→ AnyHolder(org.omg.CORBA.portable.Streamable)

ARG_IN — Java 1.2

org.omg.CORBA

This interface defines a value constant that is used to specify an input method argument when creating a named value with the ORB.create_named_value() method. The last argument to this method is an integer flag that indicates the argument mode for the named value as it is used in a dynamic method invocation. The integer flag can be either ARG_IN.value, ARG_OUT.value, or ARG_INOUT.value, to indicate what type of method argument the named value represents. Here's an example that assumes you have a reference to an ORB named myOrb and an Any object named myAny that holds the argument value:

```
org.omg.CORBA.NamedValue inArg =
  myOrb.create_named_value("MethodArg1", myAny, org.omg.CORBA.ARG_IN.value);
```

The inArg named value can now be used in a Dynamic Invocation Interface call to a method that has an in argument named MethodArg1. See also ARG_INOUT and ARG_OUT.

```
public abstract interface ARG_IN {
// Public Constants
   public static final int value;                                    =1
}
```

ARG_INOUT — Java 1.2

org.omg.CORBA

This interface defines a single constant used with the ORB.create_named_value() method. See ARG_IN for details.

```
public abstract interface ARG_INOUT {
// Public Constants
   public static final int value;                                  =3
}
```

ARG_OUT — Java 1.2

org.omg.CORBA

This interface defines a single constant used with the ORB.create_named_value() method. See ARG_IN for details.

```
public abstract interface ARG_OUT {
// Public Constants
   public static final int value;                                  =2
}
```

BAD_CONTEXT — Java 1.2

org.omg.CORBA — *serializable unchecked*

A standard CORBA exception thrown when a context object cannot be processed.

```
public final class BAD_CONTEXT extends org.omg.CORBA.SystemException {
// Public Constructors
   public BAD_CONTEXT();
   public BAD_CONTEXT(String s);
   public BAD_CONTEXT(int minor, CompletionStatus completed);
   public BAD_CONTEXT(String s, int minor, CompletionStatus completed);
}
```

Hierarchy: Object→ Throwable(Serializable)→ Exception→ RuntimeException→ org.omg.CORBA.SystemException→ BAD_CONTEXT

BAD_INV_ORDER — Java 1.2

org.omg.CORBA — *serializable unchecked*

A standard CORBA exception thrown when methods are called out of order. For example, if you call the arguments() method on a ServerRequest object, then try to reset the arguments by calling the method again, a BAD_INV_ORDER exception is thrown.

```
public final class BAD_INV_ORDER extends org.omg.CORBA.SystemException {
// Public Constructors
   public BAD_INV_ORDER();
   public BAD_INV_ORDER(String s);
   public BAD_INV_ORDER(int minor, CompletionStatus completed);
   public BAD_INV_ORDER(String s, int minor, CompletionStatus completed);
}
```

Hierarchy: Object→ Throwable(Serializable)→ Exception→ RuntimeException→ org.omg.CORBA.SystemException→ BAD_INV_ORDER

BAD_OPERATION — Java 1.2

org.omg.CORBA — *serializable unchecked*

A standard CORBA exception thrown when an invalid method is invoked. If, for example, you call an extract_XXX() method on an Any object for a type it does not contain, a BAD_OPERATION is thrown.

```
public final class BAD_OPERATION extends org.omg.CORBA.SystemException {
// Public Constructors
   public BAD_OPERATION();
   public BAD_OPERATION(String s);
   public BAD_OPERATION(int minor, CompletionStatus completed);
   public BAD_OPERATION(String s, int minor, CompletionStatus completed);
}
```

Hierarchy: Object→ Throwable(Serializable)→ Exception→ RuntimeException→ org.omg.CORBA.SystemException→ BAD_OPERATION

Thrown By: Any.{extract_any(), extract_boolean(), extract_char(), extract_double(), extract_float(), extract_long(), extract_longlong(), extract_Object(), extract_octet(), extract_Principal(), extract_short(), extract_string(), extract_TypeCode(), extract_ulong(), extract_ulonglong(), extract_ushort(), extract_Value(), extract_wchar(), extract_wstring(), insert_Object()}

BAD_PARAM — Java 1.2

org.omg.CORBA — *serializable unchecked*

A standard CORBA exception thrown when an invalid argument is passed into a remote method. This exception defines a single error code value for the SystemException.minor data member:

Minor Code	*Meaning*
1	A null value was passed into a remote method.

```
public final class BAD_PARAM extends org.omg.CORBA.SystemException {
// Public Constructors
   public BAD_PARAM();
   public BAD_PARAM(String s);
   public BAD_PARAM(int minor, CompletionStatus completed);
   public BAD_PARAM(String s, int minor, CompletionStatus completed);
}
```

Hierarchy: Object→ Throwable(Serializable)→ Exception→ RuntimeException→ org.omg.CORBA.SystemException→ BAD_PARAM

Thrown By: CompletionStatus.from_int(), DefinitionKind.from_int(), SetOverrideType.from_int(), TCKind.from_int(), org.omg.CosNaming.BindingIteratorHelper.narrow(), org.omg.CosNaming.BindingType.from_int(), org.omg.CosNaming.NamingContextHelper.narrow(), NotFoundReason.from_int()

BAD_TYPECODE — Java 1.2

org.omg.CORBA — *serializable unchecked*

A standard CORBA exception thrown when an invalid TypeCode is specified.

```
public final class BAD_TYPECODE extends org.omg.CORBA.SystemException {
// Public Constructors
   public BAD_TYPECODE();
   public BAD_TYPECODE(String s);
```

```
    public BAD_TYPECODE(int minor, CompletionStatus completed);
    public BAD_TYPECODE(String s, int minor, CompletionStatus completed);
}
```

Hierarchy: Object→ Throwable(Serializable)→ Exception→ RuntimeException→ org.omg.CORBA.SystemException→ BAD_TYPECODE

BooleanHolder — Java 1.2

org.omg.CORBA

The holder class for out and inout remote method arguments that are mapped to Java boolean values.

```
public final class BooleanHolder implements org.omg.CORBA.portable.Streamable {
// Public Constructors
    public BooleanHolder();
    public BooleanHolder(boolean initial);
// Methods implementing Streamable
    public void _read(org.omg.CORBA.portable.InputStream input);
    public TypeCode _type();
    public void _write(org.omg.CORBA.portable.OutputStream output);
// Public Instance Fields
    public boolean value;
}
```

Hierarchy: Object→ BooleanHolder(org.omg.CORBA.portable.Streamable)

Bounds — Java 1.2

org.omg.CORBA — *serializable checked*

An exception thrown when a value that falls out of the valid bounds is passed into a method (e.g., when an index passed into a list object is greater than the size of the list).

```
public final class Bounds extends UserException {
// Public Constructors
    public Bounds();
    public Bounds(String reason);
}
```

Hierarchy: Object→ Throwable(Serializable)→ Exception→ UserException(org.omg.CORBA.portable.IDLEntity(Serializable))→ org.omg.CORBA.Bounds

Thrown By: ContextList.{item(), remove()}, ExceptionList.{item(), remove()}, NVList.{item(), remove()}, TypeCode.member_visibility()

ByteHolder — Java 1.2

org.omg.CORBA

The holder class for out and inout remote method arguments that are mapped to Java byte values.

```
public final class ByteHolder implements org.omg.CORBA.portable.Streamable {
// Public Constructors
    public ByteHolder();
    public ByteHolder(byte initial);
// Methods implementing Streamable
    public void _read(org.omg.CORBA.portable.InputStream input);
    public TypeCode _type();
    public void _write(org.omg.CORBA.portable.OutputStream output);
```

```
// Public Instance Fields
   public byte value;
}
```

Hierarchy: Object→ ByteHolder(org.omg.CORBA.portable.Streamable)

CharHolder — Java 1.2

org.omg.CORBA

The holder class for out and inout remote method arguments that are mapped to Java char values.

```
public final class CharHolder implements org.omg.CORBA.portable.Streamable {
// Public Constructors
   public CharHolder();
   public CharHolder(char initial);
// Methods implementing Streamable
   public void _read(org.omg.CORBA.portable.InputStream input);
   public TypeCode _type();
   public void _write(org.omg.CORBA.portable.OutputStream output);
// Public Instance Fields
   public char value;
}
```

Hierarchy: Object→ CharHolder(org.omg.CORBA.portable.Streamable)

COMM_FAILURE — Java 1.2

org.omg.CORBA — *serializable unchecked*

A standard CORBA exception thrown when a communications failure occurs during a remote operation. Sun's Java IDL defines the following minor error code values for this exception, stored in the minor data member inherited from SystemException:

Minor Code	*Meaning*
1	Unable to connect to the required remote ORB.
2	A write to a socket failed, either because the socket has been closed by the remote peer or because the socket connection has been aborted.
3	A write to a socket failed because the connection was closed on this side of the socket.
6	Multiple attempts to connect to the remote server have failed.

```
public final class COMM_FAILURE extends org.omg.CORBA.SystemException {
// Public Constructors
   public COMM_FAILURE();
   public COMM_FAILURE(String s);
   public COMM_FAILURE(int minor, CompletionStatus completed);
   public COMM_FAILURE(String s, int minor, CompletionStatus completed);
}
```

Hierarchy: Object→ Throwable(Serializable)→ Exception→ RuntimeException→ org.omg.CORBA.SystemException→ COMM_FAILURE

CompletionStatus — Java 1.2

org.omg.CORBA — *serializable*

When an org.omg.CORBA.SystemException is thrown, it contains a CompletionStatus object that indicates whether the method invocation was completed before the exception was encountered. CompletionStatus has three static instances, COMPLETED_YES, COMPLETED_MAYBE, and COMPLETED_NO, and three static int members, _COMPLETED_YES, _COMPLETED_MAYBE and _COMPLETED_NO. When you receive a CompletionStatus, you can either compare it to one of the static instances or compare its value (queried using the value() method) to one of the static int values.

```
public class CompletionStatus implements org.omg.CORBA.portable.IDLEntity {
// Protected Constructors
   protected CompletionStatus(int _value);
// Public Constants
   public static final int _COMPLETED_MAYBE;                                    =2
   public static final int _COMPLETED_NO;                                       =1
   public static final int _COMPLETED_YES;                                      =0
   public static final CompletionStatus COMPLETED_MAYBE;
   public static final CompletionStatus COMPLETED_NO;
   public static final CompletionStatus COMPLETED_YES;
// Public Class Methods
   public static CompletionStatus from_int(int i) throws BAD_PARAM;
// Public Instance Methods
   public int value();
}
```

Hierarchy: Object→ CompletionStatus(org.omg.CORBA.portable.IDLEntity(Serializable))

Passed To: Too many methods to list.

Returned By: CompletionStatus.from_int()

Type Of: CompletionStatus.{COMPLETED_MAYBE, COMPLETED_NO, COMPLETED_YES}, org.omg.CORBA.SystemException.completed

Context — Java 1.2

org.omg.CORBA

A Context object contains a list of properties, stored as NamedValue objects, that is passed along with a method request to indicate properties of the client context. Every ORB has a default context, accessed using the ORB.get_default_context() method. Contexts can be linked in a hierarchy of contexts. If a search for a property is made on a Context object, and the search within the object fails, the search is continued in the parent Context, and so on until the root context is reached. You can create a new child of a Context using its create_child() method. Other methods on the Context class let you get, set, and delete values from the Context.

```
public abstract class Context {
// Public Constructors
   public Context();
// Public Instance Methods
   public abstract String context_name();
   public abstract org.omg.CORBA.Context create_child(String child_ctx_name);
   public abstract void delete_values(String propname);
   public abstract NVList get_values(String start_scope, int op_flags, String pattern);
   public abstract org.omg.CORBA.Context parent();
   public abstract void set_one_value(String propname, Any propvalue);
   public abstract void set_values(NVList values);
}
```

Passed To: org.omg.CORBA.Object._create_request(), Request.ctx(), org.omg.CORBA.portable.Delegate.create_request(), org.omg.CORBA.portable.ObjectImpl._create_request(), org.omg.CORBA.portable.OutputStream.write_Context()

Returned By: org.omg.CORBA.Context.{create_child(), parent()}, ORB.get_default_context(), Request.ctx(), ServerRequest.ctx(), org.omg.CORBA.portable.InputStream.read_Context()

ContextList — Java 1.2

org.omg.CORBA

A ContextList is a list of context property names only (i.e., a list of String objects). A ContextList along with an NVList that contains NamedValue objects represents the relevant subset of a Context that is passed along with a remote method call.

```
public abstract class ContextList {
// Public Constructors
   public ContextList();
// Public Instance Methods
   public abstract void add(String ctx);
   public abstract int count();
   public abstract String item(int index) throws org.omg.CORBA.Bounds;
   public abstract void remove(int index) throws org.omg.CORBA.Bounds;
}
```

Passed To: org.omg.CORBA.Object._create_request(), org.omg.CORBA.portable.Delegate.create_request(), org.omg.CORBA.portable.ObjectImpl._create_request(), org.omg.CORBA.portable.OutputStream.write_Context()

Returned By: ORB.create_context_list(), Request.contexts()

CTX_RESTRICT_SCOPE — Java 1.2

org.omg.CORBA

This interface contains a static value member that can be used as a flag to the search routine accessible through the Context.get_values() method. Using CTX_RESTRICT_SCOPE.value as the flag to this method indicates that the search for context values should be restricted to the scope specified in the first method argument, or to the context object that invokes the method, if the scope is null. For example, this call to the search method:

```
Context ctx = ... // get context somehow
NVList myVals = ctx.get_values(null, org.omg.CORBA.CTX_RESTRICT_SCOPE.value, "username");
```

searches the context represented by the context object for values named "username".

```
public abstract interface CTX_RESTRICT_SCOPE {
// Public Constants
   public static final int value;                                    =15
}
```

Current — Java 1.2

org.omg.CORBA

The Current interface represents an optional feature provided by CORBA that allows the ORB and CORBA services to export information about the thread in which they are running. Sun's Java IDL does not use this feature. If an ORB or service provider decides to provide this information, it should create a concrete subclass of this interface and make it available through the ORB's resolve_initial_references() method.

```
public abstract interface Current extends org.omg.CORBA.Object {
}
```

Hierarchy: (Current(org.omg.CORBA.Object))

Returned By: ORB.get_current()

DATA_CONVERSION — Java 1.2

org.omg.CORBA — *serializable unchecked*

A standard CORBA exception thrown when the ORB fails to convert some piece of data, such as during the conversion of a stringified object reference. Sun's Java IDL defines the following minor error code values for this exception, stored in the minor data member inherited from SystemException:

Minor Code	*Meaning*
1	A bad hexadecimal character was found while converting a stringified object reference back to an object reference.
2	The byte length of a stringified object reference is odd, when it must be even.
3	The "IOR:" preface is missing from the stringified object reference passed into string_to_object().
4	The resolve_initial_references() method failed because the location (host and port number) of the remote ORB specified is invalid or unspecified, or the remote server doesn't support the Java IDL bootstrap protocol.

```
public final class DATA_CONVERSION extends org.omg.CORBA.SystemException {
// Public Constructors
   public DATA_CONVERSION();
   public DATA_CONVERSION(String s);
   public DATA_CONVERSION(int minor, CompletionStatus completed);
   public DATA_CONVERSION(String s, int minor, CompletionStatus completed);
}
```

Hierarchy: Object→ Throwable(Serializable)→ Exception→ RuntimeException→ org.omg.CORBA.SystemException→ DATA_CONVERSION

Thrown By: Any.{insert_char(), insert_string()}

DefinitionKind — Java 1.2

org.omg.CORBA — *serializable*

Used by an IRObject to indicate what type of repository object it represents (e.g., method, attribute). To determine the type of an IRObject, either compare the value member of DefinitionKind to the static int members of this class or compare the DefinitionKind object itself to the static instances defined in this class.

```
public class DefinitionKind implements org.omg.CORBA.portable.IDLEntity {
// Protected Constructors
   protected DefinitionKind(int _value);
// Public Constants
   public static final int _dk_Alias;                                    =9
   public static final int _dk_all;                                      =1
   public static final int _dk_Array;                                    =16
   public static final int _dk_Attribute;                                =2
   public static final int _dk_Constant;                                 =3
   public static final int _dk_Enum;                                     =12
   public static final int _dk_Exception;                                =4
   public static final int _dk_Fixed;                                    =19
   public static final int _dk_Interface;                                =5
```

```
    public static final int _dk_Module;                                    =6
    public static final int _dk_Native;                                    =23
    public static final int _dk_none;                                      =0
    public static final int _dk_Operation;                                 =7
    public static final int _dk_Primitive;                                 =13
    public static final int _dk_Repository;                                =17
    public static final int _dk_Sequence;                                  =15
    public static final int _dk_String;                                    =14
    public static final int _dk_Struct;                                    =10
    public static final int _dk_Typedef;                                   =8
    public static final int _dk_Union;                                     =11
    public static final int _dk_Value;                                     =20
    public static final int _dk_ValueBox;                                  =21
    public static final int _dk_ValueMember;                               =22
    public static final int _dk_Wstring;                                   =18
    public static final DefinitionKind dk_Alias;
    public static final DefinitionKind dk_all;
    public static final DefinitionKind dk_Array;
    public static final DefinitionKind dk_Attribute;
    public static final DefinitionKind dk_Constant;
    public static final DefinitionKind dk_Enum;
    public static final DefinitionKind dk_Exception;
    public static final DefinitionKind dk_Fixed;
    public static final DefinitionKind dk_Interface;
    public static final DefinitionKind dk_Module;
    public static final DefinitionKind dk_Native;
    public static final DefinitionKind dk_none;
    public static final DefinitionKind dk_Operation;
    public static final DefinitionKind dk_Primitive;
    public static final DefinitionKind dk_Repository;
    public static final DefinitionKind dk_Sequence;
    public static final DefinitionKind dk_String;
    public static final DefinitionKind dk_Struct;
    public static final DefinitionKind dk_Typedef;
    public static final DefinitionKind dk_Union;
    public static final DefinitionKind dk_Value;
    public static final DefinitionKind dk_ValueBox;
    public static final DefinitionKind dk_ValueMember;
    public static final DefinitionKind dk_Wstring;
// Public Class Methods
    public static DefinitionKind from_int(int i) throws BAD_PARAM;
// Public Instance Methods
    public int value();
}
```

Hierarchy: Object→ DefinitionKind(org.omg.CORBA.portable.IDLEntity(Serializable))

Returned By: DefinitionKind.from_int(), IRObject.def_kind()

Type Of: DefinitionKind.{dk_Alias, dk_all, dk_Array, dk_Attribute, dk_Constant, dk_Enum, dk_Exception, dk_Fixed, dk_Interface, dk_Module, dk_Native, dk_none, dk_Operation, dk_Primitive, dk_Repository, dk_Sequence, dk_String, dk_Struct, dk_Typedef, dk_Union, dk_Value, dk_ValueBox, dk_ValueMember, dk_Wstring}

DomainManager — Java 1.2

org.omg.CORBA

The DomainManager interface represents an object that manages a group of objects (a domain) under a common set of access policies. A set of policies control access to certain operations over the objects in a given domain. You can access the DomainManager for an org.omg.CORBA.Object by using its _get_domain_managers() method, which returns an array of DomainManager objects, one for each domain of the Object. DomainManagerobjects can be hierarchical, in that a domain can contain other DomainManager objects. Since the DomainManager is an Object, you can use its _get_domain_managers() method to traverse the manager hierarchy.

DomainManager defines a single method, get_domain_policy(), that allows you to get the policy of a given type for the objects in the domain. The policy is represented by a Policy object. The type of policy is indicated with an integer identifier, where the possible values are application-specific. The CORBA Security service, for example, defines its own set of policy types. If the policy type you pass into get_domain_policy() is not supported by the ORB, or if the domain doesn't define that type of policy, an BAD_PARAM system exception is thrown.

The DomainManager interface, and the corresponding methods on the org.omg.CORBA.Object interface, are really just a placeholder for future support for object domains in the CORBA standard. There are currently no interfaces defined for adding objects and policies to domains, for example. The OMG intends to provide this in a management facility specification in the future.

```
public abstract interface DomainManager extends org.omg.CORBA.Object {
// Public Instance Methods
   public abstract org.omg.CORBA.Policy get_domain_policy(int policy_type);
}
```

Hierarchy: (DomainManager(org.omg.CORBA.Object))

Returned By: org.omg.CORBA.Object._get_domain_managers(), org.omg.CORBA.portable.Delegate.get_domain_managers(), org.omg.CORBA.portable.ObjectImpl._get_domain_managers()

DoubleHolder — Java 1.2

org.omg.CORBA

The holder class for out and inout remote method arguments that are mapped to Java double values.

```
public final class DoubleHolder implements org.omg.CORBA.portable.Streamable {
// Public Constructors
   public DoubleHolder();
   public DoubleHolder(double initial);
// Methods implementing Streamable
   public void _read(org.omg.CORBA.portable.InputStream input);
   public TypeCode _type();
   public void _write(org.omg.CORBA.portable.OutputStream output);
// Public Instance Fields
   public double value;
}
```

Hierarchy: Object→ DoubleHolder(org.omg.CORBA.portable.Streamable)

DynamicImplementation — Java 1.2

org.omg.CORBA

The abstract base class for servant object implementations in the Dynamic Skeleton Interface. Derived servant classes must implement the invoke() method, which is called by the ORB to handle requests on the object represented by the servant.

```
public abstract class DynamicImplementation extends org.omg.CORBA.portable.ObjectImpl {
// Public Constructors
   public DynamicImplementation();
// Public Instance Methods
   public abstract void invoke(ServerRequest request);
}
```

Hierarchy: Object→ org.omg.CORBA.portable.ObjectImpl(org.omg.CORBA.Object)→ DynamicImplementation

Subclasses: org.omg.CosNaming._BindingIteratorImplBase, org.omg.CosNaming._NamingContextImplBase

DynAny — Java 1.2

org.omg.CORBA

The DynAny interface forms the core of CORBA's facility for the dynamic introspection of Any values for which the implementation class is not available. This facility has similar goals as Java's built-in introspection facilities, but CORBA provides it as IDL interfaces so that it can be used no matter what implementation language is chosen. The CORBA facility allows services and objects to determine the type and contents of a value passed into a method, without having access to its implementation interface. The service or object can wrap an incoming Any value with DynAny to probe its properties and structure.

DynAny objects should not be exported outside the processes in which they are created. If you attempt to create a stringified reference to a DynAny object using the ORB.object_to_string() method, a MARSHAL exception is thrown.

The DynAny interface provides a series of get_XXX() and insert_XXX() methods that can be used to access or modify the contents of the Any value if it is an IDL basic type. The TypeCode for the contents can also be accessed, using the type() method. If the Any value holds a complex data type, such as a struct, the next(), seek(), rewind(), and current_component() methods on the DynAny interface can iterate through the data members of the contents.

There are various subtypes of DynAny that provide access to the components of specific IDL complex types, such as structs, enums, and unions. These subtypes and basic DynAny objects can be created using the create_dyn_XXX() methods available on the ORB interface.

```
public abstract interface DynAny extends org.omg.CORBA.Object {
// Public Instance Methods
   public abstract void assign(DynAny dyn_any) throws org.omg.CORBA.DynAnyPackage.Invalid;
   public abstract DynAny copy();
   public abstract DynAny current_component();
   public abstract void destroy();
   public abstract void from_any(Any value) throws org.omg.CORBA.DynAnyPackage.Invalid;
   public abstract Any get_any() throws org.omg.CORBA.DynAnyPackage.TypeMismatch;
   public abstract boolean get_boolean() throws org.omg.CORBA.DynAnyPackage.TypeMismatch;
   public abstract char get_char() throws org.omg.CORBA.DynAnyPackage.TypeMismatch;
   public abstract double get_double() throws org.omg.CORBA.DynAnyPackage.TypeMismatch;
   public abstract float get_float() throws org.omg.CORBA.DynAnyPackage.TypeMismatch;
   public abstract int get_long() throws org.omg.CORBA.DynAnyPackage.TypeMismatch;
   public abstract long get_longlong() throws org.omg.CORBA.DynAnyPackage.TypeMismatch;
   public abstract byte get_octet() throws org.omg.CORBA.DynAnyPackage.TypeMismatch;
   public abstract org.omg.CORBA.Object get_reference() throws
      org.omg.CORBA.DynAnyPackage.TypeMismatch;
   public abstract short get_short() throws org.omg.CORBA.DynAnyPackage.TypeMismatch;
```

```
    public abstract String get_string() throws org.omg.CORBA.DynAnyPackage.TypeMismatch;
    public abstract TypeCode get_typecode() throws org.omg.CORBA.DynAnyPackage.TypeMismatch;
    public abstract int get_ulong() throws org.omg.CORBA.DynAnyPackage.TypeMismatch;
    public abstract long get_ulonglong() throws org.omg.CORBA.DynAnyPackage.TypeMismatch;
    public abstract short get_ushort() throws org.omg.CORBA.DynAnyPackage.TypeMismatch;
    public abstract Serializable get_val() throws org.omg.CORBA.DynAnyPackage.TypeMismatch;
    public abstract char get_wchar() throws org.omg.CORBA.DynAnyPackage.TypeMismatch;
    public abstract String get_wstring() throws org.omg.CORBA.DynAnyPackage.TypeMismatch;
    public abstract void insert_any(Any value) throws org.omg.CORBA.DynAnyPackage.InvalidValue;
    public abstract void insert_boolean(boolean value)
        throws org.omg.CORBA.DynAnyPackage.InvalidValue;
    public abstract void insert_char(char value) throws org.omg.CORBA.DynAnyPackage.InvalidValue;
    public abstract void insert_double(double value)
        throws org.omg.CORBA.DynAnyPackage.InvalidValue;
    public abstract void insert_float(float value) throws org.omg.CORBA.DynAnyPackage.InvalidValue;
    public abstract void insert_long(int value) throws org.omg.CORBA.DynAnyPackage.InvalidValue;
    public abstract void insert_longlong(long value) throws org.omg.CORBA.DynAnyPackage.InvalidValue;
    public abstract void insert_octet(byte value) throws org.omg.CORBA.DynAnyPackage.InvalidValue;
    public abstract void insert_reference(org.omg.CORBA.Object value)
        throws org.omg.CORBA.DynAnyPackage.InvalidValue;
    public abstract void insert_short(short value) throws org.omg.CORBA.DynAnyPackage.InvalidValue;
    public abstract void insert_string(String value) throws org.omg.CORBA.DynAnyPackage.InvalidValue;
    public abstract void insert_typecode(TypeCode value)
        throws org.omg.CORBA.DynAnyPackage.InvalidValue;
    public abstract void insert_ulong(int value) throws org.omg.CORBA.DynAnyPackage.InvalidValue;
    public abstract void insert_ulonglong(long value)
        throws org.omg.CORBA.DynAnyPackage.InvalidValue;
    public abstract void insert_ushort(short value) throws org.omg.CORBA.DynAnyPackage.InvalidValue;
    public abstract void insert_val(Serializable value)
        throws org.omg.CORBA.DynAnyPackage.InvalidValue;
    public abstract void insert_wchar(char value) throws org.omg.CORBA.DynAnyPackage.InvalidValue;
    public abstract void insert_wstring(String value) throws org.omg.CORBA.DynAnyPackage.InvalidValue;
    public abstract boolean next();
    public abstract void rewind();
    public abstract boolean seek(int index);
    public abstract Any to_any() throws org.omg.CORBA.DynAnyPackage.Invalid;
    public abstract TypeCode type();
}
```

Hierarchy: (DynAny(org.omg.CORBA.Object))

Implementations: DynArray, DynEnum, DynFixed, DynSequence, DynStruct, DynUnion, DynValue

Passed To: DynAny.assign()

Returned By: DynAny.{copy(), current_component()}, DynUnion.{discriminator(), member()}, ORB.{create_basic_dyn_any(), create_dyn_any()}

DynArray — Java 1.2

org.omg.CORBA

A DynAny object associated with an array. The get_elements() and set_elements() methods allow for access to the elements of the array, as Any values.

```
public abstract interface DynArray extends org.omg.CORBA.Object, DynAny {
// Public Instance Methods
    public abstract Any[ ] get_elements();
    public abstract void set_elements(Any[ ] value) throws org.omg.CORBA.DynAnyPackage.InvalidSeq;
}
```

Hierarchy: (DynArray(org.omg.CORBA.Object, DynAny(org.omg.CORBA.Object)))

Returned By: ORB.create_dyn_array()

DynEnum Java 1.2

org.omg.CORBA

A DynAny object associated with the Java mapping of an IDL enum type. The methods on the interface allow you to access the value of the enumerated type as either a String or an int.

```
public abstract interface DynEnum extends org.omg.CORBA.Object, DynAny {
// Public Instance Methods
   public abstract String value_as_string();
   public abstract void value_as_string(String arg);
   public abstract int value_as_ulong();
   public abstract void value_as_ulong(int arg);
}
```

Hierarchy: (DynEnum(org.omg.CORBA.Object, DynAny(org.omg.CORBA.Object)))

Returned By: ORB.create_dyn_enum()

DynFixed Java 1.2

org.omg.CORBA

A DynAny object associated with the Java mapping of an IDL fixed type.

```
public abstract interface DynFixed extends org.omg.CORBA.Object, DynAny {
// Public Instance Methods
   public abstract byte[ ] get_value();
   public abstract void set_value(byte[ ] val) throws org.omg.CORBA.DynAnyPackage.InvalidValue;
}
```

Hierarchy: (DynFixed(org.omg.CORBA.Object, DynAny(org.omg.CORBA.Object)))

DynSequence Java 1.2

org.omg.CORBA

A DynAny object associated with the Java mapping of an IDL sequence type.

```
public abstract interface DynSequence extends org.omg.CORBA.Object, DynAny {
// Public Instance Methods
   public abstract Any[ ] get_elements();
   public abstract int length();
   public abstract void length(int arg);
   public abstract void set_elements(Any[ ] value) throws org.omg.CORBA.DynAnyPackage.InvalidSeq;
}
```

Hierarchy: (DynSequence(org.omg.CORBA.Object, DynAny(org.omg.CORBA.Object)))

Returned By: ORB.create_dyn_sequence()

DynStruct Java 1.2

org.omg.CORBA

A DynAny object associated with the Java mapping of an IDL struct type. In addition to the DynAny methods that allow you to traverse the components of the struct, the DynStruct interface provides methods that allow you to access an array of all of the members of the struct and to access their names within the struct.

```
public abstract interface DynStruct extends org.omg.CORBA.Object, DynAny {
// Public Instance Methods
   public abstract TCKind current_member_kind();
   public abstract String current_member_name();
   public abstract NameValuePair[ ] get_members();
   public abstract void set_members(NameValuePair[ ] value)
       throws org.omg.CORBA.DynAnyPackage.InvalidSeq;
}
```

Hierarchy: (DynStruct(org.omg.CORBA.Object, DynAny(org.omg.CORBA.Object)))

Returned By: ORB.create_dyn_struct()

DynUnion **Java 1.2**

org.omg.CORBA

A DynAny object associated with the Java mapping of an IDL union type. Methods on the interface allow you to access the discriminator value of the union and the current member of the union, as a DynAny object.

```
public abstract interface DynUnion extends org.omg.CORBA.Object, DynAny {
// Public Instance Methods
   public abstract DynAny discriminator();
   public abstract TCKind discriminator_kind();
   public abstract DynAny member();
   public abstract TCKind member_kind();
   public abstract String member_name();
   public abstract void member_name(String arg);
   public abstract boolean set_as_default();
   public abstract void set_as_default(boolean arg);
}
```

Hierarchy: (DynUnion(org.omg.CORBA.Object, DynAny(org.omg.CORBA.Object)))

Returned By: ORB.create_dyn_union()

DynValue **Java 1.2**

org.omg.CORBA

A DynAny object associated with a value being passed using the proposed Objects-by-Value extension to CORBA. This extension to CORBA allows arguments to be passed by value, rather than strictly be reference, as they are in the core CORBA standard. Sun's implementation of the Java IDL binding does not yet implement the Objects-by-Value extension, but the relevant interfaces are included in the API.

```
public abstract interface DynValue extends org.omg.CORBA.Object, DynAny {
// Public Instance Methods
   public abstract TCKind current_member_kind();
   public abstract String current_member_name();
   public abstract NameValuePair[ ] get_members();
   public abstract void set_members(NameValuePair[ ] value)
       throws org.omg.CORBA.DynAnyPackage.InvalidSeq;
}
```

Hierarchy: (DynValue(org.omg.CORBA.Object, DynAny(org.omg.CORBA.Object)))

Environment — Java 1.2

org.omg.CORBA

After a Dynamic Invocation Interface Request has been invoked, any exception it may have thrown can be accessed by retrieving the Environment from the Request using its env() method. The exception that was thrown can then be retrieved from the Environment using its exception() method.

```
public abstract class Environment {
// Public Constructors
   public Environment();
// Public Instance Methods
   public abstract void clear();
   public abstract Exception exception();
   public abstract void exception(Exception except);
}
```

Returned By: ORB.create_environment(), Request.env()

ExceptionList — Java 1.2

org.omg.CORBA

This class represents a list of exceptions that can be thrown by a remote method, in the form of the TypeCode objects for the corresponding Exception classes. An ExceptionList can be created using the ORB.create_exception_list() method; the TypeCode for each required exception can be created using the ORB.create_exception_tc() method. Once completed, the ExceptionList can create a Dynamic Invocation Interface Request object.

```
public abstract class ExceptionList {
// Public Constructors
   public ExceptionList();
// Public Instance Methods
   public abstract void add(TypeCode exc);
   public abstract int count();
   public abstract TypeCode item(int index) throws org.omg.CORBA.Bounds;
   public abstract void remove(int index) throws org.omg.CORBA.Bounds;
}
```

Passed To: org.omg.CORBA.Object._create_request(), org.omg.CORBA.portable.Delegate.create_request(), org.omg.CORBA.portable.ObjectImpl._create_request()

Returned By: ORB.create_exception_list(), Request.exceptions()

FixedHolder — Java 1.2

org.omg.CORBA

The holder class for IDL fixed values, which are tentatively mapped to the java.math.BigDecimal class. A FixedHolder wraps a BigDecimal value.

```
public final class FixedHolder implements org.omg.CORBA.portable.Streamable {
// Public Constructors
   public FixedHolder();
   public FixedHolder(java.math.BigDecimal initial);
// Methods implementing Streamable
   public void _read(org.omg.CORBA.portable.InputStream input);
   public TypeCode _type();
   public void _write(org.omg.CORBA.portable.OutputStream output);
```

```
// Public Instance Fields
   public java.math.BigDecimal value;
}
```

Hierarchy: Object→ FixedHolder(org.omg.CORBA.portable.Streamable)

FloatHolder — Java 1.2

org.omg.CORBA

The holder class for out and inout remote method arguments that are mapped to Java float values.

```
public final class FloatHolder implements org.omg.CORBA.portable.Streamable {
// Public Constructors
   public FloatHolder();
   public FloatHolder(float initial);
// Methods implementing Streamable
   public void _read(org.omg.CORBA.portable.InputStream input);
   public TypeCode _type();
   public void _write(org.omg.CORBA.portable.OutputStream output);
// Public Instance Fields
   public float value;
}
```

Hierarchy: Object→ FloatHolder(org.omg.CORBA.portable.Streamable)

FREE_MEM — Java 1.2

org.omg.CORBA — *serializable unchecked*

A standard CORBA exception thrown when an attempt to free memory fails.

```
public final class FREE_MEM extends org.omg.CORBA.SystemException {
// Public Constructors
   public FREE_MEM();
   public FREE_MEM(String s);
   public FREE_MEM(int minor, CompletionStatus completed);
   public FREE_MEM(String s, int minor, CompletionStatus completed);
}
```

Hierarchy: Object→ Throwable(Serializable)→ Exception→ RuntimeException→ org.omg.CORBA.SystemException→ FREE_MEM

IDLType — Java 1.2

org.omg.CORBA — *serializable*

IDLType is an extension of IRObject that represents IDL basic types in the Interface Repository. It allows you to query the TypeCode of the type it represents. See the IRObject interface for more details on the Interface Repository.

```
public abstract interface IDLType extends org.omg.CORBA.Object, org.omg.CORBA.portable.IDLEntity,
      IRObject {
// Public Instance Methods
   public abstract TypeCode type();
}
```

Hierarchy: (IDLType(org.omg.CORBA.Object, org.omg.CORBA.portable.IDLEntity(Serializable), IRObject(org.omg.CORBA.Object, org.omg.CORBA.portable.IDLEntity(Serializable))))

Passed To: StructMember.StructMember(), UnionMember.UnionMember(), ValueMember.ValueMember()

Type Of: StructMember.type_def, UnionMember.type_def, ValueMember.type_def

IMP_LIMIT — Java 1.2

org.omg.CORBA — *serializable unchecked*

A standard CORBA exception thrown when some implementation limit has been exceeded.

```
public final class IMP_LIMIT extends org.omg.CORBA.SystemException {
// Public Constructors
   public IMP_LIMIT();
   public IMP_LIMIT(String s);
   public IMP_LIMIT(int minor, CompletionStatus completed);
   public IMP_LIMIT(String s, int minor, CompletionStatus completed);
}
```

Hierarchy: Object→ Throwable(Serializable)→ Exception→ RuntimeException→ org.omg.CORBA.SystemException→ IMP_LIMIT

INITIALIZE — Java 1.2

org.omg.CORBA — *serializable unchecked*

A standard CORBA exception thrown when an error occurs while initializing an ORB.

```
public final class INITIALIZE extends org.omg.CORBA.SystemException {
// Public Constructors
   public INITIALIZE();
   public INITIALIZE(String s);
   public INITIALIZE(int minor, CompletionStatus completed);
   public INITIALIZE(String s, int minor, CompletionStatus completed);
}
```

Hierarchy: Object→ Throwable(Serializable)→ Exception→ RuntimeException→ org.omg.CORBA.SystemException→ INITIALIZE

INTERNAL — Java 1.2

org.omg.CORBA — *serializable unchecked*

A standard CORBA exception thrown when an ORB encounters an internal error. Sun's Java IDL defines the following minor error code values for this exception, stored in the minor data member inherited from SystemException:

Minor Code	*Meaning*
3	An IIOP reply message contained a bad status.
6	The repository ID of a user exception had an incorrect length during an unmarshalling operation.
7	The ORB failed to get the local hostname through the InetAddress.getLocalHost().getHostName() method.
8	The ORB was unable to create a listener port on its designated port because the port was in use, the creation of the daemon thread failed, or a security violation occurred.
9	An IIOP locate message contained a bad status.
10	An error was encountered while creating a stringified object reference.
11	An IIOP message contained a bad GIOP v1.0 message type.

Minor Code	Meaning
14	An error occurred while unmarshalling a user exception.
18	The ORB failed during internal initialization.

```
public final class INTERNAL extends org.omg.CORBA.SystemException {
// Public Constructors
   public INTERNAL();
   public INTERNAL(String s);
   public INTERNAL(int minor, CompletionStatus completed);
   public INTERNAL(String s, int minor, CompletionStatus completed);
}
```

Hierarchy: Object→ Throwable(Serializable)→ Exception→ RuntimeException→ org.omg.CORBA.SystemException→ INTERNAL

INTF_REPOS — Java 1.2

org.omg.CORBA — *serializable unchecked*

A standard CORBA exception thrown when an error occurs while attempting to use the interface repository.

```
public final class INTF_REPOS extends org.omg.CORBA.SystemException {
// Public Constructors
   public INTF_REPOS();
   public INTF_REPOS(String s);
   public INTF_REPOS(int minor, CompletionStatus completed);
   public INTF_REPOS(String s, int minor, CompletionStatus completed);
}
```

Hierarchy: Object→ Throwable(Serializable)→ Exception→ RuntimeException→ org.omg.CORBA.SystemException→ INTF_REPOS

IntHolder — Java 1.2

org.omg.CORBA

The holder class for out and inout remote method arguments that are mapped to Java int values.

```
public final class IntHolder implements org.omg.CORBA.portable.Streamable {
// Public Constructors
   public IntHolder();
   public IntHolder(int initial);
// Methods implementing Streamable
   public void _read(org.omg.CORBA.portable.InputStream input);
   public TypeCode _type();
   public void _write(org.omg.CORBA.portable.OutputStream output);
// Public Instance Fields
   public int value;
}
```

Hierarchy: Object→ IntHolder(org.omg.CORBA.portable.Streamable)

INV_FLAG — Java 1.2

org.omg.CORBA — *serializable unchecked*

A standard CORBA exception thrown when an invalid flag is specified in a method call.

```
public final class INV_FLAG extends org.omg.CORBA.SystemException {
```

```
// Public Constructors
   public INV_FLAG();
   public INV_FLAG(String s);
   public INV_FLAG(int minor, CompletionStatus completed);
   public INV_FLAG(String s, int minor, CompletionStatus completed);
}
```

Hierarchy: Object→ Throwable(Serializable)→ Exception→ RuntimeException→ org.omg.CORBA.SystemException→ INV_FLAG

INV_IDENT Java 1.2

org.omg.CORBA *serializable unchecked*

A standard CORBA exception thrown when an invalid identifier is specified.

```
public final class INV_IDENT extends org.omg.CORBA.SystemException {
// Public Constructors
   public INV_IDENT();
   public INV_IDENT(String s);
   public INV_IDENT(int minor, CompletionStatus completed);
   public INV_IDENT(String s, int minor, CompletionStatus completed);
}
```

Hierarchy: Object→ Throwable(Serializable)→ Exception→ RuntimeException→ org.omg.CORBA.SystemException→ INV_IDENT

INV_OBJREF Java 1.2

org.omg.CORBA *serializable unchecked*

A standard CORBA exception thrown when an invalid object reference is used. Sun's Java IDL defines the following minor error code values for this exception, stored in the minor data member inherited from SystemException:

Minor Code	*Meaning*
1	A stringified object reference had no profile.

```
public final class INV_OBJREF extends org.omg.CORBA.SystemException {
// Public Constructors
   public INV_OBJREF();
   public INV_OBJREF(String s);
   public INV_OBJREF(int minor, CompletionStatus completed);
   public INV_OBJREF(String s, int minor, CompletionStatus completed);
}
```

Hierarchy: Object→ Throwable(Serializable)→ Exception→ RuntimeException→ org.omg.CORBA.SystemException→ INV_OBJREF

INV_POLICY Java 1.2

org.omg.CORBA *serializable unchecked*

A standard CORBA exception thrown when an incompatibility between Policy objects is encountered during a remote method call.

```
public class INV_POLICY extends org.omg.CORBA.SystemException {
// Public Constructors
   public INV_POLICY();
   public INV_POLICY(String s);
```

```
    public INV_POLICY(int minor, CompletionStatus completed);
    public INV_POLICY(String s, int minor, CompletionStatus completed);
}
```

Hierarchy: Object→ Throwable(Serializable)→ Exception→ RuntimeException→ org.omg.CORBA.SystemException→ INV_POLICY

INVALID_TRANSACTION **Java 1.2**

org.omg.CORBA ***serializable unchecked***

A standard CORBA exception thrown when a transaction error occurs during a remote method call.

```
public final class INVALID_TRANSACTION extends org.omg.CORBA.SystemException {
// Public Constructors
    public INVALID_TRANSACTION();
    public INVALID_TRANSACTION(String s);
    public INVALID_TRANSACTION(int minor, CompletionStatus completed);
    public INVALID_TRANSACTION(String s, int minor, CompletionStatus completed);
}
```

Hierarchy: Object→ Throwable(Serializable)→ Exception→ RuntimeException→ org.omg.CORBA.SystemException→ INVALID_TRANSACTION

IRObject **Java 1.2**

org.omg.CORBA ***serializable***

All the informational interfaces used and exported by the Interface Repository derive from the IRObject interface. The Interface Repository is a component of the ORB that stores definitions of object interfaces. These interface definitions are used by the ORB at runtime to check the correctness of method requests and to support Dynamic Invocation Interface requests. They can also be used within development tools, to provide information about remote interfaces for browsing and linking them. The Interface Repository is analogous to a table schema in a relational database, in that it describes the type of objects an ORB is supporting. The Interface Repository uses a set of IDL interfaces (e.g., InterfaceDef, AttributeDef) to represent the modules, interfaces, attributes, methods, etc., it manages. All of these interfaces derive from the IRObject interface.

The IRObject has a def_kind() method that indicates the type of definition the object represents (module, attribute, etc.).

```
public abstract interface IRObject extends org.omg.CORBA.Object, org.omg.CORBA.portable.IDLEntity {
// Public Instance Methods
    public abstract DefinitionKind def_kind();
    public abstract void destroy();
}
```

Hierarchy: (IRObject(org.omg.CORBA.Object, org.omg.CORBA.portable.IDLEntity(Serializable)))

Implementations: IDLType

LongHolder **Java 1.2**

org.omg.CORBA

The holder class for out and inout remote method arguments that are mapped to Java long values.

```
public final class LongHolder implements org.omg.CORBA.portable.Streamable {
```

```
// Public Constructors
   public LongHolder();
   public LongHolder(long initial);
// Methods implementing Streamable
   public void _read(org.omg.CORBA.portable.InputStream input);
   public TypeCode _type();
   public void _write(org.omg.CORBA.portable.OutputStream output);
// Public Instance Fields
   public long value;
}
```

Hierarchy: Object→ LongHolder(org.omg.CORBA.portable.Streamable)

MARSHAL — Java 1.2

org.omg.CORBA — *serializable unchecked*

A standard CORBA exception thrown when the ORB fails to marshal or unmarshal method arguments, return values or exceptions. Sun's Java IDL defines the following minor error code values for this exception, stored in the minor data member inherited from SystemException:

Minor Code	*Meaning*
4	An error occurred while unmarshalling an object reference.
5	An attempt was made to marshal or unmarshal an IDL type that is not supported in this implementation, such as wchar or wstring.
6	While marshalling or unmarshalling, a character not within the ISO Latin-1 set was encountered.


```
public final class MARSHAL extends org.omg.CORBA.SystemException {
// Public Constructors
   public MARSHAL();
   public MARSHAL(String s);
   public MARSHAL(int minor, CompletionStatus completed);
   public MARSHAL(String s, int minor, CompletionStatus completed);
}
```

Hierarchy: Object→ Throwable(Serializable)→ Exception→ RuntimeException→ org.omg.CORBA.SystemException→ MARSHAL

Thrown By: Any.{insert_string(), insert_Value(), insert_wstring(), read_value()}

NamedValue — Java 1.2

org.omg.CORBA

This class represents a remote method argument or return value. It consists of an argument name (as a String), its value (as an Any object), and an argument mode, which can one of ARG_IN.value, ARG_OUT.value, ARG_INOUT.value, or zero. If the argument mode is zero, the NamedValue represents a Context property value. NamedValue objects are used in Dynamic Invocation Interface and Dynamic Skeleton Interface operations (e.g., to build the argument list for a client-side method Request object).

```
public abstract class NamedValue {
// Public Constructors
   public NamedValue();
// Public Instance Methods
   public abstract int flags();
```

```
    public abstract String name();
    public abstract Any value();
}
```

Passed To: org.omg.CORBA.Object._create_request(), org.omg.CORBA.portable.Delegate.create_request(), org.omg.CORBA.portable.ObjectImpl._create_request()

Returned By: NVList.{add(), add_item(), add_value(), item()}, ORB.create_named_value(), Request.result()

NameValuePair **Java 1.2**

org.omg.CORBA ***serializable***

A DynStruct object uses NameValuePair objects to represent its data members. It consists of a String name and a value represented as an Any object.

```
public final class NameValuePair implements org.omg.CORBA.portable.IDLEntity {
// Public Constructors
    public NameValuePair();
    public NameValuePair(String __id, Any __value);
// Public Instance Fields
    public String id;
    public Any value;
}
```

Hierarchy: Object→ NameValuePair(org.omg.CORBA.portable.IDLEntity(Serializable))

Passed To: DynStruct.set_members(), DynValue.set_members()

Returned By: DynStruct.get_members(), DynValue.get_members()

NO_IMPLEMENT **Java 1.2**

org.omg.CORBA ***serializable unchecked***

A standard CORBA exception thrown when a call is made on a method that is not implemented. Sun's Java IDL defines the following minor error code values for this exception, stored in the minor data member inherited from SystemException:

Minor Code	*Meaning*
1	An attempt to use the Dynamic Skeleton Interface was made. The DSI is not implemented in Sun's Java IDL implementation.

```
public final class NO_IMPLEMENT extends org.omg.CORBA.SystemException {
// Public Constructors
    public NO_IMPLEMENT();
    public NO_IMPLEMENT(String s);
    public NO_IMPLEMENT(int minor, CompletionStatus completed);
    public NO_IMPLEMENT(String s, int minor, CompletionStatus completed);
}
```

Hierarchy: Object→ Throwable(Serializable)→ Exception→ RuntimeException→ org.omg.CORBA.SystemException→ NO_IMPLEMENT

NO_MEMORY **Java 1.2**

org.omg.CORBA ***serializable unchecked***

A standard CORBA exception thrown when insufficient dynamic memory is available to carry out a request.

```
public final class NO_MEMORY extends org.omg.CORBA.SystemException {
// Public Constructors
   public NO_MEMORY();
   public NO_MEMORY(String s);
   public NO_MEMORY(int minor, CompletionStatus completed);
   public NO_MEMORY(String s, int minor, CompletionStatus completed);
}
```

Hierarchy: Object→ Throwable(Serializable)→ Exception→ RuntimeException→ org.omg.CORBA.SystemException→ NO_MEMORY

NO_PERMISSION — Java 1.2

org.omg.CORBA — *serializable unchecked*

A standard CORBA exception thrown when a client does not have sufficient permission to make a request.

```
public final class NO_PERMISSION extends org.omg.CORBA.SystemException {
// Public Constructors
   public NO_PERMISSION();
   public NO_PERMISSION(String s);
   public NO_PERMISSION(int minor, CompletionStatus completed);
   public NO_PERMISSION(String s, int minor, CompletionStatus completed);
}
```

Hierarchy: Object→ Throwable(Serializable)→ Exception→ RuntimeException→ org.omg.CORBA.SystemException→ NO_PERMISSION

NO_RESOURCES — Java 1.2

org.omg.CORBA — *serializable unchecked*

A standard CORBA exception thrown when resources cannot be allocated to execute a request, on either the client or the server.

```
public final class NO_RESOURCES extends org.omg.CORBA.SystemException {
// Public Constructors
   public NO_RESOURCES();
   public NO_RESOURCES(String s);
   public NO_RESOURCES(int minor, CompletionStatus completed);
   public NO_RESOURCES(String s, int minor, CompletionStatus completed);
}
```

Hierarchy: Object→ Throwable(Serializable)→ Exception→ RuntimeException→ org.omg.CORBA.SystemException→ NO_RESOURCES

NO_RESPONSE — Java 1.2

org.omg.CORBA — *serializable unchecked*

A standard CORBA exception thrown when a server response to an asynchronous remote method call is not yet available.

```
public final class NO_RESPONSE extends org.omg.CORBA.SystemException {
// Public Constructors
   public NO_RESPONSE();
   public NO_RESPONSE(String s);
   public NO_RESPONSE(int minor, CompletionStatus completed);
   public NO_RESPONSE(String s, int minor, CompletionStatus completed);
}
```

Hierarchy: Object→ Throwable(Serializable)→ Exception→ RuntimeException→ org.omg.CORBA.SystemException→ NO_RESPONSE

NVList — Java 1.2

org.omg.CORBA

A list of NamedValue objects. An NVList can be created using either the ORB.create_list() method or the ORB.create_operation_list() method. The latter method initializes the list with NamedValue objects that describe the arguments to the method definition you pass into the create_operation_list() method.

```
public abstract class NVList {
// Public Constructors
   public NVList();
// Public Instance Methods
   public abstract NamedValue add(int flags);
   public abstract NamedValue add_item(String item_name, int flags);
   public abstract NamedValue add_value(String item_name, Any val, int flags);
   public abstract int count();
   public abstract NamedValue item(int index) throws org.omg.CORBA.Bounds;
   public abstract void remove(int index) throws org.omg.CORBA.Bounds;
}
```

Passed To: org.omg.CORBA.Context.set_values(), org.omg.CORBA.Object._create_request(), ServerRequest.{arguments(), params()}, org.omg.CORBA.portable.Delegate.create_request(), org.omg.CORBA.portable.ObjectImpl._create_request()

Returned By: org.omg.CORBA.Context.get_values(), ORB.{create_list(), create_operation_list()}, Request.arguments()

OBJ_ADAPTER — Java 1.2

org.omg.CORBA — *serializable unchecked*

A standard CORBA exception thrown when an error is encountered by an object adapter in the ORB. Sun's Java IDL defines the following minor error code values for this exception, stored in the minor data member inherited from SystemException:

Minor Code	*Meaning*
1	On the server, no adapter matching the one referenced in the object reference was found.
2	Same as above, but error occurred during a locate request.
4	An error occurred while attempting to connect a servant to the ORB.

```
public final class OBJ_ADAPTER extends org.omg.CORBA.SystemException {
// Public Constructors
   public OBJ_ADAPTER();
   public OBJ_ADAPTER(String s);
   public OBJ_ADAPTER(int minor, CompletionStatus completed);
   public OBJ_ADAPTER(String s, int minor, CompletionStatus completed);
}
```

Hierarchy: Object→ Throwable(Serializable)→ Exception→ RuntimeException→ org.omg.CORBA.SystemException→ OBJ_ADAPTER

Object — Java 1.2

org.omg.CORBA

This is the base interface for all CORBA objects. An Object can be either a reference (stub) to a remote CORBA object or a local object implementation. The methods declared in the Object interface allow you to create Dynamic Invocation Interface requests on the object, get its Interface Repository definition, and check the equivalence of two objects, among other things. The org.omg.CORBA.portable.ObjectImpl class provides a default, concrete implementation of the Object interface.

```
public abstract interface Object {
// Public Instance Methods
   public abstract Request _create_request(org.omg.CORBA.Context ctx, String operation, NVList arg_list,
                                           NamedValue result);
   public abstract Request _create_request(org.omg.CORBA.Context ctx, String operation, NVList arg_list,
                                           NamedValue result, ExceptionList exclist, ContextList ctxlist);
   public abstract org.omg.CORBA.Object _duplicate();
   public abstract DomainManager[ ] _get_domain_managers();
   public abstract org.omg.CORBA.Object _get_interface_def();
   public abstract org.omg.CORBA.Policy _get_policy(int policy_type);
   public abstract int _hash(int maximum);
   public abstract boolean _is_a(String repositoryIdentifier);
   public abstract boolean _is_equivalent(org.omg.CORBA.Object other);
   public abstract boolean _non_existent();
   public abstract void _release();
   public abstract Request _request(String operation);
   public abstract org.omg.CORBA.Object _set_policy_override(org.omg.CORBA.Policy[ ] policies,
                                                             SetOverrideType set_add);
}
```

Implementations: Current, DomainManager, DynAny, DynArray, DynEnum, DynFixed, DynSequence, DynStruct, DynUnion, DynValue, IDLType, IRObject, org.omg.CORBA.Policy, org.omg.CORBA.portable.ObjectImpl, org.omg.CosNaming.BindingIterator, org.omg.CosNaming.NamingContext

Passed To: Too many methods to list.

Returned By: Any.extract_Object(), DynAny.get_reference(), org.omg.CORBA.Object.{_duplicate(), _get_interface_def(), _set_policy_override()}, ORB.{resolve_initial_references(), string_to_object()}, Request.target(), org.omg.CORBA.portable.Delegate.{duplicate(), get_interface_def(), set_policy_override()}, org.omg.CORBA.portable.InputStream.read_Object(), org.omg.CORBA.portable.ObjectImpl.{_duplicate(), _get_interface_def(), _set_policy_override()}, org.omg.CosNaming._NamingContextImplBase.resolve(), org.omg.CosNaming._NamingContextStub.resolve(), org.omg.CosNaming.NamingContext.resolve()

Type Of: ObjectHolder.value

OBJECT_NOT_EXIST — Java 1.2

org.omg.CORBA — *serializable unchecked*

A standard CORBA exception thrown when a request is made of a server object that no longer exists. Sun's Java IDL defines the following minor error code values for this exception, stored in the minor data member inherited from SystemException:

Minor Code	*Meaning*
1	The target of a locate request sent back a response indicating it did not know the object.

Minor Code	*Meaning*
2	A method request was received by a server whose ID does not match the server ID referenced in the object reference.
4	The skeleton referenced in the object reference was not found on the server.

```
public final class OBJECT_NOT_EXIST extends org.omg.CORBA.SystemException {
// Public Constructors
   public OBJECT_NOT_EXIST();
   public OBJECT_NOT_EXIST(String s);
   public OBJECT_NOT_EXIST(int minor, CompletionStatus completed);
   public OBJECT_NOT_EXIST(String s, int minor, CompletionStatus completed);
}
```

Hierarchy: Object→ Throwable(Serializable)→ Exception→ RuntimeException→ org.omg.CORBA.SystemException→ OBJECT_NOT_EXIST

ObjectHolder — Java 1.2

org.omg.CORBA

The holder class for out and inout remote method arguments that are mapped to Java org.omg.CORBA.Object values.

```
public final class ObjectHolder implements org.omg.CORBA.portable.Streamable {
// Public Constructors
   public ObjectHolder();
   public ObjectHolder(org.omg.CORBA.Object initial);
// Methods implementing Streamable
   public void _read(org.omg.CORBA.portable.InputStream input);
   public TypeCode _type();
   public void _write(org.omg.CORBA.portable.OutputStream output);
// Public Instance Fields
   public org.omg.CORBA.Object value;
}
```

Hierarchy: Object→ ObjectHolder(org.omg.CORBA.portable.Streamable)

ORB — Java 1.2

org.omg.CORBA

The ORB class is at the heart of the CORBA API. The ORB class provides CORBA clients and server objects access to the basic CORBA functions needed to engage in remote object operations. The static init() methods let you initialize a reference to an ORB. ORB provides access to initial objects and service through its resolve_initial_references() method. It also provides constructor methods that allow you to create key objects needed to perform remote method requests, like Any and NamedValue objects. The ORB also allows you to convert a CORBA object reference to a portable stringified form and back again, using its object_to_string() and string_to_object() methods.

```
public abstract class ORB {
// Public Constructors
   public ORB();
// Public Class Methods
   public static ORB init();
   public static ORB init(String[ ] args, java.util.Properties props);
   public static ORB init(java.applet.Applet app, java.util.Properties props);
// Public Instance Methods
   public void connect(org.omg.CORBA.Object obj);
```

```
public TypeCode create_abstract_interface_tc(String id, String name);
public abstract TypeCode create_alias_tc(String id, String name, TypeCode original_type);
public abstract Any create_any();
public abstract TypeCode create_array_tc(int length, TypeCode element_type);
public DynAny create_basic_dyn_any(TypeCode type)
    throws org.omg.CORBA.ORBPackage.InconsistentTypeCode;
public abstract ContextList create_context_list();
public DynAny create_dyn_any(Any value);
public DynArray create_dyn_array(TypeCode type)
    throws org.omg.CORBA.ORBPackage.InconsistentTypeCode;
public DynEnum create_dyn_enum(TypeCode type)
    throws org.omg.CORBA.ORBPackage.InconsistentTypeCode;
public DynSequence create_dyn_sequence(TypeCode type)
    throws org.omg.CORBA.ORBPackage.InconsistentTypeCode;
public DynStruct create_dyn_struct(TypeCode type)
    throws org.omg.CORBA.ORBPackage.InconsistentTypeCode;
public DynUnion create_dyn_union(TypeCode type)
    throws org.omg.CORBA.ORBPackage.InconsistentTypeCode;
public abstract TypeCode create_enum_tc(String id, String name, String[ ] members);
public abstract Environment create_environment();
public abstract ExceptionList create_exception_list();
public abstract TypeCode create_exception_tc(String id, String name, StructMember[ ] members);
public TypeCode create_fixed_tc(short digits, short scale);
public abstract TypeCode create_interface_tc(String id, String name);
public abstract NVList create_list(int count);
public abstract NamedValue create_named_value(String s, Any any, int flags);
public TypeCode create_native_tc(String id, String name);
public NVList create_operation_list(org.omg.CORBA.Object oper);
public abstract org.omg.CORBA.portable.OutputStream create_output_stream();
public org.omg.CORBA.Policy create_policy(int type, Any val) throws PolicyError;
public TypeCode create_recursive_tc(String id);
public abstract TypeCode create_sequence_tc(int bound, TypeCode element_type);
public abstract TypeCode create_string_tc(int bound);
public abstract TypeCode create_struct_tc(String id, String name, StructMember[ ] members);
public abstract TypeCode create_union_tc(String id, String name, TypeCode discriminator_type,
                                         UnionMember[ ] members);
public TypeCode create_value_box_tc(String id, String name, TypeCode boxed_type);
public TypeCode create_value_tc(String id, String name, short type_modifier, TypeCode concrete_base,
                                ValueMember[ ] members);
public abstract TypeCode create_wstring_tc(int bound);
public void disconnect(org.omg.CORBA.Object obj);
public abstract org.omg.CORBA.Context get_default_context();
public abstract Request get_next_response() throws WrongTransaction;
public abstract TypeCode get_primitive_tc(TCKind tcKind);
public boolean get_service_information(short service_type, ServiceInformationHolder service_info);
public abstract String[ ] list_initial_services();
public abstract String object_to_string(org.omg.CORBA.Object obj);
public void perform_work();
public abstract boolean poll_next_response();
public abstract org.omg.CORBA.Object resolve_initial_references(String object_name)
    throws org.omg.CORBA.ORBPackage.InvalidName;
public void run();
public abstract void send_multiple_requests_deferred(Request[ ] req);
public abstract void send_multiple_requests_oneway(Request[ ] req);
public void shutdown(boolean wait_for_completion);
public abstract org.omg.CORBA.Object string_to_object(String str);
public boolean work_pending();
// Protected Instance Methods
```

org.omg.CORBA

```
    protected abstract void set_parameters(String[ ] args, java.util.Properties props);
    protected abstract void set_parameters(java.applet.Applet app, java.util.Properties props);
// Deprecated Public Methods
#   public abstract TypeCode create_recursive_sequence_tc(int bound, int offset);
#   public Current get_current();
}
```

Returned By: ORB.init(), org.omg.CORBA.portable.Delegate.orb(), org.omg.CORBA.portable.InputStream.orb(), org.omg.CORBA.portable.ObjectImpl._orb(), org.omg.CORBA.portable.OutputStream.orb()

PERSIST_STORE — Java 1.2

org.omg.CORBA — *serializable unchecked*

A standard CORBA exception thrown when a server encounters an error with its persistent storage.

```
public final class PERSIST_STORE extends org.omg.CORBA.SystemException {
// Public Constructors
    public PERSIST_STORE();
    public PERSIST_STORE(String s);
    public PERSIST_STORE(int minor, CompletionStatus completed);
    public PERSIST_STORE(String s, int minor, CompletionStatus completed);
}
```

Hierarchy: Object→ Throwable(Serializable)→ Exception→ RuntimeException→ org.omg.CORBA.SystemException→ PERSIST_STORE

Policy — Java 1.2

org.omg.CORBA

This is the base interface for objects that represent usage policies for ORBs and other CORBA services. Policies for certain objects or domains of objects can be obtained from a DomainManager, which in turn can be obtained from the Object in question using its _get_domain_managers() method. The policy_type() method on Policy provides access to an integer type indicator, where the allowable values are implementation-specific.

```
public abstract interface Policy extends org.omg.CORBA.Object {
// Public Instance Methods
    public abstract org.omg.CORBA.Policy copy();
    public abstract void destroy();
    public abstract int policy_type();
}
```

Hierarchy: (org.omg.CORBA.Policy(Object))

Passed To: org.omg.CORBA.Object._set_policy_override(), org.omg.CORBA.portable.Delegate.set_policy_override(), org.omg.CORBA.portable.ObjectImpl._set_policy_override()

Returned By: DomainManager.get_domain_policy(), org.omg.CORBA.Object._get_policy(), ORB.create_policy(), org.omg.CORBA.Policy.copy(), org.omg.CORBA.portable.Delegate.get_policy(), org.omg.CORBA.portable.ObjectImpl._get_policy()

PolicyError — Java 1.2

org.omg.CORBA — *serializable checked*

An exception thrown when an error occurs during creation of a Policy object.

```
public final class PolicyError extends UserException {
// Public Constructors
   public PolicyError();
   public PolicyError(short __reason);
   public PolicyError(String reason_string, short __reason);
// Public Instance Fields
   public short reason;
}
```

Hierarchy: Object→ Throwable(Serializable)→ Exception→ UserException(org.omg.CORBA.portable.IDLEntity(Serializable))→ PolicyError

Thrown By: ORB.create_policy()

Principal

Java 1.2; Deprecated in Java 1.2

org.omg.CORBA

This deprecated class was used in previous versions of the CORBA standard to hold the identity of a client, in the form of an array of bytes that represents the encoded name of the client. This functionality has now been assumed by the Security Service, but the class is still available in the Java IDL API to provide temporary backward compatibility with previous CORBA applications.

```
public abstract class Principal {
// Public Constructors
   public Principal();
// Deprecated Public Methods
#  public abstract byte[ ] name();
#  public abstract void name(byte[ ] value);
}
```

Passed To: Any.insert_Principal(), PrincipalHolder.PrincipalHolder(), org.omg.CORBA.portable.OutputStream.write_Principal()

Returned By: Any.extract_Principal(), org.omg.CORBA.portable.InputStream.read_Principal()

Type Of: PrincipalHolder.value

PrincipalHolder

Java 1.2; Deprecated in Java 1.2

org.omg.CORBA

This deprecated class is the holder class for out and inout remote method arguments that are mapped to Java Principal objects.

```
public final class PrincipalHolder implements org.omg.CORBA.portable.Streamable {
// Public Constructors
   public PrincipalHolder();
   public PrincipalHolder(org.omg.CORBA.Principal initial);
// Methods implementing Streamable
   public void _read(org.omg.CORBA.portable.InputStream input);
   public TypeCode _type();
   public void _write(org.omg.CORBA.portable.OutputStream output);
// Public Instance Fields
   public org.omg.CORBA.Principal value;
}
```

Hierarchy: Object→ PrincipalHolder(org.omg.CORBA.portable.Streamable)

Request **Java 1.2**

org.omg.CORBA

A Request represents a remote method request under the Dynamic Invocation Interface. Request objects are created by calling the create_request() method on the org.omg.CORBA.Object reference for the remote object that will service the method request. The Request contains the name of the method to be invoked, an NVList containing NamedValue objects that represent the method arguments, and the return value for the method, if appropriate. It can also contain a description of the exceptions the method can throw and the client context values that the method accepts.

You add method arguments to a Request by calling one of its add_XXX() methods, which all return an Any object that you can initialize with the value of the argument. Once the Request has been initialized with its arguments and any other information, the method can be invoked synchronously using the invoke() method, asynchronously using send_deferred(), or in one-way mode using send_oneway(). Immediately after the invoke() method returns, any return values or thrown exceptions are available for you to query. After calling the send_deferred() method, you can poll and retrieve the method response by calling the poll_response() and get_response() methods. If the response is ready, get_response() initializes the internal return value or exception in the Request object, and it can be retrieved using the return_value() method. After calling send_oneway(), no return value or exception is returned. You can use send_oneway() on methods even if they weren't declared as oneway in the corresponding IDL for the interface.

```
public abstract class Request {
// Public Constructors
   public Request();
// Public Instance Methods
   public abstract Any add_in_arg();
   public abstract Any add_inout_arg();
   public abstract Any add_named_in_arg(String name);
   public abstract Any add_named_inout_arg(String name);
   public abstract Any add_named_out_arg(String name);
   public abstract Any add_out_arg();
   public abstract NVList arguments();
   public abstract ContextList contexts();
   public abstract org.omg.CORBA.Context ctx();
   public abstract void ctx(org.omg.CORBA.Context c);
   public abstract Environment env();
   public abstract ExceptionList exceptions();
   public abstract void get_response() throws WrongTransaction;
   public abstract void invoke();
   public abstract String operation();
   public abstract boolean poll_response();
   public abstract NamedValue result();
   public abstract Any return_value();
   public abstract void send_deferred();
   public abstract void send_oneway();
   public abstract void set_return_type(TypeCode tc);
   public abstract org.omg.CORBA.Object target();
}
```

Passed To: ORB.{send_multiple_requests_deferred(), send_multiple_requests_oneway()}

Returned By: org.omg.CORBA.Object.{_create_request(), _request()}, ORB.get_next_response(), org.omg.CORBA.portable.Delegate.{create_request(), request()}, org.omg.CORBA.portable.ObjectImpl.{_create_request(), _request()}

ServerRequest — Java 1.2

org.omg.CORBA

The server-side equivalent of the client-side Request object. A ServerRequest is used in the Dynamic Skeleton Interface to invoke a method on a server object through its DynamicImplementation.

```
public abstract class ServerRequest {
// Public Constructors
   public ServerRequest();
// Public Instance Methods
   public void arguments(NVList args);
   public abstract org.omg.CORBA.Context ctx();
   public String operation();
   public void set_exception(Any any);
   public void set_result(Any any);
// Deprecated Public Methods
#  public void except(Any any);
#  public String op_name();
#  public void params(NVList params);
#  public void result(Any any);
}
```

Passed To: DynamicImplementation.invoke(), org.omg.CosNaming._BindingIteratorImplBase.invoke(), org.omg.CosNaming._NamingContextImplBase.invoke()

ServiceDetail — Java 1.2

org.omg.CORBA *serializable*

A component of a ServiceInformation object that describes a service available through an ORB. Each ServiceDetail stores an integer type code and an array of bytes that contains information about the service. The semantics of the type code and the format of the byte data are implementation-specific.

```
public final class ServiceDetail implements org.omg.CORBA.portable.IDLEntity {
// Public Constructors
   public ServiceDetail();
   public ServiceDetail(int service_detail_type, byte[ ] service_detail);
// Public Instance Fields
   public byte[ ] service_detail;
   public int service_detail_type;
}
```

Hierarchy: Object→ ServiceDetail(org.omg.CORBA.portable.IDLEntity(Serializable))

Passed To: ServiceDetailHelper.{insert(), write()}, ServiceInformation.ServiceInformation()

Returned By: ServiceDetailHelper.{extract(), read()}

Type Of: ServiceInformation.service_details

ServiceDetailHelper — Java 1.2

org.omg.CORBA

The helper class for the ServiceDetail class, used internally to read and write ServiceDetail objects when they are used as remote method arguments or return values.

```
public class ServiceDetailHelper {
// No Constructor
// Public Class Methods
```

```
    public static ServiceDetail extract(Any a);
    public static String id();
    public static void insert(Any a, ServiceDetail that);
    public static ServiceDetail read(org.omg.CORBA.portable.InputStream in);
    public static TypeCode type();                                    synchronized
    public static void write(org.omg.CORBA.portable.OutputStream out, ServiceDetail that);
}
```

ServiceInformation — Java 1.2

org.omg.CORBA — *serializable*

This class represents information about a service available through an ORB. You query for information about a service using the ORB.get_service_information() method, which returns a ServiceInformation object. The ServiceInformation object consists of a set of ServiceDetail objects, each representing a particular piece of information about the service.

```
public final class ServiceInformation implements org.omg.CORBA.portable.IDLEntity {
// Public Constructors
    public ServiceInformation();
    public ServiceInformation(int[ ] __service_options, ServiceDetail[ ] __service_details);
// Public Instance Fields
    public ServiceDetail[ ] service_details;
    public int[ ] service_options;
}
```

Hierarchy: Object→ ServiceInformation(org.omg.CORBA.portable.IDLEntity(Serializable))

Passed To: ServiceInformationHelper.{insert(), write()}, ServiceInformationHolder.ServiceInformationHolder()

Returned By: ServiceInformationHelper.{extract(), read()}

Type Of: ServiceInformationHolder.value

ServiceInformationHelper — Java 1.2

org.omg.CORBA

The helper class for ServiceInformation objects, used internally to read and write ServiceInformation objects when they are used as remote method arguments or return values.

```
public class ServiceInformationHelper {
// No Constructor
// Public Class Methods
    public static ServiceInformation extract(Any a);
    public static String id();
    public static void insert(Any a, ServiceInformation that);
    public static ServiceInformation read(org.omg.CORBA.portable.InputStream in);
    public static TypeCode type();                                    synchronized
    public static void write(org.omg.CORBA.portable.OutputStream out, ServiceInformation that);
}
```

ServiceInformationHolder — Java 1.2

org.omg.CORBA

The holder class for out and inout remote method arguments that are mapped to Java ServiceInformation objects.

```
public final class ServiceInformationHolder implements org.omg.CORBA.portable.Streamable {
// Public Constructors
    public ServiceInformationHolder();
```

```
    public ServiceInformationHolder(ServiceInformation arg);
// Methods implementing Streamable
    public void _read(org.omg.CORBA.portable.InputStream in);
    public TypeCode _type();
    public void _write(org.omg.CORBA.portable.OutputStream out);
// Public Instance Fields
    public ServiceInformation value;
}
```

Hierarchy: Object→ ServiceInformationHolder(org.omg.CORBA.portable.Streamable)

Passed To: ORB.get_service_information()

SetOverrideType — Java 1.2

org.omg.CORBA — *serializable*

The static instances on the SetOverrideType class are used in calls to the set_policy_overrides() method on org.omg.CORBA.Object. This method allows you to override security-related policies that are imposed on an object by a CORBA Security Service by passing in an array of Policy objects and a SetOverrideType object. There are two static SetOverrideType instances that can be passed in as the second argument to this method. SetOverrideType.ADD_OVERRIDE indicates that the policies being passed in should be added to any existing policies that apply to the object, while SetOverrideType.SET_OVERRIDE indicates that the policies being provided should replace any existing policies on the object.

```
public class SetOverrideType implements org.omg.CORBA.portable.IDLEntity {
// Protected Constructors
    protected SetOverrideType(int _value);
// Public Constants
    public static final int _ADD_OVERRIDE;                              =1
    public static final int _SET_OVERRIDE;                              =0
    public static final SetOverrideType ADD_OVERRIDE;
    public static final SetOverrideType SET_OVERRIDE;
// Public Class Methods
    public static SetOverrideType from_int(int i) throws BAD_PARAM;
// Public Instance Methods
    public int value();
}
```

Hierarchy: Object→ SetOverrideType(org.omg.CORBA.portable.IDLEntity(Serializable))

Passed To: org.omg.CORBA.Object._set_policy_override(), org.omg.CORBA.portable.Delegate.set_policy_override(), org.omg.CORBA.portable.ObjectImpl._set_policy_override()

Returned By: SetOverrideType.from_int()

Type Of: SetOverrideType.{ADD_OVERRIDE, SET_OVERRIDE}

ShortHolder — Java 1.2

org.omg.CORBA

The holder class for out and inout remote method arguments that are mapped to Java short values.

```
public final class ShortHolder implements org.omg.CORBA.portable.Streamable {
// Public Constructors
    public ShortHolder();
    public ShortHolder(short initial);
```

```
// Methods implementing Streamable
   public void _read(org.omg.CORBA.portable.InputStream input);
   public TypeCode _type();
   public void _write(org.omg.CORBA.portable.OutputStream output);
// Public Instance Fields
   public short value;
}
```

Hierarchy: Object→ ShortHolder(org.omg.CORBA.portable.Streamable)

StringHolder — Java 1.2

org.omg.CORBA

The holder class for out and inout remote method arguments that are mapped to Java String values.

```
public final class StringHolder implements org.omg.CORBA.portable.Streamable {
// Public Constructors
   public StringHolder();
   public StringHolder(String initial);
// Methods implementing Streamable
   public void _read(org.omg.CORBA.portable.InputStream input);
   public TypeCode _type();
   public void _write(org.omg.CORBA.portable.OutputStream output);
// Public Instance Fields
   public String value;
}
```

Hierarchy: Object→ StringHolder(org.omg.CORBA.portable.Streamable)

StructMember — Java 1.2

org.omg.CORBA — *serializable*

A class that represents a member of an IDL struct type. StructMember objects can create TypeCode objects for IDL struct and exception values with the ORB.create_struct_tc() and ORB.create_exception_tc() methods.

```
public final class StructMember implements org.omg.CORBA.portable.IDLEntity {
// Public Constructors
   public StructMember();
   public StructMember(String __name, TypeCode __type, IDLType __type_def);
// Public Instance Fields
   public String name;
   public TypeCode type;
   public IDLType type_def;
}
```

Hierarchy: Object→ StructMember(org.omg.CORBA.portable.IDLEntity(Serializable))

Passed To: ORB.{create_exception_tc(), create_struct_tc()}

SystemException — Java 1.2

org.omg.CORBA — *serializable unchecked*

This is the base class for all standard CORBA exceptions. A SystemException can be thrown by any CORBA remote method call. Many CORBA API methods throw SystemException objects as well. The SystemException class provides an integer minor code that can be optionally used by a subclass to indicate a more precise reason for an exception.

The class also provides a CompletionStatus object that can indicate to the caller whether the method invocation was completed or not when the exception was encountered.

Subclasses of SystemException represent the many errors that can occur while a remote method request is being processed by the client's ORB, transferred to the server ORB, executed on the server object, and having its response transferred back to the client. A SystemException can originate on the client or on the server, before, during, or after the actual execution of the method on the remote object.

Since SystemException extends java.lang.RuntimeException, these exceptions don't need to be declared in method signatures. But remember that any remote method declared in an IDL interface can throw any of the subclasses of SystemException, just as any local Java method can throw any subclass of RuntimeException during execution.

```
public abstract class SystemException extends RuntimeException {
// Protected Constructors
   protected SystemException(String reason, int minor, CompletionStatus completed);
// Public methods overriding Throwable
   public String toString();
// Public Instance Fields
   public CompletionStatus completed;
   public int minor;
}
```

Hierarchy: Object→ Throwable(Serializable)→ Exception→ RuntimeException→ org.omg.CORBA.SystemException

Subclasses: Too many classes to list.

Thrown By: org.omg.CORBA.portable.InvokeHandler._invoke()

TCKind **Java 1.2**

org.omg.CORBA

A class that represents the type of a TypeCode object. The TCKind class contains a set of static int values that correspond to the built-in IDL data types. It also contains a set of static TCKind instances that correspond to each of these IDL types. The TCKind of a TypeCode can be obtained using its kind() method, and its value can be compared to these static data members to determine the type of the TypeCode.

```
public class TCKind {
// Protected Constructors
   protected TCKind(int _value);
// Public Constants
   public static final int _tk_abstract_interface;                          =32
   public static final int _tk_alias;                                       =21
   public static final int _tk_any;                                         =11
   public static final int _tk_array;                                       =20
   public static final int _tk_boolean;                                     =8
   public static final int _tk_char;                                        =9
   public static final int _tk_double;                                      =7
   public static final int _tk_enum;                                        =17
   public static final int _tk_except;                                      =22
   public static final int _tk_fixed;                                       =28
   public static final int _tk_float;                                       =6
   public static final int _tk_long;                                        =3
   public static final int _tk_longdouble;                                  =25
   public static final int _tk_longlong;                                    =23
   public static final int _tk_native;                                      =31
   public static final int _tk_null;                                        =0
```

```
    public static final int _tk_objref;                                    =14
    public static final int _tk_octet;                                     =10
    public static final int _tk_Principal;                                 =13
    public static final int _tk_sequence;                                  =19
    public static final int _tk_short;                                     =2
    public static final int _tk_string;                                    =18
    public static final int _tk_struct;                                    =15
    public static final int _tk_TypeCode;                                  =12
    public static final int _tk_ulong;                                     =5
    public static final int _tk_ulonglong;                                 =24
    public static final int _tk_union;                                     =16
    public static final int _tk_ushort;                                    =4
    public static final int _tk_value;                                     =29
    public static final int _tk_value_box;                                 =30
    public static final int _tk_void;                                      =1
    public static final int _tk_wchar;                                     =26
    public static final int _tk_wstring;                                   =27
    public static final TCKind tk_abstract_interface;
    public static final TCKind tk_alias;
    public static final TCKind tk_any;
    public static final TCKind tk_array;
    public static final TCKind tk_boolean;
    public static final TCKind tk_char;
    public static final TCKind tk_double;
    public static final TCKind tk_enum;
    public static final TCKind tk_except;
    public static final TCKind tk_fixed;
    public static final TCKind tk_float;
    public static final TCKind tk_long;
    public static final TCKind tk_longdouble;
    public static final TCKind tk_longlong;
    public static final TCKind tk_native;
    public static final TCKind tk_null;
    public static final TCKind tk_objref;
    public static final TCKind tk_octet;
    public static final TCKind tk_Principal;
    public static final TCKind tk_sequence;
    public static final TCKind tk_short;
    public static final TCKind tk_string;
    public static final TCKind tk_struct;
    public static final TCKind tk_TypeCode;
    public static final TCKind tk_ulong;
    public static final TCKind tk_ulonglong;
    public static final TCKind tk_union;
    public static final TCKind tk_ushort;
    public static final TCKind tk_value;
    public static final TCKind tk_value_box;
    public static final TCKind tk_void;
    public static final TCKind tk_wchar;
    public static final TCKind tk_wstring;
// Public Class Methods
    public static TCKind from_int(int i) throws BAD_PARAM;
// Public Instance Methods
    public int value();
}
```

Passed To: ORB.get_primitive_tc()

Returned By: DynStruct.current_member_kind(), DynUnion.{discriminator_kind(), member_kind()}, DynValue.current_member_kind(), TCKind.from_int(), TypeCode.kind()

Type Of: Too many fields to list.

TRANSACTION_REQUIRED — Java 1.2

org.omg.CORBA — *serializable unchecked*

A standard CORBA exception thrown when a remote method that must be run within a transaction is invoked outside of any transaction.

```
public final class TRANSACTION_REQUIRED extends org.omg.CORBA.SystemException {
// Public Constructors
   public TRANSACTION_REQUIRED();
   public TRANSACTION_REQUIRED(String s);
   public TRANSACTION_REQUIRED(int minor, CompletionStatus completed);
   public TRANSACTION_REQUIRED(String s, int minor, CompletionStatus completed);
}
```

Hierarchy: Object→ Throwable(Serializable)→ Exception→ RuntimeException→ org.omg.CORBA.SystemException→ TRANSACTION_REQUIRED

TRANSACTION_ROLLEDBACK — Java 1.2

org.omg.CORBA — *serializable unchecked*

A standard CORBA exception thrown when a remote method that was invoked within a transaction could not be completed because the enclosing transaction was rolled back.

```
public final class TRANSACTION_ROLLEDBACK extends org.omg.CORBA.SystemException {
// Public Constructors
   public TRANSACTION_ROLLEDBACK();
   public TRANSACTION_ROLLEDBACK(String s);
   public TRANSACTION_ROLLEDBACK(int minor, CompletionStatus completed);
   public TRANSACTION_ROLLEDBACK(String s, int minor, CompletionStatus completed);
}
```

Hierarchy: Object→ Throwable(Serializable)→ Exception→ RuntimeException→ org.omg.CORBA.SystemException→ TRANSACTION_ROLLEDBACK

TRANSIENT — Java 1.2

org.omg.CORBA — *serializable unchecked*

A standard CORBA exception thrown when a transient (i.e., not necessarily repeatable) error occurs during a remote method call. Since the error might not occur again, it is possible to try making the same request again.

```
public final class TRANSIENT extends org.omg.CORBA.SystemException {
// Public Constructors
   public TRANSIENT();
   public TRANSIENT(String s);
   public TRANSIENT(int minor, CompletionStatus completed);
   public TRANSIENT(String s, int minor, CompletionStatus completed);
}
```

Hierarchy: Object→ Throwable(Serializable)→ Exception→ RuntimeException→ org.omg.CORBA.SystemException→ TRANSIENT

TypeCode **Java 1.2**

org.omg.CORBA *serializable*

A TypeCode object describes the IDL type of a CORBA object, analogously to how the Java Class for an object (obtained using the getClass() method on java.lang.Object) describes its Java type. At a minimum, a TypeCode object contains a TCKind element that specifies the IDL data type it represents. For structured IDL types, like struct and union, it also contains additional information about the data type. The member_XXX() methods can obtain information about the members of struct, union, enum, and exception types, while the length() method gives the length of string, sequence and array types.

```
public abstract class TypeCode implements org.omg.CORBA.portable.IDLEntity {
// Public Constructors
   public TypeCode();
// Public Instance Methods
   public TypeCode concrete_base_type() throws org.omg.CORBA.TypeCodePackage.BadKind;
   public abstract TypeCode content_type() throws org.omg.CORBA.TypeCodePackage.BadKind;
   public abstract int default_index() throws org.omg.CORBA.TypeCodePackage.BadKind;
   public abstract TypeCode discriminator_type() throws org.omg.CORBA.TypeCodePackage.BadKind;
   public abstract boolean equal(TypeCode tc);
   public boolean equivalent(TypeCode tc);
   public short fixed_digits() throws org.omg.CORBA.TypeCodePackage.BadKind;
   public short fixed_scale() throws org.omg.CORBA.TypeCodePackage.BadKind;
   public TypeCode get_compact_typecode();
   public abstract String id() throws org.omg.CORBA.TypeCodePackage.BadKind;
   public abstract TCKind kind();
   public abstract int length() throws org.omg.CORBA.TypeCodePackage.BadKind;
   public abstract int member_count() throws org.omg.CORBA.TypeCodePackage.BadKind;
   public abstract Any member_label(int index) throws org.omg.CORBA.TypeCodePackage.BadKind,
        org.omg.CORBA.TypeCodePackage.Bounds;
   public abstract String member_name(int index) throws org.omg.CORBA.TypeCodePackage.BadKind,
        org.omg.CORBA.TypeCodePackage.Bounds;
   public abstract TypeCode member_type(int index) throws org.omg.CORBA.TypeCodePackage.BadKind
        , org.omg.CORBA.TypeCodePackage.Bounds;
   public short member_visibility(int index) throws org.omg.CORBA.TypeCodePackage.BadKind,
        org.omg.CORBA.Bounds;
   public abstract String name() throws org.omg.CORBA.TypeCodePackage.BadKind;
   public short type_modifier() throws org.omg.CORBA.TypeCodePackage.BadKind;
}
```

Hierarchy: Object→ TypeCode(org.omg.CORBA.portable.IDLEntity(Serializable))

Passed To: Too many methods to list.

Returned By: Too many methods to list.

Type Of: StructMember.type, TypeCodeHolder.value, UnionMember.type, ValueMember.type

TypeCodeHolder **Java 1.2**

org.omg.CORBA

The holder class for out and inout remote method arguments that are TypeCode objects.

```
public final class TypeCodeHolder implements org.omg.CORBA.portable.Streamable {
// Public Constructors
   public TypeCodeHolder();
   public TypeCodeHolder(TypeCode initial);
// Methods implementing Streamable
   public void _read(org.omg.CORBA.portable.InputStream input);
   public TypeCode _type();
```

```
    public void _write(org.omg.CORBA.portable.OutputStream output);
// Public Instance Fields
    public TypeCode value;
}
```

Hierarchy: Object→ TypeCodeHolder(org.omg.CORBA.portable.Streamable)

UnionMember — Java 1.2

org.omg.CORBA — *serializable*

A class that represents a member of an IDL union type. UnionMember objects can create TypeCode objects for IDL union types with the ORB.create_union_tc() method.

```
public final class UnionMember implements org.omg.CORBA.portable.IDLEntity {
// Public Constructors
    public UnionMember();
    public UnionMember(String __name, Any __label, TypeCode __type, IDLType __type_def);
// Public Instance Fields
    public Any label;
    public String name;
    public TypeCode type;
    public IDLType type_def;
}
```

Hierarchy: Object→ UnionMember(org.omg.CORBA.portable.IDLEntity(Serializable))

Passed To: ORB.create_union_tc()

UNKNOWN — Java 1.2

org.omg.CORBA — *serializable unchecked*

A standard CORBA exception thrown when the ORB encounters an error it can't interpret. Sun's Java IDL defines the following minor error code values for this exception, stored in the minor data member inherited from SystemException:

Minor Code	*Meaning*
1	During unmarshalling of the response to a method request, a user exception was returned by the server implementation that is not in the set of exceptions expected by the client.
3	The server implementation threw an unknown runtime exception.

```
public final class UNKNOWN extends org.omg.CORBA.SystemException {
// Public Constructors
    public UNKNOWN();
    public UNKNOWN(String s);
    public UNKNOWN(int minor, CompletionStatus completed);
    public UNKNOWN(String s, int minor, CompletionStatus completed);
}
```

Hierarchy: Object→ Throwable(Serializable)→ Exception→ RuntimeException→ org.omg.CORBA.SystemException→ UNKNOWN

UnknownUserException — Java 1.2

org.omg.CORBA — *serializable checked*

This exception class can wrap any user exceptions that are thrown during Dynamic Invocation Interface remote method calls. If an exception is thrown by the server object during such a call, the client can call the env() method on its Request object to get the request's Environment. The exception contained within the Environment is an UnknownUserException. The actual user exception the server threw is contained in the except data member of the UnknownUserException, which is an Any object.

```
public final class UnknownUserException extends UserException {
// Public Constructors
   public UnknownUserException();
   public UnknownUserException(Any a);
// Public Instance Fields
   public Any except;
}
```

Hierarchy: Object→ Throwable(Serializable)→ Exception→ UserException(org.omg.CORBA.portable.IDLEntity(Serializable))→ UnknownUserException

UserException — Java 1.2

org.omg.CORBA — *serializable checked*

This is the base class for all user exceptions that are defined in IDL and mapped to Java. It extends java.lang.Exception directly, so it represents a Java exception that must be declared in method signatures and caught in application code that calls these methods. Unlike the SystemException, the UserException class doesn't declare any data members for describing the exception to the caller. A subclass must do this to suit the type of exception it represents. It does, however, inherit the message property from Throwable, which can store a descriptive message on the exception to describe the reason.

```
public abstract class UserException extends Exception implements org.omg.CORBA.portable.IDLEntity {
// Protected Constructors
   protected UserException();
   protected UserException(String reason);
}
```

Hierarchy: Object→ Throwable(Serializable)→ Exception→ UserException(org.omg.CORBA.portable.IDLEntity(Serializable))

Subclasses: org.omg.CORBA.Bounds, PolicyError, UnknownUserException, WrongTransaction, org.omg.CORBA.DynAnyPackage.Invalid, org.omg.CORBA.DynAnyPackage.InvalidSeq, org.omg.CORBA.DynAnyPackage.InvalidValue, org.omg.CORBA.DynAnyPackage.TypeMismatch, org.omg.CORBA.ORBPackage.InconsistentTypeCode, org.omg.CORBA.ORBPackage.InvalidName, org.omg.CORBA.TypeCodePackage.BadKind, org.omg.CORBA.TypeCodePackage.Bounds, AlreadyBound, CannotProceed, org.omg.CosNaming.NamingContextPackage.InvalidName, NotEmpty, NotFound

ValueMember — Java 1.2

org.omg.CORBA — *serializable*

A class that represents a member of an object passed by value using the proposed Objects-by-Value extension to CORBA. ValueMember objects can create TypeCode objects for values with the ORB.create_value_tc() method.

```
public final class ValueMember implements org.omg.CORBA.portable.IDLEntity {
// Public Constructors
   public ValueMember();
   public ValueMember(String __name, String __id, String __defined_in, String __version, TypeCode __type,
                      IDLType __type_def, short __access);
// Public Instance Fields
   public short access;
   public String defined_in;
   public String id;
   public String name;
```

```
   public TypeCode type;
   public IDLType type_def;
   public String version;
}
```

Hierarchy: Object→ ValueMember(org.omg.CORBA.portable.IDLEntity(Serializable))

Passed To: ORB.create_value_tc()

WrongTransaction — Java 1.2

org.omg.CORBA — *serializable checked*

A user exception thrown when an attempt is made to get the response to a deferred method request from a different transaction than the original request. If a client makes an asynchronous Dynamic Invocation Interface method request using the Request.send_deferred() method within a given transaction and then later makes a call to the Request object's get_response() method from within a different transaction, a WrongTransaction exception is thrown. This exception can also be thrown if the ORB.get_next_response() method is called from a different transaction than the original method request.

```
public class WrongTransaction extends UserException {
// Public Constructors
   public WrongTransaction();
   public WrongTransaction(String reason);
}
```

Hierarchy: Object→ Throwable(Serializable)→ Exception→ UserException(org.omg.CORBA.portable.IDLEntity(Serializable))→ WrongTransaction

Thrown By: ORB.get_next_response(), Request.get_response()

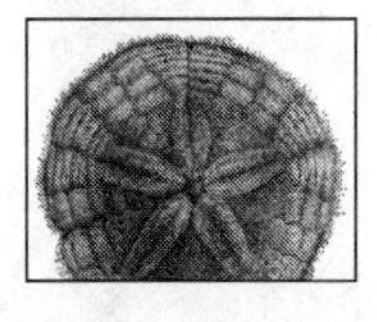

CHAPTER 31

The org.omg.CORBA.DynAnyPackage Package

The org.omg.CORBA.DynAnyPackage package defines the exceptions used by the org.omg.CORBA.DynAny interface and its subinterfaces. Figure 31-1 shows the class hierarchy of this package.

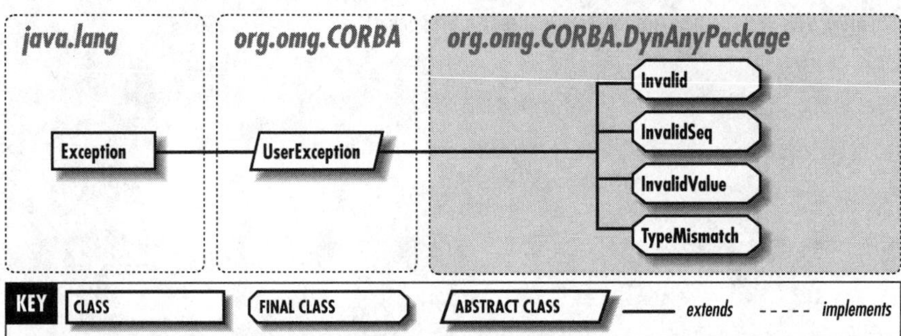

Figure 31-1: The org.omg.CORBA.DynAnyPackage package

Invalid — Java 1.2

org.omg.CORBA.DynAnyPackage — *serializable checked*

An exception thrown whenever a bad DynAny or Any object is encountered in a dynamic introspection operation.

```
public final class Invalid extends UserException {
// Public Constructors
   public Invalid();
   public Invalid(String reason);
}
```

Hierarchy: Object→ Throwable(Serializable)→ Exception→ UserException(org.omg.CORBA.portable.IDLEntity(Serializable))→ Invalid

Thrown By: DynAny.{assign(), from_any(), to_any()}

InvalidSeq **Java 1.2**

org.omg.CORBA.DynAnyPackage ***serializable checked***

An exception thrown whenever an invalid Java array is encountered in a dynamic introspection operation.

```
public final class InvalidSeq extends UserException {
// Public Constructors
   public InvalidSeq();
   public InvalidSeq(String reason);
}
```

Hierarchy: Object→ Throwable(Serializable)→ Exception→ UserException(org.omg.CORBA.portable.IDLEntity(Serializable))→ InvalidSeq

Thrown By: DynArray.set_elements(), DynSequence.set_elements(), DynStruct.set_members(), DynValue.set_members()

InvalidValue **Java 1.2**

org.omg.CORBA.DynAnyPackage ***serializable checked***

An exception thrown when a bad value is inserted into a DynAny object.

```
public final class InvalidValue extends UserException {
// Public Constructors
   public InvalidValue();
   public InvalidValue(String reason);
}
```

Hierarchy: Object→ Throwable(Serializable)→ Exception→ UserException(org.omg.CORBA.portable.IDLEntity(Serializable))→ InvalidValue

Thrown By: DynAny.{insert_any(), insert_boolean(), insert_char(), insert_double(), insert_float(), insert_long(), insert_longlong(), insert_octet(), insert_reference(), insert_short(), insert_string(), insert_typecode(), insert_ulong(), insert_ulonglong(), insert_ushort(), insert_val(), insert_wchar(), insert_wstring()}, DynFixed.set_value()

CORBA. DynAnyPkg

TypeMismatch **Java 1.2**

org.omg.CORBA.DynAnyPackage ***serializable checked***

An exception thrown when you ask for a value from a DynAny object that doesn't match the type that it contains.

```
public final class TypeMismatch extends UserException {
// Public Constructors
   public TypeMismatch();
   public TypeMismatch(String reason);
}
```

Hierarchy: Object→ Throwable(Serializable)→ Exception→ UserException(org.omg.CORBA.portable.IDLEntity(Serializable))→ TypeMismatch

Thrown By: DynAny.{get_any(), get_boolean(), get_char(), get_double(), get_float(), get_long(), get_longlong(), get_octet(), get_reference(), get_short(), get_string(), get_typecode(), get_ulong(), get_ulonglong(), get_ushort(), get_val(), get_wchar(), get_wstring()}

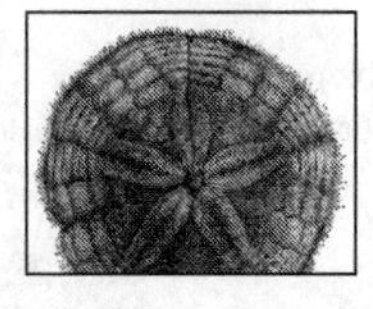

CHAPTER 32

The org.omg.CORBA.ORBPackage Package

The org.omg.CORBA.ORBPackage package defines the exceptions thrown by the org.omg.CORBA.ORB interface. Figure 32-1 shows the class hierarchy of this package.

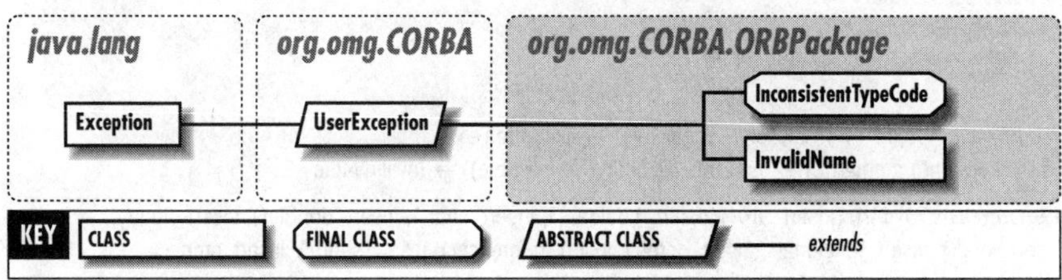

Figure 32-1: The org.omg.CORBA.ORBPackage package

InconsistentTypeCode — Java 1.2

org.omg.CORBA.ORBPackage — *serializable checked*

An exception thrown by the ORB.create_dyn_XXX() methods when the TypeCode argument does not match the type of the DynAny subclass requested.

```
public final class InconsistentTypeCode extends UserException {
// Public Constructors
   public InconsistentTypeCode();
   public InconsistentTypeCode(String reason);
}
```

Hierarchy: Object→ Throwable(Serializable)→ Exception→ UserException(org.omg.CORBA.portable.IDLEntity(Serializable))→ InconsistentTypeCode

Thrown By: ORB.{create_basic_dyn_any(), create_dyn_array(), create_dyn_enum(), create_dyn_sequence(), create_dyn_struct(), create_dyn_union()}

InvalidName **Java 1.2**

org.omg.CORBA.ORBPackage ***serializable checked***

An exception thrown by the ORB.resolve_initial_references() method when the name passed in does not have a corresponding object in the ORB's initial reference list.

```
public class InvalidName extends UserException {
// Public Constructors
   public InvalidName();
   public InvalidName(String reason);
}
```

Hierarchy: Object→ Throwable(Serializable)→ Exception→ UserException(org.omg.CORBA.portable.IDLEntity(Serializable))→ org.omg.CORBA.ORBPackage.InvalidName

Thrown By: ORB.resolve_initial_references()

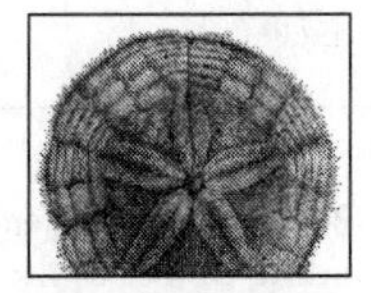

CHAPTER 33

The org.omg.CORBA.portable Package

The org.omg.CORBA.portable package contains interfaces, classes, and exceptions used by the portability layer of the CORBA API. The portability layer provides facilities that allow code to be shared between different ORB providers. Figure 33-1 shows the class hierarchy of this package.

ApplicationException — Java 1.2

org.omg.CORBA.portable — *serializable checked*

An exception is used by the Delegate and ObjectImpl layer of a stub to indicate that an exception was thrown during a remote method invocation. The ApplicationException provides an org.omg.CORBA.portable.InputStream that reads the marshalled exception object.

```
public class ApplicationException extends Exception {
// Public Constructors
   public ApplicationException(String id, org.omg.CORBA.portable.InputStream ins);
// Public Instance Methods
   public String getId();
   public org.omg.CORBA.portable.InputStream getInputStream();
}
```

Hierarchy: Object→ Throwable(Serializable)→ Exception→ ApplicationException

Thrown By: Delegate.invoke(), ObjectImpl._invoke()

Delegate — Java 1.2

org.omg.CORBA.portable

A Delegate is responsible for implementing all methods on org.omg.CORBA.Object. An Object contains a Delegate and forwards its methods to it. This allows for portability between ORB implementations, since an Object obtained from one ORB can contain a Delegate specific to that ORB, but the Object can still be used within another ORB.

```
public abstract class Delegate {
// Public Constructors
```

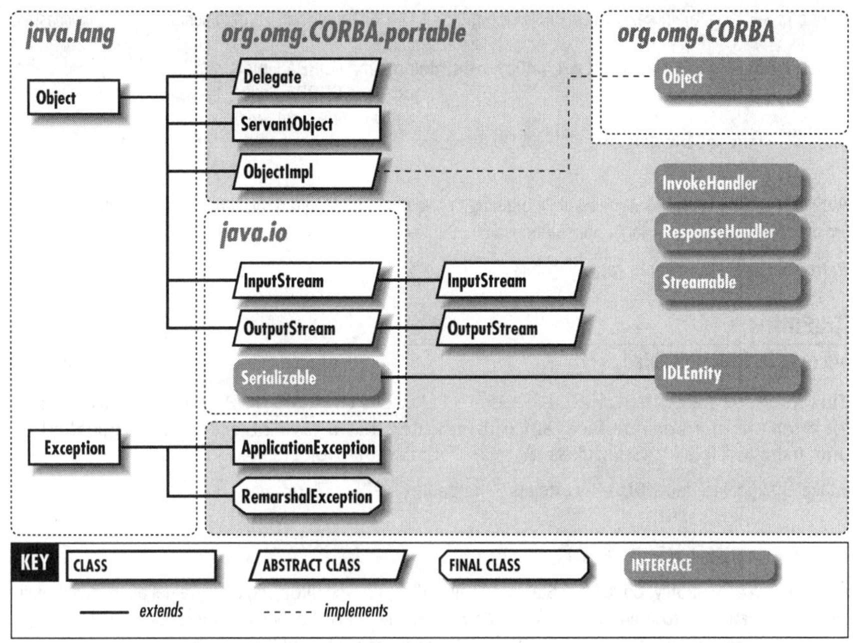

Figure 33-1: The org.omg.CORBA.portable package

```
    public Delegate();
// Public Instance Methods
    public abstract Request create_request(org.omg.CORBA.Object obj, org.omg.CORBA.Context ctx,
                                           String operation, NVList arg_list, NamedValue result);
    public abstract Request create_request(org.omg.CORBA.Object obj, org.omg.CORBA.Context ctx,
                                           String operation, NVList arg_list, NamedValue result,
                                           ExceptionList exclist, ContextList ctxlist);
    public abstract org.omg.CORBA.Object duplicate(org.omg.CORBA.Object obj);
    public boolean equals(org.omg.CORBA.Object self, Object obj);
    public DomainManager[ ] get_domain_managers(org.omg.CORBA.Object self);
    public org.omg.CORBA.Object get_interface_def(org.omg.CORBA.Object self);
    public org.omg.CORBA.Policy get_policy(org.omg.CORBA.Object self, int policy_type);
    public abstract int hash(org.omg.CORBA.Object obj, int max);
    public int hashCode(org.omg.CORBA.Object self);
    public org.omg.CORBA.portable.InputStream invoke(org.omg.CORBA.Object self,
                                                     org.omg.CORBA.portable.OutputStream output)
        throws ApplicationException, RemarshalException;
    public abstract boolean is_a(org.omg.CORBA.Object obj, String repository_id);
    public abstract boolean is_equivalent(org.omg.CORBA.Object obj, org.omg.CORBA.Object other);
    public boolean is_local(org.omg.CORBA.Object self);                              constant
    public abstract boolean non_existent(org.omg.CORBA.Object obj);
    public ORB orb(org.omg.CORBA.Object obj);
    public abstract void release(org.omg.CORBA.Object obj);
    public void releaseReply(org.omg.CORBA.Object self, org.omg.CORBA.portable.InputStream input);
    public abstract Request request(org.omg.CORBA.Object obj, String operation);
    public org.omg.CORBA.portable.OutputStream request(org.omg.CORBA.Object self, String operation,
                                                       boolean responseExpected);
    public void servant_postinvoke(org.omg.CORBA.Object self, ServantObject servant);   empty
```

CORBA. portable

```
    public ServantObject servant_preinvoke(org.omg.CORBA.Object self, String operation,          constant
                                           Class expectedType);
    public org.omg.CORBA.Object set_policy_override(org.omg.CORBA.Object self,
                                                    org.omg.CORBA.Policy[ ] policies,
                                                    SetOverrideType set_add);
    public String toString(org.omg.CORBA.Object self);
}
```

Passed To: ObjectImpl._set_delegate(), org.omg.CosNaming._BindingIteratorStub._BindingIteratorStub(), org.omg.CosNaming._NamingContextStub._NamingContextStub()

Returned By: ObjectImpl._get_delegate()

IDLEntity — Java 1.2

org.omg.CORBA.portable — *serializable*

This interface marks certain IDL-generated classes. The RMI/IIOP extensions to CORBA look for this marker interface, since it indicates that a Java object being marshalled or unmarshalled has a helper class that can serialize the object.

```
public abstract interface IDLEntity extends Serializable {
}
```

Hierarchy: (IDLEntity(Serializable))

Implementations: Any, CompletionStatus, DefinitionKind, IDLType, IRObject, NameValuePair, ServiceDetail, ServiceInformation, SetOverrideType, StructMember, TypeCode, UnionMember, UserException, ValueMember, org.omg.CosNaming.Binding, org.omg.CosNaming.BindingIterator, org.omg.CosNaming.BindingType, org.omg.CosNaming.NameComponent, org.omg.CosNaming.NamingContext, AlreadyBound, CannotProceed, org.omg.CosNaming.NamingContextPackage.InvalidName, NotEmpty, NotFound, NotFoundReason

InputStream — Java 1.2

org.omg.CORBA.portable

An InputStream is used for unmarshalling IDL-generated objects. The InputStream provides a series of read_XXX() methods for unmarshalling basic IDL types.

```
public abstract class InputStream extends java.io.InputStream {
// Public Constructors
    public InputStream();
// Public Instance Methods
    public ORB orb();
    public abstract Any read_any();
    public abstract boolean read_boolean();
    public abstract void read_boolean_array(boolean[ ] value, int offset, int length);
    public abstract char read_char();
    public abstract void read_char_array(char[ ] value, int offset, int length);
    public org.omg.CORBA.Context read_Context();
    public abstract double read_double();
    public abstract void read_double_array(double[ ] value, int offset, int length);
    public java.math.BigDecimal read_fixed();
    public abstract float read_float();
    public abstract void read_float_array(float[ ] value, int offset, int length);
    public abstract int read_long();
    public abstract void read_long_array(int[ ] value, int offset, int length);
    public abstract long read_longlong();
    public abstract void read_longlong_array(long[ ] value, int offset, int length);
    public abstract org.omg.CORBA.Object read_Object();
    public org.omg.CORBA.Object read_Object(Class clz);
```

```
    public abstract byte read_octet();
    public abstract void read_octet_array(byte[ ] value, int offset, int length);
    public abstract short read_short();
    public abstract void read_short_array(short[ ] value, int offset, int length);
    public abstract String read_string();
    public abstract TypeCode read_TypeCode();
    public abstract int read_ulong();
    public abstract void read_ulong_array(int[ ] value, int offset, int length);
    public abstract long read_ulonglong();
    public abstract void read_ulonglong_array(long[ ] value, int offset, int length);
    public abstract short read_ushort();
    public abstract void read_ushort_array(short[ ] value, int offset, int length);
    public abstract char read_wchar();
    public abstract void read_wchar_array(char[ ] value, int offset, int length);
    public abstract String read_wstring();
// Public methods overriding InputStream
    public int read() throws IOException;
// Deprecated Public Methods
#   public abstract org.omg.CORBA.Principal read_Principal();
}
```

Hierarchy: Object→ java.io.InputStream→ org.omg.CORBA.portable.InputStream

Passed To: Too many methods to list.

Returned By: Any.create_input_stream(), ApplicationException.getInputStream(), Delegate.invoke(), ObjectImpl._invoke(), org.omg.CORBA.portable.OutputStream.create_input_stream()

InvokeHandler — Java 1.2

org.omg.CORBA.portable

This interface is used during dynamic method invocations. An InvokeHandler is responsible, through its _invoke() method, for finding a named method, reading marshalled arguments from the given org.omg.CORBA.portable.InputStream, and returning the response in the form of an org.omg.CORBA.portable.OutputStream generated from the given ResponseHandler.

```
public abstract interface InvokeHandler {
// Public Instance Methods
    public abstract org.omg.CORBA.portable.OutputStream _invoke(String method,
                                                    org.omg.CORBA.portable.InputStream input,
                                                    ResponseHandler handler)
        throws org.omg.CORBA.SystemException;
}
```

ObjectImpl — Java 1.2

org.omg.CORBA.portable

ObjectImpl is the base class for all stub classes; it provides default implementations for the methods declared in the orb.omg.CORBA.Object interface. ObjectImpl contains a Delegate object that acts as a proxy for the Object methods.

```
public abstract class ObjectImpl implements org.omg.CORBA.Object {
// Public Constructors
    public ObjectImpl();
// Public Instance Methods
    public Delegate _get_delegate();
    public abstract String[ ] _ids();
```

CORBA. portable

```
    public org.omg.CORBA.portable.InputStream _invoke(org.omg.CORBA.portable.OutputStream output)
        throws ApplicationException, RemarshalException;
    public boolean _is_local();
    public ORB _orb();
    public void _releaseReply(org.omg.CORBA.portable.InputStream input);
    public org.omg.CORBA.portable.OutputStream _request(String operation, boolean responseExpected);
    public void _servant_postinvoke(ServantObject servant);
    public ServantObject _servant_preinvoke(String operation, Class expectedType);
    public void _set_delegate(Delegate delegate);
// Methods implementing Object
    public Request _create_request(org.omg.CORBA.Context ctx, String operation, NVList arg_list,
                                   NamedValue result);
    public Request _create_request(org.omg.CORBA.Context ctx, String operation, NVList arg_list,
                                   NamedValue result, ExceptionList exceptions, ContextList contexts);
    public org.omg.CORBA.Object _duplicate();
    public DomainManager[ ] _get_domain_managers();
    public org.omg.CORBA.Object _get_interface_def();
    public org.omg.CORBA.Policy _get_policy(int policy_type);
    public int _hash(int maximum);
    public boolean _is_a(String repository_id);
    public boolean _is_equivalent(org.omg.CORBA.Object that);
    public boolean _non_existent();
    public void _release();
    public Request _request(String operation);
    public org.omg.CORBA.Object _set_policy_override(org.omg.CORBA.Policy[ ] policies,
                                                     SetOverrideType set_add);
// Public methods overriding Object
    public boolean equals(Object obj);
    public int hashCode();
    public String toString();
}
```

Hierarchy: Object→ ObjectImpl(org.omg.CORBA.Object)

Subclasses: DynamicImplementation, org.omg.CosNaming._BindingIteratorStub, org.omg.CosNaming._NamingContextStub

OutputStream — Java 1.2

org.omg.CORBA.portable

An OutputStream marshals IDL-generated objects. The OutputStream provides a series of write_XXX() methods for marshalling basic IDL types.

```
public abstract class OutputStream extends java.io.OutputStream {
// Public Constructors
    public OutputStream();
// Public Instance Methods
    public abstract org.omg.CORBA.portable.InputStream create_input_stream();
    public ORB orb();
    public abstract void write_any(Any value);
    public abstract void write_boolean(boolean value);
    public abstract void write_boolean_array(boolean[ ] value, int offset, int length);
    public abstract void write_char(char value);
    public abstract void write_char_array(char[ ] value, int offset, int length);
    public void write_Context(org.omg.CORBA.Context ctx, ContextList contexts);
    public abstract void write_double(double value);
    public abstract void write_double_array(double[ ] value, int offset, int length);
    public void write_fixed(java.math.BigDecimal value);
```

```
    public abstract void write_float(float value);
    public abstract void write_float_array(float[ ] value, int offset, int length);
    public abstract void write_long(int value);
    public abstract void write_long_array(int[ ] value, int offset, int length);
    public abstract void write_longlong(long value);
    public abstract void write_longlong_array(long[ ] value, int offset, int length);
    public abstract void write_Object(org.omg.CORBA.Object value);
    public abstract void write_octet(byte value);
    public abstract void write_octet_array(byte[ ] value, int offset, int length);
    public abstract void write_short(short value);
    public abstract void write_short_array(short[ ] value, int offset, int length);
    public abstract void write_string(String value);
    public abstract void write_TypeCode(TypeCode value);
    public abstract void write_ulong(int value);
    public abstract void write_ulong_array(int[ ] value, int offset, int length);
    public abstract void write_ulonglong(long value);
    public abstract void write_ulonglong_array(long[ ] value, int offset, int length);
    public abstract void write_ushort(short value);
    public abstract void write_ushort_array(short[ ] value, int offset, int length);
    public abstract void write_wchar(char value);
    public abstract void write_wchar_array(char[ ] value, int offset, int length);
    public abstract void write_wstring(String value);
// Public methods overriding OutputStream
    public void write(int b) throws IOException;
// Deprecated Public Methods
#   public abstract void write_Principal(org.omg.CORBA.Principal value);
}
```

Hierarchy: Object→ java.io.OutputStream→ org.omg.CORBA.portable.OutputStream

Passed To: Too many methods to list.

Returned By: Any.create_output_stream(), ORB.create_output_stream(), Delegate.request(), InvokeHandler._invoke(), ObjectImpl._request(), ResponseHandler.{createExceptionReply(), createReply()}

RemarshalException — Java 1.2

org.omg.CORBA.portable — *serializable checked*

An exception thrown by the Delegate._invoke() and ObjectImpl.invoke() methods when a marshalling error occurs during the method invocation.

```
public final class RemarshalException extends Exception {
// Public Constructors
    public RemarshalException();
}
```

Hierarchy: Object→ Throwable(Serializable)→ Exception→ RemarshalException

Thrown By: Delegate.invoke(), ObjectImpl._invoke()

ResponseHandler — Java 1.2

org.omg.CORBA.portable

A ResponseHandler is responsible for generating an org.omg.CORBA.portable.OutputStream that is used by an object servant to write marshalled method responses (return value or exception).

```
public abstract interface ResponseHandler {
// Public Instance Methods
    public abstract org.omg.CORBA.portable.OutputStream createExceptionReply();
```

```
    public abstract org.omg.CORBA.portable.OutputStream createReply();
}
```

Passed To: InvokeHandler._invoke()

ServantObject **Java 1.2**

org.omg.CORBA.portable

ServantObject is a wrapper for an object that can handle method requests for a remote object. The ObjectImpl class defers method requests to a ServantObject acquired from its internal Delegate.

```
public class ServantObject {
// Public Constructors
    public ServantObject();
// Public Instance Fields
    public Object servant;
}
```

Passed To: Delegate.servant_postinvoke(), ObjectImpl._servant_postinvoke()

Returned By: Delegate.servant_preinvoke(), ObjectImpl._servant_preinvoke()

Streamable **Java 1.2**

org.omg.CORBA.portable

All holder classes extend this interface, which defines methods for marshalling and unmarshalling objects of the type corresponding to the holder class.

```
public abstract interface Streamable {
// Public Instance Methods
    public abstract void _read(org.omg.CORBA.portable.InputStream istream);
    public abstract TypeCode _type();
    public abstract void _write(org.omg.CORBA.portable.OutputStream ostream);
}
```

Implementations: Too many classes to list.

Passed To: Any.insert_Streamable()

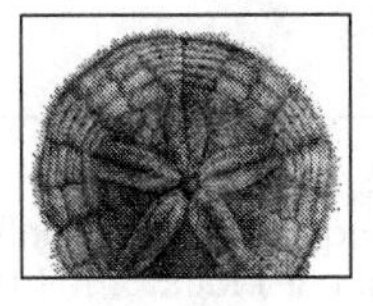

CHAPTER 34

The org.omg.CORBA.TypeCodePackage Package

The org.omg.CORBA.TypeCodePackage package defines exceptions that are thrown by the org.omg.CORBA.TypeCode class. Figure 34-1 shows the class hierarchy of this package.

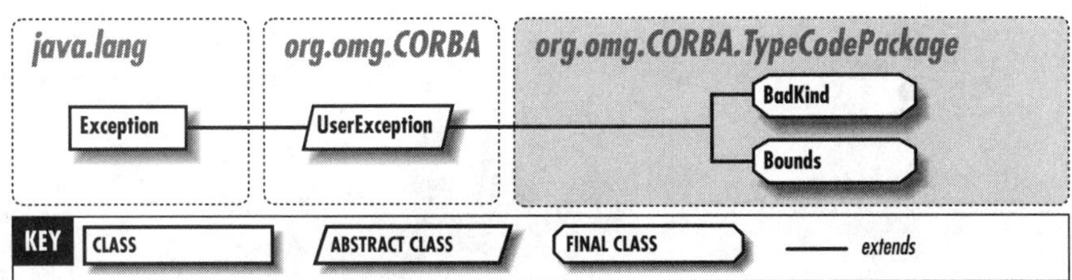

Figure 34-1: The org.omg.CORBA.TypeCodePackage package

BadKind **Java 1.2**

org.omg.CORBA.TypeCodePackage ***serializable checked***

An exception thrown when a method is called on a TypeCode object that isn't valid for the type it represents.

```
public final class BadKind extends UserException {
// Public Constructors
   public BadKind();
   public BadKind(String reason);
}
```

Hierarchy: Object→ Throwable(Serializable)→ Exception→ UserException(org.omg.CORBA.portable.IDLEntity(Serializable))→ BadKind

Thrown By: TypeCode.{concrete_base_type(), content_type(), default_index(), discriminator_type(), fixed_digits(), fixed_scale(), id(), length(), member_count(), member_label(), member_name(), member_type(), member_visibility(), name(), type_modifier()}

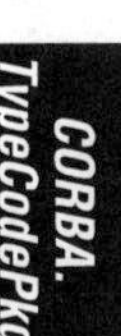

Bounds — Java 1.2

org.omg.CORBA.TypeCodePackage — *serializable checked*

An exception thrown when you request member information from a TypeCode using an index that is beyond the valid member index of the type.

```
public final class Bounds extends UserException {
// Public Constructors
    public Bounds();
    public Bounds(String reason);
}
```

Hierarchy: Object→ Throwable(Serializable)→ Exception→ UserException(org.omg.CORBA.portable.IDLEntity(Serializable))→ org.omg.CORBA.TypeCodePackage.Bounds

Thrown By: TypeCode.{member_label(), member_name(), member_type()}

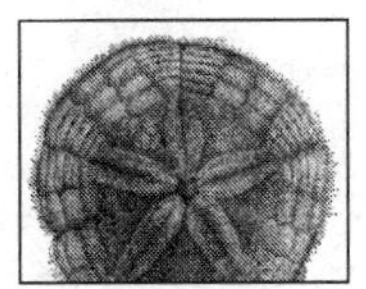

CHAPTER 35

The org.omg.CosNaming Package

The org.omg.CosNaming package is a Java mapping of the IDL interfaces defined by the CORBA Naming Service. The principal interface in the service is the NamingContext, which represents a directory of named object references. The package also contains various support classes that allow you to iterate through an NamingContext and query its contents. Figure 35-1 shows the class hierarchy of this package.

_BindingIteratorImplBase **Java 1.2**

org.omg.CosNaming *serializable*

The IDL-generated skeleton class for the BindingIterator interface.

```
public abstract class _BindingIteratorImplBase extends org.omg.CORBA.DynamicImplementation
        implements BindingIterator {
// Public Constructors
    public _BindingIteratorImplBase();
// Methods implementing BindingIterator
    public abstract void destroy();
    public abstract boolean next_n(int how_many, BindingListHolder bl);
    public abstract boolean next_one(BindingHolder b);
// Public methods overriding DynamicImplementation
    public void invoke(org.omg.CORBA.ServerRequest r);
// Public methods overriding ObjectImpl
    public String[ ] _ids();
}
```

Hierarchy: Object→ org.omg.CORBA.portable.ObjectImpl(org.omg.CORBA.Object)→ org.omg.CORBA.DynamicImplementation→ _BindingIteratorImplBase(BindingIterator(org.omg.CORBA.Object, org.omg.CORBA.portable.IDLEntity(Serializable)))

_BindingIteratorStub **Java 1.2**

org.omg.CosNaming *serializable*

The IDL-generated stub class for the BindingIterator interface.

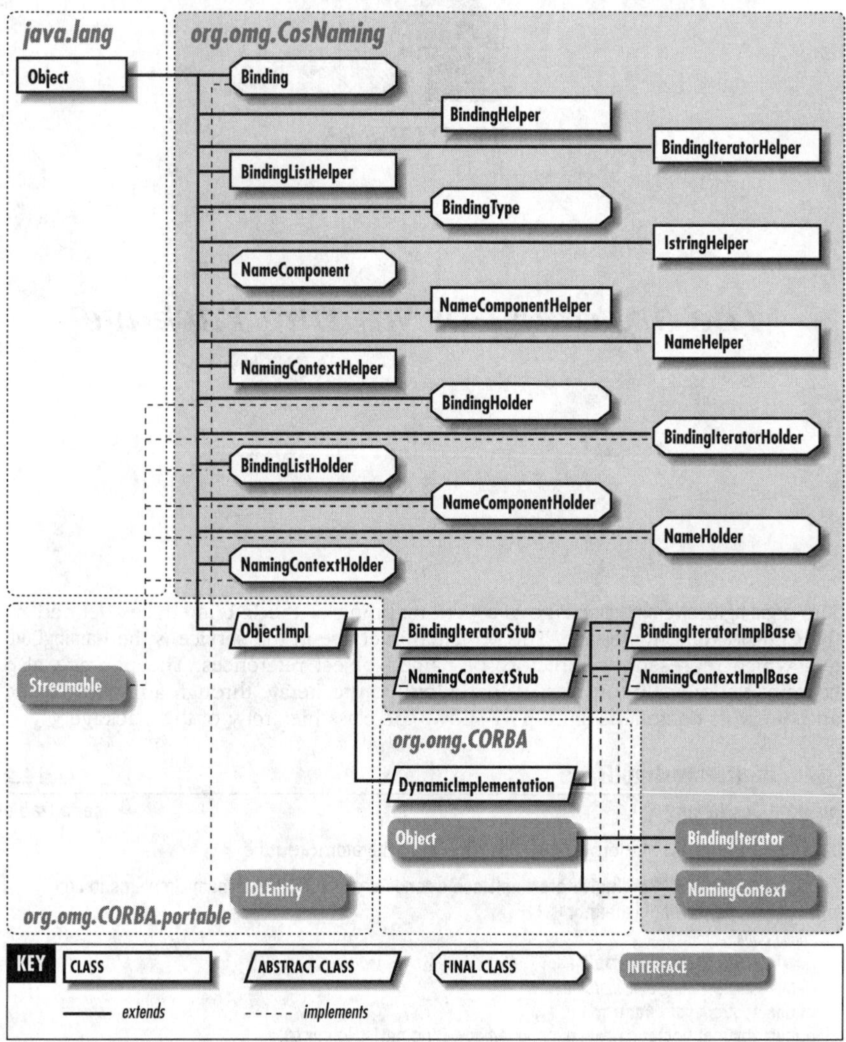

Figure 35-1: The org.omg.CosNaming package

```
public class _BindingIteratorStub extends org.omg.CORBA.portable.ObjectImpl
        implements BindingIterator {
// Public Constructors
   public _BindingIteratorStub(org.omg.CORBA.portable.Delegate d);
// Methods implementing BindingIterator
   public void destroy();
   public boolean next_n(int how_many, BindingListHolder bl);
   public boolean next_one(BindingHolder b);
// Public methods overriding ObjectImpl
   public String[ ] _ids();
}
```

Hierarchy: Object→ org.omg.CORBA.portable.ObjectImpl(org.omg.CORBA.Object)→ _BindingIteratorStub(BindingIterator(org.omg.CORBA.Object, org.omg.CORBA.portable.IDLEntity(Serializable)))

_NamingContextImplBase Java 1.2

org.omg.CosNaming *serializable*

The IDL-generated skeleton class for the NamingContext interface.

```
public abstract class _NamingContextImplBase extends org.omg.CORBA.DynamicImplementation
        implements NamingContext {
// Public Constructors
   public _NamingContextImplBase();
// Methods implementing NamingContext
   public abstract void bind(NameComponent[ ] n, org.omg.CORBA.Object obj) throws NotFound,
        CannotProceed, org.omg.CosNaming.NamingContextPackage.InvalidName;
   public abstract void bind_context(NameComponent[ ] n, NamingContext nc) throws NotFound,
        CannotProceed, org.omg.CosNaming.NamingContextPackage.InvalidName;
   public abstract NamingContext bind_new_context(NameComponent[ ] n) throws NotFound,
        AlreadyBound, CannotProceed;
   public abstract void destroy( ) throws NotEmpty;
   public abstract void list(int how_many, BindingListHolder bl, BindingIteratorHolder bi);
   public abstract NamingContext new_context();
   public abstract void rebind(NameComponent[ ] n, org.omg.CORBA.Object obj) throws NotFound,
        CannotProceed, org.omg.CosNaming.NamingContextPackage.InvalidName;
   public abstract void rebind_context(NameComponent[ ] n, NamingContext nc) throws NotFound,
        CannotProceed, org.omg.CosNaming.NamingContextPackage.InvalidName;
   public abstract org.omg.CORBA.Object resolve(NameComponent[ ] n) throws NotFound,
        CannotProceed, org.omg.CosNaming.NamingContextPackage.InvalidName;
   public abstract void unbind(NameComponent[ ] n) throws NotFound, CannotProceed,
        org.omg.CosNaming.NamingContextPackage.InvalidName;
// Public methods overriding DynamicImplementation
   public void invoke(org.omg.CORBA.ServerRequest r);
// Public methods overriding ObjectImpl
   public String[ ] _ids( );
}
```

Hierarchy: Object→ org.omg.CORBA.portable.ObjectImpl(org.omg.CORBA.Object)→ org.omg.CORBA.DynamicImplementation→ _NamingContextImplBase(NamingContext(org.omg.CORBA.Object, org.omg.CORBA.portable.IDLEntity(Serializable)))

_NamingContextStub Java 1.2

org.omg.CosNaming *serializable*

The IDL-generated stub class for the NamingContext interface.

```
public class _NamingContextStub extends org.omg.CORBA.portable.ObjectImpl
        implements NamingContext {
// Public Constructors
   public _NamingContextStub(org.omg.CORBA.portable.Delegate d);
// Methods implementing NamingContext
   public void bind(NameComponent[ ] n, org.omg.CORBA.Object obj) throws NotFound, CannotProceed,
        org.omg.CosNaming.NamingContextPackage.InvalidName;
   public void bind_context(NameComponent[ ] n, NamingContext nc) throws NotFound, CannotProceed,
        org.omg.CosNaming.NamingContextPackage.InvalidName;
   public NamingContext bind_new_context(NameComponent[ ] n) throws NotFound, AlreadyBound,
        CannotProceed;
   public void destroy( ) throws NotEmpty;
```

```
    public void list(int how_many, BindingListHolder bl, BindingIteratorHolder bi);
    public NamingContext new_context();
    public void rebind(NameComponent[ ] n, org.omg.CORBA.Object obj) throws NotFound,
        CannotProceed, org.omg.CosNaming.NamingContextPackage.InvalidName;
    public void rebind_context(NameComponent[ ] n, NamingContext nc) throws NotFound,
        CannotProceed, org.omg.CosNaming.NamingContextPackage.InvalidName;
    public org.omg.CORBA.Object resolve(NameComponent[ ] n) throws NotFound, CannotProceed,
        org.omg.CosNaming.NamingContextPackage.InvalidName;
    public void unbind(NameComponent[ ] n) throws NotFound, CannotProceed,
        org.omg.CosNaming.NamingContextPackage.InvalidName;
// Public methods overriding ObjectImpl
    public String[ ] _ids();
}
```

Hierarchy: Object→ org.omg.CORBA.portable.ObjectImpl(org.omg.CORBA.Object)→ _NamingContextStub(NamingContext(org.omg.CORBA.Object, org.omg.CORBA.portable.IDLEntity(Serializable)))

Binding — Java 1.2

org.omg.CosNaming — *serializable*

A Binding describes a name binding within a naming context. It contains a NameComponent array, which represents the name associated with the binding, and a BindingType, which indicates whether the bound object is a regular object or a NamingContext.

```
public final class Binding implements org.omg.CORBA.portable.IDLEntity {
// Public Constructors
    public Binding();
    public Binding(NameComponent[ ] __binding_name, BindingType __binding_type);
// Public Instance Fields
    public NameComponent[ ] binding_name;
    public BindingType binding_type;
}
```

Hierarchy: Object→ org.omg.CosNaming.Binding(org.omg.CORBA.portable.IDLEntity(Serializable))

Passed To: BindingHelper.{insert(), write()}, BindingHolder.BindingHolder(), BindingListHelper.{insert(), write()}, BindingListHolder.BindingListHolder()

Returned By: BindingHelper.{extract(), read()}, BindingListHelper.{extract(), read()}

Type Of: BindingHolder.value, BindingListHolder.value

BindingHelper — Java 1.2

org.omg.CosNaming

The helper class for the Binding class.

```
public class BindingHelper {
// No Constructor
// Public Class Methods
    public static org.omg.CosNaming.Binding extract(org.omg.CORBA.Any a);
    public static String id();
    public static void insert(org.omg.CORBA.Any a, org.omg.CosNaming.Binding that);
    public static org.omg.CosNaming.Binding read(org.omg.CORBA.portable.InputStream in);
    public static org.omg.CORBA.TypeCode type();                              synchronized
    public static void write(org.omg.CORBA.portable.OutputStream out,
                             org.omg.CosNaming.Binding that);
}
```

BindingHolder **Java 1.2**

org.omg.CosNaming

The holder class for out and inout IDL method arguments that are mapped to Java Binding objects.

```
public final class BindingHolder implements org.omg.CORBA.portable.Streamable {
// Public Constructors
   public BindingHolder();
   public BindingHolder(org.omg.CosNaming.Binding __arg);
// Methods implementing Streamable
   public void _read(org.omg.CORBA.portable.InputStream in);
   public org.omg.CORBA.TypeCode _type();
   public void _write(org.omg.CORBA.portable.OutputStream out);
// Public Instance Fields
   public org.omg.CosNaming.Binding value;
}
```

Hierarchy: Object→ BindingHolder(org.omg.CORBA.portable.Streamable)

Passed To: _BindingIteratorImplBase.next_one(), _BindingIteratorStub.next_one(), BindingIterator.next_one()

BindingIterator **Java 1.2**

org.omg.CosNaming ***serializable***

If you request a set of name/object bindings from a NamingContext using its list() method, the BindingListHolder you pass in is filled with any results, up to its maximum capacity. If the NamingContext contains more bound objects than the binding array you provide can hold, the BindingIteratorHolder argument is initialized to contain a BindingIterator that allows you to iterate through the rest of the bindings in the context. You can iterate through the remainder of the bindings one at a time, using the next_one() method, or in sets, using the next_n() method.

```
public abstract interface BindingIterator extends org.omg.CORBA.Object,
        org.omg.CORBA.portable.IDLEntity {
// Public Instance Methods
   public abstract void destroy();
   public abstract boolean next_n(int how_many, BindingListHolder bl);
   public abstract boolean next_one(BindingHolder b);
}
```

Hierarchy: (BindingIterator(org.omg.CORBA.Object, org.omg.CORBA.portable.IDLEntity(Serializable)))

Implementations: _BindingIteratorImplBase, _BindingIteratorStub

Passed To: BindingIteratorHelper.{insert(), write()}, BindingIteratorHolder.BindingIteratorHolder()

Returned By: BindingIteratorHelper.{extract(), narrow(), read()}

Type Of: BindingIteratorHolder.value

BindingIteratorHelper **Java 1.2**

org.omg.CosNaming

The helper class for the BindingIterator class.

```
public class BindingIteratorHelper {
// No Constructor
// Public Class Methods
   public static BindingIterator extract(org.omg.CORBA.Any a);
```

```
    public static String id();
    public static void insert(org.omg.CORBA.Any a, BindingIterator that);
    public static BindingIterator narrow(org.omg.CORBA.Object that)
        throws org.omg.CORBA.BAD_PARAM;
    public static BindingIterator read(org.omg.CORBA.portable.InputStream in);
    public static org.omg.CORBA.TypeCode type();                              synchronized
    public static void write(org.omg.CORBA.portable.OutputStream out, BindingIterator that);
}
```

BindingIteratorHolder — Java 1.2

org.omg.CosNaming

The holder class for out and inout IDL method arguments that are mapped to Java BindingIterator objects.

```
public final class BindingIteratorHolder implements org.omg.CORBA.portable.Streamable {
// Public Constructors
    public BindingIteratorHolder();
    public BindingIteratorHolder(BindingIterator __arg);
// Methods implementing Streamable
    public void _read(org.omg.CORBA.portable.InputStream in);
    public org.omg.CORBA.TypeCode _type();
    public void _write(org.omg.CORBA.portable.OutputStream out);
// Public Instance Fields
    public BindingIterator value;
}
```

Hierarchy: Object→ BindingIteratorHolder(org.omg.CORBA.portable.Streamable)

Passed To: _NamingContextImplBase.list(), _NamingContextStub.list(), NamingContext.list()

BindingListHelper — Java 1.2

org.omg.CosNaming

The helper class for the BindingList class, which is the Java mapping for Binding arrays.

```
public class BindingListHelper {
// No Constructor
// Public Class Methods
    public static org.omg.CosNaming.Binding[ ] extract(org.omg.CORBA.Any a);
    public static String id();
    public static void insert(org.omg.CORBA.Any a, org.omg.CosNaming.Binding[ ] that);
    public static org.omg.CosNaming.Binding[ ] read(org.omg.CORBA.portable.InputStream in);
    public static org.omg.CORBA.TypeCode type();                              synchronized
    public static void write(org.omg.CORBA.portable.OutputStream out,
                             org.omg.CosNaming.Binding[ ] that);
}
```

BindingListHolder — Java 1.2

org.omg.CosNaming

The holder class for out and inout IDL method arguments that are mapped to Java BindingList objects.

```
public final class BindingListHolder implements org.omg.CORBA.portable.Streamable {
// Public Constructors
    public BindingListHolder();
    public BindingListHolder(org.omg.CosNaming.Binding[ ] __arg);
```

```
// Methods implementing Streamable
   public void _read(org.omg.CORBA.portable.InputStream in);
   public org.omg.CORBA.TypeCode _type();
   public void _write(org.omg.CORBA.portable.OutputStream out);
// Public Instance Fields
   public org.omg.CosNaming.Binding[ ] value;
}
```

Hierarchy: Object→ BindingListHolder(org.omg.CORBA.portable.Streamable)

Passed To: _BindingIteratorImplBase.next_n(), _BindingIteratorStub.next_n(), _NamingContextImplBase.list(), _NamingContextStub.list(), BindingIterator.next_n(), NamingContext.list()

BindingType — Java 1.2

org.omg.CosNaming — *serializable*

A BindingType indicates what type of object is involved in a given binding, a regular object or a NamingContext. Its value() method returns an int value that can be compared to the two static int values on the class, to differentiate between these two cases.

```
public final class BindingType implements org.omg.CORBA.portable.IDLEntity {
// No Constructor
// Public Constants
   public static final int _ncontext;                                    =1
   public static final int _nobject;                                     =0
   public static final BindingType ncontext;
   public static final BindingType nobject;
// Public Class Methods
   public static final BindingType from_int(int i) throws org.omg.CORBA.BAD_PARAM;
// Public Instance Methods
   public int value();
}
```

Hierarchy: Object→ BindingType(org.omg.CORBA.portable.IDLEntity(Serializable))

Passed To: org.omg.CosNaming.Binding.Binding(), BindingTypeHelper.{insert(), write()}, BindingTypeHolder.BindingTypeHolder()

Returned By: BindingType.from_int(), BindingTypeHelper.{extract(), read()}

Type Of: org.omg.CosNaming.Binding.binding_type, BindingType.{ncontext, nobject}, BindingTypeHolder.value

BindingTypeHelper — Java 1.2

org.omg.CosNaming

The helper class for the BindingType class.

```
public class BindingTypeHelper {
// No Constructor
// Public Class Methods
   public static BindingType extract(org.omg.CORBA.Any a);
   public static String id();
   public static void insert(org.omg.CORBA.Any a, BindingType that);
   public static BindingType read(org.omg.CORBA.portable.InputStream in);
   public static org.omg.CORBA.TypeCode type();                     synchronized
   public static void write(org.omg.CORBA.portable.OutputStream out, BindingType that);
}
```

BindingTypeHolder **Java 1.2**

org.omg.CosNaming

The holder class for out and inout IDL method arguments that are mapped to Java BindingType objects.

```
public final class BindingTypeHolder implements org.omg.CORBA.portable.Streamable {
// Public Constructors
   public BindingTypeHolder();
   public BindingTypeHolder(BindingType __arg);
// Methods implementing Streamable
   public void _read(org.omg.CORBA.portable.InputStream in);
   public org.omg.CORBA.TypeCode _type();
   public void _write(org.omg.CORBA.portable.OutputStream out);
// Public Instance Fields
   public BindingType value;
}
```

Hierarchy: Object→ BindingTypeHolder(org.omg.CORBA.portable.Streamable)

IstringHelper **Java 1.2**

org.omg.CosNaming

The helper class for the Istring class. The Istring class is used in the Naming Service as a placeholder for an internationalized string type. (Note that IString is just a typedef in the CORBA specification at this point; the OMG hasn't defined an internationalized string interface yet. That's why you cannot find a definition for IString anywhere in Java IDL.)

```
public class IstringHelper {
// No Constructor
// Public Class Methods
   public static String extract(org.omg.CORBA.Any a);
   public static String id();
   public static void insert(org.omg.CORBA.Any a, String that);
   public static String read(org.omg.CORBA.portable.InputStream in);
   public static org.omg.CORBA.TypeCode type();                    synchronized
   public static void write(org.omg.CORBA.portable.OutputStream out, String that);
}
```

NameComponent **Java 1.2**

org.omg.CosNaming ***serializable***

A NameComponent represents one element in a name binding for an object. The name of an object in a NamingContext is composed of a sequence of NameComponent objects. Each NameComponent represents a subcontext that the object falls within, and the last NameComponent is the object's name within its closest context. Consider an object bound to the name apple-146 within a context bound to the name fruit within the root context. This object has two NameComponent objects in its fully qualified name within the root context: fruit, apple-146.

A NameComponent contains an id member, which represents the name associated with the component, and a kind member, which can optionally be used to further differentiate branches in a naming directory. The Naming Service does not consider the kind field on NameComponent objects when determining the uniqueness of name bindings, so each ordered list of id fields extracted from a fully qualified name binding must be unique.

```
public final class NameComponent implements org.omg.CORBA.portable.IDLEntity {
// Public Constructors
```

```
    public NameComponent();
    public NameComponent(String __id, String __kind);
// Public Instance Fields
    public String id;
    public String kind;
}
```

Hierarchy: Object→ NameComponent(org.omg.CORBA.portable.IDLEntity(Serializable))

Passed To: Too many methods to list.

Returned By: NameComponentHelper.{extract(), read()}, NameHelper.{extract(), read()}

Type Of: org.omg.CosNaming.Binding.binding_name, NameComponentHolder.value, NameHolder.value, CannotProceed.rest_of_name, NotFound.rest_of_name

NameComponentHelper — Java 1.2

org.omg.CosNaming

The helper class for the NameComponent class.

```
public class NameComponentHelper {
// No Constructor
// Public Class Methods
    public static NameComponent extract(org.omg.CORBA.Any a);
    public static String id();
    public static void insert(org.omg.CORBA.Any a, NameComponent that);
    public static NameComponent read(org.omg.CORBA.portable.InputStream in);
    public static org.omg.CORBA.TypeCode type();                          synchronized
    public static void write(org.omg.CORBA.portable.OutputStream out, NameComponent that);
}
```

NameComponentHolder — Java 1.2

org.omg.CosNaming

The holder class for out and inout IDL method arguments that are mapped to NameComponent objects.

```
public final class NameComponentHolder implements org.omg.CORBA.portable.Streamable {
// Public Constructors
    public NameComponentHolder();
    public NameComponentHolder(NameComponent __arg);
// Methods implementing Streamable
    public void _read(org.omg.CORBA.portable.InputStream in);
    public org.omg.CORBA.TypeCode _type();
    public void _write(org.omg.CORBA.portable.OutputStream out);
// Public Instance Fields
    public NameComponent value;
}
```

Hierarchy: Object→ NameComponentHolder(org.omg.CORBA.portable.Streamable)

NameHelper — Java 1.2

org.omg.CosNaming

The helper class generated for the Name typedef declared in the IDL module for the Naming Service specification. The IDL typedef associates the type Name to a sequence of NameComponent objects.

```
public class NameHelper {
// No Constructor
// Public Class Methods
   public static NameComponent[ ] extract(org.omg.CORBA.Any a);
   public static String id();
   public static void insert(org.omg.CORBA.Any a, NameComponent[ ] that);
   public static NameComponent[ ] read(org.omg.CORBA.portable.InputStream in);
   public static org.omg.CORBA.TypeCode type();                                    synchronized
   public static void write(org.omg.CORBA.portable.OutputStream out, NameComponent[ ] that);
}
```

NameHolder — Java 1.2

org.omg.CosNaming

The holder class for out and inout IDL method arguments that are typed as an IDL Name. An IDL typedef in the Naming Service specification associates the type Name to a sequence of NameComponent objects, so any in arguments using this type are mapped to NameComponent arrays in Java, and any out or inout arguments are mapped to NameHolder objects.

```
public final class NameHolder implements org.omg.CORBA.portable.Streamable {
// Public Constructors
   public NameHolder();
   public NameHolder(NameComponent[ ] __arg);
// Methods implementing Streamable
   public void _read(org.omg.CORBA.portable.InputStream in);
   public org.omg.CORBA.TypeCode _type();
   public void _write(org.omg.CORBA.portable.OutputStream out);
// Public Instance Fields
   public NameComponent[ ] value;
}
```

Hierarchy: Object→ NameHolder(org.omg.CORBA.portable.Streamable)

NamingContext — Java 1.2

org.omg.CosNaming — *serializable*

A NamingContext represents a naming directory structure, where objects are bound to unique branches, or names, in the naming directory. The full name each object is given in the NamingContext must be unique. New branches in the naming directory are created by binding a NamingContext to a name within another, root NamingContext. The child context represents a subdirectory, or subcontext, within the parent context.

Objects are bound to names in a context using the bind() and rebind() methods. The rebind() method allows you to reassign a name to a new object, if the name has already been bound. You can bind contexts using the bind_context(), bind_new_context(), and rebind_context() methods. If you want to simply create a new context without binding it to a name, use the new_context() method. Bound objects in the context can be found using the resolve() (for singular objects) and list() methods. The unbind() method lets you remove objects from their bindings in the context.

Objects can be bound to names in multiple NamingContext objects at the same time. Their names within each context are independent. The same object can also be bound to multiple, different names in a single context.

```
public abstract interface NamingContext extends org.omg.CORBA.Object,
      org.omg.CORBA.portable.IDLEntity {
```

```
// Public Instance Methods
   public abstract void bind(NameComponent[ ] n, org.omg.CORBA.Object obj) throws NotFound,
        CannotProceed, org.omg.CosNaming.NamingContextPackage.InvalidName;
   public abstract void bind_context(NameComponent[ ] n, NamingContext nc) throws NotFound,
        CannotProceed, org.omg.CosNaming.NamingContextPackage.InvalidName;
   public abstract NamingContext bind_new_context(NameComponent[ ] n) throws NotFound,
        AlreadyBound, CannotProceed;
   public abstract void destroy( ) throws NotEmpty;
   public abstract void list(int how_many, BindingListHolder bl, BindingIteratorHolder bi);
   public abstract NamingContext new_context( );
   public abstract void rebind(NameComponent[ ] n, org.omg.CORBA.Object obj) throws NotFound,
        CannotProceed, org.omg.CosNaming.NamingContextPackage.InvalidName;
   public abstract void rebind_context(NameComponent[ ] n, NamingContext nc) throws NotFound,
        CannotProceed, org.omg.CosNaming.NamingContextPackage.InvalidName;
   public abstract org.omg.CORBA.Object resolve(NameComponent[ ] n) throws NotFound,
        CannotProceed, org.omg.CosNaming.NamingContextPackage.InvalidName;
   public abstract void unbind(NameComponent[ ] n) throws NotFound, CannotProceed,
        org.omg.CosNaming.NamingContextPackage.InvalidName;
}
```

Hierarchy: (NamingContext(org.omg.CORBA.Object, org.omg.CORBA.portable.IDLEntity(Serializable)))

Implementations: _NamingContextImplBase, _NamingContextStub

Passed To: _NamingContextImplBase.{bind_context(), rebind_context()}, _NamingContextStub.{bind_context(), rebind_context()}, NamingContext.{bind_context(), rebind_context()}, NamingContextHelper.{insert(), write()}, NamingContextHolder.NamingContextHolder(), CannotProceed.CannotProceed()

Returned By: _NamingContextImplBase.{bind_new_context(), new_context()}, _NamingContextStub.{bind_new_context(), new_context()}, NamingContext.{bind_new_context(), new_context()}, NamingContextHelper.{extract(), narrow(), read()}

Type Of: NamingContextHolder.value, CannotProceed.cxt

NamingContextHelper — Java 1.2

org.omg.CosNaming

The helper class for the NamingContext interface.

```
public class NamingContextHelper {
// No Constructor
// Public Class Methods
   public static NamingContext extract(org.omg.CORBA.Any a);
   public static String id( );
   public static void insert(org.omg.CORBA.Any a, NamingContext that);
   public static NamingContext narrow(org.omg.CORBA.Object that)
        throws org.omg.CORBA.BAD_PARAM;
   public static NamingContext read(org.omg.CORBA.portable.InputStream in);
   public static org.omg.CORBA.TypeCode type( );                              synchronized
   public static void write(org.omg.CORBA.portable.OutputStream out, NamingContext that);
}
```

NamingContextHolder — Java 1.2

org.omg.CosNaming

The holder class for out and inout IDL method arguments that are mapped to Java NamingContext objects.

```
public final class NamingContextHolder implements org.omg.CORBA.portable.Streamable {
// Public Constructors
   public NamingContextHolder();
   public NamingContextHolder(NamingContext __arg);
// Methods implementing Streamable
   public void _read(org.omg.CORBA.portable.InputStream in);
   public org.omg.CORBA.TypeCode _type( );
   public void _write(org.omg.CORBA.portable.OutputStream out);
// Public Instance Fields
   public NamingContext value;
}
```

Hierarchy: Object→ NamingContextHolder(org.omg.CORBA.portable.Streamable)

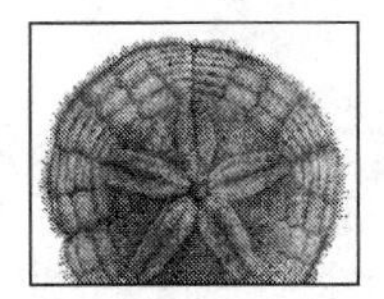

CHAPTER 36

The org.omg.CosNaming. NamingContextPackage Package

The org.omg.CosNaming.NamingContextPackage package defines the exceptions thrown by various methods on the org.omg.CORBA.CosNaming.NamingContext interface. This package consists of these exceptions, along with their helper and holder interfaces. Figure 36-1 shows the class hierarchy for the package.

AlreadyBound — Java 1.2

org.omg.CosNaming.NamingContextPackage — *serializable checked*

An exception thrown by the bind(), bind_context(), and bind_new_context() methods on NamingContext when you attempt to bind an object to a name that already has an object bound to it.

```
public final class AlreadyBound extends org.omg.CORBA.UserException
        implements org.omg.CORBA.portable.IDLEntity {
// Public Constructors
    public AlreadyBound();
}
```

Hierarchy: Object→ Throwable(Serializable)→ Exception→ org.omg.CORBA.UserException(org.omg.CORBA.portable.IDLEntity(Serializable))→ AlreadyBound(org.omg.CORBA.portable.IDLEntity(Serializable))

Passed To: AlreadyBoundHelper.{insert(), write()}, AlreadyBoundHolder.AlreadyBoundHolder()

Returned By: AlreadyBoundHelper.{extract(), read()}

Thrown By: _NamingContextImplBase.{bind(), bind_context(), bind_new_context()}, _NamingContextStub.{bind(), bind_context(), bind_new_context()}, NamingContext.{bind(), bind_context(), bind_new_context()}

Type Of: AlreadyBoundHolder.value

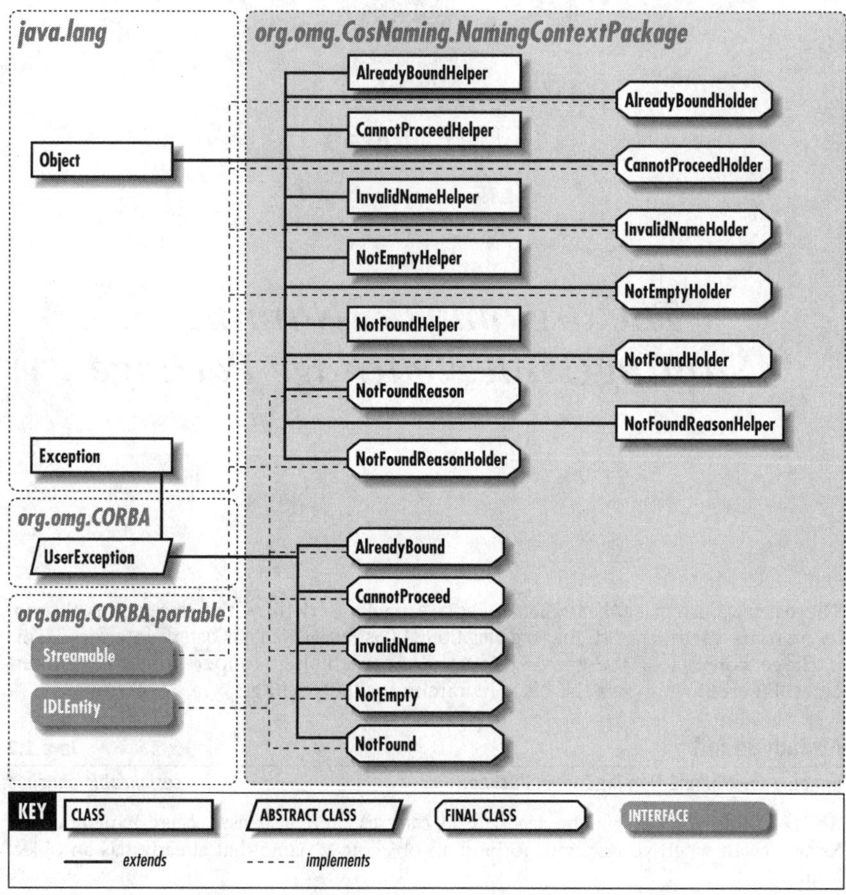

Figure 36-1: The org.omg.CosNaming.NamingContextPackage package

AlreadyBoundHelper — Java 1.2

org.omg.CosNaming.NamingContextPackage

The helper class for the AlreadyBound exception.

```
public class AlreadyBoundHelper {
// No Constructor
// Public Class Methods
   public static AlreadyBound extract(org.omg.CORBA.Any a);
   public static String id();
   public static void insert(org.omg.CORBA.Any a, AlreadyBound that);
   public static AlreadyBound read(org.omg.CORBA.portable.InputStream in);
   public static org.omg.CORBA.TypeCode type();                                    synchronized
   public static void write(org.omg.CORBA.portable.OutputStream out, AlreadyBound that);
}
```

AlreadyBoundHolder **Java 1.2**

org.omg.CosNaming.NamingContextPackage

The holder class for out and inout IDL method arguments that are mapped to Java AlreadyBound exceptions.

```
public final class AlreadyBoundHolder implements org.omg.CORBA.portable.Streamable {
// Public Constructors
   public AlreadyBoundHolder();
   public AlreadyBoundHolder(AlreadyBound __arg);
// Methods implementing Streamable
   public void _read(org.omg.CORBA.portable.InputStream in);
   public org.omg.CORBA.TypeCode _type();
   public void _write(org.omg.CORBA.portable.OutputStream out);
// Public Instance Fields
   public AlreadyBound value;
}
```

Hierarchy: Object→ AlreadyBoundHolder(org.omg.CORBA.portable.Streamable)

CannotProceed **Java 1.2**

org.omg.CosNaming.NamingContextPackage *serializable checked*

An exception thrown by any of the bind or rebind methods on the NamingContext interface, when the NamingContext has given up trying to bind the object to the name specified, for some reason not covered by the other exceptions thrown by these methods. The CannotProceed exception contains a NamingContext that is the last context it attempted to traverse, and a NameComponent array, which is the remainder of the name specified in the method call, relative to the context.

```
public final class CannotProceed extends org.omg.CORBA.UserException
      implements org.omg.CORBA.portable.IDLEntity {
// Public Constructors
   public CannotProceed();
   public CannotProceed(NamingContext __cxt, NameComponent[ ] __rest_of_name);
// Public Instance Fields
   public NamingContext cxt;
   public NameComponent[ ] rest_of_name;
}
```

Hierarchy: Object→ Throwable(Serializable)→ Exception→ org.omg.CORBA.UserException(org.omg.CORBA.portable.IDLEntity(Serializable))→ CannotProceed(org.omg.CORBA.portable.IDLEntity(Serializable))

Passed To: CannotProceedHelper.{insert(), write()}, CannotProceedHolder.CannotProceedHolder()

Returned By: CannotProceedHelper.{extract(), read()}

Thrown By: _NamingContextImplBase.{bind(), bind_context(), bind_new_context(), rebind(), rebind_context(), resolve(), unbind()}, _NamingContextStub.{bind(), bind_context(), bind_new_context(), rebind(), rebind_context(), resolve(), unbind()}, NamingContext.{bind(), bind_context(), bind_new_context(), rebind(), rebind_context(), resolve(), unbind()}

Type Of: CannotProceedHolder.value

CannotProceedHelper **Java 1.2**

org.omg.CosNaming.NamingContextPackage

The helper class for the CannotProceed exception.

```
public class CannotProceedHelper {
// No Constructor
// Public Class Methods
   public static CannotProceed extract(org.omg.CORBA.Any a);
   public static String id();
   public static void insert(org.omg.CORBA.Any a, CannotProceed that);
   public static CannotProceed read(org.omg.CORBA.portable.InputStream in);
   public static org.omg.CORBA.TypeCode type();                         synchronized
   public static void write(org.omg.CORBA.portable.OutputStream out, CannotProceed that);
}
```

CannotProceedHolder — Java 1.2

org.omg.CosNaming.NamingContextPackage

The holder class for out and inout IDL method arguments that are mapped to Java CannotProceed exceptions.

```
public final class CannotProceedHolder implements org.omg.CORBA.portable.Streamable {
// Public Constructors
   public CannotProceedHolder();
   public CannotProceedHolder(CannotProceed _arg);
// Methods implementing Streamable
   public void _read(org.omg.CORBA.portable.InputStream in);
   public org.omg.CORBA.TypeCode _type();
   public void _write(org.omg.CORBA.portable.OutputStream out);
// Public Instance Fields
   public CannotProceed value;
}
```

Hierarchy: Object→ CannotProceedHolder(org.omg.CORBA.portable.Streamable)

InvalidName — Java 1.2

org.omg.CosNaming.NamingContextPackage — *serializable checked*

An exception thrown by any of the NamingContext methods for binding, resolving, or unbinding objects, when the specified name is invalid (e.g., it contains invalid characters).

```
public final class InvalidName extends org.omg.CORBA.UserException
      implements org.omg.CORBA.portable.IDLEntity {
// Public Constructors
   public InvalidName();
}
```

Hierarchy: Object→ Throwable(Serializable)→ Exception→ org.omg.CORBA.UserException(org.omg.CORBA.portable.IDLEntity(Serializable))→ org.omg.CosNaming.NamingContextPackage.InvalidName(org.omg.CORBA.portable.IDLEntity(Serializable))

Passed To: InvalidNameHelper.{insert(), write()}, InvalidNameHolder.InvalidNameHolder()

Returned By: InvalidNameHelper.{extract(), read()}

Thrown By: _NamingContextImplBase.{bind(), bind_context(), bind_new_context(), rebind(), rebind_context(), resolve(), unbind()}, _NamingContextStub.{bind(), bind_context(), bind_new_context(), rebind(), rebind_context(), resolve(), unbind()}, NamingContext.{bind(), bind_context(), bind_new_context(), rebind(), rebind_context(), resolve(), unbind()}

Type Of: InvalidNameHolder.value

InvalidNameHelper — Java 1.2

org.omg.CosNaming.NamingContextPackage

The helper class for the InvalidName exception.

```
public class InvalidNameHelper {
// No Constructor
// Public Class Methods
   public static org.omg.CosNaming.NamingContextPackage.InvalidName extract(
                                                       org.omg.CORBA.Any a);
   public static String id();
   public static void insert(org.omg.CORBA.Any a,
                        org.omg.CosNaming.NamingContextPackage.InvalidName that);
   public static org.omg.CosNaming.NamingContextPackage.InvalidName read(
                                                       org.omg.CORBA.portable.InputStream in);
   public static org.omg.CORBA.TypeCode type();                          synchronized
   public static void write(org.omg.CORBA.portable.OutputStream out,
                        org.omg.CosNaming.NamingContextPackage.InvalidName that);
}
```

InvalidNameHolder — Java 1.2

org.omg.CosNaming.NamingContextPackage

The holder class for out and inout IDL method arguments that are mapped to Java InvalidName exceptions.

```
public final class InvalidNameHolder implements org.omg.CORBA.portable.Streamable {
// Public Constructors
   public InvalidNameHolder();
   public InvalidNameHolder(org.omg.CosNaming.NamingContextPackage.InvalidName __arg);
// Methods implementing Streamable
   public void _read(org.omg.CORBA.portable.InputStream in);
   public org.omg.CORBA.TypeCode _type();
   public void _write(org.omg.CORBA.portable.OutputStream out);
// Public Instance Fields
   public org.omg.CosNaming.NamingContextPackage.InvalidName value;
}
```

Hierarchy: Object→ InvalidNameHolder(org.omg.CORBA.portable.Streamable)

NotEmpty — Java 1.2

org.omg.CosNaming.NamingContextPackage — *serializable checked*

An exception thrown by the NamingContext.destroy() method, if you attempt to destroy a NamingContext that still has bindings within it.

```
public final class NotEmpty extends org.omg.CORBA.UserException
       implements org.omg.CORBA.portable.IDLEntity {
// Public Constructors
   public NotEmpty();
}
```

Hierarchy: Object→ Throwable(Serializable)→ Exception→ org.omg.CORBA.UserException(org.omg.CORBA.portable.IDLEntity(Serializable))→ NotEmpty(org.omg.CORBA.portable.IDLEntity(Serializable))

Passed To: NotEmptyHelper.{insert(), write()}, NotEmptyHolder.NotEmptyHolder()

Returned By: NotEmptyHelper.{extract(), read()}

Thrown By: _NamingContextImplBase.destroy(), _NamingContextStub.destroy(), NamingContext.destroy()

Type Of: NotEmptyHolder.value

NotEmptyHelper **Java 1.2**

org.omg.CosNaming.NamingContextPackage

The helper class for the NotEmpty exception.

```
public class NotEmptyHelper {
// No Constructor
// Public Class Methods
   public static NotEmpty extract(org.omg.CORBA.Any a);
   public static String id();
   public static void insert(org.omg.CORBA.Any a, NotEmpty that);
   public static NotEmpty read(org.omg.CORBA.portable.InputStream in);
   public static org.omg.CORBA.TypeCode type();                         synchronized
   public static void write(org.omg.CORBA.portable.OutputStream out, NotEmpty that);
}
```

NotEmptyHolder **Java 1.2**

org.omg.CosNaming.NamingContextPackage

The holder class for out and inout IDL method arguments that are mapped to Java NotEmpty exceptions.

```
public final class NotEmptyHolder implements org.omg.CORBA.portable.Streamable {
// Public Constructors
   public NotEmptyHolder();
   public NotEmptyHolder(NotEmpty __arg);
// Methods implementing Streamable
   public void _read(org.omg.CORBA.portable.InputStream in);
   public org.omg.CORBA.TypeCode _type();
   public void _write(org.omg.CORBA.portable.OutputStream out);
// Public Instance Fields
   public NotEmpty value;
}
```

Hierarchy: Object→ NotEmptyHolder(org.omg.CORBA.portable.Streamable)

NotFound **Java 1.2**

org.omg.CosNaming.NamingContextPackage ***serializable checked***

An exception thrown by any of the NamingContext methods for binding, resolving, or unbinding object names, when a specified name is not found as a binding within the NamingContext. The NotFound exception contains a NameComponent array, which represents the remainder of the name after the first component mismatch was found, and a NotFoundReason object, that contains an int value that indicates whether the operation failed because one of the components in the name was not found, one of the intermediate components was bound to a regular object instead of a context, or the final component was not bound to an object.

```
public final class NotFound extends org.omg.CORBA.UserException
      implements org.omg.CORBA.portable.IDLEntity {
// Public Constructors
   public NotFound();
   public NotFound(NotFoundReason __why, NameComponent[ ] __rest_of_name);
// Public Instance Fields
   public NameComponent[ ] rest_of_name;
```

```
    public NotFoundReason why;
}
```

Hierarchy: Object→ Throwable(Serializable)→ Exception→ org.omg.CORBA.UserException(org.omg.CORBA.portable.IDLEntity(Serializable))→ NotFound(org.omg.CORBA.portable.IDLEntity(Serializable))

Passed To: NotFoundHelper.{insert(), write()}, NotFoundHolder.NotFoundHolder()

Returned By: NotFoundHelper.{extract(), read()}

Thrown By: _NamingContextImplBase.{bind(), bind_context(), bind_new_context(), rebind(), rebind_context(), resolve(), unbind()}, _NamingContextStub.{bind(), bind_context(), bind_new_context(), rebind(), rebind_context(), resolve(), unbind()}, NamingContext.{bind(), bind_context(), bind_new_context(), rebind(), rebind_context(), resolve(), unbind()}

Type Of: NotFoundHolder.value

NotFoundHelper — Java 1.2

org.omg.CosNaming.NamingContextPackage

The helper class for the NotFound exception.

```
public class NotFoundHelper {
// No Constructor
// Public Class Methods
    public static NotFound extract(org.omg.CORBA.Any a);
    public static String id();
    public static void insert(org.omg.CORBA.Any a, NotFound that);
    public static NotFound read(org.omg.CORBA.portable.InputStream in);
    public static org.omg.CORBA.TypeCode type();                          synchronized
    public static void write(org.omg.CORBA.portable.OutputStream out, NotFound that);
}
```

NotFoundHolder — Java 1.2

org.omg.CosNaming.NamingContextPackage

The holder class for out and inout IDL method arguments that are mapped to Java NotFound exceptions.

```
public final class NotFoundHolder implements org.omg.CORBA.portable.Streamable {
// Public Constructors
    public NotFoundHolder();
    public NotFoundHolder(NotFound __arg);
// Methods implementing Streamable
    public void _read(org.omg.CORBA.portable.InputStream in);
    public org.omg.CORBA.TypeCode _type();
    public void _write(org.omg.CORBA.portable.OutputStream out);
// Public Instance Fields
    public NotFound value;
}
```

Hierarchy: Object→ NotFoundHolder(org.omg.CORBA.portable.Streamable)

NotFoundReason — Java 1.2

org.omg.CosNaming.NamingContextPackage — *serializable*

NotFoundReason objects are used in NotFound exceptions to indicate the reason an object binding was not found in a NamingContext. It has a value() method that returns an int which can then be compared to its three static int members to determine the reason for the failure. A value of _missing_node indicates that an intermediate component of the name specified was not found in the context, _not_context indicates that an intermediate component name was not bound to a NamingContext, and _not_object indicates that an object was not bound to the final component in the name.

```
public final class NotFoundReason implements org.omg.CORBA.portable.IDLEntity {
// No Constructor
// Public Constants
    public static final int _missing_node;                                        =0
    public static final int _not_context;                                         =1
    public static final int _not_object;                                          =2
    public static final NotFoundReason missing_node;
    public static final NotFoundReason not_context;
    public static final NotFoundReason not_object;
// Public Class Methods
    public static final NotFoundReason from_int(int i) throws org.omg.CORBA.BAD_PARAM;
// Public Instance Methods
    public int value();
}
```

Hierarchy: Object→ NotFoundReason(org.omg.CORBA.portable.IDLEntity(Serializable))

Passed To: NotFound.NotFound(), NotFoundReasonHelper.{insert(), write()}, NotFoundReasonHolder.NotFoundReasonHolder()

Returned By: NotFoundReason.from_int(), NotFoundReasonHelper.{extract(), read()}

Type Of: NotFound.why, NotFoundReason.{missing_node, not_context, not_object}, NotFoundReasonHolder.value

NotFoundReasonHelper — Java 1.2

org.omg.CosNaming.NamingContextPackage

The helper class for the NotFoundReason class.

```
public class NotFoundReasonHelper {
// No Constructor
// Public Class Methods
    public static NotFoundReason extract(org.omg.CORBA.Any a);
    public static String id();
    public static void insert(org.omg.CORBA.Any a, NotFoundReason that);
    public static NotFoundReason read(org.omg.CORBA.portable.InputStream in);
    public static org.omg.CORBA.TypeCode type();                       synchronized
    public static void write(org.omg.CORBA.portable.OutputStream out, NotFoundReason that);
}
```

NotFoundReasonHolder — Java 1.2

org.omg.CosNaming.NamingContextPackage

The holder class for out and inout IDL method arguments that are mapped to Java NotFoundReason objects.

```
public final class NotFoundReasonHolder implements org.omg.CORBA.portable.Streamable {
// Public Constructors
    public NotFoundReasonHolder();
    public NotFoundReasonHolder(NotFoundReason __arg);
// Methods implementing Streamable
    public void _read(org.omg.CORBA.portable.InputStream in);
    public org.omg.CORBA.TypeCode _type();
    public void _write(org.omg.CORBA.portable.OutputStream out);
```

```
// Public Instance Fields
   public NotFoundReason value;
}
```

Hierarchy: Object→ NotFoundReasonHolder(org.omg.CORBA.portable.Streamable)

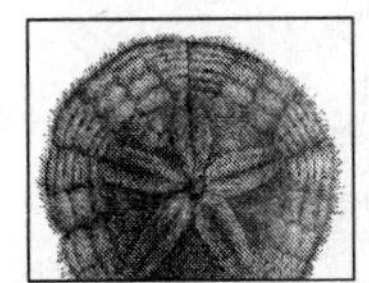

CHAPTER 37

Class, Method, and Field Index

The following index allows you to look up a class or interface and find what package it is defined in. It also allows you to look up a method or field and find what class it is defined in. Use it when you want to look up a class but don't know its package, or when you want to look up a method but don't know its class.

Symbols

_ADD_OVERRIDE: SetOverrideType
_BindingIteratorImplBase: org.omg.CosNaming
_BindingIteratorStub: org.omg.CosNaming
_COMPLETED_MAYBE: CompletionStatus
_COMPLETED_NO: CompletionStatus
_COMPLETED_YES: CompletionStatus
_create_request(): Object, ObjectImpl
_dk_Alias: DefinitionKind
_dk_all: DefinitionKind
_dk_Array: DefinitionKind
_dk_Attribute: DefinitionKind
_dk_Constant: DefinitionKind
_dk_Enum: DefinitionKind
_dk_Exception: DefinitionKind
_dk_Fixed: DefinitionKind
_dk_Interface: DefinitionKind
_dk_Module: DefinitionKind
_dk_Native: DefinitionKind
_dk_none: DefinitionKind
_dk_Operation: DefinitionKind
_dk_Primitive: DefinitionKind
_dk_Repository: DefinitionKind
_dk_Sequence: DefinitionKind
_dk_String: DefinitionKind
_dk_Struct: DefinitionKind
_dk_Typedef: DefinitionKind
_dk_Union: DefinitionKind
_dk_Value: DefinitionKind
_dk_ValueBox: DefinitionKind
_dk_ValueMember: DefinitionKind
_dk_Wstring: DefinitionKind
_duplicate(): Object, ObjectImpl
_get_delegate(): ObjectImpl
_get_domain_managers(): Object, ObjectImpl
_get_interface_def(): Object, ObjectImpl
_get_policy(): Object, ObjectImpl
_hash(): Object, ObjectImpl
_ids(): _BindingIteratorImplBase, _BindingIteratorStub, _NamingContextImplBase, _NamingContextStub, ObjectImpl
_invoke(): InvokeHandler, ObjectImpl
_is_a(): Object, ObjectImpl
_is_equivalent(): Object, ObjectImpl
_is_local(): ObjectImpl
_missing_node: NotFoundReason
_NamingContextImplBase: org.omg.CosNaming
_NamingContextStub: org.omg.CosNaming
_ncontext: BindingType
_nobject: BindingType
_non_existent(): Object, ObjectImpl

_not_context: NotFoundReason
_not_object: NotFoundReason
_orb(): ObjectImpl
_read(): AlreadyBoundHolder, AnyHolder, BindingHolder, BindingIteratorHolder, BindingListHolder, BindingTypeHolder, BooleanHolder, ByteHolder, CannotProceedHolder, CharHolder, DoubleHolder, FixedHolder, FloatHolder, IntHolder, InvalidNameHolder, LongHolder, NameComponentHolder, NameHolder, NamingContextHolder, NotEmptyHolder, NotFoundHolder, NotFoundReasonHolder, ObjectHolder, PrincipalHolder, ServiceInformationHolder, ShortHolder, Streamable, StringHolder, TypeCodeHolder
_release(): Object, ObjectImpl
_releaseReply(): ObjectImpl
_request(): Object, ObjectImpl
_servant_postinvoke(): ObjectImpl
_servant_preinvoke(): ObjectImpl
_set_delegate(): ObjectImpl
_SET_OVERRIDE: SetOverrideType
_set_policy_override(): Object, ObjectImpl
_tk_abstract_interface: TCKind
_tk_alias: TCKind
_tk_any: TCKind
_tk_array: TCKind
_tk_boolean: TCKind
_tk_char: TCKind
_tk_double: TCKind
_tk_enum: TCKind
_tk_except: TCKind
_tk_fixed: TCKind
_tk_float: TCKind
_tk_long: TCKind
_tk_longdouble: TCKind
_tk_longlong: TCKind
_tk_native: TCKind
_tk_null: TCKind
_tk_objref: TCKind
_tk_octet: TCKind
_tk_Principal: TCKind
_tk_sequence: TCKind
_tk_short: TCKind
_tk_string: TCKind
_tk_struct: TCKind
_tk_TypeCode: TCKind
_tk_ulong: TCKind
_tk_ulonglong: TCKind
_tk_union: TCKind
_tk_ushort: TCKind
_tk_value: TCKind
_tk_value_box: TCKind
_tk_void: TCKind
_tk_wchar: TCKind
_tk_wstring: TCKind
_type(): AlreadyBoundHolder, AnyHolder, BindingHolder, BindingIteratorHolder, BindingListHolder, BindingTypeHolder, BooleanHolder, ByteHolder, CannotProceedHolder, CharHolder, DoubleHolder, FixedHolder, FloatHolder, IntHolder, InvalidNameHolder, LongHolder, NameComponentHolder, NameHolder, NamingContextHolder, NotEmptyHolder, NotFoundHolder, NotFoundReasonHolder, ObjectHolder, PrincipalHolder, ServiceInformationHolder, ShortHolder, Streamable, StringHolder, TypeCodeHolder
_write(): AlreadyBoundHolder, AnyHolder, BindingHolder, BindingIteratorHolder, BindingListHolder, BindingTypeHolder, BooleanHolder, ByteHolder, CannotProceedHolder, CharHolder, DoubleHolder, FixedHolder, FloatHolder, IntHolder, InvalidNameHolder, LongHolder, NameComponentHolder, NameHolder, NamingContextHolder, NotEmptyHolder, NotFoundHolder, NotFoundReasonHolder, ObjectHolder, PrincipalHolder, ServiceInformationHolder, ShortHolder, Streamable, StringHolder, TypeCodeHolder

A

absolute(): ResultSet
acceptsURL(): Driver
access: ValueMember
AccessControlEntry: javax.ejb.deployment
AccessException: java.rmi
acknowledge(): Message
Activatable: java.rmi.activation
activate(): ActivationID, Activator
ActivateFailedException: java.rmi.activation
ActivationDesc: java.rmi.activation
ActivationException: java.rmi.activation
ActivationGroup: java.rmi.activation
ActivationGroup_Stub: java.rmi.activation
ActivationGroupDesc: java.rmi.activation
ActivationGroupDesc.CommandEnvironment: java.rmi.activation
ActivationGroupID: java.rmi.activation
ActivationID: java.rmi.activation
ActivationInstantiator: java.rmi.activation
ActivationMonitor: java.rmi.activation

Class Index

ActivationSystem: java.rmi.activation
Activator: java.rmi.activation
ACTIVATOR_ID: ObjID
activeGroup(): ActivationSystem
activeObject(): ActivationGroup, ActivationMonitor
add(): Attribute, BasicAttribute, CompositeName, CompoundName, ContextList, ExceptionList, Name, NVList, Reference
ADD_ATTRIBUTE: DirContext
add_in_arg(): Request
add_inout_arg(): Request
add_item(): NVList
add_named_in_arg(): Request
add_named_inout_arg(): Request
add_named_out_arg(): Request
add_out_arg(): Request
ADD_OVERRIDE: SetOverrideType
add_value(): NVList
addAll(): CompositeName, CompoundName, Name
addBatch(): PreparedStatement, Statement
addConnectionEventListener(): PooledConnection
addCookie(): HttpServletResponse
addRowSetListener(): RowSet
addrs: Reference
addrType: RefAddr
addToEnvironment(): Context, InitialContext
after(): Timestamp
afterBegin(): SessionSynchronization
afterCompletion(): SessionSynchronization, Synchronization
afterLast(): ResultSet
allProceduresAreCallable(): DatabaseMetaData
allTablesAreSelectable(): DatabaseMetaData
AlreadyBound: org.omg.CosNaming.NamingContextPackage
AlreadyBoundException: java.rmi
AlreadyBoundHelper: org.omg.CosNaming.NamingContextPackage
AlreadyBoundHolder: org.omg.CosNaming.NamingContextPackage
altName: CannotProceedException
altNameCtx: CannotProceedException
Any: org.omg.CORBA
AnyHolder: org.omg.CORBA
appendRemainingComponent(): NamingException, ResolveResult
appendRemainingName(): NamingException, ResolveResult
ApplicationException: org.omg.CORBA.portable
ARG_IN: org.omg.CORBA
ARG_INOUT: org.omg.CORBA
ARG_OUT: org.omg.CORBA
arguments(): Request, ServerRequest
ARRAY: Types
Array: java.sql
assign(): DynAny
Attribute: javax.naming.directory
AttributeInUseException: javax.naming.directory
AttributeModificationException: javax.naming.directory
Attributes: javax.naming.directory
attrID: BasicAttribute
AuthenticationException: javax.naming
AuthenticationNotSupportedException: javax.naming
AUTHORITATIVE: Context
AUTO_ACKNOWLEDGE: Session

B

BAD_CONTEXT: org.omg.CORBA
BAD_INV_ORDER: org.omg.CORBA
BAD_OPERATION: org.omg.CORBA
BAD_PARAM: org.omg.CORBA
BAD_POLICY: org.omg.CORBA
BAD_POLICY_TYPE: org.omg.CORBA
BAD_POLICY_VALUE: org.omg.CORBA
BAD_TYPECODE: org.omg.CORBA
BadKind: org.omg.CORBA.TypeCodePackage
BasicAttribute: javax.naming.directory
BasicAttributes: javax.naming.directory
BATCHSIZE: Context
BatchUpdateException: java.sql
before(): Timestamp
beforeCompletion(): SessionSynchronization, Synchronization
beforeFirst(): ResultSet
begin(): TransactionManager, UserTransaction
bestRowNotPseudo: DatabaseMetaData
bestRowPseudo: DatabaseMetaData
bestRowSession: DatabaseMetaData
bestRowTemporary: DatabaseMetaData
bestRowTransaction: DatabaseMetaData
bestRowUnknown: DatabaseMetaData
BIGINT: Types
BINARY: Types
BinaryRefAddr: javax.naming
bind(): _NamingContextImplBase, _NamingContextStub, Context, DirContext, InitialContext, InitialDirContext, Naming, NamingContext, Registry
bind_context(): _NamingContextImplBase,

_NamingContextStub, NamingContext
bind_new_context(): _NamingContextImplBase, _NamingContextStub, NamingContext
Binding: javax.naming, org.omg.CosNaming
binding_name: Binding
binding_type: Binding
BindingHelper: org.omg.CosNaming
BindingHolder: org.omg.CosNaming
BindingIterator: org.omg.CosNaming
BindingIteratorHelper: org.omg.CosNaming
BindingIteratorHolder: org.omg.CosNaming
BindingListHelper: org.omg.CosNaming
BindingListHolder: org.omg.CosNaming
BindingType: org.omg.CosNaming
BindingTypeHelper: org.omg.CosNaming
BindingTypeHolder: org.omg.CosNaming
BIT: Types
Blob: java.sql
BLOB: Types
BooleanHolder: org.omg.CORBA
Bounds: org.omg.CORBA, org.omg.CORBA.TypeCodePackage
BRIEF: LogStream
ByteHolder: org.omg.CORBA
BytesMessage: javax.jms

C

CallableStatement: java.sql
cancel(): Statement
cancelRowUpdates(): ResultSet
CannotProceed: org.omg.CosNaming.NamingContextPackage
CannotProceedException: javax.naming
CannotProceedHelper: org.omg.CosNaming.NamingContextPackage
CannotProceedHolder: org.omg.CosNaming.NamingContextPackage
CHAR: Types
CharHolder: org.omg.CORBA
choices: DriverPropertyInfo
classFactory: Reference
classFactoryLocation: Reference
className: Reference
clean(): DGC
clear(): Attribute, BasicAttribute, Environment, Reference
clearBatch(): Statement
clearBody(): Message
clearParameters(): PreparedStatement, RowSet
clearProperties(): Message
clearWarnings(): Connection, ResultSet, Statement
CLIENT_ACKNOWLEDGE: Session
CLIENT_IDENTITY: ControlDescriptor
Clob: java.sql
CLOB: Types
clone(): Attribute, Attributes, BasicAttribute, BasicAttributes, CompositeName, CompoundName, Cookie, Name, Reference, UnicastRemoteObject
close(): Connection, ConnectionConsumer, Context, InitialContext, MessageConsumer, MessageProducer, PooledConnection, QueueBrowser, QueueRequestor, ResultSet, Session, Statement, TopicRequestor
columnNoNulls: DatabaseMetaData, ResultSetMetaData
columnNullable: DatabaseMetaData, ResultSetMetaData
columnNullableUnknown: DatabaseMetaData, ResultSetMetaData
COMM_FAILURE: org.omg.CORBA
CommandEnvironment: java.rmi.activation.ActivationGroupDesc
commit(): Connection, Session, Transaction, TransactionManager, UserTransaction, XAResource
CommunicationException: javax.naming
compareTo(): CompositeName, CompoundName, Name
completed: SystemException
COMPLETED_MAYBE: CompletionStatus
COMPLETED_NO: CompletionStatus
COMPLETED_YES: CompletionStatus
CompletionStatus: org.omg.CORBA
composeName(): Context, InitialContext
CompositeName: javax.naming
CompoundName: javax.naming
concrete_base_type(): TypeCode
CONCUR_READ_ONLY: ResultSet
CONCUR_UPDATABLE: ResultSet
ConfigurationException: javax.naming
connect(): Driver, ORB
ConnectException: java.rmi
ConnectIOException: java.rmi
Connection: java.sql, javax.jms
connectionClosed(): ConnectionEventListener
ConnectionConsumer: javax.jms
connectionErrorOccurred(): ConnectionEventListener
ConnectionEvent: javax.sql
ConnectionEventListener: javax.sql
ConnectionFactory: javax.jms

Class Index

ConnectionMetaData: javax.jms
ConnectionPoolDataSource: javax.sql
contains(): Attribute, BasicAttribute
containsHeader(): HttpServletResponse
content_type(): TypeCode
Context: javax.naming, org.omg.CORBA
context_name(): Context
ContextList: org.omg.CORBA
ContextNotEmptyException: javax.naming
contexts(): Request
ControlDescriptor: javax.ejb.deployment
Cookie: javax.servlet.http
copy(): DynAny, Policy
count(): ContextList, ExceptionList, NVList
create_abstract_interface_tc(): ORB
create_alias_tc(): ORB
create_any(): ORB
create_array_tc(): ORB
create_basic_dyn_any(): ORB
create_child(): Context
create_context_list(): ORB
create_dyn_any(): ORB
create_dyn_array(): ORB
create_dyn_enum(): ORB
create_dyn_sequence(): ORB
create_dyn_struct(): ORB
create_dyn_union(): ORB
create_enum_tc(): ORB
create_environment(): ORB
create_exception_list(): ORB
create_exception_tc(): ORB
create_fixed_tc(): ORB
create_input_stream(): Any, OutputStream
create_interface_tc(): ORB
create_list(): ORB
create_named_value(): ORB
create_native_tc(): ORB
create_operation_list(): ORB
create_output_stream(): Any, ORB
create_policy(): ORB
create_recursive_sequence_tc(): ORB
create_recursive_tc(): ORB
create_request(): Delegate
create_sequence_tc(): ORB
create_string_tc(): ORB
create_struct_tc(): ORB
create_union_tc(): ORB
create_value_box_tc(): ORB
create_value_tc(): ORB
create_wstring_tc(): ORB
createBrowser(): QueueSession
createBytesMessage(): Session
createConnectionConsumer(): QueueConnection, TopicConnection
createDurableConnectionConsumer(): TopicConnection
createDurableSubscriber(): TopicSession
CreateException: javax.ejb
createExceptionReply(): ResponseHandler
createGroup(): ActivationGroup
createInitialContextFactory(): InitialContextFactoryBuilder
createMapMessage(): Session
createMessage(): Session
createObjectFactory(): ObjectFactoryBuilder
createObjectMessage(): Session
createPublisher(): TopicSession
createQueue(): QueueSession
createQueueConnection(): QueueConnectionFactory
createQueueSession(): QueueConnection
createReceiver(): QueueSession
createRegistry(): LocateRegistry
createReply(): ResponseHandler
createSender(): QueueSession
createServerSocket(): RMIServerSocketFactory, RMISocketFactory
createSocket(): RMIClientSocketFactory, RMISocketFactory
createStatement(): Connection
createStreamMessage(): Session
createSubcontext(): Context, DirContext, InitialContext, InitialDirContext
createSubscriber(): TopicSession
createTemporaryQueue(): QueueSession
createTemporaryTopic(): TopicSession
createTextMessage(): Session
createTopic(): TopicSession
createTopicConnection(): TopicConnectionFactory
createTopicSession(): TopicConnection
createXAQueueConnection(): XAQueueConnectionFactory
createXAQueueSession(): XAQueueConnection
createXATopicConnection(): XATopicConnectionFactory
createXATopicSession(): XATopicConnection
ctx(): Request, ServerRequest
CTX_RESTRICT_SCOPE: org.omg.CORBA
Current: org.omg.CORBA
current_component(): DynAny
current_member_kind(): DynStruct, DynValue

current_member_name(): DynStruct, DynValue
currentGroupID(): ActivationGroup
cursorMoved(): RowSetListener
cxt: CannotProceed

D

DATA_CONVERSION: org.omg.CORBA
DatabaseMetaData: java.sql
dataDefinitionCausesTransactionCommit(): DatabaseMetaData
dataDefinitionIgnoredInTransactions(): DatabaseMetaData
DataSource: javax.sql
DataTruncation: java.sql
DATE: Types
Date: java.sql
DECIMAL: Types
def_kind(): IRObject
DEFAULT_DELIVERY_MODE: Message
default_index(): TypeCode
DEFAULT_PRIORITY: Message
DEFAULT_TIME_TO_LIVE: Message
defaultInitCtx: InitialContext
defined_in: ValueMember
DefinitionKind: org.omg.CORBA
Delegate: org.omg.CORBA.portable
delete(): TemporaryQueue, TemporaryTopic
delete_values(): Context
deleteRow(): ResultSet
deletesAreDetected(): DatabaseMetaData
delistResource(): Transaction
DeliveryMode: javax.jms
DeploymentDescriptor: javax.ejb.deployment
deregisterDriver(): DriverManager
description: DriverPropertyInfo
Destination: javax.jms
destroy(): _BindingIteratorImplBase, _BindingIteratorStub, _NamingContextImplBase, _NamingContextStub, BindingIterator, DynAny, GenericServlet, IRObject, NamingContext, Policy, Servlet
destroySubcontext(): Context, InitialContext
detail: ActivationException, RemoteException, ServerCloneException
DGC: java.rmi.dgc
DGC_ID: ObjID
DirContext: javax.naming.directory
DirectoryManager: javax.naming.spi
dirty(): DGC
disconnect(): ORB
discriminator(): DynUnion
discriminator_kind(): DynUnion
discriminator_type(): TypeCode
dispatch(): Skeleton
DISTINCT: Types
dk_Alias: DefinitionKind
dk_all: DefinitionKind
dk_Array: DefinitionKind
dk_Attribute: DefinitionKind
dk_Constant: DefinitionKind
dk_Enum: DefinitionKind
dk_Exception: DefinitionKind
dk_Fixed: DefinitionKind
dk_Interface: DefinitionKind
dk_Module: DefinitionKind
dk_Native: DefinitionKind
dk_none: DefinitionKind
dk_Operation: DefinitionKind
dk_Primitive: DefinitionKind
dk_Repository: DefinitionKind
dk_Sequence: DefinitionKind
dk_String: DefinitionKind
dk_Struct: DefinitionKind
dk_Typedef: DefinitionKind
dk_Union: DefinitionKind
dk_Value: DefinitionKind
dk_ValueBox: DefinitionKind
dk_ValueMember: DefinitionKind
dk_Wstring: DefinitionKind
DNS_URL: Context
doDelete(): HttpServlet
doesMaxRowSizeIncludeBlobs(): DatabaseMetaData
doGet(): HttpServlet
DomainManager: org.omg.CORBA
done(): RemoteCall, RemoteRef
doOptions(): HttpServlet
doPost(): HttpServlet
doPut(): HttpServlet
doTrace(): HttpServlet
DOUBLE: Types
DoubleHolder: org.omg.CORBA
Driver: java.sql
DriverManager: java.sql
DriverPropertyInfo: java.sql
duplicate(): Delegate
DuplicateKeyException: javax.ejb
DUPS_OK_ACKNOWLEDGE: Session
DynamicImplementation: org.omg.CORBA
DynAny: org.omg.CORBA
DynArray: org.omg.CORBA

DynEnum: org.omg.CORBA
DynFixed: org.omg.CORBA
DynSequence: org.omg.CORBA
DynStruct: org.omg.CORBA
DynUnion: org.omg.CORBA
DynValue: org.omg.CORBA

E

ejbActivate(): EntityBean, SessionBean
EJBContext: javax.ejb
EJBException: javax.ejb
EJBHome: javax.ejb
ejbLoad(): EntityBean
EJBMetaData: javax.ejb
EJBObject: javax.ejb
ejbPassivate(): EntityBean, SessionBean
ejbRemove(): EntityBean, SessionBean
ejbStore(): EntityBean
encodeRedirectUrl(): HttpServletResponse
encodeRedirectURL(): HttpServletResponse
encodeUrl(): HttpServletResponse
encodeURL(): HttpServletResponse
end(): XAResource
endsWith(): CompositeName, CompoundName, Name
enlistResource(): Transaction
EnterpriseBean: javax.ejb
EntityBean: javax.ejb
EntityContext: javax.ejb
EntityDescriptor: javax.ejb.deployment
env(): Request
environment: CannotProceedException
Environment: org.omg.CORBA
equal(): Any, TypeCode
equals(): ActivationDesc, ActivationGroupDesc, ActivationGroupID, ActivationID, BasicAttribute, BinaryRefAddr, CommandEnvironment, CompositeName, CompoundName, Delegate, MarshalledObject, ObjectImpl, ObjID, RefAddr, Reference, RemoteObject, Timestamp, UID, VMID
equivalent(): TypeCode
errorCode: SystemException, XAException
except: UnknownUserException
except(): ServerRequest
exception(): Environment
ExceptionList: org.omg.CORBA
ExceptionListener: javax.jms
exceptions(): Request
execute(): PreparedStatement, RowSet, Statement
executeBatch(): Statement
executeCall(): RemoteCall
executeQuery(): PreparedStatement, Statement
executeUpdate(): PreparedStatement, Statement
ExportException: java.rmi.server
exportObject(): Activatable, ServerRef, UnicastRemoteObject
extract(): AlreadyBoundHelper, BindingHelper, BindingIteratorHelper, BindingListHelper, BindingTypeHelper, CannotProceedHelper, InvalidNameHelper, IstringHelper, NameComponentHelper, NameHelper, NamingContextHelper, NotEmptyHelper, NotFoundHelper, NotFoundReasonHelper, ServiceDetailHelper, ServiceInformationHelper
extract_any(): Any
extract_boolean(): Any
extract_char(): Any
extract_double(): Any
extract_fixed(): Any
extract_float(): Any
extract_long(): Any
extract_longlong(): Any
extract_Object(): Any
extract_octet(): Any
extract_Principal(): Any
extract_short(): Any
extract_string(): Any
extract_TypeCode(): Any
extract_ulong(): Any
extract_ulonglong(): Any
extract_ushort(): Any
extract_Value(): Any
extract_wchar(): Any
extract_wstring(): Any

F

failure(): RMIFailureHandler
FETCH_FORWARD: ResultSet
FETCH_REVERSE: ResultSet
FETCH_UNKNOWN: ResultSet
findColumn(): ResultSet
FinderException: javax.ejb
first(): ResultSet
fixed_digits(): TypeCode
fixed_scale(): TypeCode
FixedHolder: org.omg.CORBA
flags(): NamedValue
FLOAT: Types
FloatHolder: org.omg.CORBA
forget(): XAResource

forward(): RequestDispatcher
FREE_MEM: org.omg.CORBA
from_any(): DynAny
from_int(): BindingType, CompletionStatus, DefinitionKind, NotFoundReason, SetOverrideType, TCKind

G

GenericServlet: javax.servlet
get(): Attribute, Attributes, BasicAttribute, BasicAttributes, CompositeName, CompoundName, MarshalledObject, Name, Reference
get_any(): DynAny
get_boolean(): DynAny
get_char(): DynAny
get_compact_typecode(): TypeCode
get_current(): ORB
get_default_context(): ORB
get_domain_managers(): Delegate
get_domain_policy(): DomainManager
get_double(): DynAny
get_elements(): DynArray, DynSequence
get_float(): DynAny
get_interface_def(): Delegate
get_long(): DynAny
get_longlong(): DynAny
get_members(): DynStruct, DynValue
get_next_response(): ORB
get_octet(): DynAny
get_policy(): Delegate
get_primitive_tc(): ORB
get_reference(): DynAny
get_response(): Request
get_service_information(): ORB
get_short(): DynAny
get_string(): DynAny
get_typecode(): DynAny
get_ulong(): DynAny
get_ulonglong(): DynAny
get_ushort(): DynAny
get_val(): DynAny
get_value(): DynFixed
get_values(): Context
get_wchar(): DynAny
get_wstring(): DynAny
getAccessControlEntries(): DeploymentDescriptor
getActivationDesc(): ActivationSystem
getActivationGroupDesc(): ActivationSystem
getAll(): Attribute, Attributes, BasicAttribute, BasicAttributes, CompositeName, CompoundName, Name, Reference
getAllowedIdentities(): AccessControlEntry
getAltName(): CannotProceedException
getAltNameCtx(): CannotProceedException
getArray(): Array, CallableStatement, ResultSet
getAsciiStream(): Clob, ResultSet
getAttribute(): ModificationItem, ServletContext, ServletRequest
getAttributeDefinition(): Attribute, BasicAttribute
getAttributeNames(): ServletContext, ServletRequest
getAttributes(): DirContext, InitialDirContext, SearchResult, Struct
getAttributeSyntaxDefinition(): Attribute, BasicAttribute
getAuthType(): HttpServletRequest
getAutoCommit(): Connection
getBaseType(): Array
getBaseTypeName(): Array, Ref
getBeanHomeName(): DeploymentDescriptor
getBestRowIdentifier(): DatabaseMetaData
getBigDecimal(): CallableStatement, ResultSet
getBinaryStream(): Blob, ResultSet
getBlob(): CallableStatement, ResultSet
getBoolean(): CallableStatement, MapMessage, ResultSet
getBooleanProperty(): Message
getBranchQualifier(): Xid
getByte(): CallableStatement, MapMessage, ResultSet
getByteProperty(): Message
getBytes(): Blob, CallableStatement, MapMessage, ResultSet
getCallerIdentity(): EJBContext
getCatalog(): Connection
getCatalogName(): ResultSetMetaData
getCatalogs(): DatabaseMetaData
getCatalogSeparator(): DatabaseMetaData
getCatalogTerm(): DatabaseMetaData
getCausedByException(): EJBException
getChar(): MapMessage
getCharacterEncoding(): ServletRequest, ServletResponse
getCharacterStream(): Clob, ResultSet
getClassAnnotation(): RMIClassLoader
getClassName(): ActivationDesc, ActivationGroupDesc, Binding, NameClassPair, Reference
getClientHost(): RemoteServer, ServerRef
getClientID(): Connection
getClob(): CallableStatement, ResultSet
getColumnClassName(): ResultSetMetaData

getColumnCount(): ResultSetMetaData
getColumnDisplaySize(): ResultSetMetaData
getColumnLabel(): ResultSetMetaData
getColumnName(): ResultSetMetaData
getColumnPrivileges(): DatabaseMetaData
getColumns(): DatabaseMetaData
getColumnType(): ResultSetMetaData
getColumnTypeName(): ResultSetMetaData
getCommand(): RowSet
getCommandEnvironment(): ActivationGroupDesc
getCommandOptions(): CommandEnvironment
getCommandPath(): CommandEnvironment
getComment(): Cookie
getConcurrency(): ResultSet
getConnection(): DatabaseMetaData, DataSource, DriverManager, PooledConnection, RowSetInternal, Statement
getContainerManagedFields(): EntityDescriptor
getContent(): BinaryRefAddr, RefAddr, StringRefAddr
getContentLength(): ServletRequest
getContentType(): ServletRequest
getContext(): ServletContext
getContinuationContext(): NamingManager
getContinuationDirContext(): DirectoryManager
getControlDescriptors(): DeploymentDescriptor
getCookies(): HttpServletRequest
getCountLimit(): SearchControls
getCreationTime(): HttpSession
getCrossReference(): DatabaseMetaData
getCursorName(): ResultSet
getData(): ActivationDesc, ActivationGroupDesc
getDatabaseProductName(): DatabaseMetaData
getDatabaseProductVersion(): DatabaseMetaData
getDataSize(): DataTruncation
getDataSourceName(): RowSet
getDate(): CallableStatement, ResultSet, Time
getDateHeader(): HttpServletRequest
getDay(): Time
getDefaultInitCtx(): InitialContext
getDefaultSocketFactory(): RMISocketFactory
getDefaultStream(): LogStream
getDefaultTransactionIsolation(): DatabaseMetaData
getDeliveryMode(): MessageProducer
getDerefLinkFlag(): SearchControls
getDisableMessageID(): MessageProducer
getDisableMessageTimestamp(): MessageProducer
getDomain(): Cookie
getDouble(): CallableStatement, MapMessage, ResultSet
getDoubleProperty(): Message
getDriver(): DriverManager
getDriverMajorVersion(): DatabaseMetaData
getDriverMinorVersion(): DatabaseMetaData
getDriverName(): DatabaseMetaData
getDrivers(): DriverManager
getDriverVersion(): DatabaseMetaData
getEJBHome(): EJBContext, EJBMetaData, EJBObject
getEJBMetaData(): EJBHome
getEJBObject(): EntityContext, Handle, SessionContext
getEnterpriseBeanClassName(): DeploymentDescriptor
getEnumeration(): QueueBrowser
getEnvironment(): CannotProceedException, Context, EJBContext, InitialContext
getEnvironmentProperties(): DeploymentDescriptor
getErrorCode(): JMSException, SQLException
getEscapeProcessing(): RowSet
getExplanation(): NamingException
getExportedKeys(): DatabaseMetaData
getExtraNameCharacters(): DatabaseMetaData
getFactoryClassLocation(): Reference
getFactoryClassName(): Reference
getFailureHandler(): RMISocketFactory
getFetchDirection(): ResultSet, Statement
getFetchSize(): ResultSet, Statement
getFloat(): CallableStatement, MapMessage, ResultSet
getFloatProperty(): Message
getFormatId(): Xid
getGlobalTransactionId(): Xid
getGroupID(): ActivationDesc
getHandle(): EJBObject
getHeader(): HttpServletRequest
getHeaderNames(): HttpServletRequest
getHomeInterfaceClass(): EJBMetaData
getHomeInterfaceClassName(): DeploymentDescriptor
getHours(): Date
getId(): ApplicationException, HttpSession
getID(): Activatable, Attribute, BasicAttribute
getIdentifierQuoteString(): DatabaseMetaData
getIDs(): Attributes, BasicAttributes
getIds(): HttpSessionContext
getImportedKeys(): DatabaseMetaData
getIndex(): DataTruncation
getIndexInfo(): DatabaseMetaData
getInitialContext(): InitialContextFactory, NamingManager
getInitParameter(): GenericServlet, ServletConfig
getInitParameterNames(): GenericServlet,

ServletConfig
getInputStream(): ApplicationException, RemoteCall, ServletRequest
getInt(): CallableStatement, MapMessage, ResultSet
getIntHeader(): HttpServletRequest
getIntProperty(): Message
getIsolationLevel(): ControlDescriptor
getJMSCorrelationID(): Message
getJMSCorrelationIDAsBytes(): Message
getJMSDeliveryMode(): Message
getJMSDestination(): Message
getJMSExpiration(): Message
getJMSMajorVersion(): ConnectionMetaData
getJMSMessageID(): Message
getJMSMinorVersion(): ConnectionMetaData
getJMSPriority(): Message
getJMSProviderName(): ConnectionMetaData
getJMSRedelivered(): Message
getJMSReplyTo(): Message
getJMSTimestamp(): Message
getJMSType(): Message
getJMSVersion(): ConnectionMetaData
getLastAccessedTime(): HttpSession
getLastModified(): HttpServlet
getLinkedException(): JMSException
getLinkExplanation(): LinkException
getLinkName(): LinkRef
getLinkRemainingName(): LinkException
getLinkResolvedName(): LinkException
getLinkResolvedObj(): LinkException
getLocation(): ActivationDesc, ActivationGroupDesc
getLog(): RemoteServer
getLoginTimeout(): ConnectionPoolDataSource, DataSource, DriverManager, XADataSource
getLogStream(): DriverManager
getLogWriter(): ConnectionPoolDataSource, DataSource, DriverManager, XADataSource
getLong(): CallableStatement, MapMessage, ResultSet
getLongProperty(): Message
getMajorVersion(): Driver, ServletContext
getMapNames(): MapMessage
getMaxAge(): Cookie
getMaxBinaryLiteralLength(): DatabaseMetaData
getMaxCatalogNameLength(): DatabaseMetaData
getMaxCharLiteralLength(): DatabaseMetaData
getMaxColumnNameLength(): DatabaseMetaData
getMaxColumnsInGroupBy(): DatabaseMetaData
getMaxColumnsInIndex(): DatabaseMetaData
getMaxColumnsInOrderBy(): DatabaseMetaData
getMaxColumnsInSelect(): DatabaseMetaData
getMaxColumnsInTable(): DatabaseMetaData
getMaxConnections(): DatabaseMetaData
getMaxCursorNameLength(): DatabaseMetaData
getMaxFieldSize(): RowSet, Statement
getMaxInactiveInterval(): HttpSession
getMaxIndexLength(): DatabaseMetaData
getMaxProcedureNameLength(): DatabaseMetaData
getMaxRows(): RowSet, Statement
getMaxRowSize(): DatabaseMetaData
getMaxSchemaNameLength(): DatabaseMetaData
getMaxStatementLength(): DatabaseMetaData
getMaxStatements(): DatabaseMetaData
getMaxTableNameLength(): DatabaseMetaData
getMaxTablesInSelect(): DatabaseMetaData
getMaxUserNameLength(): DatabaseMetaData
getMessage(): ActivationException, RemoteException, ServerCloneException
getMessageListener(): MessageConsumer, Session
getMessageSelector(): MessageConsumer, QueueBrowser
getMetaData(): Connection, PreparedStatement, ResultSet
getMethod(): AccessControlEntry, ControlDescriptor, HttpServletRequest
getMimeType(): ServletContext
getMinorVersion(): Driver, ServletContext
getMinutes(): Date
getModificationOp(): ModificationItem
getMonth(): Time
getMoreResults(): Statement
getName(): Cookie, HttpSessionBindingEvent, NameClassPair
getNameParser(): Context, InitialContext
getNanos(): Timestamp
getNextException(): SQLException
getNextWarning(): SQLWarning
getNoLocal(): TopicSubscriber
getNumericFunctions(): DatabaseMetaData
getObject(): Binding, CallableStatement, MapMessage, ObjectMessage, ResultSet
getObjectInstance(): NamingManager, ObjectFactory
getObjectProperty(): Message
getOperation(): Operation
getOperations(): Skeleton
getOriginal(): RowSetInternal
getOriginalRow(): RowSetInternal
getOutputStream(): LogStream, RemoteCall, ServletResponse
getParameter(): DataTruncation, ServletRequest

Class Index

getParameterNames(): ServletRequest
getParameterValues(): ServletRequest
getParams(): RowSetInternal
getPassword(): RowSet
getPath(): Cookie
getPathInfo(): HttpServletRequest
getPathTranslated(): HttpServletRequest
getPooledConnection(): ConnectionPoolDataSource
getPrecision(): ResultSetMetaData
getPrefix(): CompositeName, CompoundName, Name
getPrimaryKey(): EJBObject, EntityContext
getPrimaryKeyClass(): EJBMetaData
getPrimaryKeyClassName(): EntityDescriptor
getPrimaryKeys(): DatabaseMetaData
getPriority(): MessageProducer
getProcedureColumns(): DatabaseMetaData
getProcedures(): DatabaseMetaData
getProcedureTerm(): DatabaseMetaData
getPropertyInfo(): Driver
getPropertyNames(): Message
getPropertyOverrides(): ActivationGroupDesc
getProtocol(): ServletRequest
getProviderMajorVersion(): ConnectionMetaData
getProviderMinorVersion(): ConnectionMetaData
getProviderVersion(): ConnectionMetaData
getQueryString(): HttpServletRequest
getQueryTimeout(): RowSet, Statement
getQueue(): QueueBrowser, QueueReceiver, QueueSender
getQueueName(): Queue
getQueueSession(): XAQueueSession
getRead(): DataTruncation
getReader(): ServletRequest
getRealPath(): ServletContext, ServletRequest
getReentrant(): DeploymentDescriptor
getRef(): CallableStatement, RemoteObject, ResultSet
getRefClass(): RemoteRef
getReference(): Referenceable
getReferralContext(): ReferralException
getReferralInfo(): ReferralException
getRegistry(): LocateRegistry
getRemainingName(): NamingException, ResolveResult
getRemainingNewName(): CannotProceedException
getRemoteAddr(): ServletRequest
getRemoteHost(): ServletRequest
getRemoteInterfaceClass(): EJBMetaData
getRemoteInterfaceClassName(): DeploymentDescriptor
getRemoteUser(): HttpServletRequest
getRequestDispatcher(): ServletContext
getRequestedSessionId(): HttpServletRequest
getRequestURI(): HttpServletRequest
getRequestURL(): HttpUtils
getResolvedName(): NamingException
getResolvedObj(): NamingException, ResolveResult
getResource(): ServletContext
getResourceAsStream(): ServletContext
getRestartMode(): ActivationDesc
getResultSet(): Array, Statement
getResultSetConcurrency(): Statement
getResultSetType(): Statement
getResultStream(): RemoteCall
getReturningAttributes(): SearchControls
getReturningObjFlag(): SearchControls
getRollbackOnly(): EJBContext
getRootCause(): NamingException, ServletException
getRow(): ResultSet
getRunAsIdentity(): ControlDescriptor
getRunAsMode(): ControlDescriptor
getScale(): ResultSetMetaData
getSchema(): DirContext, InitialDirContext
getSchemaClassDefinition(): DirContext, InitialDirContext
getSchemaName(): ResultSetMetaData
getSchemas(): DatabaseMetaData
getSchemaTerm(): DatabaseMetaData
getScheme(): ServletRequest
getSearchScope(): SearchControls
getSearchStringEscape(): DatabaseMetaData
getSeconds(): Date
getSecure(): Cookie
getSecurityContext(): LoaderHandler, RMIClassLoader
getServerInfo(): ServletContext
getServerName(): ServletRequest
getServerPort(): ServletRequest
getServerSession(): ServerSessionPool
getServerSessionPool(): ConnectionConsumer
getServlet(): ServletContext, UnavailableException
getServletConfig(): GenericServlet, Servlet
getServletContext(): GenericServlet, ServletConfig
getServletInfo(): GenericServlet, Servlet
getServletNames(): ServletContext
getServletPath(): HttpServletRequest
getServlets(): ServletContext
getSession(): HttpServletRequest, HttpSessionBindingEvent, HttpSessionContext, ServerSession
getSessionContext(): HttpSession
getSessionTimeout(): SessionDescriptor
getShort(): CallableStatement, MapMessage,

ResultSet
getShortProperty(): Message
getSocketFactory(): RMISocketFactory
getSQLException(): ConnectionEvent
getSQLKeywords(): DatabaseMetaData
getSQLState(): SQLException
getSQLTypeName(): SQLData, Struct
getStateManagementType(): SessionDescriptor
getStatement(): ResultSet
getStatus(): Transaction, TransactionManager, UserTransaction
getString(): CallableStatement, MapMessage, ResultSet
getStringFunctions(): DatabaseMetaData
getStringProperty(): Message
getSubString(): Clob
getSuffix(): CompositeName, CompoundName, Name
getSystem(): ActivationGroup, ActivationGroupID
getSystemFunctions(): DatabaseMetaData
getTableName(): ResultSetMetaData
getTablePrivileges(): DatabaseMetaData
getTables(): DatabaseMetaData
getTableTypes(): DatabaseMetaData
getText(): TextMessage
getTime(): CallableStatement, ResultSet
getTimeDateFunctions(): DatabaseMetaData
getTimeLimit(): SearchControls
getTimestamp(): CallableStatement, ResultSet
getTimeToLive(): MessageProducer
getTopic(): TopicPublisher, TopicSubscriber
getTopicName(): Topic
getTopicSession(): XATopicSession
getTransacted(): Session
getTransaction(): TransactionManager
getTransactionAttribute(): ControlDescriptor
getTransactionIsolation(): Connection, RowSet
getTransactionTimeout(): XAResource
getTransferSize(): DataTruncation
getType(): RefAddr, ResultSet
getTypeInfo(): DatabaseMetaData
getTypeMap(): Connection, RowSet
getUDTs(): DatabaseMetaData
getUnavailableSeconds(): UnavailableException
getUnexecutedModifications(): AttributeModificationException
getUnicodeStream(): ResultSet
getUpdateCount(): Statement
getUpdateCounts(): BatchUpdateException
getUrl(): RowSet
getURL(): DatabaseMetaData
getURLContext(): NamingManager
getURLOrDefaultInitCtx(): InitialContext
getUsername(): RowSet
getUserName(): DatabaseMetaData
getUserTransaction(): EJBContext
getValue(): Cookie, HttpSession, Lease
getValueNames(): HttpSession
getVersion(): Cookie
getVersionColumns(): DatabaseMetaData
getVMID(): Lease
getWarnings(): Connection, ResultSet, Statement
getWriter(): ServletResponse
getXAConnection(): XADataSource
getXAResource(): XAConnection, XASession
getYear(): Time
gotDefault: InitialContext

H

Handle: javax.ejb
hash(): Delegate
hashCode(): ActivationDesc, ActivationGroupDesc, ActivationGroupID, ActivationID, BasicAttribute, BinaryRefAddr, CommandEnvironment, CompositeName, CompoundName, Delegate, MarshalledObject, ObjectImpl, ObjID, RefAddr, Reference, RemoteObject, UID, VMID
hasInitialContextFactoryBuilder(): NamingManager
hasMore(): NamingEnumeration
HeuristicCommitException: javax.transaction
HeuristicMixedException: javax.transaction
HeuristicRollbackException: javax.transaction
HttpServlet: javax.servlet.http
HttpServletRequest: javax.servlet.http
HttpServletResponse: javax.servlet.http
HttpSession: javax.servlet.http
HttpSessionBindingEvent: javax.servlet.http
HttpSessionBindingListener: javax.servlet.http
HttpSessionContext: javax.servlet.http
HttpUtils: javax.servlet.http

I

id: NameComponent, NameValuePair, ValueMember
id(): AlreadyBoundHelper, BindingHelper, BindingIteratorHelper, BindingListHelper, BindingTypeHelper, CannotProceedHelper, InvalidNameHelper, IstringHelper, NameComponentHelper, NameHelper, NamingContextHelper, NotEmptyHelper, NotFoundHelper, NotFoundReasonHelper,

Class Index

ServiceDetailHelper, ServiceInformationHelper, TypeCode
IDLEntity: org.omg.CORBA.portable
IDLType: org.omg.CORBA
IllegalStateException: javax.jms
IMP_LIMIT: org.omg.CORBA
impl: CompoundName
importedKeyCascade: DatabaseMetaData
importedKeyInitiallyDeferred: DatabaseMetaData
importedKeyInitiallyImmediate: DatabaseMetaData
importedKeyNoAction: DatabaseMetaData
importedKeyNotDeferrable: DatabaseMetaData
importedKeyRestrict: DatabaseMetaData
importedKeySetDefault: DatabaseMetaData
importedKeySetNull: DatabaseMetaData
inactive(): Activatable
inactiveGroup(): ActivationGroup, ActivationMonitor
inactiveObject(): ActivationGroup, ActivationMonitor
include(): RequestDispatcher
InconsistentTypeCode: org.omg.CORBA.ORBPackage
init(): GenericServlet, ORB, Servlet
INITIAL_CONTEXT_FACTORY: Context
InitialContext: javax.naming
InitialContextFactory: javax.naming.spi
InitialContextFactoryBuilder: javax.naming.spi
InitialDirContext: javax.naming.directory
INITIALIZE: org.omg.CORBA
InputStream: org.omg.CORBA.portable
insert(): AlreadyBoundHelper, BindingHelper, BindingIteratorHelper, BindingListHelper, BindingTypeHelper, CannotProceedHelper, InvalidNameHelper, IstringHelper, NameComponentHelper, NameHelper, NamingContextHelper, NotEmptyHelper, NotFoundHelper, NotFoundReasonHelper, ServiceDetailHelper, ServiceInformationHelper
insert_any(): Any, DynAny
insert_boolean(): Any, DynAny
insert_char(): Any, DynAny
insert_double(): Any, DynAny
insert_fixed(): Any
insert_float(): Any, DynAny
insert_long(): Any, DynAny
insert_longlong(): Any, DynAny
insert_Object(): Any
insert_octet(): Any, DynAny
insert_Principal(): Any
insert_reference(): DynAny
insert_short(): Any, DynAny
insert_Streamable(): Any
insert_string(): Any, DynAny
insert_TypeCode(): Any
insert_typecode(): DynAny
insert_ulong(): Any, DynAny
insert_ulonglong(): Any, DynAny
insert_ushort(): Any, DynAny
insert_val(): DynAny
insert_Value(): Any
insert_wchar(): Any, DynAny
insert_wstring(): Any, DynAny
insertRow(): ResultSet
insertsAreDetected(): DatabaseMetaData
InsufficientResourcesException: javax.naming
INTEGER: Types
INTERNAL: org.omg.CORBA
InterruptedNamingException: javax.naming
INTF_REPOS: org.omg.CORBA
IntHolder: org.omg.CORBA
INV_FLAG: org.omg.CORBA
INV_IDENT: org.omg.CORBA
INV_OBJREF: org.omg.CORBA
INV_POLICY: org.omg.CORBA
Invalid: org.omg.CORBA.DynAnyPackage
INVALID_TRANSACTION: org.omg.CORBA
invalidate(): HttpSession
InvalidAttributeIdentifierException: javax.naming.directory
InvalidAttributesException: javax.naming.directory
InvalidAttributeValueException: javax.naming.directory
InvalidClientIDException: javax.jms
InvalidDestinationException: javax.jms
InvalidName: org.omg.CORBA.ORBPackage, org.omg.CosNaming.NamingContextPackage
InvalidNameException: javax.naming
InvalidNameHelper: org.omg.CosNaming.NamingContextPackage
InvalidNameHolder: org.omg.CosNaming.NamingContextPackage
InvalidSearchControlsException: javax.naming.directory
InvalidSearchFilterException: javax.naming.directory
InvalidSelectorException: javax.jms
InvalidSeq: org.omg.CORBA.DynAnyPackage
InvalidTransactionException: javax.transaction
InvalidValue: org.omg.CORBA.DynAnyPackage
invoke(): _BindingIteratorImplBase, _NamingContextImplBase, Delegate, DynamicImplementation, RemoteRef, Request
InvokeHandler: org.omg.CORBA.portable
IRObject: org.omg.CORBA

is_a(): Delegate
is_equivalent(): Delegate
is_local(): Delegate
isAfterLast(): ResultSet
isAutoIncrement(): ResultSetMetaData
isBeforeFirst(): ResultSet
isCallerInRole(): EJBContext
isCaseIgnored(): Attributes, BasicAttributes
isCaseSensitive(): ResultSetMetaData
isCatalogAtStart(): DatabaseMetaData
isClosed(): Connection
isCurrency(): ResultSetMetaData
isDefinitelyWritable(): ResultSetMetaData
isEmpty(): CompositeName, CompoundName, Name
isFirst(): ResultSet
isIdentical(): EJBObject
isLast(): ResultSet
isNew(): HttpSession
isNullable(): ResultSetMetaData
isPermanent(): UnavailableException
isReadOnly(): Connection, DatabaseMetaData, ResultSetMetaData, RowSet
isReentrant(): DeploymentDescriptor
isRelative(): NameClassPair
isRequestedSessionIdFromCookie(): HttpServletRequest
isRequestedSessionIdFromUrl(): HttpServletRequest
isRequestedSessionIdFromURL(): HttpServletRequest
isRequestedSessionIdValid(): HttpServletRequest
isSameRM(): XAResource
isSearchable(): ResultSetMetaData
isSession(): EJBMetaData
isSigned(): ResultSetMetaData
IstringHelper: org.omg.CosNaming
isUnique(): VMID
isWritable(): ResultSetMetaData
item(): ContextList, ExceptionList, NVList
itemExists(): MapMessage

J

JAVA_OBJECT: Types
jdbcCompliant(): Driver
JMSException: javax.jms
JMSSecurityException: javax.jms

K

kind: NameComponent
kind(): TypeCode

L

label: UnionMember
LANGUAGE: Context
last(): ResultSet
Lease: java.rmi.dgc
length(): Blob, Clob, DynSequence, TypeCode
LimitExceededException: javax.naming
LinkException: javax.naming
linkExplanation: LinkException
LinkLoopException: javax.naming
LinkRef: javax.naming
linkRemainingName: LinkException
linkResolvedName: LinkException
linkResolvedObj: LinkException
list(): _NamingContextImplBase, _NamingContextStub, Context, InitialContext, Naming, NamingContext, Registry
list_initial_services(): ORB
listBindings(): Context, InitialContext
loadClass(): LoaderHandler, RMIClassLoader
LoaderHandler: java.rmi.server
LocateRegistry: java.rmi.registry
log(): GenericServlet, LogStream, ServletContext
LogStream: java.rmi.server
LongHolder: org.omg.CORBA
LONGVARBINARY: Types
LONGVARCHAR: Types
lookup(): Context, InitialContext, Naming, Registry
lookupLink(): Context, InitialContext

M

MalformedLinkException: javax.naming
MapMessage: javax.jms
MARSHAL: org.omg.CORBA
MarshalException: java.rmi
MarshalledObject: java.rmi
MAXBQUALSIZE: Xid
MAXGTRIDSIZE: Xid
member(): DynUnion
member_count(): TypeCode
member_kind(): DynUnion
member_label(): TypeCode
member_name(): DynUnion, TypeCode

member_type(): TypeCode
member_visibility(): TypeCode
Message: javax.jms
MessageConsumer: javax.jms
MessageEOFException: javax.jms
MessageFormatException: javax.jms
MessageListener: javax.jms
MessageNotReadableException: javax.jms
MessageNotWriteableException: javax.jms
MessageProducer: javax.jms
minor: SystemException
missing_node: NotFoundReason
ModificationItem: javax.naming.directory
modifyAttributes(): DirContext, InitialDirContext
moveToCurrentRow(): ResultSet
moveToInsertRow(): ResultSet
myProps: InitialContext
mySyntax: CompoundName

N

name: DriverPropertyInfo, StructMember, UnionMember, ValueMember
Name: javax.naming
name(): NamedValue, Principal, TypeCode
NameAlreadyBoundException: javax.naming
NameClassPair: javax.naming
NameComponent: org.omg.CosNaming
NameComponentHelper: org.omg.CosNaming
NameComponentHolder: org.omg.CosNaming
NamedValue: org.omg.CORBA
NameHelper: org.omg.CosNaming
NameHolder: org.omg.CosNaming
NameNotFoundException: javax.naming
NameParser: javax.naming
NameValuePair: org.omg.CORBA
Naming: java.rmi
NamingContext: org.omg.CosNaming
NamingContextHelper: org.omg.CosNaming
NamingContextHolder: org.omg.CosNaming
NamingEnumeration: javax.naming
NamingException: javax.naming
NamingManager: javax.naming.spi
NamingSecurityException: javax.naming
narrow(): BindingIteratorHelper, NamingContextHelper
nativeSQL(): Connection
ncontext: BindingType
new_context(): _NamingContextImplBase, _NamingContextStub, NamingContext
newCall(): RemoteRef
newInstance(): ActivationGroup, ActivationGroup_Stub, ActivationInstantiator
next(): DynAny, NamingEnumeration, ResultSet
next_n(): _BindingIteratorImplBase, _BindingIteratorStub, BindingIterator
next_one(): _BindingIteratorImplBase, _BindingIteratorStub, BindingIterator
NO_IMPLEMENT: org.omg.CORBA
NO_MEMORY: org.omg.CORBA
NO_PERMISSION: org.omg.CORBA
NO_RESOURCES: org.omg.CORBA
NO_RESPONSE: org.omg.CORBA
nobject: BindingType
NoInitialContextException: javax.naming
non_existent(): Delegate
NON_PERSISTENT: DeliveryMode
NoPermissionException: javax.naming
NoSuchAttributeException: javax.naming.directory
NoSuchObjectException: java.rmi
not_context: NotFoundReason
not_object: NotFoundReason
NotBoundException: java.rmi
NotContextException: javax.naming
NotEmpty: org.omg.CosNaming.NamingContextPackage
NotEmptyHelper: org.omg.CosNaming.NamingContextPackage
NotEmptyHolder: org.omg.CosNaming.NamingContextPackage
NotFound: org.omg.CosNaming.NamingContextPackage
NotFoundHelper: org.omg.CosNaming.NamingContextPackage
NotFoundHolder: org.omg.CosNaming.NamingContextPackage
NotFoundReason: org.omg.CosNaming.NamingContextPackage
NotFoundReasonHelper: org.omg.CosNaming.NamingContextPackage
NotFoundReasonHolder: org.omg.CosNaming.NamingContextPackage
NotSupportedException: javax.transaction
NULL: Types
nullPlusNonNullIsNull(): DatabaseMetaData
nullsAreSortedAtEnd(): DatabaseMetaData
nullsAreSortedAtStart(): DatabaseMetaData
nullsAreSortedHigh(): DatabaseMetaData
nullsAreSortedLow(): DatabaseMetaData
NUMERIC: Types
NVList: org.omg.CORBA

O

OBJ_ADAPTER: org.omg.CORBA
Object: org.omg.CORBA
OBJECT_FACTORIES: Context
OBJECT_NOT_EXIST: org.omg.CORBA
OBJECT_SCOPE: SearchControls
object_to_string(): ORB
ObjectFactory: javax.naming.spi
ObjectFactoryBuilder: javax.naming.spi
ObjectHolder: org.omg.CORBA
ObjectImpl: org.omg.CORBA.portable
ObjectMessage: javax.jms
ObjectNotFoundException: javax.ejb
ObjID: java.rmi.server
ONELEVEL_SCOPE: SearchControls
onException(): ExceptionListener
onMessage(): MessageListener
op_name(): ServerRequest
Operation: java.rmi.server
operation(): Request, ServerRequest
OperationNotSupportedException: javax.naming
ORB: org.omg.CORBA
orb(): Delegate, InputStream, OutputStream
OTHER: Types
othersDeletesAreVisible(): DatabaseMetaData
othersInsertsAreVisible(): DatabaseMetaData
othersUpdatesAreVisible(): DatabaseMetaData
OutputStream: org.omg.CORBA.portable
ownDeletesAreVisible(): DatabaseMetaData
ownInsertsAreVisible(): DatabaseMetaData
ownUpdatesAreVisible(): DatabaseMetaData

P

packagePrefix: LoaderHandler, RemoteRef
params(): ServerRequest
parent(): Context
parse(): NameParser
parseLevel(): LogStream
parsePostData(): HttpUtils
parseQueryString(): HttpUtils
PartialResultException: javax.naming
perform_work(): ORB
PERSIST_STORE: org.omg.CORBA
PERSISTENT: DeliveryMode
Policy: org.omg.CORBA
policy_type(): Policy
PolicyError: org.omg.CORBA
poll_next_response(): ORB
poll_response(): Request
PooledConnection: javax.sql
position(): Blob, Clob
prepare(): XAResource
prepareCall(): Connection
PreparedStatement: java.sql
prepareStatement(): Connection
previous(): ResultSet
Principal: org.omg.CORBA
PrincipalHolder: org.omg.CORBA
print(): ServletOutputStream
println(): DriverManager, ServletOutputStream
printStackTrace(): ActivationException, RemoteException, ServerCloneException
PRIVATE_MEMBER: org.omg.CORBA
procedureColumnIn: DatabaseMetaData
procedureColumnInOut: DatabaseMetaData
procedureColumnOut: DatabaseMetaData
procedureColumnResult: DatabaseMetaData
procedureColumnReturn: DatabaseMetaData
procedureColumnUnknown: DatabaseMetaData
procedureNoNulls: DatabaseMetaData
procedureNoResult: DatabaseMetaData
procedureNullable: DatabaseMetaData
procedureNullableUnknown: DatabaseMetaData
procedureResultUnknown: DatabaseMetaData
procedureReturnsResult: DatabaseMetaData
propertyExists(): Message
PROVIDER_URL: Context
PUBLIC_MEMBER: org.omg.CORBA
publish(): TopicPublisher
put(): Attributes, BasicAttributes
putValue(): HttpSession

Q

Queue: javax.jms
QueueBrowser: javax.jms
QueueConnection: javax.jms
QueueConnectionFactory: javax.jms
QueueReceiver: javax.jms
QueueRequestor: javax.jms
QueueSender: javax.jms
QueueSession: javax.jms

R

read(): AlreadyBoundHelper, BindingHelper, BindingIteratorHelper, BindingListHelper, BindingTypeHelper, CannotProceedHelper, InputStream, InvalidNameHelper, IstringHelper, NameComponentHelper, NameHelper, NamingContextHelper, NotEmptyHelper, NotFoundHelper, NotFoundReasonHelper, ObjID, ServiceDetailHelper, ServiceInformationHelper, UID
read_any(): InputStream
read_boolean(): InputStream
read_boolean_array(): InputStream
read_char(): InputStream
read_char_array(): InputStream
read_Context(): InputStream
read_double(): InputStream
read_double_array(): InputStream
read_fixed(): InputStream
read_float(): InputStream
read_float_array(): InputStream
read_long(): InputStream
read_long_array(): InputStream
read_longlong(): InputStream
read_longlong_array(): InputStream
read_Object(): InputStream
read_octet(): InputStream
read_octet_array(): InputStream
read_Principal(): InputStream
read_short(): InputStream
read_short_array(): InputStream
read_string(): InputStream
read_TypeCode(): InputStream
read_ulong(): InputStream
read_ulong_array(): InputStream
read_ulonglong(): InputStream
read_ulonglong_array(): InputStream
read_ushort(): InputStream
read_ushort_array(): InputStream
read_value(): Any
read_wchar(): InputStream
read_wchar_array(): InputStream
read_wstring(): InputStream
readArray(): SQLInput
readAsciiStream(): SQLInput
readBigDecimal(): SQLInput
readBinaryStream(): SQLInput
readBlob(): SQLInput
readBoolean(): BytesMessage, SQLInput, StreamMessage
readByte(): BytesMessage, SQLInput, StreamMessage
readBytes(): BytesMessage, SQLInput, StreamMessage
readChar(): BytesMessage, StreamMessage
readCharacterStream(): SQLInput
readClob(): SQLInput
readData(): RowSetReader
readDate(): SQLInput
readDouble(): BytesMessage, SQLInput, StreamMessage
readFloat(): BytesMessage, SQLInput, StreamMessage
readInt(): BytesMessage, SQLInput, StreamMessage
readLine(): ServletInputStream
readLong(): BytesMessage, SQLInput, StreamMessage
readObject(): SQLInput, StreamMessage
readRef(): SQLInput
readShort(): BytesMessage, SQLInput, StreamMessage
readSQL(): SQLData
readString(): SQLInput, StreamMessage
readTime(): SQLInput
readTimestamp(): SQLInput
readUnsignedByte(): BytesMessage
readUnsignedShort(): BytesMessage
readUTF(): BytesMessage
REAL: Types
reason: PolicyError
rebind(): _NamingContextImplBase, _NamingContextStub, Context, DirContext, InitialContext, InitialDirContext, Naming, NamingContext, Registry
rebind_context(): _NamingContextImplBase, _NamingContextStub, NamingContext
receive(): MessageConsumer
receiveNoWait(): MessageConsumer
recover(): Session, XAResource
ref: RemoteObject
Ref: java.sql
REF: Types
RefAddr: javax.naming
Reference: javax.naming
Referenceable: javax.naming
REFERRAL: Context
ReferralException: javax.naming
refreshRow(): ResultSet
register(): Activatable
registerDriver(): DriverManager
registerGroup(): ActivationSystem
registerObject(): ActivationSystem
registerOutParameter(): CallableStatement
registerSynchronization(): Transaction

Registry: java.rmi.registry
REGISTRY_ID: ObjID
REGISTRY_PORT: Registry
RegistryHandler: java.rmi.registry
registryImpl(): RegistryHandler
registryStub(): RegistryHandler
relative(): ResultSet
release(): Delegate
releaseInputStream(): RemoteCall
releaseOutputStream(): RemoteCall
releaseReply(): Delegate
remainingName: NamingException, ResolveResult
remainingNewName: CannotProceedException
RemarshalException: org.omg.CORBA.portable
Remote: java.rmi
RemoteCall: java.rmi.server
remoteEquals(): RemoteRef
RemoteException: java.rmi
remoteHashCode(): RemoteRef
RemoteObject: java.rmi.server
RemoteRef: java.rmi.server
RemoteServer: java.rmi.server
RemoteStub: java.rmi.server
remoteToString(): RemoteRef
remove(): Attribute, Attributes, BasicAttribute, BasicAttributes, CompositeName, CompoundName, ContextList, EJBHome, EJBObject, ExceptionList, Name, NVList, Reference
REMOVE_ATTRIBUTE: DirContext
removeAttribute(): ServletContext
removeConnectionEventListener(): PooledConnection
RemoveException: javax.ejb
removeFromEnvironment(): Context, InitialContext
removeRowSetListener(): RowSet
removeValue(): HttpSession
rename(): Context, InitialContext
REPLACE_ATTRIBUTE: DirContext
Request: org.omg.CORBA
request(): Delegate, QueueRequestor, TopicRequestor
RequestDispatcher: javax.servlet
required: DriverPropertyInfo
reset(): BytesMessage, StreamMessage
resolve(): _NamingContextImplBase, _NamingContextStub, NamingContext
resolve_initial_references(): ORB
resolvedName: NamingException
resolvedObj: NamingException, ResolveResult
Resolver: javax.naming.spi
ResolveResult: javax.naming.spi
resolveToClass(): Resolver
ResourceAllocationException: javax.jms
ResponseHandler: org.omg.CORBA.portable
rest_of_name: CannotProceed, NotFound
result(): Request, ServerRequest
ResultSet: java.sql
ResultSetMetaData: java.sql
resume(): TransactionManager
return_value(): Request
rewind(): DynAny
RMIClassLoader: java.rmi.server
RMIClientSocketFactory: java.rmi.server
RMIFailureHandler: java.rmi.server
RMISecurityException: java.rmi
RMISecurityManager: java.rmi
RMIServerSocketFactory: java.rmi.server
RMISocketFactory: java.rmi.server
rollback(): Connection, Session, Transaction, TransactionManager, UserTransaction, XAResource
RollbackException: javax.transaction
rootException: NamingException
rowChanged(): RowSetListener
rowDeleted(): ResultSet
rowInserted(): ResultSet
RowSet: javax.sql
rowSetChanged(): RowSetListener
RowSetEvent: javax.sql
RowSetInternal: javax.sql
RowSetListener: javax.sql
RowSetMetaData: javax.sql
RowSetReader: javax.sql
RowSetWriter: javax.sql
rowUpdated(): ResultSet
run(): ORB

S

SC_ACCEPTED: HttpServletResponse
SC_BAD_GATEWAY: HttpServletResponse
SC_BAD_REQUEST: HttpServletResponse
SC_CONFLICT: HttpServletResponse
SC_CONTINUE: HttpServletResponse
SC_CREATED: HttpServletResponse
SC_FORBIDDEN: HttpServletResponse
SC_GATEWAY_TIMEOUT: HttpServletResponse
SC_GONE: HttpServletResponse
SC_HTTP_VERSION_NOT_SUPPORTED: HttpServletResponse
SC_INTERNAL_SERVER_ERROR: HttpServletResponse
SC_LENGTH_REQUIRED: HttpServletResponse

SC_METHOD_NOT_ALLOWED: HttpServletResponse
SC_MOVED_PERMANENTLY: HttpServletResponse
SC_MOVED_TEMPORARILY: HttpServletResponse
SC_MULTIPLE_CHOICES: HttpServletResponse
SC_NO_CONTENT: HttpServletResponse
SC_NON_AUTHORITATIVE_INFORMATION: HttpServletResponse
SC_NOT_ACCEPTABLE: HttpServletResponse
SC_NOT_FOUND: HttpServletResponse
SC_NOT_IMPLEMENTED: HttpServletResponse
SC_NOT_MODIFIED: HttpServletResponse
SC_OK: HttpServletResponse
SC_PARTIAL_CONTENT: HttpServletResponse
SC_PAYMENT_REQUIRED: HttpServletResponse
SC_PRECONDITION_FAILED: HttpServletResponse
SC_PROXY_AUTHENTICATION_REQUIRED: HttpServletResponse
SC_REQUEST_ENTITY_TOO_LARGE: HttpServletResponse
SC_REQUEST_TIMEOUT: HttpServletResponse
SC_REQUEST_URI_TOO_LONG: HttpServletResponse
SC_RESET_CONTENT: HttpServletResponse
SC_SEE_OTHER: HttpServletResponse
SC_SERVICE_UNAVAILABLE: HttpServletResponse
SC_SWITCHING_PROTOCOLS: HttpServletResponse
SC_UNAUTHORIZED: HttpServletResponse
SC_UNSUPPORTED_MEDIA_TYPE: HttpServletResponse
SC_USE_PROXY: HttpServletResponse
SchemaViolationException: javax.naming.directory
search(): DirContext, InitialDirContext
SearchControls: javax.naming.directory
SearchResult: javax.naming.directory
SECURITY_AUTHENTICATION: Context
SECURITY_CREDENTIALS: Context
SECURITY_PRINCIPAL: Context
SECURITY_PROTOCOL: Context
seek(): DynAny
send(): QueueSender
send_deferred(): Request
send_multiple_requests_deferred(): ORB
send_multiple_requests_oneway(): ORB
send_oneway(): Request
sendError(): HttpServletResponse
sendRedirect(): HttpServletResponse
serialVersionUID: RemoteRef, ServerRef
servant: ServantObject
servant_postinvoke(): Delegate
servant_preinvoke(): Delegate
ServantObject: org.omg.CORBA.portable
ServerCloneException: java.rmi.server
ServerError: java.rmi
ServerException: java.rmi
ServerNotActiveException: java.rmi.server
ServerRef: java.rmi.server
ServerRequest: org.omg.CORBA
ServerRuntimeException: java.rmi
ServerSession: javax.jms
ServerSessionPool: javax.jms
service(): GenericServlet, HttpServlet, Servlet
service_detail: ServiceDetail
service_detail_type: ServiceDetail
service_details: ServiceInformation
service_options: ServiceInformation
ServiceDetail: org.omg.CORBA
ServiceDetailHelper: org.omg.CORBA
ServiceInformation: org.omg.CORBA
ServiceInformationHelper: org.omg.CORBA
ServiceInformationHolder: org.omg.CORBA
ServiceUnavailableException: javax.naming
Servlet: javax.servlet
ServletConfig: javax.servlet
ServletContext: javax.servlet
ServletException: javax.servlet
ServletInputStream: javax.servlet
ServletOutputStream: javax.servlet
ServletRequest: javax.servlet
ServletResponse: javax.servlet
Session: javax.jms
SessionBean: javax.ejb
SessionContext: javax.ejb
SessionDescriptor: javax.ejb.deployment
SessionSynchronization: javax.ejb
set_as_default(): DynUnion
set_elements(): DynArray, DynSequence
set_exception(): ServerRequest
set_members(): DynStruct, DynValue
set_one_value(): Context
SET_OVERRIDE: SetOverrideType
set_parameters(): ORB
set_policy_override(): Delegate
set_result(): ServerRequest
set_return_type(): Request
set_value(): DynFixed
set_values(): Context
setAccessControlEntries(): DeploymentDescriptor
setActivationDesc(): ActivationSystem
setActivationGroupDesc(): ActivationSystem
setAllowedIdentities(): AccessControlEntry
setAltName(): CannotProceedException

setAltNameCtx(): CannotProceedException
setArray(): PreparedStatement, RowSet
setAsciiStream(): PreparedStatement, RowSet
setAttribute(): ServletContext, ServletRequest
setAttributes(): SearchResult
setAutoCommit(): Connection
setAutoIncrement(): RowSetMetaData
setBeanHomeName(): DeploymentDescriptor
setBigDecimal(): PreparedStatement, RowSet
setBinaryStream(): PreparedStatement, RowSet
setBlob(): PreparedStatement, RowSet
setBoolean(): MapMessage, PreparedStatement, RowSet
setBooleanProperty(): Message
setByte(): MapMessage, PreparedStatement, RowSet
setByteProperty(): Message
setBytes(): MapMessage, PreparedStatement, RowSet
setCaseSensitive(): RowSetMetaData
setCatalog(): Connection
setCatalogName(): RowSetMetaData
setChar(): MapMessage
setCharacterStream(): PreparedStatement, RowSet
setClassName(): NameClassPair
setClientID(): Connection
setClob(): PreparedStatement, RowSet
setColumnCount(): RowSetMetaData
setColumnDisplaySize(): RowSetMetaData
setColumnLabel(): RowSetMetaData
setColumnName(): RowSetMetaData
setColumnType(): RowSetMetaData
setColumnTypeName(): RowSetMetaData
setCommand(): RowSet
setComment(): Cookie
setConcurrency(): RowSet
setContainerManagedFields(): EntityDescriptor
setContentLength(): ServletResponse
setContentType(): ServletResponse
setControlDescriptors(): DeploymentDescriptor
setCountLimit(): SearchControls
setCurrency(): RowSetMetaData
setCursorName(): Statement
setDataSourceName(): RowSet
setDate(): PreparedStatement, RowSet, Time
setDateHeader(): HttpServletResponse
setDefaultStream(): LogStream
setDeliveryMode(): MessageProducer
setDerefLinkFlag(): SearchControls
setDisableMessageID(): MessageProducer
setDisableMessageTimestamp(): MessageProducer
setDomain(): Cookie
setDouble(): MapMessage, PreparedStatement, RowSet
setDoubleProperty(): Message
setEnterpriseBeanClassName(): DeploymentDescriptor
setEntityContext(): EntityBean
setEnvironment(): CannotProceedException
setEnvironmentProperties(): DeploymentDescriptor
setEscapeProcessing(): RowSet, Statement
setExceptionListener(): Connection
setFailureHandler(): RMISocketFactory
setFetchDirection(): ResultSet, Statement
setFetchSize(): ResultSet, Statement
setFloat(): MapMessage, PreparedStatement, RowSet
setFloatProperty(): Message
setHeader(): HttpServletResponse
setHomeInterfaceClassName(): DeploymentDescriptor
setHours(): Date
setInitialContextFactoryBuilder(): NamingManager
setInt(): MapMessage, PreparedStatement, RowSet
setIntHeader(): HttpServletResponse
setIntProperty(): Message
setIsolationLevel(): ControlDescriptor
setJMSCorrelationID(): Message
setJMSCorrelationIDAsBytes(): Message
setJMSDeliveryMode(): Message
setJMSDestination(): Message
setJMSExpiration(): Message
setJMSMessageID(): Message
setJMSPriority(): Message
setJMSRedelivered(): Message
setJMSReplyTo(): Message
setJMSTimestamp(): Message
setJMSType(): Message
setLinkedException(): JMSException
setLinkExplanation(): LinkException
setLinkRemainingName(): LinkException
setLinkResolvedName(): LinkException
setLinkResolvedObj(): LinkException
setLog(): RemoteServer
setLoginTimeout(): ConnectionPoolDataSource, DataSource, DriverManager, XADataSource
setLogStream(): DriverManager
setLogWriter(): ConnectionPoolDataSource, DataSource, DriverManager, XADataSource
setLong(): MapMessage, PreparedStatement, RowSet
setLongProperty(): Message
setMaxAge(): Cookie
setMaxFieldSize(): RowSet, Statement

Class Index

setMaxInactiveInterval(): HttpSession
setMaxRows(): RowSet, Statement
setMessageListener(): MessageConsumer, Session
setMetaData(): RowSetInternal
setMethod(): AccessControlEntry, ControlDescriptor
setMinutes(): Date
setMonth(): Time
setName(): NameClassPair
setNanos(): Timestamp
setNextException(): SQLException
setNextWarning(): SQLWarning
setNull(): PreparedStatement, RowSet
setNullable(): RowSetMetaData
setObject(): Binding, MapMessage, ObjectMessage, PreparedStatement, RowSet
setObjectFactoryBuilder(): NamingManager
setObjectProperty(): Message
setOutputStream(): LogStream
SetOverrideType: org.omg.CORBA
setPassword(): RowSet
setPath(): Cookie
setPrecision(): RowSetMetaData
setPrimaryKeyClassName(): EntityDescriptor
setPriority(): MessageProducer
setQueryTimeout(): RowSet, Statement
setReadOnly(): Connection, RowSet
setReentrant(): DeploymentDescriptor
setRef(): PreparedStatement, RemoteStub, RowSet
setRelative(): NameClassPair
setRemainingName(): NamingException, ResolveResult
setRemainingNewName(): CannotProceedException
setRemoteInterfaceClassName(): DeploymentDescriptor
setResolvedName(): NamingException
setResolvedObj(): NamingException, ResolveResult
setReturningAttributes(): SearchControls
setReturningObjFlag(): SearchControls
setRollbackOnly(): EJBContext, Transaction, TransactionManager, UserTransaction
setRootCause(): NamingException
setRunAsIdentity(): ControlDescriptor
setRunAsMode(): ControlDescriptor
setScale(): RowSetMetaData
setSchemaName(): RowSetMetaData
setSearchable(): RowSetMetaData
setSearchScope(): SearchControls
setSeconds(): Date
setSecure(): Cookie
setSessionContext(): SessionBean
setSessionTimeout(): SessionDescriptor
setShort(): MapMessage, PreparedStatement, RowSet
setShortProperty(): Message
setSigned(): RowSetMetaData
setSocketFactory(): RMISocketFactory
setStateManagementType(): SessionDescriptor
setStatus(): HttpServletResponse
setString(): MapMessage, PreparedStatement, RowSet
setStringProperty(): Message
setSystem(): ActivationGroup
setTableName(): RowSetMetaData
setText(): TextMessage
setTime(): Date, PreparedStatement, RowSet, Time
setTimeLimit(): SearchControls
setTimestamp(): PreparedStatement, RowSet
setTimeToLive(): MessageProducer
setTransactionAttribute(): ControlDescriptor
setTransactionIsolation(): Connection, RowSet
setTransactionTimeout(): TransactionManager, UserTransaction, XAResource
setType(): RowSet
setTypeMap(): Connection, RowSet
setUnexecutedModifications(): AttributeModificationException
setUnicodeStream(): PreparedStatement
setUrl(): RowSet
setUsername(): RowSet
setValue(): Cookie
setVersion(): Cookie
setYear(): Time
ShortHolder: org.omg.CORBA
shutdown(): ActivationSystem, ORB
SILENT: LogStream
SingleThreadModel: javax.servlet
size(): Attribute, Attributes, BasicAttribute, BasicAttributes, CompositeName, CompoundName, Name, Reference
SizeLimitExceededException: javax.naming
Skeleton: java.rmi.server
SkeletonMismatchException: java.rmi.server
SkeletonNotFoundException: java.rmi.server
skipReferral(): ReferralException
SMALLINT: Types
SocketSecurityException: java.rmi.server
SPECIFIED_IDENTITY: ControlDescriptor
SQLData: java.sql
SQLException: java.sql
SQLInput: java.sql
SQLOutput: java.sql

SQLWarning: java.sql
start(): Connection, ServerSession, XAResource
startsWith(): CompositeName, CompoundName, Name
STATEFUL_SESSION: SessionDescriptor
STATELESS_SESSION: SessionDescriptor
Statement: java.sql
Status: javax.transaction
STATUS_ACTIVE: Status
STATUS_COMMITTED: Status
STATUS_COMMITTING: Status
STATUS_MARKED_ROLLBACK: Status
STATUS_NO_TRANSACTION: Status
STATUS_PREPARED: Status
STATUS_PREPARING: Status
STATUS_ROLLEDBACK: Status
STATUS_ROLLING_BACK: Status
STATUS_UNKNOWN: Status
stop(): Connection
storesLowerCaseIdentifiers(): DatabaseMetaData
storesLowerCaseQuotedIdentifiers(): DatabaseMetaData
storesMixedCaseIdentifiers(): DatabaseMetaData
storesMixedCaseQuotedIdentifiers(): DatabaseMetaData
storesUpperCaseIdentifiers(): DatabaseMetaData
storesUpperCaseQuotedIdentifiers(): DatabaseMetaData
Streamable: org.omg.CORBA.portable
StreamMessage: javax.jms
string_to_object(): ORB
StringHolder: org.omg.CORBA
StringRefAddr: javax.naming
STRUCT: Types
Struct: java.sql
StructMember: org.omg.CORBA
StubNotFoundException: java.rmi
SUBTREE_SCOPE: SearchControls
supportsAlterTableWithAddColumn(): DatabaseMetaData
supportsAlterTableWithDropColumn(): DatabaseMetaData
supportsANSI92EntryLevelSQL(): DatabaseMetaData
supportsANSI92FullSQL(): DatabaseMetaData
supportsANSI92IntermediateSQL(): DatabaseMetaData
supportsBatchUpdates(): DatabaseMetaData
supportsCatalogsInDataManipulation(): DatabaseMetaData
supportsCatalogsInIndexDefinitions(): DatabaseMetaData
supportsCatalogsInPrivilegeDefinitions(): DatabaseMetaData
supportsCatalogsInProcedureCalls(): DatabaseMetaData
supportsCatalogsInTableDefinitions(): DatabaseMetaData
supportsColumnAliasing(): DatabaseMetaData
supportsConvert(): DatabaseMetaData
supportsCoreSQLGrammar(): DatabaseMetaData
supportsCorrelatedSubqueries(): DatabaseMetaData
supportsDataDefinitionAndDataManipulationTransactions(): DatabaseMetaData
supportsDataManipulationTransactionsOnly(): DatabaseMetaData
supportsDifferentTableCorrelationNames(): DatabaseMetaData
supportsExpressionsInOrderBy(): DatabaseMetaData
supportsExtendedSQLGrammar(): DatabaseMetaData
supportsFullOuterJoins(): DatabaseMetaData
supportsGroupBy(): DatabaseMetaData
supportsGroupByBeyondSelect(): DatabaseMetaData
supportsGroupByUnrelated(): DatabaseMetaData
supportsIntegrityEnhancementFacility(): DatabaseMetaData
supportsLikeEscapeClause(): DatabaseMetaData
supportsLimitedOuterJoins(): DatabaseMetaData
supportsMinimumSQLGrammar(): DatabaseMetaData
supportsMixedCaseIdentifiers(): DatabaseMetaData
supportsMixedCaseQuotedIdentifiers(): DatabaseMetaData
supportsMultipleResultSets(): DatabaseMetaData
supportsMultipleTransactions(): DatabaseMetaData
supportsNonNullableColumns(): DatabaseMetaData
supportsOpenCursorsAcrossCommit(): DatabaseMetaData
supportsOpenCursorsAcrossRollback(): DatabaseMetaData
supportsOpenStatementsAcrossCommit(): DatabaseMetaData
supportsOpenStatementsAcrossRollback(): DatabaseMetaData
supportsOrderByUnrelated(): DatabaseMetaData
supportsOuterJoins(): DatabaseMetaData
supportsPositionedDelete(): DatabaseMetaData
supportsPositionedUpdate(): DatabaseMetaData
supportsResultSetConcurrency(): DatabaseMetaData
supportsResultSetType(): DatabaseMetaData
supportsSchemasInDataManipulation():

DatabaseMetaData
supportsSchemasInIndexDefinitions(): DatabaseMetaData
supportsSchemasInPrivilegeDefinitions(): DatabaseMetaData
supportsSchemasInProcedureCalls(): DatabaseMetaData
supportsSchemasInTableDefinitions(): DatabaseMetaData
supportsSelectForUpdate(): DatabaseMetaData
supportsStoredProcedures(): DatabaseMetaData
supportsSubqueriesInComparisons(): DatabaseMetaData
supportsSubqueriesInExists(): DatabaseMetaData
supportsSubqueriesInIns(): DatabaseMetaData
supportsSubqueriesInQuantifieds(): DatabaseMetaData
supportsTableCorrelationNames(): DatabaseMetaData
supportsTransactionIsolationLevel(): DatabaseMetaData
supportsTransactions(): DatabaseMetaData
supportsUnion(): DatabaseMetaData
supportsUnionAll(): DatabaseMetaData
suspend(): TransactionManager
Synchronization: javax.transaction
SYSTEM_IDENTITY: ControlDescriptor
SYSTEM_PORT: ActivationSystem
SystemException: javax.transaction, org.omg.CORBA

T

tableIndexClustered: DatabaseMetaData
tableIndexHashed: DatabaseMetaData
tableIndexOther: DatabaseMetaData
tableIndexStatistic: DatabaseMetaData
target(): Request
TCKind: org.omg.CORBA
TemporaryQueue: javax.jms
TemporaryTopic: javax.jms
TextMessage: javax.jms
TIME: Types
Time: java.sql
TimeLimitExceededException: javax.naming
Timestamp: java.sql
TIMESTAMP: Types
TINYINT: Types
tk_abstract_interface: TCKind
tk_alias: TCKind
tk_any: TCKind
tk_array: TCKind
tk_boolean: TCKind
tk_char: TCKind
tk_double: TCKind
tk_enum: TCKind
tk_except: TCKind
tk_fixed: TCKind
tk_float: TCKind
tk_long: TCKind
tk_longdouble: TCKind
tk_longlong: TCKind
tk_native: TCKind
tk_null: TCKind
tk_objref: TCKind
tk_octet: TCKind
tk_Principal: TCKind
tk_sequence: TCKind
tk_short: TCKind
tk_string: TCKind
tk_struct: TCKind
tk_TypeCode: TCKind
tk_ulong: TCKind
tk_ulonglong: TCKind
tk_union: TCKind
tk_ushort: TCKind
tk_value: TCKind
tk_value_box: TCKind
tk_void: TCKind
tk_wchar: TCKind
tk_wstring: TCKind
TMENDRSCAN: XAResource
TMFAIL: XAResource
TMJOIN: XAResource
TMNOFLAGS: XAResource
TMONEPHASE: XAResource
TMRESUME: XAResource
TMSTARTRSCAN: XAResource
TMSUCCESS: XAResource
TMSUSPEND: XAResource
to_any(): DynAny
Topic: javax.jms
TopicConnection: javax.jms
TopicConnectionFactory: javax.jms
TopicPublisher: javax.jms
TopicRequestor: javax.jms
TopicSession: javax.jms
TopicSubscriber: javax.jms
toString(): AttributeModificationException, BasicAttribute, BasicAttributes, BinaryRefAddr, Binding, CompositeName, CompoundName, Date,

Delegate, LinkException, LogStream, ModificationItem, NameClassPair, NamingException, ObjectImpl, ObjID, Operation, Queue, RefAddr, Reference, RemoteObject, SearchResult, SystemException, Time, Timestamp, Topic, UID, VMID
toStub(): RemoteObject
Transaction: javax.transaction
TRANSACTION_NONE: Connection
TRANSACTION_READ_COMMITTED: Connection, ControlDescriptor
TRANSACTION_READ_UNCOMMITTED: Connection, ControlDescriptor
TRANSACTION_REPEATABLE_READ: Connection, ControlDescriptor
TRANSACTION_REQUIRED: org.omg.CORBA
TRANSACTION_ROLLEDBACK: org.omg.CORBA
TRANSACTION_SERIALIZABLE: Connection, ControlDescriptor
TransactionInProgressException: javax.jms
TransactionManager: javax.transaction
TransactionRequiredException: javax.transaction
TransactionRolledBackException: javax.jms
TransactionRolledbackException: javax.transaction
TRANSIENT: org.omg.CORBA
TX_BEAN_MANAGED: ControlDescriptor
TX_MANDATORY: ControlDescriptor
TX_NOT_SUPPORTED: ControlDescriptor
TX_REQUIRED: ControlDescriptor
TX_REQUIRES_NEW: ControlDescriptor
TX_SUPPORTS: ControlDescriptor
type: StructMember, UnionMember, ValueMember
type(): AlreadyBoundHelper, Any, BindingHelper, BindingIteratorHelper, BindingListHelper, BindingTypeHelper, CannotProceedHelper, DynAny, IDLType, InvalidNameHelper, IstringHelper, NameComponentHelper, NameHelper, NamingContextHelper, NotEmptyHelper, NotFoundHelper, NotFoundReasonHelper, ServiceDetailHelper, ServiceInformationHelper
type_def: StructMember, UnionMember, ValueMember
TYPE_FORWARD_ONLY: ResultSet
type_modifier(): TypeCode
TYPE_SCROLL_INSENSITIVE: ResultSet
TYPE_SCROLL_SENSITIVE: ResultSet
TypeCode: org.omg.CORBA
TypeCodeHolder: org.omg.CORBA
TypeMismatch: org.omg.CORBA.DynAnyPackage
typeNoNulls: DatabaseMetaData
typeNullable: DatabaseMetaData
typeNullableUnknown: DatabaseMetaData
typePredBasic: DatabaseMetaData
typePredChar: DatabaseMetaData
typePredNone: DatabaseMetaData
Types: java.sql
typeSearchable: DatabaseMetaData

U

UID: java.rmi.server
UnavailableException: javax.servlet
unbind(): _NamingContextImplBase, _NamingContextStub, Context, InitialContext, Naming, NamingContext, Registry
UnexpectedException: java.rmi
unexportObject(): Activatable, UnicastRemoteObject
UnicastRemoteObject: java.rmi.server
UnionMember: org.omg.CORBA
UNKNOWN: org.omg.CORBA
UnknownGroupException: java.rmi.activation
UnknownHostException: java.rmi
UnknownObjectException: java.rmi.activation
UnknownUserException: org.omg.CORBA
UnmarshalException: java.rmi
Unreferenced: java.rmi.server
unreferenced(): Unreferenced
unregister(): Activatable
unregisterGroup(): ActivationSystem
unregisterObject(): ActivationSystem
unsetEntityContext(): EntityBean
unsubscribe(): TopicSession
UNSUPPORTED_POLICY: org.omg.CORBA
UNSUPPORTED_POLICY_VALUE: org.omg.CORBA
updateAsciiStream(): ResultSet
updateBigDecimal(): ResultSet
updateBinaryStream(): ResultSet
updateBoolean(): ResultSet
updateByte(): ResultSet
updateBytes(): ResultSet
updateCharacterStream(): ResultSet
updateDate(): ResultSet
updateDouble(): ResultSet
updateFloat(): ResultSet
updateInt(): ResultSet
updateLong(): ResultSet
updateNull(): ResultSet
updateObject(): ResultSet
updateRow(): ResultSet
updatesAreDetected(): DatabaseMetaData
updateShort(): ResultSet
updateString(): ResultSet

updateTime(): ResultSet
updateTimestamp(): ResultSet
URL_PKG_PREFIXES: Context
UserException: org.omg.CORBA
UserTransaction: javax.transaction
usesLocalFilePerTable(): DatabaseMetaData
usesLocalFiles(): DatabaseMetaData

V

value: AlreadyBoundHolder, AnyHolder, ARG_IN, ARG_INOUT, ARG_OUT, BAD_POLICY, BAD_POLICY_TYPE, BAD_POLICY_VALUE, BindingHolder, BindingIteratorHolder, BindingListHolder, BindingTypeHolder, BooleanHolder, ByteHolder, CannotProceedHolder, CharHolder, CTX_RESTRICT_SCOPE, DoubleHolder, DriverPropertyInfo, FixedHolder, FloatHolder, IntHolder, InvalidNameHolder, LongHolder, NameComponentHolder, NameHolder, NameValuePair, NamingContextHolder, NotEmptyHolder, NotFoundHolder, NotFoundReasonHolder, ObjectHolder, PrincipalHolder, PRIVATE_MEMBER, PUBLIC_MEMBER, ServiceInformationHolder, ShortHolder, StringHolder, TypeCodeHolder, UNSUPPORTED_POLICY, UNSUPPORTED_POLICY_VALUE, VM_ABSTRACT, VM_CUSTOM, VM_NONE, VM_TRUNCATABLE
value(): BindingType, CompletionStatus, DefinitionKind, NamedValue, NotFoundReason, SetOverrideType, TCKind
value_as_string(): DynEnum
value_as_ulong(): DynEnum
valueBound(): HttpSessionBindingListener
ValueMember: org.omg.CORBA
valueOf(): Date, Time, Timestamp
values: BasicAttribute
valueUnbound(): HttpSessionBindingListener
VARBINARY: Types
VARCHAR: Types
VERBOSE: LogStream
version: ValueMember
versionColumnNotPseudo: DatabaseMetaData
versionColumnPseudo: DatabaseMetaData
versionColumnUnknown: DatabaseMetaData
versionNumber: DeploymentDescriptor
VM_ABSTRACT: org.omg.CORBA
VM_CUSTOM: org.omg.CORBA
VM_NONE: org.omg.CORBA
VM_TRUNCATABLE: org.omg.CORBA
VMID: java.rmi.dgc

W

wasNull(): CallableStatement, ResultSet, SQLInput
why: NotFound
work_pending(): ORB
write(): AlreadyBoundHelper, BindingHelper, BindingIteratorHelper, BindingListHelper, BindingTypeHelper, CannotProceedHelper, InvalidNameHelper, IstringHelper, LogStream, NameComponentHelper, NameHelper, NamingContextHelper, NotEmptyHelper, NotFoundHelper, NotFoundReasonHelper, ObjID, OutputStream, ServiceDetailHelper, ServiceInformationHelper, UID
write_any(): OutputStream
write_boolean(): OutputStream
write_boolean_array(): OutputStream
write_char(): OutputStream
write_char_array(): OutputStream
write_Context(): OutputStream
write_double(): OutputStream
write_double_array(): OutputStream
write_fixed(): OutputStream
write_float(): OutputStream
write_float_array(): OutputStream
write_long(): OutputStream
write_long_array(): OutputStream
write_longlong(): OutputStream
write_longlong_array(): OutputStream
write_Object(): OutputStream
write_octet(): OutputStream
write_octet_array(): OutputStream
write_Principal(): OutputStream
write_short(): OutputStream
write_short_array(): OutputStream
write_string(): OutputStream
write_TypeCode(): OutputStream
write_ulong(): OutputStream
write_ulong_array(): OutputStream
write_ulonglong(): OutputStream
write_ulonglong_array(): OutputStream
write_ushort(): OutputStream
write_ushort_array(): OutputStream
write_value(): Any
write_wchar(): OutputStream
write_wchar_array(): OutputStream
write_wstring(): OutputStream
writeArray(): SQLOutput
writeAsciiStream(): SQLOutput
writeBigDecimal(): SQLOutput
writeBinaryStream(): SQLOutput

writeBlob(): SQLOutput
writeBoolean(): BytesMessage, SQLOutput, StreamMessage
writeByte(): BytesMessage, SQLOutput, StreamMessage
writeBytes(): BytesMessage, SQLOutput, StreamMessage
writeChar(): BytesMessage, StreamMessage
writeCharacterStream(): SQLOutput
writeClob(): SQLOutput
writeData(): RowSetWriter
writeDate(): SQLOutput
writeDouble(): BytesMessage, SQLOutput, StreamMessage
writeFloat(): BytesMessage, SQLOutput, StreamMessage
writeInt(): BytesMessage, SQLOutput, StreamMessage
writeLong(): BytesMessage, SQLOutput, StreamMessage
writeObject(): BytesMessage, SQLOutput, StreamMessage
writeRef(): SQLOutput
writeShort(): BytesMessage, SQLOutput, StreamMessage
writeSQL(): SQLData
writeString(): SQLOutput, StreamMessage
writeStruct(): SQLOutput
writeTime(): SQLOutput
writeTimestamp(): SQLOutput
writeUTF(): BytesMessage
WrongTransaction: org.omg.CORBA

X

XA_HEURCOM: XAException
XA_HEURHAZ: XAException
XA_HEURMIX: XAException
XA_HEURRB: XAException
XA_NOMIGRATE: XAException
XA_OK: XAResource
XA_RBBASE: XAException
XA_RBCOMMFAIL: XAException
XA_RBDEADLOCK: XAException
XA_RBEND: XAException
XA_RBINTEGRITY: XAException
XA_RBOTHER: XAException
XA_RBPROTO: XAException
XA_RBROLLBACK: XAException
XA_RBTIMEOUT: XAException
XA_RBTRANSIENT: XAException
XA_RDONLY: XAException, XAResource
XA_RETRY: XAException
XAConnection: javax.jms, javax.sql
XAConnectionFactory: javax.jms
XADataSource: javax.sql
XAER_ASYNC: XAException
XAER_DUPID: XAException
XAER_INVAL: XAException
XAER_NOTA: XAException
XAER_OUTSIDE: XAException
XAER_PROTO: XAException
XAER_RMERR: XAException
XAER_RMFAIL: XAException
XAException: javax.transaction.xa
XAQueueConnection: javax.jms
XAQueueConnectionFactory: javax.jms
XAQueueSession: javax.jms
XAResource: javax.transaction.xa
XASession: javax.jms
XATopicConnection: javax.jms
XATopicConnectionFactory: javax.jms
XATopicSession: javax.jms
Xid: javax.transaction.xa

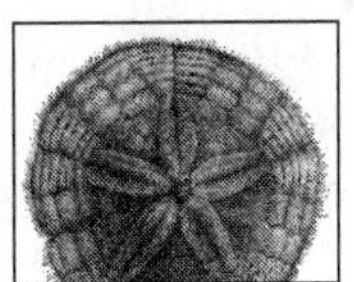

Index

Symbols

_BindingIteratorImplBase class, 519
_BindingIteratorStub class, 519
_get_domain_managers() (Object), 473, 492
_invoke() (InvokeHandler), 513
_NamingContextImplBase class, 521
_NamingContextStub class, 521
_ServerStub class, 90
(/) name components, separating, 401

A

access control, 214, 220
  container, managing, 181
  CORBA Licensing Service, 286
  CORBA Security Service, 282
  deployment attributes, 216
  exceptions, 217
  servlets, 122
Access database (Microsoft), metadata, 30
AccessControlEntry class, 369
AccessException class, 304, 307
accessor methods
  attributes (IDL interface), mapping to, 279
  unions (IDL), mapping to Java, 266–267
ACID characteristics (transactions), listed, 285
Activatable class, 55, 65–66, 313
activatable objects, 64–75
  arguments, passing before activation, 71
  assigning to groups, 73
  implementing, 67
  registering, 69
    without activating, 71
ActivateFailedException class, 315
activation
  beans, 191
    container role, 181
  entity beans, 207
    bean-managed persistence, 205
  remote objects, 64–75
  RMI activation system, 313
  session beans, 367
activation daemon (RMI), 247
  options, 248
activation groups, 65, 72
  activatable objects, assigning to, 73
  activatable objects, registering, 69
  Activator, group description, 74
  registering, 73
activation system (RMI)
  activation daemon, 74–75
  ActivationGroup, registering, 73
  objects, registering, 65–66, 69
ActivationDesc class, 70, 315

ActivationException class, 316
ActivationGroup class, 316
  entire group, becoming inactive, 73
  objects, maintaining, 72
ActivationGroupDesc class, 73, 317
  CommandEnvironment class, 318
ActivationGroupID class, 73, 318
ActivationID class, 67, 313, 318
ActivationInstantiator interface, 319
ActivationMonitor interface, 73, 319
ActivationSystem interface, 247, 320
Activator interface, 320
  activatable objects registry, 74
  active object references, transferring, 73
  inactive groups, recreating, 73
activeObject( ) (ActivationGroup), 73, 316
addBatch( )
  CallableStatement interface, 40
  PreparedStatement interface, 40
  Statement interface, 39
addCookie( ) (HttpServletResponse), 135, 440
addresses (references), 412, 414
add( )
  Attribute interface, 167
  BasicAttribute class, 419
adjacent string literals (compiler bugs), 291
afterBegin( ) (SessionSynchronization), 195, 368
afterCompletion( )
  Synchronization interface, 454
  SessionSynchronization interface, 195
aggregate functions (SQL), 239
AlreadyBound class, 531
AlreadyBoundException class, 56, 305
AlreadyBoundHelper class, 532
AlreadyBoundHolder class, 533
ANSI SQL standard, 185
ANSI-92 SQL state codes, 26
Any class, 461
AnyHolder class, 465
applets
  classes, loading, 61, 64
  deployment, Java drivers and, 18
  JDBC-ODBC Bridge requirements, 19
ApplicationException class, 510
applications
  EJB components insulating from service details, 175
  object references, 105
architecture
  CORBA, 83–86
  distributed computing (hypothetical enterprise), 11
  JDBC, 15
  JNDI, 144
  RMI, 48
ARG_IN interface, 465
ARG_INOUT interface, 466
ARG_OUT interface, 466
arguments
  initialization constructors, 66
  remote methods, 58
Array class, 339
arrays
  IDL typedef, 261
  sequences (IDL), 262
  update counts, 40
atomicity of transactions, 9
Attribute interface, 166–167, 416
AttributeModificationException class, 418
attributes
  DirContext interface, 163
  directories, specification requirements, 169
  directory services, 143, 162
  IDL interfaces, 272
    accessor methods, mapping to, 279
    identifiers, 277
    inheriting, 276
  IDL vs. Java, 88
  key, object class definition and, 164
  modifying, 167–168, 423
  searching, 170
  servlet requests, 141
  sharing, 142
  syntax definition, 164
  type definition, 164, 416
Attributes interface, 164, 167, 418

authentication
  CORBA Security Service, 282
  servlet requests, 121, 126
AuthenticationException class, 398
AuthenticationNotSupportedException class, 399
auto-commit mode (transactions), 33, 40

B

BAD_CONTEXT class, 466
BAD_INV_ORDER class, 466
BAD_OPERATION class, 467
BAD_OPERATION exception, 266
BAD_PARAM class, 104, 467
BAD_REQUEST error class, 438
BAD_TYPECODE class, 467
BadKind class, 517
BasicAttribute class, 419
BasicAttributes class, 167–168, 420
BasicServlet class, 117
batch updates (JDBC), 39
BatchUpdateException class, 40, 340
bean class (primary key, matching), 211
bean implementation, 186, 189
  classes and interfaces (deployment), 214
  entity beans, 199
    finder methods, 198–199
  JAR files, 218
  methods, home and remote interface, 187
  persistence, managing, 210, 212
  programming restrictions, 223
  remote interface, implementing directly, 190
bean-managed entity beans, 196
  (see also persistence)
beans
  insulating from service details, 175
  transaction-support attributes, 183
beforeCompletion()
  SessionSynchronization interface, 195, 368
  Synchronization interface, 454
begin() (UserTransaction), 182, 456
best effort semantics (CORBA method calls), 276
BigDecimal class, 479
binary data, transmitting (servlets), 140
binary large objects (BLOBs), 25, 41
BinaryRefAddr class, 399
bind_context() (NamingContext), 528
bind_new_context() (NamingContext), 101
binding
  IDL (early), 278
  languages to CORBA, 84
  listing (Context), 159
  name-to-objects, tracking, 403
  objects to names, 56, 146, 163
  objects to sessions, 137
Binding class, 161, 400, 522
BindingHelper class, 522
BindingHolder class, 523
BindingIterator interface, 282, 523
BindingIteratorHelper class, 523
BindingIteratorHolder class, 524
BindingListHelper class, 524
BindingType class, 525
BindingTypeHelper class, 525
BindingTypeHolder class, 526
bind()
  Context interface, 161
  Naming interface, 307
  NamingContext interface, 101, 528
  Registry interface, 56, 325
Blob interface, 341
BLOBs (binary large objects), 25, 41
BooleanHolder class, 468
Bounds class, 468, 518
branch, CORBA naming directory), 84
browsing (naming system), 157
business logic (EJB), 7
business methods
  beans, running transactions, 184
  remote interface, 179, 188
ByteHolder class, 468
BytesMessage interface, 374

C

C language
- code, wrapping with Java interface, 75
- comments (IDL), 253
- IDL interfaces, converting, 82
- IDL unions, similarity, 265
- operators (IDL support), 255
- path to preprocessor (idltojava compiler), 291

C++ language
- code, wrapping with Java interface, 75
- comments (IDL), 253
- IDL interfaces, converting, 82
- IDL modules, similarity to namespace, 271
- Java and IDL syntax, modeled upon, 87
- multithreading vs. concurrency control (CORBA), 284
- nonclass data structure definitions, 87
- operators (IDL support), 255
- path to preprocessor (idltojava compiler), 291
- unions (IDL), similarity, 265

CallableStatement interface, 21, 341
- escape sequences, 36
- stored procedures, 35

CannotProceed class, 533
CannotProceedException class, 401
CannotProceedHelper class, 533
CannotProceedHolder class, 534
case-sensitivity (attributes), 418
cast operation (remote object classes), 85
catalogs (SQL), 228
catch blocks (SQLException), 26
CGI scripts, servlets replacing, 114
chaining, servlets, 126
characters
- char strings, 77
- character sets
  - alphanumeric (ISO Latin-1), 252
  - multibyte, 254
  - servlet output streams, 121
- CLOBs, 25, 41
- IDL, 254
  - literals, 257–258
- separators (compound names), 157
- wildcard searching, 170

CharHolder class, 469
child (Context)
- children of, listing, 156
- listing, 154–159
- looking up, 148
- name and path, 155
- parent object, destroying, 160

class variables, thread safety and, 130
classes
- activatable remote objects, 66
- activation groups, 73
- definition, tracking, 248
- directory schema, determining, 162
- Dynamic Invocation Interface (DII), 111
- inner, 87
- Java, IDL interfaces vs., 87
- loading dynamically, 60–64
- loading from applets, 64
- names for (JDBC), 41
- public, 87, 190
- remote interface, implementing, 51
- remote object implementations, 54
- server, simple (IDL), 90
- service providers (JNDI), 144, 148
- stubs and skeletons, generating, 79, 245

Class.forName()
- Driver interface, 348
- DriverManager class, 349

classpath, 61
- libraries, specifying, 154
- local default class loader, 61
- RMI activation daemon, 248
- RMI registry, 63, 247
- rmic compiler, 246
- serialver utility (RMI), 249

clearBatch( ) (Statement), 40
clearBody( ) (Message), 380
clearParameters( ) (PreparedStatement), 28, 350
clear( ) (Attribute), 167
client interfaces (remote object stubs), 43
client stubs, 46, 50, 332

client stubs (cont'd)
classes, regenerating (RMI/IIOP), 79
configuring, remote class loading, 61–64
containers (EJB), generating, 180
CORBA, 83–84
remote object classes, 86
remote object references, 103
generating, 51, 55
idltojava compiler, generating, 90, 94
Java to CORBA object, 78
language-specific, generating, 81
obtaining, 220
original objects, changing, 59
remote objects, not instantiated, 71
RemoteObject class, using, 54
RMI architecture, 48
rmic compiler, generating, 245
(see also stubs)
client-initiated transactions, 184
clients, 195
cookies, storing data on, 135
CORBA
licensed services, requesting, 286
object persistence, controlling, 283
services, trading system, 287
EJB, 176
JNDI server and home interface name, specifying, 177
stubs, method requests and, 178
enterprise beans, using as, 219
host, getting name, 122
identifying, 192, 216, 220
IDL, context, 275
as Java objects (RMI), 44
remote method requests, server objects, 111
remote objects, communicating with, 52, 56–60, 98
session beans as remote extensions, 191
session tracking, 136
stateful session beans, interaction with, 193, 195
stringified object reference, using, 109
web browsers, 115
(see also client stubs)
Clob interface, 342
CLOBs (character large objects), 25, 41
cloning (remote servers), 335
close()
Connection interface, 22, 376
PooledConnection interface, 446
closing database connections, 20
clusters (SQL), 228
CODE parameter (servlet tags), 133
code, synchronized blocks, 130
CODEBASE parameter (servlet tags), 133
Collection objects, 286
Collection Service (CORBA), 288
collections, 198
types, 223
columns
ResultSet
data types, 23
values, retrieving, 23
SQL tables
adding, 232
constraints, 231
data types, 229
columns (database)
Java objects, storing (type), 41
null values, 25
COMM_FAILURE class, 469
Command interface, 152
CommandEnvironment class, 318
CommandException class, 152
commands
loading and executing (JNDI), 149
RMI registry, 247
SQL, 227
ALTER TABLE, 232
data manipulation, 233
DELETE, 239
DROP, 233
INSERT, 238
schema manipulation, 230
SELECT, 233
SUBSTRING, 241
UPDATE, 238
comments (IDL/Java mapping), 253
committing transactions, 10, 32

auto-commit mode, 33
commit()
Connection interface, 33
Session interface, 390
Transaction interface, 455
UserTransaction interface, 182, 456
XAResource interface, 459
Common Object Request Broker Architecture (see CORBA)
CommunicationException class, 401
CompletionStatus class, 469
complex data types
accessing, 475
IDL, 259
CompositeName class, 401
compound names, 156
CompoundName class, 157, 402
concurrency
support information (DataBaseMetaData), 39
transactions (EJB container management), 196
Concurrency Control Service (CORBA), 284, 286
configuration information
database metadata, 29
servlets, sharing, 142
ConfigurationException class, 403
conformance levels (SQL-92), 227
ConnectException class, 306
ConnectIOException class, 306
Connection interface, 17, 20, 342
isolation modes, listed, 33
JMS, 376
transactions (JDBC), managing, 33
connection pooling, 34
JDBC 2.0 standard extension, 42
ConnectionConsumer interface, 376
ConnectionEvent class, 444
ConnectionFactory interface, 377
ConnectionMetaData interface, 377
ConnectionPoolDataSource interface, 445
constants (IDL), 251, 255
early binding, 278
interfaces (inheritance), 277
constructors, 45
Activatable class, 66
activatable objects, 68
activation, class, 73
activation in server implementation, 65
initial context, naming systems, 146
NameComponent class, 101
public, 94
reactivation, 67
remote objects, initializing, registering, activating, 66
consumers (CORBA events), 283
container-managed entity beans, 196
(see also persistence)
containers, 180
bean management, 181
classes connecting components, 180
Context, implementing, 149
data mapping, persistent data fields, 212
deployment classes, generating, 214, 217
deployment descriptors, 179, 213, 217
EJB components and servers, 8
EJB objects, interfaces/classes, 178
EJB, role in, 176
entity beans
loading state, 199
passivation and pooling, 196
persistence, managing, 196, 208, 212, 215
finder methods, generating, 211
functions, 180
handles, 208
JAR files (bean deployment), 218
JDBC connections, providing, 184
method calls, transferring to EJB object, 179
pooling entity beans, 206–207
pooling stateless session beans, 195
primary keys
entity beans, 197
remote objects, converting to, 199
session beans, 197
public class, connecting bean to container, 190
servers vs., 180
session beans, destroying after timeout, 191

containers (cont'd)
session context, passing to bean, 192
transaction management, 222
transaction boundaries, defining, 183
containsHeader() (HttpServletResponse), 121, 440
contains() (Attributes), 167
context
IDL clients, 275
variables (IDL), Java compiler not supporting, 275
Context class (CORBA), 470
context clauses (IDL methods), 291
Context interface, 112, 144, 219
bindings, listing, 159
children, listing, 154–159
JNDI, 403
keys, properties values (JNDI), 146
naming services, interacting with, 147
service providers and, 148, 159
ContextList class, 471
ContextNotEmptyException class, 404
ControlDescriptor class, 370
Cookie class, 135, 437
cookies
manipulating, 114
Netscape specification, original, 135
CORBA, 7
architecture, 83–86
Security Services and, 282
distributed object services, 82
Dynamic Invocation Interface (DII) API, 111
Dynamic Skeleton Interface (DSI) API, 111
exceptions, standard, 269, 274
mapping to Java, 270
IDL, 82, 250–280
IIOP, 78, 86
Interoperable Object References (IORs), 108
language independence, 44
methods, best-effort semantics, 276
Naming Service, 84, 519
remote clients, connecting to, 291
server object, registering, 99
object references, narrowing, 104
objects, adding to NamingContext, 101
objects, creating, 87
ORBs (see ORBs)
org.omg.CORBA Package, 461–505
remote classes, finding, 86
remote object references, 103
RMI objects, accessing, 81
RMI vs., 83
root object class, 104
services, 281–288
Collection Service, 288
Concurrency Control Service, 284
Event Service, 282
Externalization Service, 284
Licensing Service, 286
Life Cycle Service, 283
Naming Service, 282
Persistent Object Service, 283
Property Service, 287
Query Service, 286
Relationship Service, 284
Security Service, 282
specification (OMG), 281
Time Service, 287
Trading Service, 287
Transaction Service, 284–285
create_child() (Context), 470
create_exception_list() (ORB), 479
create_exception_tc() (ORB), 479, 498
create_list() (ORB), 488
create_named_value() (ORB), 465–466
create_request() (Object), 494
create_struct_tc() (ORB), 498
createBrowser() (QueueSession), 386
createDurableSubscriber() (TopicSession), 394
CreateException class, 188, 361
createGroup() (ActivationGroup), 316
createQueueConnection() (QueueConnectionFactory), 387
createQueueSession() (QueueConnection), 387
createQueue() (QueueSession), 386
createReceiver() (QueueSession), 387

createRegistry() (LocateRegistry), 57, 324, 333–334
createSocket()
  RMIClientSocketFactory interface, 334
  RMISocketFactory interface, 334
createStatement() (Connection), 21, 36–37, 357
createSubcontext()
  Context interface, 159
  DirContext interface, 169, 420
createSubscriber() (TopicSession), 394
createTopicConnection() (TopicConnectionFactory), 393
createXATopicSession() (XATopicConnection interface), 397
create(), 189, 191
  EJBHome, matching object implementation, 188
  entity beans (container-managed persistence), 212
  stateless session beans, 195
cross-database APIs, 15
cryptography, CORBA Security Service, 282
CTX_RESTRICT_SCOPE interface, 471
Current interface, 471
cursor position (result sets), 38
customizing
  cookies, 135
  servlet initialization, 128

D

DAP (Directory Access Protocol), 162
DATA_CONVERSION class, 472
data manipulation commands (SQL), 233
data types
  binary, transmitting (servlets), 140
  binary and character (large objects), 41
  columns, returning (ResultSet), 23
  DatabaseMetaData methods, returning, 29
  IDL, 251
    declaring, 88
    typedef, 260
    user-defined, 259, 277–278
  IDL, supporting, 253
  Java/SQL mapping, 230
  large, 25
  literals (IDL), numeric, 256
  MapMessage name/value pairs, 380
  primitive, 23
    boolean, 136
    Java handling, 87
    relational databases and, 41
    serialization, 58
  servlet responses, specifying, 121
  SQL, 229, 359
  SQL and Java, 24, 28
  stored procedures output, 35
database management system (DBMS), 228
database mapping
  bean implementation (deployment descriptors), 214
  complex data structures, 212
  container-managed persistence, 215
  serialization, 213
database schema (directory schema vs.), 162
database updates, transactions, 184
DatabaseMetaData interface, 29, 343
  scrolling and concurrency, 39
databases, 5
  changes, losing, 33
  commands, database-independent (JDBC), 36
  configuration information, 29
  connections, 342
    closing, 20
    creating, 17
    pooling, 20, 133
  connections, pooling, 139
  differences among systems, 15
  enterprise applications, dependency, 15
  entries, maintaining (bean-managed persistence), 208
  interaction with JDBC, 16
  isolation levels, transactions and, 186
  Java-aware, 41
  JDBC, supporting transactions, 10
  JDBC, working with relational, 5
  mapping, container-managed persistence, 209–210
  null values, 25

databases (cont'd)
objects (Java types), inserting, 28
protocols, defining (ODMG), 283
records, mapping to Java objects, 41
rows
accessing (result sets), 37
editing data, inserting and deleting rows (ResultSet), 38
insertions, preventing (transactions), 34
null values, inserting, 39
scalar functions, 36
servlets, handling, 139
SQL statements and, 339
SQL strings, processing, 27
standardized interface (SQL), 227
stored procedures, 21, 34–36, 341
tables, displaying contents, 31
transactions, 32
update counts, getting, 22
updateable ResultSet, differences, 39
updating (atomic transactions), 13
(see also relational databases)
DataSource interface, 446
DataTruncation class, 347
date and time functions (SQL), 240
Date class, 26, 348
dates, filtering (servlets), 127
DBMS (Database Management System), 228
DCE Common Inter-ORB Protocol (DCE-CIOP), 86
debugging applications, 27
declarations
IDL interfaces, 88
IDL modules, 271
declarative language (SQL), 227
def_kind() (IRObject), 484
DefinitionKind class, 472
Delegate class, 510
delegates (CORBA object stubs), 93
DELETE (HTTP request), 120
deleteRow() (ResultSet), 39
delivery address (messages), 378
DeliveryMode interface, 377
deployment descriptors
access control, 216
bean management, specifying, 181
bean services, controlling, 175
container functions, roles in, 179
container-managed entity bean, 210
containers, generating, 217
enterprise beans, 213
format standard, lacking, 215
JAR files, 218
required information, listed, 214
XML-based, 222
DeploymentDescriptor class, 215, 371
deserialization, 6
HomeHandle, 223
Properties object, 213
(see also serialization)
Destination interface, 378
destroying cookies, 136
destroySubcontext() (Context), 160, 404
destroy(), 115
ATMServlet example, 132
GenericServlet class, 431
Servlet interface, 432
servlets, persistence, 129
DGC interface, 322
digest authentication, 122, 126
DII (see Dynamic Invocation Interface (DII) API)
DirContext interface, 144, 163, 420
Directory Access Protocol (DAP), 162
directory entries, 162
attributes, 416
modifying values, 167
names (IDs), enumerating, 166
creating, 169
directory schema, controlling, 170
LDAP servers (public), prohibiting new, 169
directory schema, 162
accessing, 420
attributes
type definition, 164
values, specifying, 166
entries, determining, 170
JNDI, supporting different, 163
modifying, 168
directory servers
JNDI and, 7
LDAP servers (online), 165

directory services
  accessing (JNDI), 162
  attributes, 166
  Context methods, supporting, 149
  JNDI SPI and, 144
  JNDI supporting (Java programs), 143
  naming services vs., 143, 162
  objects, looking up, 148
  schemas (JNDI support), 163
  searching, 170
  standard (X.500), 162
directory structure (CORBA naming service), 84
DirectoryManager class, 426
dirty reads (transactions), 33, 185
discriminators (IDL unions), 265
discriminators (idltojava compiler bugs), 291
dispatch() (Skeleton), 336
distributed applications
  with Java and non-Java components, 44
  remote interfaces, defining, 52
distributed component model, 174
distributed computing, 3
  architecture (hypothetical enterprise), 11
  complexity, 5
  Java Enterprise APIs, supporting, 5
  RMI as high-level, generic approach, 6
distributed garbage collection (DGC) 322–323
distributed object systems
  clients and servers, distinguishing, 48
distributed objects, 174
  CORBA standard services, 82
  EJB vs. regular, 174
  RMI, interacting with, 43
distributed transactions
  two-phase commit protocol, 10
distributed transactions, supporting (JDBC standard extension), 42
doDelete() (HttpServlet), 438
doGet() (HttpServlet), 117, 131, 438
Domain Name Systems (DNS), 143
domain, specifying (cookies), 136
DomainManager interface, 473
done() (RemoteRef), 331
doPost() (HttpServlet), 117, 120, 132, 438
doPut() (HttpServlet), 438
doPut() (HttpServlet), 117
DoubleHolder class, 474
Driver interface, 348
DriverManager class, 18, 349
DriverPropertyInfo class, 349
drivers
  JDBC, 5, 16, 18–19
    2.0 compliant, 37
    categories, listed, 18
    currently available, listed, 19
    data, mapping to SQL, 230
    escape sequences, translating, 35
    loading, example, 17
    null values, 25
    registering, 18
    results sets (scrollable and updateable), 39
    SQL-92 conformance, 227
    support levels, accommodating, 29
    two-phase commit, 42
  JNDI and JDBC, 144
DSI (see Dynamic Skeleton Interface (DSI) API)
duplicate records, finding, 221
DuplicateKeyException class, 361
dynamic class loading (RMI), 60–64
Dynamic Invocation Interface (DII) API, 83, 111
  asynchronous method invocation, 282
Dynamic Method Interface (CORBA), 104
Dynamic Skeleton Interface (DSI) API, 83, 111
DynamicImplementation class, 474
DynAny interface, 475
DynArray interface, 476
DynEnum interface, 477
DynFixed interface, 477
DynSequence interface, 477
DynStruct interface, 477
DynUnion interface, 478
DynValue interface, 478

E

e-commerce enterprise (example), 11
EJB, 174–224
  bean types, 179
  clients, 176
  components, naming systems and, 143
  containers, 180
  EJB object, 178
  JavaBeans and, 174
  JDBC, facilitating use, 42
  objects
    business methods, implementing, 179
    components, 174, 187
    implementing basic, 186
    JDBC connections, 185
  packaging into JAR files, 218
  roles, 176
  servers, enabled for, 175
  transaction management, 182–186
  version 1.1, changes, 222
ejbActivate()
  EntityBean interface, 191, 365
  SessionBean interface, 191–192, 367
EJBContext interface, 362
  client transaction context, 183
  environment properties, 215
  session beans, 192
ejbCreate(), 189, 191, 199–200
  EJB specification 1.1, changes, 223
EJBException class, 363
ejbFindByPrimaryKey(), 199
EJBHome interface, 187, 223, 363
EJBHome server, 175
ejbLoad(), 199
  entity beans, container-managed persistence, 212
  EntityBean interface, 365
  Properties object, deserializing, 213
EJBMetaData interface, 364
EJBObject interface, 364
  remote interface, 188
  remote interface, direct implementation, 190
ejbPassivate()
  EntityBean interface, 191, 365
  SessionBean interface, 191–192, 367
ejbPostCreate(), 199
ejbRemove(), 191, 200
  EntityBean interface, 365
  SessionBean interface, 192, 367
ejbStore(), 199
  entity beans, container-managed persistence, 212
  EntityBean interface, 365
  Properties object, serializing, 213
encodeRedirectUrl() (HttpServletResponse), 440
encodeUrl() (HttpServletResponse), 440
end() (XAResource), 459
enterprise beans
  deployment, 213
  JDBC connections, acquiring, 184
  methods, required, 190
  packaging into EJB-JAR files, 214
  RMI remote objects vs., 8
  structural information, separating from application, 222
  using as client, 219
enterprise computing, 3–5
Enterprise JavaBeans (see EJB)
EnterpriseBean interface, 190, 192, 365
entity beans, 179
  activating, 207
  bean-managed persistence, 205
  container-managed persistence
    create and remove methods, 212
    database mapping, 215
    loading and storing methods, 212
    primary key type (EJB 1.1), 223
  context, 206
  create methods, 191
  creating and finding, 220
  finder methods, 199, 206
  handles, 208
  implementation, 196, 199
  Java classes/interfaces required, 186
  life cycle, 206
  names, preventing client change, 205
  persistence, 200
  primary keys

entity beans (cont'd)
class (example), 197
container-managed persistence, 211
EJB 1.1, changes, 223
session beans vs., 179
EntityBean interface, 365
EntityDescriptor class, 215, 217–218, 372
enumerations
attributes names (directory entry), 166
binding objects, 159
finder methods, 198
IDL, 263
naming, 155, 410
environment
IDL client, 275
idltojava compiler, 291
RMI activation daemon, 248
RMI registry, 247
rmic compiler, 246
serialver utility (RMI), 249
Environment class, 479
equals()
ObjID class, 329
RemoteObject class, 54, 330
RemoteRef interface, 331
errors, 123
beans, creating, 361
binding remote objects to names, 56
I/O, 306
JDBC, handling, 26
log, output stream to, 329
marshalling, 48
messages, specifying custom, 123
remote object URLs, 57
remote sessions, 53
servlets, handling, 123–126
SQL return codes, 241–244
(see also exceptions)
escape sequences
components (JDBC), 36
dates, 26
JDBC Date, 348
JDBC Time, 358
nonprintable characters (IDL), 257
stored procedures, 35
event notification (JMS), 9
Event Service (CORBA), 282, 286
ExceptionList class, 479
ExceptionListener interface, 378
exceptions, 123
access control identities, 217
attributes, invalid, 169
bounds, data (IDL), 254
commands (JNDI NamingShell), 152
context, destroying, 160
CORBA, mapping to Java, 270
CORBA, standard, 269
helper classes, 279
home interface, 188
IDL, 88, 251, 268, 274, 277
naming (JNDI), 146
objects, binding to NamingContext, 103
primary keys, finding, 198
root cause, specifying, 141
sequences (IDL), size bounds, 262
servlets, 124
SQL return codes, 241–244
unions (IDL/Java mapping), 266
(see also errors)
exception() (Environment), 479
execute()
CallableStatement interface, 341
PreparedStatement interface, 350
ResultSet interface, 351
Statement interface, 357
executeBatch()
Statement interface, 40
PreparedStatement interface, 40
executeQuery()
PreparedStatement interface, 350
Statement interface, 21, 357
executeUpdate()
PreparedStatement interface, 28, 350
ResultSet interface, 351
Statement interface, 21, 357
execute()
Command interface, 152
Statement interface, 21
ExportException class, 327
exportObject()
Activatable class, 67–68, 313
ServerRef interface, 335

extended attributes, 169
Externalization Service (CORBA), 284

F

factory classes, 59
  custom, client and server socket, 67
  defining, example, 60
  filesystems, 147
  initial context, 219, 404
  JNDI service providers, 147
  JNDI services, 146
factory objects, 105
failure() (RMIFailureHandler), 333
fields (message headers), listed, 381
file servlet (Java Web Server), 121
files
  creating, 161
  HTML, servlets returning, 125
  IDL, converting to Java (options), 290
  .shtml extension, 133
file-serving servlets, 125
filesystems, factory class, 146
  providers, directory services and, 162
filtering
  directory searches, 170
  servlets, MIME types, 127
  search syntax, 173
findByPrimaryKey() (EJBHome), 198
finder methods
  EJB 1.1 specification, changes, 223
  EJB server providers, 212
  entity beans
    bean implementation, 199
    bean-managed persistence, 206
    container-managed persistence, 211
    home interface, 188, 198, 207
FinderException class, 198, 366
first() (ResultSet), 38, 351
FixedHolder class, 479
fixed-point literals (IDL), 256
flags, turning on and off (idltojava-compiler), 290
FloatHolder class, 480
floating-point literals (IDL), 256
forName(), 18
forward-only result sets, 37
forward() (RequestDispatcher), 141, 431
FREE_MEM class, 480
freeware database connection-pooling system, 139
functions
  scalar (databases), 36
  SQL, 239

G

garbage collection, 191
  RMI, 44, 51, 322
GenericServlet class, 116, 141, 431
  filtering servlet, implementing, 117
get_default_context() (ORB), 470
get_elements() (DynArray), 476
GET request (HTML forms), 118
get_response() (Request), 494
get_values() (Context), 471
getAll()
  Attribute interface, 167, 416
  Attributes interface, 164, 166, 418
getArray() (Array), 339
getAsciiStream()
  Clob interface, 342
getAsciiStream()
  Clob interface, 342
  ResultSet interface, 25
getAttributeDefinition() (Attribute), 416
getAttributeNames()
  ServletContext interface, 142
  ServletRequest interface, 141
getAttributeSyntaxDefinition() (Attribute), 416
getAttributes()
  DirContext interface, 164, 420
  Struct interface, 358
getAttribute()
  ServletContext interface, 142, 433
  ServletRequest interface, 435
getAuthType() (HttpServletRequest), 126
getAutoCommit() (Connection), 33, 342
getBaseType() (Ref), 351
getBinaryStream()
  Blob interface, 42
  ResultSet interface, 25

getBytes( ) (Blob), 42, 341
getCallerIdentity( ) (EJBContext), 192, 362
getCharacterEncoding( ) (ServletRequest), 435
getCharacterStream( ) (Clob), 42, 342
getClassName( ) (NameClassPair), 155
getClientHost( )
  RemoteServer class, 332
  ServerRef interface, 335
getColumnCount( ) (ResultSetMetaData), 32, 354
getColumnLabel( ) (ResultSetMetaData), 32, 354
getColumns( ) (ResultSetMetaData), 29
getColumnTypeName( ) (ResultSetMetaData), 32, 354
getConnection( )
  Connection interface, 342
  DriverManager interface, 20, 349
  PooledConnection interface, 446
getContentLength( ) (ServletRequest), 435
getContentType( ) (ServletRequest), 435
getCookies( ) (HttpServletRequest), 135, 439
getDateHeader( ) (HttpServletRequest), 439
getDefaultStream( ) (LogStream), 329
getDefaultTransactionIsolation( ) (DatabaseMetaData), 34
getDriverProperties() (DriverPropertyInfo), 349
getEJBHome( ) (EJBContext), 192, 362
getEJBMetaData( ) (EJBHome), 363
getEJBObject( ) (Handle), 366
getEnvironment( ) (EJBContext), 192, 362
getErrorCode( ) (SQLException), 26
getFailureHandler( ) (RMISocketFactory), 334
getFloat( ) (CallableStatement), 35
getHandle( ) (EJBObject), 208, 366
getHeaderNames( ) (HttpServletRequest), 122, 439
getHeader( ) (HttpServletRequest), 122, 439
getHomeHandle( ) (EJBHome), 223
getIDs( ) (Attributes), 166
getID( )
  Activatable class, 313
  HttpSession, 137
getInputStream( )
  Blob interface, 341
  RemoteCall interface, 330
  ServletRequest interface, 435
getIntHeader( ) (HttpServletRequest), 439
getLastModified( ) (HttpServlet), 118
getLog( ) (RemoteServer), 332
getMajorVersion( ) (ServletContext), 141
getMapNames( ) (MapMessage), 380
getMaxConnections( ) (DatabaseMetaData), 29
getMetaData( )
  Connection interface, 29, 342, 377
  ResultSet interface, 351
getMethod( ) (HttpServletRequest), 439
getMinorVersion( ) (ServletContext), 141
getMoreResults( ) (Statement), 22
getName( )
  HttpSessionBindingEvent class, 442
  NameClassPair class, 155
getNanos( ) (Timestamp), 359
getNextException( ) (SQLException), 26, 355
getObject( )
  Binding class, 159
  Handle interface, 208
  MapMessage interface, 380
  ResultSet interface, 41
  SearchResult class, 171
getOperations( ) (Skeleton), 336
getOutputStream( )
  RemoteCall interface, 330
  ServletResponse interface, 121, 435
getParameterNames( ) (ServletRequest), 435
getParameterValues( )
  HttpServletRequest interface, 119
  ServletRequest interface, 435
getParameter( )
  HttpServletRequest interface, 119, 133
  ServletRequest interface, 122

getPathInfo( ) (HttpServletRequest), 439
getPathTranslated( ) (HttpServletRequest), 439
getPrivileges( ) (ResultSetMetaData), 29
getProtocol( ) (ServletRequest), 122, 435
getQueue( ) (QueueReceiver), 387
getReader( )
  HttpServletRequest interface, 128
  ServletRequest interface, 435
getRegistry( ) (LocateRegistry), 57, 324
getRemoteAddr( ) (ServletRequest), 435
getRemoteHost( ) (ServletRequest), 122, 435
getRemoteUser( ) (HttpServletRequest), 126
getRequestDispatcher( )
  RequestDispatcher class, 431
  ServletContext interface, 141
getRequestURL( ) (HttpUtils), 443
getResource( ) (ServletContext), 142
getResultSet( )
  Array class, 339
  Statement interface, 21
getRollbackOnly( ) (EJBContext), 362
getRootCause( ) (ServletException), 141
getSchemaClassDefinition( ) (DirContext), 420
getSchema( ) (DirContext), 420
getScheme( ) (ServletRequest), 435
getServerName( ) (ServletRequest), 122, 435
getServerPort( ) (ServletRequest), 122, 435
getServletConfig( ) (Servlet), 432
getServletInfo( ) (Servlet), 118, 432
getServletNames( )
  deprecation, 142
  ServletContext interface, 433
getServletPath( ) (HttpServletRequest), 439
getServlets( ) (ServletContext), 433
getServlet( )
  deprecation, 142
  ServletContext interface, 433
getSession( )
  HttpServletRequest interface, 136, 439
  HttpSessionBindingEvent class, 442
get/set accessors (stateful session beans), 193
getSocketFactory( ) (RMISocketFactory), 334
getSQLState( ) (SQLException), 26
getStatus( ) (Transaction), 453
getString( ) (ResultSet), 23
getSubString( ) (Clob), 42, 342
getSystem( ) (ActivationGroup), 320
getTableTypes( ) (ResultSetMetaData), 29
getText( ) (TextMessage), 392
getTime() (Timestamp), 359
getTransactionIsolation( ) (Connection), 342
getUnexecutedModifications( ) (AttributeModificationException), 418
getUnicodeStream( ) (ResultSet), 25
getUpdateCounts( ) (BatchUpdateException), 340
getUpdateCount( ) (Statement), 22
getURL( ) (DatabaseMetaData), 29
getUserTransaction( ) (EJBContext), 362
getValueNames( ) (HttpSession), 441
getWarnings( )
  CallableStatement interface, 27, 342
  Connection interface, 27
  PreparedStatement interface, 27
  ResultSet interface, 27
  SQLWarning class, 357
  Statement interface, 27
getWriter( ) (ServletResponse), 121, 435
get( )
  Attribute interface, 416
  Attributes interface, 166
  MarshalledObject class, 306
graphs (CORBA objects), 283, 285
Greenwich Mean Time (GMT), 287
groups (activation) (see activation groups)
groups (SQL) (see SQL groups)

H

Handle interface, 208, 366
hardware (networks), server applications and, 4
hash code
- client stub and server implementation, matching, 336
- username and passwords, authenticating, 126

hashCode() (RemoteObject), 54, 330
Hashtable class, 219
- properties (InitialContext), 147

HEAD (HTTP request), 120
headers
- cookies, 135
- fields, listed (JMS messages), 381
- IDL interfaces, 88
- JNI C/C++, 76

helper classes, 91
- arrays (IDL), generating in Java, 261
- Binding class, 522
- BindingIterator class, 523
- BindingList class, 524
- BindingType class, 525
- enumerations (IDL), generating in Java, 265
- IDL/Java conversion, 89, 104, 279
- Istring class, 526
- Name (typedef), 527
- NameComponent class, 527
- NamingContext interface, 529
- sequences (IDL), generating in Java, 262
- ServiceDetail class, 495
- ServiceInformation class, 496
- unions (IDL), mapping to Java, 268

help() (Command), 152
HeuristicCommitException class, 451
HeuristicMixedException class, 451
HeuristicRollbackException class, 452
holder classes, 90, 474, 479–480, 482, 484, 490
- Any objects, 465
- arrays (IDL), generating in Java, 261
- Binding class, 523
- BindingIterator class, 524
- BindingType class, 526
- boolean values (IDL/Java mapping), 468
- byte values (IDL/Java mapping), 468
- char values (IDL/Java mapping), 469
- enumerations (IDL), generating in Java, 265
- IDL/Java conversion, 93, 279
  - objects, passing as inout, 94
- Name (IDL), 528
- NameComponent class, 527
- NamingContext interface, 529
- sequences (IDL), generating in Java, 262
- ServiceInformation class, 496
- short values, 497
- String values, 498
- structs (IDL), generating in Java, 263
- TypeCodes, 502
- unions (IDL), mapping to Java, 268

home interface, 186–187
- creating, finding and removing beans, 178
- deployment descriptor, naming, 214
- EJB containers, registering with JNDI, 180
- EJB objects, 176
- enterprise beans, 224
- entity beans
  - container-managed persistence, 211
  - example, 198
  - finder methods, 188, 198
- JAR files, 218
- JNDI, finding with, 219
- methods, 187–188
- as RMI remote interface, 187

HomeHandle interface, 223
hosts
- cookies, returning, 135
- names, authenticating (access control), 126
- ORBs, specifying, 99, 106
- RMI registry daemon, running, 56

HTML
- forms, processing results, 118
- ISO Latin-1 character set, 252

HTML (cont'd)
pages
dynamic content, adding, 133–135
JavaServer Pages, 134
servlets returning, 115
HTTP
errors, 123
form variables, 119, 134
headers
cookies, writing and reading to/from, 135
fields, manipulating, 121
requests, 120, 122
responses, 121
requests, 120, 131
servlet support, 437
stateless nature, 11
HTTPS connections (cookies), 135
HttpServlet class, 116, 438
HTTP protocol, working with, 117
HttpServletRequest interface, 118, 121, 439
HttpServletResponse interface, 118, 121, 440
HttpSession interface, 136, 441
HttpSessionBindingEvent class, 138, 442
HttpSessionBindingListener interface, 138, 442
HttpSessionContext interface, 442
HttpUtils class, 443

I

id field (NameComponent), 105
idempotent (HTTP requests), 120
identifiers (IDL), 252, 277
IDL, 82–113, 461–505
arrays, 261
character literals (IDL/Java mapping), 254, 258
comments, mapping to Java, 253
constants (IDL/Java mapping), 255
context variables (methods), 275
converting to Java, 89–97
CORBA exceptions, mapping to Java, 270
data types, 84, 253
typedef, 260
user-defined, 259
declaration language, 87
default ORB implementation, 98
early binding (constants), 278
entities, high-level, listed, 251
enumerations, 263
error codes, listed (COMM_FAILURE), 469
example, complete, 89
exceptions, 268
identifiers (IDL/Java mapping), 252
idltojava compiler, bugs, 291
initial object references, 105
interfaces
CORBA-enabled, defining, 87
declaring, 88
inheritance, 276
mapping to Java, 278
Java implementation (CORBA), 107
Java stubs to CORBA objects, 78
Java-to-IDL-mapping, 81
keywords, listed, 251
literals (IDL/Java mapping), 255–257
methods, 273
calls, semantics, 276
context clauses, ignoring (idltojava compiler), 291
mapping to Java, 279
modules, 87
declaring, 271
naming scopes, 258
Naming Service, 99–100, 291
ORBs
properties (standard), 98
properties (nonstandard), 99
reference, 250–280
remote method, inout parameter, 94
RMI vs., 82
sequences, mapping to Java, 262
strings, mapping to Java, 254
structs, mapping to Java, 262
tools, 289–291
unions, mapping to Java, 265
IDLEntity interface, 512
idltojava compiler, 82, 289
bugs, 291

idltojava compiler (cont'd)
context variable, not supported, 275
downloading from Sun, 90
environment, 291
Java classes, generating from IDL interfaces, 89
stub and skeleton classes, generating, 90
unions (IDL), mapping to Java, 266
IDLType interface, 480
IETF (see Internet Engineering Task Force)
IIOP (see RMI/IIOP)
IllegalStateException class, 141, 378
IMP_LIMIT class, 481
inactiveGroup() (ActivationGroup), 73
inactiveObject() (ActivationGroup), 73, 316
inactive() (Activatable), 313
include() (RequestDispatcher), 141, 431
InconsistentTypeCode class, 508
index (see primary keys)
initial context
changing with initctx command, 154
naming systems, 145
INITIAL_CONTEXT_FACTORY property, 146, 219, 404
initial references, listing (ORB), 105
InitialContext class, 404
browsing, use as entry point, 157
LDAP factory class, creating, 147
loading into NamingShell, 153
naming systems, 147
InitialContextFactory interface, 427
InitialContextFactoryBuilder interface, 427
InitialDirContext class, 421
initialization (see activation)
initialization constructors, 66
initialization methods (ORBs), 98
INITIALIZE class, 481
init()
GenericServlet class, 431
JDBC Connection objects, creating (servlets), 139
ORB class, 99, 490
Servlet API Version 2.1 (changes), 141
Servlet interface, 432
servlet persistence, 128
servlets, multiple invocations, 115
inner classes, 87
inner joins (SQL), 237
InputStream class, 512
insertRow() (ResultSet), 38, 351
InsufficientResourcesException class, 405
integers (IDL literals), 256
Interface Definition Language (see IDL)
Interface Description Language (see IDL)
interfaces (IDL), 251
attributes, 272
attributes and methods, inheriting, 276
constants, declaring, 255
declarations, 88, 271
Java classes and interfaces vs., 87
Java classes, generating from, 89
Java interface, converted to, 91
mapping to Java, 278
methods, mapping to Java, 279
interfaces (remote object), unknown, 111–113
INTERNAL class, 481
internal links (servlets), URL encoding, 136
Internet, distributed computing, 3
Internet Engineering Task Force (IETF) (cookies standard), 135
Internet Inter-ORB Protocol (IIOP) (see RMI/IIOP)
Interoperable Object References, 98, 108
interpreters (NamingShell, lacking), 149
InterruptedNamingException class, 406
INTF_REPOS class, 482
IntHolder class, 482
INV_FLAG class, 482
INV_IDENT class, 483
INV_OBJREF class, 483
INV_POLICY class, 483

Invalid class, 506
INVALID_TRANSACTION class, 484
InvalidAttributeIdentifierException class, 422
InvalidAttributesException class, 169
InvalidAttributeValueException class, 423
InvalidClientIDException class, 378
InvalidDestinationException class, 379
InvalidName class, 509, 534
InvalidNameException class, 406
InvalidNameHelper class, 535
InvalidNameHolder class, 535
InvalidSearchControlsException class, 423
InvalidSearchFilterException class, 423
InvalidSelectorException class, 379
InvalidSeq class, 507
InvalidTransactionException class, 453
InvalidValue class, 507
InvokeHandler interface, 513
invoke()
  DynamicImplementation class, 474
  RemoteRef interface, 331
  Request class, 494
  ServerSkeleton class, 95
IORs (see Interoperable Object References)
IRObject interface, 484
isCallerInRole() (EJBContext), 362
isNull() (ResultSet), 25
ISO date escape sequences, 26
ISO Latin-1, 252
isolation levels
  transactions, 32, 34, 185
    JDBC support, listed, 33
    database isolation levels and, 186
    deployment descriptors, specifying, 214
    listed, 186
IstringHelper class, 526

J

JAR files, 214–215, 218
  deployment descriptors, 223
jar utility (Java SDK), 218
Java
  client and server implementation, required (RMI), 6
  IDL conversion, 89–97
  IDL, differences (list), 87
  object-oriented programming, 5
  platform independence, 4
  SQL vs., 227
  versions 1.1 and 1.2, 5–6
Java 2 platform
  Enterprise Edition (J2EE), 3
  JDBC 2.0, 15, 37
  Servlet API, 9
Java archive files (see JAR files)
Java Blend (object/database mapping), 41
Java classes
  EJB client and container, providing for, 179
  EJB components, 186
  IDL interfaces vs., 87
Java Database Connectivity (see JDBC)
Java Development Kit (see JDK)
Java Enterprise APIs, 5–10
  EJB vs., 8
  heterogeneous networks, alleviating problems, 4
  Jini vs., 14
  servlets, using, 8
  SQL as key part, 15
Java IDL (see IDL)
Java language
  comments (IDL), 253
  multithreading vs. concurrency control (CORBA), 284
Java Message Service (see JMS)
Java Naming and Directory Interface (see JNDI)
Java Naming and Directory Services (see JNDI)
Java Native Interface (see JNI)
Java objects, 41
  mapping to database records (Java Blend), 41
  SQL type, mapping to, 339
Java packages (IDL modules vs.), 87
Java SDK
  jar utility, 218
Java Servlet API, 8

Java Servlet Development Kit (JSDK), 116
Java Transaction API (see JTA)
Java VM
  activation daemon, 74
  activation group, startup, 318
  activation groups, 65, 70
  libraries (native functions), loading, 77
Java Web Server (JWS), 137
Java-aware databases, 41
JavaBeans
  client GUIs, 7
  EJB and, 174
javah tool (natively implemented method), 76
java.naming.factory.initial property, 147
java.rmi package, 6, 43, 304–312
java.rmi.activation package, 65
java.rmi.dgc package, 322–323
java.rmi.registry package, 324–326
java.rmi.server package, 54, 327
java.rmi.server.codebase property, 61
JavaServer Pages (JSP), 134
java.sql package, 15, 339–360
javax.ejb package, 175, 361–368
  EJB API, 8
javax.ejb.deployment package, 215, 369–372
  EJB API, 8
javax.jms package, 373–397
javax.naming package, 7, 144, 398–415
javax.naming.directory package, 144, 416–425
javax.naming.spi package, 144, 426–429
javax.servlet package, 9, 116, 430–436
javax.servlet.http package, 9, 116, 437–443
javax.sql package, 6, 42, 444–450
javax.transaction package, 10, 451–457
javax.transactions.xa package, 10, 458–460
JDBC, 15–42, 339
  architecture, 15
  basic functions, example, 16
  batch updates, 39
  BLOB and CLOB objects, 25
  commands, database-independent, 36
  connections, 184
    Connection object, binding to sessions, 138
    container-managed persistence, 211
    pooling, 139, 185
  data types, mapping to primitive Java types, 28
  database communications, servlets, 139
  date and time classes, 26
  drivers, 16, 18–19
    (see also drivers)
  escape syntax, stored procedures, 35
  JDBC 2.0 standard extension, 20, 37–42, 444–450
  JDBC version 1.0, 15, 37, 42
  JDBC-ODBC Bridge, 19
  metadata, 29–32
  platform independence, 16
  ResultSet (version 2.0 vs. 1.0), 23
  SQL return codes, 241
  SQL statements, 21
  transactions, 32–34
  URLs, 19
    odbc subprotocol, 20
jdbc.drivers property, 18
JDBC-ODBC Bridge
  drivers, 18
  sample output (DatabaseMetaData program), 30
  Sun and Intersolv, updated version, 37
  Windows and Solaris systems, 19
JDK
  RMI registry daemon, 56
  servlets, separate distribution, 116
  version 1.0, 37
  Version 1.1 (JDBC-ODBC Bridge), 19
Jini, Java Enterprise APIs vs., 14
JMS, 9
  javax.jms package, 373–397
JMSException class, 379
JMSSecurityException class, 380
JNDI, 143–173, 398
  architecture, 144

JNDI (cont'd)
attributes
values, specifying, 169
values, working with, 166
client identity, reserved name entry, 216
CORBA Naming Service, registering with, 79
directory schemas, 163, 168
directory services, 162
searching, 170
EJB components, accessing, 143
EJB home interfaces, 177, 180
files, not creating, 159
libraries, specifying in classpath, 154
naming directory, 416–425
packages, downloading, 144
remote objects, binding to CORBA Naming Service, 79
RMI registry, binding, 50
security principal EJB/JNDI server, 220
separator characters (compound names), 157
SPI (see SPI (JNDI))
JNI, 44
JNI C/C++ header files, 76
joins (SQL), 235
multiple tables, joining, 236
tables, connecting, 235
without JOIN keyword, 236
JSDK (Java Servlet Development Kit), 116
JSP (see JavaServer Pages)
JTA, 9, 451–457
boundaries (client-side), creating, 221
EJB transaction support, 182
two-phase commit, 42
JWS (Java Web Server)
servlet chaining, 127

K

keep-alive checks, servlets, 141
key attributes, 163–164
specifying, 169
(see also attributes)
keywords
best-effort method call semantics, 276
escape sequences (JDBC), 36
IDL, 251, 272
kind field (NameComponent), 105

L

language independence
CORBA, 83
inter-ORB communications, 86
large data types, 25
last() (ResultSet), 351
layout (directories), 162
LDAP
directory servers, 165
entries, prohibiting new, 169
factory class, 147
naming systems and, 143
organizational unit and user object classes, 169
search criteria, syntax, 170
leaf, CORBA naming directory, 84, 149
Lease class, 323
length() (Blob), 341
libraries
native code, wrapping with Java, 18
native functions, loading, 77
third-party, thread safety and, 130
Licensing Service (CORBA), 286
life cycle
entity beans, 206
servlets, 115
Life Cycle Service (CORBA), 284
Lightweight Directory Access Protocol (see LDAP)
LIKE statement, 36
LimitExceededException class, 406
LinkException class, 406
LinkLoopException class, 407
LinkRef class, 407
list_initial_references() (ORB), 105
listBindings()
Binding class, 400
Context interface, 159, 403
list()
Context interface, 154, 161, 403
Naming class, 307

list() (cont'd)
  NameClassPair, 409
  NamingContext interface, 528
  NamingShell class, 155
literals (IDL)
  characters, 257
  numeric, types, 256
  strings, adjacent (compiler bugs), 291
  strings (characters), 258
loadClass() (RMIClassLoader), 333
LoaderHandler class, 327
loadLibrary() (System), 77
LocateRegistry interface, 56–57, 247, 324
logical operators (search filters), 171
LogStream class, 329
log() (LogStream), 329
LongHolder class, 484
Lookup application, 146
lookup()
  Context interface, 148, 403
  Naming class, 307
  Naming interface, 50
  Registry interface, 325
loopbacks, 215

M

main()
  RMI registry, 47
  ServerInit class, 109
MalformedLinkException class, 407
MalformedURLException class, 57
mandatory attributes, 169
manifest file (JAR file), 218
MapMessage interface, 380
mapping object-oriented languages to CORBA, 83
  MARSHAL class, 485
  MarshalException class, 48, 59
  marshalling, 49
    IDL objects, 514
    remote method arguments, 48, 254
    URL, encoding for class file, 61
    (see also unmarshalling)
MarshalledObject class, 67, 71, 304
Message interface, 381
MessageFormatException class, 384
MessageListener interface, 384
MessageNotReadableException class, 385
MessageNotWriteableException class, 380, 385
message-oriented middleware (MOM), 9
MessageProducer interface, 385
messaging
  point-to-point, 373
  publish/subscribe, 373
metadata
  EJB objects, 364
  JDBC, 29–32
  properties, querying for, 287
  result sets, SQL queries, 339
methods
  asynchronous (CORBA), 282
  calls
    return values or exceptions, 50
    semantics (IDL/Java mapping), 280
  IDL, 88, 273–276
    context variables, 275
    exceptions, 274
    identifiers, 277
    implementation, 87
    mapping to Java interface, 279
    parameters, 87, 273
  time limit, exceeding, 415
Microsoft
  Access database, metadata, 30
  ODBC (Open DataBase Connectivity), 15
  Visual C++ preprocessor, 291
MIME types
  filtering, servlets, 127
  transmitting, servlets, 139
modification types (attributes), 168
ModificationItem class, 167, 423
modifier methods, unions (IDL/Java mapping), 266–267
modifiers (IDL methods), 87
modifyAttributes()
  Attribute class, 416
  AttributeModificationException class, 418
  Attributes interface, 418
  DirContext interface, 167–168, 420
modules (IDL), 87, 251
  CORBA object relationships, 285

modules (IDL) (cont'd)
  declarations, 271
  mapping to Java, 271
  nesting within files, 87
MOM (see message-oriented middleware)
moveToCurrentRow() (ResultSet), 39
moveToInsertRow() (ResultSet), 38
multicast objects (remote object communication), 49

N

Name interface, 408
name servers, JNDI and, 7
NameAlreadyBoundException class, 408
NameClassPair class, 155, 409
NameComponent arrays (CORBA NamingContext), 282
NameComponent class, 101, 105, 526
NameComponentHelper class, 527
NameComponentHolder class, 527
NamedValue class, 112, 485
NameHelper class, 527
NameHolder class, 528
NameNotFoundException class, 146, 409
NameParser interface, 409
names
  atomic, compound vs., 163
  attributes (attribute ID), 416
  composite, 401
  compound, 156, 402
  fully qualified, 50
  how they work, 156
  invalid syntax, 406
NameValuePair class, 486
naming scope (IDL), 258, 277
naming and directory services, JNDI and, 7
naming context
  JNDI, 219
  object reference, obtaining, 105
naming conventions
  bound objects (sessions), 137
  SQL objects (within schemas), 229
  tables and schemas (SQL), 228
naming directory structure, 528
Naming interface, 46, 50, 56–57, 304
  remote objects
    looking up (example), 47
naming registry, 304
Naming Service (CORBA), 84, 99, 105, 108, 282–283, 519
  references, narrowing, 105
  (see also IDL)
Naming Service (IDL), 291
naming services
  context, 146
  directory services vs., 143
  JNDI SPI and, 144
  references to other naming services, 107
  RMI, 50, 56–58
  using multiple, 106
naming systems
  browsing, 157
  enterprise Java suppliers, JNDI accessing, 143
  initial context, 147
  naming operations (JNDI-accessible systems), 149
  objects, looking up, 145, 148
  service providers (other), 148
NamingContext interface, 84, 282, 528
NamingContextHelper class, 529
NamingContextHolder class, 529
NamingEnumeration interface, 155, 410
NamingException class, 146, 410
NamingManager class, 145, 427
NamingSecurityException class, 411
NamingShell class
  directory server, using, 165
  implementation example, 157
  JNDI commands, loading and executing, 149
  running, 154
narrow()
  NamingContextHelper class, 85
  PortableRemoteObject interface, 79–80, 224
native function libraries, 77
Native Interface API, 75
Native-API Partly-Java Drivers, 18
Native-protocol All-Java Drivers, 19
Net-protocol All-Java Drivers, 18

Netscape Directory Server (NDS), 162
network protocols
  CORBA, defining, 86
  TCP/IP, 4
networking services
  Java Enterprise APIs, supporting, 5
  Novell NDS and, 163
networks
  applications, creating with RMI, 6
  heterogeneous devices, 4
  schematic (hypothetical enterprise), 11
new_Context() (NamingContext), 528
newCall() (RemoteRef), 331
newInstance()
  ActivationGroup class, 72, 316
  ActivationInstantiator interface, 319
  Activator interface, 320
next_n() (BindingIterator), 523
next_one() (BindingIterator), 523
next()
  DynAny interface, 475
  ResultSet interface, 23, 351
NO_IMPLEMENT class, 486
NO_MEMORY class, 486
NO_PERMISSION class, 487
NO_RESOURCES class, 487
NO_RESPONSE class, 487
NoInitialContextException class, 411
nonclass data structure definitions (C++ and IDL), 87
non-HTML content (servlets), 139
non-object oriented languages (CORBA specifications and), 83
nonremote objects, remote objects vs., 59
nonrepeatable reads (transactions), 185
NoPermissionException class, 146, 411
NoSuchAttributeException class, 424
NoSuchObjectException class, 308
NotBoundException class, 308
NotContextException class, 411
NotEmpty class, 535
NotEmptyHelper class, 536
NotEmptyHolder class, 536
NotFound class, 103, 106, 536
NotFoundHelper class, 537
NotFoundHolder class, 537
NotFoundReason class, 537
NotFoundReasonHolder class, 538
notification (CORBA Event Service), 282
NotSupportedException class, 453
Novell NDS, 143
  NdsObject interface (JNDI SPI), 144
  NetWare Directory Services, 163
  service provider (JNDI), 148
null values
  database columns, 25
  inserting with PreparedStatement, 28
  rows, inserting, 39
nullsAreSortedHigh() (DatabaseMetaData), 29
numeric literals (IDL), 256
  mapping to Java, 257
NVList class, 488

O

OBJ_ADAPTER class, 488
object class definition, 164, 169
Object Data Management Group (ODMG), 283
Object interface, 489
  CORBA, 104, 279
  direct communication with remote object, 111
  remote method requests, sending, 104
  Security Service support, 282
Object Management Group (see OMG)
OBJECT_NOT_EXIST class, 489
Object Request Broker (see ORBs)
object_to_string() (ORB), 108, 490
ObjectFactory interface, 428
ObjectFactoryBuilder interface, 428
ObjectHolder class, 490
ObjectImpl class, 104, 513
ObjectMessage interface, 386
ObjectNotFoundException class, 366
object-oriented languages, mapping to CORBA, 83
  mapping to Corba specifications, 83

object-oriented programming
Java, 5, 41
RMI, extending to client-server, 6
objects
acting as clients and servers, 6
adding to NamingContext (CORBA), 101
attributes, associating with, 143
binding, 143, 161
NamingService, 101
sessions, 137–138
subcontexts, 102
CORBA, 83
creating, 87
exporting, 284
factories, 283
grouping into collections, 288
relationships, defining, 284
data types, Java handling, 87
EJB, 178
business methods, implementing, 179
components, 187
deployment descriptors for containers, 179
implementing basic, 186
JDBC connections, providing (EJB server), 185
transactions, managing, 182–183
interfaces, defining (IDL), 250
Java types, inserting into databases, 28
leaves, 149
looking up in Context, 148
remote distribution, enabled, 53
remote vs. nonremote, 59
services provided (RMI), 50
storing and manipulating, support for, 41
ObjID class, 329
ODBC, URLs, 20
URLs, example, 20
ODMG (Object Data Management Group), 283
outer join, 36
OMG
CORBA Services specification, downloading, 281
CORBA standard, defining, 7
IDL and Java mapping reference, downloading, 250
IDL to Java mapping, 289
Java IDL mapping, 84
oneway keyword, 276
onMessage() (MessageListener), 384
OODBMS (object-oriented database management systems, 41
Open DataBase Connectivity (Microsoft) (see ODBC)
Operation class, 330
OperationNotSupportedException class, 146, 412
operators
IDL. C/C++, support, 255
SQL, listed, 234
Oracle JDBC-Thin driver (URLs, type), 19
Oracle PL/SQL stored procedure (example), 34
ORB class, 490
ORBClass property, 98
ORBInitialHost property, 99
ORBInitialPort property, 99
ORBs, 84
bounds checks, data, 254
communications between ORBs, 86
stringified object references and, 108
containers (EJB) vs., 176
default implementation (IDL), 98
host and port, specifying initial, 106
initial object references, 105
initializing, 98
remote naming service reference, 108
properties, specifying (methods), 99
remote object references, 103
services provided, 105
ORBSingletonClass property, 98
org.omg.CORBA package, 82, 100, 461–505
org.omg.CORBA.DynAnyPackage package, 506–507
org.omg.CORBA.ORBPackage package, 508–509

org.omg.CORBA.portable package, 93, 510–516
org.omg.CORBA.TypeCodePackage package, 517–518
org.omg.CosNaming package, 82, 100, 519–530
org.omg.CosNaming.NamingContextPackage package, 531–539
outer joins, 36, 237
output streams (servlet responses), 121
OutputStream class, 514

P

page counter, implementing, 115
pages, redirecting (HTTP servlets), 121
<PARAM> tags, 133
parameters
  batch updates (CallableStatement), 40
  clearing or specifying (PreparedStatement), 28
  CODE (servlet tags), 133
  CODEBASE (remote servlets, loading), 133
  IDL methods, 273
    mapping to Java, 279
  initialization, activated objects, 306
  servlet requests, accessing, 122
  stored procedures, 35
parents
  Context objects and, 157
  creating new context, 159
parsePostData( ) (HttpUtils), 443
parseQueryString( ) (HttpUtils), 443
PartialResultException class, 412
passivation
  enterprise beans, container control, 181
  entity beans, 207
    bean-managed persistence, 205
  session beans, 192, 367
passwords, authenticating, 126
path, files (idltojava compiler), 290
path, specifying (cookies), 136
peer-to-peer systems, 49
performance
  precompiled SQL statements, 27
  escape-sequence processing, affecting, 36
  factory class vs. RMI registry,
  isolation levels vs., 33
  URL encoding, problems, 136
PERSIST_STORE class, 492
persistence
  container support (enterprise beans), 180–182
  container-managed, database mapping, 215
  CORBA objects, 283
  entity beans, 196, 200
    bean-managed, 196, 200, 208
    container-managed, 196, 208
    removing, 207
    session beans vs., 179
  remote references, 55, 65, 313
  servlets, 11, 114–115, 128
  session beans, 195
  tnameserv implementation, CORBA Naming Service, 291
Persistent Object Service (CORBA), 283, 286
phantom reads (transactions), 185
platform independence (JDBC), 16
point-to-point communication
  Activatable and UnicastRemoteObject objects, 313
  messaging, 373
  object references, 49
policy
  files (Java), 62–63
  security (CORBA), 82
Policy interface, 492
policy_type( ) (Policy), 492
PolicyError class, 492
poll_response( ) (Request), 494
PooledConnection interface, 42, 446
pooling
  containers (EJB)
    stateless session beans, 195
  database connections, 20, 34, 42, 139
  entity beans, 196, 206
  servlet instances, 133
  stateless session beans, 192
port, specifying (ORB), 106

PortableRemoteObject interface, 79, 224
ports
activation daemon, 75
client requests on CORBA Naming Service , 291
exceptions (already in use), 327
exported objects, specifying for, 67–68
ORBs, specifying, 69, 106
registry daemons, listening on, 56
RMI activation daemon, 247–248
servers, obtaining (servlet requests), 122
position()
Blob interface, 341
Clob interface, 342
POST (HTTP request), 120, 131
pragma directives, idltojavacompiler, 289
prepareCall()
CallableStatement interface, 35, 341
Connection interface, 35
PreparedStatement interface, 21, 27, 350
batch updates, 39
parameters, setting (example), 28
prepareStatement() (Connection), 28, 350
preprocessing directives (idltojava compiler), 289
previous()(ResultSet), 351
primary keys
class, specifying (deployment descriptors), 215
entity beans, 196–197
container-managed persistence, 211
EJB 1.1 specification, changes, 223
session beans, 197
SQL, 232
user name, storing, 205
primitive data types, 23
Principal class, 493
PrincipalHolder class, 493
println() (ServletOutputStream), 434
PrintReader, 128
printWarnings() (SQLWarning), 27
print() (ServletOutputStream), 434
privacy issues (cookies), 135
profile server, 187
properties
deployment options, settings, 175
EJB components, 174, 185
file, creating (LDAP server), 165
files, creating (naming services), 154
initial context (naming systems), 147
JMS messages, 382
naming systems, changing, 145
ORBs, 98–99
Property Service (CORBA), 287
protocol (servlet requests), accessing, 122
PROVIDER_URL properties, 146, 219
public classes, 87, 190
publish/subscribe messaging, 373
pull events (CORBA), 283
push events (CORBA), 283
PUT (HTTP request), 120
putValue() (HttpSession), 137, 441
put() (BasicAttributes), 420

Q

queries
results, treating as JavaBeans component, 42
SQL, 21
Query Service (CORBA), 286
Queue interface, 386
QueueBrowser interface, 386
QueueConnection interface, 387
QueueConnectionFactory interface, 387
QueueReceiver interface, 387
QueueRequestor interface, 388
QueueSender interface, 388
QueueSession interface, 388

R

RDBMS (relational database management system), tables, 228
reactivation constructors, 67–68
readLine() (ServletInputStream), 434
read-only result sets, 37
read() (ObjID), 329

rebind_context() (NamingContext), 528
rebind()
  Context interface, 161
  Naming interface, 307
  NamingContext interface, 528
  Registry interface, 56, 325
reentrance (deployment descriptor specification), 215
Ref interface, 351
RefAddr class, 412
Reference class, 413
Referenceable interface, 413
references, local and remote registries, 57
ReferralException class, 414
RefFSContextFactory class, 146
RefFSContxtFactory class, 147
register() (Activatable), 71, 315
registerGroup() (ActivationSystem), 73, 318
registerObject() (ActivationSystem), 320
registerOutParameter() (CallableStatement), 35
registerOutputParameters() (CallableStatement interface), 341
registerSynchronization() (Transaction), 454–455
registries
  local and remote, references, 57
  naming, 305
  RMI services provided, 50
Registry interface, 50, 56, 325
RegistryHandler class, 325
related tables (RDBMS), 228
relational database management system (RDBMS), 228
relational databases, 15
  JDBC, working with, 5
  not object-oriented, 41
  structure, 227
Relationship Service (CORBA), 283–284
RemarshalException class, 515
remote interface, 186, 224
  business methods available to client, 179
  defining, 188
  EJB, RMI vs., 178
  finder methods, 198
  implementing
    directly (EJB class), 190
    example, 45
    stub and skeleton classes, 52
  JAR files, 218
  methods
    finder methods, 198
    relation to home interface and bean implementation methods, 187
  remote exceptions, declaring, 53
  remote object, specifying, 51
  stub and skeleton classes, implementing, 245
Remote interface, 44, 53–54, 187, 304, 308
Remote Method Invocation (see RMI)
remote methods
  arguments, 58
  CORBA, out or inout arguments, 90
  declaring (remote interface), 54
  DII and DSI, executing with, 111
  IDL, inout parameter, 94
  implementation, server (IDL/Java conversion), 97
  return values, 58
remote objects
  activatable
    implementing, 66–67
    defining, 51–55, 65–69
  activation, 64–75
  activation groups, 72-73
  activation service (RMI), 50
  binding to CORBA Naming Service (JNDI), 79
  binding to names, 56
  classes
    implementation, RMI, 54
    names, finding, 73
    tracking (serialver utility), 248
    RMI registry, 56
  clients accessing, 56–60, 98
  containers (EJB), converting primary keys, 199
  CORBA
    delegates, 93
    life cycle, controlling, 283
  creating and using, 43

remote objects (cont'd)
  disassociating from beans, 207
  EJB, 176
  factory classes, 59
  finding, 103–113
  getting from other remote objects, 105
  IDL (interfaces, describing), 82
  interaction, starting, 61
  interface, defining, 44
  interfaces not available, 111–113
  looking up, 143
    JNDI, 143
    RMI registry, 57
  naming service (CORBA), 84
  native code, exporting (RMI and JNI), 78
  nonremote objects vs., 59
  nonreplicated, 337
  references as printable character strings, 108
  registering (RMI registry), 46
  remote reference, generating, 59
  server implementations, 327
  server-side implementation, 335
  session beans vs., 191
  stub and skeleton classes, generating, 245
  stubs, skeletons and objects, relationship, 51
remote references
  client stubs, 48
  clients, obtaining (IDL/Java conversion), 98
  CORBA, 103
  expiring, 51
  factory classes, 59
  finding methods (CORBA), 104
  objects, copying vs., 59
  persistence, 55, 64–65
  point-to-point, nonpersistent, 55
  reestablishing with handles, 208
  RemoteObject, containing, 54
  RMI architecture, 48
  stringified, 108
  stubs (server objects), 95
RemoteCall interface, 330
remoteEquals() (RemoteRef), 331
RemoteException class, 44, 53, 188, 198, 304, 309
remoteHashCode() (RemoteRef), 331
RemoteObject class, 54, 330
RemoteRef interface, 331
RemoteServer class, 55, 66, 313, 332
RemoteStub class, 332
remoteToString() (RemoteRef), 331
RemoveException class, 366
removeValue() (HttpSession), 441
remove(), 200
  Attributes interface, 167
  EJBHome interface, 363
  entity beans (container-managed persistence), 212
repeatable reads (transactions), 33
replication (remote objects), 49, 337
Repository interface (CORBA), Java IDL and, 289
Request interface, 112, 494
RequestDispatcher interface, 141, 431
requests (servlets), 121
  attributes, setting, 141
request()
  QueueRequestor, 388
  TopicRequestor interface, 394
reset() (BytesMessage), 374
resolve_initial_references() (ORB), 84–85, 98, 105, 490
Resolver interface, 428
ResolveResult class, 429
resolve() (NamingContext), 528
resource abstraction (servlets), 142
resource management
  bindings, listing, 159
  database connections, closing, 20
  servers (EJB), container role in, 181
  servlets, benefits, 115
  shared attributes (servlets), 142
ResponseHandler interface, 515
result sets
  multiple, 22
  structure, discovering, 29
ResultSet interface, 17, 23, 351
  BLOBs and CLOBs, 42
  cursor location (JDBC 2.0), 38
  data types, large, 25
  JDBC 1.0 vs. JDBC 2.0, 23, 37
  types, listed, 37

ResultSet interface (cont'd)
rows, inserting, deleting, editing data, 38
scroll-sensitive, updateable, 37
SQL queries, 21, 23
updating (single table without joins), 39
ResultSetMetaData interface, 29, 354
database table, contents and data types (example), 31
return codes (SQL), 241–244
return values (remote methods), 58
return_value() (Request), 494
rewind() (DynAny), 475
RMI, 43–81
activation features, listed, 64
activation daemon, 247
activation system, 55, 313
architecture, 48
classes, converting to RMI/IIOP, 79
classes, loading, 61
communication styles, remote objects, 49
CORBA distributed object API vs., 78, 83
EJB and, 174
fundamental roles, 176
IIOP, 78
interfaces (elements), 43
JNDI, looking up remote objects, 143
language dependence, 44
native method calls, 75
object services, 50
objects, accessing from CORBA, 81
registry (see RMI registry; RMI Naming registry)
stub/skeleton layer, 59
rmic compiler (see rmic)
serial version utility, 248
tools, 245–249
RMI compiler (see rmic)
RMI Naming registry, 71
JNDI, conversion, 79
(see also RMI registry)
rmi protocol (object URLs), 57
RMI registry, 50, 56–58
activatable class, registering, 65
classpath, stubs and skeletons, 63
environment (classpath), 247
factory classes, 59
naming service, 307
registering remote objects without activation, 64
remote objects, looking up, 57
remote objects, registering, 46
without activation, 64
rmic, 245–247
Skeleton interface, 336
stubs and skeletons, 46, 52
stubs and skeletons, generating, 55
updated, RMI/IIOP, 79
RMIClassLoader class, 61, 333
RMIClientSocketFactory interface, 333–334
RMIFailureHandler class, 333
RMI/IIOP
RMI communicating with CORBA remote objects, 44
servers, client compatibility with, 224
TCP/IP protocol base, 86
tnameserv utility, 81
RMISecurityException class, 309
RMISecurityManager class, 62, 304, 309
setting for remote class loading, 63
RMIServerSocketFactory class, 334
RMIServerSocketFactory interface, 334
RMISocketFactory class, 334
RollbackException class, 453
rollbacks (transactions), 32
rollback()
Connection interface, 33, 342
Session interface, 390
Transaction interface, 455
UserTransaction interface, 182, 456
XAResource interface, 459
root cause exception, specifying, 141
root (CORBA naming directory), 84
root object class (CORBA), 104
root packages (IDL/Java mapping), 289
rows
insertions, preventing, 34
ResultSet
accessing, 37
editing data, inserting or deleting, 38
navigating, 23

rows, ResultSet (cont'd)
RowSet interface, 42, 446
RowSetEvent class, 448
RowSetInternal interface, 448
RowSetListener interface, 448
RowSetMetaData interface, 449
RowSetReader interface, 449
RowSetWriter interface, 449
run-as-identity, 217
run-as-mode, 217

S

scalar database functions, 36
schemas (SQL)
  catalogs, 228
  commands, manipulating, 230
SchemaViolationException class, 424
scope (searches), setting, 171
scopes (ILD naming), 277
scrolling
  result sets, 37
  support information (DatabaseMetaData), 39
SearchControls class, 171, 424
searching
  command, 172
  controls, 171
  directories, 170
  filters, 170, 173
    logical operators, combining with, 171
  results, 171
SearchResult class, 425
search()
  DirContext interface, 170, 420, 424
  NamingShell class, 172
security
  access control, 369
  classes, loading remote, 62
  CORBA policy services, 82
  EJB containers, 216
  EJB/JNDI server interactions, 220
  HTTPS connections (cookies), 135
  JMS, 380
  naming exceptions, 411
  policies, overriding, 497
  remote objects, exporting, 337
  RMI, 304
  servlets, 126
  session IDs, exposing, 139
SECURITY_PRINCIPAL property, 220
Security Service (CORBA), 282, 286
seek() (DynAny), 475
semicolons (IDL vs. Java), 88
send_deferred() (Request), 494
send_oneway()(Request), 494
sendError() (HttpServletResponse), 121, 123, 440
sendRedirect() (HttpServletResponse), 121, 440
send() (QueueSender), 388
separator characters (JNDI compound names), 157
sequences (IDL), 262
Serializable interface, 54, 58
serialization, 6, 191
  beans (passivation), 191
  data structures (entity beans), 213
  deployment descriptors, 214
    EJB 1.1, changes, 222
  handles, 208
  HomeHandle, 223
  MarshalledObject, 73
  objects (holder class), 94
  remote methods, 48
    primitive data types, 58
  RMI objects, 306
  Streamable object (CORBA), 93
  (see also deserialization; passivation)
serialver utility, 248–249
ServantObject class, 516
server applications, network hardware and, 4
server skeletons, 46, 48, 95, 336
  classes, loading, 61
  classes, regenerating (RMI/IIOP), 79
  CORBA, 83–84
  generating (RMI), 51, 55
  idltojava compiler, generating, 90
  method invocations, forwarding to server implementation object, 111
  RMI architecture, 48
  rmic compiler, generating, 245
  (see also skeletons)
ServerCloneException class, 335
ServerError class, 310

ServerException class, 310
ServerNotActiveException class, 335
ServerRef interface, 335
ServerRequest class, 495
ServerRuntimeException class, 310
servers
  configuring, remote class loading, S
  constructing with given name, 69
  cookie support, lacking, 136
  directory (see directory servers)
  distributed garbage collection, 322
  EJB, 175
    bean instances, 178
    classes, connecting beans to container, 190
    containers and, 8, 180
    JDBC connections, providing, 185
    portability issues, 212, 223
    RMI-IIOP, compatibility, 224
    transactions, making aware of, 184
    types available, 180
  EJB/JNDI interaction, 220
  implementation, 54
  Java implementation, lacking, 78
  as Java objects (RMI), 44
  JTA, using , 10
  keep-alive checks, 141
  LDAP, 169
  methods implementation (IDL/Java conversion), 96
  native libraries, loading, 77
  objects
    loading skeleton and implementation classes, 61
    implementing in RMI, 55
    registering (CORBA Naming Service), 81
    remote activation (RMI), 50
    wrapping (holder class), 93
  obtaining information about (servlet requests), 122
  remote interface, implementing, 66
    directly (EJB class), 190
  remote requests, handling, 49
  resource management, 64
    container role, 181
  RMI, 327
  RMI/JNI or CORBA, interface to native code, 78
  server-side includes, 134, 141
  servlet state, preserving between shutdowns, 129
  session beans lifetime, dependent upon, 191
  simple class (IDL), 90
  stubs, generating (idltojava compiler), 94
  web servers, 115
ServerSession interface, 389
ServerSessionPool interface, 389
server-side implementation
  EJB interfaces, 180
  remote objects, 335
server-side Java components, accessing directly, 134
server-side programs, EJB and, 7
service provider interface (see SPI (JNDI))
service providers
  attribute values, determining, 166
  class, determining, 159
  JNDI, interacting with, 144
  listed (Sun, JNDI web page), 145
  name and directory protocols, 7
  separator characters (compound names), 157
ServiceDetail class, 495
ServiceDetailHelper class, 495
ServiceInformation class, 496
ServiceInformationHelper class, 496
ServiceInformationHolder class, 496
services
  CORBA, 281–288
  EJB objects, 174
    deployment descriptors and container roles, 179
service()
  BasicServlet class, 117
  GenericServlet class, 431
  HttpServlet class, 438
  Servlet interface, 432
services() (HttpServlet), 117
ServiceUnavailableException class, 414
Servlet API, 9, 114–142, 430–436
  cookies, 135
  core elements, 116
  exceptions, 123–124

Servlet API (cont'd)
life cycle, 115
server-side includes, support issues, 134
session tracking, 135–136
Version 2.1, 141–142
Servlet interface, 116, 432
<SERVLET> tags (HTML pages), 133
ServletContext interface, 141, 433
shared attribute methods (Version 2.1), 142
ServletException class, 124, 141, 433
ServletInputStream class, 434
ServletOutputStream class, 141, 434
ServletRequest interface, 117, 121, 435
updating with target URL, 141
ServletResponse interface, 117, 121, 435
servlets
chaining, 126
content changes, checking, 118
database connections, 139
direct access (other servlets), deprecating, 142
file-serving, 125
HTML forms and interactions, 118
information about, 118
initialization (custom), 128
non-HTML content, handling, 139
request dispatching, 141
requests and responses, 121
RMI hosts, acting as, 115
as server-side applets, 8
server-side includes and, 133
shopping cart (example), 11
threads, safety, 130
session beans, 179
create methods, 191
implementing, 191
Java classes/interfaces required, 186
methods, required implementation, 190
session context, setting, 192
stateful (see stateful session beans)
stateless (see stateless session beans)
time-out, specifying (deployment descriptors), 214
transaction boundaries, container notification of, 195
Session interface, 390
session tracking, 114, 136
objects, binding and unbinding, 138
session ID, accessing, 137
SessionBean interface, 190, 192, 367
SessionContext interface, 192, 367
SessionDescriptor class, 215, 217–218, 372
SessionSynchronization interface, 195, 367
set_elements() (DynArray), 476
set_policy_overrides() (Object), 497
setAttribute()
ServletRequest interface, 435
setAttribute()
ServletContext interface, 142, 433
ServletRequest interface, 141
setAutoCommit() (Connection), 33, 342
setBlob() (PreparedStatement), 42
setClob() (PreparedStatement), 42
setCommand() (RowSet), 446
setContentLength() (ServletResponse), 435
setContentType() (ServletResponse), 121, 435
setDateHeader() (HttpServletResponse), 121, 440
setDefaultStream() (LogStream), 329
setEscapeProcessing() (Statement), 36
setFailureHandler()
RMIFailureHandler class, 333
RMISocketFactory class, 334
set/get accessors (stateful session beans), 193
setHeader() (HttpServletResponse), 121, 440
setInitialContextFactoryBuilder() (NamingManager), 427
setIntHeader() (HttpServletResponse), 121, 440
setJMSDeliveryMode() (Message), 377
setLog() (RemoteServer), 332
setNextException() (SQLException), 355
setNull() (PreparedStatement), 28

setObject()
  MapMessage interface, 380
  PreparedStatement interface, 28, 350
SetOverrideType class, 497
setReturningObjFlag(), 171
setRollbackOnly()
  EJBContext interface, 362
  Transaction interface, 455
  UserTransaction interface, 456
setSessionContext() (SessionBean), 192, 367
setSocketFactory() (RMISocketFactory), 334
setStatus() (HttpServletResponse), 121, 440
setString() (PreparedStatement), 28
setTransactionIsolation() (Connection), 34, 342
setTransactionTimeout()
  TransactionManager interface, 455
  UserTransaction interface, 456
set() (SearchControls), 171
shared attributes (Servlet API Version 2.1), 142
shopping-cart servlet (example), 11
ShortHolder class, 497
.shtml files (HTML pages), 133
SingleThreadModel interface, 133, 436
SizeLimitExceededException class, 414
size() (Attributes), 167
Skeleton class, 336
SkeletonMismatchException, 336
SkeletonNotFoundException, 336
skeletons, 48
  (see also server skeletons)
socket programming, RMI vs., 43
sockets
  customized factories, 67
  servers (RMI), 334
SocketSecurityException, 337
Solaris C/C++ preprocessor, 291
SPI (JNDI), 144
  service providers list (Sun), 145
  web page (Sun), 148
SQL, 6, 15, 227–244
  ANSI-92 SQL state codes, 26
  ARRAY objects, 339
  data types, 24
    DATE specification, 348
    DATE, TIME, and TIMESTAMP, 26
    mapping to Java primitive types, 28
    TIME specification, 358
  database queries, 339
  date and time functions, 36
  functions, 239
  groups, 237
  joins, 235
  predicates, listed, 234
  queries, 21–23
  return codes, 241–244
  SQL-92, 16
  standard, versions, 227
  statements
    executing as batch, 40
    multiple, executing, 32
    precompiled, running repeatedly, 27
    types, 21
  stored procedures, 34
  subqueries, 235
SQLData interface, 355
SQLException class, 17, 26, 355
SQLInput interface, 355
SQLOutput interface, 356
SQLSTATE return codes, 241
SQLWarning class, 27, 347, 357
SSL encryption, authentication (web servers), 126
Standard Query Language (see SQL)
start()
  Connection interface, 376
  ServerSession interface, 389
  XAResource interface, 459
state
  entity beans, 199
  information, preserving (web sessions), 136
  servlet, preserving between server shutdowns, 129
  session beans, 192–193
stateful session beans
  as client extension, 193
  entity beans (bean-managed) vs., 205
  implementation, 193
  remote interface example, 193
  run-as-identity requirements, 217

stateful session beans (cont'd)
stateless session beans vs., 192
transaction boundaries, container notification of, 192
stateless session beans, 192
Statement interface, 17, 21, 357
PreparedStatement vs. Statement objects, 27
queries, executing multiple, 22
static methods, 89, 313
status codes
HTTP errors (servlets), 123
specifying (servlet responses), 121
Status interface, 453
stop( ), (Connection)
stored procedures (databases), 34–36
batch updates, 40
Streamable interface, 93, 516
StreamMessage interface, 391
string manipulation functions (SQL), 240
String objects (arrays), initial objects listing, 105
string_to_object( ) (ORB), 108, 490
StringHolder class, 498
stringified object references, 108, 110
StringRefAddr class, 414
strings
addresses (references), 414
adjacent (idltojavacompiler bugs), 291
arrays of (parameter values), 122
concatenation operator, 239
DatabaseMetaData methods, 29
IDL/Java mapping, 254
Java, converting to native, 77
literals (IDL), 258
read-only attribute (IDL), 88
search filters, 170
SQL, processing (databases), 27
Struct interface, 358
StructMember class, 498
structs (IDL), 262, 477
mapping to Java, 263
Structured Query Language (see SQL)
StubNotFoundException class, 311
stubs, 43
as remote references to server objects, 95
client and server, 94
converting from stringified object references, 108
RMI stub/skeleton layer, 48
subcontexts
creating, 169
destroying, 160
naming systems, 102, 146
reference, obtaining, 106
subqueries (SQL), 235
substrings (SQL), 241
Sun, CORBA implementation (Java IDL), 7
super.init( ) (servlets), 128
suppliers (CORBA events), 283
supportsTransactionIsolationLevel( ) (DatabaseMetaData), 34
supportsTransactions( ) (DatabaseMetaData), 34
switch statements (IDL unions), 265
symbols, defining with given value (idltojava compiler), 289
synchronization
servlets, service method, 133
session beans, 195
thread safety, maintaining, 130
Synchronization interface, 454
SystemException class, 454, 498

T

tables
database, modifying structure, 34
SQL
constraints, 231
creating, 231
data types, columns, 229
deleting objects, 233
deleting rows, 239
inserting data, 238
joins, 235
schemas, 228
TCKind class, 499
TCP/IP
remote references, point-to-point, 55
RMI/IIOP and, 86
TemporaryQueue interface, 391
TemporaryTopic interface, 391
TextMessage interface, 392
thin client programming , 7"

threads
  creating for ongoing tasks (servlets), 128
  database updates, performing, 34
  safety, 130
  SingleThreadModel interface, 436
ties (CORBA skeletons), 79
time
  and date functions (SQL), 240
  adjusting to SQL DATE specification, 348
Time class, 26, 358
Time Service (CORBA), 287
TimeLimitExceededException class, 415
time-out (session beans), 214
Timestamp class, 26, 359
tnameserv utility (RMI/IIOP), 81
Topic interface, 392
TopicConnection interface, 392
TopicConnectionFactory interface, 393
TopicPublisher interface, 393
TopicRequestor interface, 394
TopicSession interface, 394
TopicSubscriber interface, 394
toString() (RemoteObject), 54
TRACE (HTTP request), 120
Trading Service (CORBA), 287
Transaction interface, 455
TRANSACTION_NONE class, 33
TRANSACTION_READ_COMMITTED class, 33
TRANSACTION_READ_UNCOMMITTED class, 33
TRANSACTION_REPEATABLE_READ class, 33
TRANSACTION_REQUIRED class, 501
TRANSACTION_ROLLEDBACK class, 501
TRANSACTION_SERIALIZABLE class, 33
Transaction Service (CORBA), 284–285
TransactionInProgressException class, 395
TransactionManager interface, 455
TransactionRequiredException class, 456
TransactionRolledBackException class, 395
TransactionRolledbackException class, 456
transactions, 32–34, 362
  ACID characteristics, listed, 285
  attributes (beans), 222
  beans, support level, 214, 221
  boundaries
    defining, 183
    notification and management of, 285
    session beans and, 195
  client-initiated, 184
  client-side, 221
  concurrent (entity beans), 196
  distributed vs. simple, 9
  EJB server, awareness of, 184
  identifier, 460
  isolation levels, 32, 185
    JDBC supporting, listed, 33
    listed, 186
    setting, 34
  management, 181–186, 370
    EJB servers and, 8
  messages, 390
  run-as-identity requirements, 217
  synchronization, 367
    stateless session beans and, 195
  two-phase commit, 42
  XAConnection interface, 450
TRANSIENT class, 501
transport protocols, RMI architecture, 48
troubleshooting (see debugging)
two-phase commit protocol, 10
  JDBC drivers, 42
type (directory entry), 169
type (object class definition), 164
TypeCode class, 502
TypeCodeHolder class, 502
typedef (IDL data types), 260
  arrays, 261
TypeMismatch class, 507
Types class, 24, 359
type()
  Any class, 461
  DynAny interface, 475

U

UID class, 337
UnavailableException class, 125, 436
unbind()
  Context interface, 161
  Naming interface, 307
  NamingContext interface, 528
  Registry interface, 56, 325
UnexpectedException class, 311
unexportObject() (Activatable), 313
UnicastRemoteObject class, 45, 55, 313, 337
  nonpersistent references, 64
UnionMember class, 503
unions (IDL), 265, 478
  idltojava compiler bugs, 291
  mapping to Java, 266
unique identifier class (UID), 337
Universal Time Coordinated (UTC), 287
Unix systems, RMI registry daemon, 56
UNKNOWN class, 503
UnknownGroupException class, 321
UnknownObjectException class, 321
UnknownUserException class, 503
UnmarshalException class, 311
unmarshalling, 49
  classes, finding, 62
  IDL objects, 512
  remote method arguments, 254
  (see also marshalling)
Unreferenced class, 338
unregister() (Activatable), 313
unsetEntityContext() (EntityBean), 200, 365
updateInt() (ResultSet), 38
updateRow() (ResutSet), 38
updating
  attributes, 416, 418
  batch updates (JDBC), 39
  result sets, 37
    existing rows, editing data, 38
    support information (DataBaseMetaData), 39
  SQL tables, 238
  update counts, 22, 40
URI path, specifying, 142
URLs
  bundling into MarshalledObject, 71
  class bytecodes, storing, 70
  class file name, encoding (marshalling), 61
  class names, loading, 73
  classes, loading, 333
  encoding (session tracking), 136
  initial context filesystem service (Sun), 146
  JDBC, 19
    odbc subprotocol, 20
  JNDI server, connecting with, 219
  length limitations, exceeding (POST requests), 120
  method names, changes, 141
  object names, fully qualified, 50
  Oracle JDBC-Thin driver, 19
  resource abstraction (servlets), 142
  RMI remote objects, 57
  servlets, 118–119
  target, updating (request dispatching), 141
user access, restricting, 122
UserException class, 504
usernames, authenticating, 20, 126
UserTransaction interface, 182, 221, 456

V

value functions (SQL), 239
  date and time functions, 240
valueBound() (HttpSessionBindingListener), 138, 442
ValueMember class, 504
valueOf()
  Date class, 348
  Time class, 358
  Timestamp class, 359
valueUnbound() (HttpSessionBindingListener), 138, 442
value() (BindingType), 525
vendor naming services, RMI registry and, 50
vendors, messaging services, 9
virtual machine (see Java VM)
virtual machine identifier class (VMID), 323

W

wait(), 46
  ORB, keep running, 109
warnings (SQL), 27
wasNull() (ResultSet), 25
web applications, session tracking, 136
web servers
  cookies, 135
  GenericServlet class and, 117
  resource abstraction (servlets), 142
  servlet instances, pooling, 133
  servlet security, handling, 126
  servlets, using, 8
Web, using as development platform, 114
Weblogic/Bea Tengah server, 175
wide characters (IDL), 254
wildcard searches
  DatabaseMetaData methods, 29, 343
  directories, 170
  escape sequences
    JDBC, 36
  SQL (LIKE operator), 235
Windows systems, RMI registry daemon, 56
write() (ObjID), 329
WrongTransaction class, 505

X

X.500 directory services standard, 162
  attribute type definition, 164
  Directory Access Protocol (DAP), simplifying, 162
  object names, differing from filesystems, 163
XA API (distributed transactions standard), 10
XA interface, 458
XAConnection interface, 395, 450
XAConnectionFactory interface, 396
XAException class, 458
XAQueueConnection interface, 396
XAQueueConnectionFactory interface, 396
XAQueueSession interface, 396
XAResource interface, 459
XASession interface, 397
XATopicConnection interface, 397
XATopicConnectionFactory interface, 397
XATopicSession interface, 397
Xid interface, 460
XML deployment descriptors, 222
XOPEN specification (data types), 359
X/Open XA interface specification, 458

About the Authors

David Flanagan is the author of the bestselling *Java in a Nutshell.* When David isn't busy writing about Java, he is a consulting computer programmer, user interface designer, and trainer. His other books with O'Reilly include *JavaScript: The Definitive Guide, Netscape IFC in a Nutshell, X Toolkit Intrinsics Reference Manual,* and *Motif Tools: Streamlined GUI Design and Programming with the Xmt Library.* David has a degree in computer science and engineering from the Massachusetts Institute of Technology.

Jim Farley is a software engineer, computer scientist, and IT manager. His recent activities have included heading up the engineering group at the Harvard Business School and bringing good things to life at GE's Research and Development center. He's dealt with computing (distributed and otherwise) in lots of different ways, from automated image inspection to temporal reasoning systems. Jim has BS and MS degrees in computer systems engineering from Rensselaer Polytechnic Institute.

William Crawford got involved with web development back in 1995. He has worked at the Children's Hospital Informatics Program in Boston, where he helped develop the first web-based electronic medical record system and was involved in some of the first uses of Java at the enterprise level. He has consulted for a wide variety of institutional clients, including Boston Children's Hospital, Harvard Medical Center, and several Fortune 500 companies. Will currently heads the product development team at Invantage, Inc., a Cambridge, Massachusetts, company developing Java-based intranet tools for the pharmaceutical industry. In his spare time he is an avid photographer, writer, and economics student at Yale University

Kristopher Magnusson is the Open Source Programs Architect at Novell. He edited the original Java Directory Service Interface proposal for JavaSoft in 1996, worked on the Novell JNDI design team as the lead writer, and wrote JNDI sample code and tutorials. He earned a BS from the University of Utah in 1991 in economics, has been active in the NeXT and open source communities for years, and loves object-oriented design and computing. He lives with his partner, Kristen, in Salt Lake City, where he enjoys community activism, mountain biking, and oenophilia.

Colophon

Our look is the result of reader comments, our own experimentation, and feedback from distribution channels. Distinctive covers complement our distinctive approach to technical topics, breathing personality and life into potentially dry subjects.

The animal appearing on the cover of *Java Enterprise in a Nutshell* is a sand dollar (Echinarachnius parma). The sand dollar is a flattened, rigid, disk-shaped marine invertebrate related to sea urchins and sea stars. It is found in large numbers on the sandy bottoms in the coastal waters of many parts of the world. The sand dollar's shell, or test, is often perforated with petal-shaped slots arranged around a central point. The mouth is located in this central position on the underside of the shell. The shell is covered with spines of varying lengths. These spines aid the sand dollar in locomotion and enable it to burrow just below the surface of the sandy bottom. In this sand, the sand dollar finds the tiny organic material it feeds on, pushing the food towards its mouth with tiny tube feet. Additional tube feet on the upper side of the sand dollar are used for breathing.

The sand dollar's flower-like appearance and its abundance in many parts of the world have made it a favorite of shell collectors. Scientists have also taken an interest in this small invertebrate. The sand dollar is frequently used in the study of mitosis, the process of cell division. It is believed that a better understanding of mitosis may lead to a better understanding of cancer.

Mary Anne Weeks Mayo was the production editor and copyeditor for *Java Enterprise in a Nutshell*, Maureen Dempsey and Jane Ellin provided quality control, and Paulette Miley proofread the book. Kimo Carter provided production assistance. Lenny Muellner provided SGML support. Ellen Troutman Zaig wrote the index.

Edie Freedman designed the cover of this book, using a 19th-century engraving from the Dover Pictorial Archive. Kathleen Wilson produced the cover layout with Quark XPress 3.3 using Adobe's ITC Garamond font.

The interior layouts were designed by Edie Freedman and Nancy Priest, with modifications by Alicia Cech and Lenny Muellner implemented the layout in *gtroff*. Interior fonts are Adobe ITC Garamond and Adobe ITC Franklin Gothic. The illustrations that appear in the book were produced by Robert Romano and Rhon Porter using Macromedia FreeHand 8 and Adobe Photoshop 5. This colophon was written by Clairemarie Fisher O'Leary.

How to stay in touch with O'Reilly

1. Visit Our Award-Winning Site

http://www.oreilly.com/

★ "Top 100 Sites on the Web" —*PC Magazine*
★ "Top 5% Web sites" —*Point Communications*
★ "3-Star site" —*The McKinley Group*

Our web site contains a library of comprehensive product information (including book excerpts and tables of contents), downloadable software, background articles, interviews with technology leaders, links to relevant sites, book cover art, and more. File us in your Bookmarks or Hotlist!

2. Join Our Email Mailing Lists

New Product Releases

To receive automatic email with brief descriptions of all new O'Reilly products as they are released, send email to:
listproc@online.oreilly.com
Put the following information in the first line of your message (*not* in the Subject field):
subscribe oreilly-news

O'Reilly Events

If you'd also like us to send information about trade show events, special promotions, and other O'Reilly events, send email to:
listproc@online.oreilly.com
Put the following information in the first line of your message (*not* in the Subject field):
subscribe oreilly-events

3. Get Examples from Our Books via FTP

There are two ways to access an archive of example files from our books:

Regular FTP

- ftp to:
  ftp.oreilly.com
  (login: anonymous
  password: your email address)
- Point your web browser to:
  ftp://ftp.oreilly.com/

FTPMAIL

- Send an email message to:
  ftpmail@online.oreilly.com
  (Write "help" in the message body)

4. Contact Us via Email

order@oreilly.com
To place a book or software order online. Good for North American and international customers.

subscriptions@oreilly.com
To place an order for any of our newsletters or periodicals.

books@oreilly.com
General questions about any of our books.

software@oreilly.com
For general questions and product information about our software. Check out O'Reilly Software Online at **http://software.oreilly.com/** for software and technical support information. Registered O'Reilly software users send your questions to:
website-support@oreilly.com

cs@oreilly.com
For answers to problems regarding your order or our products.

booktech@oreilly.com
For book content technical questions or corrections.

proposals@oreilly.com
To submit new book or software proposals to our editors and product managers.

international@oreilly.com
For information about our international distributors or translation queries. For a list of our distributors outside of North America check out:
http://www.oreilly.com/www/order/country.html

5. Work with Us

Check out our website for current employment opportunites:
www.jobs@oreilly.com
Click on "Work with Us"

O'Reilly & Associates, Inc.
101 Morris Street, Sebastopol, CA 95472 USA
TEL 707-829-0515 or 800-998-9938
(6am to 5pm PST)
FAX 707-829-0104

International Distributors

UK, Europe, Middle East and Africa (except France, Germany, Austria, Switzerland, Luxembourg, Liechtenstein, and Eastern Europe)

INQUIRIES

O'Reilly UK Limited
4 Castle Street
Farnham
Surrey, GU9 7HS
United Kingdom
Telephone: 44-1252-711776
Fax: 44-1252-734211
Email: information@oreilly.co.uk

ORDERS

Wiley Distribution Services Ltd.
1 Oldlands Way
Bognor Regis
West Sussex PO22 9SA
United Kingdom
Telephone: 44-1243-779777
Fax: 44-1243-820250
Email: cs-books@wiley.co.uk

France

INQUIRIES

Éditions O'Reilly
18 rue Séguier
75006 Paris, France
Tel: 33-1-40-51-52-30
Fax: 33-1-40-51-52-31
Email: france@editions-oreilly.fr

ORDERS

GEODIF
61, Bd Saint-Germain
75240 Paris Cedex 05, France
Tel: 33-1-44-41-46-16 (French books)
Tel: 33-1-44-41-11-87 (English books)
Fax: 33-1-44-41-11-44
Email: distribution@eyrolles.com

Germany, Switzerland, Austria, Eastern Europe, Luxembourg, and Liechtenstein

INQUIRIES & ORDERS

O'Reilly Verlag
Balthasarstr. 81
D-50670 Köln
Germany
Telephone: 49-221-973160-91
Fax: 49-221-973160-8
Email: anfragen@oreilly.de (inquiries)
Email: order@oreilly.de (orders)

Canada (French language books)

Les Éditions Flammarion ltée
375, Avenue Laurier Ouest
Montréal (Québec) H2V 2K3
Tel: 00-1-514-277-8807
Fax: 00-1-514-278-2085
Email: info@flammarion.qc.ca

Hong Kong

City Discount Subscription Service, Ltd.
Unit D, 3rd Floor, Yan's Tower
27 Wong Chuk Hang Road
Aberdeen, Hong Kong
Tel: 852-2580-3539
Fax: 852-2580-6463
Email: citydis@ppn.com.hk

Korea

Hanbit Media, Inc.
Chungmu Bldg. 201
Yonnam-dong 568-33
Mapo-gu
Seoul, Korea
Tel: 822-325-0397
Fax: 822-325-9697
Email: hant93@chollian.dacom.co.kr

Philippines

Global Publishing
G/F Benavides Garden
1186 Benavides St.
Manila, Philippines
Tel: 632-254-8949/637-252-2582
Fax: 632-734-5060/632-252-2733
Email: globalp@pacific.net.ph

Taiwan

O'Reilly Taiwan
No. 3, Lane 131
Hang-Chow South Road
Section 1, Taipei, Taiwan
Tel: 886-2-23968990
Fax: 886-2-23968916
Email: taiwan@oreilly.com

China

O'Reilly Beijing
Room 2410
160, FuXingMenNeiDaJie
XiCheng District
Beijing
China PR 100031
Tel: 86-10-66412305
Fax: 86-10-86631007
Email: beijing@oreilly.com

India

Computer Bookshop (India) Pvt. Ltd.
190 Dr. D.N. Road, Fort
Bombay 400 001 India
Tel: 91-22-207-0989
Fax: 91-22-262-3551
Email: cbsbom@giasbm01.vsnl.net.in

Japan

O'Reilly Japan, Inc.
Yotsuya Y's Building
7 Banch 6, Honshio-cho
Shinjuku-ku
Tokyo 160-0003 Japan
Tel: 81-3-3356-5227
Fax: 81-3-3356-5261
Email: japan@oreilly.com

All Other Asian Countries

O'Reilly & Associates, Inc.
101 Morris Street
Sebastopol, CA 95472 USA
Tel: 707-829-0515
Fax: 707-829-0104
Email: order@oreilly.com

Australia

Woodslane Pty., Ltd.
7/5 Vuko Place
Warriewood NSW 2102
Australia
Tel: 61-2-9970-5111
Fax: 61-2-9970-5002
Email: info@woodslane.com.au

New Zealand

Woodslane New Zealand, Ltd.
21 Cooks Street (P.O. Box 575)
Waganui, New Zealand
Tel: 64-6-347-6543
Fax: 64-6-345-4840
Email: info@woodslane.com.au

Latin America

McGraw-Hill Interamericana
Editores, S.A. de C.V.
Cedro No. 512
Col. Atlampa
06450, Mexico, D.F.
Tel: 52-5-547-6777
Fax: 52-5-547-3336
Email: mcgraw-hill@infosel.net.mx